W9-CNW-909

MAGILL'S SURVEY OF AMERICAN LITERATURE

Revised Edition

10/06

MAGILL'S SURVEY OF AMERICAN LITERATURE

Revised Edition

Volume 6

Steinbeck—Zindel
Appendixes
Indexes

Edited by

Steven G. Kellman

University of Texas, San Antonio

SALEM PRESS, INC.

Pasadena, California   Hackensack, New Jersey

REF
810.9
MAG

Editor in Chief: Dawn P. Dawson

Editorial Director: Christina J. Moose

Project Editor: Tracy Irons-Georges

Copy Editors: Sarah M. Hilbert

Elizabeth Ferry Slocum

Editorial Assistant: Dana Garey

Photo Editor: Cynthia Breslin Beres

Production Editor: Joyce I. Buchea

Acquisitions Editor: Mark Rehn

Research Supervisor: Jeffry Jensen

Research Assistant: Rebecca Kuzins

Graphics and Design: James Hutson

Layout: William Zimmerman

Cover photo: Amy Tan (Hulton Archive/Getty Images)

Copyright © 2007, by SALEM PRESS, INC.

All rights in this book are reserved. No part of this work may be used or reproduced in any manner whatsoever or transmitted in any form or by any means, electronic or mechanical, including photocopy, recording, or any information storage and retrieval system, without written permission from the copyright owner except in the case of brief quotations embodied in critical articles and reviews. For information address the publisher, Salem Press, Inc., P.O. Box 50062, Pasadena, California 91115.

∞ The paper used in these volumes conforms to the American National Standard for Permanence of Paper for Printed Library Materials, Z39.48-1992 (R1997).

Library of Congress Cataloging-in-Publication Data

Magill's survey of American literature / edited by Steven G. Kellman. — [Rev. ed.].
    p. cm.
Includes bibliographical references and index.
ISBN-10: 1-58765-285-4 (set : alk. paper)
ISBN-13: 978-1-58765-285-1 (set : alk. paper)
ISBN-10: 1-58765-291-9 (vol. 6 : alk. paper)
ISBN-13: 978-1-58765-291-2 (vol. 6 : alk. paper)
 1. American literature—Dictionaries. 2. American literature—Bio-bibliography. 3. Authors, American—Biography—Dictionaries. I. Kellman, Steven G., 1947- II. Magill, Frank Northen, 1907-1997. III. Title: Survey of American literature.
PS21.M34 2006
810.9′0003—dc22

2006016503

First Printing

PRINTED IN THE UNITED STATES OF AMERICA

CONTENTS

CONTENTS

Complete List of Contents

Volume 1

Volume 2

Volume 3

Volume 4

Volume 5

Volume 6

Complete List of Contents

JOHN STEINBECK

© The Nobel Foundation

Born: Salinas, California
February 27, 1902
Died: New York, New York
December 20, 1968

Concerned with such universal themes as the meaning of life and death, Steinbeck, 1962 recipient of the Nobel Prize in Literature, employed realism to explore the lives of common people.

BIOGRAPHY

Salinas, California, over the hill from Monterey and close enough to Big Sur that John Steinbeck's mother was able to teach there, has long had the climate to grow some of the most profitable crops in the United States. When Steinbeck was born there in 1902, that part of the central California coast, some one hundred miles south of San Francisco, was quite untouched by the kind of industrial civilization that had grown up in the East, from which Steinbeck's family had come.

The father, John Ernst Steinbeck, born in Florida, had followed his parents to Hollister, California. He was a miller and served for eleven years as treasurer of Monterey County. In 1890, he married Olive Hamilton, a teacher. The Steinbecks had four children, of whom John, their third, was the only boy. He showed an early literary bent; his favorite pastime was reading, and his favorite book was Sir Thomas Malory's *Le Morte d'Arthur* (1485).

Steinbeck contributed to the school newspaper at Salinas High School, from which he graduated in 1919. He entered Stanford University as an English major. He attended Stanford in a desultory manner from 1920 until 1925 but left without a degree. A contributor to several campus publications during his years there, Steinbeck was particularly affected by his creative writing teacher, Edith

Ronald Mirrielees, for whose book, *Story Writing* (1962), he wrote the preface.

In the fall of 1925, Steinbeck went to New York City, working first as a day laborer. Before long, through the intervention of an influential uncle, Steinbeck had a twenty-five-dollar-a-week job on the New York *American,* where he had an undistinguished career as a reporter. Urged by an editor from the Robert McBride Publishing Company, Steinbeck produced a collection of short stories. When the publisher rejected the collection, a discouraged Steinbeck shipped out as a deckhand on a steamer going to California via the Panama Canal. He found work as a caretaker at a remote Lake Tahoe resort, benefiting artistically from the isolation the job assured. He wrote three novels, none ever published. In 1929, however, his novel about English pirate Henry Morgan, *Cup of Gold,* was published by McBride. Appearing only two months before the stock market crash of 1929, it sold few copies.

In 1930, Steinbeck married the first of his three wives, Carol Henning. They moved to Pacific Grove, California, where they lived in a modest house provided by Steinbeck's family, who also gave them twenty-five dollars a month on which they could live decently during the Great Depression. In the same year, Steinbeck met marine biologist Ed Ricketts, who remained his closest friend for the rest of Ricketts's life.

For his next book—and for most of his subsequent ones—Steinbeck turned to a California setting and theme. Brewer, Warren & Putnam published *The Pastures of Heaven* in 1932. Before the book could be bound, however, the publisher went out of business. Despite this, Steinbeck earned more than four hundred dollars in royalties from it, more than his first book or his third book, *To a God Unknown* (1933), brought him. Neither book sold enough copies to cover the $250 advance he had received for each.

In 1934, the year in which Steinbeck's mother died, the *North American Review* accepted the first two sections of *The Red Pony* and two short stories, one of which, "The Murder," was selected to appear in the O. Henry Prize Stories volume for 1934. It was in 1935, however, that Steinbeck's star began to rise significantly, with the publication of *Tortilla Flat*, a latter-day Arthurian legend with Danny as King Arthur and his boys as Danny's knights.

A number of publishers rejected *Tortilla Flat*, thinking its frivolity inappropriate for the mood of the Depression era. Pascal Covici, however, liked Steinbeck's writing. When he called his agent to ask whether Steinbeck had any new manuscripts for him to read, he was sent *Tortilla Flat*, which he published, thus beginning a literary relationship that lasted through Steinbeck's years of greatest celebrity. *Tortilla Flat* did not fare well with the critics, but the public liked it; Steinbeck's future was assured. Steinbeck helped people to remember that there is more to life than money.

Of Mice and Men followed in 1937 and was a Book-of-the-Month Club selection, assuring a minimum of ten thousand sales. In the same year, Steinbeck visited a camp for migrant workers. This visit led to his most celebrated work, *The Grapes of Wrath*, published in 1939. *Sea of Cortez* followed in 1941.

The next year, Steinbeck and Henning divorced, and in 1943, he married Gwen Conger, with whom he had two sons before their divorce in 1948, the same year in which Ed Ricketts was killed in an accident. *Cannery Row*, titled for the sardine factory area of Monterey, was well received in 1945, as was the novella *The Pearl* in 1947. In 1947, *The Wayward Bus* was rejected by the public. Steinbeck continued to write, but he never again attained the level of artistry he had reached in *The Grapes of Wrath*.

When Steinbeck was awarded the Nobel Prize in Literature in 1962, the academic establishment was not overjoyed, although his faithful public, recalling the work he had produced between 1935 and 1947, was less negative in its judgment. The Nobel presentation speech cited the impact of *The Grapes of Wrath*, but it also noted, among Steinbeck's later work, *Travels with Charley* (1962) and *The Winter of Our Discontent* (1961). Steinbeck died in New York in 1968. In 1974, his boyhood home in Salinas was opened as a museum and restaurant. A collection of his papers is in the Steinbeck Collection at San Jose State University, whose Steinbeck Room attracts numerous scholars.

Steinbeck's close friendship with Ed Ricketts, enduring for almost two decades until Ricketts's death in 1948, had a profound effect upon the author. Ricketts was a deeply philosophical man. Steinbeck trusted him and valued his judgment to the point that he had him read all of his manuscripts or read them aloud to him. Ricketts's judgments were not always valid—he liked *The Wayward Bus*—but were necessary to Steinbeck. Ricketts got Steinbeck to think about nature in ways that the author never had before. Steinbeck began to take on the philosophical colorations of his friend and went so far as to include in *Sea of Cortez* Ricketts's essay on non-teleological thinking, which had been circulating privately among Ricketts's friends since the 1930's.

Steinbeck wrote largely to please himself, and in so doing he often pleased vast audiences of readers as well. Seldom did he please the critics, however, after their vigorous acceptance of *The Grapes of Wrath*. Possibly this is because literary criticism was largely an enterprise of easterners or of people educated at eastern, often New England, schools. Their anti-California bias was seldom, if ever, expressed, but arguably it existed at the subconscious level.

Steinbeck resisted the inroads that the importunate tried to make upon his time. To protect his privacy, he moved away from California in 1945, buying a townhouse on the Upper East Side of New York City, where he continued to live until his death.

ANALYSIS

Although Steinbeck's first novel, *Cup of Gold*, is not much like his later work in theme, setting, or style, it supplies hints of themes that were to pervade his later work. The book is much influenced stylistically by the medieval legends with which Steinbeck had become familiar during his boyhood. The protagonist of the book, Henry Morgan, is a brigand, a rugged individualist who is as much a nonconformist as Danny is in *Tortilla Flat*. Those two protagonists, from two drastically different backgrounds, would have understood each other and sympathized with the other's outlook.

In his second and third books, *The Pastures of Heaven* and *To a God Unknown*, Steinbeck discovered the direction that most of his future novels would take. He wrote about the central California agricultural areas in which he had grown up, and, in the latter book, he also experimented with symbolism stimulated by his early reading of medieval literature. The characters in these books are memorable as individuals, but they clearly represent universal types as well.

As promising as *The Pastures of Heaven* was, it was not a commercial success. The beginning of Steinbeck's widespread national acceptance came with *Tortilla Flat*, which might not have been published at all had Covici not read Steinbeck's two preceding books and been favorably impressed by them. In *Tortilla Flat*, Steinbeck transplants the medieval legend of King Arthur and his knights to the Monterey Peninsula, where Danny and his jolly band of *paisanos* lead lives of immediate gratification and satisfaction.

The eastern establishment that essentially dominated literary criticism at that time did not always know how to handle Steinbeck's setting—California was the last frontier to the New York critics of the day—and many of them were appalled at the frivolousness and irresponsibility of Steinbeck's characters in the book. What shocked them most, however, was that Steinbeck made no value judgments about his characters. Rather, he presented them and let his readers make of them what they might.

The public accepted Danny and his boys because they represented to an economically depressed society an escape from the constraints that society had placed on many of its citizens. Danny and company lived outside those constraints. In *Tortilla Flat*, one finds the quintessential Steinbeck, the Steinbeck flexing his muscles before writing his great classic, *The Grapes of Wrath*. Steinbeck's greatest strength was his understanding and respectful depiction of people on the fringes of society.

It is important to remember that Steinbeck is not one with the people about whom he writes. He embraces them appreciatively, not with the sense that he wants to be one of them, but with a genuine respect for them as they are. In his best work, it is this disinterested, objective, yet warm presentation that entices readers. If one thinks in terms of di-

chotomies, American novelist Henry James would be at one extreme in depicting human beings, Steinbeck at the other.

This explains, in part, Steinbeck's frequent rejection by the critics. The professionals who wrote about his work had essentially been brought up in the Jamesian tradition; they had lived their lives either in the eastern establishment or outside it trying to break in. Steinbeck disoriented and threatened some of them. As a result, his writing has not received the serious and objective critical evaluation it deserves.

If Danny and his boys are a sort of lost generation transplanted to the central California coast—and they do at times put one in mind of the characters in Ernest Hemingway's *The Sun Also Rises* (1926) in that they are searching for the same universal answers that Hemingway's characters are. They are also prototypes for characters such as George and Lenny in *Of Mice and Men*, Tom Joad in *The Grapes of Wrath*, Kino in *The Pearl*, and others who live on the fringes of society.

Steinbeck's visit to a migrant workers' camp in 1937 helped to focus his energies and to give him a cause about which to write. *The Grapes of Wrath*, probably the most significant socioliterary document of the Depression era, was Steinbeck's masterpiece. Using the simple and direct language and the casual syntax that characterizes his best writing, he captured a crucial era in American history by showing the way the Great Depression and the Dust Bowl of the midwestern United States affected one family, pawns in a game so huge that they did not always realize there was a game.

Steinbeck became the darling of the Marxist critics when he published *The Grapes of Wrath* in 1939 but mostly for political reasons rather than for artistic ones. When his subsequent books failed to evince the social indignation of *The Grapes of Wrath*, critics virtually abandoned Steinbeck and often made unfeeling, superficial judgments about his work because it had failed to meet their preconceived political expectations.

Steinbeck was accused of being an intellectual lightweight and of having sold out—turning his back on his principles once he had secured his future. Actually, he had simply moved his cast of characters into new situations and shaped them to those situations, although not with consistent success. Even in the much—and justifiably—maligned

The Wayward Bus, Steinbeck was experimenting with a milieu created by imitating and modernizing the kind of microcosm with which Sebastian Brant had worked in his long medieval poem, *Das Narrenschiff* (1494; *The Ship of Fools*, 1507).

Steinbeck's work is almost wholly antiestablishment, but gently so. Every good story must have opposing forces, friends and enemies to keep the conflict moving. Steinbeck knew who his friends were: simple people such as George and Lenny, Danny and his friends, the Joad family, Kino, Jody in *The Red Pony*, and Mack and the boys in *Cannery Row*.

He had a little more trouble in deciding who the enemies were. He solved the problem, as many writers before him had, by keeping the enemy large, rich, and generalized. Upton Sinclair had taken on the impersonal giant of a meat industry in *The Jungle* in 1906. Frank Norris made the banks and the railroads the main enemies of society in *The Octopus* (1901) and *The Pit* (1903). Jack London had used greedy gold-rush speculators the same way in *The Call of the Wild* (1903). Steinbeck found his enemies in faceless bureaucracies, unfeeling governments, and grasping banks, in whose clutches the good people were held helplessly. The best they could do was to squirm a little and perhaps deal with the situation with the wry humor that characterizes Danny and his jolly cohorts.

Work remains to be done in assessing the artistry of John Steinbeck. His style reflects a mixture of influences as diverse as the Bible; the novels of Fyodor Dostoevski, Leo Tolstoy, Guy du Maupassant, Thomas Hardy, and other English and Continental writers; and the medieval texts that Steinbeck found so appealing during his childhood. Steinbeck was an uneven writer, but at his best, he was superb.

OF MICE AND MEN

First published: 1937
Type of work: Novel

The story of two men, George and Lennie, whose symbiotic relationship ends when George must kill the retarded Lennie.

The original manuscript of *Of Mice and Men* suffered a fate that gives writers nightmares: When Steinbeck and his wife were out one night, their dog, Toby, tore the first half of the finished manuscript to shreds. It was Steinbeck's only copy, so he had to rewrite half of the book. Steinbeck gave the dog meager punishment and said that he had a certain respect for the beast's literary judgment.

The book is one of Steinbeck's warmest. Lennie, a migrant ranch hand, is mentally retarded. George, also a migrant ranch hand, travels with him and looks after him. The story opens and ends on a riverbank off the main road, separated from the world of machines and impersonal technology. It is to this place that George tells Lennie to return in case of trouble. As in many of Steinbeck's novels, this riverbank, and the cave in which Lennie suggests that he and George might live away from the world, is a back-to-the-womb motif.

Lennie is large and strong. He likes soft, furry things. He likes them so much that he sometimes crushes the life out of them accidentally in showing his affection. He keeps mice in his pocket, but they do not survive his attention. Lennie lives on dreams. He longs for the day that he and George will own a little land and a house, a place where they can hide from a world that Lennie does not understand and that George does not trust. George and Lennie are different from the other ranch hands because they have each other. They conceive of a future and harbor dreams because they think that they will always be together. Their symbiotic relationship humanizes some of the other ranch hands with whom they work.

The ranch owner's son, Curley, however, is not among those humanized by George and Lennie's presence. Curley has his own problems. He is a lightweight fighter, a combative sort who resents being small but resents even more people who are larger than he. Lennie is a perfect target for his aggressions. He provokes Lennie into a fight in which he bloodies Lennie's nose, but Lennie crushes Curley's hand.

Curley's other major problem is that he is newly married to Candy, a woman of whose fidelity he is unsure. Candy goes to a local dance hall on a Saturday night and makes advances to Lennie. Lennie's fondness for soft, furry things makes him vulnerable. He strokes Candy's hair to the point that she becomes alarmed and panics. When she does, Lennie breaks her neck.

Doing as he has been told, Lennie returns to the

safety of the riverbank. He asks George to recite for him the details of how they will stay together, buy a small spread, and live out their lives happily. George, realizing that Curley will capture Lennie and make him die painfully for what he has done, puts a bullet through Lennie's head as Lennie looks out into the distance, where he envisions the future George is reciting to him.

The novel was unique in that it consisted largely of dialogue and was written so that it could also, with almost no adjustments, be acted on stage. Its popularity, particularly its acceptance as a Book-of-the-Month Club selection, surprised Steinbeck, who did not look upon the book as very significant. The original title, *Something That Happened*, reflects Steinbeck's objectivity in presenting his story; he makes no moral judgments about George and Lennie nor about the other ranch hands.

THE RED PONY

First published: 1937 (enlarged, 1945)
Type of work: Novella

The story of how Jody Tiflin moves from boyhood to adulthood.

Steinbeck, in Baja California in 1937, let it be known that he was writing a children's book, referring to what was to grow into *The Red Pony*. The first three of the four interconnected stories that make up *The Red Pony* were published in *The Long Valley* (1938). In 1945, Steinbeck added the final story, "The Leader of the People," to make the collection long enough to be published as a separate entity. The novella is not a children's book in the conventional sense; it is more accurately described as a *Bildungsroman*, a book that chronicles the education of a boy growing to manhood.

Jody Tiflin is about eleven years old. Although living on his parents' farm in the warm Salinas Valley provides him with an idyllic childhood, he learns some harsh lessons in life. Jody's first disillusionment comes in "The Gift," when the horse he has been given—the fulfillment of any boy's dream—is drenched in a rainstorm that Billy Buck, the family's farmhand, has assured the boy will not come. The horse, Gabilan, catches cold and, de-

spite all efforts to save it, dies. Billy Buck, who had been Jody's hero, is now diminished in his eyes, first because he promised fair weather when Jody took the horse out and then because Billy could not save the stricken animal.

Jody comes face-to-face with a second harsh reality relating to death in "The Great Mountains," the second story in the cycle. Gitano, an ailing old Chicano who was born on the Tiflin ranch before they owned it, walks onto the property and asks to be permitted to stay there until he dies. Carl Tiflin, ever practical and not a sympathetic character, will not permit this. The next morning Gitano rides off dejectedly—but not before he has stolen an old rapier that has been in the Tiflin family for generations.

In the third story, "The Promise," Jody is given his second horse, a newborn colt that needs care because its mother died in delivering it. Billy Buck had no choice but to kill her in order to save the colt, so, although Jody is pleased that this new life belongs to him, he grieves at the trade-off that accompanied the gift.

The last story, "The Leader of the People," is about the visit that Jody's maternal grandfather pays to the ranch. Jody adores the old man and dotes on his stories about the days when he was leader of a wagon train. Carl Tiflin hates those stories as much as Jody loves them, and he deplores the old man's visits because he knows they will be filled with reminiscences about an age in which he has little interest. The old man had a "westering" spirit, but that spirit, which helped Americans to conquer its last geographical frontier, is no longer necessary. The frontier has been conquered. Carl Tiflin must get on with his work, and he turns his back on the past that helped him to reach the point at which he finds himself.

This story ends with Jody listening to his grandfather, who confides in him that he fears the new generation no longer has the spirit of which he speaks. Jody, quite tellingly, listens and then asks his grandfather if he would like some lemonade, indicating that, for the first time, the boy is showing a sensitivity to someone else's feelings. Jody is moving toward manhood.

The Red Pony builds on Steinbeck's notion that nature is unrelenting and mysterious. Mere humans cannot thwart it any more than they can control it. When Jody's Gabilan becomes food for the vultures, Steinbeck does not suggest that commiseration is the proper emotion. It is part of the natural cycle. Living things feed on living things as inevitably as humans die.

THE GRAPES OF WRATH

First published: 1939
Type of work: Novel

The Joad family leaves the Oklahoma Dust Bowl during the Depression to find a new life in California.

In *The Grapes of Wrath*, Steinbeck vents his anger against a capitalistic society that was capable of plunging the world into an economic depression, but he does not exonerate the farmers who have been driven from the Dust Bowl of the midwestern and southwestern United States. He deplores their neglect of the land that resulted in the Dust Bowl and which helped to exacerbate the Great Depression.

The book is interestingly structured. Interspersed among its chapters are frequent interchapters, vignettes that have little direct bearing on the novel's main narrative. These interchapters contain the philosophical material of the book, the allegories such as that of the turtle crossing the road. As the animal makes its tedious way across the dusty thoroughfare, drivers swerve to avoid hitting it. One vicious driver, however, aims directly for it, clearly intending to squash it. Because this driver's aim is not accurate, he succeeds only in nicking the corner of the turtle's carapace, catapulting it to the side of the road it was trying to reach. Once the dust settles and the shock wears off, the turtle emerges and continues on its way, dropping as it does a grain of wheat from the folds of its skin. When the rains come, this grain will germinate; this is Steinbeck's intimation of hope.

As the narrative opens, Tom Joad has been released from a prison term he served for having killed someone in self-defense. On his way home, he falls in with Jim Casy, a former preacher down on his luck. Jim's initials can be interpreted religiously, as can much of the book. When Jim and Tom get to the farm where the Joads were tenant farmers, they find the place deserted, as are the farms around it, now dusty remnants of what they had been. Tom learns that his family has sold what little it owned, probably for five cents on the dollar, and headed to the promised land: California. En route, the family has paused to rest at a relative's place and to work on the antique truck they had bought secondhand for the trip. Tom and Jim catch up with them there, and they all leave—an even dozen of them—for the land in which they have placed their future hope.

The chronicle of the slow trip west, reminiscent of the turtle's arduous creep across the parched road, is recorded in such realistic detail that the reader is transported into a world peopled by hobos, stumblebums, the dispossessed, the disenchanted, and the dislocated—all of them pushing ahead to the jobs they believe exist for agricultural workers in California. Death haunts the motley band, threatening the elderly and those who are weak. The grandfather dies of a stroke the first night out; his wife dies as the family crosses the Mojave Desert. Noah, the retarded son, wanders off and is not heard from again. Ahead, however, lies hope, so the Joads bury their dead and keep going.

The land of their hearts desire, however, proves to be no Garden of Eden. The dream of a future that will offer hope and security quickly develops into a nightmare. Tom's sister, Rose of Sharon, lacks the funds for a funeral when her baby dies. She prays over it and sets it adrift in the rushes beside a river. Tom gets into trouble with the police, but Jim surrenders in his place and is taken away. By the time Tom and Jim meet again, Jim is a labor agitator. In an encounter with the police, Jim is killed and Tom is injured. The Joads hide Tom in their shack, then sneak him into a farm. There he takes up Jim's work as a labor organizer.

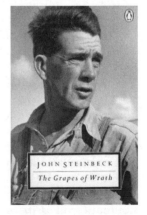

As the rains come, the Joads, who are encamped beside a river, endure floods that ruin their old truck. Having no place to live, they go into a decrepit barn, where a boy and his starving father have sought shelter. Rose of Sharon, having lost her baby, nourishes the starving man with the milk from her breasts, thereby saving his life. One is reminded again of the turtle and of the grain of wheat it deposits in the desiccated soil.

The Grapes of Wrath is a bitter tale of humans against nature and against a brutally exploitive society, but it is also a tale of nobility, of self-sacrifice, and ultimately of hope. It often offends the sensibilities, but life frequently offends one's sensibilities. The novel is a polemic, but one more detached and objective than first thought by many a critic.

CANNERY ROW

First published: 1945
Type of work: Novel

Residents of Monterey's Cannery Row plan and give a birthday party for one of their friends.

Around the sardine factories of Cannery Row in Monterey, California, lived those who worked only when they had to, preferring to talk, fight, drink, and be lazy. These are the characters of Steinbeck's *Cannery Row*, who have been compared to the rogues depicted in English artist William Hogarth's engravings and in the picaresque novels of the eighteenth century.

Monterey is only a whisper away from Pacific Grove, where Steinbeck and his first wife lived in the early 1930's. The two worlds, however, are continents apart ideologically. Pacific Grove developed as a Methodist campground. One could not buy liquor there, and the sidewalks were deserted not long after sunset. Three miles away, Monterey's bars stayed open almost until dawn. The population of each town was distinct, although the communities were virtually adjacent.

Mack presides over a band of derelicts who live from one drink to the next, one fight to the next, and one day to the next. If earlier picaros lived their irresponsible lives in ways that advanced them socially and economically, Mack's boys do not. Their progress is strictly horizontal. They live by bartering, borrowing, stealing, and conning Lee Chong, the Chinese merchant. They are the street people of an earlier age, although some of them have shacks to retreat into when they must. One of them, Malloy, lives sometimes in a huge boiler that his wife has decorated with chintz curtains.

The novel has only a loosely defined forward momentum. Mostly its characters drift laterally rather than move forward. This assortment of undistinguished humanity, however, is working together toward an outcome: getting a present to give Doc—a marine biologist, modeled on Ed Ricketts, who runs a small business supplying biological specimens to commercial distributors—at a surprise birthday party they are planning for him. One of them has taken a temporary job as a bartender, enabling him to save the dregs of people's drinks in large containers; this accumulation of leftovers constitutes their liquor supply for the party.

The boys scour the community, gathering Doc's birthday present, which is to consist of all kinds of specimens he can sell: cats, rats, frogs, dogs, anything biological enough to qualify. They invite everyone from the row to the party, including Dora, the local madam, and her girls. The climax of the novel comes in the hilarious fight that breaks out as the crowds gather and their spirits intensify. At the end of the novel, nothing has changed. The characters will go on living exactly as they have, ever good-natured, drifters who drift within the limited precincts of Cannery Row.

As he did in *The Grapes of Wrath*, Steinbeck uses interchapters to comment on the main thrust of the novel and to set it into a philosophical context. In these interchapters, one finds the strong influences of Ed Ricketts's nonteleological philosophy, which was fully explained in *Sea of Cortez*.

THE PEARL

First published: 1945, serial; 1947, book
Type of work: Novella

A poor Mexican Indian finds a rare, enormous pearl, but the find brings him suffering and heartache.

The Pearl, which its author calls a parable, was first published as "The Pearl of the World" in *Woman's Home Companion* in 1945. It was published as a novel and released as a film under the title *The Pearl* in 1947. In parables, characters exist outside and beyond their individual identities and are shaped to represent universal types.

Steinbeck's story came from a folk story he had heard and which he related in *The Log from the Sea of Cortez* (1951). The story, purported to be true, was of a simple Mexican peasant boy who had found a pearl near La Paz at the tip of Baja California. The pearl was so large that the boy was convinced he would never have to work again, that he could stay drunk forever, and that he could have his pick of women and then buy his eternal salvation after all his sinning by purchasing Masses. His dream turned sour when opportunists and thieves beset him, some of whom threatened his life. So frightened and disenchanted was this Indian boy that he eventually threw his great pearl back into the sea whence it came.

Steinbeck creates as his Indian peasant Kino, an unwed father whose chief concerns are to marry Juana, the mother of his child, Coyotito, in a church wedding and to provide for his family and for Coyotito's education. In short, Kino aspires to middle-class values to which the first readers of the story in *Woman's Home Companion* could easily relate.

Kino and Juana revel in the excitement that surrounds Kino's finding the pearl, but their elation soon turns into distrust. The brokers, through whom Kino must sell the jewel if he is to profit from it, conspire to cheat him, saying that the pearl is so big that it has no commercial potential. Kino has to hide the jewel, but while he sleeps, thieves try to rob him of it. The doctor who would not treat Kino and his family when they had no money now comes unctuously to them, proffering the best of services, to be paid for when the pearl is sold.

As the drama of Kino's situation unfolds, Kino, essentially peace-loving, is forced to kill three men and, worst of all, his adored Coyotito is killed by pursuers who shoot recklessly and strike the boy. The pearl comes to represent all that is bad in life, all that is—in the eyes of this superstitious peasant—unlucky. Finally, at Juana's urging, Kino, like the Indian boy in the original legend, heaves the jewel into the sea. He has made nothing from his find, and he has lost a great deal that is precious to him.

On an allegorical level, Kino's pearl is much like Santiago's marlin in Hemingway's *The Old Man and the Sea* (1952). It is a symbol of all the strivings of humankind. Dreams keep people going, offering them hope for the future even if the present is bleak. Steinbeck, however, like Hemingway after him, implies that human nobility comes from striving rather than from attaining.

EAST OF EDEN

First published: 1952
Type of work: Novel

This ambitious and convoluted saga follows the Trask family, residents of the Salinas Valley, and depicts human stupidity.

East of Eden is the most uncharacteristic novel in the Steinbeck canon. It is a complicated—at times convoluted—book that tries to accomplish more than it finally can. In his attempt to juggle three themes, Steinbeck at times fumbles, leaving his readers confused.

On one hand, Steinbeck is attempting to write a documentary about the Salinas Valley, which comes to represent the United States as a whole. He seeks to accomplish this by directing his attention to two complicated families, the Hamiltons and the Trasks. Upon this situation, he superimposes, quite heavy-handedly, a modern redaction of the biblical story of Cain and Abel—Caleb and Aron—in the novel.

Adam Trask and his half brother, Charles, live together in Connecticut as the story opens. They are compatible, but some rivalries exist. Adam detests his father, although he gets along with his stepmother, Charles's mother. The father has a strong militaristic bent and dreams of having a son in the Army. He handpicks Adam for this honor, leaving Charles, who adores his father, feeling rejected. In frustration, Charles beats Adam badly. After spending five miserable years in the service, Adam reenlists for another tour of duty. When it ends, he returns home to find that his father is dead. He and Charles inherit enough to make them rich. They live together in a harmony that is sometimes disturbed by violent fights.

Meanwhile, Cathy Ames is coming of age in Massachusetts. She is a confusing woman, beautiful and lovable on the surface but inherently evil in ways that few people can see. She sets fire to her parents' house, and both of them are killed in the blaze, leaving Cathy free to escape from a home she has found oppressive. She plants clues to suggest that she, too, died in the fire and runs away, becoming mistress to a man who operates a brothel.

When their relationship sours, he takes Cathy into the wilderness and beats her, leaving her there to die. She manages to get to the nearest house, which is where the Trask brothers live. They take her in and nurse her back to health. Charles divines the evil that lurks beneath Cathy's prepossessing exterior. Adam is innocent of such feelings, and he marries Cathy. She drugs him on their wedding night and steals into Charles's room, where she seduces him.

The brothers' relationship is strained by Cathy's presence, although Adam is not aware of his wife's duplicity. He decides, over his wife's protests, to go to the Salinas Valley to farm. He buys one of the best ranches in the area, and Cathy soon delivers twin sons. Unknown to Adam, they are Charles's offspring. Before names have been picked for them, Cathy shoots and wounds Adam, then flees to a bawdy house in Salinas, where she works under the name of Kate. The owner of the brothel, Faye, grows fond of Kate and decides to leave her everything she has in her will. After the will has been drafted, Kate arranges for Faye's murder and comes immediately into her money.

Meanwhile, Adam is so disconsolate at his wife's defection that he has not named the twins. Finally, goaded by his neighbor, Sam Hamilton, and several friends, he names the boys Caleb and Aron. Steinbeck interjects at this point a conversation about Cain and Abel so that there is no question about his artistic intention. Sam, who knows more about Kate than do the other principals in the novel, is aging and knows he cannot live forever. He is fully cognizant of Kate's past and knows that she has turned Faye's brothel into one in which sadism is the chief lure. He tells Adam what he

knows, and Adam visits Kate. She tries to seduce him but not before informing him that the twins are Charles's sons, not his.

Meanwhile, the two boys grow up to be quite different. Aron is blond and lovable, although quite staunch and adamant in his beliefs. Caleb, dark-haired and intelligent, is solitary but has the makings of a leader. Neither knows that Kate is alive until Aron falls in love with Abra Hamilton, Sam's daughter. Abra eventually reveals this information to Aron, who now realizes that his father has not been forthright with him. Aron does not seek to meet his mother. The story is further complicated because, at this time, Adam devises a plan for shipping lettuce to New York, iced so that it would survive the journey. When the venture collapses, Adam loses a large amount of money, causing his son Aron considerable embarrassment; he does not take well to failure in people, especially in his father.

Finally, Aron manipulates things so that Caleb finishes high school early and goes to college. Caleb has learned from Abra of Kate's existence, and he follows his mother about until she notices him and they talk. She feels threatened by him. When he finishes college, Caleb goes into the bean business with Sam Hamilton, and the two become rich because they can meet some of the food shortages brought about by World War I.

Caleb, always unsure of his father's love, tries to buy it by giving Adam money to help him recover from the loss he had on the lettuce venture. Adam, too proud to accept the money, virtually throws it back at him. To assuage his hurt, Caleb now takes Aron to meet Kate, who is intimidated by Caleb. She writes a will in which she leaves everything to Aron and shortly afterward commits suicide.

Aron, unable to cope with all that has happened, joins the Army. Sent to France to fight in World War I, he is killed. News of his death brings on a stroke that will kill Adam. Caleb blames himself for Aron's death, but as Adam nears death, at the urging of Lee, his Chinese servant, he gives Caleb his blessing and dies. Steinbeck attempted more than he could handle in this book; he was trying to produce something of epic proportions, but his greatest skill lay in working within more narrowly defined parameters.

SUMMARY

Steinbeck criticism has been generally less informed and more prejudiced than that accorded to other American writers of his stature. Current opinion supports the contention that Steinbeck will not weather well and that he will be forgotten long before contemporaries of his such as William Faulkner and Hemingway.

Further evaluation, however, may well prove the prophets incorrect. Steinbeck speaks to the general reader in ways that few American authors have. He has imbibed much of the storytelling style of medieval writers, and the folk elements that make his work appealing to a broad range of readers may be the elements that help his reputation to survive.

R. Baird Shuman

BIBLIOGRAPHY

By the Author

SHORT FICTION:
Saint Katy the Virgin, 1936
The Long Valley, 1938

LONG FICTION:
Cup of Gold, 1929
The Pastures of Heaven, 1932
To a God Unknown, 1933
Tortilla Flat, 1935
In Dubious Battle, 1936
The Red Pony, 1937, 1945
Of Mice and Men, 1937
The Grapes of Wrath, 1939
The Moon Is Down, 1942
Cannery Row, 1945
The Pearl, 1945 (serial), 1947 (book)
The Wayward Bus, 1947
Burning Bright, 1950
East of Eden, 1952
Sweet Thursday, 1954
The Short Reign of Pippen IV, 1957
The Winter of Our Discontent, 1961

DRAMA:
Of Mice and Men, pr., pb. 1937
The Moon Is Down, pr. 1942
Burning Bright, pb. 1951

SCREENPLAYS:
The Forgotten Village, 1941
Lifeboat, 1944
A Medal for Benny, 1945
The Pearl, 1945
The Red Pony, 1949
Viva Zapata!, 1952

NONFICTION:
Their Blood Is Strong, 1938
The Forgotten Village, 1941

DISCUSSION TOPICS

- What is the nature of John Steinbeck's medieval interest, especially in *Tortilla Flat*?

- What is the basis of the friendship of George and Lennie in *Of Mice and Men*?

- What distinguishes the social criticism of *The Grapes of Wrath* from Marxist-inspired social criticism of the 1930's?

- Are the Joads of *The Grapes of Wrath* typical migrant laborers?

- What factors led critics to downgrade Steinbeck's fiction after *The Grapes of Wrath*?

- What conclusions about the United States does Steinbeck reach as a result of the journey described in *Travels with Charley: In Search of America*?

Sea of Cortez, 1941 (with Edward F. Ricketts)
Bombs Away, 1942
A Russian Journal, 1948 (with Robert Capa)
The Log from the Sea of Cortez, 1951
Once There Was a War, 1958
Travels with Charley: In Search of America, 1962
Letters to Alicia, 1965
America and Americans, 1966
Journal of a Novel, 1969
Steinbeck: A Life in Letters, 1975 (Elaine Steinbeck and Robert Wallsten, editors)
America and Americans, and Selected Nonfiction, 2002 (Susan Shillinglaw and Jackson J. Benson, editors)

TRANSLATION:
The Acts of King Arthur and His Noble Knights, 1976

About the Author

Astro, Richard. *John Steinbeck and Edward F. Ricketts: The Shaping of a Novelist.* Hemet, Calif.: Western Flyer, 2002.

Benson, Jackson D. *The True Adventures of John Steinbeck, Writer.* New York: Viking Press, 1984.

French, Warren. *John Steinbeck's Fiction Revisited.* New York: Twayne, 1994.

George, Stephen K., ed. *John Steinbeck: A Centennial Tribute.* New York: Praeger, 2002.

_____. *The Moral Philosophy of John Steinbeck.* Lanham, Md.: Scarecrow Press, 2005.

Hayashi, Tetsumaro, ed. *A New Study Guide to Steinbeck's Major Works, with Critical Explications.* Metuchen, N.J.: Scarecrow Press, 1993.

Hughes, R. S. *John Steinbeck: A Study of the Short Fiction.* New York: Twayne, 1989.

Johnson, Claudia Durst, ed. *Understanding "Of Mice and Men," "The Red Pony," and "The Pearl": A Student Casebook to Issues, Sources, and Historical Documents.* Westport, Conn.: Greenwood Press, 1997.

McElrath, Joseph R., Jr., Jesse S. Crisler, and Susan Shillinglaw, eds. *John Steinbeck: The Contemporary Reviews.* New York: Cambridge University Press, 1996.

Parini, Jay. *John Steinbeck: A Biography.* New York: Henry Holt, 1995.

Shillinglaw, Susan, and Kevin Hearle, eds. *Beyond Boundaries: Rereading John Steinbeck.* Tuscaloosa: University of Alabama Press, 2002.

Tamm, Eric Enno. *Beyond the Outer Shores: The Untold Odyssey of Ed Ricketts, the Pioneering Ecologist Who Inspired John Steinbeck and Joseph Campbell.* New York: Four Walls Eight Windows, 2004.

Timmerman, John H. *The Dramatic Landscape of Steinbeck's Short Stories.* Norman: University of Oklahoma Press, 1990.

WALLACE STEVENS

Born: Reading, Pennsylvania
   October 2, 1879
Died: Hartford, Connecticut
   August 2, 1955

A meditative poet whose work drew from both European and American traditions, Stevens blended poetry and philosophy in his exploration of the relationship between the real and the imagined worlds.

Courtesy, Knopf Publishing Group

BIOGRAPHY

Wallace Stevens was born on October 2, 1879, to Garrett and Margarethe Stevens in Reading, Pennsylvania. His father's law practice was sufficient to support the large family, which included Stevens's older brother, younger brother, and two sisters, but not as well as Garrett Stevens would have wished. Constantly working to supply his family's needs, he transferred to the young Wallace Stevens his sense that a man's primary responsibility was to do well materially and support his family adequately. His mother, a strongly Christian woman who belonged to the Dutch Reformed church, provided her son with a respect for religious faith (though as a young man he rejected the practice of her religion) and a sense of the spiritual.

Growing up in Reading near the end of the nineteenth century, Stevens took part in all the activities available to the relatively privileged child. His earliest letters (home from summer camp in his teen years) show his powers of observation, his penchant for intellectual and word games, and his precocious and extensive reading. In 1897, he enrolled in Harvard College as a special student and tried to reconcile his father's wish for him to be a lawyer with his own desire (or even compulsion) to write. The excitement of the Harvard intellectual atmosphere caught him up: He took classes from Irving Babbitt, had long conversations with George Santayana, and wrote poetry for the Harvard literary magazine. In 1900, he allowed his own inclinations to rule in defiance of paternal demands and went off to New York to become a journalist.

Although he worked both for *The New York Tribune* and as a freelancer, he was not able to support himself comfortably through journalism. After some months of struggle, he enrolled in New York Law School. The year he finished his law studies and was admitted to the bar, 1904, was also the year he met his future wife, Elsie Moll. Displaying his father's prudence, he waited for years to marry her until he had enough money saved from his first position (with the legal staff of American Bonding Company) for their support. They were married on September 21, 1909.

The early years of Stevens's marriage he spent establishing himself financially while doing some writing; living in New York gave him access to the New York literary and artistic scene, with its salons and the electrifying presence of innovative artists such as Tristan Tzara and Marcel Duchamp. His first poems were published in *Trend* in 1914 and were followed by others in various small journals, including the fledgling *Poetry*. Stevens joined the Hartford Accident and Indemnity Company in 1916 and spent the rest of his life with the firm; he also moved to Hartford, Connecticut, that year. Having set himself up financially, he did so artistically in 1923 with the publication by Alfred A. Knopf of *Harmonium*, his first collection of poetry.

The rest of Stevens's life was a classic success story, despite the indifferent reviews of the first collection which may have contributed to the long silence following it. After his daughter, Holly Bright Stevens, was born in 1924, Stevens turned his attention to solidifying the position of his family. He was promoted to vice president of Hartford Accident and Indemnity in 1934, a position he held until his death. In 1935, his collection *Ideas of Order* was published by Alcestis Press; it was republished by Knopf a year later. A leftist review of Stevens which criticized him for being out of touch with the realities of the Depression resulted in two collections that attempt to justify the existence of art in hard times. *Owl's Clover* was published in 1936; *The Man with the Blue Guitar, and Other Poems* came out in 1937.

Stevens's later years underscored the divisions in his life between work and art, Hartford and New York, and public and private life. His daily office work continued even as he became more and more widely known as a poet. *Parts of a World* was published in 1942, and in 1945 he was elected to the National Institute of Arts and Letters. His grandson Peter was born in 1947, the same year that saw publication of *Transport to Summer.* The prestigious Bollingen Prize was awarded him in 1949, and in 1950 Knopf published *The Auroras of Autumn*, to be followed by *The Necessary Angel: Essays on Reality and the Imagination* in 1951 and *The Collected Poems of Wallace Stevens* in 1954. In 1955, the year of his death, he received both the National Book Award (his second) and the Pulitzer Prize. His later poems show a metaphysical drift, away from the proclaimed antireligion stance of such early poems as "Sunday Morning," and his death on August 2, 1955, was apparently preceded by a conversion to Roman Catholicism during his last illness.

ANALYSIS

In 1954, the year before his death, Stevens was asked to define his major theme. His clear, direct statement might have been taken from almost any of his earlier critics' analyses. His work, he said,

> suggests the possibility of a supreme fiction, recognized as a fiction, in which men could propose to themselves a fulfillment. In the creation of any such fiction, poetry would have a vital significance. There are many poems relating to the interactions between reality and the imagination, which are to be regarded as marginal to this central theme.

From his earliest work in *Trend* and *Poetry* to the last few poems before his death, Stevens explored the relationships between the mind and the world, sometimes setting the greater value on the imagination, verging on Romanticism, and sometimes on the actual. His final position is an attempt to balance or reconcile the two.

Stevens's first poems tend to glorify the imagination. In their energetic mental gymnastics, the poems of *Harmonium* astound by their virtuosity and their intellectual energy. It is these poems that prompted Stevens's earliest critics to call him a "dandy." Beneath the glittery surface of these early poems, however, is the first elaboration of the dynamic that would occupy him for a lifetime: the nature of the struggle between mind and world, as mind seeks to encompass and world resists.

The *Harmonium* poems return to several central propositions, including the failure of religion to satisfy the mind in the modern world, the split between human consciousness and unconscious nature, and the need for imagination to somehow replace the failed gods. The problematic role of the imagination is expounded in the various poems. The difficulty is that the mind must not simply transform reality into whatever it desires or thinks should be, but it must also enhance the world's reality through creative perception. The overall theme of Stevens's work might be described as a search for an aesthetic for his time, one which would fill the spiritual vacuum of people's lives. (Later in the poet's work, the aesthetic and the spiritual merge.) "The Comedian as the Letter C" traces the stages of discovery and disillusion in the travels of the naïve truth seeker; this early long poem explores how the mind grapples with reality and is finally consumed by it. *Harmonium* is dominated by images of the tropical and exotic, and its techniques include Poundian Imagism and orientalism.

Stevens's second collection, *Ideas of Order*, deals with the same themes, but the meditative component becomes stronger, while the imagery becomes less dense and physical. The opening poem abandons the southern paradise of *Harmonium* for a tougher northern landscape. This move north represents Stevens's desire for more involvement with the real: "My North is leafless and lies in a wintry slime / Both of men and clouds, a slime of men in clouds," he says. The negative, or at least critical, reviews of *Ideas of Order* caused him to engage even more directly with the realities of the Depression which his critics accused him of neglecting. His next collections, *Owl's Clover* and *The Man with the Blue Guitar*, are essentially apologies for art in troubled times. He develops also his theories of heroism and the heroic, a preoccupation perhaps originally linked to questions of World War I but which remains a major issue throughout the collections of his middle period.

After these collections come his most sustained discursive poems on the relationship between mind and world. His later poems describe an energetic search for a world both imagined and real, and they reflect reading of philosophy as well as poetry and poetics: His description of the grasp for experiential truth parallels the phenomenological theories of Edmund Husserl, Martin Heidegger, and other philosophers. The poems illustrate the irony of creative perception: To perceive anything is to impose an order on it and so limit it. These limitations must then be recognized as falsifications and swept away so that reality may be reinvented afresh. Thus the mind is constantly creating and de-creating the world, and to keep this reinvention in force is the creative artist's joy and taxing duty.

Stevens's last collections are preoccupied with the search for a poetry to replace religion, poetry as what he called "the supreme fiction." For Stevens, the act of creation, not the product, is the art. His poetry is concerned with the way the mind engages with reality to perceive and thus represent it. The ultimate poetry itself, as he indicates in "Notes Toward a Supreme Fiction," must be abstract, must change, and must provide pleasure. (Originally he had planned a fourth section for this long poem, "It Must Be Human.") His very last poems tend toward the mystical, raising the possibility that the truth so long sought may also be looking for the seeker: "Presence of an External Master of Knowledge" suggests this, as do some sections of "The Rock."

Stylistically, Stevens's work is powerful in its use of images of the sacred to describe the endeavors of the imagination. The tone of Stevens's work is often both exalted and elegiac: It is an elegy for the lost metaphysic, and it exalts and ennobles the search for a replacement. The later poems in particular are declamatory, using rhetorical balances and antitheses to build to a powerful conclusion which is, in his own words, "venerable and articulate and complete." His earliest poems are sometimes rhymed, sometimes blank verse, and sometimes melodic free verse.

As he developed his rhetorical, meditative style, he drifted toward a form of three-line stanzas of flexible blank verse. This form allowed him to develop theory discursively and illustrate it at once. A major characteristic of Stevens's work is the tentativity of his conclusions; "as" and "as if" appear frequently, as he approaches a position and then retreats from its finality. Although Stevens's work is filled with references to incompleteness, fragmentation, and inconclusiveness, its power and its appeal to succeeding generations of poets and readers come, in part, from the sense that the entire work is a single poem. Stevens at first intended to call his volume of collected poems *The Whole of Harmonium*; its "notes" form a letter, and its parts cohere.

"SUNDAY MORNING"

First published: 1915 (expanded version, 1922; collected in *Harmonium*, 1923)
Type of work: Poem

The faded promises of Christianity should be replaced by full participation in this world; one can reclaim one's own godhead by accepting that the only permanence is change.

"Sunday Morning" is an exploration of the position that religious piety should be replaced by a fully lived life. Part of the poem was published in 1915, but the whole was not printed until *Harmonium* came out. In its final form, "Sunday Morning" is a series of ten fifteen-line stanzas of blank verse. The argument of the poem is just that: an argument between a woman, who feels guilty about not going to church and enjoying "coffee and oranges in a sunny chair" instead, and another voice, presumably that of the poet, which tries to persuade her to give up her attachment to dead things and dead ideas. The focus alternates from what is happening in her mind—her objections and preoccupations—and his answers to her.

The woman is interrupted in her enjoyment of the "complacencies of the peignoir" by reflections on death and religion that remind her that the pleasant particulars of the moment are only transitory. Then the other voice asks, "Why should she give her bounty to the dead?" No divinity is worthwhile if it comes "only in silent shadows and dreams." One should worship where one lives: within and as part of nature. The woman should accept her own divinity as part and reflection of nature.

The woman's interlocutor then thinks about the development of godhood, from Jove, who was fully inhuman, through Christ, who was partly human, to the new god appropriate to the present, who would be wholly human. With a fully human god, heaven and earth would merge. The woman thinks about this before asking, more or less, how this system can explain away death. He responds that life is more eternal than anything promises of immortality could provide:

> There is not any haunt of prophecy,
> . . . .
> Nor visionary south, nor cloudy palm
> Remote on heaven's hill, that has endured
> As April's green endures; or will endure
> Like her remembrance of awakened birds
> Or her desire for June and evening.

The woman, though, is interested in personal immortality, which the speaker claims would not even be desirable, because, in the poem's most famous line, "Death is the mother of beauty." There is no ripeness without rot, and change, not stasis, brings fulfillment. The speaker imagines a static Paradise and the boredom that it would bring.

He then considers a possible symbol for the new perspective that life in the world would bring; it would not be a religion exactly but a religion substitute. A sun-worship image presents itself, the sun being the symbol of the real, of natural force. The people would dance naked to the sun, an image of energetic life-expending and celebrating. The woman finally accepts the speaker's proposition hearing

> A voice that cries, "The tomb in Palestine
> Is not the porch of spirits lingering,
> It is the grave of Jesus, where he lay."

Accepting the "unsponsored" and isolated ("island") human situation, she recovers her freedom

to live as part of the natural world, described in the conclusion in terms reminiscent of Romantic poet William Wordsworth:

> Deer walk upon our mountains, and the quail
> Whistle about us their spontaneous cries;
> Sweet berries ripen in the wilderness.

Human beings are like the pigeons of the closing lines, whose lives are indecipherable but beautiful in their vulnerability:

> casual flocks of pigeons make
> Ambiguous undulations as they sink,
> Downward to darkness, on extended wings.

The woman has progressed from an exaggerated seizing of experience to submission to it, and the change shows a growth in understanding. Stevens returns to the theme of this poem again and again throughout his poetic career.

"ANECDOTE OF THE JAR"

First published: 1919 (collected in *Harmonium*, 1923)
Type of work: Poem

Placing an object in the midst of a landscape rearranges the landscape.

Perhaps the most frequently anthologized of Stevens's poems, "Anecdote of the Jar" reflects Stevens's preoccupation with appearances or surfaces. "The world is measured by the eye," he said in one of his many aphoristic comments, and this difficult poem plays with the issues of what the eye measures and how. The poem's interpretation is far from agreed upon, as any identification of the jar (art? technology? any single point of reference?) tends to limit the poem unacceptably.

The poem's twelve lines describe the placement of a jar—a mason jar, as one critic suggests? a vase?—on a hill in Tennessee; once placed, the jar reorders the landscape. "It made the slovenly wilderness/ Surround that hill." The description suggests the distortions of the landscape in the curved sides of a plain glass jar. The new order is only that, a new order; it is not beauty. The jar takes over the scene: "It took dominion everywhere." Yet it is "gray and bare." The double negative in the last two lines causes confusion: "It did not give of bird or bush,/ Like nothing else in Tennessee." If the jar itself is read as the subject of the last line, the statement is clarified, but one might ask whether such a grammatical wrench is acceptable.

Read with as few limitations as possible, the poem suggests that adding an artifact or a point of focus compels a new interpretation of any scene. Moreover, there is a certain arrogance in making such rearrangements: "I placed a jar in Tennessee" has a casual affront to it, as the jar placer assumes the right to a whole state. Perhaps "I placed a jar in Tennessee" may even be read as "Eye placed a jar in Tennessee." Whatever the jar is or represents, it has made order out of chaos or "slovenly wilderness." Yet which is better—disorder or gray, bare order? If the order is not artistically preferable to the wilderness, if the net change is not a gain, what the jar represents is finally irrelevant.

Many of the *Harmonium* poems deal with changes wrought by the imagination upon reality, and these changes may alter things for the better, if the imagination is a true or honest creative perception, or for the worse, if (as in "The Ordinary Women") the imagination is limited by preconceived clichéd interpretations. "Anecdote of the Jar" is an example of perception as imagination with little judgment of its product. Only the process is defined.

"TEA AT THE PALAZ OF HOON"

First published: 1921 (collected in
  Harmonium, 1923)
Type of work: Poem

The imagination may construct a separate reality which consists of its own being.

Although many of the poems of *Harmonium* preach a yielding to reality, "Tea at the Palaz of Hoon" is an exception. Hoon is a vaguely Eastern potentate who creates a world from his mind and takes pleasure in inhabiting it.

"Hoon" may suggest "hero-moon"; in Stevens's early poems, moon and sun translate very roughly into imagination and reality. Hoon speaks about his sense of self and world, which is virtually solipsistic—he concludes that the self is the only reality. He is enclosed in trappings of royalty, "in purple." His majesty, even his divinity, is recognized by the world in which he moves: Ointment is sprinkled on his beard, and hymns are sung. The second part of the poem, however, explains the source of the recognition: "Out of my mind the golden ointment rained,/ And my ears made the blowing hymns they heard." He is enclosed in his self-made world, creator of his own landscape:

> what I saw
> Or heard or felt came not but from myself;
> And there I found myself more truly and more
>   strange.

The solipsistic world is not limited and limiting, as one might expect. Rather, to live in a world of one's own making results in a rediscovery, or reinvention, of self.

One cannot conclude, however, that Stevens is advocating solipsism in this poem. The persona of Hoon represents an extreme position on the scale of relations between imagination and reality; Stevens explores the world of a mind given over wholly to the imagination. Moreover, the speaker insists on the primacy of the imagined world, rather than the merely demonstrated. "Not less was I myself," he claims in the first stanza, and "I found myself more truly" in the last line.

This poem anticipates Stevens's later comfortable style of three-line sections. It approaches iambic pentameter, often his preferred meter, in most of the lines, but it does not use rhyme. Like others of Stevens's earlier, more formal poems (including "The Emperor of Ice-Cream"), it is divided into two rhetorical parts; in this poem, the first part poses questions about the origin of Hoon's world, and the second answers them.

"THE EMPEROR OF ICE-CREAM"

First published: 1923 (collected in *The Collected Poems of Wallace Stevens*, 1954)
Type of work: Poem

The only way to evade the proposition that death cancels out life is to live fully in the present.

A poem that Stevens once described as his favorite, "The Emperor of Ice-Cream" so puzzled its first readers that an ice cream company wrote to Stevens about it, asking whether the poem was in favor of ice cream or against it. Ice cream suggests the evanescent pleasures of life; one could answer, then, that the poem is for it.

This poem is set up as a counterpoint between a scene of a funeral and images of enjoyment. The first lines suggest a sensual celebration, as cigars, "concupiscent curds," and "wenches" are mentioned. Yet the temporary quality of all this is suggested by the lines, "let the boys/ Bring flowers in last month's newspapers." The flowers are vivid

blooms of the day, but last month's news is only history, fit to wrap flowers in. "Let be be finale of seem,/ The only emperor is the emperor of ice-cream," the first of the poem's two sections concludes. That is, one should accept whatever seems to be as what is, including flowers and history. One should not attempt to put prefabricated interpretations on life; rather, accept it in its transience and enjoy its vivid delights.

The second section presents a dead woman who, although she was poor (she had a "dresser of deal"—deal being cheap wood—and it was moreover "lacking three glass knobs"), still managed to adorn her impoverished life. She embroidered figures on her plain sheets, giving them life and color. (The "fantails" she embroidered may be either birds or goldfish.) The sheets she embroidered

should be her epitaph. The poem suggests: Let each one take pleasure in the world commensurate with his or her ability to enjoy, because there is no other world. The final line echoes, "The only emperor is the emperor of ice-cream."

The poem is memorable for its double focus—the impoverished death on one side and the wild sensual celebrations on the other. The doubleness of the poem is underscored by the two-stanza division with the shared last line, as well as by the single rhyme in the poem that concludes each section.

"THE IDEA OF ORDER AT KEY WEST"

First published: 1934 (collected in *The Collected Poems of Wallace Stevens*, 1954)
Type of work: Poem

Art, or the imagination, changes life by reordering the world and intensifying the human experience of it.

"The Idea of Order at Key West" is a discursive poem reflecting upon the work of the imagination and the relationship between the real and the imagined worlds. The poem's form is iambic pentameter with some irregular end rhymes. It begins with an unidentified woman singing beside the sea: "She sang beyond the genius of the sea." "She" is the imagination, and her voice does not change the reality it represents: "The water never formed to mind or voice." These two, then, woman and water, mind and world, are separate. Yet it would seem that reality, too, has some sort of guiding principle or spirit, a "genius." Her song does not change or "form" reality, which has its own inhuman "cry."

The second section of the poem reiterates and redefines the separation between the two: The water's sound is reflected in her song, but "it was she and not the sea we heard." She is singing in words; reality speaks its own language, that of "the grinding water and the gasping wind."

She is the "maker," and the sea is merely "a place by which she walked to sing." The listeners ask, "Whose spirit is this?" They wish to know what, or who, this secret voice, the imagination that is at the center of human nature, is. The answer is that the voice is not merely reality, "the dark voice of the sea," for if it were, the human listeners would not understand it; "it would have been deep air." Nor is the sound only humans' readings of reality, "her voice, and ours, among/ The meaningless plungings of water and the wind." Rather, her voice is the human understanding of the real—the only entrance point to it. The imagination is neither mind nor world but an act of perception that is also a blending point:

> She was the single artificer of the world
> In which she sang. And when she sang, the sea,
> Whatever self it had, became the self
> That was her song, for she was the maker.

Neither embroidery nor simple reflection, the imagination becomes a force that penetrates and incorporates.

The last two sections are addressed to "Ramon Fernandez." Stevens insisted that Ramon Fernandez was simply a made-up name and was not an allusion to the French critic by that name who was then popular, but because Stevens owned books by Fernandez, one might perhaps discount that claim. In any case, the speaker asks Fernandez (if the critic, an analyst of the imagination and its products) why the song, once ended, has reordered the world. Leaving the sea, the speaker turns back to the town and sees that the "lights in the fishing boats at anchor there" have "mastered the night and portioned out the sea,/ Fixing emblazoned zones and fiery poles." Reality has been changed by the "lights"—imagery suggesting consciousness/imagination—to something of intense and personal meaning.

The concluding five lines reach an emotional pitch seldom found in Stevens's work, as he defines the impulse of the artist/maker as a "blessed rage for order." Creative perception is necessary; it is "blessed." It is an internal imperative; it is a "rage." Moreover, it is not reality that is being ordered, finally, but words: "The maker's rage to order words of the sea." This self-defined goal is also a destiny. The words are of the "fragrant portals, dimly-starred," suggesting a mystic birth; they are "of ourselves and of our origins." As the definitions become more spiritual or mythic ("ghostlier demarcations"), the poetry, too, becomes more acute

("keener sounds"). The end of this poem may suggest that humankind's deepest, most spiritual need is for the imaginative, and that, moreover, there is a point at which mythmaking becomes discovery.

"OF MODERN POETRY"

First published: 1940 (collected in *The Collected Poems of Wallace Stevens*, 1954)
Type of work: Poem

Tradition and convention no longer produce poetry in modern times; poetry must be reenvisioned as the mind's act of self-creation.

One of the most frequently anthologized of Stevens's poems, "Of Modern Poetry" is another work that attempts to define art for a fragmented world in constant flux. Poetry is now a search, whereas it used to be a method. In the past, "the scene was set; it repeated what/ Was in the script." That is, convention and tradition defined poetry, and each poem was a modification of a pattern. Now, Stevens says, the conventions no longer apply.

The poem must reflect the world, speak its speech; it must "face the men of the time and . . . meet/ The women of the time." War, the contemporary state of affairs, must have a part in it. Most important, it must find "what will suffice," a phrase repeated twice in the poem. The search for "what will suffice" amounts to a search for satisfaction, a solace for the mind's pain of isolation. It must, in fact, express the mind to itself, so that it becomes the internal made visible. The actor must speak words that "in the delicatest ear of the mind" repeat what it desires to hear.

The imagery so far has been of the theater, but when the method of this new poetry is described, philosophy and music are interwoven with theater images to give the impression of an art that is plastic and fluid. The actor becomes "a metaphysician in the dark," suggesting a thinker concerned with first and final causes but lacking the light of any received structure for his meditations. He is, moreover, "twanging an instrument," creating a music that is "sounds passing through sudden rightnesses." These vibrations are the mind's own pulsations made audible to it.

The poem concludes by returning to the subject matter of modern poetry, which can be any action in which the self is expressed: It "may/ Be of a man skating, a woman dancing, a woman/ Combing." The subject is not the important issue, however, for the real poem is the act of creating poetry; modern poetry is finally "The poem of the mind in the act of finding/ What will suffice." This poem twists and turns in an attempt to catch a glimpse of its own creation. It is about itself: Modern poetry, and this work defining it, are self-reflexive. The poem is the creation of poetry and not the product.

This poem contains germs of the ideas that Stevens would develop and elaborate in "Notes Toward a Supreme Fiction," in which he claims that poetry must be abstract, must change, and must give pleasure.

"Chocorua to Its Neighbor"

First published: 1947 (collected in *The Collected Poems of Wallace Stevens*, 1954)
Type of work: Poem

The hero that is humankind's most central dream is half imagined, half real.

A poem that illustrates Stevens's growing preoccupation with the hero and the nature of heroism, "Chocorua to Its Neighbor" features a mountain discussing the human hero myth. "Chocorua" consists of twenty-six five-line stanzas of blank verse, and it develops the definition of the heroic through images from alchemy. The creation of the hero, then, is a mystical process, like the transmutation of the base metals into gold. Like alchemy, the creation of the hero is really a process of self-refinement.

The poem begins with an indication of the mountain's perspective. The mountain has the detachment of distance, of objectivity, of largeness. Armies and wars are perceived as mass movements of numbers, not as individual soldiers in combat. A war is "A swarming of number over number, not/ One foot approaching, one uplifted arm."

Nevertheless, there is a "prodigious shadow" which represents humankind, visible on the moun-

tain. It is "the self of selves" who is represented (in section 5) as a quintessence, or alchemical fifth essence, through references to the four elements of earth, air, fire, and water and to the "essay," a vessel for the transmutation. The figure is "the glitter of a being," half perceived, the blue "of the pole of blue/ And of the brooding mind"—that is, half real, half imagined. This figure speaks, explaining "the enlarging of the simplest soldier's cry/ In what I am, as he falls." That is, the mythic human gives meaning to an individual life. The soldier's death has its significance because of this central human.

The man-myth doubts its own reality in section 12 but then grows "strong" from new reflections in section 13. Essentially it draws its power from its source, which is human beings' desire for its existence, for something outside themselves that would dignify their lives. It now ponders the fact that there is a galaxy of myth—the captain, the cardinal, the mother, "true transfigurers fetched out of the human mountain." That the human mind has produced such beings that in some sense exist is the proposal of this poem, which then summarizes its implications about the process of creation in a section that could stand for Stevens's whole aesthetic:

To say more than human things with human voice,
That cannot be; to say human things with more
Than human voice, that, also, cannot be;
To speak humanly from the height or from the
  depth
Of human things, that is acutest speech.

This hero, this self-creating creation, is true poetry or "acutest speech." True poetry does not speak with a voice of elements beyond human experience, nor does it speak with some inhuman wisdom of human concerns. Rather, it is the human voice speaking of and within the range of human lives.

The rest of the poem explores the nature of the shadow-myth-hero. It is constantly in flux, constantly re-becoming and reinvigorating the space it inhabits: "where he was, there is an enkindling, where/ He is, the air changes and grows fresh to breathe." It is not "father"—that is, it is not an authority figure to impose its views from above—but "megalfrere"—brother and equal. It is the "common self"; moreover, it is the "interior fons. And fond." It is the spring, the baptismal well, basis of the self, and although it is "metaphysical metaphor," it is "physical if the eye is quick enough."

It is, then, both imagined and real, brought into existence by the intensity of human need for it. The mountain concludes its meditation by recognizing greatness of this presence—a human figure greater than nature, enlarged by consciousness of itself.

This poem was written during that period of Stevens's career in which his preoccupation was imagining the hero; this figure is heroic in Stevens's imaginings, in his representation of the collective imagination. As his poetics developed, Stevens turned more and more to the poetic act itself as subject. His last poems verge on an alchemical transformation of world into mind; those poems, difficult and demanding, are not usually found in more general anthologies.

SUMMARY

Stevens's lifetime search for a contemporary aesthetic, one that could satisfy the mind by filling the hole left by the lost metaphysic, sustains his poetry. His early work sets up a persuasive symbolism for the dialogue between reality and the imagination, using the repeated images of Florida and the North, summer and winter, sun and moon. His later work, in its careful analysis of experience for clues to "being," provides a poetic parallel to phe-

nomenology in philosophy. His eclectic use of techniques and ideas from other arts, as well as both European and American poetry, gives his work a sophistication perhaps unmatched among other American poets of his generation.

Janet McCann

DISCUSSION TOPICS

- What does Wallace Stevens mean by a "supreme fiction"? Do the formal divisions of the poem *Notes Toward a Supreme Fiction* offer any evidence?

- How does the inclusion of lush sensory imagery in "Sunday Morning" assist Stevens in the development of his theme?

- Several of Stevens's poems entail the "idea of order." Is "Anecdote of the Jar" such a poem? What does it say or imply about order?

- Is "The Emporer of Ice Cream" a defense of hedonism?

- Could the poem "Of Modern Poetry" have been as well titled "Of Poetry"?

- Does Stevens's poetry fall into any particular school or tradition of poetry?

BIBLIOGRAPHY

By the Author

POETRY:
Harmonium, 1923, expanded 1931 (with 14 additional poems)
Ideas of Order, 1935
Owl's Clover, 1936
The Man with the Blue Guitar, and Other Poems, 1937
Parts of a World, 1942
Notes Toward a Supreme Fiction, 1942
Esthétique du Mal, 1945
Transport to Summer, 1947
The Auroras of Autumn, 1950
Selected Poems, 1953
The Collected Poems of Wallace Stevens, 1954

DRAMA:

Three Travelers Watch a Sunrise, pb. 1916, pr. 1920
Carlos Among the Candles, pr. 1917
Bowl, Cat, and Broomstick, pr. 1917

NONFICTION:

The Necessary Angel: Essays on Reality and the Imagination, 1951
Letters of Wallace Stevens, 1966
Souvenirs and Prophecies: The Young Wallace Stevens, 1977
Three Academic Pieces, 1947

MISCELLANEOUS:

Opus Posthumous, 1957 (Samuel French Morse, editor)

About the Author

Bates, Milton J. *Wallace Stevens: A Mythology of Self.* Berkeley: University of California Press, 1985.

Bloom, Harold. *Wallace Stevens.* Philadelphia: Chelsea House, 2003.

Cleghorn, Angus J. *Wallace Stevens' Poetics: The Neglected Rhetoric.* New York: Palgrave, 2000.

Critchley, Simon. *Things Merely Are: Philosophy in the Poetry of Wallace Stevens.* New York: Routledge, 2005.

Ford, Sara J. *Gertrude Stein and Wallace Stevens: The Performance of Modern Consciousness.* New York: Routledge, 2002.

Leggett, B. J. *Late Stevens: The Final Fiction.* Baton Rouge: Louisiana State University Press, 2005.

Morse, Samuel F. *Wallace Stevens: Poetry as Life.* New York: Pegasus, 1970.

Santilli, Kristine S. *Poetic Gesture: Myth, Wallace Stevens, and the Motions of Poetic Language.* New York: Routledge, 2002.

Sharpe, Tony. *Wallace Stevens: A Literary Life.* New York: St. Martin's Press, 2000.

ROBERT STONE

Born: Brooklyn, New York
August 21, 1937

In a black humor mode of political and social satire, Stone explores humanity's heart of darkness as a reflection of national darkness.

BIOGRAPHY

Robert Stone was born in Brooklyn, New York, on August 21, 1937, the son of Gladys Catherine Grant, an elementary school teacher of Scotch-Irish origins whose schizophrenia profoundly affected her son's vision of himself and his world (he often mentions the fear of chaos his life with her instilled in him), and C. Homer Stone, a former railway detective who fled domestic responsibilities shortly after Robert's birth. Because of his mother's illness, young Robert spent time in an orphanage and in a series of Catholic boarding schools (including St. Ann's Marist Academy in Manhattan), where physical punishment was commonplace.

After his mother's release from the hospital, Stone lived with her on Manhattan's West Side; joined a street gang; read with puzzlement and then appreciation the works of Thomas Carlyle, Fyodor Dostoevski, Franz Kafka, John Dos Passos, Joseph Conrad, and F. Scott Fitzgerald; and won a New York State Regents' scholarship based on a story he wrote influenced by J. D. Salinger. However, he clashed with the Marist brothers over his drinking and his conversion of another student to atheism, and he left school before high school graduation.

In 1955, Stone joined the United States Navy and served with the amphibious force of the Atlantic Fleet. He passed his high-school equivalency test while in the military. The experiences of his childhood, captured in part in the opening to "Absence of Mercy," one of the short stories in *Bear and His Daughter* (1997), clearly influenced his interest in the rootless, the psychotic, the irresponsible, and the hypocritical. His service as a radioman aboard an attack troop carrier in the Mediterranean during the Suez Crisis of 1956 and then as senior enlisted journalist on Operation Deep Freeze Three in Antarctica prepared him to write credibly of military life, language, and style and of ships and sailing (as he does in "Under the Pitons," a story of drug smugglers who prove inept at sea, and in *Outerbridge Reach* (1992), with its transoceanic yachting competition). In the *Triquarterly* article "Me and the Universe" (1986), Stone reflected on the horrific spectacle of war that he experienced as a nineteen-year-old on Suez duty and his vision of everyday life as war.

While attending New York University from 1958 to 1960, he worked as a copy boy, caption writer, and then editorial assistant for the *New York Daily News*. On December 11, 1959, he married children's protection service worker Janice G. Burr, whom he had met in a creative writing class. Early in 1960, the Stones dropped their conventional life and migrated to New Orleans, where Stone held menial jobs (in a coffee factory, on the docks, and as a radio actor, a merchant marine seaman, a door-to-door salesman, and a census taker) and where his daughter Deidre was born at Charity Hospital. Stone read his own poetry to jazz accompaniment in a French Quarter bar and moved with the beatnik crowd, including LeRoi Jones and Gregory Corso. His experiences in that city (including trumped-up arrests) and in the South during a time of sit-ins and struggles against segregation provided material for his first novel, *A Hall of Mirrors* (1967), a work begun after reading Fitzgerald's *The Great Gatsby* (1925).

After the birth of their son, Ian, the Stones returned to New York City, where they became friends with Jack Kerouac, Allen Ginsberg, and others of the emerging bohemian scene (encountered at the Seven Arts Times Square coffee shop where Janice waitressed). She learned keypunch; he wrote advertising copy. They moved on to California when a thirty-page sample of *A Hall of Mirrors* won Stone a Stegner Fellowship in creative writing at Stanford University. While living in Menlo Park, California, he experimented with psychedelic drugs (particularly LSD) and struck up what proved to be a lifelong friendship with Ken Kesey, whom he joined on the Merry Pranksters' 1964 cross-country bus trip. (Stone later referred to them as very much like a group of fraternity boys out for a good time.) Kesey's La Honda hideaway provided a prototype for Dieter's mountain fortress in *Dog Soldiers* (1974). Stone looks back on his California experiences as "sybaritic," paradisical, life lived in "technicolor." During this period of involvement with the drug culture, Stone evolved the values that became the moral heart of the books that followed: a sense of the ambiguity of motives and of the transitory nature of moral judgments. A 1964 Houghton Mifflin Literary Fellowship helped finance his writing.

He wrote for the *National Mirror* in New York City from 1965 to 1967, then freelanced between 1967 and 1971. Having sold the film rights for his first novel, he wrote the script for its film version, *WUSA* (1970). A Guggenheim Fellowship paid his way to London, but then, as correspondent for the *London Ink* and later the *Manchester Guardian*, he traveled to Saigon, South Vietnam, where he spent two months gathering material for his second novel. Of this experience he says, "I found myself witnessing a mistake ten thousand miles long, a mistake on the American scale." He then moved on to Hollywood, where he unsuccessfully fought changes in the title and in the character of Marge in the film version of *Dog Soldiers* (the film was released as *Who'll Stop the Rain* in 1978).

Next he began a teaching career as a writer-in-residence at Princeton University from 1971 to 1972. Later, as an associate professor of English and a writer-in-residence, he taught at Amherst College, Massachusetts, between 1972 and 1978,

taking time out in the mid-1970's to travel to Central America three times, once by bus. There he went scuba diving, listened to all the stories he could about that area of the world, and began his third novel. He visited Honduras and Costa Rica, but he was particularly fascinated by Nicaragua under the Somozas and attended a party at the presidential palace in Managua—"just beyond the effective mortar distance from the nearest habitation." The parallels with his Vietnam experiences made his next novel, *A Flag for Sunrise* (1981), a continuation of his saga of Americans abroad.

His teaching has been itinerant: at Stanford University in 1979; at the University of Hawaii, Manoa, from 1979 to 1980; at Harvard University in 1981; at the University of California, Irvine, in 1982; at New York University from 1983 to 1984; at the University of California, San Diego, in 1985; and at Princeton again thereafter. His fourth novel, *Children of Light* (1986), which helped win Stone a five-year, $250,000 Strauss Living Award, grew out of his experiences with the Hollywood motion-picture scene and his 1983 participation in the Santa Cruz Shakespeare Festival production of *King Lear.*

His next novel, *Outerbridge Reach*, in turn, drew on his knowledge of the sea gained as a member of the U.S. Navy's Atlantic Fleet, a merchant marine seaman, and a yachtsman. Its protagonist, a graduate of Annapolis and a Vietnam War veteran turned advertising writer for a yacht brokerage, foolishly seeks to rediscover himself by participating in an around-the-world, single-handed yacht race in one of his own shoddy products and finds himself losing the battle of man against sea. In 1992, Stone traveled to the occupied territories of Israel, an experience that he used for *Damascus Gate* (1998). Though uneven in quality and criticized by European and Middle Eastern reviewers as too insular in its emphasis on expatriates abroad, *Damascus Gate* brings together a wealth of detail about Jerusalem, Israel, and world theologies past and present, with hair-raising vignettes of mindless hatreds expressed in very personal ways. A later trip to the Caribbean inspired *Bay of Souls* (2003) and Stone's investigation of Voodoo practices and drug running in the region. In 2004, Stone launched into new territory by directing the Magnolia Pictures documentary film *Guerrilla: The Taking of Patty Hearst.*

Stone enjoys swimming, scuba diving, walking in the woods, and engaging in aerobic exercise. He continues to write short stories and articles for popular journals (as he has throughout his career), and reads widely, though Samuel Beckett and Jorge Luis Borges remain his favorites. Trips abroad continue to provide vivid settings in which to explore themes that have intrigued him throughout his life. He thinks of himself as essentially an entertainer, though he admits that he hopes his entertainments will make his readers (whom he considers people psychologically much like himself) to reflect on the world around them. Despite his focus on damaged individuals, Stone's family is a strong stabilizing force in his life. His wife is his editorial assistant, sounding board, and first reader, one whose sensibility he trusts. The Stones have called Northhampton, Massachusetts, home for many years.

ANALYSIS

Stone, called "a beat-generation Carlyle" by Thomas Sutcliffe and "the strongest novelist of the post-Vietnam era" by Walter Clemons, writes as an American romantic, intrigued by the exotic and the faraway, by worlds that promise wealth or adventure but that prove sadly disappointing. In these alien locales, he discovers home truths as his characters obsessively pursue the American Dream in New Orleans, Vietnam, Southern California, Central America, the Caribbean, Mexico, and even Jerusalem. When they fail to accept responsibility and act unwisely, their wealth or dreams of success turn to ashes, and their personal lives disintegrate. In the face of the unknown, their nightmares overwhelm them. Dieter, in *Dog Soldiers*, claims to have "succumbed to the American dream," which he defines as "innocence" and "energy," and describes his friend Ray Hicks as "trapped in a samurai fantasy—an American one" of "the Lone Ranger" or "the great desperado" who "has to win all the epic battles singlehanded." Later Dieter claims that his mountain retreat is "[t]he last crumbling fortress of the spirit" as the world breaks down into "degeneracy and murder": "We're in the dark ages." His final line sums up part of the message in all Stone's novels—the moral vacuum in which Americans exist individually and collectively—a message Stone interprets as "an act of affirmation" amid looming catastrophe.

Stone's strength as a writer has been his ability to render true the obsessions of the baby-boom generation and the tragedy of their excesses. He has been brilliant at capturing generational *Zeitgeist*, the spirit of each benchmark decade. In the 1960's *A Hall of Mirrors* took a sharp, satirical look at romantic pessimism in the face of racial prejudice and right-wing extremism. In the 1970's he captured the naïve cynicism of failed upper-middle-class idealists and their involvement in romanticized drug-dealing and gunrunning plots—during the war in Vietnam in *Dog Soldiers* and during a would-be Latin American revolution in *A Flag for Sunrise*.

Children of Light depicts the selling out in the 1980's of the dreams of the 1960's as potential artists, novelists, and actors have lost their vision and yielded to crass commercialism. *Outerbridge Reach* captures the corporate lies and betrayals of the 1990's: a corner-cutting promoter faking a heroic exploit and unable to face the consequences. *Bay of Souls*, whose middle-American protagonist finds himself in Haiti, his mistress a Voodoo cultist with a Colombian drug connection, depicts Americans losing their souls in their obsessions with exotic Third World ways—becoming opportunistic, and driven to sleep with the devil and profit from the experience. *Damascus Gate* ushers in the new millennium with all the craziness, fears, and expectations associated with significant endings and beginnings.

Thought-provoking and emotionally engaging, Stone's works relate the individual to the trends of his or her time and raise questions about responsibility and choice. He engages in teasing pronouncements—for example, calling truth "a trick of the mind" that confounds logic in *Outerbridge Reach*, dismissing the idea of God working through history as a "delusion of the Western mind" in *A Flag for Sunrise*, and creating absurdist images like that of a blind shortwave fanatic tapping away in Morse code to unknown listeners perhaps thousands of miles away, promoting an odd assortment of goods.

His self-destructive characters pay the price of national and personal ignorance and irresponsibility. *A Flag for Sunrise* ends with the idea that "[a] man has nothing to fear . . . who understands history," yet Stone's characters continually fail to understand history in any of its contexts. Converse, in

Dog Soldiers, says, "I don't know what that guy did or why he did it. I don't know what I'm doing or why I do it or what it's like. Nobody knows. . . . That's the principle we were defending over there [Vietnam]. That's why we fought the war." Converse's personal blindness about motive and reason as representative of America's blindness is quintessential Stone.

Stone's novels define the romantic illusions of the trendsetters of the 1970's and 1980's. His characters attempt to toy with outlaws, but in a bourgeois setting; the mafiosi, the drug dealers, the gunrunners, and the revolutionaries often prove too violent and unpredictable to be tamed. Echoing an ironic 1968 French student poster, Stone suggests, "We are all undesirables," afloat morally and emotionally. His characters are cynical drifters in some way at odds with the law or the government; they are "students of the passing parade" (*Dog Soldiers*). His priests have lost their vocations and have turned to whiskey and a wishful humanism to compensate; his nuns seek a political commitment and martyrdom that will help them overcome the boredom and their doubts about their calling; his professors muse on universal meaning but have difficulty coming to terms with simple daily decisions of right and wrong. A middle-aged professor, angry at his wife for coddling their son and cold from long fruitless hours sitting in a treetop, sees in the crosshairs of his gun an equally frustrated fellow hunter cursing loudly the dead doe that repeatedly tumbles from his wheelbarrow as he struggles to haul it home and, for a moment, considers the unthinkable. Israeli soldiers threaten a Palestinian youth trapped in a cul-de-sac, and Gaza refugees stone and chop up a stranger—surely a Jew—in a spinach field.

His characters shift with the prevailing winds; caught up in movements beyond their understanding, they continually betray one another without guilt and without self-knowledge. They are rootless wanderers of mind and world—sometimes violent, often at the end of their tethers. William Shakespeare's line could well be said of each of them: "He hath ever but slenderly known himself." Michael Ahearn, having tasted the wild flavors of the Caribbean and lost his soul, returns home to hardscrabble fields of dead corn, glacial rock, derelict barns, and a "mackerel" sky, spooked by the "unimaginable."

Many of Stone's characters are burnt-out fig-

ures, at one time extremely competent but now pulled down in an inevitable spiral by irresponsible incompetents. There is a sense of a cultural breakdown, of misplaced dreams, of the despair that comes from losing hope. Often Stone sets up a dangerous fool, and someone gets killed or hurt as a result. His characters contemplate or commit suicide: Geraldine Crosby in *A Hall of Mirrors*, Marge in *Dog Soldiers*, Holliwell and Naftili in *A Flag for Sunrise*, the neurotic actress Lee Verger in *Children of Light*, Owen Browne in *Outerbridge Reach*, and the AIDS-weakened brother in *Bay of Souls*. In "Bear and His Daughter," the illegitimate daughter of a well-known poet kills her father and herself when he can neither remember a poem she thinks he wrote for her nor respond to her crank-driven need for physical confirmation of affection. Stone's characters ask one another what they are worth and find the answer depressing: "A little cinder in the wind, Pablo—that's what you are." Like Holliwell, they hover "insect-like" on the edges of societies they can never truly penetrate, like strangers from some other planet.

Often there is a truth-telling speech; therein the main character tells his audience what he really thinks, but either no one hears or they hear only what they want to hear. In *A Flag for Sunrise*, the drunken and insulting Holliwell attacks Uncle Sam and exported American popular culture as a moneymaking conspiracy to pander to the ignorant and the vulgar abroad; he warns Latin Americans that in the end "Mickey Mouse will see you dead." A further insult is his suggestion that American popular culture is no worse and is in some ways better than what was originally there. In *A Hall of Mirrors*, Rheinhardt, in an ironic parody of reactionary prose, claims that a napalm bomb dropped in Vietnam is a "bomb with a heart," the heart of "a fat old lady on her way to . . . the world's fair," innocent and motherly and pursued by a fiendish black with rape in his heart. His words are like an outrageous jazz riff played upon American fears and obsessions. His audience, however, hears nothing of his maunderings as it goes about its riot.

Influenced by Conrad, whose *Heart of Darkness* (1899) he references at the beginning of *Dog Soldiers*, Stone notes through Hicks that "The desires of the heart . . . are as crooked as a corkscrew." Stone is interested in the grammar of dominance, power plays, accommodation, and victimization.

His imagery repeatedly connects humans to fish and a bleak bottom-of-the-ocean competition—the food chain as metaphor. He captures a sense of cosmic menace—the unseen terror of the deep—in nihilism and conflict: race wars in *A Hall of Mirrors*; the Vietnam War and drug wars in *Dog Soldiers*; crazed killers and guerrilla warfare in *A Flag for Sunrise*; war against inner demons in *Children of Light*; personal disintegration in *Outerbridge Reach*; drug lords, AIDS, and military juntas in *Bay of Souls*; nihilistic apocalyptic fervor in *Damascus Gate*.

Stone's style is expressionistic and often surreal, yet his fiction is also firmly rooted in a solid sense of place. The third-person point of view often reflects the febrile imaginings of one of the central characters, with a resulting exaggeration of mood through intense emotion. Holliwell, for example, skin-dives down the sheer wall of an offshore reef, and his sensitivity toward what may or may not be a killer shark or other undersea creature (or perhaps even the watery grave of a murdered woman) transforms a casual outing into a symbol of psychological and philosophical evil, the "lower depths" where "sharks" await the adventurous. In *Damascus Gate*, the River Jordan, electrified with sunset colors, seems to reverse its course and surge uphill, a shared drug-induced hallucination of religious hysteria. These fine scenes are typical of Stone's method. Stone says of his art in *Modern Fiction Studies*, "fiction refines reality and refracts it into something like a dream [serving] to mythologize . . . in a positive way a series of facts which of themselves have no particular meaning."

Yet Stone's settings are also drawn with a sharp realism. New Orleans, Saigon, Southern California, Central America, the Caribbean, Mexico, and Jerusalem are all recognizably real places, locations one can visit and identify. It is perhaps this contradictory nature of Stone's style that has attracted filmmakers to his novels and yet has marred the two books transmuted to the screen, *A Hall of Mirrors* and *Dog Soldiers*. Paul Newman, Joanne Woodward, and Anthony Perkins could not save *WUSA*, the film version of *A Hall of Mirrors*, from critical and popular disdain, and even Rheinhardt's wonderful drunken speech scene is tame

and flat. Similarly, Nick Nolte, Michael Murphy, and Tuesday Weld could not rescue *Who'll Stop the Rain?* from being a provocative failure. The considerable strengths of both films lie in the "exteriors" they share with their respective novels—the images of New Orleans's French Quarter, lakefront, and municipal auditorium in the first book and of Dieter's mountain retreat in the second. Memorable vignettes capture emotional intensity: an Israeli smuggler stoned to death in a Muslim village, a drunken hunter at odds with his wife setting his sights on a self-righteous neighbor, a grieving mother seeing in bundles of aborted fetuses smuggled out of a local hospital (for last rites) her own dead children frozen in the thin ice through which they fell while skating.

The film lacks the gripping force of character created by Stone's prose, the sense of solidarity and identification he induces between reader and diverse, often fairly unattractive characters. Melodrama traditionally asks its audience to connect with heroic figures so perfect that the audience would like to become them; it is no mean trick to bring one into the skin and psyche of the Rheinhardts, Hickses, Holliwells, and Walkers. One guesses that Stone's novels will never make great films, as they rely so heavily on the writer's skill with prose. If Stone is right in "The Reason for Stories" that the purpose of fiction is to "expand human self-knowledge" and decrease "each individual's loneliness and isolation," then he is indeed teaching a sympathy for the "losers" of the world, the self-damned and marginal people normally ignored by mainstream fiction.

At the sentence level, Stone's prose reflects the same mixture of expressive emotion and realistic description delineated above. Stone has a journalist's eye for detail and for short, intense dramatic scenes, a poet's ear for dialogue, and an English teacher's sense of the subtle nuances of language and the importance of a complex interplay of images and scenes that gain weight and meaning from their interlocking patterns. To these he adds imaginative drive and a vision of the "convolutions and ironies of events."

A HALL OF MIRRORS

First published: 1967
Type of work: Novel

Three down-and-out characters, suffering and self-destructive, face the racism and fanatical right-wing extremism poisoning American society in the 1960's.

Winner of the William Faulkner Award for best first novel and filmed as *WUSA* in 1970, *A Hall of Mirrors*, as Stone says, takes the United States as its subject and has built into it "all . . . [Stone's] quarrels with America," but most particularly right-wing "exploitation of the electronic media." Some have called it a story of the dark night of the American soul, or more particularly a distillation of the disparate elements that made up the 1960's. Its title comes from Robert Lowell's poem "Children of Light," in which the puritan children of light become the corrupted, evil children of night, "the Serpent's seeds," and the whole world is inverted into a hideous hall of mirrors where "candles glitter," a reflected image of "might-have-beens." Thus, the children of the night in this novel, three rootless drifters seduced by illusions, must face a perverted potential, distorted and tainted. One of them, Rheinhardt, even turns the reference into a play on vampires and a bloodsucking world where all is not as it seems.

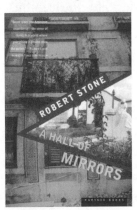

Once a brilliant classical clarinetist, now a failure and an alcoholic, Rheinhardt is down-and-out in New Orleans and happy to espouse any cause in order to be taken on as the rock disc jockey of a right-wing radio station, WUSA, whose motto, "The Truth Shall Make You Free," is perverted by the reality of its racist message. Rheinhardt's refrain is "I am not dead . . . I am—but hurt. Defend me friends, I am but hurt." Stone calls him his "scapegoat" and "alter ego." The second child of the night is a lonely, abused, and scarred country girl from West Virginia. Geraldine, who seeks love but finds only bitter alienation ("they're about to lay me low" becomes her refrain and later, to Rheinhardt, "you done undermined me, love"). She is ignorant and down-and-out, but decent, and her affair with Rheinhardt only brings her more pain and disillusionment. The third child of the night is Morgan Rainey, an idealistic but ineffectual social worker, pursued by childhood nightmares of black people tarred and feathered. He takes a room in the same rundown building as Rheinhardt and Geraldine, as he helps conduct a supposed "welfare" census, but he finds that every positive act results in pain and injury and leaves him "feeling broken" (though it is those affected by his misguided attempts to help who are truly broken).

The novel captures the conflicts and obsessions of the South in the 1960's. M. T. Bingamon, a power-hungry, right-wing demagogue, exploits the racist fears of poor white people, aided by Brother Jensen, a con man, philosopher, and supposed missionary, head of the Living Grace Mission. The comic strategies Stone develops herein to satirize the political right have served him well throughout his canon. Rheinhardt and Rainey become pawns in Bingamon's power plot. The final third of the novel is an apocalyptic Armageddon, a nightmarish description of the violent, fanatical, racist, "patriotic" rally that the radio station sponsors and of the ensuing riot, which leaves nineteen dead. Rainey is grievously wounded, and Geraldine, picked up for vagrancy, finds herself unable to face the cold, metallic solitude of her jail cell. At the end, Rheinhardt, a misfit and a drifter, is on his way out of town, a survivor who finds the battle and its losses endless. Rheinhardt, Geraldine, and Rainey's hall of mirrors reflects an American nightmare in which civilization proves a false image, actions produce unintended results, and humanity wanders confusedly without direction.

Rheinhardt's ironic, drug-inspired speech about American innocence sums up the illusions that Stone's novel negates:

> The American way is innocence. In all situations we must and shall display an innocence so vast and awesome that the entire world will be reduced by it. American innocence shall rise in mighty clouds of vapor to the scent of heaven and confound the nations!

Stone's characters have lost their innocence and their Garden of Eden, and instead blindly and mistakenly pursue their self-interests.

DOG SOLDIERS

First published: 1974
Type of work: Novel

An ex-Marine smuggling drugs from Vietnam, seeking love, "the real thing," and a drug buyer, instead finds death, betrayal, and ambiguity.

Winner of the National Book Award for Fiction in 1975 and filmed as *Who'll Stop the Rain* in 1978, *Dog Soldiers* depicts the ongoing effects of the Vietnam War back home in the United States, where heroin has become an obsession and it is hard to tell friend from enemy. Its title derives from a passage in Conrad's *Heart of Darkness*, rephrased by Ernest Hemingway, about grimly soldiering on, leading a dog's life but staying alive. A piece in the Guardian ("There It Is") had set the stage for this book, detailing the crazed violence of the war (helicopter pilots gunning down elephants, the Saigon tax office bombed). Vignettes from that piece are worked into the first forty-one pages of *Dog Soldiers.*

Despite its initial scenes in Vietnam, however, *Dog Soldiers* concentrates not on combat but on the impact of the war on the moral certainties, loyalties, and conscience of the civilian United States, where, as Stone later said, "all sorts of little bills were coming up due for payment." The novel argues that the Vietnam War most affected values back home, infecting the survivors with greed and corruption summed up in the heroin underworld. Stone calls the 1970's "a creepy, evil time" and *Dog Soldiers* his reaction to it.

John Converse, a talented but tainted journalist on assignment to Vietnam, schemes with an acquaintance, Charmian, to smuggle three kilograms of pure heroin home from Vietnam for a $40,000 profit. To do so he enlists the aid of ex-Marine Ray Hicks, a friend but also "probably a psychopath" and therefore usable. What Converse does not realize is that he has been set up from the beginning: after he handles the smuggling, the heroin is to be stolen from him.

Consequently, when Hicks contacts Converse's wife, Marge, a ticket taker for a pornographic cinema and a drug addict, he finds himself waylaid by hoods, and he and Marge must flee for their lives. When Converse arrives home, he is threatened, tortured, and then forced (by circumstances and by his ruthless father-in-law, Elmer Bender) to deal with a dishonest federal "regulatory" agent named Antheil.

As Hicks and Marge are relentlessly pursued across Southern California, they meet an array of fringe characters from Hicks's past, characters who make Hicks conclude, "It's gone funny in the states." During this flight, Hicks becomes almost as obsessed with Marge as with the heroin and is unwilling to leave her behind in order to speed up his escape. Hicks, with his cold eyes and cruel face, envisions himself as a serious man, a modern samurai with a worthy illusion, riding the wave till it crashes. Their final encounter is with Hicks's past mentor and Zen master, Dieter, a onetime hallucinatory drug advocate turned guru of the apocalypse, who lives in a mountain compound near the Mexican border and practices countercultural experimentation.

In the final shootout between Hicks and federal agents, Dieter bombards the countryside with sounds of Vietnam War battles blasted over loudspeakers, as if the war itself continued on the home front. After a confused battle scene, during which Hicks misunderstands Dieter's attempts to free him from heroin, Hicks discovers an escape route through an Indian cave but is badly wounded when he returns to rescue Marge and help reunite her with her husband. Despite this rescue, the self-centered, amoral Converse, dreaming of personal profit at the expense of friendship and loyalty, attempts to renege on his agreement to meet Hicks in the desert on the far side of the mountains and then dumps the heroin to save himself.

The moral ambiguity of the conflict continues as the crooked federal agent, Antheil, confiscates the drugs for his own profit. Hicks has said, "I'm just doing what everybody else is doing," and, in a world where the U.S. Army destroys elephants as "enemy agents," all perversities prove possible. The war's by-product, heroin, corrupts and destroys, and Stone demonstrates that its end result is nightmare and death—"a chain of victims"; both war and drugs reduce people to less than human, destroy their dreams, and annihilate their values.

A FLAG FOR SUNRISE

First published: 1981
Type of work: Novel

Americans abroad precipitate or are swept up in events that they will never fully understand but which will either consume or transform them.

An ambitious novel set in the fictional Central American country of Tecan, *A Flag for Sunrise* attacks United States interference in the economy, politics, and culture of Latin American countries. Its title derives from Emily Dickinson's question, "Sunrise, hast thou a flag for me?"—an unspoken plea by Stone's characters as they pursue something beyond themselves, a new vision to salute tomorrow. The novel continually draws parallels with the horrors and fiascoes of Vietnam through the memories of the central observer, Frank Holliwell, onetime Central Intelligence Agency (CIA) operative, now a wandering professor. It asks what blood price Americans pay daily, the distant, violent human cost of tabletop salt or sugar. The novel brought Stone the *Los Angeles Times* Book Prize, the John Dos Passos Prize for literature, the American Academy and Institute of Arts and Letters Award, and nominations for the Pulitzer Prize, the American Book Award, the National Book Critics Circle Award, and the PEN/Faulkner Award.

By exploring the fates of Americans whose lives become entangled in Tecanecan politics, Stone sums up the diverse motives that draw Americans into conflicts which he believes are none of their business and which they only vaguely understand. Characters include the bored and frustrated Roman Catholic nun, the beautiful and näive Sister Justin Feeney; the burned-out drifter, anthropologist Frank Holliwell, a would-be romantic, who only feels alive when involved in the mystery of conflicts in the threatening and oppressive tropics; and the aggressively paranoid Pablo Tabor, a demented killer who runs guns to Tecanecan revolutionaries. CIA agents, a Gnostic whiskey priest, a crazed Mennonite, journalists, an international jeweler, and resort developers suggest the multiplicity of reasons that have led to U.S. involvement in countries such as Nicaragua and El Salvador. Stone also convincingly examines the internal weaknesses of such countries that make chaos and political expediency normal.

The basic plot lines move the separate lives of different characters inexorably toward one another and toward death. The nun, ordered to close her failed mission and to return to the United States, yet "hungry for absolutes," volunteers to care for the revolutionary wounded and, after a very brief moment of glory, is senselessly battered to death by a crazed Tecanecan lieutenant, who feels justified in wiping out hippies and Communists but is disturbed by Sister Justin's final words: "Behold the handmaid of the Lord."

Pablo, after a rampage of killing, is convinced he has finally found his destiny in the ancient Indian place of sacrifice, a field of blood called "the place of the skull," where hideous ancient bloodlust still takes its toll. The toll is exacted through a lunatic Mennonite who murders children, through armed warriors destroying one another in the name of fleeting political enthusiasms, and through CIA interference in local concerns.

Holliwell, together with Pablo on a small boat, feels "alone and lost, in utter darkness without friend or faction . . . a frightening place—the point he had been working toward since the day he had come south . . . his natural, self-appointed place." With illusions stripped away, the animal within dominates, and what Holliwell had thought an aberration of nature proves normal. Like Faust, he looks to the sunrise, "where Christ's blood steams in the firmament! One drop of blood will save me," but the blood shed there reveals only "another victim of ignorance and fear," with humankind "the joke on one another" and any universal design dark and destructive.

The outsiders, as Holliwell discovers, have "no business down there." Only the revolutionaries seem to know what they are doing, and they are betrayed, tortured, and killed. Stone's final image of this world is the cold, hostile environment of the sea: at times delicate and beautiful but always predatory—the cold, gray, unfeeling monsters of the deep always at hand and always feeding. The darkest elements of William Shakespeare's *The Tempest* echo in the background.

CHILDREN OF LIGHT

First published: 1986
Type of work: Novel

Degraded and disillusioned by the Hollywood dream, an actress and screenwriter undergoing midlife crises seek unsuccessfully to recapture the romance and idealism of their youth.

Originally conceived of as *Death and the Lover,* the title *Children of Light* is uttered by Lee Verger to refer to herself and her lover, Gordon Walker. Verger is an actress of unfulfilled promise whose incredible presence and intensity are enhanced by her "dark, blue saintly . . . secret eyes." She and Walker are the filmgoing generation, sitting in darkness, high on cocaine or ecstacy, staring at a lighted screen, which becomes their only reality. Walker, once a Shakespearean actor, now a Hollywood writer, writes a screenplay of Kate Chopin's *The Awakening* (1899) and, after his wife's desertion, goes to Bahia Honda, Mexico, to see it in production.

His real interest, however, is seeing his old flame, Lee Verger. Verger, in turn, projected by her screen role into the marital and personal conflicts of Chopin's Creole character Edna Pontellier, acts out that talented woman's terrible stress as her own reality, giving up her medical treatment because it interferes with her acting; driving away her psychiatrist husband with her schizoid projects; puzzling over the trauma, inner conflicts, and turmoil that would lead the fictive character to suicide; and merging with that character as she reenacts the suicide/drowning, first for the camera and then in private for herself and her lover. The image is like that of Plato's cave allegory: The reality is elsewhere; the shadows on the screen are but projections of light, distorted and fake.

As children of light, Verger and Gordon cannot distinguish between true relationships and those projected in their art. The film world around them is a schizophrenic one of pretense, masks, and lies. Walker, the nihilist, remembers his role of King Lear as the most intense and meaningful time of his life, for he could lose himself in the mad king's vision of reality, rave against the elements, and triumph on stage. Verger, an idealist at heart, turns back to her role of Rosalind as the projected image that best captures what she would like to be but is not.

Unlike those roles, in which the microcosm of the stage provided a philosophy and a solid base for understanding character and act, the "real" Walker and Verger have lost touch with their inner realities and have buried themselves in drugs, fantasies, sex, and a wealthy lifestyle that leaves them restless, unhappy, and unfulfilled. Alienated from their marital partners, their children, and their art, they have for too long sought escape in cocaine and alcohol, and their bodies and minds bear too heavily the weight of this bitter solace.

Verger's smile quivers "between drollery and madness" as she faces the emptiness and degradation of Hollywood success and struggles to please director, producer, and press and to deal with sexual advances, blackmail, and threats, while attempting to make this one film her triumph over the mundane and the vulgar. For Walker, recapturing his bittersweet past romance with Verger and reenacting the days when they were young and fearless together can help him recapture a sense of who he was and what he can still be. When the couple escape to the distant mountain retreat of their past, their would-be religious epiphany (complete with storm, stigmata, and Gadarene swine) turns to muck.

Verger, like the mad Ophelia, understands the degree of her alienation from Walker, but she is no longer able to cope with the harshness of that reality and yields to her "immortal longings." She is a broken person for whom nothing remains. Walker, in contrast, ever the survivor—no matter the cost—asserts that living is better than dying and so returns to family, home, and shoddy career. A woman, echoing Shakespeare's Viola, has the final say: "Men have died from time to time and worms have eaten them, but not for love."

Stone denies that this novel is an attack on filmmaking per se and argues instead that it is a political study of how the United States works, with Hollywood's pretenses and self-delusions merely reflecting the larger dishonesty of American culture. Its examination of the onset of schizophrenia is unquestionably a coming to terms through art with his own devastating childhood experiences with his mother's pathology.

OUTERBRIDGE REACH

First published: 1992
Type of work: Novel

Corporate American failures weigh heavily on individuals like Owen Browne, whose pursuit of the American Dream turns to ashes because his dreams are false.

Outerbridge Reach, its title a reference to one of the New York/New Jersey channels, departs from Stone's normal crew of drug users and dropouts to focus instead on a world of junk bonds, cooked books, and shell games in which corrupt business practices (substandard materials and shoddy workmanship) endanger customers. Stone sets corporate dreams against corporate realities, as protagonist Owen Browne determines to test himself and advertise his company, Altan Marina, only to find himself not worthy, his dreams ashes, and the company on which he has set his hopes taking a dive (its CEO having already mysteriously disappeared).

A youthful success for whom combat provided a clear-cut sense of purpose, commitment, and vision, at midlife Browne, writing advertising copy for a yacht brokerage in Connecticut, feels empty and lost, estranged from his wife and daughter, unhappy with his work. The yacht race challenge to single-handedly sail around the world provides him a chance to relive the excitement of his navy days and to regain respect. Although he lacks extended solitary sailing experience, he fools himself into believing, against all odds, that winning the race will restore his youth, win back his family, and reinvigorate his working life.

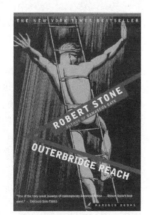

Although his daughter finds his actions frightening and doomed, his wife of twenty years, Anne, who comes from a nautical family and has a much more realistic understanding of the difficulties that Owen will face than he does, supports his plans. Yet, she is contemptuous of his occupation (Stone makes much of the educational and class differences that separate this married couple) and fascinated by documentary filmmaker Ron Strickland. Strickland's job is to create an effective advertising documentary with shots of Browne's preparation and voyage (through strategically placed cameras shipboard). Strickland, who often denigrates his subjects, plans to expose the emptiness of Browne's upper-middle-class life. The structure of the novel alternates between the Brownes and the filmmaker.

At sea, Browne listens to biblical stories of betrayals and the Morse code messages of a South African adolescent, "Mad Max," whose blindness Stone turns into a metaphor for the human condition. A storm off the coast of Argentina makes Browne realize that, by substituting plastic for wood, his company has doomed him to failure. His mast breaking up and further sailing impossible, he anchors off a small South Atlantic island, its bleached whale bones and the decaying homes of nineteenth century whalers evocative of the works of Herman Melville. His failed satellite contact hides his true position and suggests to those back home that he is ahead of the competition, not dead in the water. He cannot morally maintain this deception, however, as his two nautical logs (one fact, one lies) confirm. His dreams unrealized, his self-respect gone, he steps overboard as his ship sails slowly on. Ironically, Strickland, despite having fallen in love with Anne, employs his art to defend Browne as doing his best against difficult odds. Anne, who considers making the voyage herself as grist for a novel, asserts that the ocean sums up existence.

DAMASCUS GATE

First published: 1998
Type of work: Novel

An American novelist investigating the Jerusalem Syndrome, a tendency of newcomers to the city toward fanatical religious acts, chases an apocalyptic conspiracy that proves most deadly.

The title *Damascus Gate* refers to an ancient stone city gate, connecting Jewish and Muslim sectors of Jerusalem near sacred sites hotly contested by three faiths. That Jerusalem has incited religious and ethnic hatreds for centuries makes it the perfect setting for a millennium religious thriller in which ancient spiritual strictures, promises, and passions are reconfigured through explosive New Age sensibilities. While eruditely exploring the religious foundations of major religions, sects, and cults both modern and historical, Stone builds his story around a genuine 1980's plot to destroy the Mosque of Omar.

The novel also revisits in new ways the themes that have always driven Stone's art: religious mysticism, the drug culture and counterculturalists, competing apocalyptic visions (the products of senility, hallucinogenics, and wishful thinking), and ethnic and religious hatreds exposed and carried to bloody ends as individuals seeking meaning beyond their petty fiascoes steer, almost suicidally, toward shared disaster.

Stone's key characters are mainly displaced Americans with private visions of the Holy Land. Foremost is freelance journalist Christopher Lucas, whose Jewish father and Catholic mother have prompted both skepticism and faith and thus have indirectly led him to his latest book project, a study of the Jerusalem Syndrome—an Israeli psychiatrist's term for a form of religious mania afflicting Jewish and Christian visitors to the city, a messianic longing for epiphany often expressed through intolerant missions, for example, to destroy sites sacred to opposition faiths.

Like Lucas's fictional book, *Damascus Gate* studies religious moderates transformed into extreme fanatics in Jerusalem. Lucas's search for controversial materials and his interviews with assorted locals provide the justification for a convoluted journey that twists and turns throughout the city and is sidetracked to Tel Aviv, the Gaza Strip, the Jordan River, and Mount Hebron before returning through labyrinthine streets to the Temple Mount (at the Dome of the Rock) and a conspiracy to bomb the Muslim Al-aksa Mosque there as a step toward invoking the Second Coming and the conversion of the Jews. A visit to the Israeli Holocaust museum Yad Vashem seems at first to establish a moral center, as Lucas weeps with shame at man's inhumanity to man, but after near-death experiences at the hands of both angry Arab villagers and Jewish settlers (highly exciting sequences in a novel too often bogged down in philosophical digressions), his stoned conclu-

sion is that life is like *Alice in Wonderland*—funny, but with no justice, meaning, or mercy.

Lucas makes many of his contacts for his research through expatriate American Sonia Barnes, a Sufi acolyte and cabaret singer whose mixed-race parents (black/white) raised her as a communist in Cuba and whose relief agency work in Third World hot spots has brought her assorted friends with diverse causes. Idealistic and hopeful, despite having seen humankind at its worst globally, she seem free spirited, acting humanely where possible, hoping for a true mystical experience but finding it too often a drug high. Eclectic and syncretic in her life and beliefs, she is Lucas's guide and anchor. Her recurring motif is a song—"If you want to hear my song, you have to come with me"—and he does. Sonia lives with her Sufi master, a respected, elderly New Yorker whose death strengthens her connection with a cult concocted by a drug-driven jazz pianist, Raziel (Razz) Melker.

The son of a wealthy American congressman, Melker, formerly a junkie, a yeshiva student, and a member of Jews for Jesus, is now a mysterian, a Lurrianic Kabbalist for whom "Everything is Torah"—that is, truth is a river running through many faiths. The serpent goddess Kundalini is his guide, and an elderly former musician from New Orleans, a manic-depressive named Adam De Kuff, could be the new messiah (with a little help from Razz and his drug epiphanies). Razz contrives the plot to bomb the Al-aksa Mosque and to establish De Kuff as the new messiah (preaching "truths" that all religions share). He is responsible for the murders of United Nations Children's Foundation employees, the lovely Irish communist idealist Nuala and her local cohort Rashid, gunrunners for their cause. Other tools in Razz's scheme are the Ericksons of the House of the Galileans, a hotbed of Protestant fanatics trying to rebuild the Herodian Temple as a confirmation of biblical prophesy. Together, the band of seekers that Raziel sets in motion numbers twelve—Stone's game to infuse every incident with layers of religious associations.

Stone raises doubts about the nature of all religious experiences, as zealous Muslims chase Jews with pitchforks, Christians employ violence to fulfill the prophecies of the Book of Revelation, and Zionist extremists contrive to reignite the 1948 war to oust Arabs from Israel. The Mossad (Israeli intelligence), the Shabak (the Israeli internal security service), the Communist Party, Cypriots, Hamas, and many other groups manipulate characters and events for disparate goals (surprisingly, Stone makes the Shabak the good guys). Lucas's wished-for romance with Sonia at an end, conspiracy routed, the Mossad pressuring him to leave, man's heart of darkness confirmed, and his new book fleshed out, Lucas, as Stone's spokesman, concludes cryptically that losing something longed for or valued is "as good as having it," since longing leads to perception, definition, and a place in the heart and mind that the trials and tribulations of an adverse universe cannot take away. Stone provides no solutions, but seeming profundities roll off the tongues of many of his characters.

Summary

Stone's novels collectively have sustained a running commentary on modern American life and mores decade by decade. Stone believes that his culturally sophisticated but streetwise stories, with their literary and philosophical allusions, abet "the awareness of ironies and continuities" and show people that "being decent is really hard and that we carry within ourselves our own worst enemy." His rootless characters, hooked on alcohol, drugs, greed, or egocentricity, become intertwined, usually in sets of three, and engage in various forms of sophistry, rationalization, equivocation, and indifference. Whether passionate or withdrawn, they are corrupt and vulnerable, their lives a juxtaposing of daily banality and exotic nightmare. His true villains are casual, feckless individuals who act without thinking or feeling, who use the loyalty and affection of others, and who survive at the cost of destruction and death. The cold and ruthless survive, and the sentimental perish; moral ambiguity prevails.

Gina Macdonald and Andrew Macdonald

Bibliography

By the Author

LONG FICTION:
A Hall of Mirrors, 1967
Dog Soldiers, 1974
A Flag for Sunrise, 1981
Children of Light, 1986

Discussion Topics

- According to the philosophy of the absurd as defined by Albert Camus and Jean-Paul Sartre, among others, the absurd hero proves his heroism by asserting or creating significance even while recognizing the absolute indifference and meaninglessness of the universe. How does this definition of heroism apply to one or more of Robert Stone's protagonists?

- Stone's recurrent imagery and even his short vignettes of strangers encountering each other in dangerous circumstances convey the underlying tensions and threats inherent in a Darwinian worldview. Illustrate this notion with images or scenes from one of Stone's stories or novels.

- Despite his foreign settings, Stone's points of reference and central characters are always American. How does this fact help readers clarify his intentions and his message?

- What virtues does Stone find in his drug culture characters? How does he use these virtues to intensify his social criticism?

- Although Stone is not a comic writer, he regularly employs black humor, and his characters are sometimes caught up in somewhat comic situations. Find two examples to illustrate this point.

- Provide two examples of Stone's use of Shakespearean references in his works. What do these examples suggest about his reasons for making such references?

- Stone refers to philosophies and concepts that he expects his readers to know or learn about. Pick one of them—for example, Sufist or Kabbalist philosophies in *Damascus Gate*—and find out more about it. How does this background information help you better understand what is going on?

Robert Stone

Outerbridge Reach, 1992
Damascus Gate, 1998
Bay of Souls, 2003

SHORT FICTION:
Bear and His Daughter, 1997

SCREENPLAYS:
WUSA, 1970
Who'll Stop the Rain, 1978 (with Judith Roscoe)

About the Author

Bell, Millicent. "Fiction Chronicle." *Partisan Review* 66, no. 3 (1999): 417-430.

Finn, James. "The Moral Vision of Robert Stone: The Transcendent in the Muck of History." *Commonweal* 120, no. 19 (November 5, 1993): 9-14.

Fredrickson, Robert S. "Robert Stone's Decadent Leftists." *Papers on Language and Literature* 32, no. 3 (Summer, 1996): 315-334.

_____. "Robert Stone's Opium of the People: Religious Ambivalence in *Damascus Gate.*" *Papers on Language and Literature* 36, no. 1 (Winter, 2000): 42-57.

Halkin, Hillel. "The Jerusalem Syndrome." *The New Republic* 218, no. 21 (May 25, 1998): 29-32.

Leonard, John. "Blame It on Jerusalem." *Tikkun* 13, no. 5 (September/October, 1998): 71-73.

Pritchard, William H. "Actual Fiction." *Hudson Review* 50, no. 4 (Winter, 1998): 656-664.

Solotaroff, Robert. *Robert Stone.* New York: Twayne, 1994.

Stone, Robert. "An Interview with Robert Stone." Interview by David Pink and Chuck Lewis. *Salmagundi* 108 (Fall, 1995): 117-139.

Weber, Bruce. "An Eye for Danger." *The New York Times Magazine,* January 19, 1992, 6, 19-24.

HARRIET BEECHER STOWE

Born: Litchfield, Connecticut
June 14, 1811
Died: Hartford, Connecticut
July 1, 1896

Stowe is widely recognized as the most important writer of antislavery fiction; she shaped the genre for future antislavery writers.

Library of Congress

BIOGRAPHY

Harriet Beecher was born in Litchfield, Connecticut, on June 14, 1811, the seventh child of Lyman and Roxana Foote Beecher. Two years after her mother's death in 1816, Harriet's father married Harriet Porter of Portland, Maine. Lyman Beecher, a minister in the tradition of eighteenth century preacher Jonathan Edwards, who had attempted to breathe life into old Calvinism, dominated the household. Daily family worship and religious instruction shaped the lives of all the Beecher children. All seven brothers who reached maturity became ministers, according to their father's wishes, and the girls in the family were expected to marry ministers. Because of her father's focus on his sons' mental and intellectual preparation as future ministers, Harriet often felt neglected. Even on family activities, such as gathering and stacking firewood, Lyman Beecher was known to say that he wished she were a boy.

When Harriet was attending Litchfield Female Academy, she wrote her first essay, on the question "Can the immortality of the soul be proved by the light of nature?" It was read with those of the older students at the next exhibition. This experience of success, along with the pleasure of expressing herself freely to an extent hardly possible within her family, with so many older people holding the floor, awakened her love for writing when she was eleven.

After the death of her fiancé, Harriet's eldest sister, Catherine, opened Hartford Female Seminary together with her sister Mary. When Harriet was twelve, she was placed in the seminary under her sisters' care; as soon as she was old enough, she, too, had to assist with the teaching, a task that was a burden to her and that she did not enjoy. Catherine Beecher, who had devoted her life to female education, was said to possess the same doctrinary personality as her father, and life under her care was not a happy experience for Harriet.

In 1832, nine of the Beechers reunited and moved to Cincinnati, then the border settlement to the West. While her father was excited about the possibility of converting the West, Harriet perceived Cincinnati to be simply an uncouth town. Catherine founded and was running the Western Female Institute, and Harriet had to fall in line again, much against her own wishes. Her unhappiness became so severe that she fell ill repeatedly from the drudgery of her work and the depression accompanying it. It was there that she first visited a plantation in neighboring Kentucky and was introduced directly to issues of slavery, because in Cincinnati there were many freed and fugitive slaves.

She soon met Calvin Ellis Stowe and his wife Eliza, who became a good friend. After Eliza's death, Harriet consoled the widower, meeting with him more and more frequently until, on January 6, 1836, she found herself marrying him—without feeling much emotion. Soon her days were filled with caring for her six children who survived childhood, the last born in 1850. Constant financial problems prompted her to support her family by writing, and she published her first writings in the *Western Monthly Magazine*. She was contributing sketches to the New York *Evangelist, The Ladies' Repository,* and *Godey's Lady's Book*. Amid the household clutter and noise, she wrote her stories, mostly domestic fiction, later collected in *The Mayflower* (1843). The parlor was reserved for Mr. Stowe, who was annoyed at intrusions upon his studies. In 1850, Calvin Stowe received an appointment to Brunswick College in Maine and moved his family to New England.

After the political climate surrounding slavery changed, and the seizure and return of fugitive slaves to their owners was even preached from Boston pulpits, Harriet Beecher Stowe set out to write an antislavery story after being given an advance of one hundred dollars. Despite a long New England winter, a chaotic household, and her exhaustion from yet another birth and nursing of a child, she began poring over antislavery literature. Her main source of information was probably Theodore Weld's *American Slavery as It Is* (1839), a collection of excerpts from legal documents, advertisements, and statements from slaveholders. *Uncle Tom's Cabin* first appeared as a serial in the *National Era* (the first installment on June 5, 1851), and when it appeared in book form in 1852, fifty thousand copies were sold within eight weeks; within a year, a million copies were sold in England and the United States combined. Her second antislavery novel, *Dred: A Tale of the Great Dismal Swamp*, followed in 1856.

There never seemed to be enough time for Harriet Beecher Stowe to consider writing as art. Writing books seems to have been a substitute for the pulpit of her male minister family—a means for a moral end, not an end in itself. *The Minister's Wooing* (1859) has a religious theme that was well received during the years of public distress that accompanied the financial panic of 1857. *The Pearl of Orr's Island* (1862) is dominated by a longing nostalgia for the primitive Puritan society.

In 1862, in anticipation of her husband's retirement, Stowe moved once more—to the city of Hartford, Connecticut, where she had a large house built that would force her for the following ten years to write at a furious pace in order to keep up with the bills. After 1870, her daily load was lightened somewhat. The large, expensive house

in Hartford was sold, and a smaller one, cozy and adequate, was purchased. The Stowes spent the winters in Florida between 1869 and 1884. In 1873, Stowe published *Palmetto Leaves*, sketches describing her winter residence near Mandarin, Florida. Another novel, *Poganuc People*, with autobiographical undertones, was written for serialization in the *Christian Union* and appeared in book form in 1878. After her husband's death on August 6, 1886, Stowe began writing her testament, with her son Charley's help. Until her death on July 1, 1896, she lived once again near her father's house in Litchfield, Connecticut, surrounded by her family.

ANALYSIS

Stowe began her writing career with small sketches and stories that earned her a modest place among the minor writers. They were examples of the domestic fiction popular in many of the magazines of the time, especially in ladies' magazines and gift annuals. The characteristic elements of the sketch, with its looseness in plot and characterization, is also employed in her longer stories. Her stories and sketches are informed by personal details owed to her own experiences and to her New England background, which yielded a rich element of local color to her works.

Another earmark of most of her mature writing is also apparent in her early sketches: the need to participate in the moral debates of her time. With her story "Let Every Man Mind His Own Business," collected in *The Mayflower*, she hoped to contribute to the temperance crusade. Another important theme, the pathetic death of a perfect child, which stands at the core of *Uncle Tom's Cabin*, was already apparent in "Uncle Tim" and "Little Edward."

Her habit of writing sketches for magazines or periodicals that paid by the page, which she could write between her housekeeping chores, shaped her style. She did not cultivate the copybook English of the *Godey's Lady's Book* but wrote as she thought and talked. Because she stuck closely to topics that concerned and interested her, there was a naturalness and almost a colloquial quality about her style. Because she was always pressed for time, she never rewrote passages, corrected punctuation and grammar, or practiced the time-consuming task of stylistic refinement. Content, for her, was decidedly more important than form. She considered herself the lucky recipient of inspiration, and very often she transformed visual images directly into literary text, which is thus descriptive and lacking the proper qualities of plot.

UNCLE TOM'S CABIN

First published: 1851-1852, serial; 1852, book
Type of work: Novel

Tom, a slave, is separated from his family and sold to a plantation in the South, where he loses his life because of the abuses of his brutal owner.

Uncle Tom's Cabin was Stowe's first novel. Initially printed by installments in the *National Era*, an antislavery weekly published in Washington, D.C., from June 5, 1851, to April 1, 1852, it was a best-selling book of previously unheard of proportions. It was an instant success and soon acquired fame in many parts of the world.

It is not easy, however, to make a clear judgment of the merits of *Uncle Tom's Cabin.* Those who exclude works that cater to the taste of the masses from the realm of high culture have difficulty describing its artistry in positive terms. Moreover, Stowe has been criticized for her depiction and characterization of black people, which led to numerous stereotypical and trivial imitations on the stage, in almanacs, in songs and poems, and even in paintings.

Stowe's depiction of women has often been objectionable to modern sensibilities, because her women seem to be restricted to moral issues as they play themselves out in the domestic sphere. Underlying her portrayal of black people and women is an acceptance of the power of Christianity that is alien to modern readers. These three interwoven issues, the place of women and black people and the role of Christianity, are at the core of the novel and make it a central literary and political document of the American experience in the 1850's.

If one accepts the standards set by male writers of the American tradition, which depicted masculine confrontation with nature, as exemplified in the frontier myth of the American male, Stowe's novel seems naïvely visionary, lacking in complex philosophical content, overly melodramatic, and awkwardly plotted. It was earmarked as a book for women and children. It was not until critics such as Jane Tompkins reexamined the novel that Stowe's efforts to reorganize society from a woman's point of view came to be recognized.

The book appeared amid a growing controversy over race and religion. The author wrote in reaction to the Compromise of 1850, which admitted California to the Union as a free state, abolished the slave trade in Washington, D.C., organized the New Mexico and Utah territories without prohibiting slavery, and enacted the Fugitive Slave Law, which forced Northerners to assist in returning fugitive slaves to their owners. Although Stowe was hardly the first to point to slavery's destruction of both black and white families, her novel presented a very effective fusion of the sentimental novel with the rhetoric of an antislavery polemic.

Tom, a broad-chested, strong slave who lives with his wife and children in a small hut near the house of his master in Kentucky, is sold by his master (against the will of the master's wife) in order to pay off debts. Tom is sold "down the river" and expects the worst: to work on a Southern plantation. On the boat, he meets Evangelina (Eva), a perfect, angelic child. In her character, the tradition of children in sentimental literature and the ministerial leader of evangelical social reform are combined into a childlike female Christ figure. She persuades her father, Augustine St. Clare, to buy Tom, who is bought as Evangelina's playmate and keeper. Evangelina dies and makes her father promise to free his slaves, but before he signs the papers, St. Clare dies and thus inadvertently sets in motion Tom's demise.

Tom is sold to Simon Legree, who tortures and finally kills Tom because he is unwilling to betray two fellow slaves, Cassey and Emmelina, who fled from their brutal, sexually abusive master. Tom's death is a direct result of his aggressive nonviolence and makes him a black Christ figure. Numerous subplots and their respective characters depict various aspects and views of slavery and miscegenation.

SUMMARY

Uncle Tom's Cabin was so captivating and moving to its readers that its more subversive attacks on white male hegemony went largely unnoticed. Furthermore, positing the spiritual superiority of women and black people was not enough to disrupt the status quo. Coupled with the lack of a clear and intellectually convincing argument for the moral and intellectual identity between the races and genders, the focus on the religious vision of Christ as mother overshadows the book's possible political impact. By postulating the moral and spiritual superiority of the two suppressed groups, women and black people, instead of a vision of equal adulthood, Stowe marred the political impact of the book.

Karin A. Wurst

BIBLIOGRAPHY

By the Author

LONG FICTION:
Uncle Tom's Cabin: Or, Life Among the Lowly, 1852
Dred: A Tale of the Great Dismal Swamp, 1856
The Minister's Wooing, 1859
Agnes of Sorrento, 1862
The Pearl of Orr's Island, 1862
Oldtown Folks, 1869
Pink and White Tyranny, 1871
My Wife and I, 1871
We and Our Neighbors, 1875
Poganuc People, 1878

SHORT FICTION:
The Mayflower: Or, Sketches of Scenes and Characters of the Descendants of the Pilgrims, 1843
Sam Lawson's Oldtown Fireside Stories, 1872

POETRY:
Religious Poems, 1867

NONFICTION:
A Key to Uncle Tom's Cabin, 1853
Sunny Memories of Foreign Lands, 1854
Lady Byron Vindicated, 1870
Palmetto Leaves, 1873

CHILDREN'S LITERATURE:
First Geography for Children, 1833 (as Catharine Stowe)

DISCUSSION TOPICS

- Does *Uncle Tom's Cabin* levy blame on the North as well as on the South?

- What qualities in *Uncle Tom's Cabin* give this book so much more impact than all other antislavery literature of the time (including Harriet Beecher Stowe's own *Dred: A Tale of the Great Dismal Swamp*)?

- Is it profitable to argue about the literary merits of *Uncle Tom's Cabin*?

- Stowe wrote several novels set in New England. What are her preoccupations in these books?

- Had she lived in the twenty-first century, Stowe might very well have chosen to be something other than a novelist. On the basis of the interests displayed in her books, what occupation might she have pursued?

MISCELLANEOUS:
The Oxford Harriet Beecher Stowe Reader, 1999 (Joan D. Hedrick, editor)

About the Author

Adams, John R. *Harriet Beecher Stowe.* Updated ed. Boston: Twayne, 1989.

Boydston, Jeanne, Mary Kelley, and Anne Margolis. *The Limits of Sisterhood: The Beecher Sisters on Women's Rights and Woman's Sphere.* Chapel Hill: University of North Carolina Press, 1988.

Cognard-Black, Jennifer. *Narrative in the Professional Age: Transatlantic Readings of Harriet Beecher Stowe, George Eliot, and Elizabeth Stuart Phelps.* New York: Routledge, 2004.

Donovan, Josephine. *"Uncle Tom's Cabin": Evil, Affliction, and Redemptive Love.* Boston: Twayne, 1991.

Hedrick, Joan D. *Harriet Beecher Stowe: A Life.* New York: Oxford University Press, 1994.

Rosenthal, Debra J., ed. *A Routledge Literary Sourcebook on Harriet Beecher Stowe's "Uncle Tom's Cabin."* New York: Routledge, 2004.

Stowe, Charles Edward, comp. *Life of Harriet Beecher Stowe.* 1889. Reprint. Detroit: Gale Research, 1967.

Sundquist, Eric J., ed. *New Essays on "Uncle Tom's Cabin."* New York: Cambridge University Press, 1986.

Weinstein, Cindy, ed. *The Cambridge Companion to Harriet Beecher Stowe.* New York: Cambridge University Press, 2004.

Peter Simon

WILLIAM STYRON

Born: Newport News, Virginia
June 11, 1925

An important post-World War II novelist, Styron is considered one of the finest writers to follow in the footsteps of the great southern writer William Faulkner.

BIOGRAPHY

William Styron was born in Newport News, Virginia, on June 11, 1925, the son of William Clark and Pauline Styron. Styron's roots in the South are deep and can be traced back to the seventeenth century. He grew up steeped in stories of the Civil War and of its battlefields. Raised in Hilton Village, a semirural community several miles from Newport News, he went to segregated schools and lived in a family with black servants. His father worked in shipbuilding in Newport News. His mother, who developed cancer soon after his birth, remained an invalid for eleven years, dying in 1939, after Styron's sophomore year at Morrison High School. Around that time, he published his first story (now lost) in the school newspaper.

Styron was an active student—he was president of his sophomore class and manager of the football team—but his teachers thought he lacked discipline, and he was sent to the Christchurch School, an Episcopal preparatory school near Urbana, Virginia. In this small school of fifty students, he enjoyed the atmosphere of an encouraging extended family. He wrote for the school newspaper and yearbook, sailed, and played basketball. Although he attended chapel every day and church on Sunday, he also took up drinking, one of the traditional activities of a Virginia gentleman.

In 1942, Styron entered Davidson College, a Presbyterian institution near Charlotte, North Car-

olina. His father thought that the University of Virginia, known for its rowdy drinking parties, would be inappropriate for his son, an indifferent student. Styron joined the college newspaper and literary magazine, and he rid himself of his Tidewater accent after fellow students made fun of it.

At eighteen, Styron joined the Navy, expecting to train as an officer, but he was transferred to Duke University. There, he attended classes but was still under military discipline. Duke was a traditional campus, strict about matters of dress, with coeds wearing white gloves on off-campus dates. Again Styron proved a mediocre student, and he was put on active duty by the end of 1944.

After boot camp, Styron performed various duties and spent a few months guarding a prison camp. The dropping of the atomic bombs on Japan spared him the experience of World War II combat, and he returned to the postwar liberated atmosphere of the Duke campus in 1946. In this invigorating environment, he began to develop as a writer of fiction, winning praise from teachers and publishing several stories in the college magazine while also attending writers' conferences.

In 1947, Styron moved to New York, securing a job as an editor at McGraw-Hill, where he read reams of unsolicited manuscripts. As lax an employee as he had been a student, Styron was fired after six months. He provides a vivid portrait of himself as an aspiring writer in the character of Stingo in his novel *Sophie's Choice* (1979). Having taken a writing class at the New School for Social Research taught by Hiram Haydn, a book editor in New York, Styron began to conceive his first novel, *Lie Down in Darkness* (1951). Almost always a slow writer subject to writer's block, Styron moved back to Durham for a brief period before finishing the novel in the Flatbush section of Brooklyn and in Valley Cottage, near Nyack, New York.

In 1951, Styron was recalled to active duty in the Marines during the Korean War, and the episode became the basis of his fine novella *The Long March* (1956). His first novel had been hailed by critics, who saw him as the successor to the great southern novelist William Faulkner. About this time, he also met his future wife, Rose Burgender, and traveled in Europe. He worked on a novella he never completed (about his experiences as a prison guard) and on a novel set in Europe that was eventually published as *Set This House on Fire* (1960).

In 1953, Styron moved to Roxbury, Connecticut. He married Rose Burgender, with whom he had two daughters, Susanna (born in 1955) and Paolo (born in 1958). Active as a reviewer and a superb writer of nonfiction, Styron began work in 1962 on his most controversial novel, *The Confessions of Nat Turner* (1967), which dared to present a slave's experience not only in his own words but also within his consciousness. In spite of fierce attacks, mainly by African American writers, the novel enjoyed enormous critical and popular success, winning Styron the Pulitzer Prize in 1968.

Styron did not publish another novel until *Sophie's Choice*, in which he extended his study of human oppression to the Holocaust—another daring feat of the imagination that again brought him accolades and criticism. He also continued to work on a novel based on his experience in the Marines.

Despite his success, Styron suffered a long, desperate session of depression in 1985. An account of this episode was published by *Vanity Fair* in 1989 as an extended essay. Both *Vanity Fair* and Styron received great volumes of mail from grateful readers suffering from depression. In 1990, Random House published Styron's extended essay in a book titled *Darkness Visible*; it won critical praise and became a best seller.

ANALYSIS

Styron is a master of modern literary style. He has been compared to Faulkner because, more than any of his contemporaries, Styron has a feeling for rhythms of language that seem to embody the speech of a whole region, a lush, romantic feeling for nature and for human relationships. Styron is a painstaking writer, often spending a day per-

fecting a single page. Yet his prose flows so gracefully that his enormous effort usually remains invisible. This is especially true of *Lie Down in Darkness* and *The Confessions of Nat Turner*, both of which appear to be seamless narratives, stories that unfold without a break or flaw in style.

If there is a fault in Styron's style, some critics would say it is his perfectionism. He has been criticized for exercising too much control over his narratives, producing novels that are too meticulous, too polished. This kind of exquisite technique robs his work of a certain rough-edged life, an unruliness that should overtake the writer and ride him, so to speak. Styron's sense of language, in other words, is too precious; it can actually get in the way of the life he is trying to portray.

This tendency is perhaps most evident in *The Confessions of Nat Turner*, in which Turner's consciousness is transparently Styron's—that is, Turner is endowed with Styron's gift for language and much of Styron's literary sensibility. Some critics, however, have argued that this is precisely Styron's achievement: endowing characters such as Turner with an integrity and articulateness that is the equal of their author's. From this point of view, Styron's gorgeous vocabulary ennobles his characters and allows them to speak on a higher literary level that is the only way to reveal their full humanity and complexity. There is certainly ample precedent for Styron's sophisticated technique in Faulkner's *As I Lay Dying* (1930), in which the interior monologues use a highly elevated and baroque language to register not merely what the characters are thinking but also what they are as human beings.

Styron is also an excellent observer of social manners. In both his fiction and nonfiction, he is a shrewd reporter, rendering not only the facts of life also but how those facts are received by the senses and turned into feelings. He is a great poet of consciousness who bases his flights of rhetoric on a realistic notation of the data of life.

One of the great themes of Styron's fiction is life in the American South. *Lie Down in Darkness* surveys the modern South by focusing on the life and death of Peyton Loftis, a young woman growing up in a region still recovering from the devastation of the Civil War—psychologically more than physically. The novel suggests that World War I and the lost generation—those young Americans whose lives were interrupted by war, some of whom stayed in Europe—proved to be a crisis for those who stayed home as well, such as Peyton's father, Milton, whose lack of purpose and hollow life as a southern gentleman deprive Peyton of basic beliefs, a foundation for her future. She tells her father, in fact, that it is her generation that is lost.

The Confessions of Nat Turner, on the other hand, is Styron's self-confessed attempt to imagine what it must have been like for a slave in Virginia to revolt against his masters. As a descendant of a slave-owning class and as the product of a segregated society, Styron wrote a novel that aimed not only to understand the past but also to effect a kind of reconciliation between the races in the present. His treatment of Nat Turner as a brilliant man, a kind of genius with a gift for language equal to Styron's own, has been perceived by many critics, though by no means all, as a brilliant effort to bridge the gap between past and present. As the African American writer James Baldwin said of the novel, "He has begun the common history—ours."

Sophie's Choice represents a continuation of the themes of *The Confessions of Nat Turner.* The narrator, Stingo, is a white southerner trying to come to terms with Sophie, a survivor of the Holocaust. The novel contains passages on southern and European history, positing a historical identity that is not meant to minimize the differences between cultures but to reveal the overarching experiences, from slavery to the Holocaust, that have shaped the modern world.

Many of Styron's stories have been about survival and suicide. In writing a book about his own suicidal depression, *Darkness Visible* (1990), Styron admits that he did not realize how much these themes formed a pattern in his work, or how drinking has often been a part of this pattern, as it is in the behavior of Milton Loftis, a lawyer with a romantic, literary sensibility similar to Styron's own. Drinking immobilizes Loftis. It eases the pain of his lack of action and the harsh criticisms of his puritanical wife, and it becomes a way to negotiate the boring routines of daily existence. Loftis sees flaws in himself and in his family, but he is fatally blind to what his own daughter needs, because of his adoring, even incestuous, longing for her. Drink becomes the only lubricant that keeps him going. Though Styron has survived and become much more successful than his characters, there is a brooding, depressive sense of existence in his prose, a sense that seems related to his own titanic writer's blocks and his inability to complete work. He has begun and abandoned several novels.

In *This Quiet Dust, and Other Writings* (1982) and in *Darkness Visible,* Styron has proven himself a writer of superb nonfiction prose. In both the essay form and the memoir, his precise command of language and his candor make for compelling reading. Perhaps the best example of this is "This Quiet Dust," an account of his trip to survey the site of Nat Turner's rebellion. The essay provides a striking counterpoint to the novel, for the essay reveals not the mind of the slave but the mind of the writer approaching his material, wondering how he can recapture the past and do justice to a figure who has troubled and excited him for more than twenty years.

LIE DOWN IN DARKNESS

First published: 1951
Type of work: Novel

A woman's body is brought from New York City to her Virginia home after her suicide, and the story of her life and of her family is told in a series of flashbacks.

Lie Down in Darkness made Styron's reputation as a novelist. It was a brilliant first novel that showcased a writer in full control of his language, which fit into a perfectly shaped story, beginning on the day Peyton Loftis's body is being returned to her Virginia home. Styron describes the scene, the funeral cortege, and the characters—Peyton's father, Milton, her mother, Helen, and Milton's mistress, Dolly Bonner—who will dominate the story. It is a long day of mourning, yet Styron manages to break up the day with poignant flashbacks that gradually explain the events that led to Peyton's suicide.

Milton is inconsolable over the loss of his daughter. His one hope is that his estranged wife, Helen, will come back to him and repair their relationship, which he now believes is all that he has left in life. Helen does not even want to attend the funeral, let alone readmit Milton into her life. Through a series of flashbacks, it is revealed that Milton had always doted on his daughter and resented his wife's harsh criticism of his drinking and that Helen has been jealous of Peyton and rejected her in favor of her ailing daughter, Maudie.

Nothing Peyton does seems right in Helen's eyes. When Peyton accidentally drops Maudie, Helen accuses her of doing it deliberately. When a teenage Peyton is given a drink at a party by her father, Helen treats Peyton like a slut and excoriates Milton for turning his daughter into an alcoholic like himself. Although Helen is overly severe, she is largely right about Milton's behavior. Her unbending personality, however, is entirely devoid of humanity.

The novel's climax arrives in a flashback relating the catastrophe of Peyton's wedding. She has been away from home for years, refusing to see her mother, but she is coaxed home by her father. He has stopped drinking and become reconciled with Helen, a development that has come about partly as a result of Maudie's death. The patterns of Peyton's childhood reassert themselves at the wedding—only this time, it is Peyton encouraging her father to drink. She hurts him terribly when she confesses that she thinks he is a jerk and that she has come home only to play a role that will please her parents. She is being honest but very cruel. She has become a rather hopeless figure. She tells her father that she is a part of a lost generation because his generation has provided no substantial legacy, no repository of values that might guide her in a new, uncertain world.

In many ways, the characters of this novel are unpleasant and irredeemable. Yet they do struggle to right themselves, and Styron's deft use of flashbacks, in which the reader's knowledge of the characters increases incrementally, is riveting.

THE CONFESSIONS OF NAT TURNER

First published: 1967
Type of work: Novel

This compelling and controversial first-person story narrates the most successful slave revolt in American history.

When *The Confessions of Nat Turner* first appeared, it was acclaimed as breakthrough both in fiction and in race relations. A white southerner, steeped in the history of his region, had boldly entered the mind of a black slave, according him the dignity of an articulate voice and making him into a modern hero. Certainly, Styron's Turner is cruel in his taking of close to sixty lives, but he is nevertheless the poet of the aspirations of a people. Early reviews lauded the language and the sympathy with which Styron presented the story.

Soon, though, a group of African American writers attacked the book, accusing Styron of distorting history, of co-opting their hero, and of demeaning Turner by endowing him with love for one of his victims, a young white woman. These critics saw Styron as usurping their history, much as white people had usurped the labor and the very lives of their ancestors. They rejected the notion that a white southerner—or any white person, for that matter—could fathom the mind of a slave.

Styron defended himself admirably, for he had made a close reading of the historical record and knew exactly where he was taking liberties with history, and he was supported by several historians. Less defensible, or at least problematic, was his decision to endow Turner with a contemporary imagination. Turner does speak in the accents of nineteenth century Virginia; he thinks very much like Styron. Yet even this seeming defect in the novel may be its major strength. Styron's point is that Turner was, in many ways, ahead of his time: This self-taught slave probably had the mind of a genius, and it would be condescending to express his thoughts in language less sophisticated than the writer's own.

Quite aside from this controversy, *The Confessions of Nat Turner* can be read as a tragic love story, of a Nat Turner who learns much from white people even as they oppress him. Styron shows that tenderness was possible between the races even under the regime of slavery—a fact the historian Eugene Genovese has corroborated in his research. By thinking of Turner as his equal, Styron was able to remove the clichés from the presentation of race in fiction. That he touched a nerve in his critics, who strongly attacked him, suggests something of the power of that love story and how it might pose a threat to those who doubt the races can reconcile.

William Styron

SOPHIE'S CHOICE

First published: 1979
Type of work: Novel

Set in post-World War II Brooklyn, Sophie's
Choice *is about the maturing of a young
novelist who confronts the Holocaust in his
fascination with Sophie, a concentration camp
survivor.*

Sophie's Choice is Styron's most ambitious novel. It
contains the major themes of his previous fiction,
embodying his loves of the South and of literature,
his experience of war, and his quest to write a major
novel summing up the significant issues of his age.
His narrator, Stingo, is a callow youth who is living
in Brooklyn, as Styron did, trying to write fiction.
Stingo's sexual experience has been limited, and
he finds himself attracted to a beautiful Polish
woman, Sophie, a survivor of a concentration
camp.

It is 1947, and the incredible suffering of the
Holocaust is just beginning to be revealed and understood. The situation becomes complicated for
Stingo, who becomes the third member of a triangle when he befriends Sophie's lover, Nathan, who
is erratic and paranoic but also charismatic. Nathan flouts propriety, and his radical individualism appeals to the young Stingo, who—again, like
Styron—has fared poorly in the bureaucratic publishing world and who is looking for a way to express himself.

Sophie's behavior is puzzling to Stingo; she is
passive and willing to let Nathan abuse her. Nathan's cruelty is eventually explained in terms of
his drug addiction and mental illness. Similarly,
Sophie's willingness to be treated as a victim begins
to make sense when Stingo learns of her concentration camp experience—the way she had to make
herself available sexually to her captors, and to
make her awful choice: surrendering one of her
children to the gas ovens.

Sophie is not Jewish. In fact, her father wrote
anti-Semitic tracts. Being Polish was enough to
send her to the camps. Styron's point is an important one: Millions of non-Jews died in the camps,
and the fate of Jew and non-Jew alike is a human
tragedy that involves everyone.

Styron's decision to have Stingo narrate the
story allows him to deal with the Holocaust sensi-
tively and tactfully. His young alter ego is able to
learn gradually about these horrifying events, so
that they become a dramatic and believable part of
the novel. Yet the narrator alone does not suffice.
Styron also includes a narrator who provides essay-
like excursions into the history of the Holocaust—
a daring and perhaps not always successful addition to the novel.

Sophie's Choice is Styron's darkest vision of the
modern world. Sophie and Nathan eventually
commit suicide. Her burden of guilt is too great for
her to endure life after the war, and Nathan seems
to have chosen her for a lover to fulfill his own self-
destructive course. What redeems their lives, in a
sense, is Stingo's devotion to them, his passion to
understand what happened to them and what it
means for him. By implication, their story becomes
the writer's story, an account of why he writes, and
why others should care for lives that end in failure.

DARKNESS VISIBLE: A MEMOIR OF MADNESS

First published: 1990
Type of work: Memoir

*Styron chronicles his descent into severe
depression and explores possible reasons for it, his
treatment, and the apparent connection between
depression and creative people.*

It was in Paris in October, 1985, that Styron first realized his continuing struggle to regain his mental
equilibrium might lead to his death. He had been
fighting against a growing loss of self-esteem for
some months over the previous summer, and during that October trip to receive the Prix Mondial
Cino del Duca, which should have been a joyful
occasion, his feelings of worthlessness deepened.
He had at first ascribed his anxiety and restlessness
to alcohol withdrawal, for he had abruptly given
up whiskey and all other intoxicants the previous
June. As his moods worsened, he started to read as
much as he could on the disease of depression,
about which little was known at that time. When his
distress intensified before he had left for the Paris

trip with his wife, Rose, he had made an appointment to see a psychiatrist as soon as he returned to his home in Connecticut.

As he meditates on his own wretched mental state, Styron is reminded of the death of the existentialist writer Albert Camus and the prominence of suicide and despondency in his work. This segues into a long discussion of the suicides of the activist Abbie Hoffman and writer Primo Levi and 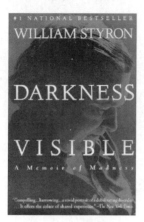 the suspected suicide of poet Randall Jarrell. Although depression afflicts an eclectic group and anyone might be a potential victim, there is some evidence to suggest that artistic types, especially poets, are unusually prone to the disease.

After returning home from Paris, Styron met with his doctor "Gold," who treated him with platitudes and large doses of drugs. He became increasingly obsessed with his own death and considered many possible methods of suicide. He disguised and then disposed of a private manuscript, rewrote his will, and attempted to write a letter of farewell but found it too difficult. Late one night, knowing he could not get through another day, he listened to the Brahms *Alto Rhapsody,* whose beauty opened his heart to all the joys that he had known in his home. The next day, he admitted himself to the hospital, in spite of the fact that his doctor had not advised it. He found the hospital a benign and stabilizing place compared to his home, with its numerous random associations, and within a few days his fantasies of self-destruction all but disappeared. Styron spent seven weeks in the hospital, and he handles his experience with such dexterity that he manages to find humor in the classes offered there, such as art therapy. More than once, he emphasizes that the disease usually runs its course, and recovery is usually possible. In his own case, he believes that the real healers were seclusion and time. This short book ends with Styron's analysis of the possible root causes of his own depression and a lovely literary illusion to Dante's *Inferno.* The memoir is marked by painful honesty and a remarkable lack of self-pity, considering the acute suffering that it recounts.

SUMMARY

Styron is the poet of human failure: Peyton Loftis kills herself, Nat Turner engages in a suicidal slave revolt, and Sophie and Nathan die in a suicide pact. In spite of these depressing stories, the author's style is uplifting, a beautiful evocation of human beings and settings. Although he himself has been subject to despair, his novels prevail in their sheer artistry. In their graceful language, they suggest that human beings are capable of grace, of a forgiveness beyond guilt. In Styron's novels, there is always the opportunity to communicate and to reconcile human conflicts, even if most such conflicts end badly.

Carl Rollyson; updated by Sheila Golburgh Johnson

BIBLIOGRAPHY

By the Author

LONG FICTION:
Lie Down in Darkness, 1951
The Long March, 1952 (serial), 1956 (book)
Set This House on Fire, 1960
The Confessions of Nat Turner, 1967
Sophie's Choice, 1979

SHORT FICTION:
A Tidewater Morning: Three Tales from Youth, 1993

DRAMA:
In the Clap Shack, pr. 1972

NONFICTION:
This Quiet Dust, and Other Writings, 1982, expanded 1993
Darkness Visible: A Memoir of Madness, 1990

About the Author

Casciato, Arthur D., and James L. W. West III. *Critical Essays on William Styron*. Boston: G. K. Hall, 1982.

Coale, Samuel. *William Styron Revisited*. Boston: Twayne, 1991.

Crane, John Kenny. *The Root of All Evil: The Thematic Unity of William Styron's Fiction*. Columbia: University of South Carolina Press, 1984.

Hadaller, James. *Gynicide: Women in the Novels of William Styron*. Madison, N.J.: Fairleigh Dickinson University Press, 1996.

Ruderman, Judith. *William Styron*. New York: Frederick Ungar, 1987.

Vice, Sue. *Holocaust Fiction: From William Styron to Binyamin Wilkomirski*. New York: Routledge, 2000.

West, James L. W., III. *William Styron: A Life*. New York: Random House, 1998.

DISCUSSION TOPICS

- How does William Styron use the theme of racism in his novels?

- Styron is considered a southern author. What are some characteristics he shares with other southern writers?

- How does Styron use historical events in his fiction?

- In *The Confessions of Nat Turner*, how does Styron arouse sympathy for his main character?

- In what ways do Styron's fictional characters reflect his own life?

GLENDON SWARTHOUT

Born: Pinckney, Michigan
April 8, 1918
Died: Scottsdale, Arizona
September 23, 1992

Swarthout's gritty, realistic novels set in the American South-west explore themes that transcend the common perception of the Western genre, revealing characters who triumph person-ally even as they suffer defeat.

Courtesy, www.glendonswarthout.com

BIOGRAPHY

Glendon Swarthout was born in Pinckney, Michigan, on April 8, 1918, the son of Fred H. and Lila (Chubb) Swarthout. He was raised and educated in Michigan, taking his A.B. in 1939 from the University of Michigan in Ann Arbor. His studies and his marriage to Kathryn Vaughn in 1940 were interrupted by the outbreak of World War II. Swarthout served in the infantry from 1943 to 1945, earning the rank of sergeant and two battle stars. After the war, he returned to his wife and to university study, this time at Michigan State University, in East Lansing, completing his M.A. in 1946. Swarthout then accepted a teaching fellowship at Michigan State. Swarthout was at the University of Maryland between 1948 and 1951. In 1951, he returned to Michigan State to accept an associate professorship in English and pursue a course of study leading to the Ph.D., which he completed in 1955. From 1951 to 1959, he was an associate professor of English at Michigan State; in 1959, the Swarthouts moved to Tempe, Arizona, where Swarthout served as a lecturer in English at Arizona State University from 1959 to 1963.

Despite the demands of a successful academic career, Swarthout was a consistently prolific and acknowledged novelist, dramatist, and writer of short stories, with sixteen novels to his credit. *Where the Boys Are* (1960), *They Came to Cordura* (1958), *Bless the Beasts and Children* (1970), and *The Shootist*

(1975) have been produced as motion pictures. Swarthout's first novel, *Willow Run* (1943), written before his stint in the infantry, established him as a writer of promise. *Willow Run* received a largely favorable review in *The New York Times Book Review*. The reviewer, Rose Feld, wrote, "Swarthout's conception of his novel is an interesting and ambitious one and his book . . . has definite rhythm and vitality." This was praise indeed for a first novel by an aspiring twenty-five-year-old writer.

After the war, Swarthout managed to keep his career as a writer alive even though he had undertaken advanced studies while supporting his family. He published short stories in such respected periodicals as *Cosmopolitan, Esquire, Collier's,* and *The Saturday Evening Post*. His efforts as a writer of short stories culminated in 1960 when he won an O. Henry Award for excellence in short fiction. The completion of his doctoral studies made it possible for him to turn again to the novel. The publication of *They Came to Cordura* brought him wide recognition and financial reward. This work was critically acclaimed and was translated into a film of the same name starring Gary Cooper. The publication of this novel marked the beginning of Swarthout's commercial success as a novelist and as a novelist whose work translates easily to the screen.

Swarthout published eleven novels from 1960 to 1979, the most successful of these and the best known to the public being *Bless the Beasts and Children* and *The Shootist,* the latter becoming the acclaimed vehicle for John Wayne's last film.

Swarthout also collaborated with his wife, Kathryn, on six books for children and young adults.

Swarthout's novels of the West appeal not only to aficionados of the Western but also to audiences as diverse as the temporal and geographic settings of his works. He was twice the recipient of the Western Writers of America Spur Award, in 1976 for *The Shootist* and in 1988 for *The Homesman* (1988). In 1991 he received the Owen Wister Award from the Western Writers of America for lifetime achievement. Other honors bestowed on him and his work include the prestigious Hopwood Award in Fiction, the O. Henry Award, and the National Society of Arts and Letters Gold Medal. More important, he produced a body of literature that has brought pleasure and insight to a generation of readers.

ANALYSIS

With the exception of *Where the Boys Are*, set in Fort Lauderdale, Florida, Swarthout's novels take place either in Michigan, where he was born and raised, or in the more spacious landscape of his adopted home in the West. Moreover, the novels tend to mirror the landscape: The ones set in the East are somewhat cribbed and confined in theme, whereas the broader backdrop of the West seems to liberate his prose and the scope of his thematic concern.

His first novel, *Willow Run*, written in 1943, reflects a United States going to war. The novel follows the story of six workers in a bomber plant who, united by ride sharing, manage to damage one another's lives during a graveyard shift filled with misunderstanding, jealousy, and violence. Much of the characterization is weak, and there are some dreadfully loose ends; however, much of Swarthout's basic promise is in evidence. *Willow Run* begins to reveal Swarthout's eye for detail, his empathy for the vulnerable, and his basic affirmation of individual dignity.

His second novel, *They Came to Cordura*, reflects Swarthout's fascinations with the testing of courage and the physical and psychic landscape of the West. Again, Swarthout juxtaposes individual effort against the dynamic of a group. Five American soldiers involved in the bloody expedition ordered against Pancho Villa have been chosen to receive the Congressional Medal of Honor. The central character, Major Thorn, had exhibited cowardice in the face of the enemy. His disgusted commanding officer assigns Thorn to select recipients for the Medal of Honor and escort them to Cordura for an awards ceremony—as an added humiliation, he is designated to make the presentations.

Swarthout handles what could have been simply melodrama with understanding and skill. The journey to Cordura proves to be full of physical and emotional pitfalls. Thorn wonders what facet of character separates the cowardly from the brave, his cowardice from the seemingly careless courage of the hero. As it turns out, the heroes are far from noble, and their bravery under fire was nothing if not serendipitous. Moreover, Thorn discovers in himself the courage that he had thought was absent. Swarthout's experience as an infantryman during World War II gives this work a ring of authenticity. Moreover, the novel fully establishes Swarthout's gift as a gripping storyteller.

When Swarthout shifts from telling a good story to social criticism, he loses narrative momentum, and his characters tend to become stereotypes. *Welcome to Thebes* (1962) and *The Cadillac Cowboys* (1964) are illustrative of these flaws. The former follows the adventures of Sewell Smith, a down-and-out writer seeking material for a pulp novel. Motivated as much by malice as by greed, Smith discovers that an eighth-grade nymphet has been dispersing her charms to the town worthies. Delighted to have the opportunity to settle old scores and pick up a little extortion money, Smith sets about ruining people's lives. The novel has a morbid fascination, but it is difficult to care about people who are essentially shallow and preoccupied with themselves.

The characters in *The Cadillac Cowboys* suffer from equally truncated development. The corruption of the plain, honest cowhand into a rich urban bumpkin is the stuff of television comedy. Moreover, what purports to be a satire is interspersed with long passages on the destruction of the environment. As much as one might sympathize with Swarthout's passion and point of view, the reader would be better advised to turn to the works of Joseph Wood Krutch or Edward Abbey.

Swarthout manages to interweave social criticism, character development, and story line successfully in *Bless the Beasts and Children*, a novel that may very well stand the test of time. Here he is at his very best; the reader shares his anger and disgust with a society that makes victims of the innocent—

the beasts and children. Swarthout does not stop to preach. Instead, he tells of the plight of the buffalo that are about to be slaughtered by so-called sportsmen and of the mission of a group of misfit boys who are out to save them. By the close of the novel, it is clear that he sees deep flaws within American society.

Swarthout has the unusual ability to involve his readers with idiosyncratic characters who are often the outcasts and misfits of a society that demands they be different. Paradoxically, his best creations are some of the most flawed characters. John Bernard Books, however, the dying gunman of *The Shootist*, is a vivid exception.

Books is a man who represents his time and place and who has outlived his circumstances. He stands tall and lives by a personal code of honor. In short, as a representative of the rugged individualism of the American frontier, he is everything that modern America is not. Books faces the circumstances of his dying with dignity and courage. When those who would seek to profit from his death move in like eaters of carrion, Books beats them at their own game. Books is not for sale, but Swarthout seems to suggest that most things in the twentieth century are.

Swarthout's most successful foray into humor is *The Old Colts* (1985), which picks up the story of Wyatt Earp and Bat Masterson when they meet again in the New York City of 1916. They encounter the likes of Damon Runyon, the bard of Broadway (whose Sky Masterson of the 1932 musical *Guys and Dolls* was, in fact, patterned on Bat, then a newspaperman and gambler in New York); Jimmy Walker, the dandy governor of New York; Arnold Rothstein, the flamboyant gangster; and Teddy Roosevelt. After geriatric escapades among the urban folk, Wyatt and Bat head for Dodge City, a town more worthy of their talents.

In *The Homesman*, Swarthout turns once again to individuals who are tested by the rigors of frontier life, a life frequently crueler to the women than to the men. Faced with isolation, hunger, and the illness and death of children, many women broke down, escaping from misery into madness. When this occurred, a homesman had to be appointed to escort the broken women home. This is the story of an unlikely couple yoked together by necessity. Mary Bee Cuddy, moved by the dementia of her best friend, offers to escort four women to meet the

Ladies Aid Society in Iowa, from there to be returned to their families.

Cuddy must team up with the reprobate George Briggs. The story of Cuddy and Briggs is central, but the flashbacks to the lives of the women who have gone insane is told with gripping power. Swarthout demonstrates again that he is able to enlist compassion for the broken, for the victims of life who, despite their personal plights, manage to affirm human worth.

Swarthout is most effective when he sticks to storytelling and abandons rhetoric. There is a repressed anger in his novels that sometimes leads him to preach or become vitriolic, and his humor tends to be heavy-handed. On the other hand, when he moves beyond social ciphers, he creates characters who engage a reader's mind and heart. Moreover, he is willing to risk writing novels that take a moral stance; at his best, he tells a good story that has a point.

BLESS THE BEASTS AND CHILDREN

First published: 1970
Type of work: Novel

A group of troubled adolescents undergoes a rite of passage at an Arizona summer camp that specializes in turning boys into cowboys.

In *Bless the Beasts and Children*, Box Canyon Boys Camp becomes a microcosm for American society; a process of "natural selection of age and cruelty and regionalism and kindred interest" divides the boys of the camp into a ranked tribal structure. The boys strive to outdo one another and to usurp the places of those higher in the social order, either by excelling in the weekly competition or by stealing the totem of another tribe. Each tribe has its special totem: the Apaches, a mounted buffalo head; the Sioux, the head of a mountain lion; the Comanches, the head of a black bear, and so on, down to the tribe of the lowest social order, designated the Bedwetters, whose totem of shame is an enameled chamber pot. The Apaches is the tribe of winners, of the biggest, toughest, and most competent boys. Swarthout writes, "Incentive was thus inherent in the system, as it was in the American way of life."

Because of their prowess in weekly competition, these boys retain their rank and the special privileges that go with it. The camp staff and the indif-ferent or desperate parents of the boys believe that this competitive system will bring about the onset of masculine maturity. Within this specially created hothouse for the development of the American male, Swarthout selects the most unlikely and apparently the least likable group for an adventure that takes them from self-loathing and infantile rage to an awakening to the promise of their own lives.

When the Bedwetters watch the annual shooting of buffalo, conducted by the Arizona Game and Fish Department to thin the herd, they are horrified by the slaughter they witness. Swarthout is relentless in presenting a description of the helplessness of the semi-domesticated beasts and the gleeful joy the "shooters" take in bringing a hideous death to the confused and terrified animals. The incompetent marksmanship creates a bloody shambles that both shocks the reader and traumatizes the boys who watch in numbed horror.

Under the halting leadership of John Cotton, the oldest of the frequently pathetic boys in the Bedwetters, the group has begun to emerge from the private world of fear and hostility into which they had withdrawn. On a subconscious level, they recognize themselves in the innocent beasts led to the slaughter. Indeed, the story opens in the middle of Cotton's nightmare in which he and the others are the buffalo who are being led to slaughter, and in that dream Cotton recognizes his mother as one of the shooters.

This shattering dream serves to merge the personal and private world of the boys with the mindless destruction encountered in the adult world of their parents. Their witnessing the killing of the buffalo returns them to desperate isolation. Only when the younger of the Lally brothers, "Lally 2," embarks on the impossible mission of returning to the buffalo range and freeing the buffalo are the boys again brought together by a purpose outside themselves, independent of their special weaknesses.

Thus, the stage is set for high adventure: The boys must escape the confines of the camp, travel across half of northern Arizona, free the buffalo penned up for the next day's shooting, and return to camp without getting caught. The task is impossible, but the boys are galvanized into action by their need to rescue the buffalo and an image of themselves as heroes: "They were mad for western movies. They doted on tales told with trumpets and ending in a pot of gold, a bucket of blood, or a chorus of the national anthem." What follows is indeed an adventure, but more important, the Bedwetters must overcome the obstacles they encounter from within.

The narrative technique Swarthout employs juxtaposes the events of the story line with events from the past that reveal the damaged and broken lives the children have led and how they have become what they are. This is some of Swarthout's most effective and poignant writing. For one reason or another, these boys have been abandoned emotionally, orphaned by their parents' insensitivity, selfishness, and immaturity. Unloved and isolated, they must work together to carry out their task.

Each boy finds something of value in himself. Teft, the perpetual juvenile delinquent and thief, turns his talent to "borrowing" a car; Lally 2 has a special way with animals; Shecker, the fat boy, is strong enough to break the wire on the bales of hay; and Cotton binds them together with dauntless courage when a turn of events seems to make their mission to free the thirty remaining buffalo impossible. The love that they failed to find at home they find in one another. The boys initially find themselves united by their misery and fear, then by the odd ferocity of John Cotton's protection and acceptance, and finally by a shared sense of purpose, triumph, and tragedy.

The triumph of misfits over a callous social order is not uncommon thematic material, but Swarthout manages to avoid the pitfalls of stereotypical villains; there are no wicked oil executives, slimy politicians, or ruthless militarists. Rather, it is the structure of society that has made the children victims. Swarthout seems to suggest that if the innocence of the beasts and children means their destruction, then the society at large is trapped in a box canyon of its own making.

THE SHOOTIST

First published: 1975
Type of work: Novel

When a gunman discovers that he is dying of cancer, he chooses to meet death on his own terms.

The Shootist is as much a story of the end of the Old West as it is the story of John Bernard Books, the last famous living gunman, whose passing will mark the end of an era. On January 22, 1901, the day of the English queen Victoria's death, Books rides into El Paso, Texas, to consult a doctor he trusts, only to discover that he is dying of cancer of the prostate—inoperable, incurable, and unimaginably painful. Books cannot move on; he has come to the end of the road in El Paso, but clearly he is an unwanted anachronism. The town, represented by Marshal Thibido, would be more comfortable if Books had picked another place to die. Like the marshal, the citizens are both fearful and fascinated by Books, royalty in his own right, a living legend of a bygone era.

Books has rented a room from Mrs. Bond Rogers, a widowed woman who is struggling to make ends meet by taking in boarders. She is unaware of the reputation of her houseguest, who in self-parody tells her he is William Hickok, United States marshal of Abilene, Kansas; however, her son knows that Hickok has been dead for more than two decades, and he recognizes the famous custom-made .44 Remingtons carried by the legendary shootist J. B. Books. The interplay between these characters as Books moves toward death gives the narrative depth and dimension.

Bond Rogers finds herself both attracted to and repelled by Books—repelled by the violence he brings to her home and attracted by his courage in the face of an adversary against whom he cannot prevail. As the word spreads that Books is in El Paso and that he is a dying man, he is plagued by parasites and reputation hunters. When a couple of would-be assassins try to ambush Books in bed,

there is a shootout that results in the bloody death of Books's assailants and the flight of the widow Rogers's remaining tenants. She upbraids Books for being a vicious killer, but Books points out, quite reasonably, that his victims were in the process of trying to kill him. She struggles with the ambivalence of her feelings and with her fear that Books will become a terrible model for her son Gillom, who already is showing signs of becoming one of the local toughs.

Books becomes remorseful for the trouble that he has brought to the Rogers's home. In an effort to make up for the lost revenue, he cleverly takes advantage of those who would seek to profit from his death. The undertaker who offers Books a free funeral in the hope of making money from putting the corpse on display finds that Books is wise to his game. Books charges him a fee for the privilege of conducting his funeral. He sees through the photographer's offer of a free portrait as well, charging him a fee for the photograph, which he is bound to copy and sell. He feels more kindly toward a secondhand man who is more candid about his motive for the purchase of his last effects.

Swarthout's cynicism is relentless, as a tenderly remembered lover from Books's past pays him a visit with an offer of marriage. It turns out that she has been offered a deal to have a book written in her name—or, rather, in the name of J. B. Books's widow. Even the preacher hopes to capitalize on Books's plight. He offers him salvation for a signed statement of repentance, for he would be the preacher who saved the soul of J. B. Books, killer and sinner extraordinaire. The shallow opportunism of the denizens of the new age is in painful contrast to the often ruthless Books, who lives by a Spartan code: "I will not be laid a hand on. I will not be wronged. I will not stand for an insult. I don't do these things to others. I require the same from them."

When Books presses Doc Hostetler into revealing the extent of the agony awaiting him, Hostetler tells Books that he will go out screaming no matter how brave he is, unless he is lucky enough to slip into a coma. Hostetler plants the seed of suicide, but Books chooses another way. Marshal Thibido had warned him that El Paso holds more than one tough who would like to make a name for himself by being the man who killed J. B. Books. Books sends separate invitations to three of the worst of El

Paso's citizens to meet him at the Constantinople Saloon: Pulford, a gambler who prides himself on having shot a man through the heart at a distance of more than eighty feet; Serrano, a cattle thief, killer, and molester of children; and Cobb, an impotent punk who hurts prostitutes. These are to be his adversaries in a final confrontation; John Bernard Books does not plan to die alone.

Throughout the novel, Books has taken grim comfort from the newspaper reporting Queen Victoria's death that he purchased as he entered El Paso. He wryly observes that it is a newspaper that he has had time to read. He perceives a parallel between his passing and the passing of an era that will later come to be known as Victorian, but he is not vain enough to think that his life has been important. As he steps through the swinging doors of the Constantinople, he takes satisfaction in the thought that even though his life did not amount to much, his death will be remembered for some time, for there is still a lot of John Bernard Books left to kill.

The Shootist reveals Swarthout at his narrative best. The action is suffused with dark humor and the revelation of characters who are both interesting and complex. Books does not prove to have a heart of gold, but he does stand above those who seek his end. His ruthlessness, flamboyance, and flinty integrity are a part of the age in which he lived.

SUMMARY

Robert Browning's famous admonition that "a man's reach should exceed his grasp" is applicable to Swarthout's central thematic concerns and perhaps to his work as well. His most successful novels employ characters who find themselves facing seemingly insurmountable obstacles. Pitted against overwhelming circumstances, they come to discover their inner strengths and weaknesses. The outcome of their efforts to prevail over forces greater than themselves is less significant than how they meet the challenge. These are the ingredients of tragedy that fundamentally affirm the human condition. When Swarthout succeeds, he succeeds in an important way; when he fails, it is usually not because the task is too small.

David Sundstrand

BIBLIOGRAPHY

By the Author

LONG FICTION:
Willow Run, 1943
They Came to Cordura, 1958
Where the Boys Are, 1960
Welcome to Thebes, 1962
The Cadillac Cowboys, 1964
The Eagle and the Iron Cross, 1966
Loveland, 1968
Bless the Beasts and Children, 1970
The Tin Lizzie Troop, 1972
Luck and Pluck, 1973
The Shootist, 1975
The Melodeon, 1977
Skeletons, 1979
The Old Colts, 1985
The Homesman, 1988
Pinch Me, I Must Be Dreaming, 1994

YOUNG ADULT FICTION:
The Ghost and the Magic Saber, 1963 (with Kathryn Swarthout)
Whichaway, 1966 (with Kathryn Swarthout)

The Button Boat, 1969 (with Kathryn Swarthout)
TV Thompson, 1972 (with Kathryn Swarthout)
Whales to See The, 1975 (with Kathryn Swarthout)
Cadbury's Coffin, 1982 (with Kathryn Swarthout)

SHORT FICTION:

Easterns and Westerns: Short Stories, 2001 (Miles Hood Swarthout, editor)

About the Author

Appel, Benjamin. "The Mystery of Courage." *The Saturday Review* 41 (February 6, 1958): 30.

Dempsey, David. "Scapegrace's Homecoming." *The New York Times Book Review*, June 17, 1962, 24.

Feld, Rose. "Building a Bomber." *The New York Times Book Review*, May 30, 1943, 18.

"Glendon Swarthout." In *The Writers Directory, 1992-1994*. Detroit: St. James Press, 1992.

"Glendon (Fred) Swarthout." In *Contemporary Literary Criticism*. Vol. 35, edited by Daniel G. Marowski. Detroit: Gale Research, 1985.

Nelson, Nancy Owen. Review of *The Homesman*. *Western American Literature* 24 (1989): 70-71.

Nordyke, Lewis. "Outbreak of Courage." *The New York Times Book Review*, February 9, 1959, 4.

Oberbeck, S. K. "High Noon." *Newsweek* 85 (February 3, 1975): 64.

Obituary. *Chicago Tribune*, September 26, 1992.

Obituary. *The New York Times*, September 26, 1992.

Richardson, Maurice. "Where the Boys Are." *New Statesman* 60 (1960): 534-541.

DISCUSSION TOPICS

- How does *Bless the Beasts and Children* present the theme of innocence?

- Compare the function of Glendon Swarthout's humor in *The Old Colts* and *The Shootist.*

- What literary techniques does Swarthout employ to capture the atmosphere of the Southwest?

- In which works of Swarthout does his social criticism work best? In which is it least effective?

- For Swarthout, what are the essential ingredients of courage?

Robert Foothorap

AMY TAN

Born: Oakland, California
February 19, 1952

Tan explores the cultural conflict between Chinese and Chinese American generations as well as the tender and difficult relationships between mothers and daughters.

BIOGRAPHY

Amy Tan (given the Chinese name of An-Mei, or "Blessing from America") was the second of three children born to Chinese immigrants John and Daisy Tan. Her father, educated as an electrical engineer in Beijing, became a Baptist minister. Daisy, child of a privileged family, was forced to leave behind three daughters from a previous marriage when she fled Communist troops.

Tan's older brother died in 1967 and her father six months later, both of brain tumors. This began a troubled time for her. At fifteen, she moved to Europe with her mother and younger brother, was arrested for drugs in Switzerland at sixteen, and nearly eloped to Austria with a German army deserter.

Daisy Tan wanted her daughter to be a neurosurgeon and a concert pianist, but Tan felt she could not live up to her mother's expectations. Although her test scores were highest in math and science, she left premedical studies to become an English major. In 1974, she earned a master's degree in linguistics from San Jose State University and married tax attorney Lou DeMattei. She began doctoral studies at the University of California at Berkeley but, after a close friend and roommate was murdered, she dropped out to become a consultant to programs for disabled children. Later she served as reporter, editor, and publisher for *Emergency Room Reports*.

Tan became a freelance business writer in 1983. She wrote sales manuals and proposals for such firms as American Telephone and Telegraph (AT&T), International Business Machines (IBM), and Apple, and by 1985 was working up to ninety hours a week. Her business writing paid well, and she could choose her projects, but, she has said, "It was death to me spiritually. It was writing that had no meaning to me."

She sought therapy, but Tan was discouraged when her psychiatrist fell asleep during her sessions. Instead, she decided to cut her work week to fifty hours, study jazz piano, and write fiction in her spare time. She had just read novelist Louise Erdrich's *Love Medicine* (1984), interwoven stories of an American Indian family, and was inspired to write her own. At the Squaw Valley Community of Writers fiction workshop, she met Molly Giles, winner of the Flannery O'Connor Award for fiction. Tan showed Giles what would become Waverly Jong's story, "Rules of the Game," in *The Joy Luck Club* (1989), and Giles became her mentor.

Tan finished three stories in three years. When *The Joy Luck Club* was sold to Putnam in 1987 on the basis of a proposal and three stories ("Rules of the Game," "Waiting Between the Trees," and "Scar"), Tan closed her business and wrote thirteen more stories in four months. She thought her acceptance was "a token minority thing. I thought they had to fill a quota since there weren't many Chinese-Americans writing."

Like the daughters in her books, Tan was ambivalent about her Chinese background. She contemplated plastic surgery to make herself look more Western, and she did not fully accept her dual culture until 1987, when she and her mother went to

China to meet her half sisters. She has remarked that, "As soon as my feet touched China, I became Chinese."

Writing *The Joy Luck Club* also helped Tan to discover how Chinese she really was. In many respects, it is her family's story. Her mother had formed a Joy Luck Club in China and again in San Francisco. Daisy Tan "was the little girl watching her mother cut a piece of flesh from her arm to make soup, and she was the little girl watching her mother die when she took opium because she had become a third concubine."

Tan's first book was a surprising best seller in both hardcover and paperback. It received the Commonwealth Club Gold Award for fiction, the Bay Area Book Reviewers Award for fiction, and the American Library Association Best Book for Young Adults Award and was a finalist for the National Book Award. *The Joy Luck Club* was made into a popular film in 1993, cowritten and coproduced by Tan, and was adapted for the stage in 1999.

For nearly a year, Tan tried to start *The Kitchen God's Wife* (1991). Again, her subjects were a Chinese mother and a Chinese American daughter, but this time she focused upon the mother's life in China. The novel, based on Daisy Tan's tumultuous past, received *Booklist*'s editor's choice honors and was nominated for the Bay Area Book Reviewers award. *The Hundred Secret Senses* (1995) followed; it told the story of Olivia Yee Bishop, a Chinese American photographer, and her irrepressible Chinese half sister Kwan, who believes that she experienced an earlier life in the nineteenth century. Tan's third novel, *The Bonesetter's Daughter* (2001), draws in part on the histories of her mother and grandmother in China.

Tan's first nonfiction work, *The Opposite of Fate: A Book of Musings* (2003), is a collection of casual writings that supplement her fiction and her life. The title essay describes her struggle with Lyme disease, which began in 1999 and for several years had a serious impact on her ability to write.

ANALYSIS

Tan uses first-person narratives as the basis of her first three books. *The Joy Luck Club* was conceived and written as a collection of short stories, but early reviewers erroneously began to call it a novel. Her publisher carefully skirted the issue by referring to Tan's "first work of fiction" on the book jacket.

The book is composed of sixteen related stories narrated by three mothers and four daughters. It recalls such loosely structured works as Sherwood Anderson's *Winesburg, Ohio* (1919), William Faulkner's *As I Lay Dying* (1930), and Erdrich's *Love Medicine*, which feature individual narratives that together reflect a culture or a period. Tan organizes *The Joy Luck Club* in terms of the contrast between generations—two sections in the voices of the Chinese-born mothers and two in the voices of their California-born daughters. The exception is June Woo, whose mother, Suyuan, founder of the Joy Luck Club, has just died. June's voice is heard in all four sections of the book.

Tan's second book, *The Kitchen God's Wife*, is constructed like a traditional novel, following one major story line. It is narrated by two voices—three chapters by daughter Pearl and all others by mother Winnie Louie, who tells Pearl of her earlier life. This is a book of revelations, illuminated vertically as well as horizontally, for things are never what they seem. When characters think they know the truth, they know only part of it. Similarly, *The Hundred Secret Senses* employs two narrators, but Tan uses a traditional third-person viewpoint in *The Bonesetter's Daughter*, a choice that sometimes distances her characters from the reader.

In books exploring emotionally intense events, Tan's humor is a pleasant surprise. June, an aspiring child prodigy, takes piano lessons from a deaf teacher. Another family names its four sons Matthew, Mark, Luke, and Bing. Some of the dialogue is priceless: June's mother calls her "a college drop-off," and another mother collects "so-so security." Tan also masters the one-line retort. Learning that Grand Auntie Du is dead at ninety-seven, Pearl asks, "What was it? . . . A stroke?" "'A bus,' my mother said."

A major theme of Tan's work is the conflict between cultures and generations. *The Bonesetter's Daughter* even traces that same conflict across three generations. Of the Chinese women, an extreme example is Winnie Louie's Old Aunt, whose feudal upbringing taught that a woman's eyes should be used for sewing, not reading; ears should listen to orders, not ideas; and lips should only be used to express gratitude or approval. When Winnie's cousin Peanut married a homosexual, her mother-in-law bought her a baby to save face. Their school-mate, forced to marry a simpleminded man and chided by her unsympathetic mother, hanged herself in despair. Winnie realizes that she has been wrong to hold such women responsible for their troubles, but, she says, "That was how I was raised—never to criticize men or the society they ruled. . . . I could blame only other women who were more afraid than I." Another woman dreams, "In America I will have a daughter just like me. But over there nobody will say her worth is measured by the loudness of her husband's belch."

These little bits of history are things of which the resentful American daughters have no awareness. They do not understand the intensity of their mothers' need to protect them from life, and they have little sense of their mothers as people. Instead, their mothers seem to be embarrassments—stingy, fussy old women. Pearl, in her old bedroom, finds her worn slippers and is impatient that her mother refuses to throw anything away. Later, Winnie, cleaning the same room, takes comfort in these traces of her daughter's childhood.

Tan explores not only the rift between mothers and daughters but also its healing. She believes in the power of love. The daughters have a desperate need to communicate with their mothers and one another which they do not even recognize, and as the barriers to communication begin to crumble, their first tentative steps toward reconciliation promise more.

Tan also examines a deeper question that she has stated as, "What in our life is given to us as fate, and what is given to us as sheer luck of the moment, and what are choices that we make?" The mothers raised in China were taught to believe in fate and luck. In *The Joy Luck Club*, An-mei Hsu's mother is the widow of a respected scholar. She is befriended by the Second Wife of a rich man who is attracted to her. Second Wife arranges the rape of An-mei's mother by this man so that he will take her as a third concubine, as she is now disgraced, and will stop spending so much money in teahouses, leaving more for the wife. When a son is born to An-mei's mother, Second Wife claims the baby as her own. The mother eats poisoned sweet dumplings, telling her daughter, "You see how this life is. You cannot eat enough of this bitterness."

An-mei points out again and again how her unhappy mother had no choice. Yet An-mei has learned from her mother's suicide that choices can be made, and she tries to teach her American daughter, whose marriage is ending, to stand up for herself: "If she doesn't speak, she is making a choice. . . . I know this, because I was . . . taught to desire nothing, to swallow other people's misery, to eat my own bitterness."

The mothers' wisdom and finely drawn characters are revealed in all of these books by a peeling away of layers down to the unblemished heart. Though their lives have been harsher, the mothers are incredibly stronger than their uncertain, unhappy daughters. If the mothers were not permitted choices, suggests Tan, perhaps the daughters are weakened by having too many.

Tan employs a world of metaphor and symbolism, especially in *The Joy Luck Club*. A thematic title and vignette introduce each section of that book. For example, "The Twenty-six Malignant Gates" section alludes to a Chinese book that warns of dangers to children, and here each daughter tells of a problem she faced as a child. In an ironically titled story, "Rice Husband," the shaky marriage of Ying-ying St. Clair's daughter is represented by a wobbly end table, designed by her husband and ready to collapse. The marriage is further symbolized by the remodeled barn that is the couple's new house, furnished in the husband's preferred minimalist style, pared down and stingy like him. Ying-ying thinks "everything . . . is for looking, not even for good-looking. . . . This is a house that will break into pieces." *The Hundred Secret Senses* adds the mystical elements of reincarnation and the World of Yin, while the vengeful ghost of Great-Granny Liu haunts the outhouse in *The Bonesetter's Daughter.*

THE JOY LUCK CLUB

First published: 1989
Type of work: Novel

These linked stories reveal the intricate lives and conflicts of four Chinese mothers and their Chinese American daughters.

The Joy Luck Club takes its title from a gathering begun in wartime China by Suyuan Woo, who met with three women in a weekly attempt to maintain their sanity and luck. They prepared special foods and played mah-jongg, even though the city was filled with horror. In 1949, in San Francisco, Suyuan resumed the tradition with three new friends.

One critic has suggested that the book is structured like the four corners of the mah-jongg table at which the women sit, with four stories in each of the book's four sections, and four mother-daughter pairs. In mah-jongg, one critic has noted, "The game starts, always, with the east wind," and June Woo, whose narrative begins and ends the book, sits on the east side, taking her dead mother's place. The game ends when one player has a complete hand, and June completes her mother's life and dearest wish when she returns to China, with a ticket paid for by the Joy Luck Club, to meet the two half sisters her mother was forced to leave behind in her flight.

Recurring motifs link the stories of each mother-daughter pair. The second mother, An-mei Hsu, bears a scar from the spilling of hot soup on her neck as a child, an accident that nearly killed her. She carries a grievous inner scar as well: Her own mother had been banished, her name never spoken. Only later does she understand how her mother dishonored the family by becoming the third concubine of a wealthy married man. Yet when An-mei's grandmother was dying, her mother returned to cut a piece of flesh from her own arm to make a magic healing broth. "This is how a daughter honors her mother," An-mei remembers. "It is *shou* [respect] so deep it is in your bones."

This same mother poisoned herself, timing her death so that her soul would return on the first day of the lunar new year to settle scores with the rich man and Second Wife, ensuring a better future for her children. Dead, she had more power than ever in life.

Lindo Jong, the daughter of peasants, was betrothed at the age of two to her first husband and became a servant in his mother's house until their marriage. Although the family nearly convinced her that a daughter belonged to her mother-in-law

and that her husband was a god, Lindo discovered herself on her wedding day: "I was strong. I was pure. I had genuine thoughts inside that no one could see, that no one could ever take away from me."

Thus, Lindo's willful and brilliant American daughter Waverly learns "the art of invisible strength" at six from her mother, who tells her, "Strongest wind cannot be seen." Waverly becomes a chess prodigy, but her early confidence falters as she tries to outwit the mother she fears. The tension between mother and daughter seems strongest with this pair. Waverly wants to become her own person, but her mother wonders, "How can she be her own person? When did I give her up?"

Little Ying-ying St. Clair, daughter of the wealthiest family in Wushi, celebrated the Moon Festival by falling off an excursion boat at night and never found herself again. After an unfortunate first marriage, she lost her "tiger spirit" and became a listless ghost. Motifs of the dark other self, of dissolution and integration, appear in her stories, yet mother-daughter love forms a stronger bond. Ying-ying's daughter struggles to rescue her mother's spirit after the devastating birth of an anacephalic child, and the mother, in turn, tries to give her daughter courage to break free of an empty marriage: "I will use this sharp pain to penetrate my daughter's tough skin and cut her tiger spirit loose. She will fight me, because this is the nature of two tigers. But I will win and give her my spirit, because this is the way a mother loves her daughter."

In the final section of the book, the mothers connect their past to their daughters' lives and encourage them to be strong. As a Chinese grandmother tells her baby granddaughter, "You must teach my daughter this same lesson. How to lose your innocence but not your hope."

THE KITCHEN GOD'S WIFE

First published: 1991
Type of work: Novel

Winnie Louie recounts her hardships in China and is reconciled with her daughter Pearl.

In *The Kitchen God's Wife*, Auntie Helen confronts her friend Winnie, who has secrets, and Winnie's married daughter Pearl, who has multiple sclerosis but is afraid to face her mother. Helen announces that they must confide in each other or she, who is dying of a "B nine" brain tumor, will tell everything. Winnie agrees and summons her estranged daughter.

Winnie's mother, born into wealth and educated in a missionary school, had met a young revolutionary and threatened to swallow gold if her family did not allow them to marry. Instead, she was made second wife to her grandfather's friend. Winnie remembers living with her mother until she was six, when her mother suddenly died or disappeared; she is never sure which. The child was sent away to relatives.

After a few years, a young man, Wen Fu, became interested in her cousin Peanut, but Winnie was a better marriage prospect because of her father's

wealth, so the Wens chose her. Though she did not love Wen Fu, she hoped for a better life. Instead, the greedy Wen family seized her dowry and sold it or used it for themselves. When Wen Fu began to brutalize and humiliate her, she was not angry: "This was China. A woman had no right to be angry."

In 1937, Wen Fu joined the Kuomintang army under his dead brother's name in order to qualify for an American-staffed flight school. There, Winnie met Helen, wife of another officer. Although popular with other pilots, Wen Fu enjoyed playing sadistic games. He was never injured in their bombing missions because, a coward, he always flew the other way.

As the Japanese army invaded China, pregnant Winnie was sent south to Kunming, where her first child was stillborn. After Wen Fu stole a jeep to impress a woman, he was partially blinded, and the woman was killed in an accident. From that time, his behavior became even more violent. He destroyed the hospital kitchen with a cleaver. His

servant, raped and impregnated, died from a self-induced abortion. Winnie's second baby, brain-damaged by his beatings, was allowed to die. Their son later died of plague.

When World War II was over, they returned to Shanghai, where Winnie's father, a collaborator with the Japanese, was viewed as a traitor. Wen Fu offered to manage his business to protect him, then took control of his money and terrified the household.

Just as Winnie decided to ask her cousin Peanut to help her leave her abusive marriage, she encountered Jimmy Louie, a kind Chinese American officer she had met in Kunming. On a pretext, she escaped her father's house and agreed to stay with Jimmy. In order to divorce Wen Fu, she hired a lawyer, but after his office was vandalized by Wen Fu's thugs, he refused to help her further.

Wen Fu had Winnie jailed for theft and desertion. Jimmy, who would become her second husband, returned to the United States because of the scandal and waited for her there. After more than a year, Helen's Auntie Du arranged Winnie's release from prison and helped her to obtain a visa and airline tickets. Wen Fu was tricked into stating publicly that they were divorced so that he could have no further control over her. He returned to rape Winnie at gunpoint before she fled China.

Pearl now realizes that she is probably Wen Fu's daughter, the secret her mother has kept from her. She tells Winnie of her own illness, and Winnie offers hope. She and Helen will go to China to find good medicine for Pearl, for Helen has confessed that she has no brain tumor. She merely pretended to be ill as a way to bring Winnie closer to her daughter.

The Kitchen God is the inhabitant of a small shrine left to Pearl by Grand Auntie Du. He was an unfaithful husband who burned in the fireplace rather than face his good wife. Winnie realizes, "I was like that wife of Kitchen God." She determines to replace his picture with a luckier one. Eventually, she finds a statue of an unnamed goddess for the shrine and names her Lady Sorrowfree, advising Pearl, "She is ready to listen. She understands English. You should tell her everything."

THE BONESETTER'S DAUGHTER

First published: 2001
Type of work: Novel

An American ghostwriter unearths the multiple secrets of her Chinese family, discovering the intense and confusing bonds of mother-daughter love.

The Bonesetter's Daughter focuses on ghostwriter Ruth Young, her present life with an almost invisible lover, and the ongoing struggle with her mercurial Chinese mother, LuLing. Fully professional as she rewrites her clients' books, Ruth is otherwise hesitant. After LuLing fries eggs with the shells on and prowls the neighborhood in her nightgown, she is diagnosed with Alzheimer's disease and cannot live alone safely. Reluctantly, Ruth moves in. LuLing, a fine calligrapher, presents her with a manuscript of her life in China, but Ruth resists reading it.

Narrated in the voice of LuLing, the manuscript reveals her story. Her nursemaid, Precious Auntie, was the daughter of a famous bonesetter, a healer who showed her a secret cave of "dragon bones" that, when powdered, would cure any pain or could be sold for profit. Liu Hu Sen, a gentle inkmaker from a neighboring village, sought the bonesetter's aid after an accident and was soon betrothed to Precious Auntie. Coffinmaker Chang, a fellow suitor, was rejected.

En route to Hu Sen's village, the wedding party was attacked by Chang, who coveted the valuable dowry of bones and left Precious Auntie's father and bridegroom dead. Because the Lius refused to believe that Chang had murdered their son, Precious Auntie, grief-stricken and already pregnant, attempted to commit suicide by drinking boiling ink. She survived, but her lower face was severely disfigured and she could no longer speak. Protected by matriarch Great-Granny Liu, she gave birth to a daughter, LuLing, and was kept on as the baby's nursemaid. LuLing was not told that Precious Auntie was her real mother.

Eventually Chang, learning that LuLing knew the location of the secret cave, sought to gain control of it by arranging her marriage to his son. Precious Auntie was helpless to intervene; LuLing alone could read her messages and understand her gestures. After writing a letter to Chang's family, threatening to haunt them forever if the marriage took place, she killed herself to protect her daughter. Only then did LuLing learn the truth. She was sent to an orphanage, where she later met her first husband, a scientist excavating nearby caves for the bones of Peking Man. When Japan invaded China, she escaped to the United States.

As Ruth reads her mother's manuscript, she understands better the bonds that connect her to her mother and grandmother. Accepting her obligation and her love for her mother, she prepares to care for LuLing.

Tan uses silence as a metaphor for loss of power. Although Ruth provides an effective voice for her clients, she frequently loses her own. LuLing briefly loses her voice at the orphanage and later forgets words, even her family name. Most significant is Precious Auntie, who speaks only with hands, eyes, and chalkboard, yet in death bequeaths her strength to her daughter and granddaughter.

The excavation of bones, as scientists come to dig for Peking Man, provides another metaphor for uncovering the past, revealing its hidden truths of identity, parentage, and name. Ruth's discovery of her heritage brings her understanding and reconciliation, allowing her to become whole.

SUMMARY

Tan's books, which have been published in more than twenty-five languages, are chiefly concerned with the troubled relationships and the conflicts of love between mothers and daughters who are separated by different cultures as well as by generations. She also covers a wide spectrum of lives and customs of Chinese women up until the postwar Cultural Revolution, and she examines the concepts of fate, luck, and choice. Although Tan does not consider herself a spokeswoman for Chinese Americans, her writing has awakened further interest in the Chinese American perspective in American literature.

Joanne McCarthy

BIBLIOGRAPHY

By the Author

LONG FICTION:
The Joy Luck Club, 1989
The Kitchen God's Wife, 1991
The Hundred Secret Senses, 1995
The Bonesetter's Daughter, 2001
Saving Fish from Drowning, 2005

NONFICTION:
The Opposite of Fate: A Book of Musings, 2003

CHILDREN'S LITERATURE:
The Moon Lady, 1992
The Chinese Siamese Cat, 1994

About the Author

Duke, Lynne. "The Secrets Silence Holds." *The Washington Post*, March 15, 2001, p. C1.

Gee, Alison Singh. "A Life on the Brink." *People Weekly* 55, no. 18 (May 7, 2001): 85-88.

Gray, Paul. "The Joys and Sorrows of Amy Tan." *Time* 157, no. 7 (February 19, 2001): 72-75.

Hamilton, Patricia L. "Feng Shui, Astrology, and the Five Elements: Traditional Chinese Belief in Amy Tan's *The Joy Luck Club*." *MELUS* 24, no. 2 (Summer, 1999): 125-146.

Lyall, Sarah. "At Home with Amy Tan: In the Country of the Spirits." *The New York Times*, December 28, 1995, p. C1.

Ma, Sheng-mei. "Chinese and Dogs in Amy Tan's *The Hundred Secret Senses*." *MELUS* 26, no. 1 (Spring, 2001): 29-45.

Mason, Deborah. "A Not-So-Dutiful Daughter." *The New York Times Book Review*, November 23, 2003, 30.

Shear, Walter. "Generational Differences and the Diaspora in *The Joy Luck Club*." *Critique: Studies in Modern Fiction* 34, no. 3 (Spring, 1993): 193-199.

DISCUSSION TOPICS

- Discuss the significance of fate, luck, and choice in Amy Tan's works.

- What sort of conflicts arise between mothers and daughters in Tan's books, and how can those conflicts be healed? Are they always the product of cultural differences?

- In what ways have some of Tan's characters been effectively silenced? How do they overcome this?

- What techniques does Tan use to make her characters come to life? Do you agree that her Chinese characters are more memorable? Why or why not?

- Some readers have complained about the one-dimensional quality of Tan's male characters. Do you find any exceptions?

- In all of her work, Tan seems to suggest that a knowledge of the past or of family history is essential to one's well-being. Do you agree?

- Is Tan's use of humor and violence effective? Why or why not?

Courtesy, Penguin Books

HUNTER S. THOMPSON

Born: Louisville, Kentucky
July 18, 1937
Died: Woody Creek, Colorado
February 20, 2005

Arguably the consummate New Journalist of the late 1960's and 1970's and certainly the paragon of "gonzo journalism," Thompson created narratives, texts, and essays that were somewhat autobiographical, somewhat political, and always laced with a bizarre and unique treatment of topic vis-à-vis alcohol, illicit substances, and popular culture.

BIOGRAPHY

It seems as if nothing known about Hunter Stockton Thompson is simple, authoritative, or goes without contention (even his birth date is occasionally contested as occurring between 1937 and 1939). Certain things are known for sure: He was born in Louisville, Kentucky, to Jack (an insurance salesman) and Virginia (a homemaker) as the oldest of three children; his father died of a heart attack before he was sixteen, and he found himself sentenced and incarcerated for sixty days for the robbery of a service-station attendant before he completed high school. Thompson only served half that time as a result of good behavior and never actually completed high school.

As such, Thompson's childhood established indicative trends that he would become synonymous with later in his adult life. As a child, Thompson reported for the *Southern Star,* a newspaper run and operated by children, where the *Louisville Courier-Journal* noted that he made approximately 10 to 15 cents an issue. Moreover, as mature as this vocational choice was at a young age, little compares to Thompson's more mature indulgences for alcohol, women, and illegal behavior. Thompson's friends and family attribute the loss of his father as being the major catalyst for his societal disregard. Others have argued that Thompson's early life has been held up to too close a scrutiny because his de-

viant behavior is often invoked, but the rigor and voracity for reading instilled in him by his mother is often overlooked.

Thompson's life took a series of missteps from that point forward. At age eighteen, Thompson enlisted and was subsequently discharged early from the U.S. Air Force in 1958. From there, he frequently was unable to hold down steady employment as a journalist at a variety of publications during the late 1950's and early 1960's. Thompson became somewhat of a vagrant and vagabond wandering the United States, trying to pen what he deemed to be the great American novel (later to become his eventually published 1998 book, *The Rum Diary*). His journalistic sojourn led him from New York to Big Sur, California, and onward from there to South America and the Caribbean islands as a reporter for the *National Observer,* a publication in its decade-long existence that, at the time, competed nationally with the likes of *Time* and *Newsweek.*

Only marriage to first wife Sandra Dawn in May, 1963, and a dispute with *National Observer* editors over covering the free speech movement ended his nomadic ways, and Thompson temporarily ended his journalistic career to focus on his novels. The work did not go well. His wife was forced into employment as a motel maid, and Thompson occasionally drove cabs to get by. However, a chance assignment in 1965 to cover the Hell's Angels for *The Nation* reinvigorated Thompson's journalism and gave rise to the voice which would resonate for the duration of his career.

It was at this juncture in his life that Thompson began to openly blur the line between investigative journalism and his own personal demons with drugs, alcohol, and deviant social behaviors. In his mind, he felt that he needed to get to the heart of the motorcycle gang's culture absent of the folklore created around them. So, armed with bourbon, beer, and unhealthy amount of narcotics (including his first experimentations with LSD), Thompson approached the Hell's Angels project and told their story from among them. The article prompted Random House to expand the article into *Hell's Angels: A Strange and Terrible Saga* in 1967, and Thompson's love affair with drugs and the drug culture began in earnest.

Following these events was a string of causality which would lead to his most widely read and critically acknowledged writing: his "fear and loathing" books. After the success of *Hell's Angels*, Thompson moved to Colorado and became involved with both local and national politics, notably by covering the riots of Chicago's Democratic Convention in 1968. In 1971, a project developed for him to cover the Mint 400 motorcycle race in the Nevada desert for *Sports Illustrated*; it became the catalyst to his masterstroke of reporting and self-reflection known as *Fear and Loathing in Las Vegas* (1972). One year later, the same approach he used in Vegas would be given a different topos: covering the presidential race in a set of serialized articles for *Rolling Stone*. The collected materials of his findings would become the starting point for *Fear and Loathing: On the Campaign Trail '72*, published in 1973.

Thompson would continue to work and develop his gonzo style of journalism throughout the 1980's and the 1990's, covering topics from the impeachment of President Bill Clinton to being a regular sports columnist for ESPN. He would continue to reprise his fear and loathing series in the late 1990's and early into the twenty-first century with a collection of letters (collected largely because of his incessant need to collect and carbon-copy every single missive he composed since he was a teenager) and two further volumes. His last written composition would come on February 17, 2005; "Football Season Is Over" was written four days prior to Thompson discharging one of his often-referenced handguns into his brain as he

committed suicide while on the phone to his second wife Anita. Thompson had been riddled with a variety of medical ailments in his last years, and the suicide note attests to his decision to end his life rather than die slowly in pain and deterioration.

ANALYSIS

Some critics have either reduced or celebrated Thompson's literary status as merely the transcriptions of a hyperbolic, deviant, or as one critic dubbed him, ritualistic writer, collecting himself within the popular, political, or cultural moment at any given time. There is truth to that. By the same token, to come to terms with Thompson's self-titled "gonzo" style and approach to composition is to come into contact with one of the cultural by-products of the 1960's counterculture movement known as the New Journalism.

Coined to some degree or another by one of its own practitioners, Thomas Wolfe, the New Journalism sought to approach journalism more from the vantage point of the literary essay. It was enamored with the free speech movement coming out of the University of Berkeley in the mid-1960's and possibly even more concerned with the idea that a nonbiased, objective journalism was veritably impossible. Thus, New Journalists sought not to even try to aim at objectivity. Rather, picking up off of the underground newspapers populating colleges, universities, and major metropolitan centers of influence, they aimed at trying to place themselves within the cultural moment being reported upon and attempted to give the most accurate description of all observable phenomena (including the feelings, emotions, and cultural ephemera that the reporter was experiencing at the time).

Oftentimes, this approach at compiling an absolute verisimilitude gave the narratives constructed a particularly nonjournalistic look: Pieces often resembled stream-of-consciousness prose reminiscent of James Joyce; conversational-styled vernacular became more pressing than strong syntax and diction; and the journalist's own "I," as a voice often used as counterpoint to actual discernable concrete fact, became imperative to get a full account of the story. The effect created by this new approach was one of meta-commentary on the events being reported on, whereby the events, themselves, almost become subservient to the narrative of the person reporting.

Thompson took this approach a step further, into a category of almost subversive decadence with what he eventually came to call gonzo journalism. The exact definition of the term is somewhat unclear as Thompson often defined and redefined the term with the same sort of flippancy that led him to call himself a doctor of journalism (a degree he bestowed upon himself when he received a mail-order "Doctor of Divinity" card from a San Francisco church). The term itself came from fellow journalist Bill Cardoso, who could only describe Thompson's writing as gonzo. Insofar as it is an actual methodology, gonzo journalism's main attributes seem to be heavily indebted to the drug culture about which Thompson avidly reported.

For, if Thompson's narratives on how to write from the gonzo perspective are to be held as accurate and instructional, then gonzo journalism demands writing under the influence of narcotics, alcohol, and a variety of illicit substances and then transferring that writing directly into print publication with virtually no substantial revision. In this effect, the construction of the narrative becomes directly indebted to the state of consciousness of the writer; for example, if the writer is operating on an ether and mescaline high, then that prose may or may not be subject to that writer's own paranoias, anxieties, or hallucinations. This can account for the dramatic shifts in narrative style and focus in Thompson's writing, in addition to his occasional use of direct transcription from audio tape to the written page (as Thompson had, on occasion, claimed no memory of the incidents except for as they were recorded).

FEAR AND LOATHING IN LAS VEGAS

First published: 1972
Type of work: Nonfiction

In search of the American Dream, Raoul Duke and Dr. Gonzo scour the Las Vegas Strip on an investigative trek into the American drug culture.

Standing posthumously somewhere behind *Fear and Loathing in Las Vegas* is the figure of Horatio Alger, Jr. A nineteenth century author of rags-to-riches fairy tales, Alger wrote stories describing how the littlest guy, through nothing more than hard work and determination, could succeed and achieve the American Dream. The conclusions to which Thompson takes that initial premise in *Fear and Loathing in Las Vegas* probably go well beyond anything Alger ever possibly conceived.

The plot itself is simple. Thompson and his lawyer, operating under the absurd pseudonyms Raoul Duke and Dr. Gonzo, respectively, are sent out to Las Vegas to cover the Mint 400, a motorcycle race across the desert. Upon receiving the assignment, both Duke and Gonzo come upon the notion that the assignment itself is really only subordinate, and is treated as such, to a much greater project: the quest for the American Dream. While Thompson often invokes Alger's thoughts and occasionally his words, to reiterate his quest, never in the narrative are any causal connections established between his assignment (proper) and his quest (conceived and undertaken).

To accomplish this more self-styled gonzo project, Duke and Gonzo formulate a plan to infiltrate the seedy underbelly of Las Vegas under the influence of a cornucopia of drugs and alcohol. What follows from here is little more than a travelogue of Duke and Gonzo's adventures over the course of a few days through Las Vegas's hotels, bars, and drug scene as they revel in their own indulgence to an unfathomable degree. Gonzo frequently teeters a line which legitimately threatens his own life, and, by the midpoint of the text, coverage of the Mint 400 largely has taken a backseat to escaping Las Vegas. In their decadence, Duke and Gonzo have possibly crossed a line by running up an absurd hotel tab that they have no intentions of paying. In Thompson's own hallucinatory state of self-disgust and paranoia, the legitimate fear and loathing of the book, he wonders if Las Vegas's reputation for settling up with welshers through lethal, if not legal, means might be employed upon him.

Part Two expands the gonzo aspects of the book and introduces, if not cements, it with irony. On the lam from seemingly everyone in Las Vegas and headed back to his California home, Thompson receives a telegram informing him that he has received a high-paying assignment to cover the National Conference of District Attorney's four-day seminar on drugs and narcotics. The idea itself of

Thompson—in his own mind a dilettante to the drug culture but a far better resource on the subject matter than district attorneys—covering the people who try to debilitate and legislate the drug scene in the United States is too tempting an opportunity to pass up.

In an instance of a Christian walking directly into the lions' den, Duke and Gonzo infiltrate the drug conference and are amazed at how far behind America's legal enforcers are to the American drug scene. Disenchanted, they both come to realize that there is no pragmatic danger of them being caught on drugs as, even though they are surrounded by the nation's drug enforcers, the attorneys are entirely clueless as to the nature of the drug user and drug culture. They leave the conference and pick up the quest for the American Dream, which, Thompson comes to find, does not exist. His final reaction and rejection leads him to believe that perhaps Alger may have been more right than he initially realized: The American Dream *can* be found in Las Vegas, as any child who grew up wanting to be part of the circus can indeed grow up to be the proprietor of Circus Circus, a low-rated resort and casino, which Thompson regards with little value. The irony for Thompson comes full circle here, as he discovers that with success can also come self-loathing.

FEAR AND LOATHING: ON THE CAMPAIGN TRAIL '72

First published: 1973
Type of work: Nonfiction

Following George McGovern on the ill-fated Democrat's run for the White House, Thompson focuses his eye on President Richard Nixon, the decrepit state of journalism, and America.

Fear and Loathing: On the Campaign Trail '72, much like its immediate predecessor *Fear and Loathing in Las Vegas*, picks up a sort of master narrative of the futile attempts of the proverbial underdog striving for and achieving the American Dream, only to be crushed at the end by the general milieu of the postmodern world. The hero that Thompson uti-

lizes in this autobiography of his coverage of the 1971-1972 presidential race is George McGovern, the idealistic Democratic candidate whom Thompson characterizes as the great underdog of the election versus entrenched Republican incumbent President Nixon.

Two points require immediate articulation. First, Thompson again writes a veritable diary of his position (both ideological and logistical as *Rolling Stone*'s political correspondent) as a chronological and cartographical narrative of what he believed to be the cultural moment. Writing in the shadows of McCarthyism and the debacle of the 1968 Democratic National Convention, he paints Richard Nixon as this narrative's villain and an entrenched evil permeating America. From Thompson's perspective, McGovern does, to a fault, represent the furthest left agenda, perhaps to a naïve degree, as he endorses extreme policies such as full amnesty for draft evaders of the  Vietnam War and total unilateral withdrawal from the conflict itself. In effect, the gonzo journalist finds a gonzo candidate. Second, given his strong polemical position regarding journalism, Thompson argues that the great mass media conglomerate largely and inappropriately dismisses McGovern as a viable candidate worth their attention (focusing rather on more notable and charismatic candidates such as Ted Kennedy). Thompson, who is literally following and critiquing McGovern, among others, in the trenches of their campaigns to almost microscopic detail, believes his perspective, no matter how biased, offers a greater degree of accuracy. For this, Thompson finds the media contemptuous for their lack of vision and objectivity—noting how the major politicians are as much indebted to "Big Media" and vice versa—and vilifies them to almost the same extent that he does the Nixon administration. Thompson finds that McGovern, without major media ties or traditional support, must largely rely upon youth platforms, grassroots politics, and the youth vote, all of which he perceives to be politically suicidal.

When McGovern rises as the Democratic front-runner and eventual presidential candidate by mid-April, Thompson's attitude (whose gonzo narrative does not take the liberty to revise his prior notions concerning McGovern, thus preserving all prior dismissals of him as even a forethought) toward him appears to take a decisively negative turn heading into October. From Thompson's perspective, McGovern's compromises and politics seem to equate to a reversal and further breakdown of the Democratic Party's political machine. His defeat at Nixon's hands seems predestined by Thompson, whose scrutiny of McGovern intensifies with every action he categorizes as mistaken, cowardly, and in total abandonment of the policies that landed him the nomination in the first place. As Thompson sees it, McGovern becomes part of the establishment that he so valiantly seemed to wish to fight. American history has recorded the resultant effect of that assessment as Thompson's underdog, McGovern, is swiftly defeated by Nixon in the presidential elections of 1972.

SUMMARY

Regardless of how seriously one considers Thompson's remarks on his own approach to writing or journalism, it is difficult not to acknowledge his own unique contributions to public inquiry. Thompson rarely minced words and less frequently chose a phrase that did not articulate exactly what his perspective was on any given matter. Whether such colorful use of metaphor, emotion, and polemic can be considered as journalistic in its integrity is a matter of some debate. Thompson's answer to that problem was simple; from the outset of his career he claimed quite vociferously that the material to be read came directly from his perspective alone. Whether or not one celebrates or declaims that perspective is open to debate.

Joseph Michael Sommers

DISCUSSION TOPICS

- How could one categorize Hunter S. Thompson's texts? Are they cases of journalism? Are they autobiographies? Could they be considered roman à clef novels?

- Given Thompson's perspective, style, and reporter's stance (or lack thereof), how could one characterize his construction of gonzo journalism, his version of New Journalism?

- Considering *Fear and Loathing: On the Campaign Trail '72*, how does Thompson characterize the American media? Nixon's administration? The Democratic Party since 1968? George McGovern? What are his primary concerns, complaints, and advocacies of any of the aforementioned?

- What does one make of Thompson's quest for the American Dream (and its subsequent abandonment) in *Fear and Loathing in Las Vegas*? How does that play into the worldview that Thompson seeks to construct in the text?

- The drug culture of the 1960's and 1970's is prominently featured and critiqued in *Fear and Loathing in Las Vegas*. How does it function as an operating discourse in the text's narrative construction?

- Where does Thompson fit in as a character within his own works (particularly in the supposed instances where the text's editors intervene and can only produce verbal transcriptions of interviews or tape recordings)? How does this comment on his analysis of the American publishing machine?

BIBLIOGRAPHY

By the Author

LONG FICTION:
The Rum Diary, 1998

SHORT FICTION:
Screw-jack, 2000

NONFICTION:

Hell's Angels: A Strange and Terrible Saga, 1967

Fear and Loathing in Las Vegas: A Savage Journey to the Heart of the American Dream, 1972 (also known as *Fear and Loathing in Las Vegas, and Other American Stories*)

Fear and Loathing: On the Campaign Trail '72, 1973

The Great Shark Hunt: Strange Tales from a Strange Time, Gonzo Papers, Volume One, 1979

The Curse of Lono, 1983 (with Ralph Steadman)

Generation of Swine: Tales of Shame and Degradation in the '80's, Gonzo Papers, Volume Two, 1988

Songs of the Doomed: More Notes on the Death of the American Dream, Gonzo Papers, Volume Three, 1990

Better than Sex: Confessions of a Political Junkie, Gonzo Papers, Volume Four, 1994

The Proud Highway: Saga of a Desperate Southern Gentleman, 1955-1967, 1997 (Douglas Brinkley, editor)

Fear and Loathing in America: The Brutal Odyssey of an Outlaw Journalist, 1968-1976, 2000 (Brinkley, editor)

The Kingdom of Fear: Loathsome Secrets of a Star-Crossed Child in the Final Days of the American Century, 2003

Hey Rube: Blood Sport, the Bush Doctrine, and the Downward Spiral of Dumbness, 2004

About the Author

Falconer, Delia. "From Alger to Edge-Work: Mapping the Shark Ethic in Hunter S. Thompson's *Fear and Loathing in Las Vegas*." *Antithesis* 6, no. 2 (1993): 111-125.

Hellmann, John. "Corporate Fiction, Private Fable, and Hunter S. Thompson's *Fear and Loathing: On the Campaign Trail '72*." *Critique: Studies in Modern Fiction* 21, no. 1 (1979): 16-30.

Johnson, Michael. "Other New Journalists: The Youth and Radical Scene and the New Muckrakers." In *The New Journalism: The Underground Press, the Artists of Nonfiction, and Changes in the Established Media*. Lawrence: University of Kansas Press, 1971.

McKeen, William. *Hunter S. Thompson*. Boston: Twayne, 1991.

Perry, Paul. *Fear and Loathing: The Strange and Terrible Saga of Hunter S. Thompson*. New York: Thunder's Mouth Press, 1992.

Sickles, Robert. "A Countercultural Gatsby—Hunter S. Thompson's *Fear and Loathing in Las Vegas*: The Death of the American Dream and the Rise of Las Vegas, USA." *Popular Culture Review* 11, no. 1 (February, 2000): 61-73.

Weingarten, Marc. *The Gang That Wouldn't Write Straight: Wolfe, Thompson, Didion, and the New Journalism Revolution*. New York: Crown, 2005.

HENRY DAVID THOREAU

Born: Concord, Massachusetts
July 12, 1817
Died: Concord, Massachusetts
May 6, 1862

With Walden *and his other nature writings, Thoreau advocated environmental awareness; as a Transcendentalist, he urged all individuals to develop their fullest potential; as a social critic, he challenged materialism and conformity and formulated the doctrine of civil disobedience.*

Courtesy, the Thoreau Institute
Research Collections

BIOGRAPHY

Many of Henry David Thoreau's writings are autobiographical, for he thought that the poet's noblest work was his life. Thoreau was born on July 12, 1817, in Concord, Massachusetts, the third of four children of John and Cynthia Thoreau. The family name is French, and Henry's paternal grandfather was a Protestant emigrant from Jersey, an island in the English Channel. His maternal grandfather was a Congregationalist minister. Thoreau was baptized David Henry but later reversed his first two names. His father, a quiet, subdued person, after failing as a shopkeeper, moved to Boston to teach school but returned to Concord when Henry was six and began to manufacture lead pencils. His mother was more energetic; active in community affairs, she was considered one of the most talkative persons in Concord.

Though a village of some two thousand people, Concord was full of intellectual ferment, being the home of Ralph Waldo Emerson and Bronson Alcott (and, later, of Nathaniel Hawthorne). To it came many literary people attracted to Emerson's Transcendentalism. After attending the Concord Academy, Thoreau went to Harvard College and graduated in 1837. While there, he heard Emerson lecture and read Emerson's "Nature," which became a seminal book for him. In the spring of 1837, Thoreau met Emerson in person, and the neighbors became friends and associates. Thoreau joined an informal group of Transcendentalists who met at Emerson's house.

At Thoreau's commencement, Emerson had given his lecture "The American Scholar," urging intellectual independence from Europe and advocating physical activity as much as book learning, and he apparently thought Thoreau exemplified such concepts. A "jack of all trades," Thoreau was an expert surveyor and a practical scientist in botany, zoology, ornithology, mineralogy, astronomy, and anthropology. Also skilled with tools, he "could outwalk, outswim, outrun, outskate, and outboat most of his contemporaries," according to his biographer Walter Harding.

Thoreau built boats and houses and invented tools, machines, and techniques that made the Thoreau pencils the best in America. Emerson, by contrast, was absolutely unhandy, even at making minor repairs, and, for all his talk of nature, was not an outdoorsman and confined himself to walks in his orchard.

After graduation, Thoreau worked for a while in his father's pencil factory, invented a superior method of mixing graphite, and began to lecture at the Concord Lyceum. In 1838, he and his brother John reopened the Concord Academy, where Thoreau was a popular and innovative teacher who took his students on frequent field trips and immersed them in local human and natural history. He stopped teaching because he would not flog students, but he later did a good deal of tutoring. In 1839, the Thoreau brothers took a boating trip on the Concord and Merrimack Rivers that became the subject of Thoreau's first book. Both brothers proposed marriage to Ellen Sewall, who rejected them both.

When the Concord Academy closed in 1841 because of John's tuberculosis, Thoreau moved into Emerson's house as resident handyman for two years. There, he had access to Emerson's library, with its extensive collection of Oriental philosophy and literature. Thoreau rejected the Oriental myths as superstition but appreciated the Eastern values of spirituality, meditation, and solitude. He also began to publish poems and essays in *The Dial*, the Transcendentalist magazine. In 1842, Thoreau met Hawthorne, then living in Concord's Old Manse, who later used him as a model for the faunlike Donatello in *The Marble Faun* (1860).

That year, John Thoreau died of tetanus, and the grieving Henry developed identical symptoms that were purely psychosomatic. Recovering, he took a position on Staten Island in New York as tutor to the children of Emerson's brother, but, homesick for Concord, he returned home after a few months and resumed working in the family pencil factory.

In 1845, Thoreau built a one-room cabin on the shore of Walden Pond on land owned by Emerson. Aside from some visits and excursions, he lived there alone for two years, two months, and two days. During his time at Walden, he was imprisoned for a night in 1846 for refusing to pay the state poll tax. In 1847, Thoreau left the Walden cabin when he was invited to take care of Emerson's house and family while Emerson lectured in Europe. The following year, Thoreau began his own career as a lecturer, though he listed his profession as surveying.

His first book, *A Week on the Concord and Merrimack Rivers*, written while he was at Walden, was published in 1849 but sold poorly. That year he took the first of three trips to Cape Cod, and the following year he made an excursion to Quebec. During the 1850's, he gathered a vast store of data on botany, zoology, and ornithology during his daily walks in the woods, donated specimens to museums, became a member of the Boston Society of Natural History, did pioneer work on pollens, and wrote a paper on "The Succession of Forest Trees" that made important discoveries about forest management.

Emerson, for whom nature (and much else) was almost entirely an abstraction, objected to Thoreau's detailed work in natural history, but it is precisely this vivid detail that makes Thoreau's work seem more meaningful today than that of Emerson. Thoreau practiced the self-reliance about which Emerson merely talked. Even Emerson acknowledged, "Thoreau gives me, in flesh and blood and pertinacious Saxon belief, my own ethics. He is far more real, and daily practically obeying them, than I." Emerson gave lip service to abolition, but Thoreau was the most active conductor on the underground railroad in Concord and wrote the militant "Slavery in Massachusetts" (1854). By 1850, Emerson had become estranged from Thoreau, who called their relationship "one long tragedy" in which the older writer had patronized the younger.

In compensation for the loss of Emerson's friendship, Thoreau became friends with Louis Agassiz and got to know most of the leading American writers of his day, including Walt Whitman, Bronson and Louisa May Alcott, Henry Wadsworth Longfellow, Henry James, Sr., and Horace Greeley, who regularly promoted his work. During the 1850's, Thoreau took several trips to the Maine woods and to Cape Cod. In 1853, he published parts of "A Yankee in Canada" in *Putnam's Monthly;* in 1854, he published his masterpiece, *Walden: Or, Life in the Woods;* and in 1855, he published his first Cape Cod essays in *Putnam's Monthly*. In 1857, he met John Brown in Concord and became a champion of his militant abolitionist activity. When his father died in 1859, Thoreau took over the family pencil factory, while continuing to give frequent lectures and to defend John Brown, executed for his raid on Harpers Ferry, Virginia.

By 1855, Thoreau had contracted tuberculosis, perhaps from too much exposure in the woods. For seven years, he fought the disease; in 1861, he visited Minnesota in a vain attempt to improve his health in a drier climate, but he died at the age of forty-four in 1862. Posthumous publications include numerous essays, including *The Maine Woods* (1864), *Cape Cod* (1865), *Letters to Various Persons* (1865), *A Yankee in Canada, with Antislavery and Reform Papers* (1866), and his *Journal* (1906).

ANALYSIS

Thoreau is a major figure in the American Transcendental movement and in what F. O. Matthiessen calls the American Renaissance of the 1840's and 1850's, when American literature came of age. Undogmatic and unsystematic, Transcendentalism was in part a heritage from Puritanism but in larger part a rebellion against it. Its American leader was Emerson, who resigned from his Unitarian ministry because even it was too dogmatic for him.

Transcendentalism rejected organized religion, biblical authority, and the concept of Original Sin in favor of pantheism and a belief in the daily rebirth of God in the individual soul. An eclectic faith rather than a systematic philosophy, it derived in part from platonic idealism, German mysticism, French utopianism, and the Hindu scriptures. Part of the Romantic movement's reaction against the Age of Reason, it stressed the instinct rather than the intellect. As Thoreau wrote, "We do not learn by inference and deduction and the application of mathematics to philosophy, but by direct intercourse and sympathy."

At first Emerson's disciple, Thoreau soon he became his own man. Emerson complained that Thoreau had no new ideas: "I am very familiar with all his thoughts," Emerson wrote, "they are my own quite originally drest." Formulating new ideas did not interest Thoreau. Emerson wrote largely in abstractions, but Thoreau did not care for abstract ideas and theorizing, stating, "Let us not underrate the value of a fact; it will one day flower in a truth." His friend Ellery Channing said that "metaphysics was his aversion." Thus F. O. Matthiessen observes that "Thoreau does not disappear into the usual transcendental vapour."

Thoreau had to test his ideas by living them and then communicating his experiences instead of declaiming abstractions. "How can we expect a harvest of thought who have not had a seed time of character?" he asked. His actions were not entirely original; Bronson Alcott had earlier refused to pay his poll tax, and Stearns Wheeler had lived in a shanty on Flint's Pond, but they did not write about these experiences in the pithy way Thoreau did, nor did they offer his profound criticism of materialism, which prevented people from realizing their own potential. Thoreau insisted that "if one advances confidently in the direction of his dreams, and endeavors to live the life which he has imagined, he will meet with a success unexpected in common hours" and will thus transcend his lower

self and his society. Doing so requires what Emerson called self-reliance, which Thoreau exemplified in his own life, writing that "If a man does not keep pace with his companions, perhaps it is because he hears a different drummer. Let him step to the music which he hears, however measured or far away."

Thoreau is the United States' first and best major writer on nature as well as one of its most trenchant social critics. His vivid, pithy prose is ultimately richer than Emerson's abstractions, and although his verse is usually second-rate, his prose poetry has made him one of the great artists of American literature.

A WEEK ON THE CONCORD AND MERRIMACK RIVERS

First published: 1849
Type of work: Essay

The contemplation of nature reveals the unity of nature and humankind and provides a health not found in diseased society.

Thoreau's first book, *A Week on the Concord and Merrimack Rivers*, is the account of a two-week boat and hiking trip he made with his brother John in 1839. Shortly thereafter, Thoreau sold the boat to Nathaniel Hawthorne. Thoreau worked on the manuscript for ten years, intending it, after John's death in 1842, to be a tribute to him. Thoreau wrote most of the work while living at Walden (writing it was part of the "private business" he planned to transact there) but continued revising it for two more years.

Despite its being promoted by Emerson, publishers would not print it unless the author underwrote the cost. James Munroe & Co. printed a thousand copies but bound only 450. Despite generally favorable reviews at home and in England, the book did not sell, and Thoreau, stuck with the unsold copies, lamented in 1853, "I have now a library of nearly nine hundred volumes, over seven hundred of which I wrote myself." A second edition came out posthumously in 1867, with additions and corrections, and the book has remained in print ever since.

In part, the work is an elegy to Thoreau's brother, who, in the elegiac tradition, is never named. Following an introductory essay, there are seven chapters—one for claiming each day of the week. About 40 percent consists of travel narrative; the rest is a combination of essays, poems, anecdotes, quotations, translations, philosophical observations on life and nature, and numerous digressions. James Russell Lowell complained that so little of it is about the trip itself, noting, "We were bid to a river party—not to be preached at."

Carl Bode somewhat agrees with Lowell, noting that "[t]he scholar is much more apparent than the traveler, for the original narrative has been weighted down with learned allusions and quotations." While the book does contain many of Thoreau's philosophical musings, however, it is by no means all preaching. Thoreau celebrates the sounds and silences, the light and shadows, of the natural world. Drifting along in their boat, he and his brother find a freedom like that of Huckleberry Finn on his raft. There are word paintings of the river and the landscape through which it flows that make it a verbal correspondence to some of the landscape paintings of the time. Thoreau celebrates the variety and vitality of nature and wildlife, "such healthy natural tumult as proves the last day is not yet at hand."

He presents part of what he calls "The Natural History of Massachusetts" in his picture of river birds, fish and fishermen, trees and wildflowers. As Robert Frost would later, Thoreau often details a scene of nature and then draws a moral or philosophical reflection from it. A neo-Platonist, he sometimes sees "objects as through a thin haze, in their eternal relations," wondering "who set them up, and for what purpose." At times, "he becomes immortal with her [nature's] immortality." Yet he also has a Darwinian awareness of the suffering in nature, the tragic end of creatures of the wild. Sometimes he recounts historical vignettes called to mind by passing locations. The book lacks the unity of *Walden* but anticipates it in many of Thoreau's concerns—a mystical relationship with nature and the life spirit, a love for wildness in nature and independence in people, and the belief that people can redirect their lives in simpler and more fulfilling ways.

WALDEN

First published: 1854
Type of work: Essay

By living alone in the woods, Thoreau set an example of how to simplify and enrich one's life.

In 1845, when he was twenty-seven years old, Thoreau built a one-room cabin on Emerson's land in the woods on the shore of Walden Pond, less than two miles from Concord. He borrowed an axe, bought the boards from an Irish railroad worker's shanty, and erected a ten-by-fifteen-foot building. He moved into his new abode on the symbolic date of Independence Day.

There he lived austerely, growing beans and doing odd jobs, living on a simple diet, and spending less than nine dollars for food during the first eight months. His plan was to simplify his life, to "live free and uncommitted," working about six weeks a year in order to have the remaining forty-six weeks free to read, write, live in intimate relationship to nature, "affect the quality of the day," and demonstrate the Transcendental belief in "the unquestionable ability of man to elevate his life by a conscious endeavor." He summed up his experiment by writing:

> I went to the woods because I wished to live deliberately, to front only the essential facts of life, and see if I could not learn what it had to teach, and not, when I came to die, discover that I had not lived. . . . I wanted to live deep and suck out all the marrow of life, to live so sturdily and Spartan-like as to put to rout all that was not life, to cut a broad swath and shave close; to drive life into a corner, and reduce it to its lowest terms, and, if it proved to be mean . . . to get the whole and genuine meanness of it, and publish its meanness to the world; or if it were sublime, to know it by experience, and be able to give a true account of it.

Feeling that most people live hurried, complicated "lives of quiet desperation," "frittered away by detail," he urged them to simplify. Citing the case of an Indian craftsman whose baskets people would no longer buy, Thoreau set an example for poor students and for would-be artists, who fear being unable to make a living by their writing, painting, music, or sculpture. Believing that many people were enslaved too much by working at unfulfilling jobs to provide themselves with material objects, he showed that if they will do with less, they can find the freedom to pursue their heart's desire. Like Thomas Carlyle, the English Transcendentalist friend of Emerson, Thoreau urged people to lower their denominator—to enrich the spiritual quality of their lives by reducing their dependence on the material by choosing "the vantage point of what we should call voluntary poverty," for "a man is rich in proportion to the number of things which he can afford to let alone."

Walden functions on several levels. As autobiography, it resembles Walt Whitman's "Song of Myself" (1855), for like Whitman, Thoreau wrote, "I should not talk so much about myself if there were anybody else whom I knew so well." Leon Edel places *Walden* among the literature of imaginary voyages. On the autobiographical and documentary level, it has affinities with Robinson Crusoe's solitary and self-reliant life on his island; its documentary detail also resembles Herman Melville's accounts of South Seas culture and of whaling, while on another level, it is like the voyage of the *Pequod* in his *Moby Dick* (1851) as a quest for ultimate spiritual reality.

Emerson complained of Thoreau's fondness for leading huckleberry parties, and as a "drop-out" from "this chopping sea of civilized life," Thoreau resembles Huckleberry Finn fleeing from "sivilization," the Walden cabin and Huck's raft both symbolizing freedom from conformity. As a work of social criticism, *Walden* challenges the abuses of capitalist materialism, for Thoreau observes that wage slaves such as the Fitchburg railroad workers laboring sixteen hours a day in poverty have no freedom to develop the artistic and spiritual side of their lives. Full of close observation of the seasons, of flora and fauna, *Walden* is finally a testament to the renewing power of nature, to the need to respect and preserve the environment, to a belief

that "in wildness is the salvation of the world"—a statement that has become a doctrine of the Sierra Club.

Thoreau never expected his readers to follow his example and live alone in a one-room hut. Such a life would make marriage difficult, if not impossible (indeed, Thoreau remained a bachelor). He himself stayed at Walden only long enough to prove that his experiment could work, after which he returned to Concord. In some ways, *Walden* is misleading. In form, it consists of eighteen essays loosely connected, in which Thoreau condenses his twenty-six-month sojourn at Walden into the seasons of a single year. In addition, he draws upon experiences there before and after his residence at the pond. Thoreau was not as solitary, austere, or remote as *Walden* suggests.

Walden was not a wilderness, nor was Thoreau a pioneer. His hut was within two miles of town, and while at Walden, he made almost daily visits to Concord and to his family, dined out often, had frequent visitors, and went off on excursions. Thoreau did not expect his readers literally to follow his example but to find applications to their own lives so that they can live more freely and intensely, with their eyes and ears more keenly attuned to the world around them, whatever it may be, and with their spirit closer to the life force behind nature.

"CIVIL DISOBEDIENCE"

First published: 1849
Type of work: Essay

In Thoreau's view, when a law is unjust it is the just person's duty to refuse to obey it.

Thoreau wrote "Civil Disobedience," first titled "Resistance to Civil Government" when it was published in the periodical *Aesthetic Papers*, in response to questions about why he had gone to jail. As an abolitionist, he had objected to the Massachusetts poll tax and refused to pay it as a protest against slavery. When the Mexican War broke out in 1846, he protested against it as an aggressive war of conquest aimed in part at adding new slave territories to the United States, and for this reason as well, he refused to pay the tax.

For several years, the authorities ignored Thoreau's nonpayment, but in July of 1846, Concord constable Sam Staples ordered Thoreau to pay up. When Thoreau still failed to comply, Staples arrested him on July 23 or 24 and imprisoned him in the Middlesex County jail. That evening some unknown person paid Thoreau's fine, but Staples kept Thoreau in jail until after breakfast before releasing him. Emerson called Thoreau's action "mean and skulking, and in bad taste," and there is an apocryphal story that Emerson, visiting Thoreau in prison, asked, "Henry David, what are you doing in there?" to which he replied, "Ralph Waldo, what are you doing out there?" Bronson Alcott, however, called Thoreau a good example of "dignified noncompliance with the injunction of civil powers."

In the essay, Thoreau argues that laws, being human-made, are not infallible, that there is a higher divine law, and that when those laws conflict, one must obey the higher law. Hence slavery, no matter how legal (and it remained legal until 1865), was always unjust in its violation of the integrity and divine soul of the enslaved. So long as the American government upheld slavery, Thoreau said, one "cannot without disgrace be associated with it. I cannot for an instant recognize that political organization as my government which is the slave's government also."

Carrying to extreme the logic of the Declaration of Independence, Thoreau argues, in effect, that each individual should declare independence from unjust laws, that citizens must never surrender their conscience to the legislators, and that "[i]t is not desirable to cultivate a respect for the law, so much as for the right." Most people, he feared, served the state as soldiers do, like unthinking machines.

He does not, however, argue for violent revolution; he advocates nonviolent resistance. (Later, Thoreau would contradict such a philosophy in three essays championing John Brown, who endorsed and practiced violence.) The disobedient must be prepared to accept punishment, if necessary: "Under a government which imprisons any unjustly, the true place for a just man is also a prison." Thoreau concludes:

> The authority of government . . . must have the sanction and consent of the governed. It can have no pure right over my person and property but what I conceded to it. There will never be a really free and enlightened State until the State comes to recognize the individual as a higher and independent power, from which all its own power and authority are derived, and treats him accordingly.

This doctrine has always been repellent to authoritarians of the far Right and Left, who tolerate no dissent and have had protesters beaten, imprisoned, and even killed. In the seventeenth century, Governor John Winthrop of the Massachusetts Bay Colony reproved his constituents for daring to criticize him, calling them naturally depraved and maintaining that the authorities are instituted by God and that to criticize them constitutes treason and atheism.

In *Billy Budd, Foretopman* (1924), Herman Melville satirically presented the authoritarian military point of view when Captain Vere insists that those in uniform must obey without question: "We fight at command. If our judgments approve the war, that is but coincidence. . . . For that law and the rigour of it, we are not responsible. Our vowed responsibility is in this: That however pitilessly that law may operate, we nevertheless adhere to it and administer it." Vere's is the defense of all war criminals—that they were only carrying out orders and cannot be expected to disobey. The rationale behind war crimes trials, however, is that even the military are subject to a higher law.

Civil disobedience is at least as old as Socrates, who preferred to die rather than yield to an order to stop asking questions that embarrassed the authorities, to whom he said, "I shall obey God, rather than you." The Christian martyrs who refused to deny their God and worship Caligula, Nero, or some other depraved Roman emperor were practicing civil disobedience. All abolitionists, members of the Underground Railroad, and those who refused to obey the Fugitive Slave Act were practicing civil disobedience. History and literature are full of examples. Huckleberry Finn resolved to defy his upbringing and "go to hell" in order to rescue his best friend, a runaway slave. Mahatma Gandhi was an admirer of Thoreau and adopted his policy of nonviolent resistance to oppose racism in Africa and imperialism in India. American civil rights leader Dr. Martin Luther King, Jr., patterned nonviolent resistance after Gandhi.

In fact, the U.S. government's system of checks and balances sometimes requires its citizens to break the law, for the only way to challenge the constitutionality of a law is to break it and try a test case, as Dr. King and his followers repeatedly did. Dr. King was frequently imprisoned and called a criminal for violating local statutes that instituted racial discrimination, but he believed in the higher law of the Constitution and wrote, "Words cannot express the exultation felt by the individual as he finds himself, with hundreds of his fellows, behind prison bars for a cause he knows is just." During the Vietnam War, an increasingly large number of people protested that the war was unjust, and many of draft age refused to serve in the armed forces and went to prison or into exile rather than be forced to kill or be killed in Vietnam. The government's position was that they were cowards or traitors, but a majority of the U.S. population came to agree with the protesters.

One problem with Thoreau's doctrine is that it is not always easy to determine whether a law is just or unjust. Thoreau never advocated the indiscriminate breaking of laws; civil disobedience applies only in cases of fundamental moral principle. Not all individuals are necessarily right in defying the government. For example, during the Civil Rights movement of the 1960's, some southern governors defied court orders to desegregate schools and other institutions, arguing that segregation was the will of God.

Frequently it is liberals who endorse civil disobedience, but in the late 1980's, members of the conservative Iran-Contra conspiracy defended their breaking of laws and lying to Congress on the grounds that they were serving a higher law. Similarly, opponents of abortion rights have argued that a higher law requires them to break laws that prohibit them from harassing those who sanction abortion rights. Thus the debate continues; through it all, Thoreau's essay remains one of the most potent and influential ever written.

JOURNAL

First published: 1906 (in *The Writings of Henry David Thoreau*)
Type of work: Journal

For twenty-four years, Thoreau recorded his thoughts and observations in his private journal.

From October 22, 1837, when he was twenty years old, until November 3, 1861, when he was suffering his fatal illness, Thoreau kept a journal. Biographer Walter Harding considers it "his major literary accomplishment," though its length of nearly two million words, fourteen volumes, and more than seven thousand printed pages makes it less accessible to the reader than *Walden* and the other shorter works that Thoreau polished for publication. A lost fifteenth volume was discovered and published in 1958. Leon Edel, who values the journal less than Harding does, calls it "discursive, sprawling, discontinuous" and complains that it is "aloof" and impersonal, with too much matter-of-factness and too little humor and feeling.

Much of the journal consists of Thoreau's reflections on nature during his daily walks and comments on his reading. In it, Thoreau often considers the problem of writing and revision as well as his observations of nature and of his neighbors in and around Concord. In his published writings, Thoreau often seems more solitary than he really was, and it is the journal that comments on his friends, his activities in Concord, and the considerable variety of people he encountered and talked with on his daily walks or who visited him at Walden.

From the journal, Thoreau mined much of the material for his lectures and the writings published during his lifetime. To it he confided many of his most intimate thoughts. As he put it:

From all the points of the compass, from the earth beneath and the heavens above, have come these inspirations and been entered duly in the order of their arrival in the journal. Thereafter, when the time arrived, they were winnowed into lectures, and again, in due time, from lectures into essays.

Some of his excursions never made it into essays and are recounted only in the journal, which is invaluable as autobiography and as a supplement to the works that he prepared for publication. Readers reluctant to plow through all fifteen volumes might instead look at *The Heart of Thoreau's Journal*, edited by Odell Shepard in 1927, or at *Men of Concord*, edited from the journal by F. H. Allen in 1936 and illustrated by N. C. Wyeth.

SUMMARY

Attacked by hostile critics such as James Russell Lowell for his nonconformity, Thoreau in some ways anticipated what came to be called the "counterculture." Despite his criticism of a materialistic society, he did not "propose to write an ode to dejection, but to brag as lustily as chanticleer in the morning, standing on his roost, if only to wake my neighbors up" to the Transcendental belief that they can elevate themselves to a fuller, simpler, more intense life.

America's greatest nature writer, Thoreau is a forefather of John Muir, Edward Abbey, and Aldo Leopold. Politically, he influenced William Morris and leaders of the British labor movement in the late nineteenth century. Leo Tolstoy called *Walden* one of the great books, and Robert Frost wrote that it "surpasses everything we have in America." Frank Lloyd Wright spoke of its positive impact on American architecture, and President John F. Kennedy spoke of "Thoreau's pervasive and universal influence on social thinking and political action." Thoreau unquestionably wrote one of the indispensable classics of American literature.

Robert E. Morsberger

BIBLIOGRAPHY

By the Author

NONFICTION:
"Civil Disobedience," 1849 (also known as "Resistance to Civil Government")
A Week on the Concord and Merrimack Rivers, 1849
Walden: Or, Life in the Woods, 1854
Excursions, 1863
The Maine Woods, 1864
Cape Cod, 1865
Letters to Various Persons, 1865 (Ralph Waldo Emerson, editor)
A Yankee in Canada, with Anti-Slavery and Reform Papers, 1866
Early Spring in Massachusetts, 1881
Summer, 1884
Winter, 1888
Autumn, 1892
Familiar Letters of Henry David Thoreau, 1894 (F. B. Sanborn, editor)
Journal, 1981-2002 (7 volumes)
Letters to a Spiritual Seeker, 2004 (edited by Bradley P. Dean)

POETRY:
Poems of Nature, 1895
Collected Poems of Henry Thoreau, 1943 (first critical edition)

MISCELLANEOUS:
The Writings of Henry David Thoreau, 1906 (20 volumes)
Collected Essays and Poems, 2001

DISCUSSION TOPICS

- What does Leon Edel mean by classifying *Walden* as an "imaginary voyage"?

- The first chapter of *Walden* is called "Economy." What meanings of the word are applicable in this chapter, and what is Henry David Thoreau's purpose in beginning the work in this way?

- How does Thoreau use time as a unifying device in *Walden*?

- How does Thoreau's concept of Transcendentalism differ from that of Ralph Waldo Emerson?

- What qualities of the essay "Civil Disobedience" have made it so extraordinarily influential?

- How did Thoreau's journal serve him?

- What has made Thoreau's journal such a popular work with dedicated Thoreauvians?

About the Author

Cain, William E. *A Historical Guide to Henry David Thoreau.* New York: Oxford University Press, 2000.

Dolis, John. *Tracking Thoreau: Double-Crossing Nature and Technology.* Madison, N.J.: Fairleigh Dickinson University Press, 2005.

Hahn, Stephen. *On Thoreau.* Belmont, Calif.: Wadsworth, 2000.

Harding, Walter. *The Days of Henry Thoreau.* New York: Alfred A. Knopf, 1965.

Harding, Walter, and Michael Meyer. *The New Thoreau Handbook.* New York: New York University Press, 1980.

Howarth, William. *The Book of Concord: Thoreau's Life as a Writer.* New York: Viking Press, 1982.

Maynard, W. Barksdale. *Walden Pond: A History.* New York: Oxford University Press, 2004.

Myerson, Joel, ed. *The Cambridge Companion to Henry David Thoreau.* New York: Cambridge University Press, 1995.

Porte, Joel. *Consciousness and Culture: Emerson and Thoreau Reviewed.* New Haven, Conn.: Yale University Press, 2004.

Richardson, Robert D. *Henry Thoreau: A Life of the Mind.* Berkeley: University of California Press, 1986.

Salt, Henry S. *Life of Henry David Thoreau.* Reprint. Hamden, Conn.: Archon Books, 1968.

Schneider, Richard J., ed. *Thoreau's Sense of Place: Essays in American Environmental Writing.* Iowa City: University of Iowa Press, 2000.

Tauber, Alfred I. *Henry David Thoreau and the Moral Agency of Knowing.* Berkeley: University of California Press, 2001.

Waggoner, Hyatt H. *American Poets: From the Puritans to the Present.* New York: Houghton Mifflin, 1968.

James Thurber

Born: Columbus, Ohio
December 8, 1894
Died: New York, New York
November 2, 1961

Thurber's short stories, essays, fables, autobiographical writings, and cartoons established him as one of America's great humorists—in the opinion of some critics the greatest since Mark Twain.

Library of Congress

BIOGRAPHY

James Grover Thurber, the second of the three sons of Charles Thurber and the former Mary Agnes Fisher, was born in Columbus, Ohio, on December 8, 1894. The family moved to the Washington, D.C., area in 1902 while his father worked as a stenographer for his representative in Congress. At a temporary residence in Falls Church, Virginia, in August of that year, a rubber-tipped arrow shot by his brother William accidentally struck James in the left eye. Several days later the eye was removed, but the delay may have affected the right eye, whose sight he also subsequently lost. An embittered Thurber certainly thought so later. Troubles with his vision plagued him throughout his life but also inspired some of his rarest humor.

The family returned to Columbus after a year, but the father's inability to find steady employment and subsequent illness kept the Thurbers poor. After graduating from Columbus East High School in 1913, the future humorist entered Ohio State University in his hometown that September. He dropped out of the university twice and never graduated, but while there he served as an editor of the daily campus newspaper and contributed to the university's monthly humor magazine. Always interested in the theater, he developed an important friendship with fellow student Elliott Nugent, an already successful actor.

After a short stint as a code and cipher clerk with the U.S. State Department, which took Thurber to Paris just after the World War I armistice, he spent four years as a reporter for the *Columbus Dispatch*. In 1922 he married Althea Adams, who encouraged him to return to Paris, where he worked on the Paris edition of the *Chicago Tribune*. Returning to the United States in 1926 to try his hand at freelance writing, he succeeded in placing his work in *The New Yorker*, whose editor, Harold Ross, soon hired him as an editor. He wrote or rewrote, in his own estimation, about a million words for the magazine's "Talk of the Town" section over the following eight years.

At *The New Yorker* Thurber established a close friendship with E. B. White, with whom he wrote a spoof of the popular manuals of advice on sexual relations. Entranced by the unique drawings with which Thurber amused the staff, White encouraged his friend to illustrate *Is Sex Necessary?* (1929), thus introducing them to the world. They did not begin to appear in the magazine until 1932. In that year Thurber's book of drawings, *The Seal in the Bedroom and Other Predicaments*, delighted a still larger audience. In 1935 Thurber resigned from *The New Yorker* staff but continued to contribute to the magazine throughout his career.

The marriage of James and Althea Thurber proved a stormy one. The couple separated in 1929, then made several only partially successful attempts to reconcile. Their daughter and only child, Rosemary, was born in 1931. In 1935 they divorced, and Thurber married magazine editor Helen Wismer, who proved a much more compatible mate. Although this union brought no children, it persisted happily to the end of Thurber's life.

Thurber's hilarious autobiography, *My Life and Hard Times*, which appeared in 1933, established him as a humorist of the first rank. The publication of his short story "The Secret Life of Walter Mitty" in *The New Yorker* in 1939 and the following year's Broadway production of *The Male Animal*, which Thurber cowrote with his friend Elliott Nugent, were also career high points, but serious decline in his eyesight at this time necessitated a series of operations in 1940 and 1941 which nevertheless failed to arrest his increasing blindness. This affliction of course threatened his cartoons and other drawings even more than it did his writing, although he managed to draw with difficulty for another decade. Other highlights of his career included two books of fables and *The Thurber Carnival*, a 1945 anthology of his most distinctive work to date.

A severe drinking problem permeated Thurber's late years, but his work continued unabated. *The Years with Ross*, originally a series of articles on the founder and editor of *The New Yorker* that appeared in the magazine, became a best-selling book in 1959. Thurber appeared in eighty-eight performances of a Broadway revue based on his works in 1960. The revue earned him a Tony Award the following year. In October of 1961, doctors discovered a brain tumor and immediately performed surgery, but the humorist died on November 8 in Doctors Hospital in New York.

ANALYSIS

No other humorist has focused on relations between the sexes as persistently as Thurber. His first book, *Is Sex Necessary?*, written in collaboration with his *New Yorker* associate E. B. White, is primarily a lighthearted satire on the psychosexual literature of the time but incidentally reflects the sexual insecurity of its young coauthors. Thus the book mocked not only a social preoccupation with Freudian psychology but also Thurber's and White's own fears and anxieties, which, in Thurber's case, also shadow much of his later work.

Thurber continued to probe the conflicts of men and women in his writings and drawings long after *Is Sex Necessary?* His cartoons characteristically depict women who prove either physically or psy-chologically overpowering to small, ineffectual men, the most extreme example being one that bears the caption "Home," showing a tiny man approaching the front steps of his house, which at the rear resolves into a huge, ominous outline of his wife. Neither of Thurber's wives were the monsters that flowed so readily from his pen, and his second wife, Helen, seems to have proved just about the ideal mate for him. He may be said to have depicted in an intensified way the common male inability to comprehend, accept, and enjoy an abiding relationship with the other sex.

The male characters of Thurber's stories tend to be mild, rather ineffectual beings, often henpecked husbands seeking victory in the eternal battle of the sexes but lacking the personal resources needed to prevail. The protagonists of "The Secret Life of Walter Mitty" and "The Catbird Seat" are both previewed in a 1935 story, "Mr. Preble Gets Rid of His Wife." Mr. Preble's scheme—to lure his oppressor into the cellar of their home and murder and bury her there—has no chance of success. The key to the humor of the situation is not so much his lack of nerve as his wife's inability to take him seriously. She has gauged him so well that she can destroy his plan with a simple offhand comment.

In "The Secret Life of Walter Mitty," published four years later, Thurber's hapless male character, rather than contrive an absurd retaliation against his oppressive spouse, responds by lapsing into a fantasy world in which he performs a variety of courageous and difficult feats, all with a coolly self-confident air. In "The Catbird Seat," the female oppressor is a coworker of the meek Mr. Martin. Again, the man's extreme solution, murder, cannot possibly come off, but he is able to turn his failure to advantage and win a rare victory.

In his work at least, Thurber was able to achieve a perspective on the ambivalent and generally unhealthy attitude toward women that clouded his social and personal life. In life he both romanticized and disdained them; in his fiction there is no romance, while the disdain is filtered through a fairly sympathetic male character. Thurber manages to enable readers to recognize in the struggles of his bickering couples amusing exaggerations of the conflicts normal to intersexual relationships.

If Thurber could transmute his sexual anxieties into art, he also could capitalize brilliantly on purely physical weaknesses such as those resulting from his childhood accident. In 1933 he shaped the difficulties caused by his poor vision and other deficiencies of his early years into a hilarious autobiography, *My Life and Hard Times.* The oft-reprinted chapter called "University Days" is also a devasting satire on the shortcomings of Ohio State University. In describing one of his specific problems—his inability to see through a microscope in botany class—he shifts the focus to his frustrated professor, who, scrupulously insistent that the young man carry out his assignment, tries "every adjustment of the microscope known to man." When he has at last seemingly succeeded but finds that Thurber has drawn not what was under the microscope but his own eyeball, the reader sympathizes more with the stupefied professor than with his student.

In the same chapter Thurber cunningly demonstrates his ability to make literary capital of his own curiously ambivalent attitude toward the priorities of his alma mater. Ohio State was caught up at the time in a fierce football rivalry with the University of Michigan. In "University Days" this takes the form of a mass effort to boost a dim-witted star tackle named Bolenciecwcz through economics class. When the athlete is baffled by a request to "name one means of transportation," his fellow students, and even the professor, prompt him shamelessly until he manages to come out with "train." Bolenciecwcz is a disguised version of a historical Ohio State football hero whose exploits Thurber raved about for years afterward—while just as frequently deploring what he saw as the university's lax academic standards. Thurber manages to recreate the same ambivalence in the reader, who roots for Bolenciecwcz even while appreciating the author's delineation of the intellectual dishonesty that made this star player available to the team.

Thurber excelled at the presentation of characters who often failed but might achieve an unexpected success—who in fact succeed through failure, as he often did in his personal life. Thus, in the literary version of his collegiate self, he becomes expert at the mandatory military drill by the mere process of failing and repeating the course so many times. The timid victim of "The Catbird Seat" converts his comically inept failure to murder his tormenter into the more socially acceptable scheme of getting her dismissed. In his fable "The Unicorn

in the Garden," a man who cannot convince his verbally abusive wife of the unicorn he has seen turns the fate she devises for him—institutionalization—against her.

Particularly in his fables and other writings featuring animals, which Thurber loved to depict, he takes satirical advantage of his skills as writer and visual artist. One of the very few great practitioners of Aesop's art, he appended morals that are both funny and profound. "The Seal Who Became Famous" captures, in its circus performer who forgets how to swim, an instantly recognizable type. A number of the fables, such as "The Very Proper Gander," which satirizes the evils of superpatriotism, reflect his concern with the desperate remedies destructive of civil liberties to which society is liable in times of war both hot and cold. Like a handful of the greatest satirists, Thurber can also level his criticism at the whole human race, as in his "Interview with a Lemming," where the lemming, in response to a scientist's puzzlement as to why lemmings rush into the sea and drown, replies that he cannot "understand why you human beings don't." Here his satire becomes truly universal.

"THE SECRET LIFE OF WALTER MITTY"

First published: 1939 (collected in *Writings and Drawings*, 1996)
Type of work: Short story

A meek, submissive, middle-aged man daydreams of a heroic, resourceful alter ego.

"The Secret Life of Walter Mitty," Thurber's best-known story, is, like most of his fiction, short, requiring only five or six pages. As Mitty and his wife are on their way to do some errands, he indulges in a daydream in which he is a brave military commander piloting a hydroplane, but his wife interrupts by exclaiming that he is driving too fast. This pattern is repeated several times. When she urges him to make an appointment with his physician, he becomes an eminent surgeon at work, until a parking-lot attendant's contemptuous commands call him back temporarily to reality. In reality, Mitty does not do anything very well.

Very little actually happens in Thurber's story. Mrs. Mitty has an appointment at a hairdresser's; Mitty himself buys a pair of overshoes. While trying to remember what his wife has asked him to buy, he becomes a cocky defendant in a murder case. He manages to buy some dog food and sinks into a chair in a convenient hotel lobby and imagines himself a bomber pilot under fierce attack. His returning wife wakes him with the admonition that she is going to take his temperature when they get home. At the end of the story, Mrs. Mitty goes into a drugstore, and he becomes a "proud and disdainful" man facing a firing squad.

Part of Thurber's technique is to present Mitty as a man who fails even as a dreamer. His daydreams are cluttered with clichés. Whether he is a murder defendant or an Army officer, he bears the same "Webley-Vickers automatic." In both of his military dreams he is an officer who can lead his men "through hell." In reality, he is a man trying to deal with the fears and difficulties of a drab and disappointing life. As such, he is only an exaggerated version of a person whom everyone will recognize.

"YOU COULD LOOK IT UP"

First published: 1941 (collected in *Writings and Drawings*, 1996)
Type of work: Short story

A baseball manager employs a midget to revitalize his team.

"You Could Look It Up" is an unusual Thurber short story in point of view: that of an illiterate trainer employed by a major league baseball team. Thurber thereby adopts a technique already made famous by Ring Lardner, in which much of the humor derives from the way the speaker fractures the English language. Unlike the typical Lardner story, Thurber's also has a strong plot. The narrator recounts a story thirty years old, which prepares the reader for an old-fashioned "yarn." It also makes more plausible the lowbrow characteristics of the trainer and the team members by placing them in an era when the men of professional baseball were usually little educated.

Manager Squawks Magrew's team has been leading the league all season but has fallen into a slump that has melted its lead almost entirely away. In a bar Magrew meets an eccentric, fifty-four-year-old midget named Pearl du Monville. Magrew comes to enjoy his company and introduces him into the dugout as a kind of mascot. As Magrew grows more and more displeased with the performance of his players, he decides to sign and outfit Pearl as a player. In the ninth inning of a crucial game, with two outs, the bases loaded, and the team needing one run to tie and two to win the game, he calls upon the midget as a pinch-hitter with instructions to wait for the inevitable base on balls that any batter with such a tiny strike zone might reasonably expect.

The midget, however, does the unthinkable. He swings at a pitch and grounds out, ending the game. Magrew is so agitated that he picks up the midget by the ankles, whirls him around, and hurls him into the outfield, where the opposing center fielder catches him. Pearl disappears into the crowd and is never seen again, but the incident somehow gives the team a new spirit, and they go on to win the pennant.

Stories seldom make specific things happen, but this one inspired Bill Veeck, the owner of the real-life St. Louis Browns, to emulate the fictional Magrew's tactic in a 1951 American League game. The midget obeyed his manager and drew a walk, after which baseball outlawed the employment of midgets as players.

"THE CATBIRD SEAT"

First published: 1942 (collected in *Writings and Drawings*, 1996)
Type of work: Short story

An unassuming office worker finds a way to defeat an obnoxious efficiency expert.

"The Catbird Seat" combines Thurber's interests in baseball and in the Walter Mitty character. The mild-mannered protagonist of this story, Mr. Martin, is afflicted in his workplace by a loud, aggressive woman named Ulgine Barrows. Although she has been hired to reduce company expenditures and thus constitutes a threat to his security, he hates most her habit of taunting him with colorful expressions drawn from the lexicon of Red Barber, the real-life play-by-play announcer of the Brooklyn Dodgers. "Are you scraping the bottom of the pickle barrel?" "Are you sitting in the catbird seat?" Pleasant enough coming from Barber, these utterances, incessantly reiterated by his nemesis, convince Martin that he must kill her.

After going home from work one evening and drinking a glass of milk, Martin walks to the woman's apartment and barges in. She, of course unafraid of him, notices his extreme nervousness and offers him a drink. While she is in the kitchen, he cannot find the weapon he had hoped to locate in her living room. He accepts the drink and a cigarette, neither of which he has ever indulged in before. Beginning to boast that he intends to murder their mutual employer, he boldly "confirms" her suspicion that he is on dope. He then leaves, uttering, "Not a word about this." When promptly the

next morning Barrows complains to their boss about her visitor's behavior, Martin denies the allegations. Growing hysterical and finally violent, Barrows must be forcibly evicted from the premises, and Martin returns quietly to his work.

That Martin will fail in his attempt to kill his tormenter there is never any doubt, but he cannily turns his failure into a triumph. In Thurber's version of the eternal war of the sexes, "The Catbird Seat" marks the signal example of a masculine victory—one that, given the bullying nature of his antagonist, the reader is inclined to celebrate.

SUMMARY

Although Thurber's ambivalent attitude toward women complicated his earlier adult life, and his increasing blindness bedeviled his later years, he managed to capitalize famously on both deficiencies in his writing and drawing. Few humorists have so successfully transmuted their phobias and afflictions, as well as the general shortcomings of society, into art.

Robert P. Ellis

BIBLIOGRAPHY

By the Author

SHORT FICTION:
Is Sex Necessary? Or, Why We Feel the Way We Do, 1929 (with E. B. White)
The Owl in the Attic, and Other Perplexities, 1931
The Seal in the Bedroom, and Other Predicaments, 1932
My Life and Hard Times, 1933
The Middle-Aged Man on the Flying Trapeze, 1935
Let Your Mind Alone!, and Other More or Less Inspirational Pieces, 1937
The Last Flower: A Parable in Pictures, 1939
Fables for Our Time and Famous Poems Illustrated, 1940
My World—And Welcome to It!, 1942
The Great Quillow, 1944
The White Deer, 1945
The Thurber Carnival, 1945
The Beast in Me, and Other Animals: A New Collection of Pieces and Drawings About Human Beings and Less Alarming Creatures, 1948
The Thirteen Clocks, 1950
Thurber Country: A New Collection of Pieces About Males and Females, Mainly of Our Own Species, 1953
Further Fables for Our Time, 1956
The Wonderful O, 1957
Alarms and Diversions, 1957

Lanterns and Lances, 1961
Credos and Curios, 1962

DRAMA:
The Male Animal, pr., pb. 1940 (with Elliott Nugent)
Many Moons, pb. 1943
A Thurber Carnival, pr. 1960 (revue)

NONFICTION:
The Thurber Album, 1952
The Years with Ross, 1959
Selected Letters of James Thurber, 1982
The Thurber Letters: The Wit, Wisdom, and Surprising Life of James Thurber, 2003 (Harrison Kinney and Rosemary A. Thurber, editors)

MISCELLANEOUS:
Writings and Drawings, 1996

About the Author

Fensch, Thomas, ed. *Conversations with James Thurber.* Jackson: University Press of Mississippi, 1989.

Grauer, Neil A. *Remember Laughter: A Life of James Thurber.* Lincoln: University of Nebraska Press, 1994.

Holmes, Charles S. *The Clocks of Columbus: The Literary Career of James Thurber.* New York: Atheneum, 1972.

Kinney, Harrison. *James Thurber: His Life and Times.* New York: Henry Holt, 1995.

Kinney, Harrison, and Rosemary A. Thurber, eds. *The Thurber Letters: The Wit, Wisdom, and Surprising Life of James Thurber.* New York: Simon & Schuster, 2003.

Rosen, Michael J., ed. *Collecting Himself: James Thurber on Writing and Writers, Humor, and Himself.* New York: Harper & Row, 1989.

Tobias, Richard C. *The Art of James Thurber.* Athens: Ohio University Press, 1970.

DISCUSSION TOPICS

- Walter Mitty and Mr. Martin both feel oppressed by individual women. Which man induces more sympathy and why?

- What is misogyny? Are James Thurber's "The Secret Life of Walter Mitty" and "The Catbird Seat" misogynistic?

- How does the use of the grammatically challenged narrator enhance "You Could Look It Up"?

- How does Thurber employ irony in his short stories?

- Are the conclusions of Thurber's stories plausible?

The Beinecke Rare Book and Manuscript Library,
Yale University Library

JEAN TOOMER

Born: Washington, D.C.
December 26, 1894
Died: Doylestown, Pennsylvania
March 30, 1967

Cane, Toomer's unusual experimental novel, is a major product of the Harlem Renaissance of the 1920's, and the poems in it rank among the best African American poetry.

BIOGRAPHY

Nathan Pinchback Toomer (by school age he was known as Eugene Pinchback Toomer) was born in Washington, D.C., on December 26, 1894, the son of Nina Pinchback and Nathan Toomer. Until he was almost eleven, he lived with his maternal grandparents, his father having left the family in 1895. Racially mixed and able to pass as white, the Pinchbacks lived in an affluent white neighborhood, though Toomer's grandfather was well known as a black and briefly had been the governor of Louisiana during Reconstruction.

When Nina Toomer was remarried (to Archibald Combes, a white man), she and her son moved to New York, where they lived until she died in 1909. Returning to the Pinchbacks, who had experienced financial reversals, the teenage Toomer lived with them and an uncle in a modest black area, attended a black high school, and was faced with confronting the issue of his racial identity. He later wrote that he was "Scotch, Welsh, German, English, French, Dutch, Spanish, with some dark blood." Having lived in both the black and white worlds, for a while he determined to consider himself simply an American, hoping to eschew any racial label.

Between 1914 and 1921, he attended five colleges in three states for brief periods and lived in Chicago, Milwaukee, New York, and Washington, D.C. He also changed his name to Jean Toomer, began writing, and in New York came to know such promising young writers as Van Wyck Brooks, Witter Bynner, Waldo Frank, and Edwin Arlington Robinson. While in Washington in 1921, caring for his ailing grandparents and writing full time, he was asked to become temporary principal of the Sparta Agricultural and Industrial Institute, a rural Georgia school for black students. Whereas his experience in Chicago and Washington served as background for parts of *Cane* (1923), the two months in Sparta introduced Toomer to black life in the South. Its spirituality, music, economic deprivation, and segregation provided him with the subjects and themes of his major literary work.

He wrote "Bona and Paul," a story in the second section of *Cane*, in 1918 during a stay in Chicago, where the story is set. The other narratives and much of the verse, however, are products of a burst of creativity that began on the train that took him back to Washington from Georgia in November of 1921. A month after his return, he had completed the first draft of "Kabnis" (the third section of *Cane*), which closely reflects his Sparta sojourn. By the end of 1922, he had finished all the pieces that would make up *Cane*, and the book was published in 1923 with a foreward by Waldo Frank, who had become Toomer's close friend and mentor. Despite favorable reviews, only about five hundred copies were sold in 1923; a small second printing was made in 1927. Shortly thereafter, the book went out of print until 1967.

In the aftermath of *Cane*'s publication, Toomer became part of New York City's avant-garde white literary circles, but he objected both to rivalries that prevailed in the fraternity of writers and to attempts to promote him as a black writer. Largely because of these factors, he departed the literary scene by 1925. Though he continued to write, he published over the following four decades only a few short stories, some poetry, a book of maxims and aphorisms, and pamphlets about the Quakers.

Much of *Cane* suggests its author's uncertainty about his identity (stemming from his mixed racial background and upbringing) and religious beliefs (he commented that he was raised "without benefit of organized religion" but that he "did have religious experiences and . . . did somehow form feelings and notions of God.") Therefore, Toomer was receptive to the philosophy of George Ivanovich Gurdjieff, a Greek-Armenian mystic who taught in Russia until the Russian Revolution and then in various Western European cities prior to opening the Institute for the Harmonious Development of Man outside Paris. Central to Gurdjieff's teachings was the need to seek a balance of mind, body, and soul through which one could develop a higher consciousness and achieve one's maximum potential. Toomer spent the summer of 1924 at Gurdjieff's schools, quickly became a disciple, and during most of the following decade led Gurdjieff groups in New York and Chicago.

Toomer married twice, both times to white women. His first wife was Margery Latimer, a novelist he met while in a Gurdjieff group in Portage, Wisconsin. Within a year, she died in childbirth, though their daughter survived. In 1934, he remarried, to Marjorie Content, an affluent New Yorker active in literary circles. They moved to Doylestown, Pennsylvania, in 1936, where they joined and became active in the Society of Friends, or Quakers. Toomer returned to the Gurdjieff philosophy in the 1950's, but inadequate funds kept him from replicating the Paris institute. Plagued by frail health and alcoholism, he spent much of the last five years of his life in a Doylestown nursing home, where he died on March 30, 1967.

ANALYSIS

Most of the fiction (at least four novels and more than a dozen short stories), drama (about a half-dozen plays), and poetry (more than eighty poems) that Toomer wrote during his lifetime remains in manuscript form, so his public reputation rests almost entirely on one work, *Cane*. Published in 1923, the slim volume includes work in all three genres and is widely recognized as a major product of the Harlem Renaissance, a 1920's flowering of African American art and literature that created intense interest among black and white intellectuals.

Cane includes six brief prose cameos, seven stories, and a play, all of which concern African Americans of the time. The book is divided into three sections, the first and last of which are set in rural Georgia. The stories of the middle unit take place in Chicago and Washington, D.C. Between the first two sections, on a separate page, is a picture of an arc that is about one-fourth of a circle. On a page between the second and third parts are two such arcs, leaving an incomplete circle. In a letter to Waldo Frank accompanying the manuscript of *Cane*, Toomer explained the curves:

> From three angles, CANE's design is a circle. Aesthetically, from simple forms to complex ones, and back to simple forms. Regionally, from the South up into the North, and back into the South again. Or from the North down into the South and then a return North. . . . Between each of the three sections, a curve. These, to vaguely indicate the design.

"Kabnis," the third part of *Cane*, is about a northern black who goes to the rural South and is unable to adapt. Toomer's explanation of the curves suggests that Kabnis will return to the North. That the circle is left incomplete also points to a continuing alienation between the black cultures of the North and the South, the inability of the old rural and the new urban to reconcile their differences.

In addition to its intrinsic merits, the book is memorable for three reasons. First, Toomer explores aspects of southern and northern black life that had not previously been examined in fiction, paying tribute to the past and concurrently showing a race and society in flux. Second, *Cane* as a whole is an exercise in self-discovery. Its sensitive, self-effacing narrator is really the author himself, who is exploring his ambivalence about his racial identity. Toomer's use of his narrator is similar to Joseph Conrad's use of the character Marlow in much of his fiction. Third, the form of the book is unusual and has been the object of much discussion. Some critics consider it a gathering of fugitives—stories, poems, and a dramatic piece previously published separately in various magazines—that are unified only by recurrent themes and settings. Most, however, label it either as a work that defies standard categorizing or call it an experimental novel, a psychological novel, a poetic novel, or a lyrical novel.

Despite such quibbles over its form, *Cane* is not at all unique. It is similar to James Joyce's *Dubliners* (1914) and Sherwood Anderson's *Winesburg, Ohio* (1919), thematically related story collections that present unified visions of societies, and it also echoes Edgar Lee Masters's *Spoon River Anthology* (1915), a collection of poems that probe the secrets and psyches of a small town's residents.

Toomer was familiar with all three works, and he knew and learned from Anderson ("*Winesburg, Ohio* opened my eyes to entirely new possibilities," he wrote). *Cane* and *Winesburg, Ohio* both have narrators who mediate between author and reader, both are made up largely of prose cameos, and both have characters who become grotesques, in Toomer's case because of the lingering social and psychological effects of slavery.

Distinguishing *Cane* from the other works is the inclusion of poems between and within the stories. Usually folk songs or ballads, the poems reinforce the action and themes of the narratives. Recalling traditional African American music, mainly pre-Civil War slave spirituals, the poems enhance the mood of wistful, even mournful, pastoralism that pervades the book. Toomer believed that spirituals helped slaves to endure their bondage, so their presence in *Cane* gives the book a historical dimension. The poems also provide thematic transition from one narrative to another and heighten the work's impressionistic style, which incorporates myth and symbol.

Because Toomer's focus in the novel is on social, racial, and economic problems in both the rural South and urban North at World War I's end, he writes both realistically and naturalistically at different times. One critic has described Toomer's style as "a mysterious brand of Southern psychological realism that has been matched only in the best work of William Faulkner." An example of this amalgam of styles is the description of Tom Burwell's lynching in the story "Blood-Burning Moon" (the title of which is taken from a folk song), which is presented both with realistic specificity and in a deliberately ritualistic manner.

"Blood-Burning Moon," and *Cane* as a whole, have meaning and significance beyond the author's concerns with racial identity and conflict in the South and North. Most of his characters, men and women, even those who love and are loved, are strangers to those with whom they live. For example, the narrator of "Fern" says, "Men saw her eyes and fooled themselves." The eyes said one thing, but men read another. "They began to leave her, baffled and ashamed," because "men are apt to idolize or fear that which they cannot understand." In "Esther," King Barlo is "slow at understanding." In "Kabnis," the old man who lives below the shop is "a mute John the Baptist of a new religion—or a tongue-tied shadow of an old." In other words, *Cane* also is about people, whatever their race may be, who are unable to communicate even with their own kind.

CANE

First published: 1923
Type of work: Novel

Black people in the rural South and urban North of the early 1920's confront the difficulties of life in a changing, but still white-dominated, society.

The first part of *Cane* consists of six prose units (only three are fully developed stories) and ten poems that separate them. All are about a segregated South of sugar cane and cotton fields, and women are the main characters in all the narratives. The first, a lyrical two-page sketch, tells of Karintha, who "ripened too soon," and whose languid beauty lures both young and old men despite her passiveness. After giving birth to an illegitimate baby, she abandons it in a sawdust pile at the local mill, sets the mill ablaze, and turns to a life of prostitution. The sadness and futility of two generations of wasted lives are the dominant note here, as in the rest of the narratives.

In the next vignette, Becky is a white woman who violates the social codes by bearing two black sons.

Maintained by secret gifts from both races—signs of communal guilt and responsibility—she is a recluse, so the community can publicly deny her existence. When her small cabin burns down one day, she (like Karintha's baby and, in a later story, Tom Burwell) is consumed by fire.

The themes of sexuality, miscegenation, and universal guilt are again merged in "Fern," the story of Fernie Mae Rosen, the illegitimate daughter of a black woman and white Jewish man. A beautiful woman of indifferent sexuality whose "body was tortured with something it could not let out," she is abandoned by her lovers, who nevertheless remain forever under her spell, "vowing to themselves that some day they would do some fine thing for her."

The religious alienation suggested in "Fern" is the thematic core of "Esther," which also dramatizes isolation and frustrated sexuality. When she is nine, introverted Esther becomes infatuated with an itinerant preacher and charlatan, King Barlo. Fourteen years later, when he returns to town, she leaves her parents' home at midnight to search for him. She finds him in a boardinghouse, drunk and with a woman who teases Esther for having a light complexion. "Jeers and hoots pelter bluntly upon her back" as she retreats, bereft of a dream that had sustained her for so long.

Following this story is the poem "Conversion," in which an African deity merges with a "white-faced sardonic god." King Barlo represents this corrupting mix of faiths from two worlds, just as Esther and Fern suffer from their biracial fusion. Dusk, a recurring descriptive motif in this first section, is a related thematic metaphor for the book as a whole.

"Blood-Burning Moon" is the last and most fully developed story in this section. Tom Burwell, a black laborer in the cane fields, becomes the lover of Louisa, who also is the lover of young Bob Stone, for whose family she works. "Strong as he was with hands upon the ax or plow," Burwell is a gentle introvert and cannot express his feelings for Louisa. Stone, ironically, is a white reflection of Burwell in actions and personality.

Their rivalry reaches a climax when Stone goes to the canebrake, where he normally meets Louisa, to confront her with Burwell. A struggle ensues, and Burwell cuts Stone's throat. In retaliation, a white lynch mob, "like ants upon a forage," traps Burwell, takes him to an abandoned cotton factory, and ties him to a stake. While the frightened black people sneak home and blow out their kerosene lamps, the mob sets Burwell afire. Louisa, in her house, senses his fate; when she looks at the full moon, she sees it as "an evil thing . . . an omen which she must sing to." Thus the first section of the novel ends as it begins, with the immolation of an African American.

Whereas the first unit of *Cane* portrays rural black people in a South still tied to antebellum mores, the second section shows them trying to cope in the North. It includes seven prose pieces (four of which are developed stories) and five poems. Two impressionistic and symbolic vignettes, "Seventh Street" and "Rhobert," introduce the theme of a white society confining and stifling black people. In a letter, Toomer described the former story as

"The song of a crude new life . . . a new people." The latter presents urban houses as a destructive metaphor, literally burying "banty-bowed, shaky, ricket-legged" Rhobert, whose northern odyssey in search of opportunity for the family he left behind ends in a lonely death.

"Avey" is the first fully developed narrative in this section. Set in Washington, D.C., it echoes tales of the first part, for it, too, is about a black woman as a remote and indifferent sex object. Avey graduates from school and becomes a teacher; however, like Karintha and Fern, she turns to prostitution. Though he does not understand her, the immaturely self-centered narrator tries without success to rekindle a boyhood passion for her.

"Theater" also is about unrequited love. Set in a Washington theater during a rehearsal, its main characters are Dorris, a dancer, and John, the manager's brother. Partly because of class differences symbolized by John's fairer skin, nothing comes of their dreams of having an affair. John also is deterred by his fear that a commitment will compromise his independence. Here, as elsewhere in *Cane*, race and social class inhibit action.

In "Box Seat," too, Dan and Muriel eventually go their separate ways because, by social standards, she is too good for him. Born in a canefield, light-skinned Dan Moore has migrated to Washington, where he is unemployed but hopefully courting Muriel, a teacher. Rejected, he follows her to a theater, where a grotesque exhibition of sparring dwarves is the feature. The winner sings a song he dedicates to Muriel, a visible presence in her box seat. When the dwarf offers her a rose, Muriel at first will not accept it, but she yields to audience pressure, a hypocritical act that ends Dan's passion for her. Serenely tweaking the dwarf's nose, he leaves the theater, "as cool as a green stem that has just shed its flower." Unfulfilled, Dan nevertheless is a kind of victor; atypical of Toomer's men, he no longer is a slave to a woman's "animalism."

In "Harvest Song," the second of two lyrics that follow "Box Seat," a reaper sings not only of his suffering but also of his determined self-control over hunger, thirst, blindness, deafness, and fatigue. "My pain is sweet," he chants, "Sweeter than the oats or wheat or corn." Set as it is between stories that take place in Washington and Chicago, the poem is a wistful glance backward to a pastoral South, where grim deprivation and hardship at least were ameliorated by a successful harvest. Life in the North does not offer any such bounty.

"Bona and Paul" closes the second section. A white woman and a black man, both southerners, meet in a Chicago physical education school. Paul Johnson, light enough to pass for white, denies that he is black; his complexion is what attracts Bona Hale to him. The climax of the story takes place at the Crimson Gardens, a nightclub featuring black music which is patronized by white customers. Paul is charmed by this blending of the two races; at the same time, he realizes "that people saw, not attractiveness in his dark skin, but difference." For the first time, he sees himself as he is and is strengthened.

Bona also seems invigorated by the experience; as they leave, however, the black doorman leers at them knowingly. Paul pauses and tells him, "Brother, you're wrong." Addressing a fellow black as "brother," Paul has come to terms with his racial identity. Bona disappears, and the story ends. Perhaps she cannot accept Paul's embrace of his blackness; perhaps the knowing, leering look of the doorman makes her realize that she cannot bridge the social gulf of race. As a southerner, she can cope with ambiguity but not with certainty. Both characters thus come to a life-altering awareness.

"Kabnis," which makes up the third part of *Cane*, is a closet drama that presents the consequences of a collision between past and present. Ralph Kabnis, a black man of mixed racial heritage, has returned from New York to his native South with an artist's zeal to improve the lot of his people. A self-styled poet, he aims to become their voice. Having accommodated to the conditions under which they live and having come to terms with who they are, however, the black Georgians are indifferent to this savior. They look upon him as a potential troublemaker who could upset a delicate social balance with which they are satisfied.

Kabnis has come to rural Sempter, Georgia, to teach at a black school, but the headmaster soon dismisses him for unspecified reasons. Fred Halsey, a blacksmith, then takes Kabnis on as an apprentice, but he is as inept at this job as he apparently was at teaching. Whereas Halsey, a master artisan, is comfortably secure with his status, Kabnis is "awkward and ludicrous, like a schoolboy in his brother's new overalls."

Halsey cannot help Kabnis. Nor can Lewis, a teacher at the school of whom Halsey says, "He strikes me as knowin a bucketful bout most things." Like Kabnis (and Paul Johnson of "Bona and Paul," and perhaps Toomer himself), Lewis must come to terms with his own ancestry. Unlike Kabnis, he embraces it, a fact demonstrated by his attraction to old Father John, "symbol, flesh, and spirit of the past."

When Kabnis rejects the connection by proclaiming, "My ancestors were Southern bluebloods," Lewis adds, "And black." To Kabnis's response, "Aint much difference between blue an black," Lewis retorts, "Enough to draw a denial from you." The next morning, Halsey's sister Carrie K., "lovely in her fresh energy," with a "calm untested confidence and nascent maternity," tries to help Kabnis climb from a cellar after a night of drinking. When she assures him that she is up to the task, he says, "twont do t lift me bodily. . . . its th soul of me that needs th risin."

By the end of the work, Kabnis has become little more than a childlike scarecrow, assailing Father John and thus rejecting his heritage and sinking to his knees before Carrie K., ashamed and exhausted. In *Essentials: Definitions and Aphorisms*, his 1931 book of maxims, Toomer wrote that "shame of a weakness implies the presence of a strength," so there may be hope for Kabnis after all. At the conclusion of "Kabnis," which also is the end of *Cane*, Toomer writes:

> Outside, the sun arises from its cradle in the tree-tops of the forest. Shadows of pines are dreams the sun shakes from its eyes. The sun arises. Gold-glowing child, it steps into the sky and sends a birth-song slanting down gray dust streets and sleepy windows of the southern town.

Given the optimistic tone of these final words, and the focus upon Father John and Carrie K., Toomer surely is not as despairing as is Kabnis. Indeed, the young woman and old man likely represent between them the past, present, and future of their race, and Ralph Kabnis may yet find his proper place.

"BLUE MERIDIAN"

First published: 1936 (collected in *The Collected Poems of Jean Toomer*, 1988)
Type of work: Poem

An optimistic vision of America flourishing from a blending of its many races is the theme of this poem, which Toomer develops in a style recalling Walt Whitman.

While still working on *Cane* in 1920 and 1921, Toomer wrote a 126-line poem he called "The First American," which was published as "Brown River, Smile" in 1932. By that time, he had expanded it considerably, and the 835-line "Blue Meridian" was included in the 1936 anthology *New American Caravan*. Toomer has written of the poem's long gestation period: "Years were to pass . . . before the germ of 'The First American' could grow and ripen and be embodied in 'The Blue Meridian.'" That germ, according to Toomer, was "that here in America we are in the process of forming a new race, that I was one of the first conscious members of this race. . . ."

Written in free verse, "Blue Meridian" is in the expansive Walt Whitman tradition, with echoes of such poems as "Song of Myself" (1855). More directly, it shows the influence of Hart Crane's longer, loosely connected sequence of poems *The Bridge* (1930), which examines America's past and present and looks ahead to the future. Crane and Toomer, who knew each other, both treat the unifying nature of human experience and Americans' relationship to country and God; in each poem, moreover, the Mississippi River is a central, almost mythic, symbol.

The three parts of Toomer's work open with references to a meridian. First is the Black Meridian, "sleeping on an inland lake." The second section begins with a stanza that tells of the White Meridian "waking on an inland lake." The third unit, consisting of the final twenty-seven lines, serves as a coda, opening with an exuberant stanza about a "*Dynamic atom-aggregate*" Blue Meridian awake and dancing. This progression from slumber to wakefulness parallels what Toomer sees as the American people's increasing awareness of their country's special quality. Tracing the historical development of the United States, he notes that whereas the "great red race was here," "wave after wave" of immigrants came from Europe, islands (Asian and Caribbean), and Africa. The use of the wave image ties in with repeated references to the Mississippi River, which Toomer calls "sister of the Ganges," India's sacred river.

Relevant, too, are the meridians' colors. Disposing of the extremes of black and white, Toomer offers "the high way of the third,/ The man of blue or purple." These are his "new people . . . called Americans." While not denying their "unbroken chain of ancestors," they "outgrow each wider limitation" and grow "towards the universal Human Being." Racial differences no longer will matter; people will be able to aspire without society's hindrance to achieve their desired goals.

Optimistic though his vision of the future is, Toomer has no illusions about the journey to the promised land. It will involve, he says, a "struggle through purgatories of many names" and will require help from the "Radiant Incorporeal" or "soul of our universe."

"Blue Meridian" and *Cane* have obvious thematic links, but although the novel concludes on a positive note, the characters are a long way from achieving the "spiritual fusion . . . of racial intermingling" that Toomer claimed to have reached for himself. The sketch of an incomplete circle between the second and third sections of the novel is emblematic of an unattained goal. By contrast, the celebratory optimism of "Blue Meridian" is signaled by its title, for the word "meridian" refers to a complete circle and also can mean the highest point of development, authority, or magnificence.

SUMMARY

Widely praised when published in 1923, *Cane* was not popular, so Toomer probably did not inspire a generation of black writers, as some have suggested. More likely, they simply were influenced by the same white figures (such as Sherwood Anderson and Waldo Frank) to whom he was drawn. His limited influence notwithstanding, he created a masterpiece of American fiction.

Cane is notable for its unusual form, which incorporates fiction, poetry and drama into a thematically and structurally unified experimental novel. It also stands apart because of Toomer's analysis of the conflicts, hardships, and aspirations of black people struggling with a legacy of slavery and with segregation. He elaborates upon these themes in his epic poem "Blue Meridian," which envisions a future of racial reconciliation and spiritual harmony in what he labels a New America.

Gerald H. Strauss

DISCUSSION TOPICS

- What early factors were responsible for Jean Toomer's identity crisis, and how is it reflected in his literary works?

- Upon what African American cultural sources did Toomer draw for his poems?

- What early twentieth century literary works does *Cane* most resemble in form?

- How does Toomer develop the theme of communication failure in *Cane*?

- In retrospect, does Toomer's optimism in "Blue Meridian" appear naïve?

BIBLIOGRAPHY

By the Author

SHORT FICTION:
"Mr. Costyve Duditch," 1928
"York Beach," 1929

POETRY:
"Banking Coal," 1922
"Blue Meridian," 1936
The Collected Poems of Jean Toomer, 1988

DRAMA:
Balo, pb. 1927

NONFICTION:
"Winter on Earth," 1929
"Race Problems and Modern Society," 1929
Essentials: Definitions and Aphorisms, 1931
"The Flavor of Man," 1949

MISCELLANEOUS:
Cane, 1923 (prose and poetry)
The Wayward and the Seeking, 1980 (prose and poetry; Darwin T. Turner, editor)

About the Author
Benson, Joseph, and Mabel Mayle Dillard. *Jean Toomer.* Boston: Twayne, 1980.

Byrd, Rudolph P. "Jean Toomer and the Writers of the Harlem Renaissance: Was He There with Them?" In *The Harlem Renaissance: Revaluations*, edited by Amritjit Singh, William S. Shiver, and Stanley Brodwin. New York: Garland, 1989.

Fabre, Geneviève, and Michel Feith, eds. *Jean Toomer and the Harlem Renaissance*. New Brunswick, N.J.: Rutgers University Press, 2001.

Ford, Karen Jackson. *Split-Gut Song: Jean Toomer and the Poetics of Modernity*. Tuscaloosa: University of Alabama Press, 2005.

Hajek, Friederike. "The Change of Literary Authority in the Harlem Renaissance: Jean Toomer's *Cane*." In *The Black Columbiad: Defining Moments in African American Literature and Culture*, edited by Werner Sollos and Maria Diedrich. Cambridge, Mass.: Harvard University Press, 1994.

Kerman, Cynthia. *The Lives of Jean Toomer: A Hunger for Wholeness*. Baton Rouge: Louisiana State University Press, 1988.

O'Daniel, Therman B., ed. *Jean Toomer: A Critical Evaluation*. Washington, D.C.: Howard University Press, 1988.

Scruggs, Charles, and Lee VanDemarr. *Jean Toomer and the Terrors of American History*. Philadelphia: University of Pennsylvania Press, 1998.

Wagner-Martin, Linda. "Toomer's *Cane* as Narrative Sequence." In *Modern American Short Story Sequences*, edited by J. Gerald Kennedy. Cambridge, England: Cambridge University Press, 1995.

SCOTT TUROW

Born: Chicago, Illinois
April 12, 1949

Beginning with a critically acclaimed memoir about legal education, Turow achieved legendary literary success by virtually inventing the modern genre of legal suspense.

BIOGRAPHY

Scott Turow was born on April 12, 1949, in Chicago, to David D. Turow, a gynecologist, and Rita Pastron Turow, an author of children's books. His early years were spent in that city in what he called a "nouveau-riche Jewish ghetto." When he was thirteen, his family moved to the wealthier, more middle-American Chicago suburb of Winnetka, Illinois.

In Winnetka, Turow endured what he characterized as a "quiet current of anti-Semitism" and failed freshman English at the prestigious New Trier High School. He responded with his first literary success, becoming editor of the school newspaper, later formulating plans to pursue a writing career and sidestepping his parents' wishes for him to become a doctor.

In 1966, Turow entered Amherst College, where, as an English major, he was influenced by Lawrence Durrell's *The Alexandria Quartet* (1962) and Robert Stone's *A Hall of Mirrors* (1967). By the end of his freshman year, Turow had completed his first novel. The manuscript was rejected by numerous publishers, but a personal response from an editor at Farrar, Straus and Giroux both encouraged him to keep writing and led eventually to a long-term relationship with the publisher.

While still an undergraduate, Turow was also encouraged by the celebrated short-story writer Tillie Olsen and by acceptance of one of his own short stories by the *Transatlantic Review.* After obtaining his B.A. from Amherst in 1970, he accepted a creative writing fellowship at Stanford University. While there, he completed a second novel, which, like the first, was roundly rejected (once again, however, Farrar, Straus and Giroux was encouraging). The plot, centering on a rent strike, reflected Turow's interest in civic policy and thus the law. After teaching creative writing at Stanford for four years and receiving his M.A., yet needing a practical career to support his family, he enrolled at Harvard Law School.

Turow had not, however, abandoned his literary ambitions. Before he entered law school, his agent negotiated a $4,000 advance from Putnam Books for a nonfiction account of his first year there. *One L,* published in 1977 just before Turow began his final year of law school, was written in the summer after his first year with the aid of a journal he had kept during the preceding eight months. Although some of Turow's professors and classmates were dismayed by their thinly disguised portraits, *One L* proved to be both a critical and popular success.

After receiving his J.D. in 1978, Turow accepted a position with the United States Attorney for the Northern District of Illinois. Returning to Chicago with his wife, the former Annette Weisberg, an artist, Turow spent eight years in the U.S. Attorney's Office, acting as prosecutor in the highly publicized series of trials known as Operation Greylord, which exposed widespread judicial corruption. During this period, he continued to write, using his half-hour train commute from Wilmette, Illinois, to work on the novel that was to make him a literary phenomenon.

Presumed Innocent was published by Farrar, Straus and Giroux in 1987, after Turow had taken off the summer of 1986 to complete it. The book made headlines even before publication, largely because of the record sums of money connected with it. Farrar, Straus and Giroux paid Turow an advance of $200,000, the largest the publisher had ever paid for a first novel. Warner Books paid $3 million for paperback rights, the highest price ever paid for reprint rights to a first novel. Film rights were sold to director Sydney Pollack for $1 million. The hardback version stayed on the best-seller list for forty-four weeks, the paperback for twenty-nine weeks.

Prior to the publication of *Presumed Innocent,* Turow had accepted a partnership position with the large Chicago law firm of Sonnenschein, Carlin, Nath & Rosenthal. During his first year and a half with the firm, he was able to write only from 6:15 to 8:15 A.M. before leaving home for his downtown office. In 1988, he reached an agreement that permitted him to spend his mornings at home with his wife and three children, Rachel, Gabriel, and Eve, and with his writing. The first product of this arrangement was a novel centered on both law and family life, *The Burden of Proof,* published in 1990. Like its predecessor, Turow's second novel quickly became a best seller and brought him great financial rewards. The appearance of a third novel, *Pleading Guilty,* in 1993 was once again evidence of Turow's singular ability to balance his dual careers as novelist and litigator.

Turow has continued his two-track career as novelist and attorney, publishing *The Laws of Our Fathers* (1996), about a trial that reunites members of a 1960's counterculture group twenty years later; *Personal Injuries* (1999), an examination of a personal injury lawyer caught up in an Operation Greylord-like sting of corrupt judges; *Reversible Errors* (2002), a fictional treatment of a death penalty conviction reversed in spite of prosecutorial zeal; and *Ordinary Heroes* (2005), a novel set during World War II that examines a court-martial and a son's search for the truth about his father. His legal work continued throughout this period, and his pro bono death penalty defenses led to the nonfiction *Ultimate Punishment: A Lawyer's Reflections on Dealing with the Death Penalty* (2003) after Turow served on Illinois governor George Ryan's commission on the death penalty.

ANALYSIS

Turow describes himself as "neurotic," driven to succeed by insecurities that originated in childhood. Despite his accomplishments, he seems to share the sentiments that his wife, Annette, expressed in a 1990 magazine interview, that his astonishing success "is all tenuous . . . not to be trusted." Indeed, even when Turow became a millionaire after the publication of *Presumed Innocent,* the couple did not move from the four-bedroom house they had bought when Turow was a $60,000-per-year public prosecutor.

This same driven quality and distrust of success is very much in evidence both in Turow's continued pursuit of demanding dual careers as lawyer and best-selling author and in his writings. Indeed, *One L* is testimony to Turow's drive and ambition. Not content merely to survive the first year of Harvard Law School, Turow took on the additional job of writing about it—and himself. His self-created persona in his law school memoir is not unlike first-year law students everywhere, but his skill at conveying angst about ambition and ethical dilemmas is unique. Turow's *One L* meditations about institutional shortcomings and the corrupting nature of ambition are echoed later in Rusty Sabich's thoughts on politics and the prosecutor's office in *Presumed Innocent* and in Sandy Stern's reflections on his successful brother-in-law's penchant for corruption in *The Burden of Proof.*

Indeed, the issues of a lawyer's civic, professional, and personal obligations dominate all the later novels as well. *Pleading Guilty* weighs self-interest against loyalty to colleagues and firm. *The Laws of Our Fathers* features a trial like that of *Presumed Innocent* in which truth takes a backseat to legal wrangling and the silent competing agendas of participants. *Personal Injuries* argues that corruptibility can coexist with likeability, and even with admirable personal behavior. *Reversible Errors* shows how the enthusiastic pursuit of one's professional duties can lead to a miscarriage of justice.

Although all of Turow's works, even *One L,* are fraught with mystery, it is his fictional heroes' moral dilemmas and especially the competing demands of family and the law that make his books so memorable. For his fictional protagonists, one dilemma always involves the competing demands of family and the law. In part, competition between home and court derives from the demands of a legal career. Rusty Sabich's wife, Barbara, is alienated and bitter, not only about her husband's affair with a coworker but also about his single-minded loyalty to his boss and to his job. Clara Stern is undone by the benign neglect with which she is treated while her litigator husband is developing his practice. In *Pleading Guilty*, Mack Malloy's home life is a disaster, as are the marriages of the characters in *The Laws of Our Fathers*. The lawyers and court officers in *Personal Injuries* and *Reversible Errors* all suffer from misshapen domestic lives. These domestic-versus-professional quandaries that the legal protagonists confront—forcing them to choose between their obligation as officers of the court and their responsibilities toward their families or even themselves—lend Turow's novels their resonance.

By way of explaining his phenomenal popularity, Turow has pointed out that the duality that characterizes his novels also characterizes American society in the early twenty-first century. The courtroom has replaced the church as the forum for dealing with the great sociological and philosophical issues of the day, such as abortion rights and surrogate motherhood. Large corporate firms have buried personal lawyer-client relationships and individual integrity under the weight of institutional procedure and the efficiencies of specialization. At the same time, Americans are wary of lawyers, who, with their knowledge of "the magic and sacred words," have developed the ability to rationalize the immoral. Such knowledge, in the hands of self-conscious and conscientious individuals such as Rusty Sabich, poses a compelling conundrum, one that is at the center of human experience. It is not too much to say that Turow's subject matter is, as William Faulkner characterized his own, "the human heart in conflict with itself."

Turow has said that he feared *Presumed Innocent* would fall between two stools, "too literary for the mystery crowd and too much a mystery to be regarded as a serious novel." Yet critics praised his first novel not only for its suspenseful plot but also for its elegant and philosophical voice. As with *One L*, Turow made good use of what he had experienced firsthand, re-creating the particulars surrounding a murder investigation and trial convincingly out of what he had learned during his career as a prosecutor. What lifts the novel above other courtroom procedurals, however, is in part Turow's choice of the telling detail, which is rendered in nearly poetic terms. For example, the "Dickensian grimness" of the prosecutors' offices is said to make the quality of light there "a kind of yellow fluid, like old shellac." Such fine turns of phrase economically set the mood and grant readers insight into the mind-set of Turow's first-person narrator and protagonist. At the same time, the fact that Rusty Sabich sometimes uses vocabulary more reminiscent of Raymond Chandler than Emily Dickinson lets readers know that Turow has not ventured too far afield from his chosen genre, the suspense thriller.

Reviews of Turow's next book, *The Burden of Proof*, were not as uniformly favorable as they had been for *Presumed Innocent*. Some criticized its style as "stodgy"; others likened its plot to Greek tragedy. To be sure, it is a very different book, more a character study of its reserved, superficially stodgy hero and his family than a thriller. The primary attribute it shares with its predecessor, however, is that it is told from the point of view of a lawyer obsessed not as much with solving a mystery as with discovering the truth of his own involvement in an ambiguous death—a truth that no legal proceeding can uncover. As in *Presumed Innocent*, such a truth can only be plumbed by an individual with a philosophical cast of mind and a penchant for self-examination.

In *The Burden of Proof*, Turow once again puts his own legal experiences to good use as background, drawing on his work as a white-collar criminal-defense counsel to create a world in which evil is personified by a wheeler-dealer commodities-firm owner who happens also to be Stern's brother-in-law, Dixon Hartnell. Although Hartnell is involved with Clara's suicide and threatens the stability of Stern's remaining family, he is still a likeable character who practices his own brand of honor. This complex characterization points to Turow's deft hand not only with character delineation but also, once again, to his insight into the ambiguous nature of morality. This insight, which seems to grow out of, even mandate, Turow's dual existence as lawyer and writer, is clearly the greatest strength of his books, helping them to rise above the conventions of the legal thriller.

ONE L

First published: 1977
Type of work: Memoir

A student at Harvard University's law school chronicles the turbulent first year of his legal studies.

One L has, for good reason, become required reading for those thinking of entering law school. Having scored in the stratosphere on the Law School Admissions Test, Turow had his choice of law schools, and he chose to enter one of the country's oldest and largest, and arguably the most prestigious, of legal education programs, Harvard Law School. What happened to Turow during his first year there, 1975-1976, is the subject of *One L*, a nonfiction account Turow reconstructed from the diary he kept during eight overwhelming months. While Turow's object is to explore emotions and

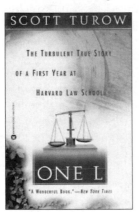

events that he personally experienced, his meditations on the system of legal education make it clear that these experiences are by no means unique, either to him or to Harvard Law School. The continuing popularity of *One L* attests to the universality of its insights.

As more than one reviewer has pointed out, part of the appeal of *One L* is that it reads like a good thriller, as Turow steers the reader through the sustained hysteria leading up to exams and the ensuing race to make Law Review. He relates his own reactions as well as those of his fellow students to the burdensome workload, to the indignities of the fabled Socratic teaching method, and to the ceaseless competition among classmates.

Along the way, he introduces some memorable personalities. Turow made only minor efforts to change names and otherwise to disguise the real-life characters who peopled his first year at law school. The most dominant of these, not unnaturally, are the professors, on whom the students'

grades—and, hence, self-definition and professional futures—depend. Turow's opinion of this small group of individuals evolves; as it does, it is hard for the reader not to speculate as to which professor will emerge as the villain of the piece. Turow does not disappoint: By the end of the book, he has given enough detail about the classroom performance of Professor Perini, who teaches the devilishly hard contracts course, that the reader fully endorses Turow's final judgment that Perini is too much the embodiment of the inhumane aspects of legal training.

In the end, Turow emerges a survivor, a kind of Everyman in the rarefied atmosphere of Harvard Law School. He does not make Law Review, but his marks are certainly respectable. Most important, he makes it through the trial of the first, formative year in the life of a lawyer with his ethics intact. He has met the enemy, the rapacity and fear inside himself, and he has prevailed.

PRESUMED INNOCENT

First published: 1987
Type of work: Novel

A public prosecutor investigates, then is tried for, the murder of his former colleague and lover.

Presumed Innocent, Turow's first published novel, was an astonishing critical and popular success. In it, he drew upon his own experiences as a prosecutor in the U.S. Attorney's Chicago office to draw a detailed and realistic portrait of the world inhabited by his hero, Rusty Sabich, a chief deputy prosecutor in a fictional Midwestern city. The particularity of this world, especially the rendition of the murder trial that is central to the book, accounts in large part for its appeal.

As the novel opens, Sabich's colleague, Carolyn Polhemus, has just been murdered, apparently after she was raped by someone she knew and trusted. The loss is especially jarring for Sabich, who only a few months before had been the victim's lover and, in part because his marriage is unsatisfactory, is still in love with her. Her murder is also a shock and an embarrassment to Sabich's boss, Raymond Horgan, who is up for reelection.

Horgan assigns Sabich to investigate the crime; when Sabich fails to uncover the murderer and Horgan consequently loses the election, Horgan conspires to frame his deputy for the murder.

As in many classic mysteries, nearly any of the characters who people *Presumed Innocent* could have killed Carolyn Polhemus, who was apparently both an unscrupulous colleague and a devotee of danger. The final revelation of the killer has frequently been attacked as contrived. Turow, though, has

stated, "We talk about literary truths as implausible, fictitious, and yet there is a way in which the mystery novel delivers a truth real life can't deliver." As with all the later Turow novels, the title resonates with meaning: There is no real innocence, only the presumption of innocence, a legal term to be sure, but also an acknowledgment of the ineffability of human motive and thus the impossibility of establishing clear-cut judgments of culpability. In large part, the truth of *Presumed Innocent* emerges not so much from the trial of Rusty Sabich but from his first-person meditations, which reveal a brooding, philosophical temperament not unlike the author's. What one reviewer saw as flawed storytelling—the fact that "the novel's resolution contains a troubling moral ambiguity"—can also be seen as another of Turow's expert renditions of verisimilitude.

THE BURDEN OF PROOF

First published: 1990
Type of work: Novel

While endeavoring to unravel the mystery surrounding his wife's suicide, a brilliant trial attorney must face his own inadequacies.

The Burden of Proof continues the story of Alejandro "Sandy" Stern, first introduced in *Presumed Innocent* as Rusty Sabich's accomplished defense counsel.

Like its predecessor, Turow's second novel opens with a death, the mystery of which is not resolved until story's end. In *The Burden of Proof,* the death is the suicide of Clara, Stern's seemingly constant, reticent wife of thirty-one years. In his effort to unravel the reasons for Clara's death, Stern must look to his own interior landscape rather than to the outside world.

The motivation for Clara's suicide is not devoid of clues; she leaves behind a note saying only, "Can you forgive me?" Stern quickly discovers that not only had Clara been unfaithful to him but also that she had picked up a venereal disease in the process. What is more, shortly before she killed herself, Clara had written a check to an unknown payee that reduced almost to nothing Stern's prospective inheritance from her estate. Stern is a brilliant lawyer in complete charge of a courtroom, but the understated attorney can only tell an investigating police officer, "Lieutenant, it should be evident that I failed to observe something I should have."

One detail Stern fails to observe until late in the book is the connection between his wife's suicide and the troubles of his brother-in-law, Dixon Hartnell. Hartnell is the owner of a brokerage house and Stern's most significant client, and throughout the course of *The Burden of Proof* Stern is occupied with defending Hartnell on charges of illegal trading. Exploring Hartnell's defense, Turow provides—as he did in *Presumed Innocent*—interesting insights into legal maneuvering; he also details the complexities of commodities trading with elegant clarity.

As in his earlier novel, however, the most compelling aspect of *The Burden of Proof* is not solving a mystery so much as it is exploring the psyche and the complex family ties of the hero. This time the tale is not told in first person voice; although the reader shares Stern's point of view, Turow rightly judged that it would not be fitting to inhabit this character, who is from first to last an outsider, a reserved, formal man, an Argentine immigrant and a Jew. Some reviewers have quibbled with Turow's endowing his middle-aged, paunchy, balding widower with a reinvigorated sex life, but it is precisely the distance the author keeps from his hero that allows Stern to find love, improbably but touchingly, with the married, pregnant federal prosecutor investigating Hartnell's case, and lively bedroom experiences with several women in his circle.

Stern's native reserve also goes a long way toward explaining his sometimes strained relationships with his three children, each of whom plays a crucial role in the unwinding of Turow's plot.

The Burden of Proof ends, in a sense, where it began, with a death in the family, this time one that ties up all the loose ends. While such a deus ex machina can be faulted for being too convenient in resolving a mystery, here it is a suitable end to what might more fittingly be labeled a domestic drama, as signaled by the novel's opening line: "They had been married for thirty-one years, and the following spring full of resolve and a measure of hope, he would marry again."

PERSONAL INJURIES

First published: 1999
Type of work: Novel

A sleazy personal injury lawyer is forced into a sting operation against corrupt judges in order to avoid a prison sentence and care for his dying wife.

Personal Injuries exploits Scott Turow's experiences as a federal prosecutor in Operation Greylord. His fictionalized version is Project Petros, a federal investigation, headed by U.S. Attorney Stan Sennett, into Kindle County judges suspected of bribery. (Sennett's Uncle Peter, *petros* in Greek, was an immigrant bankrupted by judicial corruption.) Sennett has gotten the goods on personal injury attorney Robert "Robbie" Feaver, a charming but corrupt lawyer who appears before some of the judges under suspicion: Feaver has a slush fund unreported to the Internal Revenue Service (IRS), and he faces a long prison term for tax fraud. Feaver reluctantly agrees to go undercover in a sting operation against the judges.

Federal Bureau of Investigation (FBI) agent Evon Miller will be his watchdog and controller. When Feaver hires attorney George Mason for his defense, the stage is set for an examination of the contrasting roles of prosecution and defense, and of their varying perspectives on justice versus mercy: Sennett as prosecutor views the world in black and white and is relentless in his desire to

punish; Feaver as defendant and personal injury lawyer sees shades of gray and is quick to identify mitigating circumstances. Miller has a strict Fundamentalist religious background and unbending FBI training, but she seeks a more flexible outlook to accommodate her lesbian sexual leanings; Mason is a classic observer and compromiser, a middleman both professionally and personally.

With Robbie Feaver set loose on the judges in a series of fake personal injury cases that they can be bribed to rule in favor of, the sting operation unfolds. The novel makes readers appreciate how difficult it is to gather evidence of corruption that will survive defense challengers—for example, conversations recorded in a bar could be thrown out since talk in the background might be the source of the damning statements. Television surveillance fails, various judges prove suspicious and cagey, and Feaver becomes increasingly nervous. His beautiful wife, Rainey, is dying slowly of amyotropic lateral sclerosis, or Lou Gehrig's disease, and if he fails to satisfy Sennett, he may be sent to prison when he should be caring for her. In fact, the emotional pressures on all the sting operators become increasingly difficult to bear.

Evon Miller finds herself attracted to Feaver despite his cynicism (he has trained himself to weep on cue in hospital emergency rooms in order to convince future clients of his compassion for their plight), his completely relativistic philosophy (everything is a "play," a game with no intrinsic meaning), his lies (Rainey tells Miller that he lies about everything), and his borderline criminality (besides bribing judges, Feaver has played fast and loose with his legal credentials). Yet, along with Miller, readers succumb to Feaver's charm, and his legitimate love and caring for his wife are admirable.

Once again, Turow shows the ironic inadequacy of the legal outlook, the insistence of the law that behavior and people themselves must fit into mutually exclusive categories of innocent or guilty, blameless or culpable, true or false. Robbie Feaver rivals Rusty Sabich in complexity, but Sabich is a moral exemplar in contrast to the slippery Robbie, who is among Turow's finest characters. Like Evon Miller, the reader is charmed, despite the obvious reasons for being appalled at the lawyer's dishonesty and manipulation, and ends up liking and even admiring Robbie.

Scott Turow

REVERSIBLE ERRORS

First published: 2002
Type of work: Novel

The prosecution and the defense revisit a decade-old death penalty case in which a rush to judgment led to a mistaken verdict.

Reversible Errors draws on Scott Turow's pro bono death penalty defense work to show how even well-meaning prosecutors can cause justice to miscarry. Corporate attorney Arthur Raven has been assigned the final appeal in a notorious murder, the killing of a popular restaurateur. A ne'er-do-well named Rommy Gandolph has been convicted on circumstantial evidence and a confession evoked under pressure, and since he is both marginally retarded and disagreeable, his fated end has not provoked much sympathy. Raven, however, becomes convinced of Gandolph's innocence and does battle with the two key figures in the prosecution: detective Larry Starczek, who elicited Gandolph's confession, and Muriel Wynn, the prosecutor. Starczek and Wynn were once lovers, and since their attraction endures, their professional relationship is complicated by their residual feelings. Both are competent and ambitious, unwilling to simply admit error, especially given Gandolph's confession and the absence of any other credible suspects. Their debates about the correct response to Raven shows that prosecutorial intransigence can be more than simple stubbornness, for their motives include skepticism about the defense, a righteous regard for justice and the victim's family, a yearning for closure, and a justifiable pride in what they regard as a job well done.

Raven is aided in his defense by Gillian Sullivan, the former judge who sentenced Gandolph, now disgraced after serving prison time for taking bribes. Raven consults her about the case, and they begin an affair, two lost souls united by Raven's newfound belief in himself and his professional obligation. By setting up his prosecution and defense teams as two couples in the midst of affairs, Turow

shows the human side of a process ordinarily considered dry and professional: Both Wynn and Raven are influenced by their personal and emotional states. For example, since she knows the detective as a lover, Wynn allows Starczek great leeway in his investigative conduct, a leeway not permitted a relative stranger. Raven's zeal in defense of Gandolph is at least in part fueled by his desire to demonstrate his forceful masculinity before his new lover.

As is customary in Turow's novels, the resolution of the plot is unexpected and even startling: The true culprit and motive were off the radar screen of the original investigation. As with *Presumed Innocent*, human behavior and motive are complex and murky, colored in shades of gray rather than in the black-and-white categories of guilty and innocent that the law demands. Even at the end, readers cannot be truly sure about the precise behavior of all the participants in the crime, and that is Turow's point: After ten years and the best efforts of highly competent and basically honorable people, one remains unsure. How can capital punishment be justified in the face of such doubt? While many errors, both legal and otherwise, can be reversed, the death penalty cannot. Rommy Gandolph's close call with execution—convicted on circumstantial evidence, he is exonerated only because of a series of random happenstances, such as the illness of the true culprit—is Turow's case against capital punishment.

SUMMARY

Turow's career has been characterized throughout by duality, by his twin vocations as writer and lawyer, by his ambivalent attitude toward his own success at both. His corresponding insight into the ambiguous nature of truth—particularly that of the legal variety—is what powers his work. At a time when lawyers have become the arbiters of moral dilemmas, Turow has done more than any other writer working in the genre of legal suspense to rise above cliché and stereotyping. He explores the protean nature of human experience and the ways in which the law both shapes and contradicts it.

Lisa Paddock; updated by Andrew Macdonald

BIBLIOGRAPHY

By the Author

LONG FICTION:
Presumed Innocent, 1987
The Burden of Proof, 1990
Pleading Guilty, 1993
The Laws of Our Fathers, 1996
Personal Injuries, 1999
Reversible Errors, 2002
Ordinary Heroes, 2005

NONFICTION:
One L, 1977
Ultimate Punishment: A Lawyer's Reflections on Dealing with the Death Penalty, 2003

EDITED TEXT:
Guilty as Charged: The Penguin Book of New American Crime Writing, 1996

About the Author

Klinkenborg, Verlyn. "Law's Labors Lost," *The New Republic*, March 14, 1994, 31-38.

Lundy, Derek. *Scott Turow: Meeting the Enemy: A Biography*. Toronto: ECW Press, 1995.

Macdonald, Andrew. "Personal Injuries." In *Beacham's Encyclopedia of Popular Fiction*. Vol. 13, edited by Kirk H. Beetz. Osprey, Fla.: Beacham's, 1996.

Macdonald, Andrew, and Gina Macdonald. *Scott Turow: A Critical Companion*. Westport, Conn.: Greenwood Press, 2005.

_____. "Scott Turow's *Presumed Innocent*: Novel and Film—Multifaceted Character Study Versus Tailored Courtroom Drama." In *It's a Print: Detective Fiction from Page to Screen*, edited by William Reynolds and Beth Trembley. Bowling Green, Ohio: Popular Press, 1994.

Szuberla, Guy. "Paretsky, Turow, and the Importance of Symbolic Ethnicity," *Mid-America: The Yearbook of the Society for the Study of Midwestern Literature*, 1991, 124-135.

DISCUSSION TOPICS

- Scott Turow once supported but now firmly opposes the death penalty. He voices this opposition in both his novel *Reversible Errors* and his nonfiction study *Ultimate Punishment*. What reasons does he advance for his opposition?

- *Personal Injuries* is full of descriptions and images of people who are sick, injured, or dying. Provide examples and then speculate about Turow's purpose in doing so. For instance, why does Turow include Rainey?

- Turow relies heavily on metaphorical language to define his characters. Choose a central character from *Presumed Innocent* or *Burden of Proof* and list some of the images associated with him or her. Explain what these images/pictures reveal about the character.

- Discuss narrative voice in *Pleading Guilty*. Through whose eyes do readers see events? How does that affect an understanding of the whole? Does Turow provide any other perspectives? How?

- What can readers learn about courtroom strategies from Turow's books?

- What family secrets are ultimately revealed?

- What are some of the signs that the main character in *Burden of Proof*, Sandy Stern, is learning, maturing, and discovering his own previously hidden qualities?

- Sandy Stern is an accomplished and insightful lawyer, yet he is blind to the actions of his wife, brother-in-law, and three children. What are two or three reasons for this blindness? Does Stern's background provide any explanation for his inability to "read" his family?

- Do you trust Rusty Sabich? Why or why not?

Library of Congress

MARK TWAIN

Born: Florida, Missouri
November 30, 1835
Died: Redding, Connecticut
April 21, 1910

Twain is considered one of America's greatest novelists and one of the world's greatest writers of juvenile and comic literature.

BIOGRAPHY

Mark Twain was born Samuel Langhorne Clemens in Florida, Missouri, on November 30, 1835. His father and mother both came from old Virginia families. His father was trained as a lawyer; somewhat feckless and unsuccessful in business, he moved slowly westward, involving himself in land speculation. In 1839, the family reached Hannibal, Missouri, a small town on the Mississippi River upriver from St. Louis, and it was there that Twain spent his early childhood and developed his love of the great river.

His father died when Twain was twelve years old, and Twain left school to learn the trade of printing, which his brother had entered before him. Twain spent several years as a roving journeyman printer, working as far east as New York City. In 1857, he was taken on by Horace Bixby, who trained him as a Mississippi steamboat pilot, a trade he practiced until the Civil War. The war wrecked the Mississippi River traffic, so in 1861 he went with his brother, Orion, to Carson City, Nevada, where Orion worked as a secretary in the new territorial government. Twain drifted into silver mining and eventually back to journalism with the Virginia City *Territorial Enterprise*. It was in 1862 that he first adopted the pen name Mark Twain. Within a few years, while writing for newspapers in San Francisco, his composition of short sketches and stories was encouraged by Bret Harte.

Twain was developing a minor reputation as a humorist and lecturer in the mid-1860's, but it was the publication of "The Celebrated Jumping Frog of Calaveras County" in 1865 in the New York *Saturday Press* that brought him countrywide attention. He had a further success with a series of articles about a trip to Hawaii, commissioned by the Sacramento *Union* in 1866, and from then on he was able to make a living on the lecture circuit. The first major work to come out of this was *The Innocents Abroad* (1869), which was received with considerable praise, tempered by some criticism of the author's Western lack of polish and discretion.

His experience as a Mississippi pilot and his wandering life as a printer, writer, and jack-of-all-trades gave him the raw material for a successful career as a writer and a lecturer. In 1870, he was able to marry Olivia Langdon of Elmira, New York, the daughter of a respected member of the eastern establishment. In 1870, Twain became joint owner and editor of the Buffalo, New York, newspaper the *Express*, but two years later he sold his interest, having lost a considerable amount of money in the project. He withdrew from newspaper work to Hartford, Connecticut, where he was to spend the following two decades and where he settled seriously into his career as a novelist. Some critics have suggested that this entrance into genteel social life affected the power of his work, but it was after this date that *The Adventures of Tom Sawyer* (1876), *Adventures of Huckleberry Finn* (1884), and, indeed, all of his major novels were to be written.

Twain was never to forget his past, and his greatest book, *Adventures of Huckleberry Finn*, and his greatest nonfiction work, *Life on the Mississippi* (1883), are directly related to the time and place of his early experiences as a child and a young man. However long he remained away from the Midwest, he was never to lose his allegiance to it, and the somewhat rough-cast quality of his humor, which is often seen as an integral part of his literary gift, has a rural, Western tang to it which no amount of New England gentility could ever expunge.

It is probably fair to say that his best work was done by the end of the 1880's. Certainly it is true that his work after that time becomes much more pessimistic, and the publications of the 1890's are his least read, and certainly least popular, titles, although he continued to write into the twentieth century.

The reasons for the change from comic happiness to work of misanthropic gloom are complicated. There were occasional moments of cruelty in his work from the beginning, and he could be satirically sharp, as he showed as early as *The Innocents Abroad*. There clearly is a quantitative increase in human stupidity and violence from work to work through the period prior to 1890. *A Connecticut Yankee in King Arthur's Court*, published in 1889, if still ripe with the richness of invention that was one of his gifts, is a much more violent book than anything he had produced previously, and it rejects the happy endings of many of his early novels. So the tendency was there, and the works leading through the period between the late 1860's to the beginning of the 1890's show an interesting pattern of slowly increasing seriousness and pessimism.

In the 1890's, Twain's life outside literature added to his pessimism. He lost a large amount of money early in the decade in a business proposition. His health began to fail, and the ill health and eventual deaths of his two daughters and his wife plunged him into unmitigated sorrow through the 1890's and into the early years of the twentieth century. The literature produced in this period clearly reflects not only his increasing pessimism as he grew older but also the unimpeded run of bad luck and personal sorrow that he experienced up to his own death in 1910. This is the Twain known in the main to the critics; it does not detract from his reputation as one of the great comic writers or from his reputation as the writer of, perhaps, the best book ever written about the joys of being a young boy, free at last on the great river.

Twain did, however, write a considerable amount of material during the 1890's. His financial difficulties hardly allowed him to stop working, and he spent a lot of time both in the United States and internationally on the lecture circuit, amusing audiences. *Following the Equator* (1897) reveals his feelings about the experience of appearing publicly as the smiling, professional humorist at a time when his personal life was so unhappy. The book that is best known from this period is *The Tragedy of Pudd'nhead Wilson* (1894), and it carries the stamp of Twain's deepening pessimism. He wrote a further handful of books, but the gloom was undiminished in all of his later work. He died in 1910, having lost his wife in 1904, as something of an enigma, a man of sometimes fierce misanthropic impulses who had begun his career as the sunniest of men.

ANALYSIS

Twain's general reputation as one of the most admired, and possibly the most beloved, writer in America is based, in the main, upon the work he published before 1890. After that time, his work takes on a much darker hue. *The Tragedy of Pudd'nhead Wilson*, published in 1894, though still a book of some comic mishap, marks the obvious pessimism that was to pervade his work until his death. Indeed, some materials left unpublished during his lifetime, such as "The Mysterious Stranger" stories, published posthumously, bear very little resemblance to the sunny idealization of *The Adventures of Tom Sawyer*.

Twain was, however, always more than simply a comic entertainer, and it should be remembered that as early as *The Innocents Abroad*, he responds to human error, on occasion, with quick satiric thrusts that remind one of eighteenth century English satirist Jonathan Swift. *The Adventures of Tom Sawyer* is reasonably free from such tonal darkening, but *Adventures of Huckleberry Finn* certainly is not. In order to appreciate fully the greatness of the latter novel, it is necessary to go beyond a sense of triumph in Huck's conversion to an outright defender of Jim to an understanding of the kind of world that threatens both the slave and the boy.

The confidence men of the novel, completely insensitive to the pain they cause, may be an obvious example of Twain's sense of evil in the world, but that does not circumscribe the way in which Twain suggests that human cruelty is gratuitously omnipresent—not simply among the rogues but in the center of society. Jim's greatest individual enemy is a spinster woman of scrupulous moral and religious credentials, simply because he is black.

In *The Prince and the Pauper* (1881) and *A Connecticut Yankee in King Arthur's Court*—which start out reading like amiable fairy tales—cruel acts of physical violence are dwelt upon in detail and go far beyond the ignorant "horseplay" of the rural citizens who simply do not know any better in Twain's earlier works. It is, therefore, unwise to simplify the tonal range of his oeuvre. If he is most often seen as a humorist, and often as a romantic, especially about boys and life on the Mississippi, he is often more than that. In *Adventures of Huckleberry Finn*, his best work, tonal and intellectual range is very wide indeed, leaning strongly toward serious concern about human conduct. There are ideas in that novel that Twain wants to disturb his readers quite as much as they bother Huck. Perhaps an ambition to become a writer of ideas was his from the start.

In Twain's early work he seemed to touch the core of late nineteenth century popular humor, giving Americans what they felt was the best part of their character in stories of good-natured, slightly skeptical, occasionally vulgar trickery. Twain had an eye for hypocrisy, self-interest, and pomposity, however, and his main characters, if sometimes less clever than he himself was, could not be fooled for long, even if they could be misled initially out of innocence. He certainly could have played it safe and been satisfied with a minor, lucrative career as a funnyman, but *The Innocents Abroad* showed that he could sustain a larger literary shape and, more important, that he had some things to say about human nature which could not be satisfied in the short comic story.

The other, perhaps greater, gift, was to show up in *The Adventures of Tom Sawyer*, where Twain emerges fully formed as a writer of children's fiction. The success of that work might have satisfied a lesser man and led him into a long career of repetition of the same kind of sweet-natured appreciations of childhood. *The Prince and the Pauper* looks by its title to be in that pattern, but it is loaded with comments about human stupidity and cruelty.

Adventures of Huckleberry Finn, finally out in 1884, shows a further refinement and has been recognized not simply as one of the finest juvenile novels, not simply as a book of social comment, but as one of the greatest books of American fiction. Twain was never to write a better book, but he did not rest with it. *A Connecticut Yankee in King Arthur's Court* was to show that he had not abandoned his ambition to write the novel of ideas, opposing old English inequities against the ideals and practices of a nineteenth century American and giving himself the opportunity to create political theory.

What has to be recognized in Twain's work, beyond the singular success of *The Adventures of Huckleberry Finn*, is his range—not only in his richness of fictional embellishment but also in his way of using material to make moral points with very little preaching. He can be, on too many occasions, heavy-handed (surprisingly enough, when he is being funny), and twenty-first century sensibility may find him a bit ponderous, even "corny." He can, however, be very sly and very smart. Sometimes the ideas get out in front of the fiction; this is often the case when he lets himself be personally moved by the subject. Yet he possesses a lively, quicksilver way of moving in and out of moral problems without much preaching, and he usually keeps the tale in the forefront of the work written before the dark days of the 1890's.

"THE CELEBRATED JUMPING FROG OF CALAVERAS COUNTY"

First published: 1865 (collected in *The Celebrated Jumping Frog of Calaveras County, and Other Sketches*, 1867)
Type of work: Short story

Jim Smiley, an obsessive gambler, meets his match when he bets that his trained frog, Dan'l Webster, can outjump any other frog in a Northern California mining area, Calaveras County.

Mark Twain, who had made his living as a Mississippi steamboat pilot before the Civil War and had gone on to be a printer, a journalist, and a sometime prospector, could hardly have imagined that his comic tale "The Celebrated Jumping Frog of Calaveras County," which appeared originally under the more modest title "Jim Smiley and His

Jumping Frog," was to change his life forever and establish him in a career which was to lead to him becoming one of America's greatest writers.

Certainly the tale is moderately amusing, but it seemed to catch the imagination of the American reader, and Twain was to follow it up with equally artful stories and lecture tours which were to make him well known some time before the artistic success of *The Adventures of Tom Sawyer* and *Adventures of Huckleberry Finn*. Part of the reason for the success of the story lies in its moderation, its seeming lack of artfulness. Good-natured, garrulous old Simon Wheeler tells the story to the unsuspecting Mark Twain, who is, in fact, trying to find out about an entirely different man, the Reverend Leonidas W. Smiley. What he gets is a rambling, disjointed, ungrammatical tale of Jim Smiley, who sometime back in 1849 or 1850 had provided the locals with entertainment with his antics as a gambler.

Style is a strong element in the power of the tale. Twain sets himself up as the straight man for the dead-panned raconteur, who, once he gets started, is impossible to stop. Twain (the character) provides part of the amusement in his indignation. His letter to A. Ward (which is the exterior framing device for the story) is a complaint to the effect that Ward (probably Artemus Ward, who was himself a popular humorist) had deliberately misled Twain, knowing that the surname "Smiley" would trigger the long reminiscence in Wheeler. The style of the first paragraph of the letter has a kind of prim formality about it and the sophisticated facility of an educated writer barely able to suppress his grudging suspicion that he has been made the fool.

This style of fastidious restraint continues, but when Wheeler begins to speak, the prose relaxes into a homey, genial vulgarity and sly wit which immediately establishes the old man as a master teller of tall tales. Whether the story is true hardly matters; its real power lies in the telling. The way in which the "fifteen-minute nag" fumbles her way to the finish line and the look that Andrew Jackson, the bull-pup, gives to Smiley after the defeat by a dog without hind legs are examples of how skilled Twain was in writing cleverly without seeming to be writing at all.

Twain shows equal skill in the dialogue between Smiley and his supposed victim. The repetitions, the grammatical errors, the misspellings to indicate accent, and the wary rejoinders have a seam-lessness about them which gives them an air of authenticity, of improvisational vivacity, which is part of Twain's charm as a comic writer. The story's success lies in Twain's ability to make it sound like the real thing: the loose-tongued babble of an old man who has caught another innocent fellow by the ear. Twain, the victim, twice-bitten (once by Ward and once by Smiley's narrator, Simon Wheeler), can only get away, if good-naturedly, by running for cover. The story's secret is not the trick it describes but the structure and use of style.

Beyond its technical cleverness, however, the popularity of the story lay in large part in the fact that Twain refrains from patronizing his unlettered inhabitants of Calaveras County. Smiley may have been fooled this time, but he is usually the victor and is likely to rebound. His proposed victim is to be congratulated on his quickness of mind; Simon Wheeler may be a bit long-winded, but he tells a good story. If anyone is made to look the fool, it is Twain, the aggrieved letter writer, whose proper way with grammar has not made him any less susceptible to a harmless practical joke. The story's tone, in fact, is one of generosity and good nature. The joke is ultimately on Twain, and he takes it well.

It was this kind of happy tomfoolery in the early stories, with the acceptance of rural America as a place not without its own kind of bucolic silliness and occasional quick wit, which readers and audiences liked about the young writer and performer. The tougher, sharper Twain was yet to come.

THE INNOCENTS ABROAD

First published: 1869
Type of work: Travel literature

Twain accompanies a group of affluent Americans on a tour of Europe and the Holy Land and reports on the sights and sounds and the comic and satiric confrontations between the Old and the New Worlds.

It must have seemed a clever idea to send a popular young comic journalist on a tour with a boatload of prominent citizens in order to record, as *The Innocents Abroad* did, the day-to-day experience of

Americans having a good time in the exotic old countries. When the book came out, however, the reaction was not entirely favorable. Twain had confirmed what every American already knew—that Europe was terribly run-down and was greedy for the dollars of rich Americans. He also suggested that the Americans often made fools of themselves and quite as often were downright vulgar—thereby confirming what Europeans already knew about America.

Obviously someone had misjudged Mark Twain when he was sent on the trip. His career as a literary figure was in its infancy, and he had yet to write a novel, but there was surely sufficient evidence in his newspaper work and in his short stories that he had a gift for satire that was barely controlled and that he was not quite as refined in his literary conduct as might have been expected from an East Coast journalist. He was, in short, not always as fastidious in his work as might have been expected, and this book, certainly one of the funniest (and sometimes satirically savage) works in the travel genre was to offend at the same time that it added to his reputation as a writer of promise.

The book can also be seen as an interesting anticipation of a theme that Twain is to use over and over again: the confrontation between liberal, nineteenth century ideas of politics and society with the old, sometimes savage conservatism of the Old World. The latter problem is to be used in *The Prince and the Pauper*, in which the concern for humanity and for fair treatment of citizens is manifested in the conduct of both the prince and the pauper. It becomes even more central in the later work *A Connecticut Yankee in King Arthur's Court*, where a nineteenth century American finds himself in a position of power and attempts to put his ideas about society, politics, and commerce into action—with sometimes comic but often dangerously disastrous results.

Most obvious, and perhaps most enjoyable from an American point of view, are Twain's astringently funny comments upon the limitations of European civilization. He sees how quick the Europeans and the Near Eastern citizens are to take advantage of the Americans, who are open and generous in their curiosity. He has an amusing running joke about guides who may change throughout the tour but have a kind of obvious sameness in their determination to make a meal out of the Americans. They give very little in return, usually because they hardly have any idea what they are talking about.

Twain is weakest, as he freely admits, in dealing with the art and architecture of the old countries, and he is often surprisingly insensitive, revealing himself as vulnerable to the charge that he is occasionally as stupidly stubborn as his fellow travelers. Yet that revelation gives the book a credibility which helps to keep it from becoming a tedious listing of constant complaint. It often breaks out into first-class description, particularly if Twain is moved by a scene, but its main line is that of slippery comic comment upon the discomfort of travel.

The Holy Land, in particular, fires the greatest enthusiasm in Twain and some of the most pungent complaint, caused in part by the difficulties of travel in the barren landscape. The Christian history of that area is most interesting to Twain and his fellow travelers, but Twain, who usually maintains a pose of amused indifference, is enraged by the commercialization of the biblical sites. From early in the tour there is a line of anticlerical comment which can become sharply splenetic, particularly if the Roman Catholic Church is involved.

Twain's reaction to the tawdry, profit-making manipulation of the Christian mystery was enjoyed by his American readers, but he was not afraid to suggest that Americans on the road could also be less than admirable. He could be sharply disdainful of how his fellows flashed their money, their fractured French, and, particularly, their hammers, chipping away at any monument, however sacred, that might come under their hands. Much of this is funny, and that was expected of Twain, but it can involve a strong satiric bite; Twain can be irascible. He refuses to stay within the confines of the genial, romantic idea of what a travel book "should" be.

He is often very good at showing what the foreign landscape looks like, but what really interests him is how human beings live and what the political, social, and physical implications are of the long histories of great civilizations, now less powerful and somewhat tattered and torn. Most to the point, he is fascinated by how people respond to tourists, how the experience seems to bring out the worst in both parties. He plays fair here, revealing that if the natives are often on the cheat, the Americans, acting thoughtlessly and sometimes stupidly, just as often deserved to be fleeced.

THE ADVENTURES OF TOM SAWYER

First published: 1876
Type of work: Novel

Tom Sawyer, the town's bad boy, experiences disapproval, love and hate, and imaginary and real adventure and he ends up the town hero and a boy of property.

Adventures of Huckleberry Finn is Twain's finest study of a boy's character and his best novel, but it is *The Adventures of Tom Sawyer* that is the more popular boy's tale with the public. Its simplicity, lack of psychological density, and single-minded celebration of the joys of childhood are the reasons for its attraction and the affection with which it is remembered by adults who have not read it for years and never intend to read it again. It is the American dream of ideal childhood written with unmitigated joy.

Much of its success lies with Tom, a child of lively curiosity with a mildly anarchic personality and an imagination fueled by reading (and often misreading) everything from fairy tales to the classics. He is also a boy capable of disarming affection. His relationship with Aunt Polly, swinging as it does between angry frustration and tears of loving joy, is one of the memorable child-adult confrontations in literature. For all of his strutting imitations of maleness, he has no inhibitions in his courting of Becky Thatcher. Twain has a rather crude way with feelings, but in Tom he found a character who acts out his emotions with a comic bravado that often saves the book from falling into sentimental excess.

The Tom Sawyer confidence tricks are part of the folklore of American life. The famous fence-painting game has developed a life of its own that goes beyond the novel. Tom's systematic accumulation of those yellow tickets awarded for memorizing Bible passages leads to one of those lovely moments of exposure that fall regularly into Tom's life of precarious mischief.

Beyond the individual incidents of comic chicanery, however, the novel has a strength which is often not noticed because it is carried on with such ease: It has a complicated plot that comes seemingly out of nowhere and increases in dramatic energy from its inception until the very end. The chance encounter of Tom and Huck that leads to the visit to the graveyard for the purpose of trying out a new method for curing warts leads them right into witnessing Injun Joe's murder of Doctor Robinson. Terrified by possessing a secret which they do not want, they vow to keep quiet, even after Muff Potter, a stupid, drunken companion of Injun Joe, is accused of the murder.

Tom's failure at love when Becky finds out that he had another girlfriend, his depression over the murder, and his feeling that he can do nothing right lead him to run off with Huck, but only to a nearby island, and the boys are thought to have drowned. The tale becomes complicated further as Tom and his friends return to their own funeral and Tom manages to get away with his nonsense, but the murder still hangs fire. Add to that the trial, the hunt for the pirates treasure, the discovery of Injun Joe, the picnic, Tom and Becky's misadventure in the cave, and the discovery of the hidden money, as well as the uproar that is caused in the town and the happy ending, and the reader has a deftly organized example of how adventure literature works at its very best.

At this stage in his career, Twain was most interested in telling the tale and in turning the simplicities of universal childhood play-acting into a tale of intrigue and heroism. What he never does, and this may be part of the secret of the novel's success, is expect Tom or his companions to do anything that might not be credible.

Everything that happens is probable (if unlikely to happen). More to the point, Tom is not a morally perfect character. He is hardly the ideal child: He is superstitious, he is often ignorant, boastful, and devious, and he is slow to come to Muff Potter's defense. He does, eventually, do the right thing, however, even in the face of the fact that he is still terrified of Injun Joe. What Twain has brought into children's literature is the flawed, unfocused moral sensibility of the American boy who only wants to have fun but who has in some mysterious way—through breeding, through education which he ignores and religion which he despises, through social contacts which he finds boring, and through a natural, if embryonic, fineness of character—the capacity ultimately to act with courage and firmness. Do not count on him being changed forever, however; one suspects that Tom is still susceptible to getting in and out of trouble for a long time to come.

The careful reader of *The Adventures of Tom Sawyer* will be able to watch the structure—the way Twain pulls the threads together; the way he puts on the dramatic pressure, then releases it, and puts it on again; the way seemingly separate occurrences come together in surprising ways and lead to the marvelous and dangerous discovery in the caves. Tom and Huck become rich boys, but they are not yet tamed, as Huck will prove in his own novel in which Tom once again spins a marvelous yarn of sheer comic trickery. *The Adventures of Tom Sawyer* may have the requisite happy ending necessary in juvenile fiction, but there is a slight opening left—in Huck's reluctance to settle down—which will allow Twain to go on to a more ambitious fiction.

THE PRINCE AND THE PAUPER

First published: 1881
Type of work: Novel

In the last days of English monarch Henry VIII, a London beggar boy and Crown Prince Edward change roles by chance, then attempt to undo the error.

In *The Prince and the Pauper,* Twain brought together several of his literary interests. His interest in old European civilization, which had been so successfully employed in his travel book *The Innocents Abroad* and had been essayed again in *A Tramp Abroad* (1880), is here focused on England, with emphasis upon life in London. (He will come back again to the theme in *A Connecticut Yankee in King Arthur's Court*, which also returns to the idea of taking the novel back into the past.) The novel does not forget the part of Twain's literary gift that is most celebrated: his interest in boys and how they cope in situations that are not without serious consequences. Twain also had wider ambitions for the novel, and he makes use of it to comment upon politics, social problems, and the relations between children and parents or, as often is the case in his books, surrogate parents.

The book is directly related to the fairy tale genre, and it starts simply enough with the unusual, but not impossible, idea that a London street urchin, who looks surprisingly like Prince Edward, is taken into the palace by the prince. They innocently change clothes, and the prince goes off to chide the guard who mistreated his new friend, only to be thrown out on to the street despite his claim that he is the prince. Then the real trouble starts, both for him and for Tom Canty, the beggar boy, for whom the danger is less physically obvious but potentially serious if he is discovered to be an imposter.

Twain then begins an interleaved narrative of the adventures of the two boys, both determined to get back their identities. However much they protest, they fail to impress and are considered mad. Tom, sensing how precarious his situation is in the palace, goes about accumulating as much knowledge as he can about how he ought to act, hoping to wait out the absence of the prince. His task is complicated by the death of the king and the subsequent need for the prince to take a serious role in governing the country even before he is crowned. Pleased in part by the comforts of his position, he brings his native intelligence and his guile to bear on the problem, but he is determined eventually to clear up the matter.

The prince's situation is much more difficult. Tom's brutal father catches up with him and, mistaking him for Tom, proceeds to give him his daily beating. The prince is always less flexible than Tom, and he never admits to anyone that he is not the royal child; indeed, he is determined to play the ruler even in rags. Only the chance help of Miles Hendon, a gentleman-soldier home from the wars, protects him, and even Hendon has difficulty keeping the prince out of trouble. Hendon thinks he is mad, but he likes the boy and is prepared to be patient with him, hoping that in time, he will be drawn out of his madness by kindness.

Both boys, caught in radically different situations quite beyond their former experience, respond admirably, if the prince is always somewhat less agile in dealing with problems than Tom. All the obvious problems of rags and riches are displayed, sometimes with comic intent but often with serious concern. Twain uses the switched identities for purposes beyond the study of character or comic confusion. Tom, champing at the boring nature of political duties (in a way that reminds one of Huck Finn's dislike of civilized life), is, nevertheless, aroused sufficiently to go beyond the pleasures of his position, and he begins to intrude upon the laws slowly, tempering their harshness but doing so with a care which does not alarm his courtiers.

Edward, out in the country, confronted by the harshness and violence of common life, can do little to help the unfortunate, but his reactions to a world he did not know existed are as civilized in their own way as Tom's, and he is determined to do something about the lot of the common people, particularly the cruel penal laws, if he gets out of the mess alive—which is quite often shown as unlikely.

The parallels between the two, then, go beyond their physical resemblance. They are lively, strong-willed, imaginative boys who at the beginning of the novel are captives. Tom is terrorized by his criminal father. Edward, if in an obviously comfortable position, lives a sequestered life in the palace, dominated by the dying Henry VIII.

Tom dreams of a life of royal power and plays that game with his mates in the slums, then he is given his chance. Edward is also given his chance to meet his subjects, sunk in the squalor of poverty, class privilege, and legal savagery. Both are freed of their fathers, one dying, the other disappearing into the criminal world forever, possibly also dead. What they do with their chances is central to the most serious themes in the book. What could have been simply a charming fairy tale becomes, as *Adventures of Huckleberry Finn* is to become later, a study of boys becoming men.

LIFE ON THE MISSISSIPPI

First published: 1883
Type of work: Travel literature

A loosely organized, partly autobiographical story of Mississippi steamboat life before and after the Civil War.

Life on the Mississippi is Twain's happiest book. Written early in his career, before the difficulties of his personal life had a chance to color his perception, and filled with reminiscent celebration of his time as a boy and man, as an apprentice and as a Mississippi steamboat pilot, it is a lively, affectionate tribute hardly muted by the fact that the world

of the romantic pilots of the Mississippi had disappeared forever during the Civil War and the development of the railroads.

It is a great grab-bag of a book. It starts formally enough, with a sonorous history of the river that reveals how much Twain feels for the phenomenon of the Mississippi (which will appear again in *Adventures of Huckleberry Finn*), but swiftly falls into rambling anecdotes, comic turns, and tall tales. It has, as is often the case in early Twain, a weakness for elephantine humor of the unsophisticated, midwestern rural stripe, but the obvious happiness that marks the tonality of the book manages to keep it going despite its regular habit of floundering in bathos.

The book could well have descended into an amusing shambles had it not been used to tell the very long, detailed, and sometimes hilarious story of the steamboat pilots and of how Twain as a young boy wheedles his way onto the *Paul Jones*, where Mr. Bixby, the pilot, agrees to teach him the Mississippi from New Orleans to St. Louis for five hundred dollars, which Twain is to pay him out of his first wages as a pilot. These passages are some of the best action writing done by Twain, and they anticipate the kind of exciting river narrative that is so important in *Adventures of Huckleberry Finn*.

Beyond the action, however, is Twain's ability to relate the minute-by-minute excitement of learning how to handle the great boats in their perilous journeys up and down a river that changed so rapidly, hour by hour, that charts were of limited use; the pilots had to learn to read the river, night and day, with a sensitivity that was hidden behind the hard-drinking, tough-talking braggadocio of men who possessed a high skill, improvisatory intuition, and sheer nerve.

Twain obviously fell in love with the river and with piloting, and the whole book is a joyful exercise in telling it once and for all, since it had, at the time of printing, been lost forever. Mindful of this, Twain was determined to get it down in all its detail, and he follows the trade from its height, when the pilots were kings, through the battles to unionize as a defense against the owners, to the eventual falling away of the trade during the war period.

There is a kind of broken-backed structure to the work, caused in part by the fact that earlier versions of chapters 4 to 17 originally appeared in *The Atlantic Monthly* in serial form. These, together with three further chapters, are concerned with Twain's career on the river. These were not sufficient to make a book, so the second half was added, with Twain, now the celebrity writer, touring the river and the cities along its banks. This later material is not all bad, but it has nothing like the dramatic focus or energy of the earlier chapters, and there is a feeling that Twain is sometimes at pains to pad it, despite the success of the anecdotes.

The twenty-two years that separate the later Twain from the early adventures of the boy Clemens take much of the immediacy out of the book, even when Twain tries to praise the improvements that engineering science has imposed on the river. There is a feeling that his heart is not really in it, and the latter half of the book has a melancholy air about it that Twain does not fully acknowledge but which haunts the book's conclusion. Twain, the businessman, saw the profit; Clemens, the old pilot, saw the loss.

It could be argued, however, that there is a kind of structural propriety about the book, divided as it is between Twain's early life on the river and his return many years later to discover the changes not only to his beloved river but also to the Mississippi region in general. It is certainly true that this latter material best illustrates the function of the book as a travel document, as Twain catalogs the changes in the river and in the towns along its banks. The decades that had passed between the events of the first half and the second reveal how quickly the Midwest was catching up with the East and how the village and town landscape was giving way to small cities.

ADVENTURES OF HUCKLEBERRY FINN

First published: 1884
Type of work: Novel

Huckleberry Finn, tired of being beaten by his father and of well-meaning people trying to civilize him, takes to the Mississippi on a raft and discovers that he has a runaway slave along for the ride.

Adventures of Huckleberry Finn may at first have seemed to Twain to be an obvious and easy sequel to *The Adventures of Tom Sawyer,* but this book, be-

gun in the mid-1870s, then abandoned, then taken up again in 1880 and dropped again, was not ready to be published until 1884. It was worth the delay. It proved to be Twain's finest novel—not merely his finest juvenile work but his best fiction, and a book that has taken its place as one of the greatest novels written in the United States. In some ways it is a simpler novel than *The Adventures of Tom Sawyer*; it has nothing like the complication of plot which made that earlier novel so compelling.

Huck, harassed by the Widow Douglas and her sister, Miss Watson, who want to give him a good home and a place in normal society, and by his brutal father, who wants to get his hands on the money that Huck and Tom found in *The Adventures of Tom Sawyer,* decides to get away from it all, and he runs away. This time, he does not have the tempering influence of Tom Sawyer, who was prepared to run away to a nearby island but could not resist going home for his own funeral. Tom is only an occasional renegade, eager for the romance but not the long-term reality of rebellion. Huck is of tougher stuff, and he intends to go for good. No better indication of this is to be seen than in the simple fact that Tom tries to smoke but does not have the stomach for it: Huck does not play at it. He is a real smoker and a real rebel—or so he thinks.

Kidnapped by his father and held captive by him, Huck revels at least in the freedom of the barbaric world without soap, water, or school, but he manages to get away, leaving a trail that suggests he has been murdered, and heads for an island in the Mississippi as a start on his attempt to get away from his father and from the well-meaning sisters who would turn him into a respectable citizen. He is on his way to leave all of his troubles behind him.

It is at this point that Twain adds the complication that is to be central to the ascent of this novel from juvenile fancy to the level of moral seriousness. Huck discovers that Jim, Miss Watson's Negro slave, has also run away, having overheard her plans to sell him to a southern farmer. Jim, whose wife and children have already been separated from him and sold to a southern owner, is determined to escape to the free northern states, work as a free man, and eventually buy his family out of bondage. Huck is determined to help him, but he is also unnerved by his concern for Jim's owner. Jim is property before he is a man, and Huck is deeply troubled, surprisingly, by the thought that he is going to help Jim. He sees it, in part, as a robbery, but more interestingly, he sees his cooperation as a betrayal of his obligation to the white society of which he is a member. Huck, the renegade, has, despite himself, deeply ingrained commitments to the idea that white people are superior to black people, and for all his disdain for that society, he is strongly wedded to it.

This conflict provides the psychological struggle for Huck throughout the novel. Even when the two move on, driven by the news that in the town a reward has been posted for Jim, accusing him of murdering Huck, Huck carries a strong sense of wrongdoing because he is helping Jim to escape—not from the murder charge, which can be easily refuted, but from his mistress, who clearly owns him and is entitled to do with him what she will.

Nevertheless, Huck and Jim set off on the raft, which is wedded archetypally to the Ulyssean ship and may be seen as the vehicle for Huck to find out who he is and what kind of man he is likely to become. The pattern is a common one in the history of fiction; Twain weds it to another common structure, the picaresque, which has a long literary history and in which the main characters, while traveling, encounter trials and tribulations that test their wits and ultimately their moral fiber. Twain tends to open this pattern up to include examples of human behavior that do not necessarily have any influence on Huck and Jim but rather indicate Twain's pessimism about human nature in general. The Grangerford-Shepherdson feud, for example, shows the kind of virulent stupidity that can obsess even relatively civilized human beings.

The confidence men who call themselves the Duke and the King, however, take over the raft and use Huck and Jim (and anyone else they can deceive) for profit without concern of any kind. They reveal a much deeper strain of human degradation, which anticipates the inhumanity that is to become even more common in Twain's later works. Huck fears these men but is reluctant to make a clean break from them, though it is fair to remember that they watch him and Jim very closely. The ultimate betrayal comes when Huck, who has let their confidence games be played out in several communities, draws the line when they try to defraud a family of three daughters of their inheritance. The Duke and the King escape without discovering that Huck has revealed their plan. Undismayed by their loss, they start their fraudulent games again, committing their most thoughtlessly cruel act by selling Jim for the reward money.

This is the point of no return for Huck. Jim—ignorant, superstitious, and timid but loyal and devoted to Huck—has, on the long trip down the river, shown over and over that he is a man of considerable character, despite his color and despite his disadvantaged life as a slave. Huck, in turn, discovers that however much he tries to distinguish Jim as other than an equal, however much he is bothered by his determination to see Jim as a lesser being than the white man, he cannot ignore his growing concern for him nor his deepening affection and respect for the way in which Jim endures and goes on. Disgusted by the unfeeling barbarity of the King and the Duke, Huck sets out to free Jim, believing that in so doing, he will go to Hell.

Here the novel returns to the less dangerous world of Tom Sawyer, as it turns out that Jim's new jailors are, in fact, Tom Sawyer's aunt and uncle. Huck passes himself off as Tom in order to get to Jim, who is being kept in a farm outhouse. With the arrival of Tom himself, who passes himself off as his brother Sid, the fun begins, as Tom, as wildly romantic as ever, plots to free Jim the hardest way possible. From this moment on, the novel can be said to fall away from the power that has been explored in Huck's battle to come to terms with his loyalties to society, to his own race, and, most important, to Jim. That battle has been won when Huck decides to save Jim.

All works out well in the end. Tom reveals that a repentant Miss Watson freed Jim before she died, and Aunt Sally, Tom's aunt, thinks she might have a try at civilizing Huck. Huck has other ideas. All this horseplay on the farm is irrelevant, if pleasingly so, to the real strength of the novel, which lies in the journey down the mighty Mississippi, during which Huck Finn learns to care for someone, and perhaps more important, throws off that least valuable influence of society upon him: its belief that white people are superior to black people and have a right to treat human beings as property. Huck, in a sense, comes to the end of this novel as the most civilized white person of all.

A CONNECTICUT YANKEE IN KING ARTHUR'S COURT

First published: 1889
Type of work: Novel

A nineteenth century Yankee foundry superintendent, hit over the head with a crowbar, wakes up in King Arthur's time and promptly decides to bring ancient England up to date.

A Connecticut Yankee in King Arthur's Court can be seen as looking both backward and forward in Twain's career. It is a further version of the historical fantasy that he used in *The Prince and the Pauper,* in which the commonly accepted inhumanities of early Renaissance life were exposed to civilized, liberal ideas which were not to have much support for some centuries to come. It also looks forward to the bleaker, more deeply pessimistic work which was to be so common in the Twain canon in the 1890's. Some of that savagery had been shown in *The Prince and the Pauper,* but in this book there is a predominating line of outright cruelty.

Surprisingly enough, Twain's hero, Hank Morgan, the enlightened nineteenth century man of science and democracy, is not without a tendency to violence; he may be on the right side, but he is no romantic. He does not intrude on the gratuitous cruelty of King Arthur's world unless he can do so safely, and he is often inclined to use force in ways that would make any nineteenth century reader somewhat cautious about praising him.

This change from the hero or heroes of reasonably romantic character is a mark of the darkening nature of Twain's artistic sensibility, and it is a long way from the fairly minor misconduct of a Tom Sawyer or a Huck Finn. Hank Morgan may want to civilize a vicious, savage, ignorant populace, but he has in himself disturbing inclinations to what, in the twenty-first century, would be recognized as a fascistic zeal for power, if strongly tempered by his desire to bring an entire civilization out of the Dark Ages and into the nineteenth century in one lifetime.

In Twain's previous work with the idea of confronting the modern sensibility with the ignorance of the past (which begins with his nonfiction account of Americans on tour in Europe in *The Innocents Abroad* and continues in *The Prince and the Pauper*), there was still room for the comic and the satiric to operate, although the latter book had a serious tonality. *A Connecticut Yankee in King Arthur's Court,* however, is comparatively bereft of comic effects, and its satire has a hectoring shrillness which suggests that Twain no longer finds the idea of human frailty—however fictional or, at least, long since dead and buried it may be—amusing.

The novel is a very dark one which, significantly, does not have the happy ending which draws *The Prince and the Pauper* back into the fairy tale genre with a kind of Dickensian sweetness, with the villains punished and the good people living happily ever after. No such resolution is available in *A Connecticut Yankee in King Arthur's Court,* which ends in destruction of the dream.

Along the way, however, Twain's abundant imagination is used with great skill, not only to tell an interesting tale but also to provide him the opportunity to make his points about superstition, religion, and politics with an earnestness that forces the reader to realize that this is not simply an excursion into fancy. The structure of fantasy is used to make serious comments upon human stupidity, and particularly upon people's stubborn refusal to learn, timidity, and tendencies to respond to authority with sheeplike devotion.

Hank Morgan is not simply trying to get through an unfamiliar situation with some vestige of moral integrity intact, as was often the case with previous Twain characters, including Huck Finn. He sees this accident as a chance to anticipate history, to eliminate hundreds of years of pain and suffering, and to bring Camelot kicking and screaming (as it surely does) into the enlightened nineteenth century.

The richness of incident, particularly the various ways in which Hank Morgan adjusts the scientific knowledge he possesses to the limited resources of the Arthurian times, manages to rise above the gloom of the novel, and the battle between Morgan and Merlin has a kind of comic energy that is expected in Twain's work. How his baby comes to be called "Hello, Central" reminds readers of Twain's earlier, happier works. The center of the novel is not in the fantasy, the trickery, or the adventures, however; it lies in Hank Morgan's character. Just as *Adventures of Huckleberry Finn* ultimately finds its real quality in the development of Huck's personal set of moral standards, this novel gets its strength from Hank Morgan—at first bemused, then outraged, then seizing and working his way through to the dream.

In the battle to civilize, the author is able to make Morgan his mouthpiece for Twain's concerns about society, sometimes without breaching Morgan's character (although the shrill, repetitive attack upon the clergy sometimes is more didactic than artistically appropriate). It is, however, another example of the way Twain makes obviously simple literary forms work in more than one way, and it possesses tonal range which, if sometimes excessive, indicates how ambitious and daring he can be. This book may have a title suitable for a child's bookshelf, but the book is a rough and powerful attack upon human nature, ancient and modern.

SUMMARY

Twain showed that literary art of international reputation could be made from the simplicities of rural American life and that the comic representation of that life did not necessarily have to patronize the actions and ideas of simple people trying to lead decent lives in a country still physically and intellectually unformed. He made Americans proud of his celebration of childhood innocence and childhood character and aware of the physical beauty and the psychological greatness of its midwestern landscape. He also showed that a comic writer need not eschew serious ideas and that the imagination of a writer of adventure literature could be used to consider serious human themes.

Charles H. Pullen

BIBLIOGRAPHY

By the Author

LONG FICTION:
The Gilded Age, 1873 (with Charles Dudley Warner)
The Adventures of Tom Sawyer, 1876
The Prince and the Pauper, 1881
Adventures of Huckleberry Finn, 1884
A Connecticut Yankee in King Arthur's Court, 1889
The American Claimant, 1892
Tom Sawyer Abroad, 1894
The Tragedy of Pudd'nhead Wilson, 1894
Personal Recollections of Joan of Arc, 1896
Tom Sawyer, Detective, 1896
A Double-Barrelled Detective Story, 1902
Extracts from Adam's Diary, 1904
Eve's Diary, Translated from the Original Ms, 1906
A Horse's Tale, 1906
Extract from Captain Stormfield's Visit to Heaven, 1909
The Mysterious Stranger, 1916 (revised as *The Chronicle of Young Satan*, 1969, by Albert Bigelow Paine and Frederick A. Duneka)
Report from Paradise, 1952 (Dixon Wecter, editor)
Simon Wheeler, Detective, 1963
Mark Twain's Mysterious Stranger Manuscripts, 1969 (William M. Gibson, editor)

SHORT FICTION:

The Celebrated Jumping Frog of Calaveras County, and Other Sketches, 1867

Mark Twain's (Burlesque) Autobiography and First Romance, 1871

Mark Twain's Sketches: New and Old, 1875

Punch, Brothers, Punch! and Other Sketches, 1878

The Stolen White Elephant, and Other Stories, 1882

Merry Tales, 1892

The £1,000,000 Bank-Note, and Other New Stories, 1893

The Man That Corrupted Hadleyburg, and Other Stories and Essays, 1900

King Leopold's Soliloquy: A Defense of His Congo Rule, 1905

The $30,000 Bequest, and Other Stories, 1906

The Curious Republic of Gondour, and Other Whimsical Sketches, 1919

The Complete Short Stories of Mark Twain, 1957 (Charles Neider, editor)

Letters from the Earth, 1962

Selected Shorter Writings of Mark Twain, 1962

Mark Twain's Satires and Burlesques, 1967 (Franklin R. Rogers, editor)

Mark Twains's Which Was the Dream? and Other Symbolic Writings of the Later Years, 1967 (John S. Tuckey, editor)

Mark Twain's Hannibal, Huck and Tom, 1969 (Walter Blair, editor)

Mark Twain's Fables of Man, 1972 (Tuckey, editor)

Life as I Find It, 1977 (Neider, editor)

Early Tales and Sketches, 1979-1981 (2 volumes; Edgar Marquess Branch and Robert H. Hirst, editors)

A Murder, a Mystery, and a Marriage, 2001 (Roy Blount, Jr., editor)

DRAMA:

Colonel Sellers, pr., pb. 1874 (adaptation of his novel *The Gilded Age*)

Ah Sin, pr. 1877 (with Bret Harte)

Is He Dead? A Comedy in Three Acts, pb. 2003 (Shelley Fisher Fishkin, editor)

NONFICTION:

The Innocents Abroad, 1869

Roughing It, 1872

A Tramp Abroad, 1880

Life on the Mississippi, 1883

Following the Equator, 1897 (also known as *More Tramp Abroad*)

How to Tell a Story, and Other Essays, 1897

My Début as a Literary Person, 1903

What Is Man?, 1906

Christian Science, 1907

Is Shakespeare Dead?, 1909

Mark Twain's Speeches, 1910 (Albert Bigelow Paine, editor)

Europe and Elsewhere, 1923 (Paine, editor)

DISCUSSION TOPICS

- How does Mark Twain's development of the theme of American innocents abroad differ from that of Henry James?

- In what respects is *Life on the Mississippi* a preparation for *Adventures of Huckleberry Finn*?

- What makes *Adventures of Huckleberry Finn* much more than a "spin-off" of *The Adventures of Tom Sawyer*?

- How legitimate are the concerns that have led certain school systems and libraries to ban or exclude *Adventures of Huckleberry Finn*?

- What lessons has Huck learned by the end of his adventures?

- How do you account for the growing pessimism in Twain's later books?

- Consider Twain as a practitioner of "the art that conceals art."

Mark Twain's Autobiography, 1924 (2 volumes; Paine, editor)

Mark Twain's Notebook, 1935 (Paine, editor)

Letters from the Sandwich Islands, Written for the Sacramento Union, 1937 (G. Ezra Dane, editor)

Mark Twain in Eruption, 1940 (Bernard DeVoto, editor)

Mark Twain's Travels with Mr. Brown, 1940 (Franklin Walker and Dane, editors)

The Love Letters of Mark Twain, 1949 (Dixon Wecter, editor)

Mark Twain to Mrs. Fairbanks, 1949 (Wecter, editor)

Mark Twain of the Enterprise: Newspaper Articles and Other Documents, 1862-1864, 1957 (Henry Nash Smith and Frederick Anderson, editors)

Traveling with the Innocents Abroad: Mark Twain's Original Reports from Europe and the Holy Land, 1958 (letters; Daniel Morley McKeithan, editor)

Mark Twain-Howells Letters: The Correspondence of Samuel L. Clemens and William D. Howells, 1872-1910, 1960 (Smith and William M. Gibson, editors)

The Autobiography of Mark Twain, 1961 (Neider, editor)

Mark Twain's Letters to His Publishers, 1867-1894, 1967 (Hamlin Hill, editor)

Clemens of the Call: Mark Twain in San Francisco, 1969 (Edgar M. Branch, editor)

Mark Twain's Correspondence with Henry Huttleston Rogers, 1893-1909, 1969 (Lewis Leary, editor)

A Pen Warmed-Up in Hell: Mark Twain in Protest, 1972

Mark Twain's Notebooks and Journals, 1975-1979 (3 volumes)

Mark Twain Speaking, 1976 (Paul Fatout, editor)

Mark Twain Speaks for Himself, 1978 (Fatout, editor)

Mark Twain's Letters, 1988-2002 (6 volumes; Branch et al., editors)

Mark Twain's Own Autobiography: The Chapters from the "North American Review," 1990 (Michael J. Kiskis, editor)

Mark Twain's Aquarium: The Samuel Clemens Angelfish Correspondence, 1905-1910, 1991 (John Cooley, editor)

MISCELLANEOUS:

The Writings of Mark Twain, 1922-1925 (37 volumes)

The Portable Mark Twain, 1946 (Bernard De Voto, editor)

Collected Tales, Sketches, Speeches, and Essays, 1853-1891, 1992 (Louis J. Budd, editor)

Collected Tales, Sketches, Speeches, and Essays, 1891-1910, 1992 (Budd, editor)

About the Author

Burns, Ken, Dayton Duncan, and Geoffrey C. Ward. *Mark Twain: An Illustrated Biography*. New York: Alfred A. Knopf, 2001.

Camfield, Gregg. *The Oxford Companion to Mark Twain*. New York: Oxford University Press, 2002.

Emerson, Everett. *Mark Twain: A Literary Life*. Philadelphia: University of Pennsylvania Press, 2000.

Fishkin, Shelley Fisher. *Lighting Out for the Territory: Reflections on Mark Twain and American Culture*. New York: Oxford University Press, 1997.

_____. *Was Huck Black? Mark Twain and African-American Voices*. New York: Oxford University Press, 1993.

_____, ed. *A Historical Guide to Mark Twain*. New York: Oxford University Press, 2002.

Horn, Jason Gary. *Mark Twain: A Descriptive Guide to Biographical Sources*. Lanham, Md.: Scarecrow Press, 1999.

Kaplan, Fred. *The Singular Mark Twain: A Biography*. New York: Doubleday, 2003.

Kaplan, Justin. *Mr. Clemens and Mark Twain: A Biography*. New York: Simon & Schuster, 1966.

LeMaster, J. R., and James D. Wilson, eds. *The Mark Twain Encyclopedia*. New York: Garland, 1993.

Ober, K. Patrick. *Mark Twain and Medicine: "Any Mummery Will Cure."* Columbia: University of Missouri Press, 2003.

Rasmussen, R. Kent. *Mark Twain A to Z*. New York: Facts On File, 1995.

© Diana Walker

ANNE TYLER

Born: Minneapolis, Minnesota
October 25, 1941

Tyler is admired for her skillful, sympathetic creations of extraordinary characters who courageously fight the wars of everyday existence.

BIOGRAPHY

Anne Tyler was born in Minneapolis, Minnesota, on October 25, 1941, the oldest child and only daughter of Lloyd Parry Tyler, a chemist, and Phyllis Mahon Tyler, a social worker, who later became the parents of three boys. During Anne's childhood, the family moved frequently, living in Quaker communes at various locations in the Midwest and the South and finally settling for five years in the mountains of North Carolina. As the oldest child and only girl in a large, active family, Anne Tyler recognized the feminine capacity for leadership, which is emphasized in many of her novels.

Furthermore, both within the family and within the larger context of the commune, she became aware of the tension between two human needs— one for privacy, solitude, and personal freedom, the other for membership in a group, as a defense against indecision and loneliness. By nature, though warm and sympathetic, Tyler has defined herself as an extremely private person. During childhood, she became aware of the difficulties encountered by people such as herself when groups of which they are members demand their full allegiance.

After graduating at sixteen from a secondary school in Raleigh, Tyler entered Duke University, majoring in Russian. When she picked up the enrollment card for her freshman composition class, she became the first student of a new English

teacher, Reynolds Price, who at twenty-five was already a promising novelist, experimenting with new ideas and new narrative techniques. Price recognized Tyler's talent and helped her with her writing. The importance of this early tutelage, from a novelist whose *The Surface of Earth* (1975) would later be called by some critics one of the major American novels of the twentieth century, cannot be overestimated. Tyler, however, was not yet ready to commit herself to a writing career. Instead, although she continued to write, she concentrated on her studies in Russian.

In 1961, after only three years, she graduated from Duke with a Phi Beta Kappa key and moved to New York City, where she spent a year taking graduate courses in Russian at Columbia University. The following year she was back in North Carolina, where she had accepted a position as Russian bibliographer for the Duke University library.

In 1963, Tyler married Taghi Modarressi, a psychiatrist from Iran. While she was looking for a job in Montreal, Quebec, she wrote her first novel, *If Morning Ever Comes* (1964). Although critics found it unsatisfying as a whole, lacking in character and plot development, they did see evidence of considerable talent in the book, pointing out Tyler's comic gift and her effective handling of dialogue, both of which may well have derived from her reading the works of Eudora Welty, who, along with Price, was a major influence on her work. Tyler's second book, *The Tin Can Tree* (1965), was much like the first—promising, interesting, but somehow unformed.

During her time in Montreal, Tyler held her last outside job, as assistant to the librarian at the McGill University Law Library in Montreal. In

1967, she and her husband moved to Baltimore, Maryland, which was to be their permanent home and the setting of many of her works. At this time, she developed her highly disciplined work habits, dividing her time between writing and her family, which by now included two daughters, Tezh and Mitra.

With the publication of *A Slipping-Down Life* in 1970, it was clear that Tyler had discovered how to combine realistic scenes into a novel whose complex characters would grow and change as the story progressed. This novel and *The Clock Winder,* which followed it in 1972, were praised by critics; however, it was not until the mid-1970's, when the best-selling authors Gail Godwin and John Updike publicly called attention to her works, that Tyler began to attract a large following. At the same time, her plots were developing the complexity that critics had found lacking in her early works. In *Celestial Navigation* (1974), Tyler skillfully moved from one point of view to another, interweaving the stories of a half-dozen characters, all of whom form part of the novel's thematic pattern.

The steadily increasing importance of Tyler's works is indicated by the fact that *Morgan's Passing* (1980), her eighth and perhaps her bleakest novel, was nominated for the National Book Critics Circle award and the American Book Paperback Fiction Award and received the Janet Heidinger Kafka Prize. The novel that followed, *Dinner at the Homesick Restaurant* (1982), received the PEN/Faulkner Award for fiction and was nominated for the National Book Critics Circle fiction award, the American Book Award for fiction, and the 1983 Pulitzer Prize.

The works that followed added to Tyler's reputation. In 1985, *The Accidental Tourist* was given a National Book Critics Circle fiction award. Tyler won a Pulitzer Prize for *Breathing Lessons* (1988). Her continuing popularity is evident from the fact that her works are consistently best sellers and that several of them have been made into films or adapted for television. In 1993, Tyler broke out of her usual pattern with her children's book *Tumble Tower,* which was illustrated by her daughter Mitra. However, instead of teaching, lecturing, or making public appearances, Tyler chose to continue living quietly in Baltimore, publishing a novel every three or four years and spending her spare time with her family. Her husband died in 1997.

ANALYSIS

One reason that Tyler's works are so fascinating is that they are difficult to classify. Although she was born in Minnesota, specialized in Russian, and married an Iranian, Tyler is considered a southern writer because her works are set in the South—the early ones in North Carolina, where she spent her adolescence and attended college, the later novels in Baltimore, where she has lived since the 1960's. Tyler does not fit the pattern of many southern writers, however, whose characters, often like the authors themselves, are usually an integral part of rural communities where their families have lived for generations. Although the sense of place is important in Tyler's novels, her emphasis is on the present. Instead of a rural home that a family has occupied for generations, her locale is more likely to be a house in Baltimore—perhaps rented, perhaps occupied for a generation.

Tyler is certainly in the southern tradition, however, when it comes to her emphasis on the importance of community. For example, in her second novel, *The Tin Can Tree,* she traces the ways in which the accidental death of one young girl affects not only her closest relatives but also the entire community in which the girl lived. The effect of the tragedy on this large group of interrelated people is confined, however, to the present and to the projected future. There is no conjecture as to patterns established in the past, as is found in so much southern fiction.

The protagonists in many southern novels are interesting precisely because they either refuse to accept community standards—rejecting racism, for example—or because, like the lawyer Atticus Finch in Harper Lee's *To Kill a Mockingbird* (1960), they represent principles that the community professes but which, in practice, it betrays. Tyler's protagonists are not members of the establishment who are either rebels or idealists. They tend to be eccentrics who are in flight from their societies for no particular reason other than that they possess boundless energy and unrestrained imaginations.

The energetic protagonist appears in a rather peculiar form in Tyler's first novel, *If Morning Ever Comes.* At the beginning of the story, Ben Joe Hawkes is in law school in New York City. Unfortunately, his imagination betrays him: He cannot forget the household of women he has left behind in North Carolina, women he is sure cannot manage without him. Desperately worried, Hawkes leaves law school and goes home.

There, when he finds that the women are all doing very well, he feels quite unnecessary and falls into inertia. He apparently will have the energy to move on with his own life only when he knows that a woman is truly dependent on him. Fortunately, he finds an available sweetheart from his high school days and takes her to New York with him, where one assumes he can now be dependent on her dependence.

By the time Tyler wrote *A Slipping-Down Life*, she had arrived at the peculiar combination of imagination, rebellion, energy, and even frenzy that marks many of her most interesting characters and often the protagonists in her later novels. Teenager Evie Decker loathes her school, her town, and her dull life. Her rebellion has been shown by withdrawal: She has spent most of her life hiding in her own home, merely dreaming of escape. When she falls in love with a rock musician, however, she suddenly has considerable energy. One can only call it a kind of madness when she carves his name on her forehead, thus becoming a local celebrity. It is clear that Evie intends to follow her musician out of the community and into a more exciting world. If at the end of the story Evie is moving back to her old home instead of heading for Hollywood, it is only because the situation has changed. She has a new baby, and she now desires the security of living in a home she owns. Evidently she now has an outlet for her energy.

Energetic, imaginative characters such as Evie Decker never fit easily into communities that, like most groups of people, value the comfortable virtues of moderation, conformity, and predictability. In every human being, Tyler suggests, there are two conflicting tendencies. On one hand, there is the desire for attachment, which draws Evie first toward her musician and eventually back to her own house, and which pulls the protagonist of *The Accidental Tourist* toward his childhood home, where his sister and his brothers continue to live in a tight little unit. It brings both the law student of *If Morning Ever Comes* and the long-lost Caleb of *Searching for Caleb* (1976) back to the families with whom they never did feel particularly comfortable.

On the other hand, there is also the need for privacy, for solitude, for possessing one's own soul, that the author recognizes in herself. This need may drive one inward, like the artist recluse in *Celestial Navigation*, or outward into eccentric actions such as those of the protagonist in *Morgan's Passing*, who flees from his demanding, overwhelmingly female family into disguise and a fantasy world he can control.

Because her characters keep veering from one direction to the other as one, then another, of the two needs becomes dominant, and because sometimes, like Evie, they finally return to the places where they began, Tyler's novels have been called unsatisfyingly circular in plot. In all except perhaps the first two novels, however, Tyler is so skilled in tracing the development of character that although the place may be the same, its inhabitants are clearly very different people. It is this emphasis on character that makes her readers ignore the fact that most of her incidents, though amazing and often amusing, are not earthshaking.

When the protagonist of *Breathing Lessons* slams her newly repaired car into a Pepsi truck, or even when the protagonist of *Morgan's Passing* poses as a doctor and delivers a baby, the real interest lies in the motivations of some characters and the reactions of others. Thus, if Tyler's later novels are no longer accused of formlessness, it must be emphasized that their unity derives less from plotting than from the creation of compelling characters. Tyler's greatest achievement is her skill in deferring to those characters. As an author she effaces herself, moving among her characters and reproducing their thoughts and their conversations as they rush headlong toward self-discovery.

SEARCHING FOR CALEB

First published: 1976
Type of work: Novel

A ninety-three-year-old man determinedly seeks his half brother, who disappeared sixty years before.

Searching for Caleb is unique among Tyler's novels in that it is a detective story. The first scene in the book takes place on a train from Baltimore to New York City, where Daniel Peck and his granddaughter, Justine Peck, hope to find some news of Daniel's half brother, Caleb Peck, who has been missing for sixty years. Caleb is finally found, thanks to a detective the family has hired; however, it is typical of Tyler's circuitous plotting that at the end of the story Caleb once again leaves the Peck family, with whom he had never been comfortable.

The conflict in *Searching for Caleb* is typical for a Tyler novel. The community that demands conformity is the Peck family. As Duncan Peck, the black sheep of the family, says, the Pecks have dug a moat around themselves so that from their castle they can judge and disapprove of the rest of the world. From the time of their birth, Peck children are indoctrinated with rules of behavior. Pointing out to his cousin Justine Mayhew that she is wearing a hat only because it is a Peck practice, the observant Duncan lists all the family customs, such as wearing English riding boots and refusing to develop cavities, and all the family prejudices—against golf, plastic, and emotion, for example. So extensive a code can, like the moat which Duncan mentions, effectively keep non-Pecks at a distance.

It is Justine who develops most during the novel and who, therefore, should be considered the protagonist. Once she has accepted Duncan's view of the Pecks and, incidentally, married him, Justine becomes one of Tyler's energetic heroines, whose principle of life seems to be "When in doubt, change." Because Duncan, too, is both imaginative and energetic, given to undertakings that begin with great promise and, unfortunately, soon bore him, thus ensuring their failure, it is perhaps as well that Justine can live the life of a gypsy, packing up the suitcases, giving away the cats, and moving on at a moment's notice.

Justine cannot completely forget her Peck upbringing, however, and near the end of the novel she almost succumbs. For her, Duncan offers to settle down, take a job in Baltimore, and live like the rest of the Pecks. Interestingly, it is not merely her love for him that changes Justine's original decision. It is also the feedback she gets from the Pecks, who seem less than enthusiastic about the possibility. Evidently, she discovers, the adult Pecks like to have one branch of the family living extravagant, colorful lives, just as the young Peck cousins had been delighted to have one of their number behaving like the outrageous Duncan. Both Caleb's second disappearance and Justine's arrangements for her family to travel with a carnival, then, are neces-

sary for the existence of the fixed lives of the rest of the Pecks. In this exploration of her theme, Tyler has illustrated the fact that in order for a community to remain healthy, there must be individuals who refuse to follow its rules. Perhaps, too, if individuals are to know the joys of rebellion, there must be Pecks, providing rules for them to defy.

DINNER AT THE HOMESICK RESTAURANT

First published: 1982
Type of work: Novel

A dying woman looks back on her marriage and her stormy family life.

Dinner at the Homesick Restaurant begins with Pearl Cody Tull's deathbed reflections and ends with her funeral. Like *Searching for Caleb*, this novel revolves around an unconventional family in which the mother is a central figure. While the source of Justine's energy is that of her husband, whom she imitates and even exceeds, the source of Pearl's is her misery at having been unaccountably deserted by the husband whom she dearly loved. Pearl's excesses come not from joy in freedom but from anger because she is imprisoned in a life she did not choose.

At thirty, Pearl had been facing spinsterhood. Then she met a loud, brash salesman six years her junior who admired her ladylike behavior and had the power to persuade her that anything in the world was possible. Beck Tull and Pearl hastened into marriage. Eventually, they had three children. When the oldest was entering his teens, Beck disappeared, and it was then that Pearl became almost demented. Somehow she could never tell the children that Beck was never coming back. Trapped in her lie, overburdened by responsibility, and often financially desperate, she would suddenly be over-

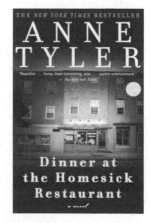

come by rage, striking out at the very children she had so desired.

Because of their mother's peculiarities, the Tull children are isolated from the community; however, unlike the eccentric Pecks in *Searching for Caleb,* they cannot take delight in their own independence. Unfortunately, because no one ever explains to them either their father's absence or their mother's furies, they come to see life as dangerous and irrational, and as they grow to adulthood, in different ways they all try to find some kind of security.

The oldest child, Cody Tull, is particularly burdened. Convinced that one of his pranks must have caused his father to leave, Cody has a profound need to control his life so that no such event will ever occur again. His choice of profession is typical of Tyler, who even in tragic stories can amuse her readers with her imaginative but unfaltering logic: Cody becomes an efficiency expert. Unfortunately, he cannot organize his own emotions as well as he can structure a factory. Jealous of his brother's success with his girlfriends, Cody marries a highly unsuitable woman simply because she is his brother's fiancée.

Cody's sister Jenny, too, seeks the rationality which her childhood denied her. The highly intelligent and completely organized Harley Baines seems perfect for her. After she marries Harley, Jenny discovers that his most well-developed faculty is the critical one, and she finds herself constantly under fire. Clearly, she had looked for intellect in a partner when she should have emphasized commitment. Through her pediatric practice, she meets a desperate widower with children of his own, and the household they set up together, though as hectic and unpredictable as that of her childhood, is extremely happy because it is founded on love, not on anger.

It is Ezra Tull, however, the middle child and his mother's favorite, whose dreams of a harmonious family life are reflected in the book title. After Ezra becomes the owner of a restaurant where he has long been working, he changes its image and its name. "The Homesick Restaurant" is intended to cater to everyone who, like Ezra, associates food with the security of a loving family. Ironically, every time Ezra brings the family together for a fine meal, they quarrel and someone walks out. The only meal that is ever completed is the feast after

Pearl's funeral, when the missing Beck Tull, who had stormed out, consents to return and finish his meal with the family he had deserted.

The excuse Beck gives for leaving his family, which caused so much pain to four people, is that Pearl could see his faults and he could not bear it. Although Tyler will never glorify conformity for its own sake, in *Dinner at the Homesick Restaurant* she makes it clear that unloving, irresponsible egotism such as Beck's cannot be justified, whatever the claims of the individual.

THE ACCIDENTAL TOURIST

First published: 1985
Type of work: Novel

A travel writer who hates to travel learns to accept the unexpected and, in the process, takes control of his own life.

Of all Tyler's characters, Macon Leary, the protagonist of *The Accidental Tourist,* is undoubtedly the one most obsessed with routine. A travel writer who hates to travel, he has developed guides for other travelers who want to reproduce their home environments as much as possible when they are abroad. Leary's life has been based on the assumption that he could outwit chance simply by planning carefully. Unfortunately, at the beginning of the novel, his only child has been killed in a random crime at a fast-food store, and, unable to cope with the death, Macon's wife, Susan, has left him.

Macon's first impulse is to order his household; however, his efforts at efficiency are less than successful, and he ends up with a broken leg. With considerable relief, he moves into the orderly household his sister, Rose, runs for their two brothers. The portrait of the four Leary children, all of whom have now returned home, symbolizes the security that Macon feels, having moved back into the unchanging past. It seems that conformity will win over the chaos that Macon so dreads.

Somewhat earlier in the story, however, Tyler has introduced one of her energetic women, Muriel Pritchett, a veterinarian's assistant with a young son and a mind of her own. Before long, Muriel is training Macon's aggressive dog and bringing Macon himself into her disorderly, fascinating world, where the unexpected is cherished. Finally, Macon must choose between returning to Susan, whose very body is comfortably familiar, and moving ahead in an adventuresome life with Muriel, where his only certainty will be her good nature.

In *The Accidental Tourist*, several characters move back and forth between individualism and conformity, disorder and order.

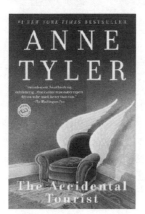

For example, Rose Leary, who is responsible for keeping the family home untouched by time, falls in love with Julian Edge, Macon's boss, a breezy, confident person who carries her away from what might seem to be a dull life. Julian has not reckoned with Rose's appetite for order, however, and before long, she returns to the family home and her old life. Only Macon's inventiveness saves the marriage; remembering the chaos of Julian's office, he suggests that Julian beg her help in getting it under control. Julian is finally the convert to conformity; the man who, Tyler says, never even consulted a consumer magazine before buying something, moves into the Leary household and happily takes part in their routine.

Two of the characters, Alexander Pritchett, Muriel's son, and Susan Leary, Macon's wife, are deeply troubled at the beginning of the novel. Allergic to everything, enthusiastic about nothing, Alexander evidently bears the burden of feeling unwanted by his father and perhaps also of his mother's eccentricity. He lacks something—the company of men, his mother thinks, but it may be a feeling of family structure as well. The turning point for Alexander comes in a scene that illustrates Tyler's subtle blend of humor and pathos. Macon decides to show Alexander how to repair a faucet; furthermore, he insists that the boy do it himself. When he succeeds, Alexander smiles for the first time. It is obvious that Alexander has a need for order which his mother cannot fulfill but which Macon can.

In the grief-stricken, gloomy Susan Leary who is introduced in the first chapter of *The Accidental Tourist*, it is hard to imagine the high-spirited young woman whom Macon married. It is not too surprising that the father and mother of the murdered boy cannot share their feelings with each other. What is surprising is the turn that Susan takes later in her life. After she goes to Paris with Macon, it seems that their marriage has been patched up; however, the once mercurial woman now seems to be clutching at order and pattern. When Susan starts to plan every detail of their trip together, Macon realizes that he must return to Muriel, who saves that kind of bossiness for the dogs she is training. At the end of the novel, everyone except Susan has learned to live in tension between order and disorder, conformity and individualism.

BREATHING LESSONS

First published: 1988
Type of work: Novel

During a one-day automobile trip on the way to a funeral, a couple recall and strengthen their twenty-eight-year marriage.

If *Dinner at the Homesick Restaurant* and *Morgan's Passing* are Tyler's darkest works, *Breathing Lessons* is one of her most optimistic. Even though many of the misadventures in all of her novels are comic, in those earlier works one cannot escape the suggestion that life consists mostly of missed opportunities. In *Breathing Lessons*, on the other hand, one feels that nothing is lost, that everything can be renewed, repaired, or redeemed.

The renewal that is central in *Breathing Lessons* is the twenty-eight-year marriage between Maggie and Ira Moran. At first glance, Maggie and Ira would seem completely unsuited to each other. Ira is rational and precise. His heroine is advice columnist Ann Landers, who personifies common sense. Maggie, on the other hand, has contempt for logic. Compassionate, ebullient, and friendly as a puppy, she moves through life as if it were a festival. In fact, that is one of the things that so annoys Ira. She does not take life seriously, he thinks; she acts as if it were all a practice for something else.

The action of *Breathing Lessons* takes place in a single day, during which Maggie, impulsive as usual, insists on going to Deer Lick, Pennsylvania, in order to attend the funeral of her girlhood friend's husband. Throughout that day, Maggie and Ira squabble, revealing their irreconcilable differences, draw apart, then forgive each other, remember how charming those differences have always been, and come back together. On the way to the wedding, for example, Maggie has an accident, forgets the road map, and stops to befriend people all along the way. When Ira, quite understandably, becomes annoyed, Maggie insists on getting out of the car. Even when Ira returns for her, things are not quite back to normal. When the friend shows some old pictures, however, Maggie gets sentimental, Ira remembers that it was her confidence about life that attracted him to Maggie in the first place, and the two start making love in the widow's upstairs bedroom, only to be discovered and kicked out of the house.

This same ebb and flow is evident in Maggie's relationship with her daughter-in-law, Fiona, who is separated from her husband, Jesse, who is busy trying to find himself. After Maggie persuades Ira to make a side trip to see their grandson, she decides to bring Fiona and Jesse together; with the help of a few blatant lies she drags Fiona and the child back to Baltimore. Throughout this adventure, Ira is appalled. He never did think that the marriage would work—but then, he is married to the same energetic, illogical woman who once recklessly pursued a purse snatcher for the sake of a few dollars. Maggie never calculates odds. She is hardly discouraged when Fiona and Jesse quarrel and part once again. The conclusion of the novel suggests that Tyler can see some victories for energetic, well-meaning, if disorderly characters such as Maggie. The widow apologizes, Ira once again falls under Maggie's spell, and undaunted, Maggie secretly begins to plan another campaign.

A PATCHWORK PLANET

First published: 1998
Type of work: Novel

The black sheep of a prominent family discovers who he really is and what constitutes a meaningful life.

Although Anne Tyler had previously used male protagonists in her fiction, until *A Patchwork Planet* she had never had a male first-person narrator. However, since the novel is about Barnaby Gaitlin's discovery of his own identity, the author's decision to let Barnaby tell his own story was a wise one.

A Patchwork Planet begins on New Year's Eve and ends on the following Christmas. Whenever the socially prominent Gaitlins have one of their ceremonial gatherings, they make it clear that they are ashamed of Barnaby. In his youth, he was arrested for housebreaking and escaped punishment only because his parents paid a hefty sum as restitution. Barnaby has never repaid them. He dropped out of college, and though his family offered him a job at their Gaitlin Foundation, instead he took a job with Rent-a-Back, which assigns employees to perform chores for those who are ill or elderly. Barnaby has not even succeeded at marriage. His wife, Natalie, left him because he lacked both money and social standing. Now remarried and living in Baltimore, she discourages his visits to their daughter, Opal, whom Natalie is rearing to be as snobbish and superficial as she is.

At thirty, Barnaby is pinning his hopes on a visitation from the Gaitlin angel, which showed one family member how to make a fortune and kept another from losing everything. At the beginning of the novel, Barnaby toys with the idea that a beautiful young woman whom he observed in the Baltimore train station may indeed be that angel. Although he later realizes that Sophia Maynard is not a supernatural being but an ordinary bank employee, he recognizes her as an energetic woman who he thinks has a loving heart. Unfortunately, he misjudges her, for when her elderly mother accuses him of stealing money from her, Sophia believes that Barnaby is guilty.

Although eventually the missing money is found, Barnaby breaks off with Sophia, who he now knows is a carbon copy of his former wife. However, the incident has shown Barnaby how many people admire him. His clients besieged his employer with requests for his services, thus making sure that he would not be fired. Moreover, one of his fellow employees, Martine Pasko, risked her own job in order to help him. Although, as the story ends, Barnaby has still not had a visitation from the family angel, he now believes that Martine may well be its earthly manifestation.

A Patchwork Planet derives its title from a quilt representing Planet Earth that Barnaby's client Mrs. Alford was determined to finish before she died. With its imperfect pieces and its uneven stitches, the quilt seemed to be a metaphor for human life. It fell as short of perfection as Barnaby Gaitlin does. To her grieving daughter, however, Mrs. Alford's quilt seemed beautiful. As Barnaby comes to see, it is loving acts, not material objects, that give life its meaning, and a person who has the skill and the inclination to perform such acts of grace is truly successful.

SUMMARY

Although Tyler's plots may seem as circular as life itself, with her characters often moving back to the places from which they came, the characters are changed by the events through which they have moved. Tyler's great gift lies in the creation and sympathetic treatment of these characters, who in their interactions produce scenes of comedy and even of farce.

DISCUSSION TOPICS

- How does place function in Anne Tyler's fiction?

- Which of Tyler's characters reject their families and their communities? What are the results?

- Which of Tyler's characters or family units represent conformity?

- How does Tyler use her eccentrics to create humor?

- How do Tyler's energetic women alter the lives of their families and especially of the men in their lives?

- Tyler acknowledges her own need for privacy. Which of her characters are motivated by that same need?

Tyler's characters and their actions may seem extreme, but the theme that they illustrate rings true. Every human being must try to harmonize such opposites as individuality and conformity, emotion and reason, and energy and restraint. Some of Tyler's novels suggest that such reconciliation is almost impossible; others indicate that the possibility exists, that energy and love can do what reason can never accomplish.

Rosemary M. Canfield Reisman

BIBLIOGRAPHY

By the Author

LONG FICTION:
If Morning Ever Comes, 1964
The Tin Can Tree, 1965
A Slipping-Down Life, 1970
The Clock Winder, 1972
Celestial Navigation, 1974
Searching for Caleb, 1976
Earthly Possessions, 1977
Morgan's Passing, 1980
Dinner at the Homesick Restaurant, 1982
The Accidental Tourist, 1985
Breathing Lessons, 1988

Saint Maybe, 1991
Ladder of Years, 1995
A Patchwork Planet, 1998
Back When We Were Grownups, 2001
The Amateur Marriage, 2004

SHORT FICTION:
"The Common Courtesies," 1968
"Who Would Want a Little Boy?," 1968
"With All Flags Flying," 1971
"The Bride in the Boatyard," 1972
"The Base-Metal Egg," 1973
"Spending," 1973
"Half-Truths and Semi-Miracles," 1974
"The Geologist's Maid," 1975
"A Knack for Languages," 1975
"Some Sign That I Ever Made You Happy," 1975
"Your Place Is Empty," 1976
"Average Waves in Unprotected Waters," 1977
"Foot-Footing On," 1977
"Holding Things Together," 1977
"Uncle Ahmad," 1977
"Under the Bosom Tree," 1977
"Linguistics," 1978
"Laps," 1981
"The Country Cook," 1982
"Teenage Wasteland," 1983
"Rerun," 1988
"A Woman Like a Fieldstone House," 1989
"People Who Don't Know the Answers," 1991

CHILDREN'S LITERATURE:
Tumble Tower, 1993 (illustrations by Mitra Modarressi)

About the Author

Bail, Paul. *Anne Tyler: A Critical Companion.* Westport, Conn.: Greenwood Press, 1998.

Croft, Robert W. *An Anne Tyler Companion.* Westport, Conn.: Greenwood Press, 1998.

Evans, Elizabeth. *Anne Tyler.* New York: Twayne, 1993.

Kissel, Susan S. *Moving On: The Heroines of Shirley Ann Grau, Anne Tyler, and Gail Godwin.* Bowling Green, Ohio: Bowling Green State University Popular Press, 1996.

Petry, Alice Hall. *Critical Essays on Anne Tyler.* New York: G. K. Hall, 1992.

_____. *Understanding Anne Tyler.* Columbia: University of South Carolina Press, 1990.

Salwak, Dale. *Anne Tyler as Novelist.* Iowa City: University of Iowa Press, 1994.

Stephens, C. Ralph. *The Fiction of Anne Tyler.* Jackson: University Press of Mississippi, 1990.

Sweeney, Susan Elizabeth. "Anne Tyler." In *The History of Southern Women's Literature,* edited by Carolyn Perry and Mary Louise Weaks. Baton Rouge: Louisiana State University Press, 2002.

JOHN UPDIKE

Born: Shillington, Pennsylvania
March 18, 1932

Widely recognized as one of the most accomplished and prolific stylists of his generation, Updike has emerged as a short-story writer and novelist of major importance in American letters.

© Davis Freeman

BIOGRAPHY

John Updike was born on March 18, 1932, in Shillington, Pennsylvania, the only child of Wesley and Linda Grace (Hoyer) Updike. His early years were spent in the Shillington home of his mother's parents, John and Katherine Hoyer. When John was thirteen, they moved to the old family farm in Plowville, ten miles outside Shillington, where John's mother had been born. These were lean years for the family, which was supported only by his father's meager salary as a mathematics teacher at Shillington High School. Though poor, his parents were well educated and had high aspirations for their son, who showed an early aptitude for art and writing.

Influenced by *The New Yorker*, the youthful Updike was determined to become a cartoonist and writer for that magazine. His mother, who had literary aspirations of her own, became determined that John should go to Harvard University. Because of his good grades, Updike won a full scholarship in 1950 to Harvard, where he majored in English and was editor of the Harvard *Lampoon*. He graduated with highest honors in 1954. He met his future wife, Mary Pennington, a Radcliffe student and daughter of a Unitarian minister, while he was a sophomore. They married in 1953, when Updike was a junior. In 1954, Updike published his first story in *The New Yorker*.

The Updikes spent a year during 1954-1955 at the Ruskin School of Drawing and Fine Art in Oxford, England, financed partly by a Knox Fellowship. Their first child, Elizabeth, was born during this time. After publishing four stories and ten poems in *The New Yorker* during that year, Updike was offered a position as *The New Yorker*'s "Talk of the Town" reporter. The Updikes settled in New York City; Updike wrote for *The New Yorker* until 1957, when he felt the need to leave the city to devote his full time to writing. In April, 1957, they moved to Ipswich, Massachusetts, where they lived for the following seventeen years. In 1958, his first book, a collection of poems called *The Carpentered Hen and Other Tame Creatures*, was published. In 1959, Updike published *The Poorhouse Fair*, his first novel, and a collection of stories, *The Same Door*. His second child, David, was born in 1957. In 1959, Updike's second son, Michael, was born; in 1960, his last child, Miranda, was born. The Ipswich years saw Updike not only as a prolific writer but also active in community affairs. He was a member of the Congregational Church and the Democratic Town Committee.

It was during that same period—the late 1950's and early 1960's—that Updike faced a crisis of faith prompted by his consciousness of the inevitability of death. His reading of the works of Danish philosopher and theologian Søren Kierkegaard and, especially, the Swiss neo-orthodox theologian Karl Barth helped him overcome this crisis and find a basis for faith. A preoccupation with the sense of death runs throughout Updike's fiction, as does an exploration of theological and religious issues.

Updike's work published in the 1960's established him as one of the United States' important writers. In 1960, he published *Rabbit, Run*, the first in a series of works about a middle-class man and his family set in a small city in Pennsylvania. Updike returned to this character at intervals of a decade, with *Rabbit Redux* appearing in 1971, *Rabbit Is Rich* in 1981 (winning the Pulitzer Prize in fiction and the National Book Award), and *Rabbit at Rest* in 1990 (again winning the National Book Critics Award and Pulitzer Prize). This tetralogy was brought together in 1995 as *Rabbit Angstrom: The Four Novels*, and in paperback in 2003 simply as *The Rabbit Novels*.

In 1962, Updike's second short-story collection, *Pigeon Feathers, and Other Stories*, appeared, and in 1963, another collection of verse, *Telephone Poles, and Other Poems*, was published. His novel *The Centaur*, also published in 1963, earned for Updike the National Book Award and election to the National Institute of Arts and Letters; he was the youngest man ever to be elected. In 1966, *The Music School*, another collection of stories, appeared, and he has continued to publish stories (often in *The New Yorker*) and to collect them, in such volumes as *The Afterlife, and Other Stories* (1994) and *Licks of Love: Short Stories and a Sequel, "Rabbit Remembered"* (2000). In 2003, he brought together *The Early Stories, 1953-1975* to much praise, including the PEN/Faulkner Award for Fiction. Likewise, he published his *Collected Poems* in 1993, and *Americana, and Other Poems* in 2001. In 2000, he edited *The Best American Short Stories of the Century*, with Katrina Kenison.

In 1964-1965, Updike traveled to Eastern Europe as part of a cultural exchange program. A number of his works reflect that experience, in particular *Bech: A Book* (1970), *Bech Is Back* (1982), *Bech at Bay: A Quasi-Novel* (1998), and *The Complete Henry Bech: Twenty Stories* (2001). In 1973, Updike traveled, under State Department auspices, to Africa; his novel *The Coup* (1978) draws upon that experience. His 1968 novel, *Couples*, caused quite a stir because of its explicit treatment of adultery in a Northeastern suburb and became a best seller. It gained for its author a cover story in *Time* and favorable treatment in *Life* as well as a large sum for the film rights.

Over the years, Updike has also published collections of his essays and reviews—*Assorted Prose* (1965), *Picked-Up Pieces* (1975), *Hugging the Shore: Essays and Criticism* (1983)—that show Updike as a fine critic and cultural commentator. As in his fic-

tion, his range is vast, from *Odd Jobs: Essays and Criticism* (1991) to *Golf Dreams: Writings on Golf* (1996). He is also a distinguished reviewer of art and has collected his essays in *Just Looking: Essays on Art* (1989) and *Still Looking: Essays on American Art* (2005).

In addition to the Rabbit quartet and *Couples*, a number of Updike's novels focus upon love and marriage and its discontents. His own marriage ended in divorce in 1974. In 1977, Updike married Martha Bernhard. Such story collections as *Museums and Women, and Other Stories* (1972), *Problems, and Other Stories* (1979), *Too Far to Go: The Maples Stories* (1979), and *Trust Me* (1987) reflect Updike's concern for marriage in various stages of decline and difficulty. The novel *Marry Me*, published in 1976 but mostly written before 1968, also focuses upon a flawed marriage. The novels *A Month of Sundays* (1975), *Roger's Version* (1986), and *S.* (1988) make up a kind of updating of Nathaniel Hawthorne's *The Scarlet Letter* (1850). *The Witches of Eastwick* (1984) attempts to explore love and marriage from a woman's perspective.

Memories of the Ford Administration (1992) continued Updike's exploration of contemporary sexual mores, against a background of American history. In *Brazil* (1994), Updike ventured into Latin American Magical Realism, *In the Beauty of the Lilies* (1996) returned to a spiritual history of four generations of Americans, *Toward the End of Time* (1997) traveled into a postnuclear future, while *Gertrude and Claudius* (2000) explored the lives of Hamlet's parents. *Seek My Face* (2002) reflected Updike's continuing interest in American art, while *Villages* (2004) returned to the Northeast in a story of suburban marriage from a male perspective. By 2005, Updike had produced more than twenty novels and an almost equal number of short-story collections. In addition to his numerous awards for individual works, he was awarded the National Medal of Arts in 1989, the National Book Foundation Medal for distinguished contribution to American letters in 1998, and the National Medal for the Humanities in 2003.

ANALYSIS

Showing remarkable versatility and range, and meeting with both critical and popular success, Updike's fiction represents a penetrating realist chronicle of the changing morals and manners of

American society. His novels continue the long national debate on American civilization and its discontents, but perhaps what is most significant about his fiction is its depiction of restless and aspiring spirits struggling within the constraints of flesh, of time and gravity, and of changing social conditions, to find something of transcendent value—all of them lovers and battlers. For Updike, as for many other writers, the conditions and possibilities of love are an index of the conditions and possibilities of faith and belief. As Updike writes in an essay: "Not to be in love, the capital N novel whispers to capital W western man, is to be dying."

Updike's versatility and range can be seen in terms of both style and subject. His first novel, *The Poorhouse Fair*, written when he was in his twenties, is cast twenty years into the future and explores the social and spiritual implications of an essentially antihumanistic socialism. The novel captures imaginatively the voices and experiences of octogenarian characters. In *The Coup*, Updike portrays the speech and sensibility of an American-educated, deposed African leader. In the Bech books, like *Bech: A Book* and *Bech Is Back*, Updike creates the persona of an urbane, sophisticated Jewish-American writer in search of his muse. In the Rabbit novels, Updike penetrates the ever-changing world of the former basketball player Harry "Rabbit" Angstrom. In such novels as *The Witches of Eastwick, S.*, and *Seek My Face*, Updike explores the feminine sensibility. Updike is still trying out new subjects and styles, in *Brazil, Toward the End of Time*, and *Gertrude and Claudius*.

In *A Month of Sundays, Couples, Roger's Version*, and *Villages*, and in such short-story collections as *Too Far to Go: The Maples Stories* (1979), *Licks of Love*, and *Problems, and Other Stories*, Updike has perhaps become the United States' supreme examiner of marriage and its discontents. Each work has a style commensurate to its subject. Updike has a fine ear for the nuances and cadences of human speech from all levels of social life. In addition, his descriptive passages are unequaled in capturing the detail and texture of modern life. For some critics, however, Updike is more style than substance, with a prose too ornate, even baroque, densely littered with perception. Nevertheless, the richness and variety of his narratives reveal a writer with extraordinary talent.

Although generalizations do not do justice to the particularities of each Updike work, there is a major predicament experienced by nearly all of Updike's protagonists—a sense of doubleness, of the ironic discrepancy of the fallen creature who yet senses, or yearns for, something transcendent. Updike's characters are creatures moving between two realms but not fully at home in either. The four novels devoted to Rabbit Angstrom illustrate this fallenness in quest of transcendence; they also portray the substitute of sexuality for religious experience.

Updike has written short stories since the beginning of his career and has published in such magazines as *The New Yorker, Esquire, The Atlantic*, and *Playboy*. He has produced a number of collections of his stories, from *The Same Door, Pigeon Feathers, and Other Stories* and *Olinger Stories: A Selection* (1964), through *The Music School, Museums and Women, and Other Stories*, and *Trust Me*, to *Licks of Love, The Complete Henry Bech* and *The Early Stories, 1953-1975*. Updike's stories (especially "A & P" and "Separating") are often anthologized in literature textbooks. His stories are generally concerned with subtle states of mind and small events; seemingly insignificant details assume an importance that is somehow sensed but is difficult to explain.

In "Separating," for example, Updike portrays well the pain of a family on the verge of divorce. The story describes Richard and Joan Maples trying to work out how their children are to be told of their impending separation but opens with detailed descriptions of household chores whose significance readers can only guess at. The final revelations at the dinner table ring painfully true. When the father tells the older son later, the son appears to take the news calmly. Yet when the father kisses him good night, the son asks the virtually unanswerable question: "Why?" Love, so often, is a painful longing for what has been lost, an irretrievable moment, an irrecoverable place.

As seen in both his nonfiction and his fiction, Updike is one of the most theologically sophisticated writers of his generation. He has read deeply in Christian theology, especially in the works of such authors as Kierkegaard and Barth. It is Updike's theological convictions that constitute the basis for his critique of modern men and women and of American society. In an interview conducted in the mid-1960's, Updike declared that "without the supernatural, the natural is a pit of horror." In

Canto IV to his long poem *Midpoint,* Updike writes: "An easy Humanism plagues the land;/ I choose to take an otherworldly stand." His characters seek passage through a decaying world, one whose traditions are disintegrating and dissolving from the pressures of secularity and materialism. Updike's fiction explores the implications of a world that is essentially post-Christian. To stay the anxiety of death, to fill the emptiness of lost or abandoned belief, Updike's characters turn to sexuality, but they are frequently disappointed. In his story "The Bulgarian Poetess" (1966), Updike writes: "Actuality is a running impoverishment of possibility." This captures well Updike's sense of human incompleteness, of the sense of discrepancy between the actual and the ideal. Problems in such a world are rarely, if ever, solved. Instead, they are endured, if not fully understood, though occasionally there are moments of grace and affirmation.

In his 1962 memoir titled "The Dogwood Tree: A Boyhood," Updike speaks of his commitment "to transcribe middleness with all its grits, bumps, and anonymities, in its fullness of satisfaction and mystery." Updike continues to fulfill that commitment in a rich and vital fiction that explores what he calls the "Three Great Secret Things: Sex. Religion, and Art," subjects that form the substance of much of his fiction, poetry, and essays.

RABBIT, RUN

First published: 1960
Type of work: Novel

In the conformity of the 1950's in the United States, a troubled quester has nowhere to go.

Rabbit, Run, a novel of a former basketball star and his floundering marriage set in the late 1950's, was the first of what has become a series of four novels about the protagonist and his family; Updike published one of them every ten years from 1960 to 1990. Together the novels form a revealing chronicle of the complex changes occurring in American culture between the 1950's and the late 1980's. In Updike's hero, Harry "Rabbit" Angstrom, the reader sees one of the author's many lapsed creatures in search of renewal, of regeneration, of something to believe in. The destructiveness of the character's actions in the first novel reflects Updike's own intense religious crisis, experienced at the time he was writing the novel.

At twenty-six, Rabbit, who got his nickname from the way he twitches his nose, finds himself in a stultifying life. He has a job selling magic-peelers in a dime store and is married to Janice, a careless and boozy woman who is pregnant with their second child. Coming home with new resolve to change his life after a brief game of basketball with some children in an alley, Rabbit finds the mess of his marital life too much to overcome. Thus begins his series of recoiling actions from the stifling experiences of his present life.

The novel captures well the sense of bottled-up frustration of the 1950's, a decade during which American society put a premium on conformity and adapting to one's environment. Hence, like so many of Updike's protagonists, Rabbit is enmeshed in a highly compromised environment, one committed to the values of the marketplace and lacking in spiritual concerns. Like a latter-day Huck Finn, Rabbit bolts from a civilization that would deny him freedom and a sense of wonder. His movement can be viewed as a kind of spiritual survival tactic.

A quote from Blaise Pascal serves as an epigraph to the novel: "The motions of Grace, the hardness of heart; external circumstances." Those three things, Updike says, describe human lives. They also describe the basic movements and conflicts in the Rabbit novels, indeed in most of Updike's fiction. Bewildered and frustrated, Rabbit wonders what has happened to his life. His disgust with his present life is deepened by his memories of when he was "first-rate at something" as a high school basketball star.

As some critics have noted, the novel is the study of a nonhero's quest for a nonexistent grail. Rabbit initially tries to escape by driving south, goaded by visions of fertility and warmth. After getting hopelessly lost, he returns to his hometown and seeks out Tothero, his old high school coach. Tothero sets Rabbit up with Ruth Leonard, a part-time prostitute, with whom Rabbit begins to live. Pursued by the do-good minister Jack Eccles, Rabbit resists returning to Janice. To Eccles, Rabbit claims that "something out there wants me to find it," though what that is he cannot say.

When Janice goes into labor, Rabbit returns, feeling contrite and resolving to restore the marriage. For nine days, their life seems to be going well. When Janice refuses Rabbit's sexual advances, however, he bolts again and looks for Ruth. Feeling abandoned, Janice starts drinking heavily and accidentally drowns the baby. Rabbit returns to Janice again, but at the funeral he outrages the family by his claims of innocence. He runs again, returning to Ruth, who reveals that she is pregnant and demands that Rabbit divorce Janice and marry her. He refuses Ruth, and the novel ends with Rabbit running the streets, resisting all claims upon his commitment.

Rabbit's back-and-forth actions create much havoc and mark him as selfish and irresponsible in the America of the 1950's, a world offering little margin for the quest for the transcendent. In place of the old revelations of religion, Rabbit substitutes the ecstasy of sex, the deep mysteries of the woman's body. Failed by his environment and its various authority figures, Rabbit registers his revolt through movement, through a refusal to stand still and be taken over by the tides of secular culture.

RABBIT REDUX

First published: 1971
Type of work: Novel

In 1969 no longer in flight, Rabbit witnesses and experiences the racial and cultural upheavals of the times.

In *Rabbit Redux*, Rabbit believes that the whole United States is doing what he did ten years earlier. Rabbit appears to have made his peace with the world and has settled down to fulfill his various obligations. He works as a typesetter in the same shop where his father has worked for more than thirty years. (He works at a trade, however, that is soon to be replaced by a new technology.) In this novel, Rabbit is more a passive listener and observer than a searcher. The racial and cultural turmoil that he sees on television literally comes into his home, and Rabbit is forced to be a student of his times. Updike uses this rather feckless working-class man in small-city Pennsylvania as a foil to the upheavals sweeping the United States during the late 1960's.

The landing of Americans on the moon, which Rabbit, like millions of others, watches on television, is a fitting analogue or metaphor for the cultural shifts of the decade. The astronauts, pioneers of the new technology and exemplars of the centrifugal movement of the West, land on a barren satellite. The implication is that America's spiritual landscape is as barren as that of the moon. Americans have gone about as far as they can, and they must now return home and make the best of things here. The gravity of Earth cannot be escaped for long.

In *Rabbit, Run*, Rabbit left Janice for a mistress. In *Rabbit Redux*, Janice leaves Rabbit to live with her lover, Stavros. Rabbit acquiesces to this affair and stays home to care for his son, Nelson. Through a strange set of circumstances—not wholly probable—Rabbit takes in Jill, a runaway flower child, and Skeeter, a bail-jumping Vietnam War veteran and black radical.

Rabbit's living room becomes the place for his encounter with the radical attacks upon America's values and policies. Skeeter's charismatic critiques of the American way of life challenge Rabbit's unquestioning patriotism and mesmerize him. As a consequence, Rabbit is helpless when disaster finally comes. His house is set on fire, probably by disgruntled neighbors; Jill is caught inside and dies in the fire. Rabbit helps Skeeter escape. Because of Stavros's heart condition, Janice gives him up to return home to Rabbit and Nelson. The novel ends with Janice and Rabbit together in a motel room asleep, in a sense rendered homeless by the forces of their time, over which they have little control.

In *Rabbit, Run*, Rabbit was a radical of sorts, a seeker for the transcendent in an entropic environment. In *Rabbit Redux*, Rabbit is a conservative, a defender of the American Dream and the war in Vietnam. He resents all the naysayers, the radicals who want to overthrow everything. He has a flag decal on his car window. In a sense, his patriotism has replaced his old religious quest for the supernatural. It is a shaky religion in a revolutionary time, when all quests are quite this-worldly.

Contrite because of the suffering his earlier quest produced, Rabbit has returned to the old rules precisely at the time most of the culture is repudiating them. Jill flees her upper-class world and seeks to overcome ego and materialism through drugs. Skeeter proclaims a radical black religion to rejuvenate an empty, "dollar-crazy" America. Janice seeks liberation through a lover. The burning of Rabbit's home represents the failure of all these quests: Jill dies, Skeeter flees, Janice returns home, and Rabbit's old dream is chastened. Significantly, it is Rabbit's sister, Mim, a Las Vegas call girl, whose visit home resolves the conflicts of the novel. Her unabashed worldliness and acceptance of an essentially empty world enable her to help the others find a way to live in the new American desert.

The novel sounds an apocalyptic note: What one sows, one reaps. The "external circumstances" become overwhelming. The televised images of flame and violence come home to destroy, perhaps to purify, like an ancient holocaust or offering. Rabbit bears witness to a disintegrating United States, even as it puts a man on the moon. Janice and Rabbit sleep, perhaps to awake to a new sense of maturity and responsibility. At least they may awake to a new beginning, which still lingers as a key element of the American Dream.

RABBIT IS RICH

First published: 1981
Type of work: Novel

In a world "running out of gas," Rabbit comes into material success, only to see it threatened by his erratic son.

Rabbit Is Rich is a novel about a middle-aged man— a fitting image for the spiritual condition of the United States at the end of the 1970's. At forty-six, Rabbit is successful, but his expansive waistline reminds him of his declining energies as well as the encroachment of death. Updike updates Sinclair Lewis's novel *Babbitt* (1922) about the ever-aspiring businessman George F. Babbitt. The remaining sparks of vitality in Rabbit seek to combat the forces of exhaustion that fill the novel. Indeed, the sense of things running down and images of falling dominate the book.

The novel is set during the summer and fall of 1979 and the first few weeks of 1980. In those last months of the Jimmy Carter administration, Americans face long lines at the gasoline pumps, high in-flation rates, and the continuing stalemate over the American hostages in Iran. Rabbit is not worried, however, for he is a co-owner of Brewer's Toyota agency, since his father-in-law, Fred Springer, died in 1974. He and Janice have been living in the Springer house since their own house was destroyed by fire in 1969. Their son, Nelson, has been going to college at Kent State University. While Rabbit struggles with his son, he is haunted by the ghosts of his past—his dead daughter, his dead mother's voice, and memories of Jill and Skeeter. Rabbit imagines that they embrace him, sustain him, and cheer him on in the autumn of his life.

In the first two Rabbit novels, Rabbit was out of step with his decade. In the complacent 1950's, he ran; in the frenetic 1960's, he watched. In *Rabbit Is Rich*, he is running again, but this time more in rhythm with the 1970's. Rabbit jogs, an activity in keeping with the fitness craze that grew in that decade. The novel begins with Rabbit thinking "running out of gas," a phrase that resonates at several levels. As a middle-aged man, Rabbit knows that his energies are diminishing. Because of the gasoline crisis, he sees America perhaps literally running out of gas.

Spiritually, the phrase suggests a running out of the old dynamism that fed the American Dream. In 1979, the American satellite Skylab was falling out of orbit—another fitting metaphor for the crises facing the Angstroms and America. Rabbit finds that his old desires and wants have shriveled. "Freedom, that he always thought was outward motion, turns out to be this inward dwindling." When asked if he has seen the film *Jaws 2* (1978), Rabbit responds in a way that reinforces the sense of entropy running throughout the novel: "D'you ever get the feeling that everything these days is sequels? . . . Like people are running out of ideas."

In his new prosperity, Rabbit plays golf at a new country club, goes to Rotary Club lunches, and reads *Consumer Reports*, the bible of his new status. Consumption is linked with sex as a way to fill the spiritual void of modern life. In a telling scene, Janice and Rabbit make love on top of their newly purchased gold Krugerrands. Ambiguously, sex represents both vitality and the void, the unfillable emptiness that constitutes death.

Rabbit lusts after Cindy, the lovely young wife of one of their new country-club friends. Janice tells Rabbit: "You always want what you don't have instead of what you do." In a wife-swapping episode during the three couples' brief Caribbean holiday, however, Rabbit must take Thelma Harrison instead of Cindy and is introduced to anal sex (arguably an appropriate image of the sense of worthlessness pervading American culture in the 1970's).

Nelson's return home is like the visit of a nightmare, of something neglected or repressed that cannot be avoided any longer. He wreaks havoc within the family's affluent complacency. Like his father, but lacking Rabbit's grace and conscience, Nelson's quest for attention and for love leads him to wreck practically everything he touches. Nelson also brings home a young woman, Pru, pregnant with his child. Their marriage is arranged, and in January of 1980, Rabbit receives a granddaughter, placed in his lap on the night of the Super Bowl. Perhaps, at last, Rabbit has the daughter he has longed for ever since Becky drowned and Jill died in his house in previous novels. He accepts his granddaughter—"fortune's hostage, heart's desire"—who represents both the hope for his future and a reminder of his mortality.

Abandoning Pru, Nelson begins the cycle of irresponsibility and bad luck that plagued his parents twenty years earlier. At one point, Rabbit tells Nelson: "Maybe I haven't done everything right in my life. I know I haven't. But I haven't committed the greatest sin. I haven't laid down and died." The statement is a good summary of the character of Rabbit throughout the novels—a man of vitality, a lover of life, an embodiment of forces running counter to entropy and death.

RABBIT AT REST

First published: 1990
Type of work: Novel

The final volume in the Rabbit tetralogy concludes the story of Harry Angstrom and continues Updike's remarkable delineation of American social and sexual mores in the last half of the twentieth century.

Rabbit at Rest ends the saga Updike began in 1960 in *Rabbit, Run* but brilliantly continues the history that Updike has been writing through the four volumes. Harry "Rabbit" Angstrom is fifty-five when the novel opens in 1989, and as the Reagan years are winding down, so is Harry. He has ballooned to 230 pounds, and his addiction to junk food foreshadows his final demise. Harry's problems are also the problems of America, for Updike is telling two complex histories here at once. In fact, readers see more of America in this final volume, for the first and last sections of the three-part novel take place in Florida, where Harry and his wife Janice live half the year in their condo.

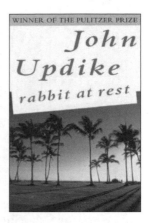

Harry is followed from the first pages by a "sense of doom" that will trail him to his end. Harry and his son are estranged, and when Nelson arrives with his family for a Florida holiday, Harry suffers his first heart attack. Things are not much better when Harry returns to Beaver, Pennsylvania. He has had angioplasty (to avoid the bypass surgery his doctors recommend), but his recovery is slow and not aided by his eating habits or his family. Nelson has been stealing from the Toyota dealership he manages (and which Janice owns) to feed a cocaine habit, and when finally confronted he reluctantly enters drug rehabilitation, and Rabbit has to return to the showroom floor. The Japanese soon take away the Toyota agency, and when Janice starts working nights on a real estate license, the drifting Rabbit ends up sleeping with his daughter-in-law, Pru. Janice finds out about the episode, and Rabbit runs again—as he did in the first volume of the tetralogy—back to Florida.

Harry senses that he has "walked through my entire life in a daze," and the self-assessment is not inaccurate. He feels betrayed by America, by his unfulfilled dreams. For all his financial success and sexual conquests, Harry is neither happy nor satisfied. Something is gnawing at this former high school basketball star. He reads history to understand his country at the same time he is trying to understand himself, but he fails in the end to penetrate either mystery. All Harry knows is that things in America have changed since he was a boy, and now they are both "drowning in debt." When he suffers another heart attack—and in another sense of closure, in a pickup basketball game in Florida—readers feel both pity and terror. Updike has written a fitting final chapter for Rabbit Angstrom and another chapter in his continuing saga of American history.

THE CENTAUR

First published: 1963
Type of work: Novel

Through the creative blending of memory and myth, an artist-protagonist recovers the meaning of his father's life as a means to recovering his own vocation.

The Centaur draws heavily upon Updike's experiences growing up in Shillington, Pennsylvania, and pays homage to his father. In many ways, the novel is Updike's most complex work, involving an interweaving of the myth of Chiron the centaur with the story of an adolescent boy and his father in the winter of 1947. The novel is part *Bildungsroman*, a novel of moral education, and part *Künstlerroman*, a novel of an artist seeking his identity in conflict with society or with his past. The nine chapters of the novel emerge as a collage, a narrative appropriate for the painter-narrator. Nearly thirty, Peter Caldwell, the artist-protagonist, is seeking to recover from his past some insight or understanding that might clarify and rejuvenate his artistic vocation. He reminisces to his black mistress in a Manhattan loft about a three-day period during the winter of 1947, fourteen years earlier.

Peter tells of his self-conscious adolescence, growing up an only child, living on a farm with his parents and Pop Kramer, his grandfather. His father is the high school biology teacher and swim coach, and his acts of compassion and charity embarrass the boy. On a mythic level, the father is depicted as Chiron the centaur, part man and part stallion, who serves as mentor to youthful Greek heroes. Chiron's life is sacrificial—he suffers for his charges, just as Peter's father suffered for (and often from) his students. Peter is eventually able to arrive at an understanding of his father's life and

death, and he finds a clarification of his own lost vocation.

In the myth, Chiron sacrifices his immortality so that Prometheus may be free to live and to create. Peter interprets his father's life in the same sacrificial terms—his father, George, in effect gives his life for Peter. While the character of George seems obsessed with death, it is doubtful that he really dies. Rather, his sacrifice is his willingness to go on fulfilling his obligation to his family. Seeing his father's life in novel, sacrificial terms, Peter, despairing over his failure to fulfill his artistic talent, asks: *"Was it for this that my father gave up his life?"* In this harsh reappraisal, Peter learns what he could not know as an adolescent about sacrificial love. He comes to see that love, guilt, and sacrifice are somehow inherent in the very structure of life. Telling the story and mythologizing his father's ordinariness reveal some truths about love to Peter. Such fatherly love liberates the son to resume his artistic vocation with courage.

The figure of the centaur captures the recurring predicament of Updike's protagonists. The centaur embodies both the godly and the bestial; he is a creature conversant with both heaven and earth, yet not fully at home in either realm. Such a figure points to faith as the way to live with courage and hope.

COUPLES

First published: 1968
Type of work: Novel

In a secular, post-Christian culture, affluent couples in a Massachusetts suburb turn to sex and adultery as the new religion.

Couples created quite a stir when it was published because of its graphic and emancipated treatment of adultery. It was on the best-seller lists for most of a year, and it led to favorable treatments of the author by *Time* and *Life* magazines. Despite the book's apparent sensationalism, the novel exhibits Updike's serious intent to explore the moral and spiritual consequences of a post-Christian world; the novel asks the question "After Christianity, what?" To Updike, the novel is "about sex as the

emergent religion, as the only thing left." Human sexuality seemed to be liturgy and sacrament of the new religion emerging in America in the 1960's—another end of innocence in a "post-pill paradise." The new religion does not truly assuage the anxiety of death, however; it leads instead to self-deception and disillusionment. Indeed, the cultic celebration of sex is the courting of disaster.

Set in the fictitious Massachusetts town of Tarbox, the novel focuses upon ten white, essentially upper-middle-class couples, most of whom have children and professional occupations. The time of the novel is from the spring of 1963 to the spring of 1964—from one season of rebirth to the next—between two pregnancies, one resulting in the birth of a child, the other in an abortion. The religion that the couples have made of one another dissolves into divorce and migration.

The main sexual pilgrim in the novel is Piet Hanema, a thirty-five-year-old building contractor, who is plagued by death anxiety and still attends church. Fearing death without immortal life, Piet finds no consolation in his marriage to the lovely Angela, who accepts death as a natural part of the cycles of life. Piet's many infidelities stem, in large part, from his inner desperation for some sort of certainty. Piet's foil is dentist Freddy Thorne, who casts himself as the priest of the new hedonism, of sensuality. To Freddy, the body is all that there is and, hence, should be celebrated and indulged.

The novel is filled with scenes of the couples' weekly gatherings at picnics, parties, and games. In the backdrop of their continuous fun and games are the growing crises in national and international affairs, but the couples have little interest in the news. Even on the night of President John F. Kennedy's assassination, they gather at Freddy's for a party. When it comes out that the assassin is a left-winger, one of the group comments, "He wasn't one of us."

The suspense of Piet's adulterous activity is broken by the arrival of a new couple: Ken Whitman, a research biologist, and his pregnant wife, Foxy.

Hired to redo their house, Piet is drawn to the very sensual Foxy, who shares his religious concerns. In Foxy, Piet finds what he lacks in Angela. After Foxy's baby is born, she gets pregnant by Piet, who goes to Freddy Thorne to arrange an abortion. For payment for the favor, Freddy asks for a night with Angela. When he gets Angela in bed, however, Freddy cannot perform; the priest of sex is impotent before the earthy and ethereal Angela.

Both men, in getting what they think they most desire, lose something vital to their identities. The loss of Angela causes Piet's fall into the earthly, to the mortal flesh. In effect, eros, physical love, defeats agape, spiritual love. Piet's church is destroyed by a fire, which Piet construes as a divine judgment upon them all. Piet and Foxy marry and move to another suburb, where they become simply another couple.

Couples shows that a certain light has gone out in the American landscape; death and decay haunt the imagination and spirit. Piet, as do the others, fails in the quest to find in the flesh what has been lost in the spirit. The church, given over to secularity and worldliness, fails them. The religion of sensuality leads to trivial and empty lives, a kind of death. Disappointment and disillusionment are the results of the failure of the new religion.

THE WITCHES OF EASTWICK

First published: 1984
Type of work: Novel

In the tumult of the late 1960's, three divorcees find a witchlike power in their friendship, encounter evil both outside and inside themselves, and end up remarried.

The Witches of Eastwick is a diabolical comedy—a novel that explores the uses and abuses of power in its diverse forms in an age of moral and social confusion and that resolves itself in marriage. Like *Rabbit Redux*, the novel is set during the first year or so of the Richard Nixon presidency, an era of protest, discontent, and polarization. The setting is a small town in Rhode Island called Eastwick. In *Rabbit Redux*, Updike portrays a rather powerless Rabbit as witness to cultural disintegration and moonlike spiritual barrenness in the context of the late 1960's. In *The Witches of Eastwick*, though he wrote the book in the early 1980's, Updike goes back to the same polarized period but explores the female perspective and the emerging new feminist synthesis. As the power of patriarchy "wastes" itself in yet another war—this time the seemingly endless war in Vietnam—women are rediscovering the old goddesses, the old sources of unity, integration, and power. Yet, like Nathaniel Hawthorne, Updike shows that power unmindful of history and exploitative of nature constitutes an evil that produces death and guilt.

The "witches" of the title refer to three divorcees, Alexandra Spofford, Jane Smart, and Sukie Rougemont, who have become close friends, meeting each Thursday and speaking often over the telephone, and who have discovered the power of sisterhood as well as some ancient feminine powers. The term "witch" is meant to refer to free women and to imply the discovery of neopagan powers—an inner direction, a sense of nature as sacred, a rejection of such dualisms as body and soul and of various political hierarchies. This hypothesis, represented by the three women, is challenged by the demonic figure of Darryl Van Horne, who takes them all as lovers and proves later to be a confidence man.

The novel is divided into three parts, "The Coven," "Malefica," and "Guilt," which suggest a progression from the women's newly found power and independence through an encounter with the demoniac to a rediscovery of responsibility. In "The Coven," the portrayal of the three women shows their neopagan, feminist convictions, their various loves and work. Alexandra calls forth a storm that clears a beach. The women tend to speak of men in ways that infantilize them. Eastwick has ecology-conscious industry, "clean" technology, and marshes where egrets rest. Male dominance is characterized as constituted of science and technology, of machine systems. Alone and free, the women have found new powers, natural powers. This gender split raises the question of whether evil is the result of technology or of nature.

"Malefica" deals with the effects of Darryl Van Horne's presence on the women and the community. Reminiscent of some of Hawthorne's scientist characters, Van Horne comes in proclaiming to be a technologist doing research in polymers and so-lar energy. Taking over the old Lenox mansion, he fills in some of the fragile wetlands for his tennis court, adds an immense hot tub, and installs fancy stereo equipment. He argues with the liberal, antiwar Unitarian minister, Ed Parsley, who later elopes with Dawn Polanski, a teenage war protester, to join the antiwar movement. Ironically, Ed Parsley blows himself up with a bomb he planned to use to bring about peace—another instance of the misunderstanding of power. The social do-gooder Felicia Gabriel, upon whom the women placed a minor curse, is killed by her frustrated husband, Clyde, who in turn commits suicide. At this point, the three witches remain caught in the solipsism of their philosophy, unable or unwilling to see or make connections between external, historical events and local events.

Like Updike's many male protagonists, the three women must come to grips with the reality of death before they can reconstitute a meaningful life. Falling for Van Horne's clumsy charms, the women develop a jealous rage when Van Horne chooses the young Jennifer Gabriel for his wife. The women use their powers to put a curse on Jennifer. When Jennifer dies, the women feel a terrible guilt, even though it is not clear that their curse caused the young woman's cancer. The women begin to sense their participation in an evil act of creation, one that cannot be reversed by a simple change of course or inner state. Jennifer's death provides the occasion for Van Horne to give a sermon on the evilness of creation, in which he excoriates a cosmos saturated with invisible parasites plaguing human life. He then leaves town with Jennifer's brother, Christopher, suggesting Van Horne's possible homosexuality.

The three women are left with the need to reflect upon all that has occurred and their responsibility for it. They move to a sense of reality that includes both the external and the internal, to an awareness of evil that is both technological and natural. The women find their ways into appropriate marriages, acts that are not meant to be seen as a capitulation to patriarchal tradition but rather as acknowledgments of their responsible connection with historical existence. In much of Updike's fiction, women and nature are associated (some of his male protagonists feel guilt because "women and nature forget"). *The Witches of Eastwick* complicates that formula by showing how guilt in the three women functions to open memory to full human responsibility.

"PIGEON FEATHERS"

First published: 1961 (collected in *Pigeon Feathers, and Other Stories*, 1962)
Type of work: Short story

David Kern finds in the perfect design of the feathers of the pigeons he has killed a temporary assurance that he will not die.

"Pigeon Feathers" showcases early several of Updike's continuing strengths, for the story wrestles with ontological issues in a prose that is stately and powerful. David is a young boy who has moved with his parents to the rural Pennsylvania farm where his mother grew up, and the move has been disturbing. He is used to his parents' bickering and his senile grandmother's nervous habits, but when he stumbles upon H. G. Wells's account of Jesus in *The Outline of History* (1920) that denies his divinity, "a stone that for weeks and even years had been gathering weight in the web of David's nerves snapped them and plunged through the page. . . . " The vague "terror" of his discovery of his mortality, "an exact vision of death," follows him everywhere, and neither his mother (who senses that something is wrong) nor Reverend Dobson (his Lutheran catechism teacher) can help him. David has experienced his first loss of faith, and the "horror" does not leave him in the next difficult months.

Relief comes for David only when his mother asks him to rid the barn of pigeons, and he takes the Remington .22 he has received for his fifteenth birthday and kills half a dozen of the birds. In burying them, he studies their feathers and "a pattern that flowed without error across the bird's body. He lost himself in the geometrical tides as the feathers now broadened and stiffened to make an edge for flight, now softened and constricted to cup warmth around the mute flesh." The discovery somehow renews David's faith in the divine design of the world, and he feels "robed in this certainty: that the God who had lavished such craft upon these worthless birds would not destroy His whole creation by refusing to let David live forever."

Throughout his career, Updike has studied what humans substitute in a post-Christian world, at a time when religion no longer seems to provide the answers. In several key works—such as the Rabbit tetralogy and *Couples*—sex is the answer, but it proves at best unsatisfying. In "Pigeon Feathers," Updike poses the dilemma and finds in the fearful mind of an adolescent boy a temporary answer. In killing the birds, David plays God, taking life almost casually, but the discovery of the perfect design of the feathers allows him to rest, if only briefly, in a renewed faith in the world and his own immortality. What awaits him in a few years, later readers of Updike suspect, is certain uncertainty. For now, Updike has captured critical moments in a young boy's life, and in a language that is almost exquisite.

"A & P"

First published: 1962 (collected in *Pigeon Feathers, and Other Stories*, 1962)
Type of work: Short story

A young protagonist's heroic gesture catapults him into the harsh reality of adult life.

"A & P" is a classic initiation story in which the young protagonist acts spontaneously and then learns something about the consequences of his actions. Sammy's conversational, comic voice is perfectly appropriate for his nineteen years and is even a little ungrammatical in its first-person narration: "In walks these three girls in nothing but bathing suits," the story abruptly begins. Little else happens: Sammy follows the three with his eyes as they wander the store to arrive at his cash register with their "Fancy Herring Snacks." The store's middle-aged manager finally notices the girls and reminds them of the store's clothing policy, and Sammy, their sudden and "unsuspected hero," defends them by quitting his job. The immature Sammy believes that "once you begin a gesture it's fatal not to go through with it," and although Lengel warns Sammy of the consequences of his act, Sammy walks out anyway. When he gets to the parking lot, the girls are gone, and Sammy suddenly realizes "how hard the world was going to be to me hereafter."

Short as it is, the story has a number of classical overtones. Like the hero of some Arthurian legend, Sammy is on a romantic quest: In the name of chivalry, he acts to save "Queenie" (and her two consorts) from the ogre Lengel. On a more Homeric level, the hero is tempted by the three Sirens (from the wealthy "summer colony out on the Point") and rejects his mentor to follow them. Such mythical possibilities point up the underlying richness of Updike's prose, but there are sociopsychological implications in this initiation story as well. Although Sammy defends the three girls against the provincial morality of his small town, he is the only one holding his outmoded romantic code; the three girls ignore him. Sammy, in other words, is a working-class hero defending a privileged upper class which does not even acknowledge his existence, and Sammy loses his job because of romantic notions to which only working-class characters, apparently, still subscribe. On another level, the story points to a generation gap in which Sammy acts to protect the young women from the world of adults, only to end up in some limbo between the two worlds himself. With a series of binary oppositions, Updike has shown readers the complex world that adults inhabit and the compromise that is needed to navigate that world. The story's many reprintings demonstrate its universal appeal.

"THE MUSIC SCHOOL"

First published: 1964 (collected in *The Music School*, 1966)
Type of work: Short story

A straightforward recital of events opens into a series of Chinese boxes revealing a disintegrating marriage.

"The Music School" is a short story encompassing all the materials of a novel, for what starts out as a simple first-person narration soon becomes a confession of marital infidelity. The story features themes and techniques Updike often uses, in particular complex metaphor and the tension between materiality and spirituality.

The story revolves around three brief incidents. The narrator, who identifies himself only as Alfred Schweigen, a writer, tells readers that the night before he heard a priest describe a change in "his Church's attitude toward the Eucharistic wafer," that what was only allowed to melt in the mouth during Communion was now to be chewed and swallowed. This anecdote is immediately followed by another, the discovery in the paper this morning that an acquaintance, a computer expert, has been murdered, shot through a window in his home as he sat at dinner with his family. The focus has already shifted, and the story is becoming increasingly confessional, as the narrator admits that he is sitting in a music school this afternoon, waiting for his eight-year-old daughter to finish her piano lesson. He loves taking her and waiting for her, he says, but he only does it "because today my wife visits her psychiatrist. She visits a psychiatrist because I am unfaithful to her," and he admits that he is also seeing a psychiatrist, who wonders "why I need to humiliate myself. It is a habit, I suppose, of confession." He goes on to describe the country church he attended as a child where every two months there was a public confession—which is what the story itself is becoming. He knew the man who was shot because he had once thought of writing a novel about a computer programmer that would develop into a story of love, guilt, and death, into what, in short, his own marriage is becoming. He watches his daughter coming from her lesson and her "pleased smile . . . pierces my heart, and I die (I think) at her feet."

The story epitomizes the technique Updike uses (as in his later story "Separating") of relating mundane events while, just beneath the surface, larger changes are going on. The writer is fixated on his daughter, not as any father might be, but in order to keep himself from thinking about the changes ahead. Like a number of Updike stories, "The Music School" is ultimately about sex and religion or, rather, how contemporary sexuality has replaced more traditional spiritual life. The two opening incidents involve "a common element of nourishment, of eating transfigured by a strange irruption," but they also involve transubstantiation, the process by which the spiritual becomes material, through the Communion wafer and through the bullet carrying "a maniac hatred."

This metaphorical complexity works throughout the story. The priest was playing the guitar at the party the night before, the music school is like a church, and for the daughter "the lesson has been a meal." Music carries its meaning as the spiritual is transcribed into notes on a score or fingers on an instrument. The Communion wafer, like the daughter's music lesson, carries nourishment, as the narrator's marriage is, in contrast, losing its spiritual meaning through the narrator's own material, sexual needs.

"MY FATHER ON THE VERGE OF DISGRACE"

First published: 1997 (collected in *Licks of Love: Short Stories and a Sequel, "Rabbit Remembered,"* 2000)
Type of work: Short story

A boy learns that to be human means to live on the edge of disgrace.

"My Father on the Verge of Disgrace," like other Updike works (for example, *The Centaur,* "Pigeon Feathers"), is an initiation story set in rural Pennsylvania before and just after World War II and typically carries a heavier weight than its slight appearance. The story is almost anecdotal in its first-person narration: A young boy living in a large house with his parents and his maternal grandparents during the Depression worries that his father will "fall from his precarious ledge of respectability." His father lost his job as a china salesman the year the boy was born, and it was three years before he found a position as a high-school chemistry teacher. The house they live in—purchased by the grandfather during better times—is too large for the family, and they have to economize. Two incidents epitomize to the boy his father's precarious position, one involving his father's relationship to a fellow teacher courting a student, the other the fact that the father sometimes has to borrow from the high-school sports receipts to cover household expenses. Although the boy is proud of his father's position in town, he shares his mother's anxiety about him.

During World War II, things ease, and the father finds summer work, but when the boy enters the high school, he discovers more to worry about. The father is "the faculty clown," the boy discovers, confirmed in the annual faculty-assembly program when the father plays Thisbe in a scene from William Shakespeare's *A Midsummer Night's Dream,* to the delight of students. "This had to be ruinous, I thought. This was worse than any of my dreams." After the war, the family moves to a smaller house in the country, and the boy and his father become "a kind of team, partners in peril, fellow-sufferers on the edge of disaster" driving to and from school every day. The boy survives adolescence and its fears, he concludes, and "By the time I went off to college I no longer feared—I no longer dreamed—that my father would be savaged by society." The boy has learned an important lesson for adulthood, that "part of being human is being on the verge of disgrace."

The story was selected for the *Best American Stories, 1998,* and it is easy to see why. Updike's prose carries readers through a recital of some of childhood's pitfalls and sketches out the Oedipal conflict, all in a style that is at once elegant and amazingly physical. The details of Updike's fiction just nail down even more forcefully the significance of this story of the uneasy journey to adulthood.

SUMMARY

Updike is rightfully acclaimed as one of the most accomplished stylists and prolific writers of his generation. In both thematic seriousness and narrative range, he has produced a body of writing of the highest order.

His fiction constitutes a serious exploration and probing of the spiritual conditions of American culture in the late twentieth century and early twenty-first, and it reflects a vision of life informed by his protestant Christian convictions. Like the work of Nathaniel Hawthorne, in whose steps Updike ably follows, Updike's fiction continues the long conversation concerning the plight of innocence and its loss that has been so central to the American tradition. In a world no longer supported by traditional beliefs, Updike's fiction explores the possibilities of love as the basis for a gracious and responsible life.

John G. Parks; updated by David Peck

BIBLIOGRAPHY

By the Author

SHORT FICTION:

The Same Door, 1959

Pigeon Feathers, and Other Stories, 1962

Olinger Stories: A Selection, 1964

The Music School, 1966

Museums and Women, and Other Stories, 1972

Problems, and Other Stories, 1979

Three Illuminations in the Life of an American Author, 1979

Too Far to Go: The Maples Stories, 1979

The Chaste Planet, 1980

Bech Is Back, 1982

The Beloved, 1982

Trust Me, 1987

Brother Grasshopper, 1990 (limited edition)

The Afterlife, and Other Stories, 1994

Licks of Love: Short Stories and a Sequel, "Rabbit Remembered," 2000

The Complete Henry Bech: Twenty Stories, 2001

The Early Stories, 1953-1975, 2003

LONG FICTION:

The Poorhouse Fair, 1959

Rabbit, Run, 1960

The Centaur, 1963

Of the Farm, 1965

Couples, 1968

Bech: A Book, 1970

Rabbit Redux, 1971

A Month of Sundays, 1975

Marry Me: A Romance, 1976

The Coup, 1978

Rabbit Is Rich, 1981

The Witches of Eastwick, 1984

Roger's Version, 1986

S., 1988

Rabbit at Rest, 1990

Memories of the Ford Administration, 1992

Brazil, 1994

In the Beauty of the Lilies, 1996

Toward the End of Time, 1997

Bech at Bay: A Quasi-Novel, 1998

Gertrude and Claudius, 2000

Seek My Face, 2002

Villages, 2004

DISCUSSION TOPICS

- What is the initiation process like for John Updike's protagonists? What do they learn while growing up? What epiphanies do they experience?

- How does the family function as a unit in an Updike work? Do individuals find support in their families, conflict, or both?

- What are the characteristics of Updike's use of language? Is his style poetic? Metaphorical? Lyrical? Dense? Abstract?

- How does Updike characterize contemporary American society in his stories and novels? What is the American Dream like in his fiction, and how easy is it to reach?

- What is the state of marriage in Updike's works? Are couples happy and fulfilled, or constrained and unsatisfied?

- Updike has been called the foremost chronicler of the mores of Middle America. What is the portrait that emerges from his accounts?

DRAMA:

Three Texts from Early Ipswich: A Pageant, pb. 1968
Buchanan Dying, pb. 1974

POETRY:

The Carpentered Hen, and Other Tame Creatures, 1958
Telephone Poles, and Other Poems, 1963
Dog's Death, 1965
Verse, 1965
The Angels, 1968
Bath After Sailing, 1968
Midpoint, and Other Poems, 1969
Seventy Poems, 1972
Six Poems, 1973
Cunts (Upon Receiving the Swingers Life Club Membership Solicitation), 1974
Query, 1974
Tossing and Turning, 1977
Sixteen Sonnets, 1979
Five Poems, 1980
Jester's Dozen, 1984
Facing Nature, 1985
Mites, and Other Poems in Miniature, 1990
Collected Poems, 1953-1993, 1993
A Helpful Alphabet of Friendly Objects, 1995
Americana, and Other Poems, 2001

NONFICTION:

Assorted Prose, 1965
Picked-Up Pieces, 1975
Hugging the Shore: Essays and Criticism, 1983
Just Looking: Essays on Art, 1989
Self-Consciousness: Memoirs, 1989
Odd Jobs: Essays and Criticism, 1991
Golf Dreams: Writings on Golf, 1996
More Matter: Essays and Criticism, 1999
Still Looking: Essays on American Art, 2005

EDITED TEXT:

The Best American Short Stories of the Century, 2000

About the Author

Bloom, Harold, ed. *John Updike: Modern Critical Views*. New York: Chelsea House, 1987.

Boswell, Marshall. *John Updike's Rabbit Tetralogy: Mastered Irony in Motion*. Columbia: University of Missouri Press, 2000.

Greiner, Donald. *John Updike's Novels*. Athens: Ohio University Press, 1984.

Luscher, Robert M. *John Updike: A Study of the Short Fiction*. New York: Twayne, 1993.

Miller, D. Quentin. *John Updike and the Cold War: Drawing the Iron Curtain*. Columbia: University of Missouri Press, 2001.

Newman, Judie. *John Updike*. New York: St. Martin's Press, 1988.

Schiff, James A. *John Updike Revisited*. New York: Twayne, 1998.

Updike, John. *Self-Consciousness: Memoirs*. New York: Knopf, 1989.

Uphaus, Suzanne Henning. *John Updike*. New York: Frederick Ungar, 1980.

LUIS MIGUEL VALDEZ

Born: Delano, California
June 26, 1940

One of the most influential Chicano playwrights of his time, Valdez created a drama dedicated to social progress and to the full exploration of Chicano identity.

Courtesy, UCLA Library/Alice Greenfield
McGrath Papers

BIOGRAPHY

Luis Miguel Valdez was born on June 26, 1940, in Delano, California, the second of ten brothers and sisters. His mother and father were migrant farmworkers, and Luis began working in the fields at the age of six. Because his family traveled to the harvests in the San Joaquin Valley, Luis received little uninterrupted schooling.

In an interview, Valdez discussed one significant, and ultimately fortunate, consequence of such a disruptive early life: His family had just finished a cotton harvest; the season had ended, the rains begun, but because their truck had broken down, the family had to stay put. Leaving school one day, Luis realized he had left behind his paper lunch bag, a precious commodity in 1946, given the paper shortages and the family's poverty. When he returned to get it, however, he found his teacher had torn it up. She was using it to make papier-mâché animal masks for the school play. Luis was amazed by the transformation. Although he did not even know what a play was at the time, he decided to audition and was given the leading role as a monkey. The play was about Christmas in the jungle, and the following weeks of colorful preparation were exhilarating. A week before the show was to begin, however, his father got the truck fixed, and the family moved away. Valdez has said of the experience: "That left an unfillable gap, a vacuum I've been pouring myself into ever since."

The pang of that early disappointment sparked a fascination for the theater and a wealth of creative energy that was to bring Valdez remarkable success in the years ahead. Despite his intermittent schooling, he won a scholarship to San Jose State College in 1960. There he studied theater history and developed a lasting enthusiasm for classical Greek and Roman drama. His own work also began to take shape, and his first one-act play, *The Theft*, won a regional playwriting award. In 1965, he directed his first full-length play, *The Shrunken Head of Pancho Villa*, which audiences greeted warmly.

After receiving a degree in English in 1964, Valdez spent several months traveling in Cuba before joining the San Francisco Mime Troupe. In 1965, he returned home to Delano and joined the newly formed United Farm Workers Union under the leadership of César Chávez. During this time, Valdez began fully to explore drama as a vehicle for social justice. He developed a form suitable for his migrant-worker audiences: a short skit, or *acto*, designed to inspire Chicanos to political action.

These *actos*, often improvised on flatbed trucks for workers in the fields, proved so powerful as political weapons that Valdez's life was threatened during the grape strike of 1967. Immensely popular with the workers, the *actos* aroused hostility in the growers, whose exploitative labor practices the plays satirized. Valdez has recalled being "beaten and kicked and jailed. . . . essentially for doing theater." Still, he persisted, and the *actos* gained so much attention that the Teatro Campesino, or Farmworker's Theater, toured the United States performing the works in 1967.

From then on, Valdez's work began to reach increasingly larger audiences. He left the fields late in 1967 for Del Rey, California, where he founded the Centro Campesino Cultural. Between 1969 and 1980, the troupe toured Europe four times and won an Obie Award. Despite such acclaim Valdez remained true to his Chicano, migrant-worker roots. Moving the troupe to Fresno, California, in 1969, Valdez founded an annual Chicano theater festival and began teaching at Fresno State College. As its audience grew, the troupe became more technically sophisticated but continued its efforts to "put the tools of the artist into the hands of the humblest, the working people." The troupe moved in 1971 to rural San Juan Bautista, from which it toured widely among college campuses, while remaining deeply involved with the concerns of its own community.

Having spent his entire career well outside mainstream, commercial theater, Valdez decided in 1978 to reach for a still larger audience. The result was *Zoot Suit*, a Broadway-style dance musical about the Sleepy Lagoon murder trial and the riots that followed in Los Angeles in 1943. Though still quite political, the play succeeds in being genuinely entertaining, particularly in its film adaptation. Like *Zoot Suit, Bandido!* (1981) and *"I Don't Have to Show You No Stinking Badges!"* (1986) both reach for more general audiences and explore the Chicano struggle for identity against the limiting stereotypes imposed by an Anglicized history and American media. Such plays, as well as the successful 1987 film *La Bamba*, which Valdez wrote and directed, speak not only for Chicanos but also to white audiences, forcing them to reexamine their preconceptions about who Chicanos really are. These works also testify to Valdez's extraordinary journey from migrant farmworker to one of the most vital Chicano voices in American drama.

ANALYSIS

From the earliest and simplest *actos* to the complex sophistication of *"I Don't Have to Show You No Stinking Badges!"* nearly three decades later, Valdez's plays have displayed a remarkable consistency of theme and purpose. Certainly, his work has evolved in scope, depth, and technique, but his basic objectives have remained constant: to expose social injustice, to satirize the oppressors, and to dramatize, in all of its fullness and variety, the struggle to achieve a viable Chicano identity.

Born into a family of migrant farmworkers,

Valdez knew firsthand the effects of oppression and exploitation. It was therefore quite natural that his first short plays would deal with the struggles of the farmworkers to unionize. These early *actos* were improvised using a unique collaborative method: Valdez would simply ask striking workers to show what had happened to them during the day. Employing masks or crude signs to indicate different characters—workers, scabs, growers, and so forth—the strikers, under Valdez's direction, produced skits of engaging immediacy, broad humor, and a pointed political message. Their purpose was to raise consciousness, deflate the opposition's authority, and point to a solution. Yet the plays were quite entertaining as well, often transforming and releasing the workers' immediate feelings of fear and frustration through comedy and withering satire.

Though some of the *actos*, such as *Vietnam campesino* (1970), can seem too bluntly didactic, Valdez learned much from them about making theater a vehicle for inspiring social action. He also sensed, eventually, the need to ground the Chicano experience in something more enduring than immediate political struggle. He returned to the ancient wellsprings of Aztec and Mayan culture to provide such a groundwork for the contemporary Chicano identity.

In his introduction to *Aztlan: An Anthology of Mexican American Literature* (1972), Valdez frames the problem of Chicano marginalization explicitly:

> His birthright to speak as Man has been forcibly stripped from him. To his conqueror he is patently sub-human, uncivilized, or culturally deprived. The poet in him flounders in a morass of lies and distortions about his conquered people. He loses his identity with mankind, and self-consciously struggles to regain his one-to-one relationship with human existence. It is a long way back. . . . Such is the condition of the Chicano.

That "long way back" took Valdez to pre-Columbian Mexico. What he found there were the achievements of Aztec and Mayan civilization, their astonishing developments in medicine, art, poetry, hygiene, urban planning, and religion, all of which he compares favorably to their European counterparts of the time. To combat the degradation of centuries of Anglo racism, of being seen as "foreigners in the continent of their birth," Valdez wants to reconnect Chicanos to an ancient, proud, and venerable culture. Chicanos must, in his view, revive this connection and rethink their history if they are to maintain an identity in Anglo society.

Valdez attempts this reconnection in a variety of ways. In *Bernabé* (1970), he creates a character, the village lunatic, who physically and metaphorically marries La Tierra (the Earth) and thus reestablishes the Mayan reverence for it. In *Zoot Suit* and *Bandido!*, Valdez reexamines history from the Chicano and Mexican perspective. Thus Tiburcio Vasquez, whom history had portrayed as a mere bandit working the California countryside from 1850 to 1875, becomes in *Bandido!* a revolutionary bent on political rebellion. *Zoot Suit* retrieves for the American conscience an overlooked period of intense racism culminating in the Sleepy Lagoon murder trial and the riots that followed. Both plays try not only to set the record straight but also to discover a source of pride for Chicanos in a history that has been unjustly debased.

The consequence of Chicanos being cut off from the life-giving power of their history and culture is brilliantly dramatized in *"I Don't Have to Show You No Stinking Badges!,"* in which Valdez explores the deeply problematic nature of assimilation into Anglo culture. In their desire to fit in with middle-class America, the members of the Villa family find themselves silenced and marginalized. Bit-part actors who rarely receive speaking roles, Buddy and Connie Villa have achieved a comfortable success, but their only connection with their own culture is the stereotyped Mexicans they portray on film. Their son, who enrolled in Harvard Law School at age sixteen, represents the possibility for the epitome of Anglo success. Yet he rebels against this assimilation and drops out of school, only to discover just how rigid the limitations are for Chicanos who reject an Anglo identity.

Stylistically, Valdez is clearly not a realist, though some of his plays—those, for example, depicting actual historical events—employ elements of realism. In all of his plays, however, Valdez takes pains (often in the manner of Bertolt Brecht) to ensure that his audiences never forget that they are watching a play. He does not want to create the illusion of reality or to manipulate the audience into emotional identification with the characters. Plays within plays, characters who speak directly to the audience, radical shifts in time, and many other de-

vices all serve to disrupt the illusion of reality and focus the audience's attention on the artifice before them. Such strategies serve Valdez's purposes well, for he wants audiences to maintain the necessary distance to reflect on the problems that his plays present and to relate them to the world outside the theater. Often the plays are open-ended or have multiple endings, and in this way, too, the audience must actively engage the play and resolve it for themselves. These methods do not provide a comfortable or easy theatrical experience, but the rewards of thinking hard about Valdez's plays are indeed worth the effort.

LAS DOS CARAS DEL PATRONCITO

First produced: 1965 (first published, 1971)
Type of work: Play

The boss trades places with one of his farmworkers and discovers how exploited they are.

Las dos caras del patroncito (the two faces of the little boss) typifies, in many ways, Valdez's early *actos*. The piece grew out of a collaborative improvisation during the grape strike of 1965 and dramatized the immediate and intense feelings of its audience. Like all the *actos*, it is brief, direct, didactic, intending not only to express the workers' anger and urge them to join the union but also to satirize the growers and reveal their injustice. The play succeeds brilliantly by enacting a total reversal of what Friedrich Wilhelm Nietzsche termed the master/slave relationship.

The play begins with an undocumented Mexican worker being visited by his *patroncito*, or "little boss," who appears wearing a pig mask and smoking a cigar. Initially, both play their assumed roles of intimidating master and cowering slave to perfection. Soon, though, the *patroncito* waxes poetic over his Mexicans. Seeing them "barreling down the freeway" makes his "heart feel good; hands on their sombreros, hair flying in the wind, bouncing along happy as babies." "I sure do love my Mexicans," he says. The patroncito reveals a typical condescension, romanticizing the migrant workers' lives and regarding them essentially as children. When the farmworker responds by putting his arm around him, however, the *patroncito* says; "I love 'em about ten feet away from me."

Their conversation takes a peculiar turn as the *patroncito* verbally coerces the farmworker into agreeing that the workers have it easy, with their "free housing" (labor-camp shacks), "free transportation" (unsafe trucks), and "free food" (beans and tortillas). The boss asserts that he himself suffers all the anxiety that comes from owning a Lincoln Continental, an expensive ranch house, and a wife with expensive tastes. At one point, he asks the farmworker, "Ever write out a check for $12,000?" The audience of migrant workers struggling to raise their wages to two dollars an hour would have felt the irony of such a question; the agony of writing out such a check is not something they would experience anytime soon, given their exploited condition.

Yet the *patroncito* actually envies the farmworkers' "freedom" and wishes to trade places. After some coaxing, the farmworker agrees, and the *patroncito* gives him his pig mask, whereupon the power relations between them are reversed. The farmworker now gives the boss a taste of his own medicine. He insults him and proceeds to claim his land, his house, his car, and his wife. The *patroncito* soon realizes that the game has gone too far. He does not want to live in the rat-infested shacks he so generously provides for his workers, or ride in his death-trap trucks, or work for such low wages.

By the play's end, the farmworker has so thoroughly abused his *patroncito*, calling him a "spic," "greaseball," and "commie bastard"—all the slurs the workers endured—that the *patroncito* calls for help from union activist César Chávez and screams "huelga" ("strike"). Thus the play brings him full circle from callous owner to union supporter and suggests that if the oppressors could put themselves in the place of the oppressed, they would see their own injustice.

ZOOT SUIT

First produced: 1978 (first published, 1992)
Type of work: Play

The Sleepy Lagoon murder trial of 1943 shows young Chicanos to be the victims of prejudice.

Zoot Suit, though perhaps Valdez's most commercial play, retains the political spirit of the early *actos* and anticipates the struggle for Chicano identity of Valdez's later works. Because it is a musical, with terrific song and dance throughout, it is his most conventionally entertaining play, but because it dramatizes an overlooked episode in American history that reveals a pervasive racism against Chicanos, it is also one of his most powerful and socially relevant plays.

Set in Los Angeles in the early 1940's, the play centers around the trial and wrongful murder conviction of Henry Reyna and three other Chicano gang members, or *pachucos*. Act 1 explores the trial and, through flashback, the violence that leads up to it; act 2 deals with the efforts to appeal the conviction and free the *pachucos*. Throughout the play, Valdez gives the action an added dimension through the use of two extraordinary devices. One is the mythic figure of El Pachuco. He is larger than life, the zoot-suiter par excellence, the embodiment of Chicano pride, machismo, and revolutionary defiance. He dominates the play, though he is seen only by Henry and the audience. Indeed, he may be understood as a layer of Henry's personality externalized, a kind of alter ego who continually advises Henry and comments on, at times even controls, the play. The second device is El Pachuco's counterpart and antagonist, The Press. In *Zoot Suit*, the news media functions as an actual character who symbolizes the racist hysteria of public opinion during World War II. Significantly, it is The Press, rather than a prosecutor, that tries and convicts Henry.

This racist hysteria ("EXTRA! EXTRA!, ZOOT-SUITED GOONS OF SLEEPY LAGOON! . . . READ ALL ABOUT MEXICAN BABY GANGSTERS!") provides a crucial context for understanding the play. As the United States fought Nazis abroad, it imprisoned Japanese Americans at home, denied African Americans basic human rights, and harassed Mexican Americans in Los Angeles. The irony of Henry's being arrested on trumped-up charges the night before he is to report to the Navy to join the fight against racist Germany is cynically pointed out by El Pachuco, who says that "the mayor of L.A. has declared all-out war on Chicanos." In this climate, racial stereotypes, media-inspired fear, and repressive forces unleashed by war are quite enough to convict the *pachucos*, even in the absence of any real evidence.

The trial itself is a mockery, a foregone conclusion, and thus Henry finds himself at the mercy of forces he did not create and cannot control. Even those who try to help him—his lawyer, George, and Alice, a reporter from the *Daily People's World*—earn Henry's resentment, for they, too, seem to be controlling his fate. In this sense, El Pachuco represents a compensating fantasy. He is always in control and indeed is able to freeze the action of the play, speak directly to the audience, rerun dialogue, or skip ahead at will. He is a kind of director within the play, and however vulnerable the other young *pachucos* are, El Pachuco remains invincible. Even when he is tripped and beaten by Marines, he rises up undaunted, clad only in a loincloth, like an Aztec god.

Henry Reyna and the other *pachucos* are vindicated in the end, winning their appeal and a provisional kind of freedom. Yet Valdez presents multiple endings to Henry's life story. He does so to make the audience see that Henry's character still exists, as do the forces of racism that torment him, and the defiant spirit and cultural pride that will not allow his will to be broken.

"I Don't Have to Show You No Stinking Badges!"

First produced: 1986 (first published, 1986)
Type of work: Play

In a rebellious attempt to create his own identity, a young Chicano finds himself trapped by stereotypes.

"I Don't Have to Show You No Stinking Badges!" is Valdez's most complex, ambitious, and satisfying play. Satirical, comic, filled with puns and painful insight, the play explores the search for an authentic Chicano identity against the limiting stereotypes and restricted possibilities afforded Mexican Americans in the 1980's United States.

The play is set in Los Angeles in the home of Connie and Buddy Villa, middle-aged Chicano bitpart actors. The conflict is sparked by the unexpected return of Sonny, their son. Defying his parents' dreams for him, Sonny quits Harvard University Law School and thus forfeits his chance at the kind of Anglo success his parents have not been able to achieve. His return home, with his Chinese American girlfriend, and his announced intention to become an actor, writer, producer, and director—"the newest superstar in Hollywood" and "the next Woody Allen"—creates a crisis in the family that the rest of the play tries to resolve. In a tempestuous family quarrel, Sonny derides his parents' acting; they have made careers playing stereotyped nonspeaking parts as maids, gardeners, bandits, and prostitutes.

He proclaims his desire to surpass them. *"I Don't Have to Show You No Stinking Badges!"* then moves to a play within a play. Sonny films his parents and his girlfriend, Anita, but when his parents are called off to a Latino Actors Guild meeting, he decides to act in another way. He takes his father's gun and holds up several fast-food restaurants. The climax of the play occurs when police and news crews arrive at the Villa home; a standoff ensues, replete with gunfire, bullhorns, and live coverage. The play then offers three completely different endings, with Sonny either killing himself, becoming a television director, or returning to Harvard, via spaceship, to finish his law degree.

Valdez gives the play's most compelling theme, the struggle against racial stereotypes to find a viable Chicano identity, a complex and layered treatment. Even the characters' names—Buddy, Connie, and Sonny Villa—suggest a divided identity. "Villa" recalls the Mexican revolutionary Pancho Villa, but their first names are all too typically Anglo. Their cultural frame of reference, moreover, is almost exclusively that of white films and film stars. Throughout the play, they compare themselves and one another to Otto Preminger, Woody Allen, James Bond, Marlon Brando, Al Pacino, and many others. Their understanding of themselves and their world seems to have been defined not by Chicano role models but by Hollywood film stars.

Sonny alone recognizes this problem, and he rebels against it. He sees that his parents' roles as "silent" actors signify their powerlessness, their marginalized stature in Hollywood, and the invisibility of Chicanos generally. Sonny also understands that by acting the film roles of Mexican stereotypes, his parents have achieved in their private existence nothing more than a "low rated situation comedy" and "a cheap imitation of Anglo life," with a comfortable home, swimming pool, and all the other trappings of middle-class America. Sonny wants no part of it. Yet he knows how limited his options are:

> Here's the main event: the indispensable illiterate cholo gang member-heroin-addict-born-to-lose-image, which I suppose could account for 99 percent of my future employment in TV land. Just look hostile, dumb, and potentially violent. Preferably with rape on the mind, know what I mean?

Thus Sonny's decision to leave Harvard and create his own films is an attempt to create and control his own identity, not as an imitation Anglo but as a Chicano. For all of his insight and ambition, however, Sonny feels trapped. When his parents abandon his home movie, titled *Types in Stereo*, Sonny decides to make his acting real. Yet he merely assumes another role, and a stereotypical one at that, of the Chicano bandit. He robs fast-food restaurants, symbols of the emptiness he sees in American life, and thus gives in to the pressures against which he had fought.

The play's multiple endings leave readers and audiences perplexed. Clearly, though, Valdez wants audiences to step back and reflect on the relationship between acting and reality and to consider the options open, or perhaps closed, to someone like Sonny. Ultimately, the play forces audiences to think deeply about their own stereotypes and to see, in all of its painful complexity, the damage such stereotypes can do.

SUMMARY

Unlike many of his contemporaries who prefer to explore psychological conflicts or the complexities of personal relationships, Valdez has devoted his work to dramatizing social problems. His plays, early and late, expose the injustice endured by Chicanos—not to elicit pity or to portray them as victims but to focus attention on the forces of oppression and to make Chicanos fully visible in American society. In plays that are satirical, unconventional, unpredictable, painful, and often hilarious, Valdez succeeds in abolishing the stereotypes and showing not only what Chicanos have suffered but also who they really are.

John Brehm

BIBLIOGRAPHY

By the Author

DRAMA:
The Theft, pr. 1961
The Shrunken Head of Pancho Villa, pr. 1965, pb. 1967
Las dos caras del patroncito, pr. 1965, pb. 1971
La quinta temporada, pr. 1966, pb. 1971
Los vendidos, pr. 1967, pb. 1971
Dark Root of a Scream, pr. 1967, pb. 1973
La conquista de México, pr. 1968, pb. 1971 (puppet play)
No saco nada de la escuela, pr. 1969, pb. 1971
The Militants, pr. 1969, pb. 1971
Vietnam campesino, pr. 1970, pb. 1971
Huelguistas, pr. 1970, pb. 1971
Bernabé, pr. 1970, pb. 1976
Soldado razo, pr., pb. 1971
Actos, pb. 1971 (includes *Las dos caras del patroncito, La quinta temporada, Los vendidos, La conquista de México, No saco nada de la escuela, The Militants, Vietnam campesino, Huelguistas,* and *Soldado razo*)

Las pastorelas, pr. 1971 (adaptation of a sixteenth century Mexican shepherd's play)

La Virgen del Tepeyac, pr. 1971 (adaptation of *Las cuatro apariciones de la Virgen de Guadalupe*)

Los endrogados, pr. 1972

Los olivos pits, pr. 1972

La gran carpa de los rasquachis, pr. 1973

Mundo, pr. 1973

El baille de los gigantes, pr. 1973

El fin del mundo, pr. 1975

Zoot Suit, pr. 1978, pb. 1992

Bandido!, pr. 1981, pb. 1992, revised pr. 1994

Corridos, pr. 1983

"I Don't Have to Show You No Stinking Badges!," pr., pb. 1986

Luis Valdez—Early Works: Actos, Bernabé, and Pensamiento Serpentino, pb. 1990

Zoot Suit, and Other Plays, pb. 1992

Mummified Deer, pr. 2000

SCREENPLAYS:

Zoot Suit, 1982 (adaptation of his play)

La Bamba, 1987

TELEPLAYS:

Fort Figueroa, 1988

La Pastorela, 1991

The Cisco Kid, 1994

EDITED TEXT:

Aztlan: An Anthology of Mexican American Literature, 1972 (with Stan Steiner)

MISCELLANEOUS:

Pensamiento Serpentino: A Chicano Approach to the Theatre of Reality, 1973

DISCUSSION TOPICS

- Compare Luis Miguel Valdez's use of history in *Zoot Suit* and *Bandido!*

- What does *"I Don't Have to Show You No Stinking Badges!"* say about American society's view of Chicanos? What does it say about the effect of American popular culture on ordinary lives?

- How do Valdez's plays show the influence of the dramatic methods of Bertolt Brecht?

- How does *Zoot Suit* continue and expand upon the themes of Valdez's *actos*?

- In *Zoot Suit*, how does El Pachuco embody Chicano pride?

- Does Valdez's film *La Bamba* look at Chicano culture differently from his plays?

About the Author

Cizmar, Paula. "Luis Valdez." *Mother Jones* 4 (June, 1979): 47-64.

Davy, Daniel. "The Engimatic God: Mask and Myth in *Zoot Suit*." *Journal of American Drama and Theatre* 15 (Winter, 2003): 71-87.

Elam, Harry Justin. *Taking It to the Streets: The Social Protest Theater of Luis Valdez and Amiri Baraka*. Ann Arbor: University of Michigan Press, 1997.

Gross, Steven. "Intentionality and the Markedness Model in Literary Codeswitching." *Journal of Pragmatics: An Interdisciplinary Journal of Language Studies* 32 (August, 2000): 1283-1303.

Huerta, Jorge A. *Chicano Theater: Themes and Forms*. Ypsilanti, Mich.: Bilingual Press/Editorial Bilingue, 1982.

Noriega, Chon A. "Fashion Crimes." *Aztlán: A Journal of Chicano Studies* 26 (Spring, 2001): 1-13.

Shank, Theodore. "A Return to Aztec and Maya Roots." *The Drama Review* 18 (December, 1974) 56-70.

Valdez, Luis. Interview. In *In Their Own Words: Contemporary American Playwrights*, edited by David Savran. New York: Theatre Communications Group, 1988.

MONA VAN DUYN

Born: Waterloo, Iowa
     May 9, 1921
Died: University City, Missouri
     December 2, 2004

Van Duyn's examination of everyday experience, including marriage and family relationships, has earned her work much critical praise.

AP/Wide World Photos

BIOGRAPHY

Mona Van Duyn (pronounced "van dine") was born in Waterloo, Iowa, on May 9, 1921. She has said that neither of her parents was interested in poetry. She recalls that she read constantly as a child, particularly fairy tales, in spite of the fact that her father would take books out of her hands to urge her to play outdoors. At school, she saw poetry used as a punishment for badly behaved students who had to stay after school to memorize it. Still, she developed an early love for poems. Although her father did not want her to attend college, she was allowed to go (on a scholarship she had won) after carrying out a long campaign of nerves to persuade him.

It was only in college, at Iowa State Teachers College (now the University of Northern Iowa), that Van Duyn received encouragement to write. One of her English teachers, Burt Boothe, took her writing seriously, encouraged her to publish, and focused her reading. She received a B.A. in 1942 and an M.A. from the University of Iowa in 1943. In 1943, she married Jarvis A. Thurston, a professor of English.

Van Duyn held several teaching positions from the 1940's to the 1960's, notably at the University of Iowa, the University of Louisville, and Washington University in St. Louis. With her husband, Van Duyn founded and edited *Perspective: A Quarterly of Literature* between 1947 and 1967. She gave up teaching in 1967, saying that teaching took too much of the same energies she needed for writing; she subsequently confined her teaching to summer writing courses. She also gave many poetry readings.

Van Duyn's first book of poems, *Valentines to the Wide World*, was published in 1959. Her second was *A Time of Bees* (1964), followed by *To See, to Take* (1970), *Bedtime Stories* (1972), *Merciful Disguises* (1973), and *Letters from a Father, and Other Poems* (1982). All of her work up to *Near Changes: Poems* (1990) has been collected in a volume called *If It Be Not I: Collected Poems, 1959-1982*, published in 1993. *Firefall* was also published in 1993.

Recognition for Van Duyn's work has taken the form of several important grants, prizes, and appointments, including service as poetry consultant for the Olin Library Modern Literature Collection at Washington University (where her papers are housed). She was one of the first five American poets to win a grant from the National Endowment for the Arts (1966), and she has also received a Guggenheim Fellowship (1972). In 1970, she won the prestigious Bollingen Prize for Poetry.

In 1971 *To See, to Take* won the National Book Award. In her acceptance speech, Van Duyn talked about the nature of poetry and the poet's work, saying that in poetry's concern for both sound and sense, it pays tribute to language refined by patterns. Poets inform those patterns with their own voices in an effort to share their experiences with others. To do that requires a caring about others, "which is a form of love." Her volume *Near Changes* won the Pulitzer Prize in poetry in 1991.

In 1992, Van Duyn was appointed poet laureate by the Library of Congress. In an interview, she commented on the position's requirements, saying that her first task was to give a public reading of her work and later a public lecture. Additionally, she hoped to give recognition to young poets by inviting them to read in the Library of Congress's reading series. She noted that her wide experience as a contest judge would prepare her well to make decisions about potential readers' merits. In the same interview, she protested the label "poetess," but she also noted that of the thirty-one poetry consultants named by the Library of Congress before "poet laureate" was added to the title in 1985, only six had been women. She was the first woman to have been named U.S. poet laureate.

In talking about her work habits, Van Duyn commented that she did extensive revising during the composition of a poem, writing a few lines out in longhand, typing the lines, revising them, and then going on to the next lines. Van Duyn said that she wrote only when she had ideas, although she admitted that the system of a daily writing schedule had some appeal for her when ideas seemed scarce. In her later career, she said she no longer relied on feedback from other writers about her work in the way she did as a beginning writer, before she had established her voice. The poet succumbed to bone cancer in 2004.

ANALYSIS

Van Duyn protested the application of the label "domestic" to her work, noting that male writers who write about their spouses and the events of their daily lives, as she often did, are never labeled that way. In fact, she frequently found her subjects in literature, including the subject of poetry itself, as well as in history, mythology, and even newspaper items. Nevertheless, her subject matter frequently came from her daily life, its various events, her family, her travels. At the heart of her achievement is the fact that those domestic events, even those she treats with considerable humor, become metaphors for the complex statements she makes about the world and the place of people in it.

Van Duyn is a formal writer, almost always using rhyme (often slant rhyme) and frequently using regular stanzas. The volume *Firefall* (1993) may serve to illustrate the diversity she achieves. The first poem in the collection, "A Dog Lover's Confes-

sion," is prefaced by a lengthy note that identifies it and several other poems in the book as "Minimalist sonnets." She explains that she has kept the Petrarchan or Shakespearean conventions in these works while shortening the conventional ten-syllable line length. She sometimes also added an extra quatrain.

"Miranda Grows Up" works like a sort of inverted Petrarchan sonnet with two-syllable lines, and several similar poems are included in a section called "Minimalist Sonnet Translations of, or Comments on, Poems by Auden, Eliot, Yeats, Frost, Hopkins, Arnold." The collection also contains works in quatrains and other stanza forms as well as some poems partly in prose.

Rhyme is everywhere in Van Duyn's work. In "Christmas Present for a Poet," for example, she manages to find seventeen rhymes for the word "hornet" (after originally claiming she can find only "hairnet"); they range from "hornat" ("horn at") to "howornate" to "hearnot" to "hernit" (in the phrase "her nit-wit"). The poem is partly a joking apology for a Christmas-gift shirt that made the recipient look like a hornet, but, typically, the work becomes more than that. Van Duyn considers the implications of the shirt's golden bars on the dark background to suggest that they are like forms in poetry, like the strands of a hairnet that keep neat what they confine. The shirt was bought as a bargain, she claims, and is not the miraculous weave she would like to have sent, but, like life, it is a bargain of which the best must be made.

Poetry that uses humor and a modest subject to talk about something more serious is typical of Van Duyn. In "Mockingbird Month" (from *Near Changes*), for example, she describes a July in which, apparently ill, she is confined to a house where she spends her time listening to a mockingbird. At first she admires its virtuosity, reads about its abilities to imitate, and notes that it bullies the neighbor's cowardly cat. By the end of the month, however, her feelings have changed. She says the lesson is both for art and art lover: When the bird sings all night, she begins to long for silence and concludes that she should also husband her own "apprentice words."

In "In Bed with a Book" (from *Near Changes*), Van Duyn uses the detective novel, her favorite sort of escape reading, to talk about death. The first stanza of the poem describes the novel's crimes;

bodies are found everywhere. The second stanza asks a serious question: What difference does it make that these dead are denied the joys of human experience? In the third stanza, the speaker notes that all the novel's mysteries will be answered with the detective's solution tomorrow night. Meanwhile, surrounded by her loved ones, the speaker is falling asleep, a sleep she calls a "little rehearsal," evidently a rehearsal for the same death that fills the novel.

Van Duyn's work is filled with pictures of family life—an aunt in Texas who describes her apocalyptic religious visions in her chatty letters, a grandmother's series of memories of immigrant life in the Middle West in the late nineteenth century, a speaker's sudden awareness of her love for her husband of many years. By the same token, Van Duyn also makes generous references to the literature of others, to history, and to mythology. Christopher Smart, Alexander Pope, Plato, and Graham Greene all find places in her work, sometimes alongside more immediate references to the speaker's private life.

The nature of love and its place in people's lives is one of Van Duyn's most compelling themes. In "Three Valentines to the Wide World," from her first collection, an eight-year-old child asks whether God's hobby is love. Van Duyn's later poems repeatedly answer that question affirmatively and suggest that humans are at their best when they, too, share love, however raggedly they manage to do it.

"Quebec Suite" concludes with the speaker identifying the loon, which is lonely in its solitude and spends its days calling across the water to its mate, as her favorite bird. In "The Stream," the speaker recalls her mother, who died a night after she and the daughter had shared a special lunch. Now the speaker knows that she will never be able to talk to her mother about love, that she can no longer be sure even what love is. Yet she knows that although love may be stained by abuse, still, like a narrow underground stream, its existence hidden and even unsuspected, it continues to press its way to the surface.

"THREE VALENTINES TO THE WIDE WORLD"

First published: 1959 (collected in *Valentines to the Wide World*, 1959)
Type of work: Poem

The three parts of this long poem attempt to define the interrelationship between love, beauty, and art.

"Three Valentines to the Wide World" is the first poem in Van Duyn's first book. In looking at the poem's three parts, the reader should remember that a valentine is a short love message, and Van Duyn has addressed these messages to the world, emphasizing in her title the world's vastness.

Part 1 is written in twelve-line stanzas, each stanza composed of three rhymed quatrains. That the rhyme is often slant rhyme (listening is rhymed with chastening, for example) does not diminish its effect.

The first stanza describes an eight-year-old child, awkward and graceless, who stands scratching a scab on her knee. In the second stanza, she asks her profound question without even looking up from her knee: "Mother, is love God's hobby?" The speaker believes that the girl has not yet noticed that suffering and death inhabit the world, that she thinks of God as a gardener who will eventually create new leaves from dead stems. The child receives no answer, and the speaker takes her mind back to her own childhood, when anything seemed possible, including the idea that love sustains the world. Section 1 ends with a sort of prayer that the child will be able to maintain her sense of a world eternally recreated as she grows into "the grace of her notion."

The second section is composed of seven four-line rhymed stanzas. The tone of this section is more reserved than that of the first; the section forms a sort of meditation on beauty and the function of poetry. The speaker begins by saying that she has never liked landscapes that are huge vistas, the kind one sees from roadside overlooks. They are too divorced from the immediacy of specifics. That loss of awareness of the specific must affect truck drivers, she thinks, as they roll along in a world where everything below the cabs of their trucks must blur into abstraction.

The antidote to this distance is the poem, the speaker says; its function is to create a sort of pressure. "To find some spot on the surface/ and then bear down until the skin can't stand/ the tension and breaks under it. . . ." Only a poem is strong enough to do that, and when it does, the result is both discovery and reminiscence—just what the speaker experienced in the first section. The writer's joy is to use discovery and reminiscence to create, rather like God the gardener.

Section 3 is composed of three eight-line rhyming stanzas and is introduced by a quotation from Geoffrey Chaucer in which the poet says that he cannot bear the beauty of a certain lady's eyes; they will slay him. The speaker here says that, like the lady's eyes, the beauty of earth seems merciless, powerful enough to kill, except when it is tempered by love and art—things in which compassion resides.

"LETTERS FROM A FATHER"

First published: 1982 (collected in *Letters from a Father, and Other Poems*, 1982)
Type of work: Poem

These "letters" picture an elderly couple who find solace for their declining health in the pleasure of watching a bird feeder.

The six sections of the title poem of *Letters from a Father* record the slow growth into health and peace of an elderly couple, presumably the speaker's parents, as they find increasing pleasure in a bird feeder the speaker has given them. The voice throughout most of the poem is that of the father. Throughout, the stanzas are composed of rhymed quatrains.

In the first section, the speaker offers a long list of his pains—an ulcerated tooth, pressure sores from a leg brace, a bad prostate gland, and a bad heart. He feels ready to die. His old wife is in even worse shape: She falls down and forgets her medicines; her ankles are swollen, and her bowels are bad. This letter concludes with the old man chastising his daughter for wasting good money on a bird feeder; better to poison the birds and be rid of their diseases and mess, he says.

The next section notes that the daughter has brought her parents a bird feeder of their own—a waste of money, the old man says, as they will surely live no more than a few weeks. Still, he confesses that they are enjoying it. In this section, the old man's physical complaints are still vivid—deafness, a bad heart, and belching—and he has added complaints about the birds. They are not even good for food, like the ones the father used to hunt years ago.

The third section creates a sort of transition; its tone is far more positive than that of the first two. The old man is evidently pleased at the large numbers of birds coming to the feeder, and he asks the daughter for a bird book so that he and "Mother" can identify them. They have even sent "the girl" (evidently a household helper) to buy more feed, although the old man tempers the hopefulness of this remark by noting that she had to go to town anyway (the reader suspects that the father is rationalizing).

In the fourth section, the reader learns that, in their feeding frenzy, some of the birds are flying into the old couple's window and knocking themselves out. The old man recounts how a visitor rescued one unconscious bird and brought it in to be restored by the old man's stroking. His joy in the little bird's recovery is evident. He adds that the bird book has arrived.

The fifth section records the old man's delight in the great variety of birds that frequent the feeder. He has names for all the species and describes their habits with pleasure (reminding the reader of Van Duyn's assertions about the beauty of the specific in "Three Valentines to the Wide World"). He even has a kind word for squirrels. At the end of the section, he notes that he has pulled his ulcerated tooth himself and, despite his predictions, he did not bleed at all.

Section 6 continues to record the old man's newfound joy; moreover, he is full of plans for feeding his birds all summer and next winter, too. Mother is doing well, too. She still forgets her medicine, but her bowels are fine. The old man takes some sly pleasure in noting that he has learned that some birds have three wives.

The last line is in the daughter's voice: "So the world woos its children back for an evening kiss." The kiss is the healing pleasure the old couple take in the specific beauties of the world's birds.

"THE STREAM"

First published: 1982 (collected in *Letters from a Father, and Other Poems*, 1982)
Type of work: Poem

Shortly after her mother's death in a nursing home, the speaker reflects on their relationship and compares her mother's love to an underground stream.

"The Stream" is a narrative poem, written in rhymed couplets, which relates the events of the speaker's last four days spent with her mother. The time is three months after the death of the speaker's father; her mother is in a nursing home and hates it. The mother's memory is failing, with the result that, by mistake, she makes a huge effort and dresses herself for a special lunch with her daughter. The lunch is really tomorrow, but the daughter is touched that her frail mother has made so much effort on her own, even fastening to her blouse a pin the daughter once brought her from Madrid.

The daughter has arranged for a special lunch in a lounge in a distant wing of the home, and when they arrive, the mother is uneasy. She does not like it here, she says, and she worries about finding a bathroom if she needs one. Yet when the lunch arrives with its special tablecloth and dishes, she calms herself and enjoys it. She eats more than she has in months, finishes her soup, and eats her own cakes and the daughter's, too, with the daughter feeding her. The daughter remembers that her mother used to like restaurants, although her husband refused to spend the money for them, and that memory, along with her mother's urgent thanks, brings tears to the daughter's eyes.

On their last night together, the daughter helps her mother get ready for bed and watches her go through the rituals of a lifetime—finding the nightgown, washing her face. She looks at the work of age on her mother's body and, as she prepares to leave, tries to reassure her mother that she will call and write; however, she is stopped by tears. Her mother takes the daughter's face in her hands, tells her not to cry, and says that the daughter will never know how much she loves her.

At this point, the reader realizes that the relationship between mother and daughter has not been an affectionate one. The speaker's recognition that the mother makes this gesture as if she had done it all her life makes the reader aware that, in fact, she has not done it. When the daughter says that the statement about love felt true, it is clear that she has not always believed it. The day after the speaker arrives home, the mother dies.

The poem then moves to its central idea: What is love? The speaker compares it to an underground stream, held beneath the surface by pressures no one can understand, perhaps the pressures of the mother's own youth, her parents and husband. Aboveground, others would like to locate that stream of love, like dowsers searching for water for a well. Even dowsers, though, are helpless until at last the stream finds its own way to the surface, just as the mother's love was finally articulated when she spoke to her daughter on their last night. It may happen, Van Duyn notes, too slowly, but after sixty years there is a gathering of water at last; to it, the speaker says, she adds her own tears. They are tears of loss and regret, of course, but also tears of love and joy. The combination, Van Duyn implies, is inevitable in this world.

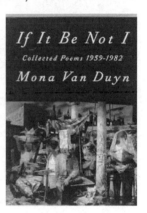

SUMMARY

Mona Van Duyn's poems frequently assert the difficulty of experiencing love in a world where so much goes wrong. Nevertheless, she champions the value of the effort to love, and she implies that art is what helps people to understand love and the world's beauty.

These concerns are linked to Van Duyn's definition of poetry as necessarily involving art and beauty—patterned language, the poet's voice—and the poet's love for those who read the poems. Such affection is betokened by the poet's desire to share meaningful experience with others.

Ann D. Garbett

BIBLIOGRAPHY

By the Author

POETRY:
Valentines to the Wide World, 1959
A Time of Bees, 1964
To See, to Take, 1970
Bedtime Stories, 1972
Merciful Disguises, 1973
Letters from a Father, and Other Poems, 1982
Near Changes, 1990
If It Be Not I: Collected Poems, 1959-1982, 1993
Firefall, 1993
Selected Poems, 2002

About the Author

Augustine, Jane, and William T. Hamilton. "Mona Van Duyn." In *Critical Survey of Poetry*, edited by Philip K. Jason. 2d rev. ed. Pasadena, Calif.: Salem Press, 2003.

Burns, Michael, ed. *Discovery and Reminiscence: Essays on the Poetry of Mona Van Duyn.* Fayetteville: University of Arkansas Press, 1998.

Hall, Judith. "Strangers May Run: The Nation's First Woman Poet Laureate." *The Antioch Review* 52, no. 1 (Winter, 1994): 141.

Prunty, Wyatt. *"Fallen from the Symboled World"*: *Precedents for the New Formalism*. New York: Oxford University Press, 1990.

DISCUSSION TOPICS

- What caused Mona Van Duyn to object to the adjective "domestic" in critics' references to her writing?

- What indications of independence mark Van Duyn's traditional verse forms?

- Consider "Letters from a Father" as an example of successful artistic compression of a life process.

- What does Van Duyn have to say about the nature of love?

- What makes "The Stream" an effective metaphor for conveying her theme of love?

© Jane Bown

GORE VIDAL

Born: West Point, New York
October 3, 1925

As a principal literary figure in the post-World War II era, Vidal has achieved success as a novelist, short-story writer, essayist, playwright, and television and film scriptwriter.

BIOGRAPHY

Gore Vidal, named Eugene Luther Vidal at birth, was born on October 3, 1925, at the United States Military Academy, West Point, New York. His father, Eugene Vidal, was an instructor in the new science of aeronautics; he later founded airlines and in the 1930's was director of air commerce for President Franklin D. Roosevelt. Gore's mother, Nina, was the beautiful and socially prominent daughter of Oklahoma senator Thomas P. Gore.

Soon after Gore's birth, his family moved to Washington, D.C., and lived with his grandfather. Senator Gore was blind; in exchange for young Gore's reading to him, the senator allowed his grandson to use his huge library. Gore began to educate himself at age five, when he could read and write. When the Vidal marriage ended in divorce in 1935, Nina married Hugh D. Auchincloss, a wealthy investment banker. Gore moved to the huge Auchincloss estate in Virginia, only a few miles from his grandfather Gore.

Young Gore grew up among the United States' political, economic, and journalistic elite. He attended good private schools with other young men from prominent families, spending the happiest three years of his life at Phillips Exeter Academy in New Hampshire. After he graduated in 1943, during World War II, he immediately went into the Army. He never went to college but is considered one of the most learned literary figures of his generation.

Before he left the Army in 1946, Vidal finished writing his first two published novels, *Williwaw* (1946) and *In a Yellow Wood* (1947). These established him as one of the best of the young postwar writers. By 1954 he had published eight novels, but it was his third novel that would affect the rest of his life: *The City and the Pillar* (1948) dealt with homosexuality. Homosexuality was a shocking subject in 1948, made doubly so because Vidal made his protagonist a normal, all-American boy, not a bizarre or doomed figure, as such characters usually were in American fiction.

Vidal would himself be labeled homosexual, which would influence reaction to him in the literary and political world. Vidal does not believe that anyone is homosexual or heterosexual. He believes that all humans feel sexual desires for both males and females but that most societies try to socialize their members into suppressing their desire for their own sex. Sexual acts are homosexual or heterosexual, Vidal says, but a person is neither.

His next few books were ignored, and Vidal found himself in financial trouble. In 1954, he began writing for television, in the so-called Golden Age when television broadcast many live dramas. He also became a Hollywood figure, writing screenplays, including *The Catered Affair* (1956) and, with Tennessee Williams, *Suddenly Last Summer* (1959). He wrote several plays, including two Broadway hits: *Visit to a Small Planet: A Comedy Akin to a Vaudeville* (1957) and *The Best Man: A Play About Politics* (1960). He also wrote three mystery novels under the name Edgar Box.

By the early 1960's, Vidal had built a secure financial base and had established himself as a well-known public figure. He was an outspoken social critic, and he offered a scathing indictment of United States leadership and policy. The turmoil produced by the Civil Rights movement, the Vietnam War, and the Watergate scandal made a large segment of the educated public receptive to his message. In 1960, Vidal ran for a seat in the House of Representatives; in 1982, he ran for the Senate. He did not win either race but received greater percentages of the votes than observers had thought he could.

In 1964, Vidal published *Julian*, a historical novel about a fourth century Roman emperor, Julian the Apostate, who had tried to stop the spread of Christianity. This was Vidal's first novel in ten years and was a critical and financial success. After this, Vidal turned out a succession of bestselling novels, including more historical fiction and such famous and controversial forays into popular culture as his novel *Myra Breckinridge* (1968).

Vidal remains a scathing critic of almost every aspect of American life. He lives much of each year in Italy, where he has a beautiful villa overlooking the Bay of Salerno. He returns periodically to the United States to make the talk-show circuit on television and to release his newest novel or book of essays.

ANALYSIS

Great diversity in subject matter, narrative structure, and style characterizes Vidal's fictional work. His first eight novels, written before he was thirty years old, typically depicted young men in search of proper and fulfilling lives. For example, young men at war on a ship have to work out moral and ethical problems in a small group under stress; other young men examine the meaning of friendship and love; some are caught up in historical events, such as a revolution in Central America; some face dilemmas of choosing careers and lifestyles. Young men who choose what appear to be secure positions or socially acceptable and conforming lifestyles often find themselves destroyed. Vidal's message is that to live fully, one must defy social pressures and choose to live a life of personal freedom.

Author Ernest Hemingway greatly influenced Vidal's writing style, as he did that of many other young writers in the postwar years. Vidal's seventh and eighth novels were particularly important to his development. In *The Judgment of Paris* (1952),

he began to develop his own stylistic voice, marked by wit and irony. In the ancient Greek myth, Zeus forces a young man, Paris, to choose the most beautiful among three goddesses. In Vidal's story, a modern young man confronts three women, each offering him a different gift: political power, knowledge, or love. He chooses love—not static, possessive love with one person but the stance of remaining open to love and friendship as he moves through life.

In *Messiah* (1954), regarded by some as a small masterpiece awaiting discovery, Vidal took up a subject to which he would return in several future novels. *Messiah* is a journal narrated by an old man, Eugene Luther, who had helped found a new religion based on the teaching of John Cave. "Cavesword" had displaced Christianity. Figures in the book correspond to Jesus, Mary, Saint Paul, Martin Luther, and other religious figures. Vidal shows how the needs of the organized church suppress and distort the message of a religious founder such as John Cave (or Jesus Christ).

Lack of money during the ten years that followed *Messiah* forced Vidal to write for a mass audience on Broadway and in televison and films. He continued to explore the proper role of the individual in modern civilization, but he also learned to entertain and to lace his social criticism with biting satire and flashing wit.

In 1964, Vidal turned back to the novel and proved to be a master of historical fiction. *Julian* and *Creation* (1981) won applause from historians because of Vidal's fidelity to the historical record. Vidal turned his historical probing to the United States by writing a cycle of seven novels, in order by the period covered: *Burr* (1973), *Lincoln* (1984), *1876* (1976), *Empire* (1987), *Hollywood: A Novel of America in the 1920's* (1990), *The Golden Age* (2000), and *Washington, D.C.* (1967). Vidal believes that the United States is a deeply flawed society, a garrison state that manages a worldwide empire, a society run by a small, wealthy, elite removed from any concern with the masses of American people. The genius of the American ruling class, he says, is that the people do not even know they have one.

In his historical cycle, Vidal studies this ruling class as it evolves over two centuries. He believes that the democratic promise of American society was lost at the very beginning of United States history. The Founding Fathers, such as George Washington, Thomas Jefferson, and Aaron Burr, he depicts as opportunists who built a nation not from some great sense of national purpose but to secure their fortunes and to gain political power. Lincoln is shown as a great man, but his greatness is in creating a centralized and unified nation, not in achieving the nation's proclaimed democratic promise. In *Empire* and *Hollywood*, set in the early twentieth century, the United States' rulers create an overseas empire which will serve as the foundation of the military-industrial complex. The nation's rulers use modern mass media, such as newspapers and films, to manipulate the people. *Washington, D.C.*, shows the emptiness of a John Kennedy-like politician whose only goal is to win power. In *The Golden Age*, Vidal examines the same period but with a different focus: The destruction of a cultural golden age by the suppressive atmosphere unleashed by the Cold War. Vidal typically provokes and angers readers, but he also edifies.

Vidal's historical fiction provides a foundation for understanding some of his "campy" literature: *Myra Breckinridge*, *Myron* (1974), *Kalki* (1978), *Duluth* (1983), *Live from Golgotha* (1992), and *The Smithsonian Institution* (1998). These are studies of sexuality—of the "heterosexual dictatorship," in Vidal's terms—the nature of religious movements, and the role of mass media, especially television and films, in shaping people's sense of reality.

JULIAN

First published: 1964
Type of work: Novel

In the fourth century, Roman emperor Julian tries to stop the spread of Christianity.

Julian was Vidal's first venture into historical fiction. History fascinates him, and he has read as widely in the field as most professional historians. Vidal adheres closely to the historical record, but as a novelist he can do two things that professional historians cannot: He can invent facts when the facts are not known, and he can ascribe motives to historical figures. In both cases, Vidal carefully invents facts and motives that seem most likely to have been true historically. Vidal intends to enter-

tain, but he also intends to instruct: He gives a historically accurate portrait of Julian and explores with his readers the origins of Western civilization.

The novel opens in 380 C.E., seventeen years after Emperor Julian's death during an invasion of Persia. Two old friends of Julian, the philosophers Libanius of Antioch and Priscus of Athens, learn that the Emperor Theodosius has declared an end to toleration of Christian and non-Christian "heresy." Libanius has heard a rumor that Priscus possesses the only copy of a memoir written by Julian. He proposes that they publish the memoir to remind the world of Julian's previous attempt to stop the spread of Christianity. The novel, then, consists of Julian's memoir, interspersed with letters and comments by Libanius and Priscus, who were eyewitnesses to the events described by Julian. They "correct" his version of events and add their own perspectives.

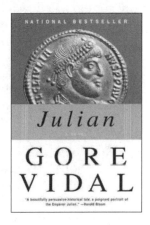

Julian (Flavius Claudius Julianus), born about 331, is a descendent of the Christian emperors Constantine the Great and Constantius II. Constantius kills all the other members of Julian's family to prevent any challenge to his authority. Julian saves himself by making sure he is not seen as a threat. He lives a secluded life, aiming first to be a priest and later studying philosophy with some of the greatest minds of his age.

Yet Julian loses his faith in Christianity, even though he has a religious mentality and personality. His friends say that at another time Julian might well have been a Christian saint. He leads a life of asceticism and, after his wife's death, maintains sexual celibacy. His faith breaks because he grows up in an age when church bureaucrats gain control of Christianity and rob it of its mystery by carrying on dry and learned battles over esoteric matters. They engage in political intrigues that neglect or distort Jesus's simple message of love. Julian is drawn to Jesus but detests the church that speaks in his name. As a young boy, Julian witnesses Christians beating and killing other Christians. He cannot square Christian violence and brutality with Jesus's message of peace and love. Simultaneously, he reads the works of non-Christian scholars, who teach pre-Christian Greek philosophy and religion.

Meanwhile, Constantius brings Julian out of seclusion to play a role in governing the huge Roman Empire. In 355 C.E., Constantius places Julian in control of the Roman provinces beyond the Alps. The young, ascetic scholar proves to be a military genius and quickly wins the love of his troops. In 361, Constantius dies, and Julian becomes emperor.

As emperor, Julian proclaims religious toleration for both Christians and non-Christians. Julian says that he is going to punish Christians by forbidding them to do what they enjoy most—persecuting one another. He sacrifices to the old gods of Mount Olympus and tries to revive the pagan temples and rituals. He lays plans to breathe new life into Hellenism, the civilization inherited from Greece. He also, Vidal believes, is captivated by Alexander the Great's vision of conquering the known world.

Julian invades Persia and drives deep into the heart of that empire. He wins many victories but is killed—murdered, Vidal believes, by one of his Christian soldiers. "With Julian, the light went, and now nothing remains but to let the darkness come," says Libanius. Now nothing stands in the way of the spread of Christianity, and Western civilization enters a thousand-year decline, later called the Dark Ages.

One of Vidal's biographers asked two outstanding historians of the fourth century Roman Empire to evaluate *Julian*. The historians agreed that Vidal's work is probably the best portrait of Julian that exists. Vidal sees the era as crucial to the evolution of the West. If Julian had lived, Vidal believes, Christianity would be only one of several religions in Western civilization.

BURR

First published: 1973
Type of work: Novel

The activities of the Founding Fathers of the United States were aimed at gaining wealth and power for themselves, not at any idealistic concept.

Vidal's iconoclastic portrait of the American Founding Fathers in *Burr* would have shocked an earlier generation. In 1973, however, the United States had just emerged from the tumult of the Civil Rights movement and was still torn by controversy over the Vietnam War and by the Watergate scandal that would soon force President Richard Nixon to resign from office. As one reviewer of *Burr* pointed out, to the millions of Americans who believed that the ancient verities of the republic had become hollow, Vidal explained that they always had been. If many readers were surprised that Vidal's history was not what their teachers had taught them, his description of the Founding Fathers did not shock professional historians. As usual, Vidal had done excellent research and had based his work solidly in the interpretative tradition of such great American historians as Henry Adams and Charles Beard as well as the young revisionist historians of the 1960's and 1970's.

Burr opens in 1833 and ends in 1840, four years after Aaron Burr's death at age eighty. It is narrated by Charles Schuyler, a twenty-five-year-old law clerk in Burr's office, who wants to give up the legal profession to be a writer. He is intrigued by Burr, a dark figure of the heroic period of American history, who is still very much alive and active. Burr is witty, cosmopolitan, and sophisticated. He is willing to talk to Charlie about the past. Meanwhile, several friends of Charlie are plotting against Vice President Martin van Buren, whom they expect will try for the presidency in 1836, after Andrew Jackson's second term in office. Van Buren's enemies see Charlie's project with Burr as a possible way to carry out their political schemes. They know that Burr and Van Buren had been close; in fact, there is a rumor that Van Buren is Burr's illegitimate son. If Charlie finds evidence of that in his research on Burr, they can use it to defeat Van Buren.

Burr provides Charlie with copies of his journal on the Revolutionary War, in which he was an officer, and dictates additional material to fill out his memoirs. Charlie is quickly captivated by the old man, who makes the famous figures of the past, his friends and acquaintances, come alive: George Washington, Thomas Jefferson, Benedict Arnold, James Madison, James Monroe, John Marshall, Alexander Hamilton, John Adams, Andrew Jackson, and many more. Burr had been a leader among the Founding Fathers, a man who sparkled even among that glittering elite. He was Jefferson's vice president, and he assumed, as did many others, that he would someday be president. Yet he got in the way of powerful interests in New York, represented by Hamilton, and seemed to threaten the Virginia clique headed by Jefferson. Burr killed Hamilton in a duel. His political career in ruins, he went westward, probably with plans to break Mexico away from Spain. Perhaps he intended to become king of Mexico. Jefferson accused him of attempting to break up the union; he had Burr arrested and tried for treason. Despite pressure from Jefferson, however, Burr was not convicted.

Burr brings to life one of American history's important and neglected figures, but it does more. It entertains and titillates as Burr turns his irreverent wit against the holy figures of the past. Washington is a plump figure who has difficulty getting on a horse without splitting his pants. As a general, he displays "eerie incompetence"; he is a man of courage and will, not military ability. His real genius is for business and for political intrigue. Jefferson is a hypocrite who rattles on about inalienable rights yet denies them to slaves, Indians, women, and poor white men. He is an empire builder who doubles the size of the United States.

Burr is not an embittered old man who has nothing good to say about his contemporaries, however; he likes Adams, Madison, and Jackson. His point is that the Founding Fathers were like all political leaders: They were opportunistic men out for money and power. They did not create the United States out of some idealistic concern for the masses. When they wrote the United States Constitution, they built a governmental structure designed to benefit themselves personally. Burr sees nothing wrong with that; he simply dislikes the hypocrisy with which many of his contemporaries, especially Jefferson, cloaked their intentions.

When Charlie Schuyler finishes his work with Burr, he loves the old man. He finds evidence that Burr is indeed Van Buren's father, but he does not use it; Van Buren rewards him with a government position overseas. In a final twist, Charlie learns that Burr is his own father (a wish fulfilled), making Van Buren his big brother.

LINCOLN

First published: 1984
Type of work: Novel

Abraham Lincoln creates a new centralized and unified nation that goes far beyond the vision of the Founding Fathers.

Lincoln surprised some readers, who expected Vidal to turn his iconoclastic wit on the Great Emancipator, as he had Washington and Jefferson. Instead, Vidal draws an admiring portrait of the Civil War president. In this long, rich study of Lincoln during the Civil War, Vidal describes the interwoven lives of a variety of people surrounding Lincoln in the war-besieged capital: Young John Hay, Lincoln's personal secretary (and later one of the greatest American secretaries of state); Lincoln's rivals for power in the Republican party, including wily Secretary of State William Seward and staid Secretary of the Treasury Salmon P. Chase; arrogant generals such as George McClellan, who struts prettily in his uniform but never gets around to fighting battles; and plotters determined to kill Lincoln, including young David Herold and actor John Wilkes Booth, who finally does assassinate the president.

Vidal shows deep sympathy for the president's wife, Mary Todd Lincoln, so often portrayed as a horrible shrew, another burden for the beleaguered president to carry. Vidal presents Mary Lincoln as an intelligent and decent woman going insane. Lincoln is the mystery. Vidal does not take the novelist's liberty of getting inside Lincoln's mind to show what he was thinking; he presents Lincoln only from an exterior viewpoint, as described and interpreted by those around him. Vidal emphatically rejects the popular view of Lincoln, the view largely shaped by poet and Lincoln biographer

Carl Sandburg. The folksy, man-of-the-people figure presented by Sandburg was only a mask created by Lincoln, Vidal believes, to hide his real self. The real Lincoln was a cold, brilliant, ruthlessly determined man, a man who did not shrink from exercising dictatorial power during the Civil War crisis, becoming the most powerful president in American history.

In *Lincoln*, William Seward, another master of power and of masks, most clearly understands the president. Seward knows what later generations tended to forget: Lincoln did not step out of a log cabin directly into the White House. He had served in Congress and had been a successful railroad lawyer. Lincoln heads the Republican Party, which Seward has helped create. This is not a party of backwoods farmers but of industrial capitalism. After the war starts, Seward tells Lincoln that he has a chance to re-create the republic and to achieve greatness. Lincoln, startled, freezes with attention.

Seward says that he had looked at an old Lincoln speech, given when he was twenty-eight years old. Lincoln had mentioned Alexander the Great, Julius Caesar, and Napoleon. The Founding Fathers had gotten all the glory of great deeds, Lincoln said in his speech; those who came afterward, such as Lincoln himself, would be mere office holders. The Founding Fathers had left little room for an eagle or lion. Now, Seward implies, the war crisis gives Lincoln a chance to soar, to achieve greatness.

Lincoln understands one terrible fact. Despite the squabbling of Republican politicians and the incompetence of northern military leaders, if he can hold the nation together, the North will inevitably win. Because it has more people than the South, the South will run out of men before the Union does. Seward finally fully understands that "there had been, from the beginning, a single-minded dictator in the White House . . . by whose will alone the war had been prosecuted." Seward understands Lincoln's political genius: "He had been able to make himself absolute dictator without ever letting anyone suspect that he was anything more than a joking, timid backwoods lawyer."

Lincoln achieves his destiny. He leads the nation to victory and, like a hero in an ancient myth, is swept away at his moment of success. In 1867, while in France, John Hay meets Charles Schuyler, the narrator of *Burr*, who has not returned from overseas since 1837. Hay tries to explain to the curious Schuyler Lincoln's place in history. Lincoln had superseded Washington, Hay said, because he had led the greatest war in human history and had put the Union back together. More than that, he had created a new country not envisioned by the Founding Fathers, a unified, centralized power. He was the American Bismarck, Hay and Schuyler agree, referring to Otto von Bismarck, who was at that time creating a unified Germany.

EMPIRE

First published: 1987
Type of work: Novel

Presidents William McKinley and Theodore Roosevelt seize Spanish colonies and create an overseas American empire.

Empire opens in 1898, just as the Spanish-American War ends. Charles Schuyler, the engaging young narrator of *Burr*, is dead, but his granddaughter, Caroline Sanford, is the protagonist of this book. Her half brother, Blaise Sanford, works for publisher William Randolph Hearst, and Caroline defies the Victorian era gender code and buys her own newspaper, in Washington, D.C. She copies Hearst's style of yellow journalism, featuring murders on the front page of her newspaper, preferably of beautiful half-naked young women. Blaise later joins her as part owner of the *Tribune*, which gives them access to the power brokers who make history, as does Caroline's affair with a rising southern politician, James Burden Day.

Much of the story is told from the point of view of Caroline's friend, John Hay, once Abraham Lincoln's young aide, now secretary of state. Hay's circle includes Presidents McKinley and Roosevelt, whose geopolitical intrigues are wryly observed by Hay's close friends, historian Henry Adams and author Henry James.

Hay, Adams, and James dissect the world scene as the United States continues its evolution from republic to empire. Vidal traces the path from the republic established by men such as George Washington and John Adams through the creation of an internal empire by Presidents Thomas Jefferson, Andrew Jackson, and James Polk—expansionists who grabbed vast tracts of land from Native Americans, Mexicans, and others. Lincoln created a unified nation with a powerful central government. McKinley then uses that new power to destroy the Spanish empire. He seizes Cuba, Puerto Rico, and the Philippines, which, along with other island bases, transform the Caribbean and Pacific into American lakes. Roosevelt adds the Panama Canal to the American empire, which allows Washington to move its fleet quickly from one geopolitical hotspot to another.

Washington becomes the dynamic hub of the new empire, a place where politics and the media merge in ways that transform both. Caroline and Blaise Sanford both admire and are appalled by Hearst. Rather than contenting himself with just reporting the news, they believe that he is assuming immense power as an inventor of reality. Hearst believes that he, almost alone, created the war with Spain, which in its wake gave the United States an overseas empire. He says he invented the nation's newest hero, Theodore Roosevelt, by sending him off to war surrounded by reporters.

There were limits to this new form of power. Hearst decides to go into politics himself but is shoved aside by his invention, Roosevelt, who becomes vice president in March, 1901, and then president, after McKinley's assassination in September. The book ends with an angry confrontation between Hearst and Roosevelt. The publishing tycoon tells Roosevelt that he is a Hearst creation. History made me, not you, Roosevelt says. However, true history, Hearst muses, is the final fiction, and he is author of that.

HOLLYWOOD: A NOVEL OF AMERICA IN THE 1920'S

First published: 1990
Type of work: Novel

Powerful political and business interests scent the potential political significance of new forms of media, especially of the film industry.

Hollywood opens in 1917. The three brilliant observers who added intellectual bite to *Empire* are gone. John Hay and Henry James are dead, and Henry Adams, frail and isolated, makes only brief appearances before his own death. Caroline Sanford, now forty years old, observes the maneuvers of President Woodrow Wilson. She is publisher, with her half brother Blaise Sanford, of the Washington *Tribune*. She watches Wilson push the United States toward entry into World War I, despite the fact that he had just been reelected using the slogan "He kept us out of war," implicitly promising to continue doing so.

The United States, in Vidal's view, had long been evolving from a republic into an imperial power. Wilson provides the rationale for this new American global imperialism, a rationale used by his successors to justify all future American wars. American wars are noble enterprises, Wilson said, not undertaken to benefit America itself, but to make the world safe for democracy and to establish global peace and freedom.

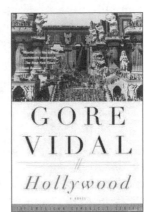

Wilson's wartime propaganda managers send Caroline to Hollywood to draw the film industry into the war effort. Her mentor, William Randolph Hearst, has already sensed the potential of motion pictures. Most Chinese people cannot read my newspapers, he tells Caroline, but they flock to see my serial, *The Perils of Pauline*. Film embodies power more basic than the written word, he believes. As a lark, Hearst puts Caroline in one of his films, and, to her surprise, she emerges a star. Caroline, excited by Hearst's vision of the power of the film industry, decides to cast her lot with Hollywood.

Meanwhile, Wilson has used the war to expand American power, at the expense of European allies, drained by years of carnage. He persuades the Europeans to accept the League of Nations, but, blinded by self-righteousness, he fails to realize how far out of step he is with American public opinion. He collapses during his losing battle to swing the American people behind the League.

Blaise Sanford and Senator James Burden Day closely observe the new president, Warren Harding. Underneath Harding's dull exterior, they detect a shrewd politician who successfully engineers a comprehensive disarmament treaty that cools an overheated arms race among the great powers. Still, Harding's shrewdness fails when it comes to his crooked friends, who bring his administration down in ruins.

Caroline remains a major film star until she loses her battle with age. She has watched Washington use the film industry to demonize the Germans and then to whip up a postwar Red Scare, ferreting out Bolsheviks who supposedly were about to subvert the nation. She asks herself, why not deliberately use films to alter reality? This country or any country, she believes, exists only as a product of people's dreams. She starts a film production company and sets out to furnish the world with dreams.

WASHINGTON, D.C.

First published: 1967
Type of work: Novel

Political insiders vie for power and influence during the administrations of Presidents Franklin D. Roosevelt, Harry Truman, and Dwight Eisenhower.

Vidal has said that he was born to be a writer but was trained to be a politician; he grew up in the environment he describes in *Washington, D.C.* The origins of the United States fascinate him, and he uses his historical novels to trace the evolution of the nation's history. Vidal keeps his focus on the elite, as he believes that the masses of people have little to do with shaping the course of American national history. He confronts one of the oldest and hardest questions that historians face: Do individuals (the "great" men and women) shape history, or do impersonal forces (such as the rise of nationalism or the intertwining of global economies) shape history and sweep individual leaders along with the tide? Vidal says, "A good ruler in a falling time falls, too, while a bad ruler at a time of national ascendancy rises," then adds, "But, men certainly affect events. . . . the only moral life is to act as if whatever one does is of great moment."

Washington, D.C. moves through the years of the Great Depression, World War II, the beginning of the Cold War, the Joseph McCarthy period of anti-

communist hysteria, and the Korean War. It opens in July, 1937. A fictitious southern senator, James Burden Day, has successfully led the fight to block an attempt by President Franklin D. Roosevelt (FDR) to pack the Supreme Court with supporters of his New Deal program. Day, who has similarities to Vidal's grandfather, Senator Gore, is being pushed for the presidency by anti-Roosevelt conservatives, and he wants to save the republic from FDR. He and the president represent two opposing principles, Day says: FDR believes that government must do everything for the people, while he, Senator Day, believes it cannot do much more than it is doing if individuals are going to retain any sort of private freedom.

Day is a decent, restrained man. He does not have much idealistic feeling for others, although "he tried, for he truly believed that one ought to be good." In his quest for the presidency, he is supported by his smart, cold assistant, Clay Overbury, and by Blaise Sanford, a ruthless newspaper publisher who wants to make someone—anyone— president. Burden Day has a major problem, however: He lacks money to run a campaign, as he has not used his office to enrich himself. Blaise introduces him to a man who represents oil interests. He offers Senator Day money in return for a favor that will benefit those interests. Day agrees, but in the contest for the presidency, Roosevelt outmaneuvers him and goes on to win the 1940 and 1944 elections.

Burden Day remains senator but finds himself on the periphery of power as Roosevelt and his successors, Harry Truman and Dwight Eisenhower, move the United States into a new arena as a world imperial power and leader of the so-called free world during the Cold War with the Soviet Union. A central point in the mind of Day (and Vidal) is that the American empire is no different from any other empire. The republic, based on the ideal of a small government with limited power and on the dignity of the individual, is submerged within a militarized empire that operates on a global scale.

As an old man who has served in Washington since the days of Woodrow Wilson, Day decides in the early 1950's to run for one last term in the Senate. Overbury, however, now the son-in-law of Sanford, uses his knowledge of the bribe to force his friend Day to withdraw from the race. Overbury takes Burden's seat in the Senate. If Day is a decent, modest, flawed man, Overbury, with some similarities to John F. Kennedy, is an empty man without belief in friends, ideals, or issues. He only wants power. At the end, Overbury has his power and Burden Day dies, perhaps by suicide. As Burden dies, he tells a ghostly vision of his father, "It has all gone wrong." Presumably he means that not only his life has gone wrong but the promise of the American republic has also been lost.

The Golden Age

First published: 2000
Type of work: Novel

Peter Sanford believes that the mid-twentieth century experienced a brief golden age of cultural creativity, a renaissance choked off as the United States cemented its global economic and military power.

Caroline Sanford provides the central focus of *The Golden Age* as it begins in 1939, but she soon gives way as protagonist to her young nephew and heir, Peter Sanford. Peter meets President Franklin D. Roosevelt and Harry Truman and most of the other political insiders of his time, as well as such cultural figures as playwright Tennessee Williams, composer Leonard Bernstein, and even a young novelist named Gore Vidal.

Sanford family relationships are tangled, although death simplifies matters as the years pass. Peter's father, Blaise Sanford, champions the ruthlessly ambitious Clay Overbury in his relentless drive for power. Overbury forces his benefactor, Senator James Burden Day, into retirement so that Overbury can take Day's Senate seat.

However, the Sanford domestic entanglements take a backseat to the geopolitical maneuvers that begin in 1939. Caroline observes the drama firsthand, through her friendship with Harry Hopkins, Roosevelt's alter ego. Hopkins mocks the blindness of isolationists who oppose Roosevelt's attempts to support France and Great Britain, under assault from Nazi dictator Adolf Hitler. Hopkins says that the unspoken reality is that Americans have a world

empire and that Great Britain is America's client state, which must be protected for American self-interest. Peter and his friend Gore Vidal later speculate about Roosevelt's role in the Japanese attack on Pearl Harbor. They believe that Roosevelt deliberately provoked Japan into an attack, allowing the United States to enter World War II and establish itself as the dominant global power.

After World War II, Peter and his friend Aeneas Duncan publish a journal, *American Idea*, which becomes a major force in American intellectual and cultural life, and marks the beginning, they believe, of a postwar golden age, in literature, dance, music, and art.

The American renaissance flared and then quickly dimmed. Everything takes a backseat to the Cold War. The two wartime allies, the United States and Soviet Union, divide the world between them and face off in a potentially deadly confrontation. President Truman puts the finishing touches on the American empire. He uses the people's fear of the Soviet Union to build a national security state, creating the Department of Defense, Central Intelligence Agency, and the National Security Council. His newly militarized national government then inaugurates a loyalty program that quashes dissent and ends the brief golden age.

The book skips ahead to the millennium. On New Years Day, 2000, Peter meets a young man, Aaron Burr Decker, Caroline's great-grandson. Aaron asked Peter to participate in a televised dialogue with Peter's friend, Vidal, which takes place in Vidal's home in Italy. The two old men, Gore and Peter, try to make sense of the era they had lived in. Peter finally reminds Gore that he, Peter, is only a made-up character in a Vidal novel. Why, he asks, did you not give me a better world in which to live?

Summary

Gore Vidal has proved to be the master of historical fiction in the post-World War II era. His concern with the nature of Western civilization and with the way people gain and use power has led him to explore history from sixth century B.C.E. Athens to modern Washington, D.C. Wit, irony, and deep pessimism about the human estate characterize his work.

William E. Pemberton

BIBLIOGRAPHY

By the Author

LONG FICTION:
Williwaw, 1946
In a Yellow Wood, 1947
The City and the Pillar, 1948, revised 1965
The Season of Comfort, 1949
A Search for the King: A Twelfth Century Legend, 1950
Dark Green, Bright Red, 1950
The Judgment of Paris, 1952, revised 1965
Death in the Fifth Position, 1952 (as Edgar Box)
Death Before Bedtime, 1953 (as Box)
Death Likes It Hot, 1954 (as Box)
Messiah, 1954, revised 1965
Julian, 1964
Washington, D.C., 1967
Myra Breckinridge, 1968
Two Sisters: A Memoir in the Form of a Novel, 1970
Burr, 1973
Myron, 1974
1876, 1976
Kalki, 1978
Creation, 1981
Duluth, 1983
Lincoln, 1984
Empire, 1987
Hollywood: A Novel of America in the 1920's, 1990
Live from Golgotha, 1992
The Smithsonian Institution, 1998
The Golden Age, 2000

SHORT FICTION:
A Thirsty Evil: Seven Short Stories, 1956

DRAMA:
Visit to a Small Planet: A Comedy Akin to a Vaudeville, pr. 1957
The Best Man: A Play About Politics, pr., pb. 1960
Romulus: A New Comedy, pr., pb. 1962
An Evening with Richard Nixon, pr. 1972

SCREENPLAYS:
The Catered Affair, 1956
Suddenly Last Summer, 1959 (with Tennessee Williams)
The Best Man, 1964 (adaptation of his play)
Last of the Mobile Hot-Shots, 1969
Caligula, 1977

DISCUSSION TOPICS

- What does Gore Vidal mean when he says that the genius of the American ruling class is that the people do not even know they have a ruling class?

- Vidal believes that the American republic was soon destroyed and replaced by an empire—first an internal empire (seized from Native Americans, Mexicans, and others) and then an overseas one (based mainly on dominating countries rather than owning them as colonies). How do Americans maintain an empire without owning many foreign colonies? Why does Vidal believe that the avowed American policy of exporting its concepts of democracy and freedom is a key to the creation and maintenance of an empire?

- Aaron Burr and his descendants figure in each of Vidal's American historical fictions. Why does he center on Burr, the "bad boy" among the Founding Fathers?

- Vidal's portraits of George Washington, Thomas Jefferson, Abraham Lincoln, and Franklin D. Roosevelt often shock readers, although many professional historians believe that his interpretations are accurate and convincing. Discuss.

- Vidal has an insider position within various American elites: the wealthy, political, celebrity, and creative. How does his insider status give his descriptions of the American ruling class particular force and flavor?

- Why does Vidal believe that if the Emperor Julian had lived and achieved his goals, then American history would have been quite different (and better)?

TELEPLAYS:
Visit to a Small Planet, and Other Television Plays, 1956
Dress Gray, 1986

NONFICTION:
Rocking the Boat, 1962
Reflections upon a Sinking Ship, 1969
Homage to Daniel Shays: Collected Essays, 1952-1972, 1972
Matters of Fact and of Fiction: Essays, 1973-1976, 1977
The Second American Revolution, and Other Essays, 1976-1982, 1982
At Home: Essays, 1982-1988, 1988
The Decline and Fall of the American Empire, 1992
Screening History, 1992
United States: Essays, 1952-1992, 1993
Palimpsest: A Memoir, 1995
Virgin Islands, A Dependency of United States: Essays, 1992-1997, 1997
Gore Vidal, Sexually Speaking: Collected Sex Writings, 1999
The Last Empire: Essays, 1992-2000, 2000
Dreaming War: Blood for Oil and the Cheney-Bush Junta, 2002
Perpetual War for Perpetual Peace: How We Got to Be So Hated, 2002
Imperial America, 2004

MISCELLANEOUS:
The Essential Gore Vidal, 1999 (Fred Kaplan, editor)
Inventing a Nation: Washington, Adams, Jefferson, 2003
Conversations with Gore Vidal, 2005 (Richard Peabody and Lucinda Ebersole, editors)

About the Author

Dick, Bernard F. *The Apostate Angel: A Critical Study of Gore Vidal.* New York: Random House, 1974.

Ebersole, Lucinda, and Richard Peabody, eds. *Conversations with Gore Vidal.* Jackson: University Press of Mississippi, 2005.

Kaplan, Fred. *Gore Vidal: A Biography.* New York: Doubleday, 1999.

Stanton, Robert J. *Gore Vidal: A Primary and Secondary Bibliography.* Boston: G. K. Hall, 1978.

Stanton, Robert J., and Gore Vidal, eds. *Views from a Window: Conversations with Gore Vidal.* Secaucus, N.J.: Lyle Stuart, 1980.

White, Ray Lewis. *Gore Vidal.* New York: Twayne, 1968.

Courtesy, Penguin Putnam Inc.

HELENA MARÍA VIRAMONTES

Born: East Los Angeles, California
February 26, 1954

Viramontes is one of the most important Latina writers to emerge at the end of the twentieth century, a short-story writer and novelist who addresses some of the most significant American issues, particularly for Latinos.

BIOGRAPHY

Helena María Viramontes was born in East Los Angeles, California, on February 26, 1954, one of six daughters and three sons born to a construction worker and a homemaker. After graduation from Garfield High School, Viramontes earned her B.A. degree in English literature at Immaculate Heart College, also in Los Angeles, where she was one of only five Latinas in her class, graduating in 1975. She enrolled in the Master of Fine Arts Creative Writing Program at the University of California at Irvine in 1981 but left and completed her M.F.A. requirements after the publication of her first collection of short fiction, *The Moths, and Other Stories*, in 1985. In 1989, she received a National Endowment for the Arts fellowship which allowed her to attend a workshop given by the famed Columbian writer Gabriel García Márquez at the Sundance Institute in Utah. Viramontes has not been a prolific author, but she has published consistently over her career. In 1988, with María Herrera-Sobek, she coedited *Chicana Creativity and Criticism: Charting New Frontiers in American Literature* (second edition, 1996), a collection of both creative work (including Viramontes's short story "Miss Clairol") and criticism inspired by a literary conference held at U.C. Irvine; in 1995, the two writers edited a similar collection titled *Chicana (W)rites: On Word and Film*. In 1995, she published her short novel *Under*

the Feet of Jesus and in 2000, a second novel *Their Dogs Came with Them*, about the brutality of the Spanish conquest of the Americas. By the early twenty-first century, she had been a visiting professor at a number of universities but lived in Ithaca, New York, with her husband, the well-known environmental biologist Eloy Rodriguez, and their children. She also serves on the faculty at Cornell University, where she teaches creative writing. Her stories have appeared in a number of periodicals and anthologies, and she has won numerous awards, including the John Dos Passos Prize for Literature in 1996. As her fiction grapples with contemporary social issues, Viramontes herself has gotten involved in a number of cultural and educational projects, including as literary editor of *XhistmeArte* in the early 1980's; cofounder of the nonprofit group Latino Writers and Filmmakers, Inc.; and coordinator for the Latino Writers Association.

ANALYSIS

In most of her fiction, Viramontes focuses on the struggles of Latina characters within the family, their culture, and the larger society. All of these institutions can be seen as oppressive, usually retarding the growth of the central characters. In "The Moths," for example, it is the family unit from which the young protagonist must break free; in "The Cariboo Café," it is poverty, racism, and abusive governmental policies; and in *Under the Feet of Jesus*, it is economic, familial, and social injustices in the Central Valley of California. Viramontes's stories, in short, communicate the overwhelming trials that Latina mothers, wives, and daughters face as they attempt to grow up, raise families, and discover their own identities, but her dual focus is always on the cultural and social values by which these women attempt to live as well. The narrative technique in these fictions is not always easy to follow, and the writing can be dense with poetic imagery. Viramontes uses shifting points of view, and it is sometimes difficult to reconstruct the temporal sequence of actions within the rapid changes in narration (as in "Cariboo Café"), but characters define themselves by their speech and thought in vivid and revealing ways (not only Latina protagonists such as Estrella in *Under the Feet of Jesus*, but Anglo characters such as the café owner in "Cariboo Café" as well), and in language that is often personal and poetic. Viramontes's focus on the larger social and cultural context that her characters inhabit resembles the viewpoint of many contemporary Latina writers: Viramontes's "Miss Clairol," for instance, is a harsh indictment of consumer culture and its underpinning of the American Dream for Latinos and it reminds readers of stories by Sandra Cisneros, such as her often-anthologized "Barbie-Q." As with most Latina writers (including poets like Cherrie Moraga and Lorna Dee Cervantes), Viramontes is never far from the social reality that Mexican Americans and other immigrant cultures have experienced in the twentieth century—not only the economic injustices, but also the discrimination and prejudice that often follow. On the other hand, her young women characters are capable of spiritual acts which carry her fiction to another, often mystical level. Her fiction has created a unique voice in American literature.

"THE CARIBOO CAFÉ"

First published: 1985 (collected in *The Moths, and Other Stories*, 1985)
Type of work: Short story

Illegal immigrants and other disoriented characters collide violently in a city diner.

"The Cariboo Café" is a powerful short work that is representative of many of Viramontes's fictional concerns and techniques. The story is complicated by a shifting point of view, which moves from past to present without explanation, and readers may have

some difficulty following the plot initially. However, this technique is exactly what Viramontes wants the reader to feel in order to experience the kind of displacement and alienation that her characters share. The first section of the three-part story is told from somewhere within six-year-old Sonya, who is supposed to be taking care of her younger brother, Macky, after she comes home from school. Sonya has lost the key to her apartment, however, and does not notice the loss until after she picks up Macky from Mrs. Avila, who watches him during the day. Sonya and her brother are immigrants, both their parents work to support the family in this adopted country, and the story portrays powerfully the dangers of this new life. Sonya decides to walk back to Mrs. Avila's to wait for her parents to return, but she only knows the route the other way, and she and her brother are easily lost in the garment district of Los Angeles. When the police stop a man on the street, Sonya and Macky—following their parents' iron rule—run and hide and are further lost in "a maze of alleys and dead ends, the long abandoned warehouses shadowing any light." Across some railroad tracks, Sonya sees "the zero-zero place" and drags Macky toward it.

Part 2 of the story moves to the perspective of the owner of the Cariboo Café where the story's action will take place, a run-down diner whose sign has been reduced to "the double zero" of its original name, a symbol which comes to stand for all the losses in the story. The café owner describes himself as "honest" and "fair," but readers hear the anger and bitterness in his voice. Like all the characters in this story, he is oppressed by the conditions of his life and blames the outcasts and misfits, the "scum" around him, with whom he shares more than he admits.

Beneath this recital of his woes, readers learn what has happened in his café. A woman has brought the two children into the place for something to eat. (Readers assume that the three met outside in the interstice between the first two parts of the story.) The owner does not like the watchful Sonya, but he is immediately attracted to her brother, whom he dubs "Short Order," and he brings hamburgers for them all. He later learns from the television news that the children have been reported missing by their parents, but he does nothing except drink beer and fall asleep.

The owner had a son himself, "JoJo," who was killed fifteen years before in Vietnam, and thus his attraction to Macky. A drug addict overdoses in the café bathroom the next morning, and the police swarm in—further reason, the owner explains, why he never told them about the woman and the missing children. A few hours later, three other illegal immigrants run into the café to hide from the immigration authorities in the bathroom, but the police find them. After they are arrested, the woman and the two children return to the café, and part 2 ends.

The last third of the story is narrated from several shifting perspectives. The first part comes from within the old woman who, it turns out, is herself an illegal alien from Central America who has come to the United States because her young son was taken by the military authorities. Part 3 is, if anything, murkier than the first two parts, because this narrator has become unhinged by recent events in her life and moves between past and present with no transitions. She clearly confuses Macky with her five-year-old son Geraldo (the same way, ironically, that the café owner confuses the boy with his dead son JoJo). She has left El Salvador because, "Without Geraldo, this is not my home; the earth beneath it, not my country," and now she sees Macky as a returned Geraldo. She takes the children back to her hotel room, bathes Macky, and watches both children sleep.

With no break (except a new paragraph), the narrative shifts back to the consciousness of the café owner. He cannot believe how the three have cleaned themselves up this morning, but he takes their orders and goes into the kitchen to prepare the meal. There, suddenly, "For the first time since JoJo's death, he's crying"—in anger for his son, for his wife Nell who apparently left after JoJo was killed, even for the old woman who is going to bring more trouble on him. "Children gotta be with their parents, family gotta be together, he thinks." At this point, he apparently calls the police.

Again with no noticeable break, the story shifts back to the deranged woman as two black-and-white police cruisers pull up to the café, and officers enter, guns drawn. She grabs Macky, thinking that she is reenacting the terror in her home country when Geraldo was taken. She throws hot coffee on the police, but the story ends when she hears

"something crunching like broken glass against my forehead and I am blinded by the liquid darkness." Still, she will not release Macky/Geraldo's hand; "you see, I'll never let go. Because we are going home. My son and I." Evidence in the beginning of part 2 indicates that she has been shot and killed.

The story has been anthologized often, including in one of the most popular college literary surveys titled *The Heath Anthology of American Literature*, and for good reason, as the story not only raises a number of relevant social issues but at the same time is representative of the concerns of many Latinos living in the United States. U.S. authorities are seen as threatening collaborators with those in Central America, immigration becomes a dangerous choice, and all the characters are victims of exploitation and oppression. Sonya and the old woman are the focus here, but even the male characters—Macky, the café owner, the drug user—share the oppression and alienation.

"THE MOTHS"

First published: 1985 (collected in *The Moths, and Other Stories,* 1985)
Type of work: Short story

A young Latina finds her own identity as she nurses her dying grandmother and holds her in the bathtub as the soul escapes.

"The Moths," the story that would become the title work in Viramontes's first collection of short fiction, is even more representative of her central concerns and develops more deeply her feminist themes. Again two women play central roles: an older woman and her fourteen-year-old granddaughter. The technique of the story is less complex than "The Cariboo Café," for the girl is the narrator throughout the short piece, and the structure of her story is fairly straightforward. However, the story is full of rich sensory detail (of sight, sound, smell, and touch), as well as the magic realism that infuses so much of Latin American fiction and that influences so many Latino and other writers.

Essentially this is a coming-of-age story, of a young girl who, in rebellion against her own patriarchal family, seeks comfort in the company of her grandmother and, in easing the grandmother through death, finds her own spiritual core. It is clear from the opening of the story that the girl is different, not "pretty or nice," she admits, nor even "respectful." She clashes with her family often, especially with the older sisters who try to bully her, and with a father who tries to make her fit a conventional mold, as by attending church. Her grandmother has requested her help, however, as the girl says in the story's first sentence, for Abuelita is dying. Traditional religion is no solace here: The girl goes into a local chapel but only feels "alone" there; in her Abuelita's house, by contrast, she feels "safe and guarded and not alone. Like God was supposed to make you feel." The girl's mother is hardly able to cope with her mother's imminent death, but the narrator rises to become the caretaker, bathing Abuelita and holding her hand for hours. When her grandmother dies, the girl cleans her body and then, in a mystical ritual of ablution, undresses herself and carries the naked body of the grandmother into a full bathtub and holds her. "There, there, Abuelita, I said, cradling her . . . ." At this point in the last paragraph of the story, the Magical Realism takes over:

> Then the moths came. Small gray ones that came from her soul and out through her mouth fluttering to light . . . . The bathroom was filled with moths, and for the first time in a long time I cried, rocking us, crying for her, for me, for Amá, the sobs emerging from the depths of anguish, the misery of feeling half-born. . . .

She is "half-born" but she is in the process of giving birth to herself through her devotion to her Abuelita. In a powerful and complex poetic metaphor (for the bath is also a kind of baptism), Viramontes has imagined the emergence of this young girl through her grandmother's death (as the moths emerge from Abuelita). It is a spiritual image which defies translation, but beneath the image, readers can sense Michaelangelo's "Pieta," the statue of the Virgin Mary holding the dead body of Christ, another image of death and transfiguration. (Viramontes has acknowledged the influence of W. Eugene Smith's famous 1972 *Life* magazine photograph, "Tomoko in the Bath," of a Japanese woman holding her child deformed by

industrial poisoning.) Viramontes's fiction is ripe with this kind of religious imagery. The girl and her grandmother have created a separate, alternative, and sacred family based on love, and Viramontes draws on Christian iconography to confirm it. In contrast to her own home (where her father abuses the women), the girl finds her true self here.

UNDER THE FEET OF JESUS

First published: 1995
Type of work: Novel

A young girl holds her fragmented and exploited family of migrant farmworkers family together after one of them is sickened by pesticides.

Under the Feet of Jesus is a novella telling a powerful story about California's migrant farmworkers. Viramontes has dedicated this work to her parents, who met while picking cotton, and to the memory of César Chávez, the revered leader of the United Farm Workers. The work centers on Estrella, a thirteen-year-old girl traveling with her family from job to job in California's central San Joaquin Valley. Estrella's father has abandoned the family of five children, and her mother is pregnant again by the seventy-three-year-old Perfecto Flores, who drives them to their new job in his aging car but dreams of getting away himself. The family moves into a dilapidated house near an aging barn, works picking grapes, and befriends two cousins, Alejo and Gumecindo. Estrella and Alejo have an immediate attraction, and the novella's drama builds when Alejo is sprayed by pesti-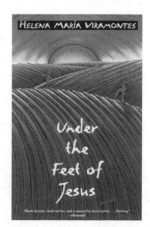cides one night while he and Gumecindo are stealing apples from a nearby orchard to sell. Alarmed by his worsening illness, the family drives him to a clinic, where a nurse takes their money, only to direct them to a nearby hospital. Knowing they need their money for gas, Estrella takes a crowbar from the car and shatters the nurse's glass-topped desk. It is Estrella's symbolic rite of passage; the nurse gives back their money, and Estrella and her family drive Alejo to the hospital. Estrella comes out of the hospital entrance to her waiting family, and Viramontes underlines the religious imagery she employs throughout the novella: "she stepped forward and the glass doors split open before her as if obeying her command. . . . Estrella parted the doors like a sea of glass and walked through . . . ."

When they return to their camp, Estrella climbs onto the roof of the old barn, and, in a continuation of this rich religious imagery, the shingles feel like "the serpent under the feet of Jesus" and Estrella stands on the roof "as immobile as an angel standing on the verge of faith." In this symbolism that Viramontes has taken from Christian iconography, Estrella has gained the strength, not to save Alejo, perhaps, but to hold her family together. She has become a star, like her name, and a savior.

Readers may be reminded here of another Latino coming-of-age classic, Rudolfo Anaya's *Bless Me, Ultima* (1972), and there are a number of similarities, including the mixed use of religious and folk images. *Under the Feet of Jesus* is even closer in subject and sympathy to John Steinbeck's *The Grapes of Wrath* (1939), however. Estrella's migrant farm family, Viramontes assures readers—as Steinbeck did with the migrant Joads a half century earlier in the same region—has its spiritual figures and power in spite of what society does to it, how it is pummeled and poisoned. Estrella's growth to young adulthood at the end of the novella, like much of the symbolism in Steinbeck's work (both books end in barns, for example), gives a power to the migrant family and its transformative potential. "If we don't take care of each other, who would take care of us?" her mother asks earlier. "We have to look out for our own."

SUMMARY

In the last decades of the twentieth century, Helena María Viramontes became one of a handful of Latina writers to voice the concerns of a growing Latino population. Her fiction deals with issues such as immigration and farm labor, but her particular focus is on the women in the Latino family and the ways in which they find their identity in spite of the oppressive institutions they inhabit. Viramontes, in short, is recognizable for the ways she merges her feminism with ethnic consciousness.

Her stories are not always easy to follow, but her language is poetic and powerful, and her message is unmistakable. In a Long Beach, California, Women Writers Conference in 1984, Viramontes read aloud the story she had just completed writing, "The Cariboo Café." She felt foolish because she could not stop crying as she read it, she later said, but when she finished she looked up and everyone in the room was crying as well.

David Peck

BIBLIOGRAPHY

By the Author

LONG FICTION:
Under the Feet of Jesus, 1995
Their Dogs Came with Them, 2000

SHORT FICTION:
The Moths, and Other Stories, 1985
"Miss Clairol," 1987
"Tears on My Pillow," 1992
"The Jumping Bean," 1993

NONFICTION:
"Nopalitos: The Making of Fiction," 1989
"Why I Write," 1995

EDITED TEXTS:

Chicana Creativity and Criticism: Charting New Frontiers in American Literature, 1987, revised 1996 (with María Herrera-Sobek)

Chicana (W)rites: On Word and Film, 1995 (with Herrera-Sobek)

About the Author

Carbonell, Ana Maria. "From Llorona to Gritona: Coatlicue in Feminist Tales by Viramontes and Cisneros." *MELUS* 24, no. 2 (Summer, 1999): 53-74.

Lawless, Cecilia. "Helena María Viramontes' Homing Devices in *Under the Feet of Jesus.*" In *Homemaking: Women Writers and the Politics and Poetics of Home,* edited by Catherine Wiley and Fiona R. Barnes. New York: Garland, 1996.

Rodriguez, Ana Patricia. "Refugees of the South: Central Americans in the U.S. Latino Imaginary." *American Literature* 73, no. 2 (June, 2001): 387-412.

Saldivar-Hull, Sonia. *Feminism on the Border: Chicana Gender Politics and Literature.* Berkeley: University of California Press, 2000.

_____. "Helena María Viramontes." In *Chicano Writers, Second Series.* Vol. 122 in *Dictionary of Literary Biography.* Detroit: Gale, 1992.

Viramontes, Helena Maria, and Maria Herrera-Sobek, eds. *Chicana Creativity and Criticism: New Frontiers in American Literature.* Rev. ed. Albuquerque: University of New Mexico Press, 1996.

_____. *Chicana (W)rites: On Word and Film.* Berkeley, Calif.: Third Woman Press, 1996.

DISCUSSION TOPICS

- What is the role that institutions, such as government, church, and family, play in the fiction of Helena María Viramontes?

- How do protagonists find their identity in the stories of Viramontes—through traditional assimilation into these institutions or through resistance and rebellion?

- What is coming-of-age like for Viramontes's young protagonists?

- What role does gender play in these stories? Social class? Ethnicity?

- What characterizes the structure and style of Viramontes's stories?

GERALD VIZENOR

Born: Minneapolis, Minnesota
October 22, 1934

Vizenor has preserved the folkways of the Chippewa Indians in poetry and prose, highlighting their exploitation by the dominant culture and simultaneously contributing to their tradition.

BIOGRAPHY

Gerald Robert Vizenor, son of Clement William and LaVerne Peterson Vizenor, is a crossblood member of the Chippewa tribe. Vizenor invented the term "crossblood" to refer to American Indians of mixed heritage, and he uses the term frequently in his writing.

Born in Minneapolis, the author had a difficult childhood. His father was murdered when Gerald was less than two years old and his step-father, Elmer Petesch, fell to his death in an elevator shaft one Christmas Eve as the boy, not yet ten, waited for him to come home to celebrate the holiday. His mother had deserted Petesch and her son. The boy, who survived by his wits, did not complete high school, but became the prototypical trickster who appears in much of his writing.

Vizenor attended New York University after completing three years of military service (1952-1955), part of it served in Japan. In the army, he earned his high school equivalency certificate. After one year at New York University, he transferred to the University of Minnesota, from which he received a bachelor's degree in 1960. He pursued graduate study there from 1962 until 1965.

In 1959, Vizenor married Judith Helen Horns, an instructor at the University of Minnesota; they were divorced in 1969. They had one son, Robert Thomas. Vizenor married Laura Jane Hall in 1981. Immediately before and during his years at the University of Minnesota, he was a group worker and later a corrections agent at penal institutions in Minnesota, where he confronted many of the social tensions that exist between Native American cultures and the dominant culture.

Vizenor was a staff writer for the *Minneapolis Tribune* from 1968 until 1970. His books sometimes include items he wrote for the newspaper. In 1971, Vizenor became a trainer of teachers for the Park Rapids public schools in Minnesota and taught at Lake Forest College and Bemidji State University.

In 1976, Vizenor became a lecturer at the University of California at Berkeley, where he remained until 1980, when he moved to the University of Minnesota as a professor of American Indian studies. By 1987, however, he had returned to the University of California system, this time to the Santa Cruz campus, as professor of literature and American studies. He served in this capacity for several years before returning to Berkeley as professor of ethnic studies.

Vizenor also taught at the University of Tianjin in China during part of 1983. Out of this experience grew his book *Griever: An American Monkey King in China* (1987). This teaching stint in post-Maoist China helped Vizenor understand better some of the Native American myths with which he had been raised.

Generally considered among the most productive and avant-garde of modern American Indian writers, Vizenor gained considerable respect within the sophisticated circles of the literary establishment. Although his writing is sometimes diffuse and difficult for mainstream American readers to comprehend, it remains true to its sources, which is Vizenor's fundamental aim.

Vizenor's screenplay for the short film *Harold of Orange* (1984) won him the Film-in-the-Cities National Award for screenwriting, and the picture was chosen as best film at the San Francisco American Indian Film Festival. Although his first novel, *Darkness in Saint Louis Bearheart* (1978), received meager attention and confounded many who read it, Vizenor's second novel, the more conventional *Griever*, was widely read and won both the American Book Award of the Before Columbus Foundation and the New York Fiction Collective Prize.

Vizenor's collection of stories *Wordarrows: Indians and Whites in the New Fur Trade* (1978) also helped to secure his literary reputation. Vizenor's *The Trickster of Liberty* (1988) is a biting satire about a huge monument conceived as a Native American counterpart to the Statue of Liberty but abandoned at crotch level. This book, which received widespread attention, struck out at so many of the social ills that afflict Native Americans that scarcely any major institution in the dominant culture escaped Vizenor's trenchant invective.

Dedicated to preserving American Indian culture through literature, Vizenor helped to found and is general editor of the American Indian Literature and Critical Studies series of the University of Oklahoma Press. The second offering in the series, Vizenor's *Dead Voices: Natural Agonies in the New World* (1992), reflects the animistic nature of Chippewa mythology and relates to similar animistic cross-currents in other mythologies.

ANALYSIS

Vizenor, a heterodox and demanding writer consistently produces work that is important for its social commentary (which is usually stinging), for its subtle use of story lines (which are sometimes so subtle as to be almost indiscernible), and for its linguistic invention (which is still in the formative stages). A postmodern, poststructuralist writer, Vizenor does not concentrate much attention on individual characters in his novels. Their motivations and development are secondary to Vizenor's other, more pressing artistic concerns, which have to do with the broader culture and with the conflict between the two major societies upon which his work focuses. The influence of his growing up on the White Earth Reservation in northern Minnesota is evident in most of his writing.

Readers probably absorb Vizenor's novels best if they read them in chronological order. This is partly because characters recur from novel to novel but also, more cogently, because occurrences from the earlier novels are alluded to meaningfully but with little edifying detail in the later novels. Not having read the earlier novels can limit one's comprehension of the later ones.

Having suggested a sequential reading, one can then say that in a novel such as *The Trickster of Liberty* it is not necessary to read the various episodes within the work sequentially. Many of the chapters are independent essays that can be read in any order without reducing the reader's comprehension and appreciation of the work as a whole. These chapters fall within a narrative frame of prologue and epilogue, but the structure reflects a non-Western mind-set, which the author consciously strives to depict.

The American Indian frame of reference is a bewildering one for most members of the dominant culture. Such readers struggle with Vizenor's books until they begin to understand Vizenor conceptually. He does not aim to write Native American stories adapted to the sensibilities of Anglo culture; rather, he attempts to be true to the culture he is depicting and from which he sprang.

Vizenor is not the sort of literary purist who confines his writing to the oral sources through which so much Native American culture has been transmitted and preserved. He uses his extensive literary background to draw upon sources from many ages and from many cultures as he develops his stories. He does so unabashedly and without apology. His writing is much more than a mere extension of the oral tradition of his forefathers.

In conventional American and European literature, actions are expected to result from specific, identifiable sources. In Vizenor's work, however, the causes are often neither articulated nor hinted at, a fact that can create problems for uninitiated readers who approach his novels. The literary reference points on which most readers rely are often absent or, at best, considerably distorted in Vizenor's writing, as he strives relentlessly and intelligently toward developing new modes of expression.

In his first novel, *Darkness in Saint Louis Bearheart*, Vizenor chooses an apocalyptic setting several decades in the future. This cautionary novel foresees the environmental destruction of the

United States and, with it, the complete economic collapse of society. Here Vizenor displays the extremes of irony of which he is capable and demonstrates as well his considerable gift for satire. He interweaves Native American culture with sociopolitical elements of the dominant society, producing a chilling effect. His biting social satire and keen sensitivity to the contradictions and absurdity of much of modern life—particularly when viewed from the Chippewa perspective—continues in his later novels and is most strident, perhaps, in *The Trickster of Liberty*, where the humor has an underlying element of sadness.

Vizenor does not avoid sexuality or violence in his writing and has been criticized for his concentration on both. He has confirmed in interviews that he includes violence and sexuality in his work because he believes it is unhealthy to suppress these aspects of the human experience. He claims that to deny violence is to create victims who can be controlled by the symbolic appearance of violence: People cannot fight things that they do not know.

In its presentation of violence, Vizenor's work does not depart significantly from much of the folk literature of the past—the tales of the Brothers Grimm, the Mother Goose rhymes, many of the stories in Greek and Roman mythology. In approaching Vizenor's novels, one must keep in mind the philosophical reasons for the violence that pervades the author's writing.

Judging from some of his public utterances, Vizenor has given considerable thought to developing new ways to work with the English language. He would like to break the bonds of grammatical convention, to imagine ways in which language can be pushed to new extremes. He has experimented with using an intermixture of tribal languages with the English in which he writes. He first attempted such experiments in his collection of stories *Wordarrows*, with results that left many readers confused and frustrated. In *Griever*, Vizenor introduced elements of Chinese into the mix with moderately successful results, perhaps because *Griever* is structurally a more conventional novel than any of his other work.

In *The Heirs of Columbus* (1991), Vizenor exercised his authorial prerogative to bend history to his own fictional ends, an approach that distressed some of his more literal readers and critics. Vizenor,

however, is indisputably daring, interesting, and enticing in everything he writes. If his literary experiments do not always succeed, he must nevertheless be admired for the originality of his attempts.

GRIEVER: AN AMERICAN MONKEY KING IN CHINA

First published: 1987
Type of work: Novel

The story of a Native American teacher, a trickster, who teaches in China.

In order to comprehend *Griever: An American Monkey King in China*, Western readers must consider Vizenor's statement that tragedy is a Western invention. Native American tales emphasize the comic with little overlapping toward the tragic. With this in mind, one can consider Griever de Hocus (as in Hokus-Pokus) the sort of trickster protagonist Vizenor set out to create.

Griever, a Native American teacher, himself a consummate trickster, finds himself teaching at Tianjin University in China, just as Vizenor, also a consummate trickster, did for a while in 1983. Griever considers himself a reincarnation of the legendary Chinese Monkey King. He has arrived in China at the precise moment that a surge toward Western-style capitalism and consumerism has been loosed upon the country, transforming it from a communistic to a capitalistic state.

Having little allegiance either to Western values or the communist state, Griever, in a series of lively adventures, has a light-hearted affair with the daughter of a government official. The affair takes an ominous turn when the young woman becomes pregnant and is murdered.

Vizenor, well schooled in ancient literature, employs his broad background to shape his story. He draws on a classical Chinese story, "Journey to the West," and a version of the story, "Monkey," to structure his own tale. In "Monkey," the title character is born when a huge boulder the gods have impregnated bursts open and releases him. He develops into a religious person who goes to India in quest of sacred writings. This story has been influential not only in Vizenor's writing but also in Ishmael Reed's *Reckless Eyeballing* (1986) and in Maxine Hong Kingston's *Tripmaster Monkey: His Fake Book* (1989).

Much of *Griever* involves dream sequences in which truths are revealed to Griever, although Vizenor does not always identify crucial actions in his novel as being dreams or reality. In one such sequence, which is obviously a product of a dream, Griever, his face painted to make him look like a monkey, performs acts of charity and heroism like freeing the chickens from a large market. In two other such acts, he frees a bird from its cage only to have it fly back in, and he frees prisoners on their way to execution from the truck carrying them to their doom only to have many of them refuse to flee.

As such acts prove futile, Griever, who has constructed a tiny, ultralight airplane, flies it across China with Kangmei, the sister of Griever's dead lover, a crossblood. This flight ends in a mixed-blood marriage between the two. Despite such fantastic turns, *Griever* is a satirical indictment of communist rule in China. It comments on everything from bound feet to governmentally sanctioned murders.

THE TRICKSTER OF LIBERTY: TRIBAL HEIRS TO A WILD BARONAGE

First published: 1988
Type of work: Novel

Using language daringly and intermixing the Chippewa language with English, Vizenor creates a stinging satire which the trickster controls.

Creating a framing device of prologue and epilogue, Vizenor presents vignettes, some stingingly satirical and many based on his experiences in the academic world. In the prologue, Vizenor's protagonist, Sergeant Alex Hobriser, a name that is clearly satirical, comments on Eastman Shicer, who is both a cultural anthropologist and an aerobics instructor. This juxtaposition of professions provides a clue of what will follow.

Vizenor warns that academic attempts to "harness the trickster in the best tribal narratives and to discover the code of comic behavior, hindered imagination and disheartened casual conversation." From this iconoclastic base, the author proceeds to use language so unique yet so reflective of Chippewa communicative patterns that it may bewilder Western readers.

The narrative, enclosed in the envelope pattern that creates its structural frame, consists of a selection of vignettes about the grandchildren of Novena Mae Ironmoccasin and Luster Browne and of memoirs by these two. Luster is a caring trickster who tells his tales more to amuse than to inform.

As in most of Vizenor's writing, characters from previous works recur. Griever de Hocus is a de facto member of Luster Browne's family, accorded family membership by decree rather than birth. The stories, imbued with a sense of the magical, the mythical, and the mystical, can be read in random order.

Vizenor sets the early vignettes in Bejing or Tianjin, where he taught during part of 1983. He shifts focus from China to Patronia, the imaginary baronetcy on the White Earth Reservation that Luster Browne received from President Theodore Roosevelt. This far-reaching baronetcy extends to an anthropological museum at the University of California at Berkeley.

Vizenor obviously is not constrained here by reality or by an attempt to depict actual or fictional events in ways that seem reasonable to Western readers. Luster's land holdings also include the Native American Indian Mixedblood Studies Department of the University of California, a take-off of the Department of Native American Studies with which Vizenor was affiliated at the University of California at Berkeley.

Vizenor uses the trickster to release the stereotypical, frozen mind-sets of Westerners, to free them from the linear thinking that they consider rationality. Vizenor's presentation of life is not structured in consistent, rational patterns, but that is not to imply that it is deficient any more than the world that an author such as Lewis Carroll created in *Through the Looking Glass, and What Alice Found There* (1872) is deficient. Rather, it is refreshing and liberating to readers who surrender themselves for transportation to a new universe.

CROSSBLOODS

First published: 1990
Type of work: Essays

This collection of essays and articles concentrates on the major issues that confront Native Americans in modern America.

This volume shows the range of Vizenor's work over a twenty-year span. The pieces included present him as the investigative reporter he was in the early 1970's and as the creative and academic writer he became. The collection is somewhat ragtag, but it is significant for showing the author's development.

The book is divided into two major sections. The first, "Crossblood Survivance," deals with the problems of those who, like Vizenor, are not pureblooded. These "crossbloods" constitute the largest group among those who claim to be Native Americans. To survive in their Native American environments, Vizenor says, these people sell out much that their forbears held sacred. They redefine treaties, reaching compromises that promise short-term gains. They are instrumental in bringing gambling to reservations, and they abrogate the hard-won fishing and hunting rights for which their ancestors fought.

With the money these compromises generate come the problems that accompany gambling and other easy-money schemes. Vizenor implies that American Indians are losing their selfhood or, more accurately, are selling out to the highest bidder. Tribal pride, once the hallmark of the reservation, is being subordinated to immediate gain.

"Crossbloods and the Chippewa," one of the more recent contributions to the volume, focuses compellingly on some of the major problems facing Indians. Some of these problems are caused by the Bureau of Indian Affairs, which exerts pressure to have tribal children attend federal boarding schools, effectively removing them from their families and their cultures. What is done in the name of education, Vizenor argues, is essentially a form of tribal genocide imposed by a paternalistic government that thinks it best to homogenize Native Americans, to draw them into the dominant culture at any cost.

The second half of this book consists largely of investigative articles written by Vizenor during his days as a journalist. "Capital Punishment," a detailed report of Thomas White Hawk's murder of a South Dakota jeweler, shows Vizenor at his journalistic high point. Vizenor might have updated this contribution to reflect the commutation of White Hawk's prison sentence and his reintroduction into the outside community.

Perhaps the most poignant of the essays in this book is "Bone Courts: The Natural Rights of Tribal Bones," in which Vizenor writes about a matter that he discusses in many of his books: the robbing of Indian grave sites in the name of archeology or anthropology. Vizenor cites Thomas Echo-Hawk, an attorney for the Native American Rights Fund, who contends that a Native American who desecrates a white person's grave is imprisoned but that a white person who desecrates a Native American burial mound wins a doctorate.

THE HEIRS OF COLUMBUS

First published: 1991
Type of work: Novel

Stone Columbus, who claims direct descent from Christopher Columbus, attempts to establish a sovereign Native American nation.

Although Vizenor and his publisher call *The Heirs of Columbus* a novel, it takes an act of faith to accept it as such. The book, an occasional piece written to mark the quincentenary of Christopher Columbus's arrival in the New World, is fanciful, taking great liberties with the facts that historians have unearthed. The concept of the book and the social problems it poses, which are similar to those on which Vizenor has often focused, are significant. Also important are his use of Native American mythology and his emphasis on the trickster tradition that is a fundamental part of Native American lore.

Stone Columbus is a talk-show host made rich by his floating bingo parlor on the Mississippi River—a riverboat destroyed by fire—whose activities were protected by treaties Stone's forefathers forged with the white invaders of their land. Stone claims direct lineage from Christopher Columbus, whom he declares to be a crossblood with Mayan ancestors who visited Europe before Columbus visited the New World.

Stone claims his lineage through Samana, a "hand talker," among the first people to greet Columbus when he landed in San Salvador. The explorer was burdened by an incredibly large, deformed penis, twisted in such a way that any sexual experience was excruciatingly painful to him, a fact substantiated by historians, some of whom Vizenor cites in his book. Samana, nevertheless, engages in intercourse with Columbus, who impregnates her. It is through that union that Stone claims his Columbian lineage.

Stone, financially secure and well known, attracts around him a band of followers with whom he hopes to establish a Native American nation in the northwestern United States. His followers hope that they can reproduce the healing genes of the Mayan people and use them to save the world from cataclysm. The symbol of Stone's new sovereignty is the half-completed Trickster of Liberty statue, the subject of Vizenor's earlier novel, *The Trickster of Liberty*. Standing in a harbor, visible from toe to crotch—which is where construction terminated—the statue becomes a bitter, mocking emblem of the straits in which Native Americans find themselves.

The great irony of *The Heirs of Columbus* is that the explorer sets in motion the forces that landed American Indians in their present state. Columbus does not emerge from this book as a real character, although Vizenor has researched his material well. Nor is Stone Columbus much more real than his ancestor; rather, he is the symbol of a genocide that a Eurocentric culture has visited upon an indigenous people.

DEAD VOICES: NATURAL AGONIES IN THE NEW WORLD

First published: 1992
Type of work: Novel

Players in a card game actually become the animals depicted on the cards they turn over ritualistically.

White men hear the "dead voices" to which Vizenor refers in his title, the voices of the printed word or carefully prepared lecture. These are the voices not of a ritualistic, storytelling tradition but the desiccated croakings of a literature apart from nature. In this novel, Vizenor focuses on American Indians who live in urban Oakland, California, rather than on a reservation.

Bagese, a shaman, engages in the tarotlike game of wanaki with the seemingly autobiographical narrator. The game extends from December, 1978, until December, 1979, with a prologue dated February, 1982, and an epilogue dated February, 1992. Vizenor has important things to say; he must say them even at the cost of losing some of his Eurocentric audience. His message becomes a moral imperative.

In wanaki, the participants, over an extended period, turn over cards bearing representations of bears, fleas, squirrels, mantises, crows, and beavers. When a card is turned, a participant becomes the creature on the card; accepting this demands a cognitive leap that people raised outside Native American traditions may not comfortably make. The tales that make up this novel—which is perhaps actually more a collection of short fables than a novel—are creation stories. They have to do with the quintessential forces of the universe, but Chippewa forces are far different from those considered quintessential in the Eurocentric world.

Bagese, a "tribal woman who was haunted by stones and mirrors," warns the narrator never to publish the stories in this collection or to reveal the location of her apartment in Oakland. At the end of the year-long wanaki meditation, she disappears without a trace.

Bagese considers the best listeners for her stories to be "shadows, animals, birds, and humans, because their shadows once shared the same stories." This suggestion of intergenerational continuity suggests a Native American concept of reincarnation. Like most of Vizenor's writing, *Dead Voices* is witty, infused with a pervasive humor that distinguishes the author's work from that of such other Native American writers as N. Scott Momaday and Sherman Alexie.

HOTLINE HEALERS: AN ALMOST BROWNE NOVEL

First published: 1997
Type of work: Novel

This novel satirizes modern culture and invokes many autobiographical elements as it unfolds.

"Almost Browne" is a play on words suggesting the crossbloodedness of the story's protagonist. Almost received his name because he was born in the back of a car that was almost within Minnesota's White Earth Indian Reservation. A crossblood, a term Vizenor invented, Almost is not quite Native American (brown), not quite white. He is the son of a native nun, Eternal Flame Browne, and a native priest, Father Mother Browne, whose trickster activities are motivated by the conviction that he is born to torment authority figures.

Like Vizenor, Almost is a trickster. Also like Vizenor, he teaches at the University of California at Berkeley as a member of the Transethic Situations Department. All goes well for him until the honor of delivering a commencement address befalls him. Almost, in full trickster form, gives a ribald speech that leaves students and faculty astounded.

Vizenor intersperses the novel with satirical chapters. In one such chapter, he has Almost establish a telephone call-in service that will connect troubled callers with Native American healers. This chapter is an obvious burlesque of the New Age and of the call-in psychic telephone services available at a price to troubled people.

In one of the novel's few flashbacks, Almost has an offer from President Richard Nixon to become vice president provided that he will organize a Na-

tive American invasion that will free Cuba from communist rule and will bring down its president, Fidel Castro. Vizenor uses this proposal to explain the eighteen-minute gap in the Watergate tapes that caused so much consternation during the hearings in the early 1970's and that forced Nixon's resignation from the presidency.

Vizenor loved taking pot shots at Nixon, whose attraction to Native Americans involved only his own political ambitions. In this novel, he takes similar pots shots at luminaries as diverse as Henry Louis Gates, Jr., the guru of black literary criticism whose seminal book *The Signifying Monkey* (1988) touches on some of Vizenor's interests; Ishmael Reed, the black poet and novelist, who also uses the monkey tradition in some of his writing; Gloria Steinem, the feminist activist, whose calls for gender equality shook the nation; and Claude Levi-Strauss, the celebrated French anthropologist and linguist.

Among the novel's more hilarious chapters is one that focuses on a typically silly faculty meeting of the English department at Oklahoma University. In this chapter, Vizenor satirizes several of the colleagues who annoy him and indirectly lauds the few whom he considered his supporters.

Although this novel includes a great many references to Vizenor's earlier writing, making it desirable for readers to be familiar with his earlier work, the novel can be read by first-time Vizenor readers for its sheer comic impact. Vizenor's own activities as a trickster throughout his life, particularly during his tormented early life following the death of his father and stepfather within a short period, inform this work with an authenticity that readers will immediately glean and appreciate.

SUMMARY

Vizenor's work captures the unique spirit of a people who hold a worldview closely attuned to animism. Many Eurocentric people find this worldview incomprehensible; talking stones and plants that react to human commands lie outside their conceptual contexts. Vizenor nevertheless has devoted his life to tapping into this worldview, bent on informing a broad reading public without debasing native materials upon which any legitimate Native American writing is necessarily predicated.

Vizenor tempers his presentations with a sardonic wit and a raucous humor, both of which help the uninitiated to relate to this literature. His standing as one of the foremost writers of haiku in English helps to explain the sharpness of imagery in much of his prose. Added to his broad and deep understanding of the American Indian themes and legends about which he writes is Vizenor's comprehensive understanding of conflict between Native American and the dominant culture. One of the most prolific—although not the best-known—Native American writers, Vizenor heads the avant-garde of this genre.

R. Baird Shuman

BIBLIOGRAPHY

By the Author

LONG FICTION:
Darkness in Saint Louis Bearheart, 1978, revised 1990 (as *Bearheart: The Heirship Chronicles*)
Griever: An American Monkey King in China, 1987
The Trickster of Liberty: Tribal Heirs to a Wild Baronage, 1988
The Heirs of Columbus, 1991
Dead Voices: Natural Agonies in the New World, 1992
Hotline Healers: An Almost Browne Novel, 1997
Chancers, 2000
Hiroshima Bugi: Atomu 57, 2003

SHORT FICTION:
Anishinabe Adisokan: Stories of the Ojibwa, 1974
Wordarrows: Indians and Whites in the New Fur Trade, 1978
Earthdivers: Tribal Narratives on Mixed Descent, 1981
Landfill Meditation: Crossblood Stories, 1991
Wordarrows: Native States of Literary Sovereignty, 2003 (originally pb. as *Wordarrows: Indians and Whites in the New Fur Trade*)

SCREENPLAY:
Harold of Orange, 1984

POETRY:
Matsushima: Pine Islands, 1984 (originally pb. as four separate volumes of haiku during the 1960's)

NONFICTION:
Thomas James White Hawk, 1968
The Everlasting Sky: New Voices from the People Named the Chippewa, 1972
Tribal Scenes and Ceremonies, 1976
Crossbloods: Bone Courts, Bingo, and Other Reports, 1990
Interior Landscapes: Autobiographical Myths and Metaphors, 1990
Manifest Manners: Postindian Warriors of Survivance, 1994
Fugitive Poses: Native American Indian Scenes of Absence and Presence, 1998
Postindian Conversations, 1999

DISCUSSION TOPICS

- Discuss Gerald Vizenor's use of names in the works that you have read.

- The stories that Vizenor writes are often set in either Minnesota or China. Does the author make significant connections in his writing between these two locales?

- To what effect does Vizenor employ academic settings in the stories that you have read?

- After reading some of Vizenor's stories, how would you now define the term "trickster"?

- Vizenor is very well read. Discuss some evidence in his stories that he consciously uses stories from past ages and literatures to illuminate some of his writing.

- Vizenor has said in interviews that tragedy is an invention of the West. Despite this theory, do you find evidence in any of his writing of elements of tragedy?

- What do you think Vizenor's feelings are toward modern technology?

EDITED TEXTS:

Summer in the Spring: Ojibwe Lyric Poems and Tribal Stories, 1981 (revised as *Summer in the Spring: Anishinaabe Lyric Poems and Stories,* 1993)

Native American Perspectives on Literature and History, 1992 (with Alan R. Velie)

Narrative Chance: Postmodern Discourse on Native American Indian Literatures, 1993

Native American Literature: A Brief Introduction and Anthology, 1995

MISCELLANEOUS:

The People Named the Chippewa: Narrative Histories, 1984

Shadow Distance: A Gerald Vizenor Reader, 1994

About the Author

Blaeser, Kimberly M. *Gerald Vizenor: Writing in the Oral Tradition.* Norman: University of Oklahoma Press, 1996.

Hochbruck, Wolfgang. "Breaking Away: The Novels of Gerald Vizenor." *World Literature Today* 66 (Spring, 1992): 274-278.

Isernhagen, Hartwig. *Momaday, Vizenor, Armstrong: Conversations on American-Indian Writing.* Norman: University of Oklahoma Press, 1999.

Lee, A. Robert, ed. *Loosening the Seams: Interpretations of Gerald Vizenor.* Bowling Green, Ohio: Bowling Green University Press, 2000.

Owens, Louis, ed. *Studies in American Indian Literatures* 9 (Spring, 1997). Special issue devoted to Vizenor.

Vizenor, Gerald. *Interior Landscapes: Autobiographical Myths and Metaphors.* Minneapolis: University of Minnesota Press, 1990.

KURT VONNEGUT

Born: Indianapolis, Indiana
November 11, 1922

Short-story writer and novelist Vonnegut is noted for his satiric humor, social commentary, frequent use of science fiction, and increasingly postmodern techniques.

© Jill Krementz

BIOGRAPHY

Kurt Vonnegut was born in Indianapolis, Indiana, on November 11, 1922, the son of Kurt and Edith Vonnegut. He was the youngest of three children. His ancestors had come from Germany in 1855. They were prosperous, originally as brewers and merchants, down to Kurt's grandfather and father, who were both architects, and they were prominent in the heavily German Indianapolis society. Then World War I left a residue of anti-German feeling in the United States and prohibitions on the use of the German language, dimming the family's pride and its cultural heritage. Prohibition brought an end to the brewing business, and the Great Depression of the 1930's left Vonnegut's father without work for essentially the rest of his life. Vonnegut writes frequently of the Depression and repeatedly portrays people who, like his father, are left feeling purposeless by loss of occupation.

At Shortridge High School, Vonnegut wrote for the *Shortridge Daily Echo*. The rigor of writing daily to deadlines helped shape his habits as a writer. In 1940, he went to Cornell University in Ithaca, New York, where he majored in biochemistry and wrote for the *Cornell Sun*. By January, 1943, Vonnegut was a private in the United States Army. In May of that year, his mother committed suicide, an event of which he would write as having left him a "legacy of suicide." Soon thereafter, the Army sent him to Europe, where he was captured and held as a prisoner

of war in Dresden, Germany. There he experienced the event that forms the basis of his novel *Slaughterhouse-Five* (1969), the firebombing that virtually destroyed Dresden on the night of February 13, 1945.

After discharge from the Army, Vonnegut undertook graduate studies in anthropology at the University of Chicago. He also married his former high school sweetheart, Jane Cox. While a student, he worked as a police reporter for the Chicago City News Bureau. Vonnegut left Chicago without a degree, although in 1971 his novel *Cat's Cradle* (1963) was accepted in lieu of a thesis, and he was awarded an M.A.

In 1947, Vonnegut moved to Schenectady, New York, where he worked as a public relations writer at the General Electric Research Laboratory. There he began writing fiction, and his first published short story, "Report on the Barnhouse Effect," appeared in *Collier's* in February, 1950. Encouraged by his success as a short-story writer, he resigned from General Electric and moved to Provincetown, Massachusetts, to devote himself full time to writing. He continued to publish in popular magazines such as *The Saturday Evening Post, Ladies' Home Journal, Collier's,* and *Cosmopolitan,* but he also placed stories in science-fiction journals such as *Galaxy* and *Fantasy and Science Fiction Magazine.* His first novel, *Player Piano* (1952), was reissued by Bantam in 1954 with the title *Utopia 14.* Largely because of his success with short stories, which often paid well, Vonnegut did not produce his second novel, *The Sirens of Titan* (1959), until seven years after *Player Piano.* Those first two novels, together with a number of the short stories, earned for Vonnegut identification as a science-fiction writer, a label with which he was not always happy, because that genre was disdained in many quarters. During this time, Vonnegut faced personal hardships. In October, 1957, his father died, and in 1958, his sister Alice was stricken with cancer. Days before her death, her husband, John Adams, was killed when his commuter train crashed from a bridge. After this double tragedy, Vonnegut adopted three of their four orphaned children, doubling the size of his family.

The 1960's began as difficult times for Vonnegut but then saw his gradual emergence to fame. Television dried up the magazine market for short stories, and he turned to the paperback book market, first publishing a collection of short stories called *Canary in a Cat House* (1961), then the novel *Mother Night* (1961). Neither achieved great sales. The next two novels, *Cat's Cradle* and *God Bless You, Mr. Rosewater* (1965), appeared in hardcover. In 1965, he went to teach at the Writers' Workshop at the University of Iowa, where he met other writers and critics who influenced him, particularly in encouraging him to enter his fiction more personally. This led to his adding a new and highly personal preface to the 1966 hardcover edition of *Mother Night*; in many of his subsequent works, such autobiographical introductions have become a popular feature.

In 1966 and 1967, Avon and Dell reissued all of his novels in paperback, and *Player Piano* and *Mother Night* were reprinted in hardcover. The coincidence of these events brought greater public attention to his work, and his fame began to build. A new collection of his short stories, *Welcome to the Monkey House*, appeared in 1968. Meanwhile, Vonnegut had won a Guggenheim Fellowship to revisit Dresden and research the event he had struggled to write about for years, the great air raid he had experienced. This led to *Slaughterhouse-Five*. The novel, and the film that followed it, brought Vonnegut broad popularity and financial security.

Success, however, brought its own difficulties. Having faced in fiction the event that had motivated so much of his writing, Vonnegut now struggled. He even considered abandoning the novel for other forms, writing the play *Happy Birthday, Wanda June* (1970). A compilation from his works appeared as a teleplay called *Between Time and Timbuktu* (1972). His marriage to Jane foundered, and he moved alone to New York City. At last, in 1973, he published another novel, *Breakfast of Champions*,

different in form from his previous work and illustrated with his own drawings. It drew mixed reviews but achieved excellent sales, with a first printing of a hundred thousand copies.

In 1974 came the publication of a collection of Vonnegut's essays, speeches, stories, and biography called *Wampeters, Foma, and Granfalloons (Opinions)*. Two more novels, *Slapstick* (1976) and *Jailbird* (1979), followed, in what Vonnegut has asserted was a difficult decade for him as a writer. He achieved a feeling of completion with *Slaughterhouse-Five*, he said, and found little that provided stimulation in the society of that period. By 1979, however, Vonnegut had remarried, to the photographer Jill Krementz, and adopted a baby daughter, Lily. Also in 1979, he had a return to the stage when his daughter Edith produced a musical adaptation of *God Bless You, Mr. Rosewater* in New York. He wrote the text of a children's Christmas story, *Sun Moon Star* (1980), illustrated by Ivan Chermayeff. *Palm Sunday: An Autobiographical Collage* (1981) was another collection, and it was followed by the novels *Deadeye Dick* (1982), *Galápagos* (1985), *Bluebeard* (1987), *Hocus Pocus* (1990), and *Timequake* (1997). Also, *Bagombo Snuff Box*, a collection of Vonnegut's early stories, was published in 1999, as was *God Bless You, Dr. Kevorkian*, a collection of fictional interviews, and *Like Shaking Hands with God: A Conversation About Writing*. Finally, a collection of essays, *A Man Without a Country*, was published in 2005.

Having become a major figure in the American literary establishment, Vonnegut has been much in demand as a speaker, frequently using the title "How to Get a Job Like Mine" to embark upon a rambling and highly entertaining evening something in the manner of Mark Twain. He has also been much in demand for articles in magazines and even for advertisements—an ironic echo of his beginnings as a public relations writer for General Electric.

ANALYSIS

Vonnegut has spoken of his experience of being in Dresden in 1945, when that city was firebombed and perhaps a hundred thousand lives were lost, as being an early motivation to write. Although it was not until his sixth novel, *Slaughterhouse-Five*, that he actually based a book on that experience, his first five novels point in that direction. Notably, there is an apocalyptic event involved in each of those novels. There is also the descent into an underground place—much as he went underground to survive Dresden—from which the protagonist emerges with a new view of the world. In this way, Vonnegut weaves together personal experience with the mythic pattern of descent (Jonah into the belly of the whale, Orpheus into the underworld) as prelude to rebirth, transformation, or new knowledge.

Other patterns discernible in Vonnegut's novels clearly draw on personal history. Vonnegut's father was a retiring person who, after his prolonged unemployment, became reclusive. The novels contain numerous father-son relationships in which the father is distant. Vonnegut's mother committed suicide, and he speaks frankly of his "legacy of suicide" and his proneness to depression. He repeatedly treats the themes of isolation, depression, mental illness, and suicide in his characters as manifestations of the stresses of society.

Vonnegut was very close to his sister Alice—in *Slapstick*, he speaks of her as the imaginary audience to whom he writes—and her death touched him deeply. Perhaps the early loss of the two women closest to him gave rise to a fear of entrusting love to women, as seen in his earlier fiction, in which women frequently withdraw, die, or betray. Certainly a triangle of two men and a woman, reflecting his family structure of the two brothers and the sister, is repeated.

Apart from Dresden, Vonnegut speaks of the Great Depression as being the other shaping event in his life. It gives rise to his interest in socioeconomic topics such as how to achieve full employment, how to distribute the wealth of the nation equitably, how to preserve a sense of individual worth in an automated system, and how to ensure that technology is applied with thought for human needs. Novels such as *God Bless You, Mr. Rosewater* and *Jailbird* make issues of economics and ethics their main themes, and these issues also make up one of the most persistent themes throughout Vonnegut's work.

Because his prewar education had a science emphasis, because his brother was a scientist, and because he worked for General Electric's Research Laboratories, his interest in science and technology was always considerable. In fact, he has said that he did not write science fiction but simply wrote about the world he saw, which was a techno-

logically sophisticated one. He is the product of a generation that saw science produce the atomic bomb and hoped-for breakthroughs such as the insecticide DDT prove poisonous. Science, technology, and the moral and ethical issues raised by their uses occupy a major place in Vonnegut's fiction. As early as his college years, Vonnegut wrote antiwar columns, and his subsequent works continued such antiwar sentiments as themes, most conspicuously in *Slaughterhouse-Five*.

Other recurrent motifs bear on social issues: how to overcome individual loneliness in an indifferent urban society; the treatment of African Americans, Native Americans, and women in American history; the plight of the homeless; and the inadequacy of the small nuclear family to deal with the stresses of modern life. Vonnegut describes himself as being like a shaman who responds to and comments on the flux of daily life. This description makes him sound solemn, whereas he is, for many, a comic writer. Much of his humor is satire, mocking the foibles of human behavior and ridiculing aspects of modern society. He sees himself in the tradition of previous satirists such as Voltaire, Jonathan Swift, and Twain.

Such mythic humor is often barbed. At other times, Vonnegut is farcical, finding humor in odd-sounding words, ludicrous situations, comical names, oddly proportioned bodies, and almost anything that might provoke laughter. It is laughter, he sees, that helps people through many testing moments in life. Growing up in the Depression, he saw how the comedy of such entertainers as Stan Laurel and Oliver Hardy, W. C. Fields, and Jack Benny boosted public morale. Vonnegut has even described his books as being like mosaics, where each tile is a separate little joke.

A characteristic of the slapstick comedians such as Laurel and Hardy whom Vonnegut applauds is that they "bargain in good faith with destiny." They are decent people who honestly try and who naïvely expect fair return. Vonnegut sees most people as being like that, which is one reason why there are few villains in his books. Romantic love, he argues, is overestimated, but what is important is treating other people with "common human decency," a phrase he often repeats. That also may account for the kindly tone that persists in Vonnegut's fiction, however sharp the satire.

Stylistically, Vonnegut's work suggests the influence of his early work in journalism. There is little flourish, elaborate description, or prolonged psychological characterization. His prose is compressed, functional, and curt. In the middle novels, notably *Cat's Cradle* and *Breakfast of Champions*, exaggeratedly short sentences, paragraphs, and chapters are conspicuous.

Vonnegut's mature fiction also displays characteristics associated with postmodernism, such as declaring its own fictionality, refusing to be consistent in form, and not trying to order a chaotic world. Such elements are seen in the chopped-up and shuffled chronology of *Slaughterhouse-Five*; Vonnegut's own appearance in *Breakfast of Champions* as the author, discussing what he will do next with the characters; his use of drawings and his mixing of history and fantasy in that same book; his basing the world of *Deadeye Dick* on the characters and setting of his previous work *Breakfast of Champions*; and the number game ending of *Hocus Pocus*, in which the reader must unravel a sequence of numerical puzzles to learn the answer to questions posed by the novel's narrator.

Such characteristics add up to a highly individualized style. This effect is heightened by the way in which Vonnegut enters many of his novels directly and personally. Often there is a character who seems partly autobiographical, standing for some aspect of Vonnegut: Billy Pilgrim, the soldier and prisoner of war in *Slaughterhouse-Five*, or the science-fiction writer Kilgore Trout, for example. Frequently there is also an autobiographical preface or introduction in which Vonnegut discusses his life and how it relates to the present story. Hence the reader may sense an unusually overt connection between the fiction and the author when reading Vonnegut's work.

MOTHER NIGHT

First published: 1961
Type of work: Novel

A former American double agent comes to suspect that he really was the Nazi he pretended to be.

Mother Night, Vonnegut's third novel, differs from its predecessors in having no emphasis on technol-

ogy or use of a fictional future. It is the first to be written with a first-person narrator, which deepens the characterization of the protagonist and intensifies the soul-searching, both on his part and the author's, that goes on in this novel. *Mother Night* is also the first of his novels to have an autobiographical introduction, added to the 1966 edition, in which Vonnegut ruminates about his own wartime experience and his being of German origin. He notes: "If I'd been born in Germany, I suppose I would have *been* a Nazi, bopping Jews and gypsies and Poles around, leaving boots sticking out of snowbanks, warming myself with my secretly virtuous insides. So it goes." That thought illustrates the moral that Vonnegut sees in this novel: "We are what we pretend to be, so we must be careful about what we pretend to be."

The pretense in this story concerns Howard Campbell, an American playwright living in Germany with a German wife as World War II breaks out. Campbell is persuaded to remain in Germany, cultivate the Nazis, and become an American agent. He becomes increasingly successful as a Nazi propagandist, although his broadcasts contain coded information vital to the Allies. At war's end he is spirited back to New York because his secret role cannot be revealed and he is generally thought to be a Nazi. He is hunted by vengeful patriots and by admiring neo-Nazis racists—and by the Israelis, to whom he eventually delivers himself.

Campbell's narrative is written in an Israeli prison as he searches himself for the answers to the question of whether he was really the Nazi he pretended to be or the secret spy, whether he did more to further Nazi crimes than he needed to, and what he would have done if the Germans had won. He had always believed that his propaganda was too ludicrous to believe and that he could remain detached from the horrors around him, yet the fact remained that many Nazis found him inspirational. What sustained Campbell during the war was the love of his actress wife, Helga Noth. They would retreat into a private world of love, defined by their big double bed, and become a separate "Nation of Two." That escape is denied when Helga disappears while entertaining German troops.

Clearly, this novel raises questions of the "good Germans" who opposed the Nazis but never spoke out against them or their atrocities, and it probably looks back to the Joseph McCarthy hearings of the early 1950's, when the American government was involved in a "witch-hunt" for suspected Communists. Almost certainly it reflects some doubts on Vonnegut's part about his former role as a public relations person at General Electric. It also prompts readers to ask themselves about those situations in which they may have believed they remained inwardly loyal to certain values while doing nothing publicly to oppose their violation. The novel takes a hard look at how people survive in such times as the Nazi reign, either believing themselves secretly aloof or escaping into narrow personal worlds, or by what Vonnegut calls "schizophrenia"—simply obliterating a part of their consciousness.

In the end, Campbell commits suicide, condemning himself for "crimes against myself." He is unable to unravel the pros and cons of his public role; what he does know is that he betrayed his conscience and misused both his love for Helga and his integrity as a writer. The issue of a writer's integrity comes up in several of Vonnegut's novels, starting with *Player Piano*. His writers frequently have to decide whether to compromise in order to achieve sales, for example, or determine what responsibility they bear for actions to which they may prompt their readers.

Campbell goes from being a romantic playwright dealing in pure fantasy to a propagandist contributing to hideous atrocities. *Mother Night* also extends the moral issue to include everyone, inasmuch as they may try to author parts of their lives, create illusions for themselves, and manipulate others like characters. *Mother Night*, especially with its added introduction, reflects Vonnegut's ruminations about Dresden and about the contradictions implicit in his being a German American fighting against Germans, who then is nearly killed by the Americans. It reflects his concerns about the Allies' destruction of historic, nonmilitary Dresden and thousands of civilian lives in the name of a noble cause. It also shows him moving to a first-person voice, which enables him to explore directly the inner doubts such issues raise. The novel is especially compelling because its questions are not easy to resolve. Howard Campbell's dilemma is no easier for the reader to resolve than it is for him. He remains one of Vonnegut's most complete characterizations, the more haunting because the reader may think, on a smaller scale, that "there, but for the grace of God, go I."

CAT'S CRADLE

First published: 1963
Type of work: Novel

A careless scientific genius leaves his children crystals that turn all the world's water into ice.

Cat's Cradle is narrated by "Jonah," or John, who originally intends to write a book about the atomic bombing of Hiroshima called "The Day the World Ended." The book he ends up writing is the present one, which could have the same title, although it is about a different apocalypse. John sets out to interview "Newt," the son of the late Dr. Felix Hoenikker, one of the "'Fathers' of the first atom bomb."

There are three Hoenikker children: Frank, the oldest; Angela, a tall musician; and the diminutive Newt. The father has left each of his children a vial of crystals of ice-nine, a compound that turns water to ice at room temperature. Angela has used hers to buy a "tom cat husband" who turns out to be a United States agent, Newt has turned over his to a tiny dancer from the Bolshoi Ballet who is a Soviet agent, and Frank uses his to gain his position as chief adviser to Papa Monzano, dictator of the island of San Lorenzo, where most of the plot is set.

Also on San Lorenzo is a fugitive preacher named Bokonon, founder of a religion called "Bokononism," which has been invented as a panacea for the population of an island so destitute that no economic system can possibly help them. Bokononism is outlawed but practiced by virtually everyone on the island. Its tenets are contained in the Books of Bokonon, which begin, "All of the true things I am about to tell you are shameless lies." Vonnegut, the former anthropology student, obviously enjoys inventing this religion, parodying the way religions are shaped to fit the needs of particular times, places, and populations. He also has fun inventing the language made up of the dialect of San Lorenzo and the vocabulary of Bokononism. To Bokononists, nations are "granfalloons," lies are "foma," and one's inevitable destiny is one's "Zah-mah-ki-bo."

Ultimately, Papa Monzano uses his ice-nine crystals to commit suicide, thus starting the chain reaction that turns all the world's water to ice and dooms humanity. Those islanders not already killed join Bokonon in suicide. Jonah plans to write his story of "The Day the World Ended" before he, too, takes ice-nine.

While *Cat's Cradle* takes a view of religions that is at once spoofing and anthropologically valid, it also comments on the nature of fiction. In so doing, it draws analogies between preachers and writers. Both use words to persuade audiences of the truth of the visions of the worlds they create. Both, this novel seems to say, may be like the maker of the cat's cradle, who tells the child it sees the cat and sees the cradle, where there is only string. Bokonon makes a religion of a fiction, just as the writer makes up a plausible world out of words. Bokonon, however, admits his religion is "shameless," if helpful, lies. In *Cat's Cradle*, Vonnegut essentially does the same, prefacing it with the epigraph "Nothing in this book is true" and beginning with a borrowing of Herman Melville's opening of *Moby Dick* (1851), possibly the most conspicuous sentence in American literature. He then spoofs serious fictional forms with 127 "chapters," each with its own joke title, made-up words, calypsos, and poems; a digressive, rambling plot; and a bizarre array of slapstick characters.

While *Cat's Cradle* typifies earlier Vonnegut with its ending in mass suicide and the end of the world, it is irresistibly comic and light in tone. In the previous three novels, Vonnegut had worked with recognizable forms: the dystopian novel in *Player Piano*, the space opera with *The Sirens of Titan*, and the confessional novel in *Mother Night*. *Cat's Cradle* is strikingly different and shows the author emerging with a style that is uniquely his own. The blend of serious social commentary and irreverent lampooning, of cynicism and compassion, of caricature figures and staccato style, would become Vonnegut's trademark.

GOD BLESS YOU, MR. ROSEWATER

First published: 1965
Type of work: Novel

An alcoholic philanthropist tries to prove that his obsession with the needy does not mean he is insane.

God Bless You, Mr. Rosewater: Or, Pearls Before Swine is the story of a multimillionaire who, traumatized by a wartime experience, tries to compensate with philanthropy and by treating the underprivileged with kindness. He seeks to enact the slogan, "God damn it, you've got to be kind," which some have seen as the essence of Vonnegut. This proves to be difficult and complicated, however, in a society that equates riches with merit and morality, and poverty with sloth and undeservingness. Eliot Rosewater's egalitarian efforts cause universal doubt about his sanity, drive his wife to a breakdown, infuriate his father to the point of obsession, and eventually lead to his own mental collapse.

Vonnegut writes that a sum of money, the Rosewater fortune, is the central character of the novel. The distribution of wealth and its social and psychological consequences is certainly the novel's central theme. One can see the impact on Vonnegut's life of the Great Depression behind this novel. Through prolonged unemployment, his father became purposeless and reclusive, while his mother could not live in the style in which she had been raised, and she was anguished to the point of suicide.

A second major theme of this book is neurosis. Almost every character suffers some degree of mental affliction, often accompanied or caused by physical malaise. The craziness contributes to both the poignancy that occurs in this novel and the humor that dominates it, but through the wacky characters and events, Vonnegut examines troubling social issues that he sees pervading America: excessive wealth alongside dire poverty; attitudes that make the poor despised, even by themselves; purposelessness, bred alike by unemployment and unearned riches; and the loneliness, depression, and suicidal complexes generated by such an economic and moral structure.

The trigger for Eliot's neurosis seems to be that in the war he killed some German soldiers who were actually noncombatant volunteer fire fighters. For Eliot, volunteer fire fighters are the perfect symbolic saviors. Without pay, they will go to the point of risking their own lives to help anyone, regardless of who or what they are. Eliot's philanthropy seems an effort to atone for his mistake and to become a kind of social fire fighter, rescuing those suffocating in the flames of the economic system. At first he tries giving money to charities, museums, and other causes but feels no satisfying consequences of his actions and sinks into alcoholism. He then moves back to Rosewater County, Indiana, his ancestral home, where he organizes fly hunts for the unemployed and dispenses aspirin, sympathy, and glasses of wine to the distraught. He becomes a slovenly slum saint, to the despair of his conservative, hygiene-obsessed senator father, while his wife, Sylvia, breaks down under Eliot's neglect of her and his obsession with the needy.

An avaricious attorney named Norman Mushari (first seen in *The Sirens of Titan*) tries to overturn Eliot's inheritance by proving him insane, but Eliot is rescued by Kilgore Trout, Vonnegut's shabby science-fiction writer who reappears in several novels and is perhaps his best-known character. Trout argues that Eliot is not insane—what he has done is to conduct a social experiment. "The problem is this," says Trout: "How to love people who have no use?" The answer, he says, is to find a way of "treasuring human beings because they are *human beings.*" That is what volunteer fire fighters do and what Eliot has tried to do in a society in which such a response is rare.

Vonnegut once said in an interview that the Dresden firebombing was less of an influence on him than the Great Depression. True or not, he is certainly deeply concerned with the kinds of socioeconomic issues stamped in his memory in those years; this novel emphasizes those issues (as does the later *Jailbird*). It offers no easy answers, but its implications seem almost as religious as political and may owe as much to the Sermon on the Mount as to the political or economic theories of Karl Marx or John Maynard Keynes. At the end, Eliot is echoing biblical language and might be seen as a kind of modern saint or Christ figure. The novel asks what this acquisitive age would make of someone who advocated giving everything to the poor. Where limitless greed is condoned and approved, a new Christ would seem crazy unless a crafty Trout could help out.

God Bless You, Mr. Rosewater has some of Vonnegut's most interestingly developed characters. The interactions between Eliot, his father, and his wife are psychologically complex. The rest of the cast are caricatures, but they are just what is needed for the novel's moral commentary—and for the broad comedy that stops it from becoming too didactic.

At the point that Eliot's mind snaps, he imagines that he sees Indianapolis consumed by the Dresden firestorm. Other than the references to fires and fire fighters, there is little other allusion to the apocalypse that is to dominate Vonnegut's next novel, *Slaughterhouse-Five*. Yet the story of a man who returns from the war haunted and changed by what he has seen parallels the author's experience and paves the way for his next protagonist, Billy Pilgrim.

SLAUGHTERHOUSE-FIVE

First published: 1969
Type of work: Novel

An American prisoner of war witnesses the firebombing of Dresden during World War II and time-travels to the planet Tralfamadore.

In full, the title, *Slaughterhouse-Five: Or, The Children's Crusade, a Duty-Dance with Death*, says much about Vonnegut's sixth novel. This is the novel in which Vonnegut confronts his traumatic experience of having been in Dresden when, on February 13, 1945, it was bombed by the Allies, producing a firestorm that virtually destroyed the city and killed perhaps 130,000 people. He survived the raid in the underground meat locker of a slaughterhouse, to spend the following days exhuming corpses from the ruins and cremating them. For him, Dresden becomes the symbol of the senseless horror of war, of humankind's self-destructive propensities, and of how events arbitrarily overrule the lives of individuals.

"The Children's Crusade" comes from the wife of a wartime buddy's having said, "You were just *babies* then!" Vonnegut reflects that they were indeed very young, and the soldiers in his novel are swept along as helplessly as the hapless children of the original medieval Children's Crusade, many of whom were, in fact, sold into slavery. "A Duty-Dance with Death" expresses Vonnegut's need to encounter in words his experience with death, to wrestle with its meaning, or rather, lack of meaning.

In *Slaughterhouse-Five*, the wartime experience is undergone by his protagonist, Billy Pilgrim. As his name implies, Billy is a kind of universal man-child going through the pilgrimage of life. In this way, Vonnegut is able to embody directly his personal experience in an autobiographical character, while universalizing its meaning through the use of an Everyman figure.

Similarly, Vonnegut speaks directly as himself in the first and last chapters and interjects periodically throughout, "That was I. That was me," permitting him both to express intensely personal emotions and to make detached editorial comment. He avails himself of the chance to be in the story and outside it, so that he can tell his personal experience and perhaps come to a catharsis. Yet Vonnegut does not entirely want to make sense of Dresden or to make his book an explanation. Dresden is, for him, an event without sense, and it becomes an emblem of the senseless and arbitrary in life. Those qualities are emphasized when the Germans shoot one of the American prisoners as

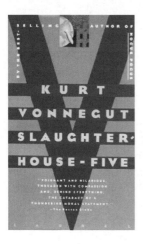

a looter when he picks up a teapot from among the ruins. Such strict and arbitrary justice in the midst of the carnage is the crowning irony of the novel.

Part of Vonnegut's resistance to ordering and rationalizing the events of his story is to chop them up, fragment them, and displace them chronologically. Billy Pilgrim becomes "unstuck in time," which means that his mind constantly shifts between times and places, as, then, does the novel. Because the story recounts Billy's postwar life up to his death, and his adventures, real or imagined, on the planet Tralfamadore, there is considerable disjunction. The reader is jerked from a childhood memory to the war years to a middle-aged Billy (an optometrist) to the preacher Pilgrim's death, and from Ilium, New York, to Dresden to Tralfamadore.

The style of the novel emphasizes its disjunction. Each of the ten short chapters is divided into short segments, each of three or four paragraphs, which may themselves be no more than a sentence long. A fragment of one scene succeeds a fragment of another, not ordered by time, place, or theme, but hurled together almost as a collage. Looked at

all together, however, the parts add up to a moving depiction replete with ethical implications and emotional impact, if shorn of the kind of direct moral summations Vonnegut supplies in *Mother Night.*

Slaughterhouse-Five sees the return of Kilgore Trout, Vonnegut's fictional science-fiction writer, and also of Eliot Rosewater and Howard Campbell, so that, in part, the novel builds upon preceding ones. This is not the novel's only metafictional characteristic; it mixes fact and fiction, history and fantasy. It includes quotations from actual documents by President Harry Truman and Air Marshal Sir Robert Saundby and from the fictional Trout and Campbell as if equally authentic. There are quotations of all kinds, from mildly off-color jokes to the Serenity Prayer, scattered throughout the book. There is the world of Tralfamadore, presented right alongside the historical events of World War II.

An often-noticed trait of this novel is its repetition of the phrase, "So it goes." This occurs every time anything or anyone dies. The repeated phrase has annoyed some readers, who see it as inappropriately flippant. Its repetition drums home the amount of death there is in this story and in the world, constantly calling attention to that, while at the same time reflecting a weary recognition that the author can do little to change things. Although *Slaughterhouse-Five* has earned an enduring reputation, much of its initial popularity was related to the climate of the times. In the late 1960's, protest of U.S. involvement in the Vietnam War was at its height. There was a large, receptive audience for an antiwar novel. The young, among whom Vonnegut was already popular, were intensely active politically. The legions of students who campaigned for antiwar presidential candidate Senator Eugene McCarthy in 1967 and 1968 were frequently called "the Children's Crusade" in the press, and that allusion in Vonnegut's subtitle was not missed by readers of the time. *Slaughterhouse-Five*, then, is remarkable in its ability to evoke pathos and laughter together, to simultaneously voice antiwar outrage and philosophical acceptance, and to combine the story of personal experience with a broader social commentary. The novel's unique form, which enables it to accomplish so much, is the culmination of Vonnegut's experiments with narrative technique in the five preceding novels.

SLAPSTICK

First published: 1976
Type of work: Novel

A giant neanderthaloid twin becomes president and creates artificial extended families to end Americans' loneliness.

In the prologue to *Slapstick: Or, Lonesome No More!* Vonnegut writes, "This is the closest I will ever come to writing an autobiography." That may seem surprising, given that the protagonist is a seven-foot, six-inch neanderthaloid with seven fingers on each hand and six nipples, but he clarifies his point by saying: "It is about what life *feels* like to me." He calls it "grotesque situational comedy," and that seems an apt description of the bizarre content of this novel. He also dedicates the novel to comedians Laurel and Hardy, who "did their best with every test." There is a lot of that spirit in the novel, too.

Wilbur Swain and his twin, Eliza, are born so abnormal that their parents send them to be raised in a distant, obscure mansion. While they learn to behave like idiots in public because that is expected of creatures who look like them, they are actually capable of great intelligence so long as they are together. Separated, they become dull. Yet separated they are for most of their lives. Wilbur goes on to become president of the United States on the campaign slogan "Lonesome No More!" (which is also the novel's subtitle). As president, Wilbur institutes a system of artificial extended families, wherein everyone is issued a new middle name by the government and thus inherits a whole set of new relatives of the same name. Wilbur, however, comes to preside over a country which, under the impact of variable gravity, the Albanian flu, and the "Green Death," is disintegrating into warring dukedoms and states. He ends his days living among the ruins of Manhattan.

The world of this novel is one of hyperbolic distortion. In that respect it is heightened slapstick, the world rendered in manic-depressive surrealism. Vonnegut has amused with invented religions before, but the Church of Jesus Christ the Kidnapped, whose believers constantly snap their heads to look over their shoulders in the hope of

seeing their abducted savior, seems peculiarly suited to this novel, in which so much of the humor is visual. Similarly, the Chinese experiments that vary gravity, so that on some days bridges collapse and elevator cables snap, while on others all men have erections and can toss a manhole cover like a discus, emulate the broad, often painful comedy of slapstick.

Vonnegut's "grotesque situational comedy" includes an impression of his personal life as well as the national. He speaks of how his sister Alice loved slapstick comedy and describes how, when she heard that her husband had been killed as she herself was dying of cancer, commented, "Slapstick." That situation, with both parents dying within days of each other in tragic circumstances and leaving four young children, is a good example of the kind of real-life grotesquerie that contributes to Vonnegut's vision in *Slapstick*. The close relationship of Eliza and Wilbur may be seen as a play on Vonnegut's closeness to Alice, whom he describes as still the imagined audience for most of his writing. Similarly, Wilbur's dependence on "tri-benzo-Deportamil" may be a slapstick rendition of the author's own use of antidepressant drugs at one point in his life.

"Lonesome No More!" is a slogan Vonnegut actually suggested that vice presidential candidate Sargent Shriver might use during the 1972 election campaign. Believing that the large, extended family of relatives living in proximity has virtually ceased to exist in America and that the small nuclear family is incapable of fulfilling the same role, Vonnegut has argued seriously that other kinds of social groupings are needed to support the individual. When he went to Biafra during the Nigerian civil war, he was most impressed with how tribal families operated, and this experience gave rise to the artificial extended families presented in *Slapstick*. The idea is treated humorously and shown with limitations, but the problem of individual isolation and loneliness within American society is one Vonnegut has always taken seriously.

His return to the theme of love in this novel is also familiar. Eliza's argument that saying "I love you" to someone leaves them no option but the obligatory "I love you, too" echoes those exchanges in the same words and the same tone in *Player Piano*. Romantic love—and here, sibling love becomes erotic—remains volatile, emotional, and undependable. Vonnegut again reasserts the superiority of "common human decency," of treating others with respect and consideration. There are other reiterations from earlier work. The name Bernard O'Hare—actually that of a wartime buddy—is used again, and Norman Mushari reappears. There is even the reappearance of a boring Paradise. These "in jokes" become part of the humor of the novel.

Some of the humor has aroused criticism of *Slapstick* as being cavalier with serious issues and carelessly dismissive. The repeated, interspersed uses of "Hi ho" and "And so on" particularly draw ire. They are the words of a first-person narrator, however, and one who is frequently high on "tribenzo-Deportamil" and having to describe cataclysmic events beyond his control. The phrases and the tone are as much an invocation of the slapstick films of Laurel and Hardy, to whom the book is dedicated, as are the caricatures and exaggerated actions. That tone changes in the ending, where Wilbur has died and a third-person narrator takes over. The account of his granddaughter Melody's journey to share Wilbur's old age is a touching and affirmative one. Her act is one of family love, and the story of how she is helped along the way by other people, not only those of her extended family, and by birds and animals, is a warmly affirmative one. Closing the novel with *"Das Ende"* is Vonnegut's gesture to the large, close-knit, German-speaking family that once existed in Indianapolis, as described in the prologue.

GALÁPAGOS

First published: 1985
Type of work: Novel

The last survivors of the human race escape to the Galápagos Islands and evolve over a million years into furry amphibians.

Galápagos is narrated from a future one million years hence by the ghost of Leon Trout, son of Vonnegut's frequently used character, science-fiction writer Kilgore Trout. Leon was beheaded while working as a shipbuilder, and his ghost inhabits a cruise ship bound for Guayaquil, Ecuador, to carry tourists to the Galápagos Islands.

While the ship is awaiting its maiden voyage, the world economic system breaks down under the burben of global debt, and World War III is triggered. Those events, however, which contain typical Vonnegut warnings about contemporary conditions, do not end the human race; what does is a corkscrew-like microorganism that destroys ovaries.

As order breaks down in the port of Guayaquil, ten people escape in the cruise ship. They reach Santa Rosalia, one of the Galápagos Islands. At this point there is only one male, the ship's captain, and the women include an Indianapolis schoolteacher who eventually becomes the mother of the new human race. She transmits the captain's sperm to six Indian girls and impregnates them. The male line survives in the baby of a Japanese woman. He is born furry as the result of a genetic mutation caused when his grandparents were caught in the atom bombing of Hiroshima.

Over the succeeding million years, as the descendants of these original survivors reproduce, they adapt to their largely marine life by developing flippers, instead of hands and feet, and smaller, streamlined heads. They also inherit the fur of the Japanese mutant ancestor. Thus they evolve as seal-like "fisherfolk."

Charles Darwin and evolutionary theory are major themes in this book, and evolution is even reflected in the form of *Galápagos*. The novel has fifty-two chapters, as the year has weeks. The first part of the book is called "The Thing Was," capturing the colloquial way to refer to complications in a narrative as well as alluding to the original form of the human animal. The second part's title is "And the Thing Became," recounting the adaptation to aquatic life. Having *Galápagos* narrated by the son of Vonnegut's fictional alter ego, Kilgore Trout, makes it seem as if the novel itself has evolved out of Vonnegut's own earlier fiction.

Vonnegut recognizes that evolutionary theory is often misunderstood and that it leaves unanswered questions. He points out that evolution is not simply an inevitable progression of constant improvement. Contingency often shapes the course of events, such as the occurrence of a new virus that destroys female reproductive organs or the mutation caused by the Hiroshima bomb. Moreover, evolution is not always toward the better. For example, in the Irish elk, the deer family's defense mechanism of antlers was taken to such an extreme that it ultimately led to the extinction of the species.

Some of these ideas Vonnegut treats with typical humor. The convoluted development of the first part of the book, with its many characters, digressions, histories, and coincidences, creates its own kind of whimsical evolution into the main plot concerning the few who reach Santa Rosalia. The short chapters, chopped into subsections, end with suspenseful jokes. It is as if *Galápagos* itself, like evolution, is shaped not by grand design but by chance and coincidence.

One of the central ideas, comical but pointed, that the novel presents is that the huge human brain has become as burdensome an evolutionary step for humans as the Irish elk's huge antlers were. Humans' brains, with their capacity to invent, imagine, and hold opinions, have become their greatest enemies. One problem, Vonnegut posits, is that it has proved impossible for humans to imagine something that could happen without trying to make it happen, often with disastrous results. Similarly, opinions, not necessarily grounded in fact, become so firmly held that they drive humans to irrational acts. In *Galápagos*, then, Vonnegut reverses the general supposition that as people evolve to higher intelligence they improve. His fisherfolk develop flippers and lose the manual dexterity to make tools or weapons, and as their skulls shrink, their brains diminish, and they become harmonious and content.

Implicit in *Galápagos*, despite its humor, are some grim warnings. Among the most obvious are warnings about the world economic situation, with its inequalities resulting in massive starvation and in debts that threaten the monetary system. There are warnings about the possibilities of accidental war, of conflict over "opinions," and of new viruses made dangerous by environmental damage to immune systems. Behind all these ideas, though, looms the overriding danger of what humans are themselves, here presented as the danger posed by their oversized brains.

Galápagos is dominated by a positive tone, however, not only because of its humor but because it ultimately is affirmative about human decency. It is notably affirmative about women. While many of the men are impaired or incompetent, the women, particularly the central mother figure, Mary Hepburn, cope, survive, and nurture. Even the ghostly narrator rejects his father's cynicism and his own tormented past to become reconciled. The epigraph, borrowed from Anne Frank, is appropriate: "In spite of everything, I still believe people are really good at heart."

"HARRISON BERGERON"

First published: 1961 (collected in *Welcome to the Monkey House*, 1968)
Type of work: Short story

A married couple epitomize loss of fundamental humanity by witnessing and failing to respond to the murder of their exceptionally gifted son.

First published in *Fantasy and Science Fiction Magazine*, "Harrison Bergeron" is set in 2081, when equality has finally been achieved by elimination of the exceptionally gifted or by controlling them via technology. Such methods of control include mental handicap radios in ears which emit ghastly sounds to interrupt and control thought, masks which conceal exceptionally attractive faces and clothing which does the same for bodies, and weights that the physically strong carry at all times, like handicaps for horses. However, George and Hazel Bergeron's son, Harrison, is so exceptionally gifted physically, artistically, and mentally that the HG (Handicapper General) men come and take him away. Harrison escapes, though, and enters a television station where a dance program is being broadcast (which his parents are watching), throws off his physical handicaps, declares himself emperor, and encourages one exceptionally beautiful (and onerously handicapped) female dancer to throw off her handicaps and dance with him and be his empress. During the dance by these two beautiful and gifted people, and at the moment of their kiss, the dancers are shot dead by the Handicapper General. Harrison's parents, too handicapped and controlled to be able to focus clearly on or understand or respond to the death of their son, simply continue watching television, although George's ear radio noises are drastically increased to impede comprehension and reaction, and Hazel cries because of "something real sad on television." She just cannot remember what it was.

"Harrison Bergeron" effectively renders Vonnegut's vision of the unethical, misguided use of scientific and technological advancements in the future, a frequent theme in his later fiction, such as in *Cat's Cradle* in 1963. Under the guise of an admirable equality, those in power in 2081 use technology to maintain their power and the status quo by controlling, by force if necessary, the evolutionary progression of human abilities. Vonnegut would return to this theme of evolutionary interference in *Galápagos* in 1985, with more subtle examination of the ambiguous permutations. Although a creative and ironically humorous story in which the laughter is, as always in Vonnegut, a painful response to an absurd world, "Harrison Bergeron" lacks the originality and technical creativity of Vonnegut's best fiction, particularly since Aldous Huxley had more realistically and effectively dramatized the same themes and ideas in *Brave New World* (1932) nearly thirty years earlier.

BLUEBEARD

First published: 1987
Type of work: Novel

An aging painter meditates upon his ancestry, his war experiences, his problematic relationships, and his artistic failures, and achieves catharsis by his final artistic endeavor.

Bluebeard is Kurt Vonnegut's most extensive examination of artistic endeavor, namely painting by abstract expressionists, but in reality all artistic activity, including literature. Although precursors of this artistic meditation are elements of earlier works, including the questioning of the truth-telling capacity of literature in *Cat's Cradle*, nowhere else has Vonnegut directly faced the fundamental issue of whether art at its highest is representational of reality or is a self-enclosed, nonrepresentational medium for presentation of the artist's emotions. The narrator, Rabo Karabekian, an elderly artist of Armenian ancestry who began as a copyist but becomes an abstract expressionist, can copy anything but is frustrated by the criticism that his representational painting lacks "soul," or emotional profun-

dity. Then, his work as an abstract expressionist is condemned as so subjectively nonrepresentational as to be meaningless. His abstract expressionist work is also jeopardized by modern technology, as he uses a paint, Sateen Dura-Luxe, which is supposedly a significant improvement on earlier paints but which literally disintegrates after a few months, sabotaging virtually all of Karabekian's expressionist paintings, including a huge one on public display in New York City. Thus, again, Vonnegut satirizes the blind faith of the modern world in technology, a theme throughout his fiction.

Humiliated by his failings as both representational painter and abstract expressionist and motivated by the suicide of abstract expressionist friends and by the death of his wife, like several Vonnegut narrators, Karabekian emerges from his personal underground of tragic loss of loved ones and personal failure to make a final, successful attempt at art. Realizing that the greatest painting, and by implication literature, is representational of and commentary on life, the narrator turns to his most powerful life experience, the view of the valley where he and other World War II prisoners were taken at the end of the war and released. With thousands of people present, of virtually all nationalities, conditions of health, occupations, and mentalities, and including even remnants of Hitler's armies with their killing machines, the sight is unforgettable, reflecting the customary Vonnegut premise that war and its aftermath are the fundamental, defining realities of human existence. Karabekian renders that scene on the panels of his largest failed abstract expressionist painting, and it is a success, the catharsis that reunifies his life and art. As with the paintings of little girls in his house, representing human beauty prior to the pain and horror of real life and which cause visitors to leave saying "no more war," the greatest art, as Karabekian realizes and as Vonnegut believes and practices in his fiction, is art that shows the tragedy, the pain, of war and related destructive human actions, as well as art that shows the courage, humor, and kindness that are the only means to combat the horror. Vonnegut's fiction reflects a lifetime devoted to showing the horror and encouraging resistance to it, and *Bluebeard* is a powerful addition to that tragic depiction and lifetime of comic resistance, a novel worthy to be counted among Vonnegut's best work.

HOCUS POCUS

First published: 1990
Type of work: Novel

A former Vietnam military officer, college and prison teacher, and now jailbird contemplates his disastrous life and a schizophrenic, disintegrating America in the near future.

Hocus Pocus is perhaps Vonnegut's grimmest and most powerful indictment of Americans and American life, indicative of why fifteen years later he would title his collection of essays *A Man Without a Country*. This novel is set in 2001, enabling Vonnegut a decade earlier to project his vision of what America would soon become. What he sees is revealed by his first-person narrator, his typical war veteran; this time, it is a veteran of the Vietnam War—fittingly for this novel, America's most humiliating military venture. The narrator is presented as the last person to leave by helicopter from the top of the U.S. embassy in Saigon, and the experience enables him to emerge from this personal underground a changed man, convinced that all pro-war propaganda is "hocus pocus," of which he was an admitted master as a military spokesman himself and dedicated to trying to tell the truth, without self-serving deception.

What America has become in the near future is a schizophrenic, disintegrating world, symbolized both by the college for the wealthy but learning-disabled where the narrator finds postwar employment and by the prison for impoverished and uneducated minorities directly across a lake from the college. The U.S. Supreme Court has reinstituted segregation, at least in prisons, and while the number of learning-disabled wealthy students has remained a constant number at three hundred, the prison population has grown constantly, to ten thousand. Also, America is basically under absentee ownership, having been sold bit by bit to foreign nations and individuals by wealthy Americans who "take the money and run," unwilling to be responsible for America's future. Race- and class-based uprisings are prevalent, including in the South Bronx, and gasoline is so scarce and expensive that it is to be found only in semisecret locations.

In his role as teacher of physics, the narrator attempts to expose the overweening pride and abysmal ignorance that have generated much of the disintegration of America, both represented by the failed perpetual motion machine created by the college's founder and prominently placed in the foyer of the college's library, proof of blind faith in technological solutions by humans who are, in the words of the narrator's dead war buddy, "1,000 times dumber and meaner than they think they are." The narrator's efforts only get him fired as a college teacher, though, with the firing orchestrated by a college trustee who is a conservative television talk-show host and whose daughter uses the technology of voice recording to take the narrator's statements out of context and thereby convict him of anti-American teaching. As the narrator notes, a history professor at the college says much worse but only about the distant past; however, the narrator, Eugene Debs Hartke (aptly named), talks about America's present inequalities, injustices, and delusional destructiveness.

After being fired, the narrator is hired by the prison, whose director is a Hiroshima survivor by the mere chance that he went into a ditch to retrieve a ball when the explosion occurred, with all around him incinerated, reflecting Vonnegut's belief that time and chance are the prime movers of the universe. Inevitably in a race- and class-divided world, a prison break occurs, and the minority prisoners (who are not rehabilitated but only watch television reruns) attack the college and kill the faculty and staff who are present (the students are away on vacation) and are themselves killed when enough American military finally arrive from the Bronx and other intracountry battle fronts to address the prison revolt. Then, since he is Caucasian and educated, and under the assumption that no members of a minority could have planned the break, the narrator is arrested, charged with being the ringleader, and imprisoned, from which location and viewpoint he putatively authors the novel.

Unlike in *Galápagos* and *Bluebeard*, there is very little optimism in *Hocus Pocus*, aside from the narrator's humane insight and understanding. The novel conveys Vonnegut's conviction that humans will ultimately destroy themselves, probably sooner than they think, given their arrogance and ignorance and self-deception—their hocus pocus. Vonnegut has admitted that he struggled mightily in writing one more novel, *Timequake*, and one reason is probably because he subconsciously realized that he said it all in *Hocus Pocus* and said it incredibly well. *Hocus Pocus* is the powerful culmination of Vonnegut's fiction.

SUMMARY

Vonnegut has likened his role as writer in society to that of the canaries in the coal mines of old—to give alarm of danger. He has also spoken of himself as a shaman, responding to and speaking about what goes on in society. Yet he remains a comic novelist. His novels, as a result, are full of warning, social commentary, and, frequently, moral judgment, but in their humor and compassion escape heavy didacticism. Vonnegut has evolved a distinctive style. His often fragmented, tragicomic renderings have struck a chord in the readers of his time.

Peter J. Reed; updated by John L. Grigsby

BIBLIOGRAPHY

By the Author

LONG FICTION:
Player Piano, 1952
The Sirens of Titan, 1959
Mother Night, 1961
Cat's Cradle, 1963
God Bless You, Mr. Rosewater: Or, Pearls Before Swine, 1965
Slaughterhouse-Five: Or, The Children's Crusade, a Duty-Dance with Death, 1969
Breakfast of Champions: Or, Goodbye Blue Monday, 1973
Slapstick: Or, Lonesome No More!, 1976
Jailbird, 1979
Deadeye Dick, 1982
Galápagos, 1985
Bluebeard, 1987
Hocus Pocus, 1990
Timequake, 1997
God Bless You, Dr. Kevorkian, 1999 (novella)

SHORT FICTION:
Canary in a Cat House, 1961
Welcome to the Monkey House, 1968
Bagombo Snuff Box: Uncollected Short Fiction, 1999

DRAMA:
Penelope, pr. 1960, revised pr., pb. 1970 (as *Happy Birthday, Wanda June*)

TELEPLAY:
Between Time and Timbuktu: Or, Prometheus-5, a Space Fantasy, 1972

NONFICTION:
Wampeters, Foma, and Granfalloons (Opinions), 1974
Palm Sunday: An Autobiographical Collage, 1981
Conversations with Kurt Vonnegut, 1988
Fates Worse than Death: An Autobiographical Collage of the 1980's, 1991

Like Shaking Hands with God: A Conversation About Writing, 1999 (with Lee Stringer)
A Man Without a Country, 2005

CHILDREN'S LITERATURE:
Sun Moon Star, 1980 (with Ivan Chermayeff)

About the Author
Bloom, Harold, ed. *Kurt Vonnegut.* Philadelphia: Chelsea House, 2000.
Boon, Kevin Alexander, ed. *At Millennium's End: New Essays on the Work of Kurt Vonnegut.* Albany: State University of New York Press, 2001.
Broer, Lawrence. *Sanity Plea: Schizophrenia in the Novels of Kurt Vonnegut.* Ann Arbor: University of Michigan Press, 1989.
Giannone, Richard. *Vonnegut: A Preface to His Novels.* Port Washington, N.Y.: Kennikat Press, 1977.
Klinkowitz, Jerome. *Kurt Vonnegut.* London: Methuen, 1982.
_____. *"Slaughterhouse-Five": Reforming the Novel and the World.* Boston: Twayne, 1990.
_____. *The Vonnegut Effect.* Columbia: University of South Carolina Press, 2004.
_____. *Vonnegut in Fact: The Public Spokesmanship of Personal Fiction.* Columbia: University of South Carolina Press, 1998.
Klinkowitz, Jerome, and Donald L. Lawler, eds. *Vonnegut in America.* New York: Delacorte/Seymour Lawrence, 1977.
Klinkowitz, Jerome, and John Sorner, eds. *The Vonnegut Statement.* New York: Delacorte/Seymour Lawrence, 1973.
Lundquist, James. *Kurt Vonnegut.* New York: Frederick Ungar, 1976.
Merrill, Robert, ed. *Critical Essays on Kurt Vonnegut.* Boston: G. K. Hall, 1990.
Morse, Donald E. *The Novels of Kurt Vonnegut: Imagining Being an American.* Westport, Conn.: Praeger, 2003.
Pieratt, Asa B., Julie Huffman-Klinkowitz, and Jerome Klinkowitz. *Kurt Vonnegut: A Comprehensive Bibliography.* 2d ed. Hamden, Conn.: Shoe String Press, 1987.
Reed, Peter J. *Kurt Vonnegut, Jr.* New York: Thomas Y. Crowell, 1976.
Schatt, Stanley. *Kurt Vonnegut, Jr.* Boston: Twayne, 1976.
Tomedi, John. *Kurt Vonnegut.* Philadelphia: Chelsea House, 2004.

DISCUSSION TOPICS

- In *Player Piano,* is technological advancement part of the problem, part of the solution, or both? Explain what the novel indicates about Kurt Vonnegut's likely attitude toward modern technology.

- In *Mother Night,* what does Vonnegut show about how and why human beings are prone to self-deception? Does he offer any ideas about how self-deception can be minimized, if not avoided?

- How does Billy Pilgrim's being "unstuck in time" affect how the novel *Slaughterhouse-Five* is structured or constructed? In which of Vonnegut's other novels is this "unstuck in time" technique utilized? Is there a valid psychological basis for this technique? If so, what is it?

- What view of religion is reflected in *Cat's Cradle*?

- How is the structural technique or characterization device of descent into a psychological underground and then emergence with a new, and better, understanding of the world involved in three of Vonnegut's novels? In each instance, what has the main character learned by the experience?

- Based upon *Bluebeard,* what makes a great painting and, by implication, a great novel? How does *Bluebeard* itself embody or fail to embody the qualities of great literature?

- Based upon *Hocus Pocus,* what are Vonnegut's beliefs about the Vietnam War, and about war in general?

- Did the main character in *Hocus Pocus* deserve to be fired as a teacher? Justify your opinion with specifics from the novel, and with explanation of what personal qualities and intellectual abilities a good teacher possesses.

Courtesy, *The Eatonton Messenger*

ALICE WALKER

Born: Eatonton, Georgia
February 9, 1944

Accomplished in several literary genres, Walker has achieved most recognition for her novels, especially her Pulitzer Prize-winning novel The Color Purple *and her innovative, challenging* The Temple of My Familiar.

BIOGRAPHY

Alice Walker was born on February 9, 1944, in Eatonton, Georgia, the eighth and youngest child of Willie Lee and Minnie Grant Walker. Eatonton was a small, poor town, and the Walkers made their living by sharecropping cotton, a way of life that earned the family about three hundred dollars a year. Walker learned early the oppression of economic deprivation coupled with the southern reality of white domination.

Despite adverse circumstances, Walker developed into a pretty, precocious child who excelled in school. Her self-image received a life-changing blow, however, when she was eight years old and her brother accidentally shot her in the right eye with a BB gun during a game of cowboys and Indians. Although rendered blind in that eye, Walker experienced more emotional trauma from the wound's disfiguring scar tissue. Her vivaciousness gave way to reticence as society responded to her scarred eye. Accustomed to admiration, Walker began to retreat emotionally and physically. She hung her head; although she turned to books for solace, she began to do poorly in school. She wrote her first poetry during this difficult period.

Six years after the accident, Walker visited her brother in Boston. He took her to a local hospital, where the hated scar tissue was removed. Walker's head came up, she made friends, and she became high school prom queen and class valedictorian. Although many years would pass before Walker could make peace with the injury, she ultimately came to attribute much of her inner vision to the suffering it caused. The experience of overcoming physical deformity, in some cases by its acceptance, is reflected in Walker's art.

Walker's education continued when she received a scholarship to attend Spelman College, a black women's school in Atlanta. Her mother gave her three practical gifts to take with her—a suitcase, a sewing machine, and a typewriter—all suggestive of a liberated, self-sufficient, artistic life. Walker's Spelman experience juxtaposed freedom with restriction. Through her studies, she discovered the intellectual liberation inherent in education. Simultaneously, she became active in the Civil Rights movement, which was particularly concentrated around Atlanta during her two years (1961-1963) at the college. Spelman advocated turning out "proper" young women and discouraged political activism among its students. The school's attitudes and the students' frustration with them are suggested by Meridian Hill's experiences at the fictional Saxon College in Walker's novel *Meridian* (1976).

Having had a taste of the larger world and desiring a less restricted involvement in it, Walker accepted a scholarship to Sarah Lawrence College, a prestigious women's college in Bronxville, New York. There, another traumatic event in her life led to a positive result. Between her junior and senior years, Walker became pregnant. Having entertained thoughts of suicide during her years of disfigurement, she once again contemplated taking her life and kept a razor blade under her pillow. Her immediate anguish was relieved when a friend found an abortionist for her. As her body recovered, she reclaimed her emotional health by incessantly writing poetry. She slid the poems under the door of teacher and poet Muriel Ruykeyser, who gave them to an editor at Harcourt Brace Jovanovich. The collection, *Once*, was published in 1968.

After Walker graduated from Sarah Lawrence College in 1965, she worked for the welfare department in New York City and in voter registration projects in Georgia. In 1966, she received a writing fellowship and spent that summer working in civil rights programs in Mississippi, where she met and fell in love with Melvyn Rosenman Leventhal, a white civil rights lawyer. During the year they lived together in New York City, she published her first story, "To Hell with Dying," and her first essay, "The Civil Rights Movement: What Good Was It?" After their marriage on March 17, 1967, they moved to Jackson, Mississippi. Walker worked with Head Start programs and served as writer-in-residence at Tougaloo College and Jackson State University. During those seven years in the South, Walker and Leventhal's daughter, Rebecca Grant, was born, and Walker wrote her first novel, *The Third Life of Grange Copeland*, published in 1970 by Harcourt Brace Jovanovich.

In 1973, Walker left the South to accept temporary positions teaching at Wellesley College and the University of Massachusetts, Boston. Leventhal remained in Mississippi. In 1973, Walker published *Revolutionary Petunias, and Other Poems*, as well as a collection of stories titled *In Love and Trouble: Stories of Black Women* and a children's biography, *Langston Hughes: American Poet*. *In Love and Trouble* won the Rosenthal Award of the National Institute of Arts and Letters in 1974.

Walker and Leventhal returned in 1974 to New York, where Walker went to work for *Ms.* magazine as a contributing editor. In 1976, the year her second novel, *Meridian*, was published, Walker and Leventhal were divorced. During this period, Walker wrote the book of poems *Goodnight, Willie Lee, I'll See You in the Morning* and edited an anthology of work by Zora Neale Hurston titled *I Love Myself When I Am Laughing . . . and Then Again When I Am Looking Mean and Impressive*, both of which were published in 1979.

Following her divorce, Walker moved to San Francisco, then to a nearby farm. Her second book of short stories, *You Can't Keep a Good Woman Down*, was published in 1981 while she was living there. The characters of her third novel, *The Color Purple* (1982), could not develop in an urban setting, emerging fully only after Walker found a place to live that reminded her of rural Georgia. Heeding her creative instincts produced a novel that earned Walker fame, money, and literary recognition. *The Color Purple* won the Pulitzer Prize and the American Book Award, was on *The New York Times* bestseller list for six months, and was made into a popular, although somewhat controversial, film by Steven Spielberg.

In 1983, Walker published *In Search of Our Mothers' Gardens*, a series of essays concerning her life, literature, the Civil Rights movement, and black women, among other subjects. Her fourth book of poetry, *Horses Make a Landscape Look More Beautiful*, was published in 1984. Her second collection of essays, *Living by the Word: Selected Writings, 1973-1987* (1988) addresses global concerns as well as feminist and political issues and also contains excerpts from Walker's journal. Her fourth novel, *The Temple of My Familiar*, was published in 1989; it includes some of the characters from *The Color Purple* and again pushes the envelope of experimental writing in what critic Bernard Bell called "a colorful quilt of many patches."

Her fifth novel, *Possessing the Secret of Joy* (1992), is a controversial exploration of female sexuality, a subject also analyzed in the 1998 novel *By the Light of My Father's Smile*. At the beginning of the new century, she seemed to be returning to other genres, her 2003 collection *Absolute Trust in the Goodness of the Earth* being her first poetry book in a decade. She came back to her most familiar literary form with *Now Is the Time to Open Your Heart* (2004), the story of an aging African American female novelist in search of meaning—a less challenging and also less controversial story than her earlier novels. Her place as a writer who crosses boundaries, however, is assured.

ANALYSIS

Walker is at home in many literary forms, managing originality and innovativeness in whatever genre she chooses, be it poetry, essay, or long or short fiction.

Walker identifies diverse literary influences as well: Zora Neale Hurston, Jean Toomer, Thomas

Hardy, Flannery O'Connor, and the nineteenth century Russian novelists among them. Walker's style is characterized by clarity and experimentation. In particular, the language of her characters marked Walker early in her career as a careful listener and later as a medium through whom the characters speak.

Walker's experience with the novel form began with *The Third Life of Grange Copeland*, a straightforward, chronological novel. *Meridian* moved away from strict chronology, using vignettes as puzzle pieces. Those two novels show the conception of character and language development that bore unique fruit in *The Color Purple*. Using for that novel a common nonfiction form, a collection of correspondence, Walker functions as a medium through whom two sisters tell the novel, each in changing language that reflects her life's experience. *The Color Purple* epitomizes Walker's control of believable dialogue. Similarly, in *The Temple of My Familiar*, the characters share narration, which gives the effect of storytelling and reveals much of their personalities through their use of language.

The reader of Walker's work finds that the common thread binding the varied genres is Walker's genius of kneading the personal into the political, the unique into the universal. Most of the drama experienced by Walker's characters points to a larger issue. For example, her black female characters experience much in common with the larger black female population: the search for self-reliance and self-confidence and the embrace of a black feminist stance referred to by Walker as "womanism."

Although Walker's characters do not function as autobiographical vehicles for her personal experience as a black woman in the South, neither are they homogeneous composites. Walker strives not to sacrifice character for stereotype merely to fulfill an African American or "womanist" agenda. Instead, she creates believable heroines. Ruth, Meridian, Celie, and Shug are made fine, in part, by their flaws; from their believable experiences, a light may be brought to bear on more universal truths.

Hand in hand with the recurring theme of the black woman's struggle in a white-dominated society is Walker's controversial representation of the black man and the black woman's struggle against him. In *The Third Life of Grange Copeland, Meridian*, and *The Color Purple*, black men react against their economic and social oppression by dominating their wives, lovers, and daughters. Walker has received criticism for these repeated "negative" portrayals, but she creates from a primary moral responsibility to what she believes to be the truth—part of that truth being that, through honesty, understanding and change come. Particularly in *The Third Life of Grange Copeland*, Walker dissects her black male characters' violence in an attempt to understand the frustrations and results of repressed anger. Not an apologist, Walker ultimately demands that black men assume responsibility for their actions.

The tension between black men and women usually takes precedence in Walker's fiction over the issue that, in large part, precipitates it: the oppression of black people by white people. In the tradition of Hurston's fiction, Walker's black characters do not think about white people constantly. Walker focuses far more on the internal struggles of black people and the black community than on the relationship between the races. As Walker demands the assumption of responsibility by black men, so she commands all of her black characters to look to themselves, to find their inner strengths and talents and thereby improve their lives. This is not to say that civil rights issues and political activism do not play a role in Walker's fiction, only that civil rights must begin with personal growth and family relationships.

Ruth is introduced to the Civil Rights movement in *The Third Life of Grange Copeland*, but *Meridian*, in particular, portrays one woman's discovery of the sanctity of change offered by the Civil Rights movement. Meridian realizes that the best way she can help people is to put them before the movement that, to her, becomes a separate entity whose radicalism she cannot embrace; moral integrity overrides a political agenda.

The importance of the family unit is another theme on which Walker varies throughout her fiction and nonfiction. Given the dysfunctional marriages and relationships between black men and women presented in her work, the hope of sanctuary in the family may at first appear absurd. The contradictions fade, however, when Walker's broader definition of family is understood. In *The Third Life of Grange Copeland*, for example, Ruth and her grandfather form a family unit based on trust and reciprocity. In *The Color Purple*, the two sisters' faith in their relationship, even when separated by years and miles, takes them farther spiritually than God can; Celie's family expands to embrace Shug and even Albert. Slavery destroyed family relationships for the African American; Walker suggests reclaiming the family as an important element of black self-determinism.

Religion as a theme also appears in Walker's fiction and nonfiction, religion as a broad concept embracing self-determined redemption, as in the case of Grange Copeland, as well as Nettie's Christian missionary stance in *The Color Purple*. In the latter novel, Shug's belief that God is in everything allows Celie to begin to make peace with the heinous wrongs done to her. The concept of a "womanist" God is further developed in *The Temple of My Familiar*, in which Shug and her notion of a continually self-renewing female creative principle reappear. The idea of personal integrity and independence becomes a religious concept in *The Color Purple* and elsewhere in Walker's work. Walker's personal spiritual journey toward harmony with the earth's environment (involving becoming a vegetarian) and with the universe is described and celebrated in *Living by the Word*.

The concept of the ever-present capacity to change runs through Walker's life and work. The theme of change accompanies each of the already discussed themes: race, the oppressed and oppressive black male, "womanism," civil rights, the black family, religion, even the language by which Walker's characters express themselves.

THE THIRD LIFE OF GRANGE COPELAND

First published: 1970
Type of work: Novel

A black tenant farmer achieves integrity from a life of oppression, and redemption through love and sacrifice.

The Third Life of Grange Copeland, Walker's first novel, is the chronological story of three generations of a black sharecropping family in the South. The novel addresses several issues that occupy

Walker's career: the abuse of black women by their husbands and fathers, the Civil Rights movement, and the necessities of self-reliance and moral responsibility.

Grange Copeland begins his married life with Margaret as an optimistic sharecropper. By the time their son Brownfield is born, however, the white landowner's exploitation of Grange's labor, resulting in irreversible indebtedness, has spawned hopeless frustration. Grange's feelings of inadequacy precipitate a rage that finds misdirected expression in the abuse of his wife and son. He drinks heavily and begins a sexual relationship with a prostitute. When Margaret retaliates by having sex with white men, which results in a light-skinned baby, Grange abandons Margaret and the children, going north. Completely demoralized, Margaret kills the baby and herself, leaving Brownfield alone.

Brownfield determines not to work for the same white man who controlled his father, but even as he tries to break from Grange's behavior pattern, he unknowingly becomes involved with Josie, his father's mistress. This ironic situation takes a positive turn, however, when Brownfield falls in love with and marries Mem, Josie's educated niece. Walker explains in a later afterword to the novel that she named this character from the French word *la meme* for "the same," and Mem proves to be the same kind of victim Brownfield's mother was and that countless other black women have been.

Mem dreams of a middle-class life for them, and Brownfield believes, as did Grange, that working as a sharecropper will be a stepping-stone to this better life. As was the case with his father, a growing family and indebtedness work against him. Mem's attractiveness and education, the very traits that drew Brownfield to her, become symbols of his failure, and he sets out to destroy her so she will be the ruined woman that he believes he deserves. Mem, no matter how Brownfield batters her, manages always to hold up her head and tries to improve their situation. Mem's persistent hope, a trait long gone from Brownfield, finally enrages him so much that he murders her.

Grange had returned from the North before that happened and made an effort to help his son and Mem, but Brownfield bitterly refused the atonement. After Brownfield murders Mem, Grange takes his youngest granddaughter, Ruth, to raise. The reader is told at this point in the novel that Grange's experiences in New York were no better than life in the South. The crisis of trying to save a drowning white woman, only to have her refuse his hand because it is black, proved a pivotal point for Grange. The woman's death triggers his active hostility toward all white people, and having finally taken an indirect revenge against them, Grange feels renewed and vindicated. Purged from the old, defining victimization, Grange chooses sanctuary from white people and a self-determined life. He marries Josie, buys a farm, and vows to give Ruth a nurturing environment away from white people and the violence born of frustration.

Ruth matures into an independent young woman who, having been sheltered by Grange, does not share his bitterness toward society. Through the media and the local activities of civil rights workers, Ruth comes to believe in the possibility of social change. Grange humors Ruth's ideals, but he still cannot bear the thought of a white woman under his roof, civil rights worker or not.

Grange's greatest battle must still be fought on the home front when Brownfield is released from prison and seeks custody of Ruth, not because of love but in rage against his father. A corrupt white judge gives Ruth to Brownfield, but Grange, having suspected the outcome, shoots his son in the courthouse to prevent Brownfield's sure destruction of Ruth. Grange and Ruth escape to the farm, where Grange prepares to defend his autonomy to the death. Educated, self-reliant, and full of a hope that Grange himself had lost, Ruth emerges the black woman that Margaret and Mem could have been.

Walker's novel delivers an ultimately hopeful message of the possibility of change through love and moral responsibility. Grange finds a productive way out of his anger by himself; his reclusive solution allows Ruth to reenter the world with the inner strength imperative to a black woman's survival. Walker's attempts to understand the reasons behind Grange and Brownfield's violence do not condone it; rather, the motives revealed serve to clarify the means to change it.

MERIDIAN

First published: 1976
Type of work: Novel

A young, black, single mother becomes involved with the Civil Rights movement, coupling self-determinism with a commitment to poor black people in the South.

Walker's second novel, *Meridian*, explores one black woman's experience in the Civil Rights movement, the psychological makeup of which fascinates Walker more than the political and historical impact it had. *Meridian* exemplifies Walker's ability

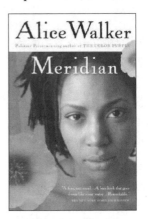

to combine the personal and the political in fiction. Whereas Walker's first novel, *The Third Life of Grange Copeland*, moves chronologically, *Meridian* is constructed of smaller "chapters" that make up the novel, as Walker has said, much as pieces of cloth compose a quilt.

Meridian Hill grows up in the South, marries a high school boyfriend, becomes pregnant, and has a son. She experiences mixed feelings about motherhood, often fantasizing about killing the baby. After her husband leaves her, Meridian lives in emotional limbo, daydreaming and watching television—on which, one morning, she sees that the nearby house where the voter registration drives are organized has been bombed. She decides to volunteer to work with the movement, more out of curiosity about what the people are like than from any political ideology. One of the workers is Truman Held, a man with whom Meridian will have an ongoing, although stormy, relationship.

Because of her unusually high intelligence, Meridian is offered a scholarship to Saxon College, and when she discovers that Truman attends college in Atlanta, his potential proximity becomes a motivating factor in her decision to accept it. Against the protests of her mother, Meridian gives away her baby, believing that he will be better off with someone else, and leaves for Saxon College. As a former wife and mother, Meridian is not the socially preferred virginal Saxon girl. Much as Walker's experience at Spelman proved paradoxical, so Meridian feels the pull of her former life, feminism, and the Civil Rights movement.

The world beyond Saxon seems to contradict itself as well. Truman becomes involved with a white exchange student, Lynne, a baffling development to Meridian. Walker's story explores the difficulties an interracial relationship encounters; the reactions it causes in families, friends, and society in general; and the confusion of a political statement with love.

Throughout Truman's fascination with Lynne and other white women, he periodically returns to Meridian for spiritual and physical comfort. One of those homecomings leaves Meridian pregnant, and she suffers a subsequent abortion alone, never telling Truman. Although Meridian ultimately reconciles spiritually with Truman, she must learn to love and accept him and Lynne in the act of letting them go.

Letting go becomes a discipline that Meridian perfects as her purpose matures. When the movement demands that she vow to kill for it if need be, Meridian cannot comply. She realizes her willingness to sacrifice and even die for the cause, but when she cannot say what the group wants to hear, Meridian lets them go. She returns to the South, where she lives a spartan life of emotional wealth, working for poor black people in small, everyday ways. Such seemingly insignificant protests, in fact, come to define the Civil Rights movement for many people. Again, Walker extracts the political from the personal.

Meridian's almost saintly qualities magnify Walker's belief in the power of personal discipline. Meridian is not perfect, however; her physical maladies and her guilt concerning her mother and child combine effectively to cripple her until she determines to move toward a life of work with which she is morally comfortable. Only then does her strength return. By her example, Truman comes to see the power in her life and dedicates himself to similar work.

Meridian proclaims that true revelation comes from personal change and growth. Although the novel deals with a particular political time period, implications of moral responsibility, love, and sacrifice transcend the specific, making *Meridian* a novel of timely worth.

THE COLOR PURPLE

First published: 1982
Type of work: Novel

Celie's letters to God and to her sister Nettie illustrate her metamorphosis from oppression to confidence; Nettie's letters from Africa record her experience as a missionary.

Walker's third novel, *The Color Purple*, made her famous, winning both the Pulitzer Prize and the American Book Award. The novel takes the form of letters: from Celie to God and Nettie, from Nettie in Africa to Celie. The letters afford the characters the opportunity to speak in their own voices, their own unique language. Not only does the language enhance the storytelling qualities of the novel, but the changes in Celie's language also illustrate her emotional growth.

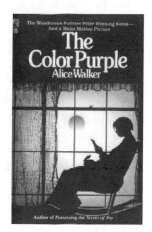

Warned by her father to tell "nobody but God" about his sexual abuse of her, Celie writes letters to God that tell of repeated rape resulting in the births of two babies, of the babies' removal by her father, and of being married off to Mr. _____, a man whose name Celie will not speak. Woven into the letters as well are details of day-to-day farming life in the South that involves racism and economic hardship. Celie's life of mistreatment and drudgery continues unabated until Shug Avery, a blues singer and Mr. _____'s former lover, appears. Shug is beautiful, stubborn, and independent—traits that Celie has never seen in a woman. Their unlikely friendship changes Celie's life. Shug convinces Mr. _____ to stop beating Celie and encourages her to see herself as a worthwhile person. The feeling between them intensifies, and Shug and Celie become lovers for a time.

It is Shug who discovers and procures the years of letters from Nettie hidden in Mr. _____'s trunk. From Nettie's letters, written in a language illustrating her education, Celie learns that the man who raped her was not her biological father and that her two children were adopted by the same missionaries with whom Nettie lived and traveled to Africa. Although it intensifies her hate for Mr. _____, the culmination of this knowledge, coupled with loving Shug, frees Celie from the guilt and poor self-image she had developed at the hands of men.

Exemplifying Walker's theme of self-determinism, Celie, at Shug's urging, exhibits a "womanist," entrepreneurial streak and begins to create and sell pants for men and women. The pants allow her a creative expression and suggest Celie's liberation from men on an economic as well as a physical level. Through Shug's belief of God's existence in everything, Celie reclaims her spirituality as she reclaims her body and soul by becoming comfortable with herself, a transformation that occurs in her language as well. This new Celie eventually makes peace with Mr. _____, whom she comes to call Albert. Albert's maturation and Celie's forgiveness reflect Walker's recurrent theme of the possibility of change—that there can be respectful relationships between black men and women.

Nettie, her husband, Samuel, and Celie's children return from Africa to reunite the family, their missionary work having proved futile. Much as Celie's was, Nettie's God has been transformed to an immediate, internal spirituality. Nettie's faith in Celie, shown through years of unanswered letters, coupled with Celie's reciprocal faith, even after Nettie's supposed drowning on the return ship, underscores the kindred spirit of the long-separated sisters.

For all the praise it received, *The Color Purple* also received much criticism for its negative portrayals of black men. The optimism of the novel outweighs its negativity, however, and Celie's triumphant embrace of a vital existence reflects Walker's hope for humanity.

"1955"

First published: 1981 (collected in *You Can't Keep a Good Woman Down*, 1981)
Type of work: Short story

A white rock-and-roll singer becomes famous by singing a song purchased from a black woman blues singer, but he never understands the song's meaning.

The story "1955" appears in Walker's collection of stories *You Can't Keep a Good Woman Down*; it is a creative depiction of one incident of black musicians' exploitation by the white-dominated entertainment industry. Elvis Presley made Mama Thornton's "Hound Dog" a hit; similarly, in "1955," Traynor sings Gracie Mae Still's song into stardom.

The story clearly addresses a political issue, but Walker's approach transcends the political theme by creating multidimensional characters, drawn together by what separates them. Traynor becomes a pitiable character, as victimized by the entertainment industry as Gracie Mae—more so, in that he lacks her sense of self-worth. The greatest irony involves Traynor's lack of understanding of the song; never being in emotional possession of the song brings Traynor repeatedly to Gracie Mae, who cannot explain what lies beyond his understanding.

Over the years, Traynor gives Gracie Mae a car, a farm, a house, and countless other presents in an attempt to return some of the wealth her talent helped him attain. Traynor's success debilitates him spiritually, while Gracie Mae maintains a wisdom and integrity that Traynor cannot attain. Walker's "womanist" message is clear in Gracie Mae's inner strength and compassion that is great enough to embrace the man she so easily could have hated.

"A SUDDEN TRIP HOME IN THE SPRING"

First published: 1981 (collected in *You Can't Keep a Good Woman Down*, 1981)
Type of work: Short story

A black student returns South from her northern college for her father's funeral and sees new worth in what she left behind.

"A Sudden Trip Home in the Spring" appears in Walker's collection of stories *You Can't Keep a Good Woman Down*. The story examines a turning point in the psychological development of a black college student who has left Georgia for an exclusive northern college, a scenario reminiscent of Walker's personal experience, and employs recurring themes of family dynamics, racism, and feminism.

Sarah Davis feels better suited to her northern home and is not pleased with the idea of going South for her father's funeral. Her opinion of the South and of her father in particular has inhibited her growth as an artist; she cannot render black men on paper at all, not having the strength to draw what she sees as complete defeat. While she is home, however, interactions with her brother and grandfather, made more meaningful by her recent distance from them, open her eyes to her grandfather's innate dignity and her brother's youthful promise. Free from a single, oppressed image of all black men, Sarah feels she may now portray her grandfather in stone.

Mirroring Walker's own diverse experiences, the story underscores the significance of recognizing the worth in one's diversity. As Walker's writing is influenced by everything from her sharecropper beginning to the Civil Rights movement, so Sarah's work is broadened by reopening a door she thought closed. Sarah's pivotal trip home allows her to see the narrowness of the northern college as well. Choosing not to allow one environment to define her gives her the freedom to define herself.

TO HELL WITH DYING

First published: 1967 (collected in *In Love and Trouble*, 1973); republished with illustrations in 1988
Type of work: Short story, then children's book

An old man is loved by the children of his community, who find his company a special gift.

Mr. Sweet is a sick old man whose multiple ailments bring him often to the brink of death; the narrator's father and the children would call him back from his deathlike state by calling "To hell with death!" and surrounding him with affection. The story describes Mr. Sweet lovingly so that the reader can see that someone others might reject as a person of no account (he gets drunk on his own home brew and chews tobacco) is in fact important to the family and to the town. The "resurrections" in which the children participate hide from them the reality that death is permanent. Finally, when the narrator is away at college, Mr. Sweet gets sick again, and this time no one can call him back. After his death, the family celebrates him, and the narrator accepts the gift of Mr. Sweet's guitar, which she plays in his memory.

Published originally as adult short fiction and included in Walker's collection *In Love and Trouble*, this clear, gentle short story needed only the addition of some fine illustrations to become a children's book, where its message of acceptance and inspiration is transparent. It is different from other children's stories of death because it does not hide the unacceptable parts of the main character and because it does not offer any traditional consolations, only that of remembered affection. It represents a child's viewpoint (remembered, as the narrator is now grown up) of a society in which affection and tolerance for difference are important values.

Alice Walker

"Everyday Use"

First published: 1973 (collected in *In Love and Trouble*, 1973)
Type of work: Short story

A decision over who gets the family quilts helps to define heritage.

The speaker in this story is the mother of two very different girls, Maggie and Dee. Maggie has stayed home with her mother and lived an old-fashioned, traditional life, while Dee has gone off to school and become sophisticated. Dee comes home with a new name, Wangero, and a new boyfriend; she claims that she wants to take the family heirlooms along as a part of claiming her true identity as an African American. She especially wants the quilts, which she plans to display on the wall as artworks because of their fine handiwork. Maggie, on the other hand, had been promised the quilts for her marriage; she loved them because they reminded her of the grandmother who made them. Dee feels entitled to them, but the speaker chooses to give them to Maggie—not to show but, as Dee says scornfully, "for everyday use." Dee sweeps off with her other trophies, and the mother and Maggie remain together, enjoying a heritage that is experience and memory, not things to put on display.

"Everyday Use" is probably Walker's most frequently anthologized short story. It stresses the mother-daughter bond and defines the African American woman's identity in terms of this bond and other family relationships. It uses gentle humor in showing Dee/Wangero's excess of zeal in trying to claim her heritage, and her overlooking of the truth of African American experience in favor of what she has read about it. Dee has joined the movement called Cultural Nationalism, whose major spokesman was LeRoi Jones (Amiri Baraka). In fact, however, Dee's understanding of the movement's basics is flawed, and she is using bits of African lore rather than a coherent understanding of it. Walker doubtless intended this misinterpretation. The contrast is clear—the snuff-dipping, hardworking mother who tells the story has passed her true inheritance, not quilts but love, to the daughter who is not book-educated but who belongs to the tradition.

"The Revenge of Hannah Kemhuff"

First published: 1973 (collected in *In Love and Trouble*, 1973)
Type of work: Short story

An old African American woman seeks revenge through Voodoo for the needless, careless destruction of her family years ago.

The speaker is the apprentice of Tante Rosie, a Voodoo practitioner consulted by Hannah Kemhuff, a sick, elderly African American woman who desires revenge. Her family was lost because help was refused them during the Depression when they were starving. Because the family seemed too well dressed, having been given some hand-me-downs, a woman would not give them the meager food that was being handed out to the hungry. The woman who turned the family away is now wealthy and self-satisfied, attended by her servant. Tante Rosie offers to help Hannah Kemhuff and prepares to go through the Voodoo ritual, which involves the collection of such objects as fingernails and hair clippings. Her apprentice, the narrator, goes to visit the woman who had caused the disaster, Sarah Marie Holley, and makes her purpose of collecting the physical materials for the ritual clear. Hannah Kemhuff dies of her illness, and Sarah Marie Holley, trying to avoid the Voodoo threat, dies shortly afterward, basically of a wasting illness brought on by terror.

Voodoo brings Hannah her revenge through natural rather than supernatural means. This story creates suspense as to whether its conclusion will affirm a belief in Voodoo, but it does not have the depth of character or sense of community evident in many of the other stories that appear in the collection *In Love and Trouble*. Its main interest is that, in preparing for the story and researching Voodoo, Walker found the works of Zora Neale Hurston, which opened new doors for her. The story is dedicated to the memory of Hurston.

Summary

Walker's recurrent, controversial themes—violence in the black family, racism, and "womanism" among them—will always draw her mixed attention. The broad social scope of her work, from Georgia to Africa, from folklore to civil rights philosophy, will continue to influence the way readers perceive black women. Her bold literary experimentation and clarity of vision have earned acclaim for her work in spite of controversy. Above all else, Walker strives for honest portrayals in her work, believing that truth makes even the painful tellable, and curable in the telling.

Claudia Emerson Andrews; updated by Janet McCann

BIBLIOGRAPHY

By the Author

SHORT FICTION:
In Love and Trouble: Stories of Black Women, 1973
You Can't Keep a Good Woman Down, 1981
The Complete Stories, 1994
Alice Walker Banned, 1996 (stories and commentary)

LONG FICTION:
The Third Life of Grange Copeland, 1970
Meridian, 1976
The Color Purple, 1982
The Temple of My Familiar, 1989
Possessing the Secret of Joy, 1992
By the Light of My Father's Smile, 1998
Now Is the Time to Open Your Heart, 2004

POETRY:
Once: Poems, 1968
Five Poems, 1972
Revolutionary Petunias, and Other Poems, 1973
Goodnight, Willie Lee, I'll See You in the Morning: Poems, 1979
Horses Make a Landscape Look More Beautiful, 1984
Her Blue Body Everything We Know: Earthling Poems, 1965-1990 Complete, 1991
Absolute Trust in the Goodness of the Earth: New Poems, 2003
A Poem Traveled Down My Arm, 2003

NONFICTION:
In Search of Our Mothers' Gardens: Womanist Prose, 1983
Living by the Word: Selected Writings, 1973-1987, 1988
Warrior Marks: Female Genital Mutilation and the Sexual Blinding of Women, 1993 (with Pratibha Parmar)
The Same River Twice: Honoring the Difficult, 1996
Anything We Love Can Be Saved: A Writer's Activism, 1997
The Way Forward Is with a Broken Heart, 2000
Sent by Earth: A Message from the Grandmother Spirit After the Attacks on the World Trade Center and Pentagon, 2001

DISCUSSION TOPICS

- What is the spiritual element in Alice Walker's work? How is God envisioned in *The Color Purple?* In *The Temple of My Familiar?*

- What forces does Walker identify as hostile to African American women?

- What characteristics identify her later novels as experimental?

- What is Walker's definition of a good community, from the descriptions in her novels of community building?

- Do Walker's stories have villains? What characterizes her "worst" people?

CHILDREN'S LITERATURE:
Langston Hughes: American Poet, 1974
To Hell with Dying, 1988
Finding the Green Stone, 1991

EDITED TEXT:
I Love Myself When I Am Laughing . . . and Then Again When I Am Looking Mean and Impressive: A Zora Neale Hurston Reader, 1979

About the Author

Banks, Erma Davis, and Keith Byerman. *Alice Walker: An Annotated Bibliography, 1968-1986.* New York: Garland, 1989.

Christian, Barbara. "Novel for Everyday Use: The Novels of Alice Walker." In *Black Women Novelists: The Development of a Tradition, 1892-1976.* Westport, Conn.: Greenwood Press, 1980.

Lauret, Maria. *Alice Walker.* New York: St. Martin's Press, 1999.

McMillan, Laurie: "Telling a Critical Story: Alice Walker's *In Search of Our Mothers' Gardens." Journal of Modern Literature* 23, no. 1 (Fall, 2004): 103-107.

Noe, Marcia. "Teaching Alice Walker's 'Everyday Use': Employing Race, Class, and Gender, with an Annotated Bibliography." *Eureka Studies in Teaching Short Fiction* 5, no. 1 (Fall, 2004): 123-136.

Parker-Smith, Bettye J. "Alice Walker's Women: In Search of Some Peace of Mind." In *Black Women Writers (1950-1980): A Critical Evaluation,* edited by Mari Evans. Garden City, N.Y.: Anchor, 1984.

Tate, Claudia. *Black Women Writers at Work.* New York: Continuum, 1983.

Willis, Susan. "Black Woman Writers: Taking a Critical Perspective." In *Making a Difference: Feminist Literary Criticism,* edited by Gayle Greene and Coppelia Kahn. London: Methuen, 1985.

MARGARET WALKER

Born: Birmingham, Alabama
July 7, 1915
Died: Chicago, Illinois
November 30, 1998

Courtesy, Chicago Public Library

Walker's 1942 Yale Award for New Poets made her the first nationally recognized modern African American woman in American letters. Her novel Jubilee *authentically records the Civil War history of African Americans.*

BIOGRAPHY

Margaret Abigail Walker Alexander was born in Birmingham, Alabama, on July 7, 1915. Her Methodist minister father was Sigismund Constantine Walker. Her mother was Marion Dozier, a musician and teacher. Her maternal grandmother, Elvira Ware Dozier, was the source of Walker's deep sense of participating in the history of African Americans. The family moved to New Orleans in 1925, and she attended Model School, part of New Orleans University. She began writing when she was twelve, filling a "datebook" given to her by her father. She went to New Orleans University (now Dillard University) and then on to Northwestern University for a B.A. in English in 1934. Edward Buell Hungerford at Northwestern was among her most influential writing teachers. Her first poem was published in W. E. B. Du Bois's magazine, *The Crisis*. In March, 1935, she began an important time in the South Side (Chicago) Writers' Group of the Federal Writers' Project of the Works Progress Administration (WPA). Here she met James T. Farrell, Studs Terkel, Frank Yerby, and Saul Bellow. She finished "For My People" in 1937, publishing it in *Poetry* that same year. In these years, she would come to know Dudley Randall, Stephen Vincent Benet, Gwendolyn Brooks, and Richard Wright, a biography of whom, *Richard Wright: Daemonic Genius*, she would publish in 1987. In 1939, she went to the University of Iowa Writers' Workshop for an

M.A. Accepted as her thesis was a collection of poems, *For My People*, published as the winner of the Yale Award in 1942. She married Firnist James Alexander in 1944 and later had four children. In these years, she taught at Livingston College in North Carolina and West Virginia State College, moving to take a position at Jackson State College (now University) in 1949, where she remained until she retired in 1979. She returned to the University of Iowa to earn a Ph.D. in 1965. Her dissertation was *Jubilee* (1966), which showed great debts to African American folklore and to numerous writers such as James Weldon Johnson, Roland Hayes, Paul Robeson, Zora Neale Hurston, and Arna Bontemps. She read the Bible and the holy works *Mahabharata*, *Bhagavad Gita*, *Gilgamesh*, *Book of the Dead*, and *Sundiata*. She also read Civil War history and once announced that her choice of the five greatest thinkers of the twentieth century were Karl Marx, Sigmund Freud, Søren Kierkegaard, Albert Einstein, and Du Bois. *Jubilee* was commercially published in 1966 and would eventually sell more than two million copies in seven languages. *For My People* and *Jubilee* brought her prestige, fame, and eventually a certain amount of money. Moreover, she was one of the voices of the African American revolution in the United States during the 1960's that produced so many leaders and martyrs. The poems she wrote were published in *Prophets for a New Day* (1970). More books followed: poetry in *October Journey* (1973), and *A Poetic Equation: Conversations Between Nikki Giovanni and Margaret Walker* (1974). The Walker-Giovanni contrast represents the transformation of the themes of African American writing from brooding to militance in the 1970's. Walker established at Jackson State University the Institute for the Study of Black Life and Culture, which was later renamed to commemorate her. In 1989, she brought out a collection of her poems, *This Is My Century: New and Collected Poems*. Other late books were *How I Wrote "Jubilee," and Other Essays on Life and Literature* (1990) and *On Being Female, Black, and Free: Essays by Margaret Walker, 1932-1992* (1997). The posthumous publication of *Conversations with Margaret Walker* in 2002 is as close as Walker got to the publication of the autobiography she intended to write. Though Walker died in Chicago, where she had moved in 1998 to be in the care of her daughter, she lived in Mississippi and in the American South, because, she said, it was her home.

ANALYSIS

Walker called herself a "visionary" and stated that she was committed to a life as an artist for the people, especially in "the public statement poem." Her poetry was intuitive and brooding. She intended a realism, and she succeeded to the degree that realism can be commingled with didacticism and what she named "orphic" discourse. Her poetry, her fiction, and her essays were transformations of Walker's lyric sensibility. The poetry prophesied, witnessed, celebrated, and grieved with personal immediacy. The fiction was a distillation of her maternal family history for four generations, an apostrophe to her own ancestry as an African American. The essays were by a teacher speaking determinedly in the first person. Above all, her writing was meant to be recited, to be oral; it was made for telling, saying, and declamation, combining the forms of folk sermon and the story of common people, a proletariat, with a great deal of inventory and repetition, which roll-calls the wealth and certainty in the goals of African Americans.

Walker saw on Earth a sublime beauty of nature and a utopian potential for humankind. The natural beauty, especially of rural or small-town settings, is the frame of the history of slavery in *Jubilee*. The utopian potential is the closing declamation of "For My People," which chants into possibility the end of hate and injustice and the triumph of a once-enslaved and someday morally heroic hu-

mankind. She believed in the existence and efficacy of the culture hero—epiphanic, messianic, self-sacrificial persons: Frederick Douglass, Du Bois, Malcolm X, Martin Luther King, Jr.—people who endured and were inspirational before they died, were killed, or exiled.

Walker also privileged history. Only historical fact dissolved the lies of a U.S. national mythology that denied culpability, denied inherited responsibility, refused retribution and reparation, and resisted the moral transformation that would grant justice to a race not yet fully delivered from the slavery that exploited it. In *Jubilee*, the tapestry of the interconnectedness of every American to every event of the past is inventoried.

Biblical signature is everywhere in Walker's writings but not in support of institutional religion. The narratives of *Jubilee* and of "Prophets for a New Day" are biblical in selection of detail so that they become new parables. There is not much humor in Walker's writing. Even "Poppa Chicken" is too sinister to allow much levity. Her writing is also biblical in appropriation of the tropes of banishment and national exile and the resultant enslavement, as well as the continuation of hope when reason predicted despair. Moreover, Walker's writing methodically logs violence, yet she said could not take up the subjects of the Vietnam War and the African American culture of the 1970's, which she saw filled with the discourses of violence, profanity, drugs, and racial nationalism. She narrated also the episodes of fickle deliverance, such as the Emancipation Proclamation and the victory of the Union in the Civil War and the civil rights acts of 1954 and 1964. Freedom as reality and as chimera is also a subtext in virtually all of Walker's writing. For Walker, it is a precious legality. It is also a feeling.

As a poet of the people, Walker used the sonnet to acknowledge the formal events and occasions of their progress. She had deaths and victories and anniversaries to commemorate. "For Malcolm X" is illustrative. She used the ballad to distill the personalities and behavior of the folk characters in her people's experience, such as in "Poppa Chicken," the pimp. She used what she called "the long line of free verse punctuated with a short line" to make the oracular discourse of poems such as "For My People." It gives multiplied detail a ritual coherence that reveals the integrity of the culture of Walker's

African American audience. With her fiction, she corrected the historical record. With her essays, she explained her fiction and the method of the authentication of her vision.

"FOR MY PEOPLE"

First published: 1937 (collected in *For My People*, 1942)
Type of work: Poem

A ten-stanza, free-verse apostrophe to the collective culture of African Americans announces an epic hope.

"For My People" was mostly written in a fifteen-minute burst of brilliant inspiration. Its principal tactics are inventory—a concretization of the feeling—and repetition, a concentration and intensification of the poem's passion and political resolve, especially tuned for oral presentation.

Stanza I begins the chronology of African American history with the first of six incantations of "for my people," recalling the songs of an enslaved race—of sadness, of verbal play, of grief, of the rare times of joy, and of supplication and submission to whatever God has willed.

Stanza II describes the tasks of slavery, performed in uncompensated and blind hope: "washing, ironing, cooking, scrubbing, sewing, mending, hoeing, plowing, digging, planting, pruning, patching."

Stanza III goes from the ancestral past to Walker's childhood with a list of her places and acts of play in Alabama—baptizing, preaching, doctor, jail, soldier, school, mama, cooking, concert, store, hair, and "Miss Choomby and company," Walker's childhood code for African American grown-up women.

Stanza IV remembers the experience of going to a segregated school to learn the bitter truth of how being black in America was to be poor and politically ignored.

Stanza V celebrates the youth who bravely grew to maturity against these obstacles, had some fun and joy, married and had children, and then died of "consumption and anemia and lynching."

Stanza VI cameos the African American neigh-borhoods of Chicago, New York, and New Orleans, where the lack of money and property form a back-drop for African Americans who dream their hope in spite of their disenfranchisement.

Stanza VII evokes the manic-depressive state of African Americans made crazy by the social forces and manipulation of a majority race "who tower over us omnisciently and laugh."

Stanza VIII is a mini-chronicle of the sincere and unceasing attempts by African Americans to join American society, in churches, schools, clubs, societies, associations, councils, committees, and conventions—only to be cheated and deceived in money and religious association by the white ruling majority—the "facile force of state."

Stanza IX declares admiration "for my people," hoping to make a world of universal brotherhood to replace the fascist one that suppresses African Americans.

Finally, stanza X closes the litany of pain, endurance, grief, and relentless hope with the poem's famous incantation, calling for a new world, born of a "bloody peace," peopled by a courageous and freedom-loving new generation, a race of people—perhaps an alliance of Caucasians and African Americans—that will "rise and take control."

"POPPA CHICKEN"

First published: 1942
Type of work: Poem

An African American subcultural folk-type—Poppa Chicken, the pimp—progresses from his prime to his decline.

"Poppa Chicken" is a caricature of a pimp. He has style. He is a commodifier of sex. He is violent. He is an outlaw who has paid off the authorities to shorten the prison time he ultimately must serve. Then he gets old. He has sinister heroic status. The ballad has twelve four-line stanzas, rhymed *abcb*, with lines from five to eight syllables.

Poppa Chicken was a "sugar daddy" in his time, with a stable of many women. He made lots of money, and he harried his women "employees," who said he was swell (probably out of well-grounded fear of reprisal for disrespect). Poppa

Chicken's face was "long and black" with a wide grin. When he went on show, his women heralded his progress with hysterical shouts. Inexorably, Poppa Chicken brutalized the women to command their obedience—the poem's line "Treat 'em rough and make them say/ Poppa Chicken's fine!" is a euphemism that might mask his viciousness. Poppa also carried guns and knives and inevitably killed a "guy"; jailed, he bought himself a short sentence, and released, his ambivalent folk-hero status grew, and he seemed unchanged by his experience. Poppa's personality is one of conspicuous consumption, especially of custom cigars and large diamonds. In his post-jail life, he boldly carries no gun and swears at police officers (whom he has likely bribed). He eventually meets a woman with whom he actually falls in love, thereby acquiring a poignant and ominous vulnerability. However, soon "her man Joe"—perhaps her pimp of more youthful strength than Poppa—ends the affair, a poetically just denial of the experience of a love relationship for a person who forbade sentiment in the relationships between his employees and their customers. Poppa survives, but the reader now understands him to be the victim of his business as much as the women are and their "johns" who work for him in the soulless grapplings of prostitution.

JUBILEE

First published: 1966
Type of work: Novel

Jubilee is the fictionalized history of Walker's maternal great-grandmother, Margaret Duggans Ware Brown, and her daughter, Walker's grandmother, Elvira Dozier, from 1837 to about 1890, framing the crucial years of the U.S. Civil War.

"Jubilee" is the biblical name for amnesty and forgiving of money debts every forty-nine years. The novel is organized in three parts. Chapter 1 (1837) is titled "Sis Hetta's Child—The Ante-Bellum Years." The novel opens with the birth of Vyry in 1837, Hetta's last child, on the John Morris Dutton plantation, in Dawson, Georgia. The thirty-five-year-old

Dutton was her father. Vyry would be able to pass for white. Hetta then died in pregnancy when Vyry was two. Mothered by Mammy Sukey until she is old enough to work at the age of seven, Vyry looks like the twin of Miss Lillian, Dutton's child with his wife, Salina. In this chapter, nearly all the important characters of the story are introduced.

Chapter 2 takes place in 1844. At age seven, Vyry becomes a house servant, to be brutalized by the jealous Dutton wife, Big Missy Salina. Grimes, the plantation overseer, is a poor, white man. Vyry breaks a dish and is punished by Big Missy by being hung by her wrists in a closet. The beautiful natural landscape of Georgia is described once again.

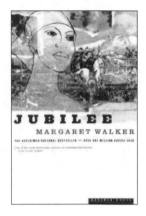

Chapter 3 (1847) describes ten-year-old Vyry's world of work, often using the inventories of things such as food, work tasks, animals, sicknesses, and children's games to go with the folk songs and slave songs that regularly punctuate the narrative and make *Jubilee* into a discourse for oral telling. The religion of the slaves has a biblical connection, but it is not the same as that of the Southern whites. The slave Brother Ezekiel can read and write. Near the Dutton plantation, white antislavery agitators appear in the late 1840's.

Chapters 4 through 7, taking place around 1851, depict Ezekiel the minister, who is also an agent of the Underground Railroad. Vyry is more warmly dressed and better fed in winter than many poor whites. Randall Ware, a freeman blacksmith with his own smithy in Dawson, appears and begins to court Vyry. Among white people, watchfulness for possession of weapons and evidence of the ability to read by the slaves is increased. The cook, Aunt Sally, whom Vyry has come to love, is peremptorily sold. The signature lie of slave owners of how the plantation's slaves are loved and well-treated enters the narrative as irony razored with anger.

Chapters 8 through 14, circa 1853, tell how the courtship of Randall Ware and Vyry progresses. A courtship and marriage of Miss Lillian and the rather sensitive Kevin MacDougall has as context the punishment of slave Lucy by branding an "R" on her face. The Fourth of July is celebrated with the hanging murders of women slaves who poisoned their master. Fall canning and the cotton harvest are described. Two old slaves are beaten to death by Grimes with a whip. The year ends with a description of a typical Christmas on the plantation: For one day of the year, the field hands get enough to eat and may rest. Dutton refuses to let Randall Ware buy Vyry's freedom, and the reader learns that Vyry is pregnant.

Chapters 15 through 18, from 1854 to 1858, chronicle the growth of Vyry's family. Her first child, James, is born. Minna is born in 1858. Vyry is threatened with being auctioned and is shown stripped to slavers but not sold. She tries to escape to freedom with Ware but is caught and given seventy-five lashes, which scar her grotesquely for life. In the narrative, the experience of the slaves, with Vyry as the central personality, is often reminiscent of the experience of Jesus in the New Testament.

Part 2 of the book, titled "Mine Eyes Have Seen the Glory—The Civil War Years," takes place from 1861 to 1866. John Dutton dies. The South believes it will win the war easily and quickly. Young John Dutton dies in 1863, the year of the Emancipation Proclamation. Early in 1864, Kevin MacDougall dies. The Union Army's victories in Georgia are too much for Big Missy, who dies of a heart attack. Confederate soldiers arrive to trash the Dutton plantation in January, 1865. Innis Brown, an escaped slave, arrives at the Dutton plantation, where the slaves, led by Vyry, are now in charge. Vyry and Innis leave the plantation in January, 1866.

The final section of the book—"Forty Years in the Wilderness—Reconstruction and Reaction" follows Vyry and her family between 1866 and 1870. They reach Henry County, below Abbeville, but they must leave. After more attempts, they settle in Greenville, Alabama, in spring, 1870, where they finally are able to make a permanent home. Randall Ware finds them. Vyry displays the scars of her whipping to Innis and Ware, declaring that she would still feed the person who whipped her.

"FOR MALCOLM X"

First published: 1965 (collected in *Prophets for a New Day*, 1970)
Type of work: Poem

Walker salutes all who mourned the assassination of Malcolm X, and includes a fervent address to Malcolm himself.

For Malcolm X joined the river of elegiac discourse elicited by Malcolm X's bloody murder in 1965 by Nation of Islam congregation members. Walker's sonnet expresses collective African American grief. Its loose Petrarchan form uses the first eight lines (octet) to describe the mourners, who gaze upon the dead Malcolm in the climactic six lines (sestet) that resolve the poem.

Line 1 to 8 address the "Violated ones," the African Americans who may enact the internecine violence of brothers killing brothers. They are street people who hate the white oppressors and the middle-class black people economically sealed off from the African American underclass. The stanza's final line summons the hearers to Malcolm's coffin to feel the great loss of a beautiful surrogate for them—a "swan."

Lines 9 to 14 frame the dead body of Malcolm as it lies in state. His message to his mourners was difficult. Christ-like blood and water of the mourners flow from them and from Malcolm's wounds. In Walker's earthy diction, Malcolm is credited with having entered the hearts and minds of his mourners—"cut open our breasts and dug scalpels in our/ brains." Malcolm is irreplaceable, and there is a profound desire to see him incarnate in someone new.

Margaret Walker

"PROPHETS FOR A NEW DAY"

First published: 1970 (collected in *Prophets for a New Day*, 1970)
Type of work: Poem

A formal voice announces another suffering-and-death experience in progress like that of Jesus Christ; however, this time, it is not for one person but for a number of people—for "us."

Prophets for a New Day reprises the heroic sacrifice of the revolutionary 1960's in the United States, a decade which featured the assassinations of President John F. Kennedy, Martin Luther King, Jr., Malcolm X, and Robert Kennedy, as well as the Watts riots and the American forces in Vietnam, where a disproportionate number of those who died were African American.

Stanza I appropriates the Old Testament personalities and narrative of the Hebrew captivity and ordeal in a modern discourse that is homiletic and exhortative. It announces the threshold of an apocalyptic time. The gravity of the proclamation is suggested by its association with the tropes of heroic Old Testament personalities—Moses and the burning bush, Isaiah's lips purified with a hot coal, the portentous wheels of fire that accompanied Ezekiel's dire prophesies, and Amos, who prophesied the fall of the Hebrew kingdom. Like the biblical audience, the modern African American one lives in poor places and jails, in the worthless lands and the roads between inns. A composite prophetic leader delivers a message to all who are tired and in pain because they are denied creature comforts and safety.

The second stanza connects the biblical and the modern population of believers who have no political power. They kneel by an iconic river and around the world. Prophecy is proclaimed, signaled by "flaming flags of stars," "a blinding sun," "the lamp of truth" that burns the "oil of devotion." The prophet personalities—now no longer composite—chant the spell of an apocalyptic vision. Upon the prayerful throng of faces that are racially dark descends "the Word," accompanied by an energy of freedom that is felt like the weather of a great storm coming.

However, in stanza III, the terrible means of deliverance is the biblical "beast," reincarnated in modernity to destroy order and the rational as well as the creatures and landscape of the temporal world. The beast—a male, anthropomorphic personality of chaos, the sum of the extreme possibility of perversion of humankind—destroys everything, individually, genocidally, and ecologically. The beast is humanity run amok, a cannibal. War, Famine, Pestilence, Death, Destruction, and Trouble, unceasingly, day and night, eat humankind and its defenders. It is a coward whose genius is to know humanity's cowardice, who slanders the possibility of freedom and virtue. Its lie is that the people who have died in the slavery that built modern civilization are not worth remembering, acknowledging, and repenting. Then the beast reenacts Calvary transmogrified and drives the people from the city to a new Golgatha, "to be stabbed" in a virtual forest of crucified people. Escape from the beast and deliverance will come with an apocalyptic ending of the world as it is.

SUMMARY

Margaret Walker set out to have a significant life as writer and spokesperson for African Americans and humanity in general. With the advantage of extraordinary parents, great natural talent, early discovery by cultural leaders, and intense personal discipline, she succeeded. Her discourse is personal and oral and proletarian. In her writing, from poetry to fiction, literary and cultural criticism, and formal biography, she constructs a lyric presence, making herself, as much as African Americans and all other races, the subject of her writing with an art rarely equaled in the canon.

John R. Pfeiffer

BIBLIOGRAPHY

By the Author

LONG FICTION:
Jubilee, 1966

POETRY:
For My People, 1942
The Ballad of the Free, 1966
Prophets for a New Day, 1970
October Journey, 1973
For Farish Street Green, 1986
This Is My Century: New and Collected Poems, 1989

NONFICTION:
How I Wrote "Jubilee," 1972
A Poetic Equation: Conversations Between Nikki Giovanni and Margaret Walker, 1974
Richard Wright: Daemonic Genius, 1987
How I Wrote "Jubilee," and Other Essays on Life and Literature, 1990
God Touched My Life: The Inspiring Autobiography of the Nun Who Brought Song, Celebration, and Soul to the World, 1992
On Being Female, Black, and Free: Essays by Margaret Walker, 1932-1992, 1997 (Maryemma Graham, editor)
Conversations with Margaret Walker, 2002 (Graham, editor)

MISCELLANEOUS:
Margaret Walker's "For My People": A Tribute, 1992

DISCUSSION TOPICS

- Margaret Walker's description of the landscape of Georgia in *Jubilee* is stunningly beautiful. What is the purpose of this emphasis on the beauty of nature?

- How does Walker represent sexual behavior in *Jubilee* and "Poppa Chicken"?

- How does Walker use biblical references in each of the works discussed in the analysis above?

- Show how Walker's writing is both optimistic and pessimistic about the moral progress of humankind.

- One of the principal narrative tactics in Walker's writing is the use of inventories—of flowers, smells, foods, emotional states, medicines, and so on. Locate some examples and explain their function where they appear.

- In spite of her hope, Walker depicts significant violence in her writing. Identify some examples and explain the purpose of such descriptions where they are found.

About the Author

Barksdale, Richard K. "Margaret Walker: Folk Orature and Historical Prophecy." In *Black American Poets Between Worlds, 1940-1960,* edited by R. Baxter Miller. Tennessee Studies in Literature 30. Knoxville: University of Tennessee Press, 1986.

Berke, Nancy. *Women Poets on the Left: Lola Ridge, Genevieve Taggard, Margaret Walker.* Gainesville: University Press of Florida, 2001.

Buckner, B. Dilla. "Folkloric Elements in Margaret Walker's Poetry." *CLA Journal* 33 (1990): 367-377.

Carmichael, Jacqueline Miller. *Trumpeting a Fiery Sound: History and Folklore in Margaret Walker's "Jubilee."* Athens: University of Georgia Press, 1998.

Graham, Maryemma, ed. *Conversations with Margaret Walker.* Jackson: University of Mississippi Press, 2002.

_____. *Fields Watered with Blood: Critical Essays on Margaret Walker.* Athens: University of Georgia Press, 2001.

Klotmas, Phyllis. "'Oh Freedom'—Women and History in Margaret Walker's *Jubilee.*" *Black American Literature Forum* 11 (1977): 139-145.

Miller, R. Baxter. "The 'Intricate Design' of Margaret Walker: Literary and Biblical Re-Creation in Southern History." In *Black American Poets Between Worlds, 1940-1960,* edited by Miller. Tennessee Studies in Literature 30. Knoxville: University of Tennessee Press, 1986.

Ward, Jerry W., Jr. "A Writer for Her People: An Interview with Dr. Margaret Walker Alexander." *Mississippi Quarterly* 41, no. 4 (Fall, 1998): 515-527.

ROBERT PENN WARREN

Born: Guthrie, Kentucky
April 24, 1905
Died: West Wardsboro, near Stratton, Vermont
September 15, 1989

Warren, the first American poet laureate, is known primarily as a prolific poet and novelist; with Cleanth Brooks, Jr., he significantly influenced the teaching of literature.

Robert A. Ballard, Jr.

BIOGRAPHY

Robert Penn Warren was born to Anne Ruth Penn Warren on April 24, 1905, in Guthrie, a tiny community of twelve hundred people in southwestern Kentucky. His father, Robert Franklin Warren, was a banker—according to Warren, a "misplaced" person who gave up early aspirations of a literary nature for more practical aims of making money. Warren's relationship to his father was a subtle and important one for its impact on his fiction and poetry, which often dramatized father-son relationships. Warren had a deep admiration for his father's rectitude, especially his humane resolution of the conflicts between personal desires and family duty. This admiration was coupled with a curious feeling of guilt because he, Robert Penn Warren, lived the literary aspirations that his father had abandoned.

Warren's summers were spent on his maternal grandfather's tobacco farm, an environment supporting his deep love of nature. His grandfather's personality, however, was fully as important as the rural setting for Warren's development. Gabriel Thomas Penn had been a Confederate cavalryman as well as an ardent reader of military history and poetry. He could, and did, quote poetry vigorously and told exciting stories of the Civil War. The young Warren considered the Civil War the great American epic, analogous to the Trojan War for

the Greeks. This gift of spontaneous storytelling had a profound effect upon Warren's writing style in both prose and poetry. Though Warren had no literary aspirations at all when he was growing up, he was absorbing the traditional tales of the South, the characters, and the dialects, which would emerge years later in fiction and poetry.

In his early years, Warren wanted to become an outdoorsman or an adventurer on the high seas. He might have done so, for his father was getting him an appointment at the U.S. Naval Academy at Annapolis—the first step, Warren hoped, to being an admiral of the Pacific Fleet. Unfortunately, a childhood accident when he was fifteen years old destroyed one of Warren's eyes. Although it was tragic at the time and contributed to feelings of depression for several years, it may have been crucial to America's gaining a great literary artist instead of a naval officer.

Warren enrolled instead in Vanderbilt University, where he became friends with Allen Tate, another gifted young man who would become a writer, and the well-known poet and teacher John Crowe Ransom, who perceived Warren's talent with words and encouraged him to write poetry. Warren became the youngest recruit to a literary group called "the Fugitives," who published some of his first verse. The Fugitives had some notion of creating a new Southern literary tradition, in opposition to the stereotyped, romantic "magnolia image" of the South found in popular, cheap fiction.

After graduating from Vanderbilt in 1925, Warren earned an M.A. from the University of California at Berkeley and started postgraduate work on a scholarship at Yale University. That program was interrupted, however, by his being chosen to be a Rhodes scholar. He earned a bachelor of letters at the University of Oxford in 1930. Meanwhile, he had published his first book, a historical study, *John Brown: The Making of a Martyr* (1929), and his first short story, "Prime Leaf," which he would expand into his first novel, *Night Rider* (1939). During his training at Oxford, Warren also contributed to the Southern Agrarian writers manifesto, *I'll Take My Stand: The South and the Agrarian Tradition, by Twelve Southerners* (1930).

Warren started his teaching career as assistant professor of English at Southwestern College in Memphis. The next year, he returned to his alma mater, Vanderbilt, and taught there for three years. In 1934, he moved on to Louisiana State University, where he taught until 1942. There Warren watched at first hand the political demagogue Huey Long, who provided the germ of the character Willie Stark in *All the King's Men* (1946). When Warren was actually writing the novel several years later (first as verse drama), he was living in Italy on a Guggenheim Fellowship, watching another popular people's choice, Benito Mussolini, the Fascist dictator, rise to power.

At Louisiana State, Warren began one of the most genial and fruitful partnerships in American letters—his professional relationship with Cleanth Brooks, Jr. He and Brooks cooperated first to create and edit the literary magazine *Southern Review.* Their most lasting contributions to the profession of teaching, however, were the textbooks *An Approach to Literature* (with John Thibaut Purser, 1936), *Understanding Poetry: An Anthology for College Students* (1938), and *Understanding Fiction* (1943). These did more than anything else to propagate the New Criticism, which emphasized a close examination of works of literary art to see what makes them effective.

Warren taught at the University of Minnesota between 1942 and 1950, with one year out to occupy the chair for poetry at the Library of Congress in Washington, D.C. Warren's friend, the novelist Katherine Anne Porter, who occupied the chair for fiction at the Library of Congress at that time, brought his attention to a peculiar document she had found in the archives. It was the confession of Jeremiah Beauchamp, who had been hanged for murder in Kentucky in 1826. This was the genesis of Warren's longest and most complex novel, *World Enough and Time: A Romantic Novel* (1950). Warren's last academic appointment was as professor of play writing at Yale University.

Warren was married twice, first in 1930 to Emma Brescia; they were divorced twenty years later. In 1952, he married the writer Eleanor Clark, with whom he had two children. His enchantment with his new family reawakened his poetic abilities, which had been seriously blocked for ten years. In 1953, he published his unique *Brother to Dragons: A Tale in Verse and Voices*, then, in 1957, *Promises: Poems, 1954-1956*, inspired by his children. His poetic output, winning numerous literary honors and awards, continued into the 1980's.

ANALYSIS

Warren's poetry and fiction often meditate on the twin mysteries of time and identity. Childhood is half remembered and half mythologized as a time of ignorance and innocence, sometimes expressed in terms borrowed from religion. It is a remembered paradise from which one inevitably falls from grace through original sin—that is, some malicious act or an insight into the moral ambiguity of oneself and others.

Original sin, as Warren uses the term, is not traceable to evil inherited from Adam's initial disobedience, as Christian myth describes it, but is a normal development in the process of growing up. In that sense, guilt is inevitable, and the need for redemption is a psychological state peculiar to the human psyche. There is some element of inheritance in the nature of one's individual burden of guilt, however, as the time and place of one's birth help determine the kind of illusion, sin, or temptation one encounters. Like many southern writers of Warren's generation, his being engrossed later in the history of the South, with its double jeopardy of inherited racial conflicts and defeat in the Civil War, adds a special depth to more personal family and individual problems. In this affinity for regional sorrows and predicaments, he is akin to his contemporary William Faulkner.

In some cases, the problem of identity and its moral implications are dramatized as a quest involving fathers and sons. The protagonist is often a young man in search of his father—that is, the source of his being. He may reject his biological father and choose a surrogate father whom he admires more. The ambitious protagonist of *At Heaven's Gate* (1943) despises his lowborn parent and idealizes a successful but unscrupulous business tycoon.

The romantically deluded young man in *World Enough and Time* kills the surrogate father who has been his friend and benefactor. The protagonist of *A Place to Come To* (1977, a title suggesting a spiritual home) has both envied and despised his father but, in retirement, becomes reconciled to his childhood roots in the South and befriends the foster father that he had never acknowledged. In *All the King's Men*, Jack Burden, whose very name may suggest unresolved guilt, does not even know who his father is. Moreover, Willie Stark in that novel is at least partially responsible for the death of his own son.

In some poems using a very young persona, such as "Court Martial," the child gains a foreboding insight into the darker side of an idealized older man—in this case, Warren's beloved grandfather. The episode is both historical and autobiographical, as well as a striking symbolic image of the frightening shadow-self that lurks in the unconscious mind. The moment when the child first glimpses the dark side of a loved person may pave the way for an understanding of his own capacity for evil. That self-recognition is necessary for emotional and moral maturity.

Trained as he was in the classical tradition of Greek, Shakespearean, and Jacobean drama, which he often taught, Warren was very conscious of the tragic sense of life. While human destiny may seem fated or inevitable, it is nevertheless self-chosen and rooted in individual character. One learns through error and suffering. The self-knowledge gained in this process may end in disaster or, in more fortunate circumstances, may result in a reconciliation and renewed love for life. Warren noted how, in his classes at Louisiana State (which was Huey Long's alma mater) the students' attention sharpened as he discussed the political background of William Shakespeare's *Julius Caesar.*

Tragedy came alive when Huey Long was assassinated, almost on the steps of the state capitol, in a seeming replay of historical drama.

Warren often used local legends or adapted historical events for literary purposes. He made no claims for literal accuracy. He disclaimed any actual knowledge of Huey Long, for example, but he listened to the endless legends that circulated among the common people who thought they had found a champion at last against the aristocratic, wealthy families who controlled southern politics.

Physical deformity was sometimes used by Warren to suggest or symbolize the human character flaw that afflicts all people. Such flawed characters are not necessarily bad persons; in fact, in some cases, such a visible sign of imperfection seems to help the sufferer to avoid inordinate pride and attain a measure of redemption. In the poem "Original Sin," the defect is first associated with an old man's disfiguring wen, later with some foolish monster, and still later rather fondly with an old dog, scratching at the door, or a tired horse put out to pasture. Warren has even used a glass eye, which he himself wore, as indicative of some secret flaw. Sometimes the sign is more obvious, such as the clubfoot of the idealistic young immigrant who comes to America to help free the slaves in the Civil War novel *Wilderness: A Tale of the Civil War* (1961).

In his long career, Warren sought to reconcile some of the most contradictory elements of American intellectual life, particularly the inheritance of eighteenth century optimism about humankind's essential goodness and social progress with the darker, romantic consciousness of good and evil advanced by such American writers as Nathaniel Hawthorne and Herman Melville. Although Warren may lean heavily on the symbolism and imagery of romanticism, he does so with an irony that recognizes illusion and myth as necessary parts of human consciousness. Warren believed that the self is not synonymous with the ego alone but must include irrational elements of the subconscious, through which the individual is bound to all humanity and to nature.

ALL THE KING'S MEN

First published: 1946
Type of work: Novel

Jack Burden, former newspaperman and former graduate student of history, gains self-knowledge through his association with a charismatic politician.

All the King's Men, which won the Pulitzer Prize in fiction, has sometimes been called the best political novel written in the United States. Nevertheless, its emphasis is on the private psychological roots of action that is played out on a public political stage. The social milieu is authentically drawn, with redneck farmers pitted against entrenched aristocratic families.

Jack Burden is in between the political forces, initially simply a spectator and a reporter from an upper-middle-class background, watching with curiosity and a certain fascination as a man from the farm becomes a self-taught lawyer and moves into politics. Plain-speaking Willie Stark, who hardly looks like a hero, learns to capture an audience of poor dirt farmers and small-town businessmen, in whom he inspires almost fanatical devotion. He is a cunning, hardworking, expedient politician, promising to build roads and bridges in the isolated rural areas and hospitals for the common people.

It is a story of men who do not know themselves. Willie Stark thinks he can use evil means to achieve good ends. Jack Burden tries to avoid guilt by running away from it or simply not seeing it, and he does not recognize his own father and inadvertently kills him. Judge Irwin, representative of the old genteel tradition, literally forgets his original sin. Adam Stanton, the puritan idealist, suddenly casts off all restraints to kill Willie Stark.

Stark attains power partly by understanding and controlling other men. He recruits Jack for his personal staff, partly for his skill in research. Jack's first task at the outset of their relationship is to "find something" on an old friend of his father, Judge Irwin, who had been like a father to Jack in his younger days. The reason for the investigation is that Judge Irwin has come out for Stark's opponent in the upcoming election.

Jack pursues this inquiry into Judge Irwin's background with a curious objectivity, convinced, on one hand, that there can be no hint of wrongdoing in what he calls "the case of the upright judge" and, on the other hand, wondering whether Stark's assessment of human nature may, after all, be accurate.

Stark's answer to Jack's assurances that there could be nothing dishonorable in the background of Judge Irwin is reiterated three times in the novel: "Man is conceived in sin and born in corruption and he passeth from the stink of the didie to the stench of the grave. There is always something." Burden does, in fact, find "something" in the forgotten past. Not only did the upright judge once accept a bribe, but he was also protected by the equally immaculate Governor Stanton, father of Adam and Anne, Jack's dearest childhood friends. Anne had been Jack's first love.

The career of Willie Stark quickly becomes, to Jack, more than an interesting spectator sport, and his employment becomes more than a convenient job serving a dynamic personality. Burden becomes enmeshed in a complex web of relationships and circumstances that involve his own past, as well as the uneasy present and the dubious future. Burden holds on to his knowledge about the judge until Anne herself asks him to convince her brother Adam, now a celebrated surgeon, that he should accept the directorship of the new medical center that Willie wants to build.

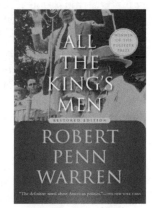

Jack understands that the only way to influence Adam in this respect is to change his mind about the moral nature of the world—to break his conviction that good and evil can be kept separate. How better to achieve this than to reveal that the idealized father and the irreproachable judge were themselves guilty of political crimes?

The bitter knowledge of his father's expedient compromise with honor has the desired effect on the puritanical Adam. He makes an uneasy alliance with Stark (whom he despises) for the sake of doing good. Stark seems to have made his point—

good must be made out of evil, because, he says, that is all there is from which to make it. Even Stark, expedient and pragmatic as he is, has a vision of the hospital, which is to be free to anyone who needs medical service, as an unsullied oasis in a grimy world, a monument of his own submerged idealism. This tension between persons who seem unalterably opposed, yet are drawn to a common purpose, is one of Warren's favorite devices for revealing the moral ambiguity of human motivations.

Burden, still withholding from Stark the information about Irwin, suffers a profound shock when he learns from Stark's secretary and sometime mistress that Stark has become Anne Stanton's lover. Burden precipitously drives out West until he is stopped by the Pacific Ocean. There he drops into what he calls the "Great Sleep," a neurotic reaction which has afflicted him before—once when he walked out on his Ph.D. studies in history and once when he walked out on his wife.

From the Great Sleep, Jack is born again into a bleak but emotionally insulating belief in the "Great Twitch"—an understanding of the world as completely amoral and mechanistic, wherein nobody has any responsibility for what happens. He returns to his job as if nothing had happened. He hardly hesitates at all when Stark wants to use the evidence against Judge Irwin. Burden's education in hard reality has only begun, however, and the shell of indifference is irrevocably broken with even more unexpected revelations. It is a lesson in tragedy that involves several families, with Jack Burden, Anne Stanton, and Willie Stark's faithful wife as survivors.

Quite aside from the dramatic elements of political chicanery, adultery, suicide, and murder that make this an exciting story, the novel suggests a more subtle observation about a symbiotic psychological dependency between people. No one is complete and self-sufficient—not even Anne, though the narrator, Jack, early in the book assumes that she is peculiarly integrated and whole. Anne actually shares with Jack an essential passivity that makes them both feed emotionally on the dynamic energy of Willie Stark. The gravitation of the passive personality to the active man also has its political expression, accounting for the success of the demagogue with his constituency, who feel themselves to be socially and politically helpless.

"THE BALLAD OF BILLIE POTTS"

First published: 1943 (collected in *The Collected Poems of Robert Penn Warren*, 1998)
Type of work: Poem

A rascally innkeeper fails to recognize his own son, who is returning home from the Western frontier, and murders him for his gold.

"The Ballad of Billie Potts" is perhaps the most striking of Warren's early poems. In a little over thirteen pages, it brings together several of the themes that would concern him for a lifetime: the passage from childhood innocence into guilt, the journey that ends with a return to the father or to the place of origin, the undiscovered self, and a certain mysticism that unites each person with humankind and with nature.

Warren prefaced the poem with this note: "When I was a child I heard this story from an old lady who was a relative of mine. The scene, according to her version, was in the section of Western Kentucky known as 'Between the Rivers,' the region between the Cumberland and the Tennessee." According to legend, Billie Potts kept an inn on one of the popular frontier routes along which early travelers to the West passed. He communicated regularly with bands of cutthroats, notifying them of the routes his guests were taking into the wilderness. The robbers shared with him any booty that they could acquire from ambushing the travelers.

Billie Potts and his wife have a son whom they both adore. The son, thinking he will prove his worth to his father, attempts to kill and rob a stranger by himself instead of conveying the information to more experienced killers, as he was told to do. He botches the job and returns home in humiliation. His father, in anger, turns him out to make his fortune as best he can.

Years later, the son, having prospered out West, returns in triumph, sporting a heavy beard, a handsome coat, and a bag of gold. He conceals his identity for a while, hoping to tease his parents, but they, thinking he is only another traveler, murder him for his money. The parents learn too late, through an identifying birthmark, that they have killed the only person they ever loved. Warren captures the rhyming, lilting, occasionally uneven rhythm of folk ballad, its colloquial language combined with an occasionally oracular tone.

The comment upon the action, which universalizes the legend, appears in parentheses. Warren uses the second-person voice, as he does in a number of poems, to indicate the conscious self, which does not recognize the unconscious shadow-self. What at first seems a simple device to show what it was like in the nineteenth century West—a guided tour of the past, so to speak—becomes a way of involving the reader, as conscious ego, in a somber psychodrama. The final meditation is almost a benediction, likening the wanderer's return (not only Billie's now, but also the reader's own) to the mysterious natural forces that direct the salmon's return to the "high pool" of its birth, with its ambiguous implications of both innocence and death.

> The salmon heaves at the fall, and wanderer, you
> Heave at the great fall of Time, and gorgeous,
>   gleam
> In the powerful arc, and anger and outrage like
>   dew,
> In your plunge, fling, and plunge to the
>   thunderous stream:
> Back to the silence, back to the pool, back
> To the high pool, motionless, and the
>   unmurmuring dream.
> . . . .
> And the father waits for the son.

BROTHER TO DRAGONS

First published: 1953
Type of work: Poem

Characters from the past and present, including Thomas Jefferson and Robert Penn Warren, comment upon the brutal murder of a slave.

After a ten-year period of writing prose, during which he found poems impossible to finish, Warren emerged as a poet of peculiar power and originality with the publication in 1953 of *Brother to Dragons: A Tale in Verse and Voices*, a book-length

poem unlike any in American literature. The subject was a shocking real-life murder perpetrated by Lilburne Lewis, a nephew of Thomas Jefferson (primary author of the Declaration of Independence and the third president of the United States).

Warren invented a unique mode of presentation for this work. It is neither narrative poem nor play but a discussion by characters long dead (except for one, the poet himself, designated as RPW), who try to understand the grisly event that occurred in the meat house when Lilburne Lewis hacked a teenage slave to pieces with an ax for breaking a pitcher belonging to Lilburne's late mother, Lucy Jefferson Lewis. The other slaves witnessed this performance. As Warren explains in a brief preface: "We may take them to appear and disappear as their urgencies of argument swell and subside. The place of this meeting is, we may say, 'no place,' and the time is 'any time.'" Besides the victim, the main characters include Lilburne, the killer; Isham Lewis, who watched his older brother commit the murder; their mother, Lucy; her brother, Thomas Jefferson; Letitia, Lilburne's wife; Aunt Cat, Lilburne's Negro mammy; Meriwether Lewis, Lilburne's cousin, who went West on the Lewis and Clark expedition; and RPW.

The central character, if the poem can be said to have one, is not the hapless victim, who has only one brief speech in the first edition (three in the 1979 revision). It is not even Lilburne, the moral monster, but Thomas Jefferson, inheritor of the eighteenth century optimism about the perfectibility of humankind. The poem examines the hideous event and ponders why it occurred, but it is Jefferson who develops and changes in the poem. There is no evidence that the historical Thomas Jefferson ever discussed or even acknowledged the murder, a fact which suggested to Warren that he could not face the thought of such barbarity in one of his own blood.

Actually, the stance of Jefferson in the poem is initially quite grim and cynical. He has already recognized that he had been overly optimistic in his view of human nature. The moral project of the poem is not to convince Jefferson of the reality of evil, which he affirms from the first, but to convince him that he himself shares that burden of human evil. This humbling of Jefferson is achieved primarily by burdening him with some guilt for the fate of

Meriwether Lewis, who had once been his secretary; this part of the poem is not completely convincing. The real Meriwether Lewis committed suicide when he was governor of the Louisiana Territory, but the reader does not know, from the poem itself, what happened or why Jefferson should share any guilt in the matter. Jefferson ultimately achieves some kind of universalized feeling for his fellows that includes even the despised Lilburne.

The discussion and the narrative action of the first hundred pages are gripping, both mentally and emotionally. At the psychological level, Warren suggests that the act of murder was a ritualized attempt to purge Lilburne's own evil. The slave is Lilburne's shadow-self, the scapegoat whose elimination will bring order in a chaotic world or in Lilburne's chaotic psyche. The butcher block, on which the boy lies curled in the fetal position with eyes tightly closed, suggests an altar to some savage god.

The death of Lilburne repeats the psychological ritual, with Lilburne playing victim, the dark shadow of his brother Isham. Lilburne forces Isham into a suicide pact, whereby they will shoot each other at the count of ten over their mother's grave. He counts to ten very slowly, knowing full well that Isham will panic and shoot first, then try to escape. During this melodramatic scene, there is a great earthquake. This event may seem like a piece of gothic fiction, but, in fact, there was such an earthquake at about that time—one of the biggest ever recorded in that area.

Jefferson observes in the poem that slain monsters and dragons are innocent. All heroes, whether Hercules, David with his sling, or Jack of the beanstalk, are playing "the old charade" in which man dreams that he can destroy the objectified bad and then feel good: "While in the deep/ Hovel of the heart the Thing lies/ That will never unkennel himself to the contemptible steel."

"TO A LITTLE GIRL, ONE YEAR OLD, IN A RUINED FORTRESS"

First published: 1957 (collected in *Promises: Poems, 1954-1956,* 1957)
Type of work: Poems

His child's innocent delight in natural beauty helps a father to accept the suffering that life brings.

Warren broke away from his somewhat morose obsession with evil with his sparkling *Promises,* winner of his first Pulitzer Prize in poetry. The first five poems of *Promises* are dedicated to Warren's daughter Rosanna under the general title "To a Little Girl, One Year Old, in a Ruined Fortress." The setting is the imposing ruin overlooking the Mediterranean Sea where Warren and his second wife, Eleanor, lived in Italy—Cesare Borgia's hunting ground, said Warren, who always knows his history—"those blood-soaked stones." The first poem of the series, "Sirocca," speaks of Philip of Spain, "the black-browed, the anguished,/ For whom nothing prospered, though he loved God." His arms, carved in stone, which once stood over the drawbridge, have long since fallen into the moat, buried in garbage. Yet the blue blooms of rosemary and the gold bloom of thistle flourish there, bringing gay laughter to the golden-haired child.

The poem establishes a contrast of perception, maintained through the five poems, between the innocence and delight of the child's view of the world and the darker awareness of the father, who knows the evil and suffering enacted here—and which still goes on in the world. Nevertheless, because he participates in and marvels at the child's innocent joy in nature, the speaker becomes reconciled to the world, believing, or at least praying, that all can be redeemed.

The second and third poems introduce some of the human misery existing in this beautiful setting. The pathetic, defective child next door has cried all night; her disabilities are the result of an unsuccessful attempt at abortion. The "monster's" twelve-year-old sister, who is "beautiful like a saint," has taught the disabled child to make the Italian sign for *ciao.* The speaker, galled at the assumption that suffering and tragedy have any such simplistic solution as a catchword for "okay," is moved to metaphysical rebellion, like Russian novelist Fyodor Dostoevski's Ivan Karamazov, who refused salvation at the price of the suffering of children.

The fourth poem, "The Flower," is the climax, where the little daughter's joy in a natural ritual dispels the speaker's rebellion against the world's injustice and pain. He is carrying the child up the cliff from the beach, where in the past she has been given a white flower to hold and a blue one for her hair. As it is now fall, the parents are hard put to find a white bloom not sadly browned and drooping, but the child accepts gladly the best one they can find, "as though human need/ Were not for perfection." The lyrical joy of this hour seems to transfigure time itself. The parents look back and see a single gull hovering on a saffron sunset. They note that the white gull looks black, but it swings effortlessly as it descends, changing from black to white and back, according to its background and the direction of light, suggesting to the poet that at least some aspects of reality are matters of human perception. Context determines meaning.

The final poem in this sequence, "Colder Fire," is less serene than "The Flower," with its sense of exaltation. It begins humbly, re-admitting, so to speak, the persistent negative. Though the speaker knows that "the heart should be steadfast," he is often helpless to command his own moods. The speaker sits in the sun with his child on his lap, watching the white butterflies, soon to die, in their "ritual carouse," nature's assurance of an immortality of the flesh; the butterflies reflect the father's sense of immortality in his child. Warren achieves a remarkable fusion of thought, passion, and concrete imagery in this to form a vision of spiritual transcendence without violating or misrepresenting actual human experience, with its reality of pain and death.

SUMMARY

Warren, the first poet laureate of the United States, produced ten novels and eighteen books of poetry as well as short stories, plays, biography, social commentary, and literary criticism. His best novels are probably *All the King's Men* and *World Enough and Time*; his best-known short story is "Blackberry Winter." He won his third Pulitzer Prize when he was seventy-three years old for *Now and Then: Poems, 1976-1978*. At age seventy-eight, he produced his last book-length poem, *Chief Joseph of the Nez Percé* (1983). A colleague at Yale University once called Warren the "most complete man of letters we've ever had in this country."

Katherine Snipes

BIBLIOGRAPHY

By the Author

SHORT FICTION:
Blackberry Winter, 1946
The Circus in the Attic, and Other Stories, 1947

LONG FICTION:
Night Rider, 1939
At Heaven's Gate, 1943
All the King's Men, 1946
World Enough and Time: A Romantic Novel, 1950
Band of Angels, 1955
The Cave, 1959
Wilderness: A Tale of the Civil War, 1961
Flood: A Romance of Our Time, 1964
Meet Me in the Green Glen, 1971
A Place to Come To, 1977

POETRY:

Thirty-six Poems, 1935
Eleven Poems on the Same Theme, 1942
Selected Poems, 1923-1943, 1944
Brother to Dragons: A Tale in Verse and Voices, 1953
Promises: Poems, 1954-1956, 1957
You, Emperors, and Others: Poems, 1957-1960, 1960
Selected Poems: New and Old, 1923-1966, 1966
Incarnations: Poems, 1966-1968, 1968
Audubon: A Vision, 1969
Or Else—Poem/Poems, 1968-1974, 1974
Selected Poems 1923-1975, 1976
Now and Then: Poems, 1976-1978, 1978
Brother to Dragons: A New Version, 1979
Being Here: Poetry 1977-1980, 1980
Ballad of a Sweet Dream of Peace, 1980 (with Bill
    Komodore)
Rumor Verified: Poems, 1979-1980, 1981
Chief Joseph of the Nez Percé, 1983
New and Selected Poems, 1923-1985, 1985
The Collected Poems of Robert Penn Warren, 1998 (John Burt, editor)

DRAMA:

Proud Flesh, pr. 1947
All the King's Men, pr. 1958 (adaptation of his novel)

NONFICTION:

John Brown: The Making of a Martyr, 1929
Modern Rhetoric, 1949 (with Cleanth Brooks)
Segregation: The Inner Conflict in the South, 1956
Selected Essays, 1958
The Legacy of the Civil War: Meditations on the Centennial, 1961
Who Speaks for the Negro?, 1965
Democracy and Poetry, 1975
Portrait of a Father, 1988
New and Selected Essays, 1989
Cleanth Brooks and Robert Penn Warren: A Literary Correspondence, 1998 (James A. Grimshaw, Jr., editor)
Selected Letters of Robert Penn Warren, 2000-2001 (2 volumes; William Bedford Clark, editor)
Conversations with Robert Penn Warren, 2005 (Gloria L. Cronin and Ben Siegel, editors)

EDITED TEXTS:

An Approach to Literature, 1936 (with Cleanth Brooks and John Thibault Purser)
Understanding Poetry: An Anthology for College Students, 1938 (with Brooks)
Understanding Fiction, 1943 (with Brooks)
Faulkner: A Collection of Critical Essays, 1966
Randall Jarrell, 1914-1965, 1967 (with Robert Lowell and Peter Taylor)
American Literature: The Makers and the Making, 1973 (with R. W. B. Lewis)

DISCUSSION TOPICS

- Who were the Fugitives, and what was Robert Penn Warren's contribution to their activities?

- What generalizations can be made about the relationships of fathers and sons in Warren's fiction?

- What does Jack Burden learn from his association with Willie Stark in *All the King's Men*?

- Consider *Brother to Dragons* as a psychological study of guilt.

- What is New Criticism? What roles did Warren play in this critical movement?

About the Author

Blotner, Joseph. *Robert Penn Warren: A Biography.* New York: Random House, 1997.
Bohner, Charles. *Robert Penn Warren.* Rev. ed. Boston: Twayne, 1981.
Burt, John. *Robert Penn Warren and American Idealism.* New Haven, Conn.: Yale University Press, 1988.

Clark, William Bedford, ed. *Critical Essays on Robert Penn Warren.* Boston: G. K. Hall, 1981.

Grimshaw, James A. *Understanding Robert Penn Warren.* Columbia: University of South Carolina Press, 2001.

Justus, James H. *The Achievement of Robert Penn Warren.* Baton Rouge: Louisiana State University Press, 1981.

Madden, David, ed. *The Legacy of Robert Penn Warren.* Baton Rouge: Louisiana State University Press, 2000.

Ruppersburg, Hugh. *Robert Penn Warren and the American Imagination.* Athens: University of Georgia Press, 1990.

Szczesiul, Anthony. *Racial Politics and Robert Penn Warren's Poetry.* Gainesville: University Press of Florida, 2002.

Watkins, Floyd C., John T. Hiers, and Mary Louise Weaks, eds. *Talking with Robert Penn Warren.* Athens: University of Georgia Press, 1990.

WENDY WASSERSTEIN

Born: Brooklyn, New York
October 18, 1950
Died: New York, New York
January 30, 2006

As a successful comic playwright, Wasserstein gave voice to the dilemmas and triumphs of modern women.

Courtesy, Dartmouth College

BIOGRAPHY

Wendy Wasserstein was born in Brooklyn, New York, on October 18, 1950. She was the youngest of the five children of Morris W. Wasserstein, a textile manufacturer, and Lola Scheifer Wasserstein, an amateur dancer, both immigrants from Central Europe. An awkward young girl and a less than elegant dresser, Wendy developed a sense of humor as a survival skill. When she was thirteen, her family moved to the fashionable East Side of Manhattan, where she attended the Calhoun School, an exclusive girls' prep school. In order to be excused from athletics, she wrote the school's musical revue for the mother/daughter luncheons. She also studied at the June Taylor School of Dance and frequently attended Broadway shows.

Wasserstein attended Mount Holyoke College, where she studied to be a congressional intern. Her interest in theater, however, was sparked by a summer playwriting course at Smith College and by her junior year excursion at Amherst College, where she participated in theatrical productions. After earning a bachelor of arts degree in history from Mount Holyoke, she received a master of arts in creative writing from the City University of New York, where she studied under novelist Joseph Heller and playwright Israel Horowitz. In 1973, her play *Any Woman Can't*, a satire about a woman whose failure as a tap dancer leads her to marry an egotistical sexist, was produced Off-Broadway at Playwrights Horizons, a theater that would play a significant part in her career.

In 1973, Wasserstein was accepted by both the Columbia School of Business and the Yale University School of Drama, and she chose to attend Yale. While at Yale, she wrote *Happy Birthday, Montpelier Pizz-zazz* (1974), a cartoonish caricature of college life focusing on male domination of women, and she collaborated with Christopher Durang on *When Dinah Shore Ruled the Earth* (1975), a parody of beauty contests. These early plays about the suppression of women display an absurdist humor depending on comic caricatures and a broad use of irony.

In her 1975 one-act thesis production at Yale, *Uncommon Women, and Others*, Wasserstein's style moved closer to realism. During a summer at the Eugene O'Neill Memorial Theater Center, she expanded the play into a full-length comedy that was eventually produced Off-Broadway in 1977. In 1978, the play appeared on public television. Critics now hailed Wasserstein as a promising new playwright, and her play was produced throughout the United States, winning her an Obie Award, a Joseph Jefferson Award, and an Inner Boston's Critics Award.

After adapting John Cheever's short story "The Sorrows of Gin" for a television production on public television, Wasserstein opened her next play, *Isn't It Romantic*, Off-Broadway in 1981. Critics found the play loosely constructed and full of unnecessary jokes. After seven revisions, she reopened the play in 1983 at Playwrights Horizons, where it achieved critical acclaim and was a box-office success, running for 733 performances.

In 1983, her one-act play *Tender Offer,* about a father who misses his daughter's dance recital, was produced by the Ensemble Studio Theater. In 1986, *The Man in a Case,* her one-act adaptation of an Anton Chekhov short story, was produced by the Acting Company. Her 1986 musical *Miami* received only a workshop production. After writing for television and finishing several unproduced screenplays, she rocketed back into national prominence in 1988 with *The Heidi Chronicles,* the play that would establish her as both a noted playwright and a popular success. *The Heidi Chronicles* won the New York Drama Critics Circle Award, the Outer Critics Circle Award, and the Drama Desk Award. The play also made Wasserstein the third woman in a decade to win the Pulitzer Prize in drama and the first woman to win a Tony Award for an original drama.

Continuing her success, Wasserstein published a collection of essays, *Bachelor Girls* (1990), and opened *The Sisters Rosensweig* at Lincoln Center in 1992. As both a critical and a box-office success, the play moved to Broadway's Ethel Barrymore Theater and was nominated for a Tony Award.

Wasserstein became a single mother in 1999 and continued to write plays. She was hospitalized with lymphoma in December, 2005, however, and died a month later at the age of fifty-five.

ANALYSIS

Wasserstein ventured into playwriting partially because she felt that there was more comedy in her life than on the television situation comedies she saw as a girl. Primarily, though, she began writing plays because she believed that the women in the plays she saw were stereotypes that did not reflect the women that she knew. She set out to write meaningful comedies about women; Wasserstein's plays thus deal primarily with the relationships among intelligent, educated, and often highly successful women who are trying to come to terms with both their own identities and society's expectations. In *Uncommon Women, and Others,* all the women characters are graduates of Mount Holyoke College, a prestigious women's college for the academically superior. Harriet in *Isn't It Romantic* is an up-and-coming executive with an M.B.A. from Harvard University, and the protagonist of *The Heidi Chronicles* is an art professor with a degree from Yale. Wasserstein deals with exceptional women.

Wasserstein's exceptional heroines are asked to live up to new expectations for women, but the pressure to be exemplary has left them confused and uncertain about their identities. Much of modern drama focuses on characters who have lost their sense of purpose and cannot figure out who they are or where they belong. Wasserstein works out this theme by exploring the lives of troubled women who are trying to discover what they want in the age of women's liberation. Both Holly in *Uncommon Women, and Others* and Janie in *Isn't It Romantic* wish that they were somebody else. Susan in *The Heidi Chronicles* has been so many different people that she does not know who she is anymore.

Outside forces bear down on Wasserstein's heroines as they try to sort out their many choices. They are often torn between their inner yearnings and the many models that are given them by society. Janie and Heidi, like most of Wasserstein's women, are deciding if they want to "have it all" (a husband, children, a career, an active social and community life)—and whether having it all will even make them happy.

Wasserstein's characters are haunted by a sense of loneliness and alienation. In a world of many options, they often do not want to choose, or they become self-absorbed, always questioning their choices. Janie is afraid of living alone, but she feels that she must be true to herself and must not marry a man out of sheer desperation. Heidi, who has fulfilled her potential as a historian of women's art, feels stranded and adopts a child.

The characters in Wasserstein's plays, like those in most modern dramas, are waiting for life to change and for someone or something to transform their worlds. At a party, Holly says she has two months for something to happen before she goes out in the world; six years later, however, she is still exploring her options. Desperate not to find herself living alone like her mother, Harriet marries the first man who comes along, hoping that he will change her life. Often, fulfillment seems to lie in a distant future. In college, Rita says that she will be amazing by the age of thirty. As time passes and she has still accomplished nothing, she keeps pushing the age of success back. Heidi can see hope only in her daughter's future somewhere in the twenty-first century.

Although Wasserstein deals with the characteristic themes of modern drama, her plays do not display the harsh violence and crude realities of a world gone mad, as many contemporary dramas do. Instead, she creates nostalgic memory plays and romantic comedies focusing on rapidly changing events in which both society and individuals are in a permanent state of transition. Though inwardly confused, her characters are always witty and literate. To break the tension, they play games and act out roles. Frequently, they create romantic fantasies. For example, Heidi and Peter act out a melodramatic romance scene at their first meeting, and Mervyn in *The Sisters Rosensweig* fictionalizes a romantic night of lovemaking out of his past. In Wasserstein's plays, the pain and loneliness of life is broken up by harmless fantasies, and intense emotional confessions are followed by singing and dancing, often to corny romantic and nostalgic music.

Wasserstein's plays are built on episodic scenes that have a cinematic quality. Often she used framing devices, beginning her dramas in the present and then flashing back to the past, thus juxtaposing present realities with past expectations. Her plots depend less on strong central conflicts than on impressionistic glimpses of characters sorting out their lives. Her dialogue is full of one-liners, witty comebacks, and clever put-downs. Although she employed stereotyped characters, she gave them a sense of believability. Her comedy is often charged with a sense of feeling that either masks the pain that the characters are feeling or helps them to celebrate a moment of joy. Often, tense moments that can turn into nasty confrontations are broken up by humorous lines.

Wasserstein's satire of modern life may be brittle, but it is rarely caustic. Like her favorite playwright, Chekhov, Wasserstein tried to skirt a fine line between comedy and tragedy. Her Chekhovian characters—wacky, neurotic, but thoroughly human—are lost in their self-reflective worlds, entangled in hopeless relationships, reminiscing about past events, and looking forward to some vague future. As a playwright, Wasserstein was committed without being preachy, serious in her view of the world but comic in her expression of it.

UNCOMMON WOMEN, AND OTHERS

First produced: 1975, one act; 1977, two acts (first published, 1978)
Type of work: Play

Amid the social changes of the 1970's, a group of young women express their confusion about their goals in life.

Uncommon Women, and Others traces the choices and frustrations of a group of young women attending an exclusive women's college in the early 1970's, a time of social change in which the traditional family expectations for young women were giving way to new possibilities. The women are confused by the options open to them after graduation. The play depends less on plot than on character groupings. The characters form a spectrum of women, with Susie on one end of the spectrum and Carter on the other. Susie is a cheerleader and organizer who, without reflecting on life, bounces through a world of elegant teas, steady boyfriends, and career plans. Carter, on the other hand, is a withdrawn woman who lives solely in the world of the imagination.

Between these two peripheral characters are the five main characters, who are confused about their purposes and goals in life. On one side of the group is Kate, who wants to be a lawyer but feels that such a career choice will compel her to accept a lifetime of boring routines. On the other side is Samantha, a child/woman who will settle for marriage to a man whom she can encourage and stand behind. In the middle is the attractive Muffet, who does not know whether to wait for her prince or to strike out on her own. Balancing Kate and Samantha are two women who do not know what they want. The raunchy Rita does not want to live through a man, nor does she want the business world to transform her into the duplicate of a power-hungry man. The self-conscious Holly, pressured by her parents to lose weight and marry well, keeps postponing her choices.

The drama opens on a reunion of the five women and then flashes back six years to their senior year in college. This device allows for a contrast between the women's present conditions and their past expectations. A man's voice representing the male-dominated world spouts ambiguous clichés about the responsibilities of educated women; at the same time, scenes of the women's college gatherings, ranging from formal teas to late-night chats, are depicted onstage. These scenes are punctuated by three rambling and confused monologues delivered by Muffet, Kate, and Holly.

The contrasts in the play's structure are heightened by the contrast among the women and their lives. Samantha is celebrating the birthday of a stuffed animal, while Holly is putting cream into a diaphragm. The women sip sherry and fold their napkins at formal gatherings, then go off and discuss masturbation and the possibilities of male menstruation. These contrasts are further reflected in the women's inner turmoil. Sometimes they are self-assured; at other times, one woman wishes she were like another. These contrasting moods are captured in the play's tone, which balances sensitive moments with sharp comic exchanges.

Although they have seen the frilly world of feminine charm classes come to an end, the women are still baffled six years out of college. Holly is still collecting options that range from having a baby to becoming a birdwatcher, and Rita is waiting until she is forty-five to achieve success. *Uncommon Women, and Others* brings to the stage a series of sympathetic and ingratiating young characters, a community of women who can share their emotions, express their insecurities, and play out their fantasies together as they march off into an uncertain future.

THE HEIDI CHRONICLES

First produced: 1988 (first published, 1988)
Type of work: Play

A middle-aged art professor relives the hope and disillusionment of the women's movement.

Wasserstein was inspired to write *The Heidi Chronicles* by the image she had of a woman telling a group of other women how unhappy she feels. The play arose partially out of Wasserstein's anger that the search for personal fulfillment had led to the abandonment both of shared ideals and of a mutual acceptance of different lifestyles. At a crucial moment in the play, Heidi Holland delivers a speech to her prep school alumnae, telling them that she feels stranded.

The Heidi Chronicles, however, is not an argumentative play; it is a nostalgic journey through one woman's life. The play opens with Heidi's lecture on women's art. Heidi discusses a picture that symbolizes the brevity of youth and life. The picture reminds Heidi of a young girl at a high school dance who does not know whether to leave or stay and who simply waits for something to happen. In act 2, Heidi, still lecturing, notes that the detached woman in the painting is a spectator, not a participant. Surrounded by flashbacks, these two scenes in the present highlight the play's major themes: the passing away of youthful idealism and the isolating of an outsider who feels increasingly alienated in a changing world.

Heidi's position as an outsider structures almost every scene in the play. The flashbacks begin at a high-school dance in 1965, with Heidi sitting on the side until she meets Peter, who says that if they cannot marry they will still be friends for life. While clinging to the food table at a political gathering, she meets the charismatic  Scoop and goes off with him. Later, she accompanies her friend Susan to a women's group. She tries to remain an observer, but she confesses her inability to detach herself from Scoop. As the years flash by, Scoop goes from revolutionary to trendsetter, marrying a woman who cannot compete with him and his career. Susan moves from being a caretaker in a women's commune to working as a fast-talking television producer; her sharing sessions with other women turn into hurried executive lunches.

The play closes with an intermingling of the past and present. The play began with Heidi's meeting with Peter, followed several years later by her meeting with Scoop. The last two scenes follow the same pattern, as the sad and confused Heidi reenacts the two romantic meetings of her youth. The play opens on a nostalgic view of the past and ends with a view of a distant future in which Heidi's adopted daughter will not feel stranded and inferior.

The Heidi Chronicles provides a comic yet wistful view of the passing of a generation. It is a play about the search for identity, the vanishing of ideals, and the effects of isolation and loneliness. It is also a dreamlike play filled with songs of a bygone era, recurring images, and relived moments. Wasserstein was always aware of the history of her generation, a generation caught in the sweep of social change but forever on a journey toward self-discovery.

THE SISTERS ROSENSWEIG

First produced: 1992 (first published, 1993)
Type of work: Play

Three Jewish American sisters examine their lives and explore their future options during a birthday weekend in London.

The Sisters Rosensweig is something of a departure from Wasserstein's earlier dramas. The play takes place in one locale during a single weekend in 1991, at a time when the Soviet Union is dissolving. The action is more limited than in Wasserstein's earlier work; the play, though, is still a series of mixed-up encounters that are held together less by a tight plot than by a series of counterbalancing interactions.

The play follows the structure of Chekhov's famous play *Tri sestry* (1901; *Three Sisters*, 1920). Like Chekhov's play, it begins with the birthday party of one of the sisters, in this case the fifty-four-year-old Sara Goode. As in *Three Sisters*, the birthday gifts given are eccentric or inappropriate. Both plays take place not long after the death of a parent who has set goals for the sisters' lives—the father in Chekhov's play and the mother in Wasserstein's. Like Chekhov's play, moreover, Wasserstein's drama is built on a series of arrivals and departures, fanciful monologues, rambling retrospectives, unlikely relationships gone awry, and absurd mishaps occurring at moments of tension. The play captures the Chekhovian view of a society on the brink of change and depicts a group of insecure people who are desperately trying to find a moment of happiness in a world that is falling down around

them. Like Chekhov's plays, *The Sisters Rosensweig* mixes comedy with a feeling of sadness and a promise of hope that lies somewhere in the future. Like Wasserstein's *The Heidi Chronicles*, moreover, the play ends with a mother anticipating a brighter future for her daughter.

The characters in the play are eccentric but believable. Sara Goode, an American Jew living in London, is an executive officer with the European division of a Hong Kong bank. She has one romantic night with Mervyn Kant, a widower who has made his fortune in synthetic furs while retaining his Jewish roots. Pfeni Rosensweig, an international journalist who has set aside her work on the plight of oppressed women to write travelogues, accepts a marriage proposal from Geoffrey Duncan, a flamboyant, bisexual theater director who leaves her for a man. The third sister, Gorgeous Teitelbaum, a forty-six-year-old housewife who has become an amateur psychiatrist on a radio talk show, is taking a group of women from her temple on a tour to see England's crown jewels.  Pfeni has seen a relationship slip away, and Gorgeous has to go home to her unemployed husband, who writes mysteries in their basement.

Although the play is set against the backdrop of social and political upheaval, the larger social world is kept at a distance. Characters struggle with their identities, examine their life choices, and try to seize a moment of happiness. After the social activism they saw in *The Heidi Chronicles*, some critics were disappointed that Wasserstein had moved toward traditional drawing-room comedy. *The Sisters Rosensweig*, however, is consistent with her other plays. It is less a play about issues than a play about people.

SUMMARY

Wasserstein brought to the stage the hopes and frustrations of modern American women. Her plays are about the quest for identity and the struggle of women to fulfill their personal ambitions without being molded by social pressures; she depicted a generation reflecting on its lost ideals and examining new possibilities. Wasserstein's dramas focus on character instead of plot and are thought-provoking without being preachy, comedic without sacrificing sentiment, and theatrical without losing believability. Critics who favor more revolutionary dramas about women find her plays too traditional and trivializing, but those who champion her works find them stimulating as well as entertaining.

Paul Rosefeldt

BIBLIOGRAPHY

By the Author

DRAMA:
Any Woman Can't, pr. 1973
Happy Birthday, Montpelier Pizz-zazz, pr. 1974
When Dinah Shore Ruled the Earth, pr. 1975 (with Christopher Durang)
Uncommon Women, and Others, pr. 1975 (one act), pr. 1977 (two acts), pb. 1978
Isn't It Romantic, pr. 1981, revised pr. 1983, pb. 1984
Tender Offer, pr. 1983, pb. 2000 (one act)
The Man in a Case, pr., pb. 1986 (one act; adaptation of Anton Chekhov's short story)
Miami, pr. 1986 (musical)
The Heidi Chronicles, pr., pb. 1988
The Heidi Chronicles, and Other Plays, pb. 1990
The Sisters Rosensweig, pr. 1992, pb. 1993
An American Daughter, pr. 1997, pb. 1998
Waiting for Philip Glass, pr., pb. 1998 (inspired by William Shakespeare's Sonnet 94)
The Festival of Regrets, pr. 1999 (libretto)
Old Money, pr. 2000, pb. 2002
Seven One-Act Plays, pb. 2000

NONFICTION:
Bachelor Girls, 1990
Shiksa Goddess: Or, How I Spent My Forties, 2001

CHILDREN'S LITERATURE:
Pamela's First Musical, 1996
Sloth, 2005

SCREENPLAY:
The Object of My Affection, 1998 (adaptation of Stephen McCauley's novel)

TELEPLAYS:
The Sorrows of Gin, 1979 (from the story by John Cheever)
"Drive," She Said, 1984
The Heidi Chronicles, 1995 (adaptation of her play)
An American Daughter, 2000 (adaptation of her play)

DISCUSSION TOPICS

- How did Wendy Wasserstein use humor to comment on the status of American women?

- How did Wasserstein use music to support her themes?

- Discuss Wasserstein's use of flashbacks. Is this device more effective than presenting events in chronological order?

- How does *Uncommon Women, and Others* reflect the social changes of the 1970's?

- *The Heidi Chronicles* deals with the search for identity. What does Heidi discover about herself over the course of the play?

- Compare the characters and themes of *The Sisters Rosensweig* to those of Anton Chekhov's *The Three Sisters* (1901).

- Wasserstein's plays have been characterized as too traditional. Defend or attack this view.

About the Author

Balakian, Jan. "Wendy Wasserstein: A Feminist Voice from the Seventies to the Present." In *The Cambridge Companion to American Women Playwrights*, edited by Brenda Murphy. New York: Cambridge University Press, 1999.

Barnett, Claudia. *Wendy Wasserstein: A Casebook.* New York: Garland, 1999.

Becker, Becky K. "Women Who Choose: The Theme of Mothering in Selected Dramas." *American Drama* 6 (Spring, 1997): 43-57.

Betsko, Kathleen, and Rachel Koenig. "Wendy Wasserstein." In *Interviews with Contemporary Women Playwrights*. New York: Beech Tree Books, 1987.

Ciociola, Gail. *Wendy Wasserstein: Dramatizing Women, Their Choices, and Their Boundaries*. Jefferson, N.C.: McFarland, 1998.

Franklin, Nancy. "The Time of Her Life." *New Yorker* 73 (April 14, 1997): 62-68, 70-71.

Homes, A. M. "Wendy Wasserstein." *BOMB* 75 (Spring, 2001): 34-39.

Hubbard, Kim. "Wendy Wasserstein." *People Weekly* 33 (June 25, 1990): 99-106.

Rosen, Carol. "An Unconventional Life." *Theater Week* 6 (November 8, 1992): 17-27.

Wasserstein, Wendy. "Holidays on the Keyboard." In *The Writing Life: Writers on How They Think and Work*, edited by Marie Arana. New York: PublicAffairs, 2003.

Whitfield, Stephen J. "Wendy Wasserstein and the Crisis of (Jewish) Identity." In *Daughters of Valor: Jewish American Women Writers*, edited by Jay Halio and Ben Siegel. Newark: University of Delaware Press, 1997.

© Marc Hefty

JAMES WELCH

Born: Browning, Montana
November 18, 1940
Died: Missoula, Montana
August 4, 2003

Welch, a poet, novelist, and historian of American Indian ancestry, offers a view of life in the nineteenth and twentieth century American West through the eyes of its original inhabitants.

BIOGRAPHY

James Phillip Welch was born in Browning, Montana, the administrative center of the Blackfeet Indian Reservation, and attended school on the Blackfeet and Fort Belknap reservations as a boy. His father, James, Sr., a member of the Blackfeet, was a rancher, welder, and hospital administrator for the Indian Health Service. His mother, Rosella O'Bryan Welch, a member of the Gros Ventre tribe, worked for the Bureau of Indian Affairs.

Welch attended the University of Minnesota and Northern Montana College before completing a bachelor of arts degree at the University of Montana in 1965. The following year he began a master's program in creative writing with poet Richard Hugo. In an interview, Welch credited Hugo, who became a close personal friend, with helping him find his way as a writer. Hugo "opened up a world" to him with some simple advice: "Write about what you know. Where'd you grow up, what was your Indian heritage, what kind of landscape was there?" Welch taught briefly at the university in Missoula and in 1968 married Dr. Lois Monk, a professor of comparative literature.

Although Welch was not raised in a traditional way, he had grown up around reservations, listening to stories and absorbing knowledge that would later inform his writing. One example of this can be found in the title of his first book and only collection of poems, *Riding the Earthboy Forty* (1971); the title refers to the fact that, as a youngster, Welch spent time working on a forty-acre field on a ranch owned by neighbors, the Earthboy family. The Earthboy ranch also appears in Welch's second book, the novel *Winter in the Blood* (1974), which opens with a quotation from his poem "In My Lifetime" and a description of the "Earthboy place," fictionalized as a cabin near the narrator's home.

In 1976, Welch held the Theodore Roethke Chair in Poetry at the University of Washington. He later served as a visiting professor there and at Cornell University. After the publication of *The Death of Jim Loney* in 1979, he wrote the historical novel *Fools Crow* (1986), which would become his most successful book, especially in Western Europe. It also won the *Los Angeles Times* Book Prize for fiction, the American Book Award, and the Pacific Northwest Booksellers Award.

A fourth novel, *The Indian Lawyer,* followed in 1990, suggested in part by Welch's ten-year service on the Montana State Board of Pardons. In 1992 he was asked to coauthor the script of the documentary "Last Stand at Little Bighorn," for the public television series *The American Experience.* This film script, and the tribal research it required, inspired his only nonfiction book, *Killing Custer: The Battle of Little Bighorn and the Fate of the Plains Indians* (1994), with Paul Stekler, which presented an account of the 1876 massacre of General George Custer's army from an Indian perspective. Author Sherman Alexie praised this as "the first history book written for Indians."

Welch was named a Chevalier of the Order of

Arts and Letters by the French government for *Fools Crow* in 1995; in later years, the Welches traveled often in France. His final novel, *The Heartsong of Charging Elk* (2000), based on a historical incident, replaced his customary Montana setting with nineteenth century France. At his death from a heart attack in 2003, he had been working on a sequel to bring Charging Elk home.

ANALYSIS

Welch's situation as a writer is characterized in three lines of his poem "In My First Hard Springtime."

> My horse, Centaur, part cayuse,
> was fast and mad and black. Dandy in flat hat
> and buckskin, I rode the town and called it mine.

The poet's horse has a name imported from Greek mythology, but the animal with the European name is neither white nor assimilated. It is "fast and mad and black" and of Native American ancestry, for it is "part cayuse," a breed developed by Indians.

Welch's ethnic background is Native American, but the language he uses and the education that helped him to become a writer are European in style. His writing thus poses a question: Is it possible to do justice to Native American themes using the language of the invasion?

This poem answers by showing a poet proud to "ride the town" outfitted in the clothes of two cultures: European American flat hat, Indian buckskin. In the iconography of the West, "the town" is the definitive European American space, and the townspeople are on top of it. In Welch's poem, the poet is on top. He rides triumphantly, flaunting his Indian heritage, claiming this imported space for himself, reversing the convention that says it is always Europeans who "discover" and claim territory owned by Indians.

Early in his career, Welch stated that he wanted to be known as a poet, not as an "Indian poet." He believed that writers of Indian heritage have some advantages in the presentation of Indian themes. "Whites have to adopt a stance to write about Indian material," he explained. "For Indian writers that material is much more natural."

Natural or not, Indian themes are challenging for a serious writer. At the time Welch was beginning his career, few literary models were available. Clichés abounded in classical American literature; fantasy Indians such as Henry Wadsworth Longfellow's Hiawatha or James Fenimore Cooper's Uncas reflected the European stereotype of the "noble savage," once described by Welch in an ironic poem ("Directions to the Nomad") as a "mad decaying creep."

The most useful model Welch had to work with was N. Scott Momaday's *House Made of Dawn* (1968), the story of a Pueblo Indian who returns from World War II suffering from culture shock and alcoholism. Complex, severe, and lyrical, this Pulitzer Prize-winning story appeared capable of defining "the Indian novel" for all time.

With each of his novels, Welch tried to do something different. His first two, *Winter in the Blood* and *The Death of Jim Loney*, owe much to Momaday. The protagonists are comparable: alienated Indian men in their early thirties (although one is full-blooded and one is not), unable to relate to families, estranged from mainstream and reservation cultures, threatened by alcoholism. Welch's style, especially his restraint and understatement in the presentation of emotionally charged themes, also appears to have been influenced by Momaday.

Welch's third and fourth novels, *Fools Crow* and *The Indian Lawyer*, move in new directions. *Fools Crow* is a finely detailed historical novel set in the last days of traditional high plains Indian culture around 1870. *The Indian Lawyer* describes the psychological and social distance that isolates an urban Indian who achieves success in mainstream terms. The protagonist, Sylvester Yellow Calf, is a respected lawyer with a promising future, but his success distances him from his Blackfeet origins, while his background distances him from the white world in which he moves professionally. Welch's last book, *The Heartsong of Charging Elk*, traces the life of an Oglala Sioux who travels with Buffalo Bill's Wild West Show in France, becomes ill with influenza, and is left behind.

From the beginning, however, Welch's writing has had its own complex, often paradoxical character. He uses restraint to show emotion, surrealism to serve the purposes of realism, lyrical nuance to reveal alienation, and ironic humor to develop serious, perhaps tragic, themes. The subtlety of his writing has given rise to a broad range of interpretation. Some critics, focusing on the theme of alienation, see Welch as a grim existentialist. Others, taken by his quirky humor, portray him as a comedian.

In Welch's works, however, humor and seriousness are not mutually exclusive. Welch uses irony to fend off sentimentality. Near the end of *Winter in the Blood*, for example, at the moment when the protagonist achieves an important insight about his Indian heritage, his horse loudly passes gas. This comic "comment" deflates the pathos of a moment of insight but does not devalue it.

As Welch pointed out, his third novel, *Fools Crow*, provides background for understanding his other books. In *Fools Crow*, the pressure brought to bear on traditional Pikuni (Blackfeet) culture by the white invasion is made starkly clear, but the Pikuni are not glorified, nor are the white characters dehumanized. Both cultures appear three-dimensional, as people with families in the background and hopes for the future; Welch presents both groups without moralizing, but he does depict the foibles, weaknesses, and other typically human limitations of all his characters. Welch's attention to human nuance helps him to present the communal nature of traditional Pikuni society without nostalgia. By showing how each individual is rooted in overlapping social, cultural, and ecological contexts, Welch makes it easier to understand the isolation described in his other books.

Welch uses landscape to illustrate alienation. In his first two novels, the Montana plains appear, in the words of one critic, as a "bleak, vast, nondescript space with a few cheap houses and bars thrown in." *Fools Crow* is set in the same geography but in another world. In the first chapters, when the settlers' influence still seems minimal, culture and nature are parts of a single pattern, consisting of story, ritual, and seasonal change. Winter, for example, signifies the return of Cold Maker, the mythological figure who brings the frigid wind from his home in the North. Fearsome but approachable, he was familiar to the Pikuni from appearances in myths and dreams.

When Fast Horse, a young Pikuni, becomes a renegade, severing ties to his immediate and extended tribal family, the traditional world collapses for him, and the land loses familiarity. He finds himself "a solitary figure in the isolation of a vast land." Cold Maker is gone, and Fast Horse has become a stranger in an empty, frozen world. This impersonal, sightless face is the same one that the land turns toward Welch's contemporary protagonists. The nameless cold that haunts them is the "winter in the blood," a season of the soul that yields to no spring or summer. This alienation is intensified in *The Heartsong of Charging Elk*, when the Sioux protagonist finds himself abandoned in a Marseilles hospital, without funds, friends, or even a common language.

WINTER IN THE BLOOD

First published: 1974
Type of work: Novel

A Blackfeet man, haunted by memories of his deceased father and brother, drifts through arbitrary adventures, chancing, finally, upon a living piece of his own history.

Winter in the Blood, Welch's first novel, met with almost unanimous critical acclaim, establishing its author as a major novelist. Narrated by its unnamed protagonist, a thirty-two-year-old Blackfeet Indian man, the story develops in a series of aimless adventures in dusty towns and bars on the edge of the reservation. The narrator, searching halfheartedly for the girlfriend who has run off with his rifle and electric razor, appears only marginally interested in his own actions. His father and brother, the only people with whom he had ever been close, are both dead, but he is more aware of their absence than of the world around him. By reliving the painful memories of their deaths, the narrator begins to come to terms with their demise. The novel's ending is ambivalent about the protagonist's future, but he appears to be moving to take control of his life.

The book's central theme is alienation. The narrator, whose namelessness underscores his estrangement, describes himself as a "servant to a memory of death." Indeed, memories of death are the only events in which he fully participates: First Raise, his father, froze on his way home from Dodson, where he drank with the white ranchers and made them laugh; Mose, his brother, was killed in an automobile crash while herding cattle.

A solitary protagonist preoccupied with death, dusty towns, and a bleak and endless landscape—

such elements seem to describe a Montana version of the alienated, half-real, half-surreal worlds portrayed by writers Albert Camus and Franz Kafka. There is, however, a starkly lyrical element in Welch's language that sets his work apart from the tradition of European surrealism. The landscape may be harsh and distant, but it is not without grace or voice. Detached as he is, Welch's narrator is still aware of the vastness of the land. He is close, so to speak, to its distance. When the night sky clears, he wonders about the stars: "One looked at them with the feeling that he might not be seeing them, but rather obscure points of white that defied distance, were both years and inches from his nose."

The ghosts and memories that haunt the land allow an echo of familiarity, a slight intimacy so frag-

ile that it can only tolerate oblique, ironic reference, as in the case of the vanishing fish. The muddy river that runs past the narrator's home has as much difficulty sustaining natural life as the narrator's psychological environment has in sustaining emotional life. The fish, trucked in by "the men from the fish department," simply disappear, until, finally, the men from the fish department disappear, too. Still, the narrator goes to the river and fishes. He catches nothing, but when he loses his lure to a fallen tree, the landscape responds: A magpie squawks "from deep in the woods on the other side of the river." Nature may be losing its ability to nurture, but it is not totally witless. It has preserved a sense of irony.

The narrator's relationship to his home is similarly complex. It is a place to which he returns, though he feels only emptiness toward the people who live there: mother, grandmother, girlfriend. "None of them counted; not one meant anything to me." Here, too, Welch uses irony to indicate a dimension of awareness in the narrator's consciousness that belies the layered indifference. The narrator remembers that his grandmother, too infirm to move out of her rocking chair, saw only the ancient tribal enemy in his Cree girlfriend and spent days plotting to murder her with a paring knife

concealed in her stocking. The girlfriend, oblivious to the old woman's scheming, spent her time reading film magazines and imagining that she looked like Raquel Welch.

The scene is ludicrous, but the author is not ridiculing these people. Along with her senility, the scene reveals the old woman's fierceness of spirit and rootedness in tradition. Despite her physical incapacity, she has a power and presence lacking in the younger woman.

The narrator takes several steps toward reclaiming his Blackfeet heritage, but each such step is interwoven with ironic and realistic elements that dispel both nostalgia for the past and unguarded optimism for the future. He discovers who his grandfather was and learns more about his grandmother's courage, but the same discovery reveals the harsh treatment she received in the traditional Blackfeet culture.

In one of the book's closing moments, the narrator throws himself into a furious, mock-epic struggle to rescue a cow stuck in a mudhole. The cow is rescued. Despite its muddy, slapstick intonations, this gesture of involvement indicates a shift away from the old habit of indifference. This bit of progress has its price: the narrator's old horse, the last living tie to the time when his father and brother were living, succumbs. Perhaps the connection was no longer necessary.

THE DEATH OF JIM LONEY

First published: 1979
Type of work: Novel

A half-breed living in a small Montana town finds both strands of his ancestry inaccessible and brings about his own death.

The theme and setting of Welch's second novel, *The Death of Jim Loney*, are similar to those of his first. Loney is a thirty-five-year-old half-breed living in Harlem, a small Montana town near the reservation. The differences between Loney and the narrator of *Winter in the Blood*, however, are considerable. The earlier book's narrator lives on the reservation and visits the towns. Jim Loney resides in town and visits the reservation, but he is not at home anywhere. He is a "breed," half non-Indian, half nonwhite, neither here nor there. His Indian mother is absent, perhaps insane; his white father is physically present in Harlem, near enough for Loney to know he is "the worst sort of dirt."

Even more than *Winter in the Blood*, this is the story of absolute isolation. Even the protagonist's name is a play on "lone" and "lonely," a fact underscored by his nickname, "The Lone Ranger." The narrator of *Winter in the Blood* felt nothing for the people in his home but realized that at least there was a place called home. The relationships seemed empty but still carried memories.

In contrast, Loney and his sister, Kate, were abandoned by their mother as infants. Their father, now a sixty-two-year-old barfly living on pasteurized cheese and scrounged beer, abandoned them as children. Kate has made a career in education and wants to bring Loney to Washington, D.C., to live with her. Loney's girlfriend, Rhea, a teacher from a wealthy family in Dallas, dreams of escaping with him to Seattle.

Kate, determined and competent, sees the extent of Loney's danger more clearly than Rhea, but Kate has clamped down her own emotional life as the price of her own survival. Rhea feels Loney's vulnerability, but she is out of her depth, lacking the experience to see the implications. "Oh, you're so lucky to have two sets of ancestors," she exclaims. "You can be Indian one day and white the next."

Loney takes some steps to try to uncover his past, but these yield nothing he can start from or move toward. The two strands of his past haunt him in memories and dreams he cannot penetrate: an ominous Bible verse from Loney's European American side ("Turn away from man in whose nostrils is breath, for of what account is he?") and daily visions of a dark bird, which Loney thinks must be something "sent by my mother's people."

Death finds its occasion when the dynamic between Loney and a hunting companion generates an accidental shooting. Loney's companion, a childhood acquaintance and successful, assimilated Indian who learned ranching from "white men from down the valley," is killed. Loney did not shoot him intentionally, but he feels that the intention was near him. He claims responsibility in order to stage his own execution at the hands of the reservation police.

FOOLS CROW

First published: 1986
Type of work: Novel

In this historical novel, an isolated band of Pikuni Indians lives in the twilight of traditional high plains Indian culture.

Each of Welch's first two novels focused on one character and fragments of immediate families. *Fools Crow*, however, is as much about the protagonist's extended family, band, and tribe as about the protagonist himself. The author has not abandoned one theme for another, replacing alienation with community; rather, he continues to work the same theme turned inside out. The interrelatedness shown in this narrative makes it possible to understand the isolation of the first two novels. Mainstream readers tend to see individualism and a certain amount of isolation as normal. This book makes it clear that the experiences of American Indians are different.

As the story begins, the main character is an uncertain adolescent, named White Man's Dog, who has no standing among his people. After he conducts himself well on a horse-stealing raid against the Crow tribe, he gains a new name, Fools Crow, and growing status as a healer and leader.

To this extent, *Fools Crow* is a traditional *Bildungsroman*, a story of transition from youth to adulthood. Yet this work is exceptional in that as the protagonist grows, his world contracts, collapsed by white encroachment, smallpox, and repeating rifles. Survivors are left sorting through the traditional ways of thinking and healing, looking for explanations that still make sense.

Several options are shown. One Pikuni chief, Heavy Runner, chooses assimilation. He allows his desire to do what is best for his people to deceive him into believing that the white people, too, want the best for them. Owl Child, on the other hand, leads a renegade group of young Pikuni men who plunder, rob, and murder. Their actions provide the white soldiers with a convenient justification for a brutal attack on a Pikuni village of mostly women and children, in what is known historically as the Marias River Massacre. (As a side note, Welch's paternal great-grandmother was one of the few Pikuni who escaped this slaughter in 1870, six years before General Custer's defeat at the Little Bighorn. Welch includes a further account of both events in *Killing Custer.*)

Fools Crow and his father reject both these options. Heavy Runner's way is based on self-deception, Owl Child's on self-destruction. Owl Child's renegades break ties with family and tribe, become dependent on the plunder they take, and fight among themselves. Despite their talk of driving out the white people, they come increasingly to reflect, in appearance and behavior, the norms of the culture they hate.

Owl Child and his followers are the nineteenth century ancestors of Welch's twentieth century protagonists. Fools Crow has a vision in which he sees Pikuni children "quiet and huddled together, alone and foreign in their own country." It is easy to imagine a young Jim Loney or the narrator of *Winter in the Blood* huddled among them.

Fools Crow hopes that the Pikuni will find a way that leads further than assimilation or suicidal resistance. Is this possible? The novel ends on a somber but resolute note: "Burdened with the knowledge of his people, their lives and the lives of their children, he knew they would survive, for they were the chosen ones."

THE INDIAN LAWYER

First published: 1990
Type of work: Novel

A modern, assimilated Blackfeet lawyer who has achieved success in the mainstream world finds that it is not what he expected.

The Indian Lawyer, perhaps Welch's least rewarding novel, follows the career of Sylvester Yellow Calf, a successful urban attorney in an otherwise white firm. He is the descendant of earlier Welch characters, *Fools Crow*'s outcast Yellow Kidney and *Winter in the Blood*'s blind Yellow Calf. Even as a respected member of the Montana State Board of Pardons and the newest partner in a prestigious Helena law firm, Sylvester feels alienated. He is not completely comfortable in either the white or the Indian world and is viewed suspiciously by many.

Abandoned by his alcoholic parents, Sylvester grew up on the Blackfeet reservation, where he was cared for by loving grandparents—although his grandmother, a tribal elder, felt ashamed that the boy preferred the outside world to the tribal. He became the star of his high school championship basketball team, but his life changed abruptly when a white sportswriter, praising his leadership and intelligence, called him a "winner for all minorities." This well-meaning salute shattered the team's unity by setting Sylvester above and apart from the others, thus violating the Indian sense of community, and his teammates grew resentful. While basketball earned him a scholarship to the University of Montana, he ultimately graduated from Stanford Law School. In many respects, Sylvester has rejected his heritage, symbolized by the medicine pouch of his warrior great-great-grandfather and the green Saab that separates him from tribal land.

Sylvester is dating the daughter of a prominent senator. She and Sylvester's wealthy law partner arrange for him to meet a party official from Washington, D.C., who urges him to consider running for Congress. Sylvester is at first stunned, then guilt-stricken by his good fortune. When he recalls a ragged little boy playing a solitary game of marbles in an empty lot, however, he realizes that his entry into politics could inspire Indian youths to make something of themselves rather than yield to hopelessness. He accepts the offer.

A parallel plot develops as the state parole board, on which Sylvester sits, convenes to hear the petition of convict Jack Harwood. Bright, manipulative, and thoroughly selfish, Harwood commits crimes for the thrill of it. He does not like Indians, and when his parole is denied he blames Sylvester. Harwood recruits his naïve young wife to blackmail the Indian lawyer and force him to reconsider his vote. Sylvester soon finds himself involved romantically with two (or perhaps three) attractive women, and the plot then deteriorates into predictability. Eventually, he withdraws his candidacy to become a legal advocate for tribal cases, yet in the final scene, he stands alone on a school playground, shooting hoops. The irony of the popular young lawyer now reduced to a solitary basketball player is not lost on him, as he goes "one on one against the only man who ever beat him."

SUMMARY

James Welch, whose books have been published in nine languages, drew his material from his Native American heritage, and his work is most power-ful whenever he maintains that focus. A central theme of his work is alienation. Although he offers an unsparing examination of Indian history and contemporary life, his style is frequently restrained and understated. He develops ideas through attention to detail and nuance in a way that is often a lyrical reminder of his poetic roots. As his wife Lois commented, he was "a major spokesman for Native American issues, the subject of all his writing."

Ted William Dreier; updated by Joanne McCarthy

BIBLIOGRAPHY

By the Author

POETRY:
Riding the Earthboy Forty, 1971, revised 1975

LONG FICTION:
Winter in the Blood, 1974
The Death of Jim Loney, 1979
Fools Crow, 1986
The Indian Lawyer, 1990
The Heartsong of Charging Elk, 2000 (also known as *Heartsong*, 2001)

NONFICTION:
Killing Custer: The Battle of Little Bighorn and the Fate of the Plains Indians, 1994 (with Paul Stekler)

About the Author

Charles, Jim. "'A World Full of Bones and Wind': Teaching Works by James Welch." *English Journal* 93, no. 4 (March, 2004): 64-69.

Curwen, Thomas. "The Book of Dreams." *Los Angeles Times*, October 1, 2000, p. 7.

Gish, Robert Franklin. *Beyond Bounds: Cross-Cultural Essays on Anglo, American Indian, and Chicano Literature*. Albuquerque: University of New Mexico Press, 1996.

Lee, Don. "About James Welch." *Ploughshares* 20, no. 1 (Spring, 1994): 193-199.

_____. *James Welch: A Critical Companion*. Westport, Conn.: Greenwood Press, 2004.

McFarland, Ron. *Understanding James Welch*. Columbia: University of South Carolina Press, 2000.

Nixon, Will. "James Welch." *Publishers Weekly* 237, no. 40 (October 5, 1990): 81-82.

Saxon, Wolfgang. Obituary. *The New York Times*, August 9, 2003, p. B6.

Seals, David. "Blackfeet Barrister." *The Nation* 251, no. 18 (November 26, 1990): 648-650.

Welch, James. "Interview with James Welch (1940-2003)." Interview by Mary Jane Lupton. *American Indian Quarterly* 29, nos. 1/2 (Winter/Spring, 2005): 198-211.

DISCUSSION TOPICS

- What differences do you find between Indian and mainstream culture? Between nineteenth and twentieth century American Indian life?

- How does the conflict between traditional and modern ways lead to misunderstandings?

- Compare the alienation experienced by James Welch's characters. Are there any Native American characters who do not display alienation?

- What role does prejudice play in Welch's work?

- Considering that Welch began his career as a poet, can you still find examples of lyricism or poetic language in his fiction?

- Comment on the significance of landscape in Welch's writing.

- Comment on his use of irony. What effects does it produce?

EUDORA WELTY

Born: Jackson, Mississippi
April 13, 1909
Died: Jackson, Mississippi
July 23, 2001

Welty is ranked high among southern fiction writers because of her unique kind of realism, which is detached but compassionate and always holds out hope that the conflicting claims of society and of the individual can be resolved for the benefit of both.

Frank Hains/Courtesy, Mississippi Department
of Archives and History

BIOGRAPHY

Eudora Welty was born in Jackson, Mississippi, on April 13, 1909. Her father, Christian Webb Welty, was originally from rural Ohio; he had met Mary Chestina ("Chessie") Andrews when he was working in West Virginia, where she was a teacher in the mountain schools near her home. To the dismay of her five adoring brothers, the new bride and her husband decided to move to Jackson. There Christian became a successful businessman. Eudora was their second child. As she recalls in *One Writer's Beginnings* (1984), her parents did not speak freely of the baby boy who had died at birth, but Eudora was aware of being cherished and even sheltered.

Welty was an observant child. Sounds and sights, musical harmonies and the cadences of human voices, the coming and the fading of the seasons, the subtle changes in human beings—all were fascinating to her. With her two younger brothers, Welty could disappear into the world of the imagination. There were also trips north and east to visit both of her parents' families. Her world was filled with stimuli, yet it was safe; the serenity that is evident in her fiction began with a happy childhood in a family filled with love.

Encouraged by her mother, Welty read a wide variety of books. Soon she was also writing. Her gifts were not only literary, however; in high school and later in college, she took lessons in drawing and painting. This visual gift was to be utilized in her photographs as well as in the memorable descriptive passages in her fiction.

After she graduated in 1925 from Central High School in Jackson, Welty spent two years at Mississippi State College for Women. In 1927, she transferred to the University of Wisconsin, where she majored in English. In *One Writer's Beginnings*, she recalls the moment when she knew that literature must be her life; as she explains it, a poem by William Butler Yeats so imbued her with passion that she believed she could live within it, possessing it and possessed by it.

However, after Welty graduated from college in 1929, she followed her father's advice: She went to New York City and entered the School of Business at Columbia University, studying advertising, so that she would be able to get a job. Unfortunately, when the Depression hit, there were no jobs in New York. In 1931, Welty returned to Jackson. That year, she suffered a great loss in the death of her father, who called himself the family optimist.

During the next several years, Welty worked for a radio station, several newspapers, and, perhaps most important, as a junior publicity agent for the Works Progress Administration. This job took her all over Mississippi; she interviewed ordinary people, wrote articles, and took photographs. Although she was writing regularly, it was her photographs that Welty first tried to sell. In 1936, she had a one-woman show of them in New York; that same year marked the appearance of her first published story, "Death of a Traveling Salesman." It was not the work of an apprentice but of a polished, mature writer whose vision and approach were uniquely her own.

After "Death of a Traveling Salesman," Welty's stories began appearing regularly in *The Southern Review* and in mass-circulation magazines such as *The Atlantic*. In 1941, her first book-length collection, *A Curtain of Green, and Other Stories*, was published. This volume was followed by a novel, *The Robber Bridegroom* (1942), the story of a magical romance that ends when the lovers see each other as the ordinary people they really are.

Now a full-time writer, Welty entered her most productive period. She published *The Wide Net, and Other Stories* (1943); a novel, *Delta Wedding* (1946); another short-story collection, *The Golden Apples* (1949); the novella *The Ponder Heart* (1954); and *The Bride of the Innisfallen, and Other Stories* (1955). A number of the works produced during this time were singled out for literary honors. For example, in 1942, "The Wide Net" won an O. Henry Award, and "Livvie Is Back" won the same prize in 1943. *The Ponder Heart* won the William Dean Howells medal; it was dramatized and became a Broadway hit in 1956.

During the next three decades, Welty published less frequently. She spent a great deal of time working on what was to be her most complex novel, *Losing Battles* (1970). She also had to deal with family problems, her mother's long illness and death and the death of a brother. One outcome of these experiences was her Pulitzer Prize-winning novel *The Optimist's Daughter* (1972). In 1980, her short fiction was brought together in a single volume entitled *The Collected Stories of Eudora Welty*, which won the American Book Award. In 1978, Welty published *The Eye of the Story*, a collection of essays and reviews that reveals much about her views of art. Two other important nonfiction works of Welty's later years were the autobiographical *One Writer's Beginnings* (1984) and *A Writer's Eye: Collected Book Reviews* (1994). Two posthumous works were *On Writing* (2002), which consisted of seven essays about literature, and *Some Notes on River Country* (2003).

The people of her native state often demonstrated their pride in Welty's accomplishments. The governor proclaimed May 2, 1973, to be Eudora Welty Day, and on April 13, 1984, the whole state joined in a celebration of the writer's seventy-fifth birthday. Welty's achievements were also recognized nationally and internationally. In 1980, she received both the National Medal of Literature and the Presidential Medal of Freedom, and in 1996, she was awarded the French Legion of Honor.

Eudora Welty died of pneumonia on July 23, 2001, in Jackson, Mississippi. She had spent her life in her native state, observing ordinary people and writing about ordinary events. In the process, she had become one of America's most important writers and one of the most beloved.

ANALYSIS

In *The Eye of the Story*, there is an essay called "Reality in Chekhov's Stories," which explains as much about Eudora Welty as it does about Anton Chekhov. Welty comments that one of Chekhov's most important contributions to fiction was his redefining of reality. Before Chekhov, there was one viewpoint in fiction, directly or obliquely the author's; after Chekhov, the writer felt free and even compelled to present various viewpoints as versions of reality. This approach necessitates a determined detachment on the part of the fiction writer. As Welty frequently explained, she does not consciously manipulate her characters; instead, she creates them and lets them speak for themselves. As a result, her short stories and novels often have the quality of a stage play.

In "A Visit of Charity," for example, Welty begins with a brief mention of the time of day; she proceeds to describe the appearance of a young girl and to give the directions for her coming onstage—in this case, into the Old Ladies' Home. Although the point of view of this story is that of fourteen-year-old Marian, who notices everything, even the smell of the room that she has chosen to enter, the minute the two old women begin to talk, there are two additional versions of reality. The old women do not agree about anything. One says that another girl has visited them, and the other says she did not; one says that her roommate is sick, and the roommate denies it; one begins to speak of her school days, and the other interrupts with a tirade to the effect that the first speaker had no life whatsoever before she came to the home to torture her roommate.

With all the controversy going on, it is no wonder that the girl herself feels as if she is in a dream; in other words, her own view of reality becomes shaky. In the final scene, after escaping from the Old Ladies' Home, Marian bites into an apple. The implication is clear: She is returning to the single and simple reality of her own appetite.

Welty's dramatic structure, then, is her way of stressing a major theme: that each character is living in a unique world. Furthermore, although Marian shuts out the past and the future by focusing on her apple, most characters live in memory and in anticipation as well as in observation of the present. In *One Writer's Beginnings*, Welty explains her idea of the basic pattern of life. Everyone is involved, she says, in a continual process, moving from memories of the past to discoveries about the present and then again back to memories. There are, however, occasions when the memories and discoveries converge in a single moment, annihilating the conventional divisions between past and present, the living and the dead. Welty calls these times "confluences."

In Welty's fiction, the confluences are usually both healing and strengthening, at least for the characters who pay attention to them, such as the naturalist James Audubon in "A Still Moment" and Phoebe in "Asphodel," who finds in the retelling of an old love story, an appearance of a naked hermit, and an attack by hungry goats the occasion for joy. The theme of confluence is reflected in the final sentence of the story, as Phoebe's reaction is described:

> She seemed to be still in a tender dream and an unconscious celebration—as though the picnic were not already set rudely in the past, but were the enduring and intoxicating present. still the phenomenon. the golden day.

Even though Welty emphasizes the uniqueness of each individual's perception, she does not therefore assume that there can be no connections between people. Indeed, most of her stories and all of her novels stress the need for acceptance, for tolerance, for a sustaining community. Welty often chooses a ceremonial gathering as the setting for a story or a novel. The title of *Delta Wedding* suggests that occasion; *Losing Battles* takes place at a birthday celebration; *The Optimist's Daughter* involves a deathbed vigil and a funeral. Even the student recital in the short story titled "June Recital" and the weekly meeting in the beauty shop described in "Petrified Man" are times when human beings come together to deal with their uncertainties and to resolve their conflicts.

As a writer, Welty was conscious of the joys of solitude; however, as a human being, she believed that there was also strength in community. The revelation that comes too late to the protagonist of "Death of a Traveling Salesman" is that his life was a waste because he never chose to become involved with other people. Although Welty never minimizes the difficulties that arise from being subject to the rules and customs of any group, she chooses to have her characters work out their own independence without rejecting their ancestors, their extended families, their neighbors, and their communities.

DELTA WEDDING

First published: 1946
Type of work: Novel

A young girl, visiting relatives who are preparing for a wedding on their Mississippi plantation, finds her own identity as part of the family.

Delta Wedding is a study of the relationships among the individual members of the Fairchild family and between that family and the rest of the world. The setting for the story is Shellmound, the Mississippi plantation that is the home of Battle Fairchild; his wife, Ellen Fairchild; and their eight children, as well as of various female relatives and black servants. Shellmound is not merely a backdrop; it is the center of family life. The sound of Shellmound is the sound of conversation; this is a place where people gather to talk. The conversations at Shellmound may appear to be superficial, examples of the southerners' need to fill every silence, yet they serve important purposes. They enable family members to explore their own feelings and to understand those of others, to connect living people with those who are dead, and to comprehend the events taking place in the present by recalling similar occasions in the past.

It is therefore not mere provinciality or possessiveness that causes the Fairchilds to consider it a tragedy when one of them moves away from that sustaining influence. They mention the young woman who married a northerner and moved far away from them; obviously, she understood what she had left behind, because she returns to her parents' home to have her babies.

To its credit, the Fairchild family is willing to change, to open its ranks to those who would once have been considered outsiders. The wedding for which they are gathering is an example of the family's flexibility, for they will be celebrating the marriage of Battle's daughter, seventeen-year-old Dabney Fairchild, to the plantation overseer, Troy Flavin, an outsider from the hill country. If the Virginian Ellen Fairchild is still somewhat ill at ease in the family, Troy, who is socially and culturally inferior to the Fairchilds, should feel totally rejected. However, he does not. The Fairchilds have come to appreciate his virtues, his diligence, his love of the land, and his understanding of Dabney's need to remain near her roots.

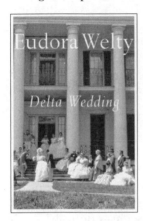

In contrast, Robbie Reid Fairchild is jealous of the family into which she has married. Early in the novel, Robbie's husband, George Fairchild, who is Battle's brother, arrives from Memphis with a fine little filly for Dabney's wedding present but without his wife. Robbie has left George. The cause of the breach was an action that the family sees as heroism but that Robbie sees as George's desertion of her.

Two weeks before, the family had gone fishing. As they crossed a railroad trestle on the way back, George's mentally handicapped niece, Maureen, got her foot caught. Even though a train was coming, George stayed with her, working to free her. The train stopped in time; however, Robbie interpreted the incident as George's choosing his family instead of his wife, and therefore she has left him. If one movement of the novel is toward the family's complete acceptance of Troy, another is toward Robbie's acceptance of her husband and of his needs for his family. Halfway through the book,

Robbie arrives, still furious, but by the end of the novel, she has realized that George's love for her is not diminished by his sense of duty toward the Fairchilds, and she agrees to move back home with George.

Most of the events in *Delta Wedding* are reflected through the eyes of another outsider, nine-year-old Laura McRaven, who has come from Jackson to visit the relatives of her dead mother. Laura is fascinated by Shellmound—the constant motion, the talk, the exclamations, the laughter, the embraces. She desperately needs the security that Shellmound offers her, desperately needs to replace the love of her dead mother with the love of her mother's family. On the other hand, she notices that Shellmound can be restrictive; it is a difficult place to read, she observes, and is in some ways a difficult place to find oneself. Laura manages to achieve a balance between her conflicting needs. When the assigned flower girl gets chicken pox, Laura takes her place, thus becoming part of the wedding and, she believes, of the family. George, whom she adores, assures her that she is truly a Fairchild. When Laura returns to Jackson, she can take with her all that is best at Shellmound. She will always be a part of it, yet she will always have her own secrets and her own identity.

LOSING BATTLES

First published: 1970
Type of work: Novel

A clan gathers to celebrate the ninetieth birthday of a matriarch and to avenge the imprisonment of one of its finest young men.

Losing Battles is a book-length illustration of Welty's theory of confluence. When the Beechams, the Renfros, and the Vaughns gather to celebrate Granny Vaughn's ninetieth birthday, they all talk. In the southern social tradition, this talk involves a great deal of storytelling and reminiscence. In this way, people long dead appear among the living, and past events are revived to determine present actions.

As the title implies, there are many conflicts in the novel. Many involve an outsider's attempt to deal with a highly structured society—in this case, the large, extended family present at the reunion. Aunt Cleo Webster is one of the characters who has a problem with the family into which she has recently married. Early in the novel, it is clear that her questions show her ignorance of the family heritage and, worse, her slightly different perspective. Because she is from southern Mississippi and the reunion takes place in the hill country of northern Mississippi, there is a geographical explanation; however, when the family discovers that she was previously married to a member of the Stovall clan, the hereditary enemies of the Beechams and the Renfros, Aunt Cleo becomes, to a degree, the object of suspicion. Fortunately, by the end of the novel, Aunt Cleo has been taught much about family history and, by learning the correct responses in the never-ending conversations, has become a part of the family.

Another outsider is Gloria Renfro, who is waiting for the return of her husband, Jack Renfro, from the penitentiary, where he had been sent because of an altercation involving a Stovall snatching a family ring from Jack's young sister. Because Jack is the family hero and Granny's favorite, after his return Gloria has difficulty getting him alone. The family demands that he avenge himself on the judge who sent him to the penitentiary. Desperately, Gloria plays every card she holds in order to keep Jack from getting in trouble and being sent away again. She tries to focus his attention on their baby, on her own physical charms, and on their future life together.

However, the family does not want to let go of the past. They would rather have another mythic character to tell stories about than have a real Jack Renfro, happy at home. It is chance, Gloria, and the Renfro sense of honor that unite to keep Jack at home. When Judge Moody, who had sentenced Jack, sacrifices his wife's beloved car in order to keep from hitting the baby and Gloria, Jack cannot harm him; instead, he invites him and his wife to the reunion.

During the celebration, Gloria undergoes a kind of initiation into Jack's family. At one point, several of the women hold her down and force watermelon into her mouth; at another, they criticize her wedding dress, which she has worn to welcome back her husband, and finally cut it up because they say it has far too much material in it. For a time, Gloria feels that Jack must choose between his family and her; eventually, however, she realizes that the love between them is so strong that she can afford to share him with his family.

These main plot lines indicate the importance of the theme of reconciliation in *Losing Battles*. In all these cases, individuals become accepted by a society that had initially viewed them as outsiders. Yet there is another character in the novel who has chosen to remain an outsider—Miss Julia Mortimer, the influential schoolteacher, who has just died. Although she appears at the reunion entirely through anecdote, nonetheless she is a very real presence. Early in the novel, Gloria has to choose whether to go to the funeral of Miss Julia, her friend and mentor, or to stay and wait for Jack. She chooses Jack, as she had chosen him when she left teaching to marry him. In her battle for Gloria, Miss Julia loses, as she had lost most of the battles that she had waged against ignorance. At the end of her life, she was still fighting, but she had come to the conclusion that if her students did learn anything, it would be more or less a miracle rather than anything she had consciously done.

Despite its length, its structural complexity, and the innumerable characters, living and dead, that crowd its pages, *Losing Battles* is considered one of Welty's most interesting novels. Superficially, it appears to be little more than a record of conversations, yet it is a superb exploration of the subjects and themes that dominate Welty's works.

THE OPTIMIST'S DAUGHTER

First published: 1972
Type of work: Novel

A young woman must face the death of her beloved father and her conflicts with his vulgar, greedy second wife.

The Optimist's Daughter deals with family relationships, as do the earlier novels *Delta Wedding* and *Losing Battles* and many of Welty's short stories. *The Optimist's Daughter*, however, focuses on a family of only three people: Laurel McKelva Hand, a widow, the protagonist; her ill father, Judge Clinton McKelva; and his second wife, Fay Chisom McKelva, who is even younger than Laurel. It is not the difference between generations that causes conflict in this novel, however; as in "Moon Lake" and "A Memory," it is the difference in attitude and in conduct between two social classes, a difference that cannot easily be reconciled.

The old, educated southern aristocracy, connected by common memories and by generations of intermarriage and marked by the restraint that they show in times of crisis, is represented by Judge McKelva, his dead wife Becky McKelva, and their daughter, Laurel. Fay comes from a lower social level, one that people such as the McKelvas generally view with embarrassment and distaste. People of Fay's class, whatever their income, can be counted on to be loud, aggressive, and insensitive to social nuances.

Although it would seem that the hospital room in New Orleans where the story begins would be a neutral ground in the class conflict, it is not. The Judge's doctor is at ease with the Judge and Laurel; a native of Mount Salus, Mississippi, where the McKelvas live, he behaves as the Judge and Laurel do—they become more and more controlled as the Judge's health declines. It is not surprising that the doctor is appalled by Fay's behavior. Evidently she is convinced that if she pouts and complains enough about how bored she is, the Judge will rise from his bed and take her around New Orleans. Laurel, remembering her own refined, dead mother, loathes Fay. The family of the Judge's roommate, however, whose background is the same as Fay's, understand that her temper tantrums are simply the appropriate way for people of her class to respond to stress. It is to these people that Fay turns for comfort when the Judge dies.

In Mount Salus, as in New Orleans, there are two distinct groups of people. The friends of the McKelvas have one code; Fay's relatives, who come to attend the funeral, have another. From the vantage point of Laurel, with whom Welty clearly sympathizes, Fay is an intruder who intends to take the Judge's effects and, more important, to destroy the memories that are still present for Laurel in her childhood home.

For Laurel, the turning point of the story comes after the funeral, when Fay tries to appropriate a breadboard that Laurel's dead husband had made for her mother. In a moment of fury, Laurel very nearly hits Fay over the head with the breadboard;

however, Laurel realizes that such an action would be typical of Fay, not of the McKelvas. She also realizes that whatever material things Fay may claim, she cannot take either Laurel's sense of the family

past or her memories of her husband, her mother, and her father.

At the end of the story, although she may not realize it, Fay has been defeated. She will always be an outsider in the society that she had hoped to enter by marrying the Judge. However much she mocks and attacks the aristocrats, she has a deep sense of inferiority when she is around them, based, Laurel sees, on Fay's very real defects, not simply on Laurel's distaste for her. Fay does not have enough imagination to understand a person of intelligence and of sensitivity. Therefore, she can neither love nor defeat such a person.

The Optimist's Daughter is different from Welty's other novels in that Fay comes close to being a real villain, rather than simply a person whose perceptions are different from those of others. Unlike the other novels, it ends without a reconciliation between characters in conflict, without the family's incorporating unlike people into their society. Instead, there is a personal victory for Laurel. After her experience of confluence, her assurance of the presence of the dead she mourns, she knows that Fay and her like can never defeat her.

"A MEMORY"

First published: 1937 (collected in *The Collected Stories of Eudora Welty*, 1980)
Type of work: Short story

A young girl at the beach finds her proper, orderly world threatened by the antics of a vulgar family.

In "A Memory," her second story to be published, Welty shows how difficult life with others can be. As in her earlier story, "Death of a Traveling Salesman," she emphasizes the appeal of human contact. In both stories, the family that the solitary protagonist encounters is a very ordinary one. In "Death of a Traveling Salesman," the salesman perceived a natural mannerliness in the young couple who offered him their hospitality. In "A Memory," however, the girl who is telling the story perceives only ugliness in the people who come to disturb her daydreams.

One reason for her reaction, she admits, is the fact that she is suffering from first love, cherishing the memory of an accidental touch by a boy whom she does not even know. The result of this condition, she says, is that she lives a life of heightened observation at the same time that she is creating a world of dreams. This is essentially the pattern Welty later described in *One Writer's Beginnings*; certainly the symptoms are those of the creative artist. What this protagonist wishes to do, however, is to select only the most beautiful memories and observations for her private world. When the boy she loves gets a nosebleed at school, she faints. Fearing another shock, she takes care not to find out where he lives or who his parents are. The world that she has created will not admit the world that, in the course of human life, she is take bound to encounter.

It is this rejection of the whole of life that makes the protagonist's encounter with the vulgar family such a shock to her. The strangers on the beach do not even speak to her, but she is offended by their ugliness, their noisiness, even their energy. When they leave, she is overcome by pity, not for them but for the little pavilion that had to endure them. At the end of the story, she recognizes how difficult it is to fit anything distasteful into an ideal world that one has invented and in which one wishes to dwell.

"PETRIFIED MAN"

First published: 1939 (collected in *Selected Stories of Eudora Welty*, 1954)
Type of work: Short story

A conversation between a beautician and her customer reveals insecurities that they do not mean to admit.

The title "Petrified Man" refers to one of the oddities in a traveling freak show that has stopped off in a small southern town. However, the title character never appears in person, nor is he even the main topic in the conversation between Leota, a beautician, and her customer, Mrs. Fletcher. The story takes place in a beauty shop, where Leota is giving Mrs. Fletcher a shampoo and set. During the hour that it takes to complete the process, the two women engage in what appears to be polite conversation. The external action in "Petrified Man" is minimal; the real drama takes place in the dialogue.

Mrs. Fletcher strikes the first blow by suggesting that the permanent Leota gave her on a previous visit may have made her hair fall out. Leota replies that the cause is more likely to be Mrs. Fletcher's being pregnant. Upon finding out that people are gossiping about her, Mrs. Fletcher becomes furious. From that time on, she is defensive about her own life and nasty about everyone whom Leota likes. Though she has never seen any of them, she finds fault with Leota's new friend Mrs. Pike, with Mr. Pike, with a fortune-teller whom Leota has found, and even with the petrified man. Mrs. Fletcher is especially irritated by Billy Boy, Mrs. Pike's rambunctious three-year-old son, who is running loose in the beauty shop.

However, after Leota completes her story, Mrs. Fletcher feels better. It seems that Mrs. Pike recognized the rapist pictured in one of Leota's magazines as the petrified man and got a $500 reward for turning him in. Mrs. Pike's good fortune is more than Leota can stand, and this time when little Billy misbehaves, she paddles him with a hairbrush.

"Petrified Man" differs from many of Welty's other works in that it does not end with a reconciliation. Although Mrs. Fletcher is no longer angry with Leota, now Leota loathes the Pikes. Little

Billy's final wisecrack reinforces what Leota now knows: that her life has been one long disappointment.

"A WORN PATH"

First published: 1941 (collected in *Selected Stories of Eudora Welty*, 1954)
Type of work: Short story

An elderly African American woman walks to town in order to get her grandson the medicine that he needs.

"A Worn Path" is a simple story about a difficult journey. The protagonist, Phoenix Jackson, is an elderly African American woman who lives in the country. On a cold December day, she is walking to town along the path that she always takes. Along the way, she encounters various obstacles: thorny bushes, a creek, a barbed-wire fence, a swamp. Then she waves her cane to drive away a dog, loses her balance, and falls. Fortunately, a white man happens along and helps her up. Without knowing it, he drops a nickel, and she pockets it, though she feels guilty about stealing.

After arriving in town, Phoenix gets a lady to lace up her shoe, explaining that she must be properly dressed to go into a big building. Once in the doctor's office, she has to be reminded that she has come to get medicine for her grandson, who swallowed lye several years before. The receptionist offers her some pennies, and Phoenix hints that five of them would be a nickel. With her two nickels, Phoenix will buy her grandson a little paper windmill. The story ends with her making her way laboriously back down the stairs.

In "A Worn Path," the author utilizes the conventions of the heroic journey to describe the adventures of a woman who is unaware of her own heroism. The simple style that Welty uses for her account of Phoenix Jackson's odyssey makes the story even more effective and poignant.

"WHY I LIVE AT THE P.O."

First published: 1941 (collected in *Selected Stories of Eudora Welty*, 1954)
Type of work: Short story

The narrator explains why she left the family home and moved into the back of the post office where she works.

"Why I Live at the P.O." is a monologue in which the narrator, whom the other characters call "Sister," explains how she came to leave the family home in China Grove, Mississippi. In the process, she reveals her own character and a good many family secrets.

According to Sister, her life with her grandfather, her Uncle Rondo, and her mother had been harmonious until the Fourth of July holiday, when her younger sister, Stella-Rondo, left her husband and came home, bringing with her a two-year-old child named Shirley-T, who was supposedly adopted. Sister immediately made it clear that she did not believe that story. Stella-Rondo avenged herself that night by persuading their grandfather, "Papa-Daddy," that Sister wanted him to cut off his beard. When Uncle Rondo got drunk and wrapped himself in Stella-Rondo's kimono, Sister insists that she came to his defense. She also sees herself as the heroine of a confrontation with her mother. After Sister insisted that Stella-Rondo had given birth to Shirley-T and then mentioned a disgraced female relative, Mama slapped her. Sister lost her last ally when Stella-Rondo persuaded Uncle Rondo that Sister had made fun of him for wearing the kimono.

Defeated, Sister collected everything that she could possibly claim and moved to the post office. She comforts herself with the the knowledge that as long as her family members refuse to enter the post office, they will not get their mail.

"Why I Live at the P.O." is funny because all the characters in the story, including the narrator, use warped logic to justify their irrational behavior. Sister's down-to-earth language in describing her family is another source of humor, and the fact that Sister has her own agenda makes her comments even more amusing. It is hardly surprising that "Why I Live at the P.O." has been called a comic masterpiece.

"THE WIDE NET"

First published: 1942 (collected in *Selected Stories of Eudora Welty*, 1954)
Type of work: Short story

A young husband spends a long day looking for his pregnant wife, who supposedly had run away to drown herself.

"The Wide Net" is a story about the conflict between the needs of the individual and the claims of the community. Young, pregnant Hazel Jamieson feels that the primary allegiance of her husband, William Wallace Jamieson, should be to her. When he stays out all night drinking with his friends, Hazel interprets his action as a rejection of her and of their marriage. She decides to take action.

When he arrives home, William Wallace finds a note from Hazel indicating that she has gone to drown herself. He is shocked. All he can think of is to turn once again to his friends, to the very people who got him into difficulty in the first place. Because they are used to the unfathomable ways of women, they have a remedy for every kind of trouble that women can cause men, even the threat of suicide. Although they cannot prevent Hazel from killing herself, the men can provide the necessary procedure for recovering the body: They must gather by the river and drag it with a wide net until Hazel is found.

At first, the mood is suitably gloomy; however, as the day progresses, the atmosphere becomes festive. Other people join them. With the net, they bring up a baby alligator and an eel. They swim. They feast. At times, even William Wallace forgets the occasion of the gathering in the general excitement.

At the end of the day, the gathering disperses, and William Wallace must go home. He has cut his foot, and he needs someone to take care of it for him. When Hazel comes out of hiding, the two are reconciled. Even though she pretends submission, what Hazel now knows is that she can always find a way to throw William Wallace off balance. The day he has spent searching for her is proof of his love.

What she does not realize is that the strength of the male community was demonstrated when he turned to his friends for help, and that even before she came forward to relieve his apprehensions, William Wallace had undergone a healing ceremony in the company of those friends. There need not be a conflict, however; as long as William Wallace comes home early enough to convince Hazel that he loves her, she will not object to the rituals which involve his male friends. The story is resolved in Welty's usual pattern: Her characters settle their differences without withdrawing from the community which, though flawed, is needed to sustain its members.

"MOON LAKE"

First published: 1949 (collected in *The Collected Stories of Eudora Welty*, 1980)
Type of work: Short story

During a week at summer camp, upper-class girls try to understand what it would be like to be people other than themselves.

"Moon Lake" illustrates how complex the relationships within a group can be and how subtly the distinctions between insider and outsider can be drawn. The story begins by pointing out that the girls at summer camp on Moon Lake are very much aware of lifeguard Loch Morrison's deliberate dissociation from them. Although Loch must work as their lifeguard, he does not intend to become a member of their group. The group of girls is split into two segments: the regular, paying campers from Morgana, Mississippi, three miles away, and the charity campers, who are orphans from the county home. The two groups dress differently and behave differently. The Morgana girls swim confidently, while the orphans, who cannot swim, simply stand nervously in the water until they are allowed to come out.

As the story progresses, Welty makes it clear that different people have different perceptions of social acceptance. For example, from Loch's lonely eminence as the only male in camp, all the girls are beyond the pale; he is secure in his society of one. To the leaders of the Morgana group, Nina Carmichael and Jinny Love Stark, it is the orphans who are outsiders. The Morgana girls automatically stick out their tongues at the orphans, only occasionally shifting from contempt into condescending pity. Easter, however, the leader of the orphans, scorns the soft girls from town, who do not even own jackknives, must less know how to throw them.

One example of the difference in viewpoint is the lengthy discussion among Nina, Jinny Love, and Easter about their names. Because no one around Morgana is named Easter, Jinny says, Easter's name is not a real name. Troubled, Nina tries to convince Easter that her name is merely misspelled; if it is in fact Esther, she says, it could be a real name, because there are other people around Morgana who are named Esther. Nevertheless, Easter will not be renamed. While the girls from Morgana derive their senses of identity from their senses of family and community, Easter is proud of being her own creation. She has no father, and her mother has abandoned her. She was free to name herself, and now she is free to choose her own future, in a way that Nina and Jinny Love cannot be. If Easter goes off to become a singer, as she plans, no one will argue with her.

The girls from Morgana are always alert for outward signs of social deficiency, such as the dirt ring at the back of Easter's neck and the mispronounced words of the Yankee counselor, Mrs. Gruenwald. They accept the fact that Loch is different; after all, he is a boy. When, at the end of the story, they see him silhouetted in his tent, stark naked, they speculate as to whether he has been beating his chest, Tarzan-like. Nina is fascinated enough by these outsiders to wish that she could slip into their skins, if only briefly, in order to know how they really feel. One night in the tent, Nina touches Easter's hand. Again, when Easter is unconscious, Nina comes so close to her that she faints. Ironically, it is the outsiders Loch and Easter who are symbolically united when he resuscitates her, while Nina and Jinny Love once more become simply Morgana girls.

Summary

In Welty's fiction, there is great variety as to point of view, structure, and the degree of complexity. In some works, the focus is on the experience of one person, who, though an accepted member of society, has retreated enough from it to view the world with a certain detachment. In others, Welty presents a number of different perceptions, maintaining a dramatic detachment and refusing to take sides in the conflicts she presents.

Sometimes the individual comes to terms with a sense of alienation. More often, the resolution involves an individual's learning to preserve some independence, while at the same time he or she is incorporated into a society that at first had been intolerant, a society that nevertheless should be valued for its preservation of the rich past.

Rosemary M. Canfield Reisman

Bibliography

By the Author

LONG FICTION:
The Robber Bridegroom, 1942
Delta Wedding, 1946
The Ponder Heart, 1954
Losing Battles, 1970
The Optimist's Daughter, 1972

SHORT FICTION:
A Curtain of Green, and Other Stories, 1941
The Wide Net, and Other Stories, 1943
The Golden Apples, 1949
Short Stories, 1950
Selected Stories of Eudora Welty, 1954
The Bride of the Innisfallen, and Other Stories, 1955

The Collected Stories of Eudora Welty, 1980
Moon Lake, and Other Stories, 1980
Retreat, 1981

NONFICTION:
Music from Spain, 1948
The Reading and Writing of Short Stories, 1949
Place in Fiction, 1957
Three Papers on Fiction, 1962
One Time, One Place: Mississippi in the Depression, a Snapshot Album, 1971
A Pageant of Birds, 1974
The Eye of the Story: Selected Essays and Reviews, 1978
Ida M'Toy, 1979
Miracles of Perception: The Art of Willa Cather, 1980 (with Alfred Knopf and Yehudi Menuhin)
Conversations with Eudora Welty, 1984 (Peggy Whitman Prenshaw, editor)
One Writer's Beginnings, 1984
Eudora Welty: Photographs, 1989
A Writer's Eye: Collected Book Reviews, 1994 (Pearl Amelia McHaney, editor)
More Conversations with Eudora Welty, 1996 (Prenshaw, editor)
Country Churchyards, 2000
On William Hollingsworth, Jr., 2002
On Writing, 2002 (includes essays originally pb. in *The Eye of the Story*)
Some Notes on River Country, 2003

CHILDREN'S LITERATURE:
The Shoe Bird, 1964

MISCELLANEOUS:
Stories, Essays, and Memoir, 1998

DISCUSSION TOPICS

- Some of Eudora Welty's characters are called "grotesques," or exaggerated to the point of caricature. Which characters seem to fit that definition?

- How does Welty use humor in her works?

- How does Welty's fiction reflect her belief in the continuing presence of the past?

- What evidence do you find in Welty's works of her belief in the value of the family?

- How do Welty's characters deal with community pressures?

- Welty typically uses several points of view in a single work in order to show how differently people see reality. In which works is that technique especially effective?

About the Author

Champion, Laurie. *The Critical Response to Eudora Welty's Fiction.* Westport, Conn.: Greenwood Press, 1994.

Gygax, Franziska. *Serious Daring from Within: Female Narrative Strategies in Eudora Welty's Novels.* New York: Greenwood Press, 1990.

Gretlund, Jan Nordby. *Eudora Welty's Aesthetics of Place.* Newark: University of Delaware Press, 1994.

Gretlund, Jan Nordby, and Karl-Heinz Westarp, eds. *The Late Novels of Eudora Welty.* Columbia: University of South Carolina Press, 1998.

Johnston, Carol Ann. *Eudora Welty: A Study of the Short Fiction.* New York: Twayne, 1997.

Kreyling, Michael. *Understanding Eudora Welty.* Columbia: University of South Carolina Press, 1999.

McHaney, Pearl Amelia, ed. *Eudora Welty: Writers' Reflections upon First Reading Welty.* Athens, Ga.: Hill Street Press, 1999.

Montgomery, Marion. *Eudora Welty and Walker Percy: The Concept of Home in Their Lives and Literature.* Jefferson, N.C.: McFarland, 2004.

Waldron, Ann. *Eudora: A Writer's Life.* New York: Doubleday, 1998.

Weston, Ruth D. *Gothic Traditions and Narrative Techniques in the Fiction of Eudora Welty.* Baton Rouge: Louisiana State University Press, 1994.

Courtesy, New Directions Publishing

NATHANAEL WEST

Born: New York, New York
    October 17, 1903
Died: El Centro, California
    December 22, 1940

West's fiction depicts the loneliness and frustration of urban life and reflects the destructiveness of lives based on empty illusions; his work prefigured the existentialism and black humor of works of the 1960's.

BIOGRAPHY

Nathanael West was born Nathan Weinstein in New York City on October 17, 1903, the only son of Russian Jewish immigrants. His father, Max Weinstein, was a prosperous building contractor, and his mother, née Anna Wallenstein, was from a cultivated family. West was devoted to his father and to the younger of his two sisters, Lorraine.

An ungainly boy, West attended public schools in Manhattan, where he showed no academic distinction. According to his sisters' reports, he spent much of his time reading. He irregularly attended DeWitt Clinton High School, where he was a weak student and left without graduating. His summers were spent in a camp in the Adirondacks, where he liked baseball but proved more talented as arts editor of the camp newspaper, printing his own cartoons satirizing his fellow campers.

In 1921, West entered Tufts University on the strength of an apparently forged high school transcript and flunked out during his first term. The following year he was admitted to Brown University as a transfer student from Tufts, probably on the basis of someone else's advanced grade record. There West became a serious student and graduated in two and a half years with a bachelor's degree in English.

At Brown, West revealed a sociable nature. He dressed fashionably, engaged in campus social life despite nonacceptance by Gentiles-only fraterni-

ties, and enjoyed a circle of friends including S. J. Perelman (the future humorist and columnist for *The New Yorker* who later married West's sister Lorraine). Having great college success as an aesthete, West studied medieval Catholicism and the lives of saints, and he avidly read the works of Irish writer James Joyce, the French Symbolist poets, and Euripides. As the editor of the Brown literary magazine, he designed its first cover and contributed a poem and an article.

After graduation, West legally changed his name to Nathanael West and intermittently worked for his father, who, then suffering setbacks in his business, eventually accepted his son's rejection of a commercial career and was persuaded to secure funds to send West to Paris in 1925 for a short stay. Once there, he affected the look of the expatriate bohemian writer and became intrigued by dadaism, with its foundation of cynicism and despair, and surrealism, with its Freudian connections.

Returning to New York, West (through a family connection) secured a job as night manager at a hotel in 1927 and later moved on to a fancier hotel. During his stint as a night clerk from 1927 to 1930, he put up indigent writers at reduced rates, including Dashiell Hammett, who finished *The Maltese Falcon* (1930) as West's bootleg guest. West wrote not-to-be published short stories and revised his first novella, begun in college.

The latter, a surrealist fantasy about a young man's abortive search for life's meaning, was published in 1931 as *The Dream Life of Balso Snell* in a limited edition by a small press. The short novel, drawing only one journal review, caused no stir. In that same year, West became co-editor of a little magazine called *Contact* and published articles and chapters of the then-unpublished but completed *Miss Lonelyhearts* (1933) in it. He also became associate editor of the magazine *Americana*, which published a West short story about Hollywood titled "Business Deal."

Miss Lonelyhearts was published in 1933 and received largely positive reviews, but only two hundred copies of the edition appeared, because the publisher went bankrupt. By the time West got the work republished, the reviews were forgotten; fewer than eight hundred copies were sold. Shortly after, however, the novel was purchased by a Hollywood studio, and an offer to write an original screenplay followed from Columbia Pictures. West accepted and worked in Hollywood for $350 a week on two projects, which did not materialize into films, before his contract was terminated.

After seeing *Miss Lonelyhearts* twisted into a murder thriller film titled *Advice to the Lovelorn* (1933) starring Lee Tracy, a disillusioned West returned to New York, impressed with the idea that both Hollywood and life generated the lie of false dreams. He enlarged this notion in two still unpublished short stories: "Mr. Potts of Pottstown" and "The Sun, the Lady, and the Gas Station." In 1934, West published his third short novel, *A Cool Million: The Dismantling of Lemuel Pitkin*, a black comedy satirizing the Horatio Alger myth and the American Dream. The book was unfavorably reviewed and sold poorly.

Returning to Hollywood in 1936, West was first hired as a writer for Republic Productions and later worked until 1940 for other studios, turning out a number of undistinguished screenplays, alone or in collaboration. Because of his facile script-writing ability, West was able to make a securely comfortable living for the first time since 1929. With many of his fellow artists of the 1930's, West assumed a leftist outlook, becoming active in social causes and joining the embryonic Screen Writers Guild, then considered leftist by Hollywood executives. As early as 1935, West had espoused liberal views by signing the manifesto of the 1935 American Writers Congress, which had advocated a proletarian revolution.

Continuing to be well paid as a screenwriter, West completed his fourth novel, *The Day of the Locust* (1939), based on West's perceptions of Holly-

wood. Despite some good reviews, it was a commercial failure, selling fewer than fifteen hundred copies. The author's disappointment was forgotten when, in 1940, he fell in love with and married Eileen McKenney, celebrated as the protagonist of Ruth McKenney's *My Sister Eileen* (1938). This happy period in West's life was brief. On December 22, 1940, the Wests, returning from a hunting trip in Mexico, were both killed in an automobile crash in El Centro, California. West was thirty-seven. He was buried in a Jewish cemetery in New York City.

West's posthumous reputation has expanded considerably. His two major novels, when reprinted, sold thousands of copies. Scholarly articles about West multiplied. *The Day of the Locust* was made into a successful film in 1974. In 1957, the collected four novels were published to favorable reviews and critical recognition of West as an important 1930's writer. The black-comedy tone of his work had a demonstrable influence on many writers who succeeded him.

ANALYSIS

West shared with his fellow writers of the 1930's a disillusionment with the American Dream in the wake of the upheaval of World War I and the worldwide Great Depression. While most expressed their protest in realistic form, West developed an oblique vision of reality less overtly concerned with sociopolitical causes than with aesthetic and psychological ones. It tended toward bleakness and surrealism. For West, life presents a masquerade of false dreams concealing a reality that grotesquely contradicts the expectation.

In each of his four novels, this pattern emerges. In *The Dream Life of Balso Snell*, the dream of art is exploded. In *A Cool Million*, the Horatio Alger myth that good intentions and virtuous hard effort will win the day is proved ineffective. *Miss Lonelyhearts* exposes a reality that will not permit living by the Golden Rule and Christ-like behavior. *The Day of the Locust* unmasks the deceptiveness of Hollywood. In the latter two major novels, the protagonist of each embarks on a quest for self-fulfillment, lured initially by a dream that ultimately turns to dust; the effort leads to grotesque revelation.

In addition to the myth pattern of the quest (for Holy Grail or golden fleece), other classical motifs found in myth and literature appear in West's work. Most evident are the scapegoat, who takes on the community's sins and becomes a sacrificial victim; the holy fool, a lowly person raised to an elevated state and allowed to partake of saturnalian pleasures for a limited time and then symbolically or literally killed in a rite of purgation; and the medieval concept of the Dance of Death, which allegorically represents the triumph of Death reminding people of their mortality and the need for repentance. Such motifs are found in the action and climax of both major novels.

Painter-protagonist Tod Hackett in *The Day of the Locust* provides a thematic statement when he observes that the need for beauty and romance, however "tasteless, even horrible" the result, cannot easily be laughed at; it is "easy to sigh. Few things are sadder than the truly monstrous." West's ability is to delineate the monstrous in a grotesque world that hangs ambiguously between the laughably ridiculous and the heartbreakingly sad.

Not unlike poet T. S. Eliot's *The Waste Land* (1922), which presents a world of disassociated fragments suggesting the broken pieces of the past, West's work is hallucinatory, but it is more pessimistic and more comic. It is indebted to the techniques of surrealism, with its focus on dreams, and to psychoanalysis, which West especially develops in *Miss Lonelyhearts*. Also in his work is a moral irritation, possibly stemming from his experience as an assimilated American Jew who discovered at college the uncomfortable ambiguity of that status.

In both *Miss Lonelyhearts* and *The Day of the Locust*, West cultivates a compact, cinematic style, advancing his narrative in a sequence of intense and fragmented scenes. West's skills and discipline as a Hollywood screenwriter in the last years of his life were compatible with his inclination for constructing stories out of dominantly visual images. Like a film script, which often contains less dialogue than directions regarding visualization, West's short fiction is terse and usually describes character and action in terms of movement, activity, and visual impressions.

To portray his landscapes of a desolate American wasteland of decay and pain, West employs images of the grotesque. Such images encompass violence, animalistic sexuality, the mechanical, and death. Among the inhabitants of these landscapes are the malformed—a cripple, a dwarf in a Tyrolean hat, a young girl without a nose—and the victimized—women who have suffered rape or domestic sexual brutality or a loveless marriage. The spiritually dead are described in mechanical terms such as "a poorly made automaton," "a phallic Jack-in-the-box," "a wound-up cowboy toy," "a mechanical woman self-created from bits of vanished film heroines," or a face like a frozen and cubistic clown mask.

An uncontrolled mob, first peaceably gathered to ogle celebrities at a film premiere, becomes a nightmarish group of figures akin to those in a Hieronymous Bosch (a fifteenth century Dutch painter) painting of hell. A character subconsciously retreating from reality experiences distorted perceptions, seeing a man's cheeks as rolls of toilet paper or a woman's buttocks as enormous grindstones. Such images are stylistically influenced by the nihilistic side of surrealism, destroying the world of rationalism with the surrealistic world of individual perceptions.

Evident in West's work is the influence of dadaism and surrealism, cubism, the French Symbolists, Freudian psychoanalysis, the lives of saints, and such individual writers as James Joyce, Fyodor Dostoevski, and Euripides. Such influences can be seen in the structure, character delineation, depiction of events, overall images, tone, and thematic outlook of West's fiction.

The world of West's novels is a pessimistic one exuding a pervasive atmosphere of failure and defeat and peopled by the lost and the victimized. West describes this world with a darkly comic vision which recognizes that it holds humor, if little real joy. His fiction not only foreshadowed the existentialism of 1960's writers such as Samuel Beckett but also introduced "black humor" as an influence over a number of American writers when, after World War II, his works were republished. In that sense, West was a most modern American writer.

MISS LONELYHEARTS

First published: 1933
Type of work: Novel

A columnist advising the lovelorn finds that Christ-like behavior will neither assuage their misery nor effect his salvation in a callous and spiritually bankrupt world.

Miss Lonelyhearts, the author's first major novel, stands as West's most critically successful, influential, and representative work. The short novel clearly reflects West's pessimistic view of the world and his characteristic narrative technique, employing graphic and often surreal visual images in describing characters and events. The work's expressionistic approach, coupled with its nihilistic outlook and sardonic tone, foretold the existentialism of 1960's writers and became recognized as an early example of black comedy, serving as a model of stimulation to such American writers as Carson McCullers, James Purdy, Flannery O'Connor, and John Hawkes.

Miss Lonelyhearts is the pseudonym of a bachelor newspaper columnist assigned to advise the lovelorn, whose desperation he first finds amusing. His initial attitude fades as he becomes obsessed with his correspondents' misery, cynically illuminated by the city editor, and sees his own helpless condition in that of his supplicants.

He embarks on a self-perceived Christ-like pilgrimage to attain salvation for himself by helping the hopeless. His messianic quest only serves to exacerbate the impotence of his own relationships and alienates him from those around him who view such a search as insanely futile. When his perceptions of reality become increasingly surreal, he meets a ludicrously ironic death as he intervenes in the life of one lovelorn supplicant whom he thinks he has redeemed, only to be shot by her confused husband. His death becomes a futile sacrifice added to the novel's world of unhelped humanity.

The single work most representative of West's style, *Miss Lonelyhearts* shares features with his other novels. Like his immediately preceding first novella, *The Dream Life of Balso Snell*, it introduces a lost protagonist set on an abortive quest to find meaning in an American wasteland masked by false dreams and devoid of beauty, charity, and love. The novel's metaphor for that wasteland is New York City's seedy apartments, bars, and newspaper offices. (In West's second major novel, it is Hollywood.)

While the overall tone of West's novels is a sardonic one, here the fevered messianic religiosity of the nameless Miss Lonelyhearts lends the story distinctiveness and intensity, as that central figure pursues a once powerful dream now rendered puerile and powerless in a modern America. No longer operative in West's world, the Christ dream will betray and ultimately destroy the dreamer.

Similar to his first novel, *Miss Lonelyhearts* follows an episodic narrative pattern. Here the work refines an abbreviated cinematic style that spills the story out in an expressionistic sequence of fragmented scenes, described in terms of visual images somewhat like a cartoon strip or the storyboards used in preparing a screenplay for filming. The scenes externalize the inner state of the protagonist's mind—an expressionistic technique—as he progresses from reality, often perceiving people and events in surrealistically grotesque images that mirror the ugliness and lovelessness of West's world.

It is a surrealist world, as seen through the eyes of the protagonist, governed by individual perceptions that contradict the world of rationalism. A woman is seen as a tent, veined and covered with hair, and a man as a skeleton in a closet. West offers objective correlatives for human fears, perverted love, ambivalent sexuality, ineffective concern for suffering, and other problems of modern consciousness. Apparent in *Miss Lonelyhearts* is the theme that the quest for either personal salvation or Christ-like ministration to others is impossible in a morally and spiritually decaying world in which the dreams that people employ to contend with misery have become false and powerless.

THE DAY OF THE LOCUST

First published: 1939
Type of work: Novel

In the dream factory of Hollywood, a young studio designer finds neither beauty nor romance but only falsity, desperation, and the emptiness of the American Dream.

The Day of the Locust (originally titled *The Cheated*) is the last, the longest, and the most realistic of West's novels. Set in 1930's Hollywood, the novel, drawing on West's experiences as a studio screenwriter, won critical recognition and, upon its republication in the 1950's, popular success that was capped by a 1974 motion picture that was faithful to the original. Less surreal in style and slightly more comic in tone than *Miss Lonelyhearts*, the story depicts a similarly bleak world.

Hollywood, with its masquerade of beauty and romance, contains neither but conceals frustrated hopes and false dreams of success. Unlike other Hollywood novels (commonly focusing on the successful and the powerful), *The Day of the Locust* chiefly concentrates on the unsuccessful, the untalented, and the impotent: the bit players, the hangers-on, the displaced persons from mid-America, all of whom represent disillusioned or lost searchers cheated of their romantic expectations and fantasies stimulated by films.

Observing those lives is the novel's protagonist, a college-educated painter named Tod Hackett. He finds success as a studio designer but comes to realize the frustration and the spiritual and moral emptiness of Hollywood, where the natural is the artificial. Hackett, himself cheated in the pursuit of romance with an artificial and ungifted bit player incapable of returning his love, ultimately leaves the dream capital. The characters are seen by the painter-protagonist's eyes as often-grotesque images that parallel their needs for meaningful emotional lives. Their unfulfilled needs lead to actual and vicarious violence and lust and to an ultimate feeling of spiritual and emotional death with the realization of betrayal. Their lives are ones of desperation, boredom, and frustrated search.

Stressing the failure of dreams, the novel culminates in the violent, orgiastic riot of frenzied movie fans at a Hollywood premiere. The riot embodies Hackett's progressive panoramic painting of the city depicting an apocalyptic vision of terrified citizens facing fiery destruction. It epitomizes the novel's indictment of the destructiveness of false dreams in modern America.

The novel's principal themes are the tension between disillusion and romance and the impact of the realization of betrayal. *The Day of the Locust* is a trenchant exposure of the decay and violence arising from the betrayal of dreams. Life as an illusion, implies West, masks a discontent capable of explosion. Conveying the dilemma of the modern American psyche, the work is a savage satire on America and its dreams.

SUMMARY

In his two major novels, West created a sardonic vision of a moral and spiritual American wasteland disguising its emptiness with romance and dreams. Sadly, the seekers after such dreams are doomed to frustration. West's early existential vision foreshadowed the mood of the 1960's as well as subsequent literary views of life.

Miss Lonelyhearts represents the best expression of West's vision. Both of West's major novels together constitute a distinctive and powerful body of work marking their author as an American writer ahead of his time.

Christian H. Moe

BIBLIOGRAPHY

By the Author

LONG FICTION:
The Dream Life of Balso Snell, 1931
Miss Lonelyhearts, 1933
A Cool Million: The Dismantling of Lemuel Pitkin, 1934
The Day of the Locust, 1939

SCREENPLAYS:

Follow Your Heart, 1936 (with Lester Cole and Samuel Ornitz)

The President's Mystery, 1936 (with Cole)

Ticket to Paradise, 1936 (with Jack Natteford)

It Could Happen to You, 1937 (with Ornitz)

Born to Be Wild, 1938

I Stole a Million, 1939

Five Came Back, 1939 (with Jerry Cady and Dalton Trumbo)

Men Against the Sky, 1940

MISCELLANEOUS:

Novels and Other Writings, 1997 (includes long fiction, letters, and unpublished writings)

About the Author

Bloom, Harold, ed. *Nathanael West.* New York: Chelsea House, 1986.

_____. *Nathanael West's "Miss Lonelyhearts."* New York: Chelsea House, 1987.

Martin, Jay, ed. *Nathanael West: A Collection of Critical Essays.* Englewood Cliffs, N.J.: Prentice-Hall, 1971.

Siegel, Ben, ed. *Critical Essays on Nathanael West.* New York: G. K. Hall, 1994.

Veitch, Jonathan. *American Superrealism: Nathanael West and the Politics of Representation in the 1930's.* Madison: University of Wisconsin Press, 1997.

Widmer, Kingsley. *Nathanael West.* Boston: Twayne, 1982.

Wisker, Alistair. *The Writing of Nathanael West.* New York: St. Martin's Press, 1990.

DISCUSSION TOPICS

- What is surrealism, and what is surreal in Nathanael West's *Miss Lonelyhearts* and *The Day of the Locust*?

- Which characteristics of West's writing translated most effectively to the motion picture screen?

- What effect did the film version of *Miss Lonelyhearts* have on its author?

- West's writing was done mainly in the Depression decade of the 1930's. What aspects of this decade most depressed him personally?

- Why does the practice of altruism not work in *Miss Lonelyhearts*?

EDITH WHARTON

Born: New York, New York
January 24, 1862
Died: St. Brice sous Forêt, France
August 11, 1937

Best known for her realistic novels of manners depicting the upper classes in late nineteenth and early twentieth century New York society, Wharton is one of America's most distinguished writers.

Library of Congress

BIOGRAPHY

Edith Wharton was born Edith Newbold Jones on January 24, 1862, into the wealthy "aristocracy" of the old New York society which would become the focus of much of her fiction. Her mother and father, George F. and Lucretia Stevens Rhinelander Jones, both traced their family lines back three hundred years; their ancestors were mentioned in Washington Irving's history of the Hudson River.

Wharton spent most of her childhood in Europe, where her family fled to avoid post-Civil War inflation. Returning to the United States in 1872, the Whartons followed the pattern common among their social set, wintering in New York City and summering in Newport, Rhode Island. As was the practice for a girl of her social status, she was educated primarily by governesses and tutors, made her debut to society at eighteen, and then traveled abroad.

In 1882, Wharton's father died, and she lived in New York City with her mother. During this period, she met Walter Berry, a wealthy lawyer, and began one of the most important relationships of her life—it was to last more than thirty years. Berry acted as Wharton's unofficial editor and literary adviser, beginning with her first book, *The Decoration of Houses* (1897), a volume on interior decoration inspired by her reaction against the ornate fashions then popular in the United States. Their

relationship continued throughout Wharton's career until Berry's death in 1927. Although controversy exists as to both the quality and extent of Berry's effect on her work, it remains clear that his influence was strong.

In 1885, Wharton married Edward R. "Teddy" Wharton, a member of socially well-connected families from Boston and Philadelphia. Although Teddy loved to travel as much as his wife did, the two had little else in common; he shared none of her love of the arts or the life of the mind. They spent the early years of their marriage traveling abroad, but in the early 1890's Wharton suffered from a depressive illness which lasted until 1902, at which time Teddy began to show signs of the mental disorder that would plague him for the rest of his life.

Because of Teddy's unstable condition and the financial difficulties which ensued, the couple curtailed their travels and settled into a pattern of wintering in Paris or New York and summering at The Mount, a home in Lenox, Massachusetts, designed by Wharton. There she found the solitude necessary to pursue her writing. Teddy's mental condition was diagnosed as incurable in 1910, and in 1913 Wharton divorced him.

Wharton began to pursue a writing career seriously, partly as a cure for the depressive illness she suffered. She first gained recognition for short stories such as "The Greater Inclination" (1899), "Crucial Instances" (1902), and "The Descent of Man" (1904). Also during this period she followed her popular first book with *Italian Villas and Their Gar-*

dens (1904). She experimented with novellas early in her career, producing *The Touchstone* (1900) and *Sanctuary* (1903). Her greatest success with that form would come later with the publication of *Ethan Frome* (1911). Her first novel, *The Valley of Decision* (1902), a historical romance set in eighteenth century Italy, received mixed reviews, but her second novel, *The House of Mirth* (1905), was a critical and commercial success. It marked the beginning of her career as a prominent literary figure.

The publication of *The House of Mirth* began a very productive period in Wharton's career, during which she wrote the novellas *Madame de Treymes* (1907) and *Ethan Frome* and the novels *The Reef* (1912) and *The Custom of the Country* (1913). During this period, she developed a long-standing friendship with American author Henry James, with whom she has often been compared. James's influence on Wharton is especially evident in *The Reef* but is present throughout her work.

Wharton was extremely active during World War I, living in Paris and performing extensive volunteer work for the Red Cross, serving as the head of the American Committee of the Acueil Franco-Americain, which by 1918 was caring for five thousand refugees settled in Paris. Wharton also founded the Children of Flanders Rescue Committee to send 650 orphans and children displaced by the war to families who lived away from the battle zones. She cared for six children in her own apartment, finding permanent homes for them after the war. Wharton was decorated with the Cross of the Legion of Honor in 1917 for these activities. Her war experiences produced *Fighting France, from Dunkerque to Belfort* (1915), which describes her inspection tour of hospitals in the battle zone, and a novel, *A Son at the Front* (1923).

Following the war she continued to reside permanently in France, making only one trip to the United States, in 1923, to receive an honorary doctorate from Yale University. In 1920, she moved from Paris to the eighteenth century Pavillon Calombe outside Paris; she also restored an ancient monastery on the French Riviera, in which she spent her ensuing summers. During this period she produced *The Age of Innocence* (1920), generally considered her best work, for which she received a Pulitzer Prize in 1921. She also became the first woman gold medalist of the American Society of Arts and Letters in 1924.

Her work after *The Age of Innocence* did not achieve the critical or popular success of her earlier books, although she remained prolific. Two novels, *The Glimpses of the Moon* (1922) and *The Mother's Recompense* (1925), were not up to her usual standards and did not enhance her reputation, but with *Old New York* (1924), a collection of novellas, she regained her form. She published five more novels before her death in 1937, including *Hudson River Bracketed* (1929), her autobiography *A Backward Glance* (1934), and the promising but unfinished *The Buccaneers* (1938). Wharton died of a stroke at the age of seventy-five and was buried next to the ashes of Walter Berry in the Cimetière des Gonards at Versailles, France.

ANALYSIS

Too often known only as "that society lady author," a writer of irrelevant and obsolete books, Wharton cannot be dismissed so easily. Although primarily dealing with a narrow social range and short historical span—the upper echelons of New York society from the 1870's to the 1920's—she mines verities about the whole of human nature from these small, seemingly unrepresentative samples of humanity. Far from being anachronistic or irrelevant, Wharton's novels go deeper than their surface manners and mores to reveal universal truths about individuals in relation to their society, and she explores themes relevant to any era.

Regarded as one of America's finest realists, along with her friend and literary inspiration Henry James, Wharton emphasized verisimilitude, character development, and the psychological dimensions of experience, all of which placed her in this tradition, although with some significant variations. Some of her fiction, such as *Ethan Frome*, owes a greater debt to romantics such as Nathaniel Hawthorne than to the realists, and most of her work deals with the upper rather than the middle classes more common to realist fiction; critic Blake Nevius remarks: "She was destined from the beginning to be a realist. As a child in Paris, she used to . . . make up stories about the only people who were real to her imagination—the grownups with whom she was surrounded. . . . Mother Goose and Hans Christian Andersen bored her."

The United States premiere novelist of manners, Wharton employs intricately detailed descriptions of outward form, including manners, customs, fashion, and decor, to reveal the inner passions and ideals of her characters. Using manners to register internal events as well as external circumstances allows her to indicate deeper emotions indirectly. The constricting effect of an elaborate and confining set of behavioral guidelines on the human psyche and the human spirit's survival within these narrow boundaries provides one of the overriding themes of her fiction.

This emphasis on the power of environment over the individual sets her apart from the writer to whom she is most often compared, Henry James. Frequently mentioned in the same breath, the two indeed have many similarities. They traveled in the same social circles, wrote about similar kinds of people, held the same values, and dealt with many of the same themes, particularly innocence versus experience. James, however, placed more emphasis upon the individual within the society than on the society itself. Perhaps the strongest bond between these two writers lies in their mutual devotion to the art of fiction, their continual study of the novel's form, and their interest in the technique and processes of art.

As a realist, Wharton describes the houses, fashion, and social rituals of "old New York" in minute detail, studying this small stratum of society as an anthropologist might study a South Sea island. *The Age of Innocence*, for example, abounds in anthropological terminology, as the protagonist, Newland Archer, reveals when reflecting that "there was a time when . . . everything concerning the manners and customs of his little tribe had seemed to him fraught with world-wide significance." He describes his own wedding as "a rite that seemed to belong to the dawn of history." Archer's use of this anthropological jargon reveals Wharton's almost scientific fascination with the social milieu.

Similarly, in *The House of Mirth*, structured as a series of scenes that reflect the social status of its heroine, Lily Bart, Wharton meticulously records even the finest lines between classes, noting that "the difference [between them] lay in a hundred shades of aspect and manner, from the pattern of the men's waistcoats to the inflexion of the women's voices." Although no such subtlety of detail exists in the very different world of *Ethan Frome*, a nevertheless fixed and immovable social structure offers the novel's protagonist no avenue of escape from his equally barren business and mar-

riage. In all these novels, the elaborate rituals that sustain a culture protect tradition and stabilize the society, but they also constrict the freedom of the individual within that society.

Often victims of society's narrow definition of acceptable behavior, Wharton's multifaceted, psychologically complex characters are also victimized by their own weaknesses. Lily Bart, one of Wharton's most fully realized characters, suffers under the limitations placed on women in her circumstances, but she falls equally victim to her own selfishness and snobbery. Similarly, Newland Archer, imprisoned within the narrow behavioral confines of old New York, is also imprisoned by prejudices and lassitude. The eponymous character of *Ethan Frome*, as a result of his own and society's limitations, also fails to escape a suffocating town, business, and marriage in order to seek intellectual and emotional fulfillment.

Although not involved in the feminist movement of her day, Wharton's preoccupation with the limiting effects of societal restrictions on the human soul necessarily invokes feminist issues, for women especially suffered under this society's narrow boundaries. Lily Bart, for example, finds her options severely limited because of her gender; even taking tea alone with a man in his apartment results in social condemnation.

Newland Archer often muses on the peculiar demands and expectations placed on women. When he declares, "Women ought to be free—as free as we are," Wharton notes that he is "making a discovery of which he was too irritated to measure the terrific consequences." May Welland Archer is yet another victim—in this case, of her husband's narrow definition of her character—and Ellen Olenska is the victim of society's preconceptions of a woman's behavior.

The principal theme of Wharton's fiction involves the individual in society: how personal relationships are distorted by societal conventions, the clash between changing characters and fixed society, and the conflict between nature and culture. Wharton therefore stands a bridge between an older, more established nineteenth century world and the world of the twentieth century, which placed increasing emphasis on individual experience.

Edith Wharton

THE HOUSE OF MIRTH

First published: 1905
Type of work: Novel

A young woman falls from the heights of New York society to the depths of poverty and despair when she fails to conform to society's expectations.

The House of Mirth, Wharton's second full-length novel, not only guaranteed her literary reputation but also established the setting and themes she would explore throughout her career. Set in the early twentieth century New York society with which she was so intimately familiar, the novel offers an angrier and more bitter condemnation of this social milieu than Wharton's later work, which mellowed with the passage of time. Both a meticulously thorough examination of a complex social structure and a brilliant character study, it offers a compelling exploration of the effects of social conformity upon the individual.

As the novel opens, its heroine, twenty-nine-year-old Lily Bart, has achieved the height of her powers: Beautiful, intelligent, charming, and sought after, she has nevertheless reached a turning point, knowing too well that society has no place for an unmarried woman past her prime. Her parents having left her no legacy but an appreciation for the finer things in life, Lily occupies a precarious social position under the protection of her dreary, socially prominent Aunt Peniston, and she must rely on the favors of the wealthy ladies and gentlemen who find her company amusing.

Lily's craving for the secure foothold that only marriage can provide cannot entirely overcome her distaste for the hypocrisy and insensitivity of her class. Hardly lacking for opportunities to marry well, Lily nevertheless manages to sabotage her best chances, as she does in bungling her courtship with Percy Gryce, an eminently eligible but overwhelmingly boring pillar of the community.

Lily's unique place in New York society—simultaneously insider and outsider—makes her one of Wharton's most fascinating creations and offers the reader a privileged perspective on this world. A product of her society, "at once vigorous and exquisite, at once strong and fine . . . [who] must have cost a great deal to make," Lily is also "so evidently the victim of the civilization which had produced her that the links of her bracelet seemed like manacles chaining her to her fate."

Lily's need to be surrounded by the beautiful things that only immense sums of money can buy and her distaste for the common and ugly enslave her to those she might otherwise find at best ridiculous and at worst repellent; they cause her to reject the only person for whom she feels genuine emotion, Lawrence Selden, a cultivated lawyer of modest means. As Lily can neither totally accept her society's values nor be hypocritical enough to survive without doing so, she finally must perish.

Lily's fall from social grace is incremental rather than precipitous, occurring gradually as she makes small compromises in order to survive. The novel opens with one of many small lapses in judgment, as she accepts Lawrence Selden's impromptu invitation to take tea alone at his apartment. An ill-advised financial arrangement with Gus Trenor, the husband of her friend and social arbiter, Judy Trenor, leaves Lily further compromised, as does her well-intentioned effort to keep socially powerful Bertha Dorset's husband occupied while Bertha conducts an affair. Ostracized by the aristocracy and the nouveau riche, she then fails to succeed as a milliner's apprentice and finally finds herself alone and nearly penniless.

Paradoxically, as Lily descends through these various layers of society, her strength of character grows, as evidenced by her determination to use the entirety of her meager inheritance to repay her debt to Gus Trenor and by her unwillingness to accept a handout from rich industrialist Simon Rosedale. Yet her fragile new sense of self cannot survive unsupported. She has "the feeling of being something rootless and ephemeral, mere spindrift of the whirling surface of existence, without anything to which the poor little tentacles of self could cling before the awful flood submerged them," before succumbing to an overdose of sleeping pills.

Far from creating a clear-cut good versus evil or spirit versus materialism dialectic, Wharton establishes a more subtle and interesting conflict. Many of the novel's characters embody such antithetical attributes, as, for example, the social worker Gerty Farish, who reveals more "good" attributes than Lily, including honesty, generosity, and devotion to good works. Nevertheless, she is not a particularly attractive or sympathetic figure, lacking Lily's charm, perceptions, and sensitivity to beauty.

Simon Rosedale, on the other hand, a ruthless businessman and ambitious social climber, is one of the rare characters who shows genuine sympathy for Lily when she descends to the bottom of the social heap. Lawrence Selden, although largely sympathetic, exhibits a weakness of character that proves fatal for Lily; he is unwilling to relinquish his safe niche in the social order for her sake until too late. Like Lily, he senses that life holds more than exists in his narrow social milieu, but also like Lily he is loathe to give up his social acceptance to explore the possibilities. Lily, while too self-centered and elitist to be a conventional heroine, still possesses many qualities that attract the reader.

More naturalistic than her other novels, *The House of Mirth* contains too many coincidental plot twists to make Lily's fall entirely believable. Wharton's portrayal of the lower classes, as illustrated by her portrait of Nettie Struthers, the poor shop girl, possesses none of the subtlety or believability of her presentation of the upper classes; it often descends to melodrama. Despite these minor flaws, however, *The House of Mirth* portrays a small stratum of society and one character within that society to perfection, brilliantly illustrating the power of social conformity over individuality.

ETHAN FROME

First published: 1911
Type of work: Novella

In the bleak landscape of New England, an outsider pieces together the tragic history of the town's most striking character.

Ethan Frome, neither a commercial nor a critical success when first published, actually offended many of Wharton's contemporaries by its harsh portrayal of New England life and its characters' failure to triumph over adversity. Nevertheless, its popularity gradually increased until, by 1920, it had become the best-known and most widely read of Wharton's works. Wharton herself believed that too much attention was paid to *Ethan Frome* at the expense of her other novels. Indeed, to judge her

career solely by this single novella would prove misleading, because it is very unlike her other major works in setting, tone, and characterization. Like much of her other work, however, it deals with the relationship between an individual and that individual's society.

Structured as a frame tale, the story unfolds from the point of view of Lockwood, a young engineer on assignment in the isolated New England village of Starkfield. His curiosity about one of the town's characters, the physically deformed but striking Ethan Frome, drives him to construct a "vision" of Ethan's history, assembled from information gathered in conversation with various townspeople and from his own observations of the fifty-two-year-old farmer.

The significance of this structure cannot be overestimated; Wharton even adds an uncharacteristic introduction to explain her decision to employ this literary device, which achieves perspective by creating an educated, observant narrator to intercede between the simple characters and the more sophisticated reader. Wharton also adds poignancy by setting the novella twenty-four years after the main action occurs.

Lockwood relates the simple but compelling story of twenty-eight-year-old Ethan Frome, a farmer and mill owner left nearly destitute after the death of his parents, both of whom suffered mental disorders. After enduring lonely years of silence with his mother, who was too busy listening for imagined "voices" to converse with him, Frome marries Zenobia Pierce, seven years his senior, who had nursed Mrs. Frome in her dying days. The sound of Zeena's voice in his house is music to Ethan's starved ears, and by marrying her he hopes to escape further loneliness.

Soon after their marriage, however, Zeena becomes obsessed with her various aches and pains, and she concerns herself solely with doctors, illnesses, and cures, falling as silent as his mother.

At her doctor's advice, Zeena takes in her homeless young cousin, Mattie Silver, to help with the housework. Although a hapless housekeeper, Mattie brings a vitality to the Frome house that has been absent for years, and she and Ethan fall in love. Trapped by circumstances, as well as by Ethan's strong sense of responsibility toward Zeena, the two foresee no future together.

On the evening that Zeena sends Mattie away for good, Ethan and Mattie decide to aim their sled straight for a giant elm tree so that they might find mutual solace in death. Both, however, survive the plunge, which paralyzes Mattie and disfigures Ethan. Zeena takes responsibility for caring for Mattie and Ethan, and the three live on in the Frome house, as Mattie becomes as querulous and unpleasant as Zeena and Ethan attempts to scratch out a living from his failing farm and mill.

In Ethan, "the most striking figure in Starkfield, though he was but the ruin of a man," Wharton fashions a character of heroic proportions. He is a country man who would have preferred the intellectual stimulation of the city, a sociable man doomed to silent suffering, a man whose misshapen body mirrors his thwarted intellectual and emotional life. Like Lily Bart in *The House of Mirth*, he is "more sensitive than the people about him to the appeal of natural beauty" but finds little of it in his own life. Like Lily, he feels trapped by society's demands on him: "The inexorable facts closed in on him like prison-wardens handcuffing a convict. There was no way out—none. He was a prisoner for life."

As always in Wharton's work, setting figures prominently, but in *Ethan Frome* the stark landscape of New England, rather than the elegant brownstones of New York City, provides the background. Wharton draws a close parallel between the action and the emotions of the characters and the bleak landscape; the two are inextricably intertwined. Ethan "seemed a part of the mute melancholy landscape, an incarnation of its frozen woe, with all that was warm and sentient in him fast bound below the surface." Even Frome's house, lacking the "L" wing common to New England farm structures, reflects the emotionally stunted life existing inside, and the withering orchard of starving apple trees and crazily slanting gravestones in the family plot also mirror Frome's blighted life.

Wharton uses irony, as well as landscape and imagery, to great effect in this work, often juxtaposing scenes for ironic effect. When Zeena greets Ethan at the kitchen door in the evening, "The light . . . drew out of the darkness her puckered throat and the projecting wrist of the hand that clutched the quilt, and deepened fantastically the hollows and prominences of her high-boned face under its ring of crimping-pins." Later, however, when Mattie stands "just as Zeena had stood, a lifted lamp in her hand, against the black background of the kitchen. . . . [I]t drew out with the same distinctness her slim young throat and the brown wrist no bigger than a child's." *Ethan Frome*'s ultimate irony lies in the suicide pact which ends not in the mutual release of death but in endless years of pain and suffering and in the transformation of the vibrant young Mattie into a mirror image of the whining Zenobia.

THE AGE OF INNOCENCE

First published: 1920
Type of work: Novel

In "old New York" society a young man must choose between his innocent young fiancé and her more worldly sophisticated cousin.

The Age of Innocence, often considered Wharton's masterpiece, takes a nostalgic look at the New York society of her childhood, which had undergone enormous changes by 1920. In a mood tempered from that expressed in the 1905 *House of Mirth*, Wharton criticizes many aspects of this society, especially its hypocrisy and tendency to stifle creativity and genuine emotion. In this retrospective she also finds value in its stability and traditions. At the height of her powers in this novel, Wharton brilliantly uses plot, character, dialogue, point of view, and irony to express her themes, including the needs of the individual versus the claims of the society and the tenuous balance between the values of innocence and experience and between tradition and change.

The novel's plot revolves around the choice the protagonist, Newland Archer, must make between two women—his fiancé, May Welland, a flower of New York society, and her cousin, Countess Ellen Olenska, recently separated from her abusive husband and settled in New York. The Welland family enlists Newland to talk the countess out of seeking a divorce in order to avoid scandal and pain to her family. Newland soon falls in love with Ellen and, reversing his position, asks her to divorce her husband to marry him. Ironically, Ellen refuses, persuaded too well by Newland's arguments against divorce, and Newland marries May. Ellen eventually returns to Europe, May announces her pregnancy, and Newland's fate is sealed. Twenty-five years later,

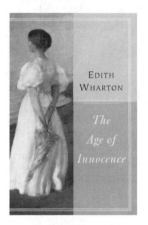

after May's death, Newland passes up an opportunity to see Ellen in Paris, realizing that his dreams have become more important to him than reality.

The society Wharton describes in *The Age of Innocence* values conformity over originality, superficial pleasantness over reality, and respectability over individual freedom. Newland understands that "they all lived in a kind of hieroglyphic world, where the real thing was never said or done or even thought, but only represented by a set of arbitrary signs," but he does not disapprove. Smugly self-satisfied, he feels intellectually and culturally superior to his social set but nevertheless embraces most of its moral doctrines and values, never fully realizing the extent of his own conformity.

In fact, Newland's attraction to May is indicative of his acceptance of the establishment's values. Initially, "[n]othing about his betrothed pleased him more than her resolute determination to carry to its utmost limit that ritual of ignoring the 'unpleasant' in which they had both been brought up." May's innocence, which Newland initially finds appealing, becomes oppressive, however, and Newland feels trapped by this creature he helped to create. Ironically, although May does represent the weaknesses of the old guard—innocence, hypocrisy, and stifling propriety—she also embodies its strength: stability and respect for tradition. Yet for twenty-five years, Newland fails to look beyond his own preconceptions of his wife to appreciate these qualities.

Ellen Olenska, on the other hand, embodies experience, intellect, freedom, and individuality. Separated from her husband, a stranger in her own country, and largely ignorant of the strict codes of the society she was born into, she symbolizes disintegration of tradition and lack of stability. At the same time, she offers honesty and genuine emotion to a culture sorely lacking these qualities.

Wharton invests the novel's minor characters with symbolic weight as well. The van der Luydens, the social establishment's judges of morals and taste, appear in terms of death and dying. Mrs. van der Luyden "struck Newland Archer as having been rather gruesomely preserved in the airless atmosphere of a perfectly irreproachable existence, as bodies caught in glaciers keep for years a rosy life-in-death."

At the other end of the social spectrum, the immensely wealthy Julius Beaufort represents the threat of the new materialism. Tolerated only because he married into aristocracy, his open philandering and questionable business dealings typify the crass vulgarities of those breaking down society's barriers. Mrs. Manson Mingott, combining both the old and new, stands for the stability of class combined with the vigor and independence of the nouveau riche, and Newland's two companions, the gossiping Sillerton Jackson and womanizing Lawrence Lefferts, symbolize the establishment's most hypocritical aspects.

Wharton also employs irony and symbolism to great effect in *The Age of Innocence*, particularly to describe the romance of Ellen and Newland. Although their passion for each other is evident and genuine, Wharton never allows the romance to descend into the tragic or melodramatic. Each of the couple's interludes is somehow ironically undercut: Newland tenderly kisses what he believes to be Ellen's pink parasol, only to discover it is not hers at all; the couple boards a ferry for a romantic tête-à-tête, only to be surrounded by a gaggle of schoolteachers on holiday; and, finally achieving solitude, they cannot forget that they are alone together in May's wedding carriage.

Rich in characterization, symbolism, and irony, the novel deals with several powerful themes, including the balance between innocence and experience, tradition and change, and individual and society. It also addresses the repression of women, the role of marriage and family, and the conflict between sexual passion and moral obligation. In *The Age of Innocence*, Wharton perceives the repression of the self in the old ways, and fragmentation of the self in the new. Wharton's alter ego, Newland Archer, feels comfortable with neither the old nor the new order; he inhabits a lonely middle ground, searching for a workable compromise between individual freedom and the claims of society.

SUMMARY

No other writer of her time knew the upper classes of the United States more intimately or detailed their lives more movingly or convincingly than did Wharton. Her attitude toward "old New York" was one of both anger and nostalgia—anger at its stifling hypocrisies and moral passivity and nostalgia for the stability and sense of tradition which were being assaulted by the rise of the new industrial classes at the beginning of the twentieth century. The tension between these two conflicting emotions provides the subject matter for most of Wharton's work. Torn between scorn and admiration for the old ways and fear of the chaos she saw accompanying the new, her fiction stands at the threshold of the twentieth century, a harbinger of the changes to come in American life.

Mary Virginia Davis

BIBLIOGRAPHY

By the Author

SHORT FICTION:
The Greater Inclination, 1899
Crucial Instances, 1901
The Descent of Man, 1904
The Hermit and the Wild Woman, 1908
Tales of Men and Ghosts, 1910
Xingu, and Other Stories, 1916
Here and Beyond, 1926
Certain People, 1930
Human Nature, 1933
The World Over, 1936
Ghosts, 1937
The Collected Short Stories of Edith Wharton, 1968
Collected Stories, 1891-1910, 2001 (Maureen Howard, editor)
Collected Stories, 1911-1937, 2001 (Howard, editor)

LONG FICTION:
The Touchstone, 1900
The Valley of Decision, 1902
Sanctuary, 1903
The House of Mirth, 1905
Madame de Treymes, 1907
The Fruit of the Tree, 1907
Ethan Frome, 1911
The Reef, 1912
The Custom of the Country, 1913
Summer, 1917
The Marne, 1918
The Age of Innocence, 1920
The Glimpses of the Moon, 1922
A Son at the Front, 1923
Old New York, 1924 (4 volumes; includes *False Dawn*, *The Old Maid*, *The Spark*, and *New Year's Day*)
The Mother's Recompense, 1925

Twilight Sleep, 1927
The Children, 1928
Hudson River Bracketed, 1929
The Gods Arrive, 1932
The Buccaneers, 1938

POETRY:
Verses, 1878
Artemis to Actæon, 1909
Twelve Poems, 1926

NONFICTION:
The Decoration of Houses, 1897 (with Ogden Codman, Jr.)
Italian Villas and Their Gardens, 1904
Italian Backgrounds, 1905
A Motor-Flight Through France, 1908
Fighting France, from Dunkerque to Belfort, 1915
French Ways and Their Meaning, 1919
In Morocco, 1920
The Writing of Fiction, 1925
A Backward Glance, 1934
The Letters of Edith Wharton, 1988
The Uncollected Critical Writings, 1997 (Frederick Wegener, editor)
Yrs. Ever Affly: The Correspondence of Edith Wharton and Louis Bromfield, 2000 (Daniel Bratton, editor)

DISCUSSION TOPICS

- How did the life Edith Wharton lived up to the age of eighteen prepare her for her writing career?

- Do Wharton's novels give the lie to those who see a preoccupation with manners as a superficial interest?

- What are the significant differences between Wharton's presentation of character and that of her admired friend Henry James?

- In *The House of Mirth*, what traits in Lily Bart make it possible to view her sympathetically despite her many faults?

- Discuss Wharton's attitude toward social conformity.

- Do the socially elite characters in Wharton's novels deserve the downfall that many of them experience?

About the Author

Ammons, Elizabeth. *Edith Wharton's Argument with America*. Athens: University of Georgia Press, 1980.

Beer, Janet. *Kate Chopin, Edith Wharton, and Charlotte Perkins Gilman: Studies in Short Fiction*. London: Macmillan, 1997.

Bell, Millicent, ed. *The Cambridge Companion to Edith Wharton*. Cambridge, England: Cambridge University Press, 1995.

Bendixen, Alfred, and Annette Zilversmit, eds. *Edith Wharton: New Critical Essays*. New York: Garland, 1992.

Benstock, Shari. *No Gifts from Chance: A Biography of Edith Wharton*. 1994. Reprint. Austin: University of Texas Press, 2004.

Dwight, Eleanor. *Edith Wharton: An Extraordinary Life*. New York: Abrams, 1994.

Fracasso, Evelyn E. *Edith Wharton's Prisoner of Consciousness: A Study of Theme and Technique in the Tales*. Westport, Conn.: Greenwood Press, 1994.

Gimbel, Wendy. *Edith Wharton: Orphancy and Survival*. New York: Praeger, 1984.

Lewis, R. W. B. *Edith Wharton: A Biography*. 2 vols. New York: Harper & Row, 1975.

Lindberg, Gary H. *Edith Wharton and the Novel of Manners*. Charlottesville: University Press of Virginia, 1975.

McDowell, Margaret B. *Edith Wharton*. Boston: Twayne, 1975.

Nettels, Elsa. *Language and Gender in American Fiction: Howells, James, Wharton, and Cather*. Charlottesville: University Press of Virginia, 1997.

Pennel, Melissa McFarland. *Student Companion to Edith Wharton*. Westport, Conn.: Greenwood Press, 2003.

Singley, Carol, J., ed. *Edith Wharton's "The House of Mirth": A Casebook*. New York: Oxford University Press, 2003.

_____. *A Historical Guide to Edith Wharton*. New York: Oxford University Press, 2003.

PHILLIS WHEATLEY

Born: West coast of Africa, possibly the Senegal-
Gambia region
1753(?)
Died: Boston, Massachusetts
December 5, 1784

*Brought to America as a child slave, Wheatley was educated
by her owners and began composing poetry at the age of twelve;
a volume of her work,* Poems on Various Subjects, Religious and Moral, *was the second book published by an American woman and the first by a black American.*

Library of Congress

BIOGRAPHY

Born in western Africa, Phillis Wheatley was kidnapped by slave traders in 1761 when she was about seven years old. Named for the *Phillis*, the slave ship on which she was transported, the child was taken to Boston and put up for sale. Susannah Wheatley, wife of prosperous Boston tailor John Wheatley, picked out the child, and her husband bought her as a servant for his wife. As customary, the slave girl took the surname of her new owners.

The African girl spoke no English, but her intelligence was obvious to the Wheatleys, and they educated her, finding her to be a quick learner. The family became very fond of her, and when they observed her trying to form letters, the Wheatleys' adolescent children, twins Mary and Nathaniel (Nat), taught Phillis to read and write, remarkable in a time when literacy was forbidden for slaves. Phillis was soon reading the Bible, classical mythology, ancient history, geography, astronomy, and literature. The Wheatley twins also tutored her in Latin.

Introduced to Christianity soon after her arrival, she embraced it fervently; salvation and Christian duty loomed large in the poetry she would write later. Charmed by her intelligence and sweet disposition, Susannah Wheatley doted on the child, keeping her always at her side. Although still in bondage, Phillis lived apart from the other slaves and was not required to share their labor. When

she began to compose poetry around the age of twelve, Susannah Wheatley encouraged her and made sure that Phillis was well supplied with writing materials and all the time she desired for her compositions. On December 21, 1767, *The Newport* (Rhode Island) *Mercury* published Phillis's first poem.

The unusual circumstances of the young poet—her gender, age, race, and unexpected literacy—drew the attention of many notables of the day, including Benjamin Franklin, John Hancock, John Adams, and George Washington. Wheatley continued to write and publish poems for the next couple of years, most of them for special occasions and about public events, and she was often asked by the Wheatleys and others to read her poetry at social gatherings.

One of her most famous poems was an elegy for the popular British evangelical minister George Whitefield, who frequently preached in the colonies. Whitefield was chaplain to the countess of Huntingdon in England, so Wheatley sent a copy of the elegy to the countess, which proved fortunate. Although the Wheatleys promoted Phillis's work in every way, they were unable to find a publisher in Boston. At Susannah Wheatley's request, a friend found an English printer who was interested, providing it could be proved that such an unlikely person was indeed the author. Thus, in a preface to Wheatley's collected poems is a statement affirming that she is the true author, signed by prominent men of Boston, including some who were later to sign the Declaration of Independence.

Because the countess of Huntingdon was a woman of influence whose patronage could be important to the book's success, Wheatley wisely dedicated the book to her; the countess suggested that Wheatley's portrait be placed in the book. The picture shows a contemplative young woman seated at her writing table. The artist is believed to have been Scipio Moorhead, also an African slave, to whom Wheatley wrote a poem included in the collection. The book aroused significant interest both in Massachusetts and in England.

However, Wheatley's health, which had always been delicate, seemed to decline. Susannah Wheatley thought a trip to England would restore Phillis's health, so in May, 1773, Phillis accompanied Nat Wheatley on a business trip to England. London society was quite taken with the young poet and entertained her with respect and honor. There was even talk of her meeting King George III. This was not to occur, however, because Phillis received news that her mistress, Susannah Wheatley, had become ill. Phillis set sail for America immediately without seeing her book, *Poems on Various Subjects, Religious and Moral,* published on September 1, 1773. The book, a collection of thirty-nine poems, was enthusiastically received in England but less positively reviewed in America. Thomas Jefferson was one of its most outspoken critics.

More good fortune was to befall Wheatley; shortly after her return to America, the Wheatleys released her from slavery. She continued to live with the family, but for the first time she wrote openly about the injustice of slavery. In a letter to friend Sampson Occom, an American Indian Christian convert and missionary, Wheatley condemned slavery in strong terms. Her letter was published in newspapers throughout New England and was considered an important contribution to the abolitionist movement. Although Wheatley had much to be happy about, her fortunes were to turn and decline for the rest of her life.

Early in 1774, her former mistress and most ardent supporter, Susannah Wheatley, died. The world outside the Wheatley home paralleled the disruption within. War between England and the American colonies was brewing; British warships filled Boston harbor, and British soldiers filled the

city. With America on the brink of war, Wheatley fled Boston to stay with Mary Wheatley, now married, in Rhode Island. While there, Phillis wrote a poem praising George Washington, commander in chief of the Continental Army. The poem resulted in an invitation for the poet to meet the general, an invitation Phillis happily accepted.

In 1776, after the British had left Boston, Wheatley returned to the shattered city and discovered that most of her friends had died or fled. Goods were hard to come by, and life was a struggle for everyone in Boston, especially a young, unmarried woman of limited finances. Wheatley's circumstances worsened as the war continued, and then she suffered another blow; her friends John Wheatley and his daughter Mary died within close succession. The only surviving family member, Nat, had remained in England. The family she had been so close to most of her life was now lost to her. It was then, in 1778, whether out of necessity or genuine feeling, that Wheatley chose to marry John Peters.

Like her, Peters was a freed slave. After their marriage, Peters worked at a series of occupations ranging from grocer to lawyer, while Wheatley continued to write her poetry and attempted to have a second book published. However, in a country consumed by war and where money and goods were scarce, books of poetry generated little interest. A few of her patriotic poems and letters were published in newspapers and magazines, but she never published a second book. The Peters family suffered financial problems, and the two children to whom Wheatley gave birth perished. She was obliged to work as a seamstress and maid in a boardinghouse to support herself when her husband abandoned her or was sentenced to debtors' prison. The final days of her life were marked by deprivation and hardship. She did not live to see her final poem, a celebration of American independence, published. She and her third child died, hours apart, on December 5, 1784; she was around thirty-one years old.

ANALYSIS

No one could deny Wheatley's remarkable achievement in being the first African American of either sex to publish a book in colonial America, a time and place where slaves' very humanity was questioned. The publication of a slave girl's poems attested to the spiritual and intellectual capacities of Africans kept in bondage. However, while the accomplishment is noteworthy, the poetry itself has always received an ambivalent response, from both her contemporaries and from some modern readers.

Some of the early criticisms can be attributed to a lack of ease with the poetry's source; for example, Jefferson's dismissal of Wheatley's work suggests his unwillingness to credit the idea of art from the hand of a slave. Nonetheless, even her supporters have observed that her poetry was good but not exceptional. Although the quality of her work has long been debated, it is an unfair judgment to suggest that her interest lies primarily in her unusual circumstances and historical significance.

European culture was a heavy presence in early American writing, and the neoclassical influence is clearly seen in Wheatley's poetry in its polished poetic diction, conventional figures of speech, classical allusions, decorum, and emotional restraint. The works of Alexander Pope, one of the great neoclassical poets, were an important part of Wheatley's early education, and his translation of Homer's *Iliad* (c. 725 B.C.E.) was her favorite piece of literature. She modeled her poems on Pope's heroic couplets.

Many of Wheatley's works were occasional poems, verse written to celebrate public events and achievements or to mourn the deaths of, usually, public figures. Whatever emotion is expressed in such poems is restrained. She emphasized morality and duty—both Christian duty and duty to one's country and its leadership. The subject matter and the audience of the poetry are the white people of Boston, the society in which she lived. Her fellow slaves, denied education, could not have read her work.

Although Wheatley has been criticized for not striking a blow for the emancipation of her people and denouncing slavery in her poetry, this charge ignores the fact that the poet could publish only what was permissible in the world she inhabited. However charmed members of the privileged class of Boston were by her accomplishments, to a large extent she published her works by their indulgence. Nonetheless, there is a certain subversion in her poems. Wheatley often draws the reader's attention to her African heritage and servitude. She implies, however, that it is God alone who owns her and to whom she must ultimately submit, the impli-

cation being that her masters, too, will someday have to account for themselves as slave owners.

She does not overtly confront the establishment but employs irony and ambiguity in her poetry and takes lessons from Scripture and popular sermons to overturn the racial assumptions and expectations of her readers. Additionally, the irony of a people fighting for their liberty from a tyrannical government while at the same time exercising the tyranny of slavery over another race was not lost on the poet. In subtle ways her poetry points out the hypocrisy of Christians who condone slavery. Divine and social justice are thus linked in her work.

"To the Right Honorable William, Earl of Dartmouth"

First published: 1773 (collected in *Poems on Various Subjects, Religious and Moral*, 1773)
Type of work: Poem

The poet congratulates the earl on being appointed by King George III as secretary of state for North America, then lays out her hopes for his leadership.

Wheatley, a slave, had met William Legge, the earl of Dartmouth, when she was in England for the publication of her collected poems. She knew him to be a friend of the countess of Huntingdon, a supporter of Wheatley's work. Because the countess also supported the abolishment of slavery, Wheatley's hopes were that the earl would share these abolitionist sensibilities. Putting her faith in this hope, she makes a frank personal appeal to him in this poem.

Because the earl had opposed the Stamp Act, he was considered a friend of the colonists, and the poem opens with a picture of New England's joy at his new political appointment. The reins of authority will be, in his hands, "silken," suggesting relief from the tyranny colonists had experienced at the hands of England's monarch. Wheatley expresses her—and America's—confidence that past wrongs will be made right.

The second stanza moves from the perspective of all New England to a personal one. The poet suggests that Dartmouth may wonder about the source of her love of freedom. Her answer is uncharacteristically outspoken. She refers to the "cruel fate" of being kidnapped from her African homeland and of the anguish this would have caused her parents in losing their "babe belov'd." As a slave, she truly knows the value of liberty. Having suffered so much, she wants to spare others the pain she has known in her loss of freedom; thus her hopes are that New England will be spared further tyranny. The emotional restraint of most neoclassical poetry is set aside in this poem, and Wheatley speaks from the heart. The decision to express her feelings about her bondage was a risky one.

"TO THE UNIVERSITY OF CAMBRIDGE, IN NEW ENGLAND"

First published: 1773 (collected in *Poems on Various Subjects, Religious and Moral,* 1773)
Type of work: Poem

Wheatley admonishes the students of Harvard to shun sin and seek salvation.

In the ringing tones of a sermon, the slave poet draws a clear distinction between the backgrounds of herself and the Harvard College students she addresses. Wheatley opens with a statement about how recently she was brought from Africa, "land of errors." In contrast, the students have had the benefit and privilege of studying the world's best wisdom. Calling them "sons of science," the poet reminds them, however, that the most important knowledge they will ever have is that Jesus died to redeem them and all other sinners. She exhorts them to be ever vigilant against evil and to shun sin in its smallest manifestations.

The two major notes that Wheatley strikes repeatedly in the poem are her race and the urgency of renouncing sin. A devout Christian, she does more than serve as witness to God's mercy and humans' need for salvation. She testifies to the power and glory of the merciful God who brought her safely from a dark place; it is possible that she is referring to Africa, but she may well be referring to the dark slave ship that transported her to America where, though well treated, she is still enslaved. Again she draws attention to her race and servitude by reminding the students that an "Ethiop" (African) is warning them that sin leads to ruin and damnation. By implication, she seems to be leading them to the conclusion that enslaving fellow humans is one such deadly sin.

"TO S. M., A YOUNG AFRICAN PAINTER, ON SEEING HIS WORKS"

First published: 1773 (collected in *Poems on Various Subjects, Religious and Moral,* 1773)
Type of work: Poem

Wheatley's only poem explicitly about art praises the work of a fellow African and artist— and slave.

The poem opens with praise for the art of Scipio Moorhead, slave of a Presbyterian minister, who was both an artist and a poet. It was he who drew Wheatley's portrait which appeared in her book of poems. As a fellow artist, she strives to comprehend the creative process that achieves his purposes and also gives her, as the audience of his work, such pleasure. The artist's pencil gives life to figures born of his imagination and intent, and the speaker praises the power of imagination which bestows on the painter and the writer the ability to transcend the limitations of their world. For these two slave artists, those limitations would have been great indeed.

She encourages Moorhead to make the most of his gifts and to enjoy any fame that comes to him, but at the same time she fixes her thoughts on the afterlife, suggesting that what the earth offers as glory is paltry by comparison to Heaven's glory. In paradise, where they will both be free, their celestial gifts will be nobler and purer, and they will no longer write about or paint "Damon" or "Aurora," subjects that are worldly as well as being products of Western culture rather than the artists' African culture.

"THOUGHTS ON THE WORK OF PROVIDENCE"

First published: 1773 (collected in *Poems on Various Subjects, Religious and Moral,* 1773)
Type of work: Poem

In lofty tones, the poet praises God, who manifests himself through the majesty and orderliness of the created universe.

SUMMARY

Wheatley's poems record, celebrate, or mourn the public events and figures of her day. They do so in language that is formal and draws on familiar classical images and themes; emotion is restrained except for the religious fervor which permeates her work. Her poetry reveals a race consciousness that grows out of her status as a slave.

Linda Jordan Tucker

The speaker of the poem urges her soul to rise and contemplate the majesty of God through the vastness and orderliness of his creation. Though God himself is unseen, he is made manifest in the heavens and the earth through such powerful objects as the sun. Wheatley takes the grandeur of the cosmos as proof of God's sublime, divine imagination. The poem is shaped by the pattern of day's light being following by night's darkness and the return of daylight on the following morning. Humans and the vegetative world require the productive light of the day and the restorative darkness of night, so God is not only powerful but also merciful. The poem ends with Reason and Love, personified, asking what most shows forth almighty God. The poet's answer is that everywhere one looks one sees God's infinite love made visible; humans know him through their senses. Reason falters and fails in the face of the Eternal. All that is left is for humans to praise and worship.

DISCUSSION TOPICS

- What neoclassical influences can be found in Phillis Wheatley's subjects and styles?

- How does Wheatley use classical mythology in her poetry?

- What statements about Christian faith does Wheatley make in her poetry?

- What statements does Wheatley's poetry make about the responsibilities of an artist?

- Who was the audience for Wheatley's poetry—white colonists or her fellow slaves?

- How would you explain Wheatley not strongly opposing slavery in her poems?

- In which poems does Wheatley draw attention to her being African? What is her purpose in doing so?

- Compare three or more of Wheatley's elegies. Is there a pattern in the poems? Identify and discuss it.

BIBLIOGRAPHY

By the Author

POETRY:
Poems on Various Subjects, Religious and Moral, 1773
The Poems of Phillis Wheatley, 1966, 1989 (Julian D. Mason, Jr., editor)

MISCELLANEOUS:
Memoir and Poems of Phillis Wheatley: A Native African and a Slave, 1833
The Collected Works of Phillis Wheatley, 1988 (John Shields, editor)

About the Author
Bassard, Katherine Clay. *Spiritual Interrogations: Culture, Gender, and Community in Early African American Women's Writing.* Princeton, N.J.: Princeton University Press, 1999.

Carretta, Vincent, and Philip Gould, eds. *Genius in Bondage: Literature of the Early Black Atlantic.* Lexington: University Press of Kentucky, 2001.

Lasky, Kathryn. *A Voice of Her Own: The Story of Phillis Wheatley, Slave Poet.* Cambridge, Mass.: Candlewick Press, 2003.

Renfro, G. Herbert. *Life and Works of Phillis Wheatley.* The Black Heritage Library Collection. Plainview, N.Y.: Books for Libraries Press, 1970.

Richmond, Merle. *Phillis Wheatley.* American Women of Achievement. New York: Chelsea House, 1988.

Robinson, William H., ed. *Critical Essays on Phillis Wheatley.* Boston: G. K. Hall, 1982.

Shields, John C. "The American Epic Writ Large: The Example of Phillis Wheatley." In *The American Aeneas: Classical Origins of the American Self.* Knoxville: University of Tennessee Press, 2001.

WALT WHITMAN

Born: West Hills, Long Island, New York
May 31, 1819
Died: Camden, New Jersey
March 26, 1892

Regarded by many as America's greatest poet, Whitman employed an innovative verse form in visionary celebrations of personal liberation and American democracy.

NARA

BIOGRAPHY

Walt Whitman was born on May 31, 1819, in West Hills, near Huntington, Long Island, New York, the second child of Louisa and Walter Whitman. His father was a carpenter who later speculated unsuccessfully in real estate. The family moved to Brooklyn in 1823, and Whitman attended school until the age of eleven, after which he worked as an office boy in a law firm. The owner of the firm enrolled him in a library, and Whitman was soon engrossed in reading, particularly the novels of Scottish writer Sir Walter Scott. The following year, he worked in the printing office of a newspaper, and by 1835 he had found work as a typesetter in New York. He was also contributing conventional poems to an established Manhattan newspaper.

The poor economic situation in New York compelled Whitman to seek work elsewhere, and in 1836 he began teaching at a school on Long Island. This was the first of several poorly paid, short-term teaching positions that Whitman held, on and off, for four years. His interest in journalism continued, and in 1838, with financial support from his family, he founded, published, and edited a newspaper, *The Long Islander*, which continued under his stewardship for a year. Whitman had also developed an interest in politics; in 1840, he campaigned for President Martin Van Buren, and the following year he addressed a Democratic political rally in New York. In 1841, he published eight short

stories in the Democratic Party paper, the *Democratic Review.*

Over the following decade, Whitman remained active in politics and continued his journalistic career, editing the *Brooklyn Daily Eagle* from 1846 to 1848. Fired from the *Eagle* for being a Free-Soiler (the Free-Soilers opposed slavery in newly annexed territories), he edited the *Brooklyn Freeman,* a Free-Soil journal, until September, 1849. From 1850 to 1854, Whitman operated a printing shop and worked as a part-time journalist and building contractor. He followed an irregular routine, spending much time walking and reading. His family was puzzled by his apparently aimless life, not realizing that Whitman was developing the knowledge and aesthetic vision that would shortly burst forth in spectacular fashion.

In July, 1855, the first edition of *Leaves of Grass,* containing twelve untitled poems and a preface, was printed in Brooklyn at Whitman's expense. Ralph Waldo Emerson, one of the most eminent men of letters in America, received it with enthusiasm, but others were shocked by Whitman's bold celebration of the pleasures of the senses and his sometimes coarse language. The following year, Emerson and Henry David Thoreau, the author of *Walden* (1854), visited Whitman at his home, and a second edition of *Leaves of Grass* appeared. Twenty new poems were added, as was Whitman's poetic manifesto, under the guise of a letter to Emerson.

From 1857 to mid-1859, Whitman was editor of the *Brooklyn Daily Times.* After leaving this post he continued to write; he also became a member of a bohemian circle that met at Pfaff's Restaurant in

New York City. In 1860, Whitman traveled to Boston to oversee the printing of the third edition of *Leaves of Grass*, containing sixty-eight new poems, by the young firm of Theyer & Eldridge, Whitman's first commercial publishers. During Whitman's visit, Emerson advised him not to include the sexually oriented "Children of Adam" poems, but Whitman would not be persuaded.

In 1861 the Civil War broke out, and in December, 1862, Whitman traveled to Falmouth, Virginia, to seek out his brother George, who had been slightly wounded at the battle of Fredericksburg. He returned to Washington, D.C., and worked part time as a copyist in the paymaster's office. He also served for several years as a visitor and volunteer nurse to soldiers in hospitals. His tender, fatherly concern and unselfish dedication to his task made a profound impression on the soldiers.

In January, 1865, Whitman became a clerk in the Department of the Interior, and in March he attended the second inauguration of President Abraham Lincoln. A month after Lincoln's assassination in April, 1865, Whitman's poems of the war, *Drum-Taps*, were printed at his own expense. A sequel to *Drum-Taps*, containing the great elegy to Lincoln, "When Lilacs Last in the Dooryard Bloom'd," followed in September. In the meantime, however, Whitman had been fired from his job on the grounds that *Leaves of Grass* was indecent. After a friend intervened, Whitman was employed the next day in the attorney general's office.

In 1867, Whitman's reputation began to develop internationally, stimulated by the interest of William Michael Rossetti in England, who published an expurgated edition of the fourth edition of *Leaves of Grass* (which Whitman had printed in 1867). In 1871, *Democratic Vistas*, consisting of essays on democracy, social philosophy, and literature, was published.

In January, 1873, Whitman became partially paralyzed after a stroke, and in the summer he moved into the house of his brother George, in Camden, New Jersey. With financial support from distinguished writers in England, a centennial edition of *Leaves of Grass* and the volume *Two Rivulets* appeared in 1876. Whitman could now count Alfred, Lord Tennyson, the poet laureate of England, as an admirer, but he was still underappreciated in his own country. His publishing difficulties resurfaced in 1882, when the district attorney threatened to prosecute the Boston firm of James R. Osgood for its publication of the seventh edition of *Leaves of Grass*. In the same year, Whitman began publishing *Specimen Days and Collect*, much of which consists of diary notes of his experiences during the Civil War.

In 1884, Whitman bought a small house on Mickie Street in Camden, where he lived for the remainder of his life. After years of declining health, he died on March 26, 1892.

ANALYSIS

When Whitman first thrust *Leaves of Grass* on an unsuspecting and unresponsive American public, it was clear that he viewed himself as a national bard who would inject something "transcendent and new" into the poetic veins of his country. In the preface, which was strongly influenced by Emerson's essay "The Poet" (1844), Whitman discussed the kind of American bard he envisioned and the kind of poetry that such a bard would write.

Believing that "Americans of all nations . . . have probably the fullest poetical nature" and that "the United States themselves are essentially the greatest poem," Whitman's ideal was a poet whose "spirit responds to his country's spirit. . . . [H]e incarnates its geography and natural life and rivers and lakes." The truly American poet, like the American people, must embrace both the old and the new but must not be bound by conventional poetic forms, whether of rhyme and meter or subject matter. (Whitman had in mind both the didactic verse of American poet Henry Wadsworth Longfellow and the work of the "graveyard school.") Rather, the poet must seek to incarnate that which lies deeper than form and which reflects the laws and realities that are implanted in the human soul. Advocating a poetry of simplicity and genuineness, Whitman's advice to his reader was to "dismiss whatever insults your own soul."

In successive editions of *Leaves of Grass*, Whitman undoubtedly succeeded in his attempt to articulate an authentic American poetic voice, one which was not dependent on models derived from English literature. Further, by applying the central premises of Romanticism and Transcendentalism in a wider and more daring form than any American poet had done, he created a visionary and prophetic book which ranks as one of the great achievements of nineteenth century literature.

Perhaps the most startling aspect of Whitman's poetry for the modern reader is not its free-verse form, to which readers have become accustomed, but the extraordinary metaphysical thought that underlies so much of it. Whitman is the supreme poet of the expanded self. His poetic persona continually celebrates, as a fait accompli, the achievement of the goal to which Romanticism and Transcendentalism aspired: a state of being in which humankind's sense of separateness and isolation in the universe is overcome, a state in which subject and object are unified, and the perceiving self feels deeply connected, emotionally and spiritually, with the rest of creation. The "I" in Whitman's poems, like the figure of Albion in English Romantic poet William Blake's epic poem *Jerusalem* (1804-1820), merges with all things and contains all things. Whitman expressed this succinctly in his poem "There Was a Child Went Forth":

> There was a child went forth every day,
> And the first object he look'd upon, that object he
>   became,
> And that object became part of him for the day or a
>   certain part of the day,
> Or for many years or stretching cycles of years.

Whitman's poetry thus abolishes "otherness." Although English novelist D. H. Lawrence complained that Whitman had accomplished this only by suppressing his own individuality, this was not Whitman's intention.

Thoreau was more appreciative, stating that Whitman's philosophic vision was "Wonderfully like the Orientals," and several modern scholars have analyzed Whitman's poetry in the light of the Vedic literature of India. According to this analysis, Whitman's understanding of the self can best be understood by reference to doctrine probably found in the Upanishads and *Bhagavad Gita*, that the "atman," the essence of the individual self, is identical to Brahman, the universal self. It is not known for certain how well Whitman was acquainted with Eastern thought, and it may be that his philosophy was based as much on personal experience as on the reading of books. "Song of Myself" is notable for its denigration of book learning in favor of the direct intercourse of the self with the natural world.

The doctrine of the self sheds light on another leading theme in *Leaves of Grass*, Whitman's celebration of American democracy. He admired democracy because it combined individualism with the needs of the whole society, and he believed unreservedly in the wisdom of the common man and woman. The "I" of Whitman's poetry sees in all people the same divine status that he experiences within himself. Whitman's poetic program was essentially a democratic one, as is clear from the following passage from the preface to the first edition of *Leaves of Grass*: "The messages of great poets to each man and woman are, Come to us on equal terms, Only then can you understand us, We are not better than you, What we enclose you enclose, What we enjoy you may enjoy."

Equally important for a full picture of Whitman's poetry is his attitude toward sex, which shocked his early readers. Whitman did not regard sex as an inappropriate subject for poetry, and he insisted that it was central to the design of *Leaves of Grass*. He rejected a dualistic view of human life that would relegate the body to an inferior place; on the contrary, he honored sexual desire as a pure expression of the life force that flows through all things. The act of procreation, Whitman believed, furthered the evolution of the human race, and he looked forward to the emergence in America of a race of sturdy, physically healthy human beings who would build a civilization free of the disease and degeneration that, in this view, afflicted the old civilizations of Europe.

As a complement to the love between men and women, Whitman also celebrated, in the "Calamus" poems, comradely love between men, which he called "adhesiveness." Many readers have taken these poems to be expressions of homosexual feelings, although in *Democratic Vistas* Whitman insisted that such love would help to spiritualize the nation and offset the vulgar aspects of American democracy. The Calamus poems, therefore, take their place in the grand vision that Whitman held of *Leaves of Grass* as a new bible, with every leaf contributing to a new heaven and a new earth.

"SONG OF MYSELF"

First published: 1855 (collected in *Leaves of Grass*, 1855)
Type of work: Poem

A celebration of the human self and all that it can see, hear, touch, taste, smell, intuit, and contemplate in the human and natural world.

"Song of Myself," the longest poem in *Leaves of Grass*, is a joyous celebration of the human self in its most expanded, spontaneous, self-sufficient, and all-embracing state as it observes and interacts with everything in creation and ranges freely over time and space. The bard of the poem, speaking in the oracular tones of the prophet, affirms the divinity and sacredness of the entire universe, including the human body, and he asserts that no part of the universe is separate from himself—he flows into all things and is all things.

The "I" of the poem is quite clearly, then, not the everyday self, the small, personal ego that is unique and different from all other selves. Rather, the persona who speaks out in such bold terms is the human self experiencing its own transcendental nature, silently witnessing all the turbulent activity of the world while itself remaining detached: "Apart from the pulling and hauling stands what I am, . . . Both in and out of the game and watching and wondering at it." This "I" is immortal and persists through numberless human generations and through all the changing cycles of creation and destruction in the universe. It cannot be measured or circumscribed; it is blissful, serenely content with itself, and needs nothing beyond or outside itself for its own fulfillment.

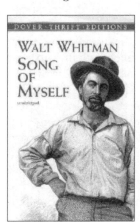

In "Song of Myself," this large self continually floods into and interpenetrates the small, personal self, including the physical body, and becomes one with it. It is this union of the absolute self with the relative self that allows the persona of the poem to express such spontaneous delight in the simple experience of being alive in the flesh. "I loafe and invite my soul,/ I lean and loafe at my ease observing a spear of summer grass," announces the persona in the very first section of the poem. This is a state of being that does not have to perform any actions to experience fulfillment; it simply enjoys being what it is: "I exist as I am, that is enough,/ If no other in the world be aware I sit content,/ And if each and all be aware I sit content."

It is in this context that the persona's celebration of the pleasures of the body should be understood. Lines such as "Walt Whitman, a kosmos, of Manhattan the son,/ Turbulent, fleshy, sensual, eating, drinking and breeding," do not signify mere sensual indulgence. The human body is a microcosm of its divine source, in which there is always perfection, fullness, and bliss. There is no dualism of soul and body, because, as William Blake put it in *The Marriage of Heaven and Hell* (1790), a prophetic work which bears a strong resemblance to "Song of Myself," "that call'd Body is a portion of Soul discern'd by the five senses."

Hence the Whitman persona can declare that "I am the poet of the Body and I am the poet of the Soul"; he will not downgrade one in order to promote the other. The senses are "miracles," no part of the body is to be rejected or scorned, and sexual desire should not be something that cannot be spoken of: "I do not press my fingers across my mouth,/ I keep as delicate around the bowels as around the head and heart,/ Copulation is no more rank to me than death is."

This perception of the divine essence in the physical form extends to everything in the created world, however humble its station:

> I believe a leaf of grass is no less than the journey-
>   work of the stars,
> And the pismire is equally perfect, and a grain of
>   sand, and the egg of the wren,
> And the tree-toad is a chef-d'œuvre for the highest,
> And the running blackberry would adorn the
>   parlors of heaven.

Heightened perception such as this also extends to other human beings, all of whom are viewed as equally divine by the persona. It is this conviction of the shared divinity of the self that enables the persona repeatedly to identify and empathize with other human beings, as in section 33: "I do not ask the wounded person how he feels, I myself become the wounded person."

In the worldview of the persona, humankind and nature interpenetrate each other in the most intimate way. The cycle of death, rebirth, and transformation is endless and unfathomable. The grass may, the persona muses, be made from the breasts of young men or from the hair of old people; he bequeaths himself to the earth and counsels the curious reader to look for him "under the boot-soles." This points to a paradox, one of many in the poem. The self is immortal, yet it will also go through many transformations ("No doubt I have died myself ten thousand times before"); similarly, the universe is complete and perfect at every moment, yet it is also perpetually flowing onward in dynamic transformation and evolution. Finally, the self merges with everything in the world yet also stands aloof and apart from the world. Paradoxes such as this cannot be rationally explained, but they can, the persona would argue, be spontaneously lived through.

Scholars have discussed whether "Song of Myself" has its origins in Whitman's own mystical experiences or whether the persona is solely a literary invention designed to embody the kind of universal, all-seeing American bard that Whitman believed was appropriate for a vast and still expanding land. Such questions are impossible to answer with any certainty; however, it might be noted that in section 5, the Whitman persona records a significant moment when the transcendent soul seemed to descend and envelop him in an intense, almost sexual embrace, as a result of which "Swiftly arose and spread around me the peace and knowledge that pass all the argument of the earth." He then knows, as an immediate fact of awareness, that his own spirit is a brother of the spirit of God, that all humankind are his brothers and sisters, and that the whole universe is bound together by love.

Attempts have also been made to discern a structure to the poem, but these have not, in general, proved satisfactory. Rather than trying to find a linear progression of themes, it is perhaps more useful to think of each of the fifty-two sections as spokes of a wheel, each expressing the same theme or similar themes in diverse ways, from diverse angles. As the persona states, "All truths wait in all things."

"The Sleepers"

First published: 1855 (collected in *Leaves of Grass*, 1855)
Type of work: Poem

In a dream vision, the persona moves among a varied group of people as they sleep, sympathetically identifying with their inner lives.

"The Sleepers" has been called a surrealistic poem. Although it certainly possesses the disconnected incidents and imagery characteristic of dreams, however, it also has a discernible, tripartite structure that suggests a myth of initiation, death, and rebirth. In the first part, which consists of the first two sections, the persona wanders freely at night and sympathetically identifies with a wide variety of sleeping people; in part 2 (sections 3-6) the persona experiences vicariously the destructive and painful aspects of human experience; part 3 (sections 7-9) celebrates the night world of restoration, rebirth, and cosmic unity.

In section 1, as the persona overlooks the sleepers—drunkards, idiots, the insane, a married couple, a mother and child, a prisoner, and others—the night in which they sleep is presented almost as a mystic presence which "pervades them and infolds them," rather like the Oversoul in the thought of Emerson. The speaker then undergoes

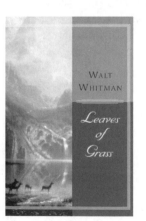

some kind of initiation: He pierces the darkness, new beings appear, and he dances and laughs in a bacchanalian whirl, accompanied by divine spirits. The result is that he is able to become the people he is observing and dream their dreams with them. This mystic expansion of the self into all things is similar to the central idea in "Song of Myself."

Part 2 consists of three unconnected visions. First, a beautiful, nude, male swimmer is caught in a tide which draws him to death; there is also a shipwreck, and the persona desperately tries to effect a rescue, but no one survives. Second, the persona goes back in time to the defeat of General George Washington at Brooklyn Heights in August, 1776. He pictures Washington on two occasions: weeping in defeat with a group of officers around him, and embracing his officers in a tavern when peace was declared. The third vision is a memory from the persona's early life, when a beautiful Indian woman came to the family homestead one breakfast time. She was received with warmth by the persona's mother, who regretted having no work to give her. The squaw left in the afternoon, never to return, much to the mother's regret.

Perhaps this incident was meant to symbolize the loss of an old way of life, in which pure and generous social intercourse was the norm.

In the first version of the poem, it is clear that at this point in his experience, the persona is in a state of psychic disintegration. Three verse paragraphs followed, including the line "Now Lucifer was not dead . . . or if he was I am his sorrowful heir." All three paragraphs were omitted in the version of the poem published in *Leaves of Grass* in 1871.

Part 3 marks a change of atmosphere, beginning with images of sunlight, air, summer, and the burgeoning fullness of nature. Travelers of all nations are returning to their homelands, including the lost swimmer, the Indian squaw, and others with whom the persona has earlier identified. Sleep and the night have restored them and made them all equal, peaceful, and beautiful. The speaker realizes that such is the true state of things.

Section 9 presents a fine vision of the night as an experience of transcendental unity. As the sleepers lie at rest, people of all nations "flow hand in hand over the whole earth from east to west as they lie unclothed": The chain of unity includes the learned and the unlearned, father and son, mother and daughter, scholar and teacher. All those who were diseased have been cured. The poem concludes with the serene thoughts of the persona, who is happy to take part in the day world of conscious activity but feels no fear at the thought of returning to the secret regenerative powers of the night, now suggestive of a nourishing earth mother.

"CROSSING BROOKLYN FERRY"

First published: 1856 (as "Sun Down Poem"; collected in *Complete Poetry and Selected Prose*, 1959)
Type of work: Poem

Observing the sights and sounds of a mass of people crossing from Brooklyn by ferry, the poet contemplates the link between past and future.

"Crossing Brooklyn Ferry" is a subtle, oblique attempt to transcend time and persuade the reader of the simultaneity of past, present, and future. Whitman shed light on the poem in the preface to the 1855 edition of *Leaves of Grass*: "Past and present are not disjoin'd but joined. The greatest poet forms the consistence of what is to be from what has been and is. . . . He . . . places himself where the future becomes present." The poem is also rich in imagery that suggests the coexistence of opposite values, such as fixity and motion, rest and activity, time and eternity.

"Crossing Brooklyn Ferry" is divided into nine sections. In the first section, the poet observes the crowds of people crossing the East River to Manhattan by ferry and thinks of those who will be making the crossing in years to come. He develops this thought in section 2, as he contemplates the ties that bind him to the people of the future. In a hundred years, others will be seeing the same landmarks, the same sunset, the same ebb and flow of the tides. The speaker also hints that the scene he contemplates forms part of a grand, spiritual "scheme" of life, in which everything possesses its own individuality yet is part of the whole. That sense of wholeness has power to impart glory to all the poet's daily activities and sense perceptions. The poet makes this hint explicit at the end of the poem.

Having evoked the passage of time and underscored it with images of flux—the tide, the sunset—the poet in section 3 does everything he can to negate it: "It avails not, time nor place—distance avails not,/ I am with you, you men and women of a generation, or ever so many generations hence." Whatever future generations might see, the poet has also seen. He recalls the many times he has crossed the river by ferry, and he catalogs the sights that met his gaze: steamboats and schooners, sloops and barges, circling seagulls, sailors at work, the flags of many nations, the fires from the foundry chimneys on the shore. Most notable in this section are the images that combine motion and stasis and that reinforce the theme of time which is no-time. The poet pictures the people who stand still on the rail of the ferry "yet hurry with the swift current," and he observes the seagulls "with motionless wings, oscillating their bodies." Underlying the whole section (indeed, the whole poem) is the great central symbol of the river, forever flowing, yet forever appearing the same.

After the recapitulation that makes up the fourth section, sections 5 and 6 take the theme to a more intimate level. The poet again asserts that time and place do not separate. Now, however, instead of evoking sense perceptions only, he asserts that the thoughts and feelings experienced by future generations have been his, too. His soul knew periods of darkness and aridity; he, too, experienced self-doubt, and he committed most of the sins of which humanity is capable. In this respect he was one with everyone else, whether present or future.

Section 7 is a direct address to the reader of the future. The poet's tone becomes increasingly intimate and personal as he suggests that he is drawing ever closer to the reader. Three rhetorical questions follow, the last of which suggests a linking of past and future that is at once mysterious and mystical: "Who knows, for all the distance, but I am as good as looking at you now, for all you cannot see me?" This implies that the fullest human self is part of a larger entity which is not subject to the limitations of time or space and which endures through all things. Because of this, the awakened consciousness of the poet (or of any man or woman) may perceive past, present, and future fused into a single enlightened moment.

The rhetorical questions continue in section 8, at the end of which the poet hints cryptically and conspiratorially that his purpose has been accomplished obliquely: The reader has accepted what the poet promised, without him even mentioning what it was. Poet and reader have accomplished what could not be accomplished by study or preaching.

The final section begins with an apostrophe to the river—which also symbolizes the world of time and change—urging it to continue its eternal ebb and flow. More apostrophes follow, in excited and exclamatory vein—to the clouds at sunset, to Manhattan and Brooklyn, to life itself. This section is both a recapitulation and a renewed celebration of what the poet has earlier described—the everyday sights and sounds encountered while crossing the river—but now with the separation between past and future irrevocably broken (or so the poet would believe) in the reader's mind.

In the final lines of the poem, the poet reveals the deepest reasons for his wish that the myriad phenomena of the natural and human world should continue to flourish, with even greater intensity, in the vast sea of time. They are all "dumb, beautiful ministers": Through the material forms of temporal life, the poet and the reader (now no longer referred to as "I" and "you" but as "we"), having engaged in the process of revelation which is the poem, are able to perceive the eternal, spiritual dimensions of existence. This conclusion has already been suggested by a marvelous image in section 3, when the poet, looking into the sunlit water, sees "fine centrifugal spokes of light round the shape of my head." In section 9 the image is repeated and universalized: Those who gaze deeply into the flux will also see their own heads aureoled in splendid, radiating light.

"OUT OF THE CRADLE ENDLESSLY ROCKING"

First published: 1859 (as "A Child's Reminiscence"; collected in *Complete Poetry and Selected Prose,* 1959)
Type of work: Poem

The poet describes an incident from his childhood in which he first realized that his destiny was to become a poet.

"Out of the Cradle Endlessly Rocking" is a poem of reminiscence, in which the poet, at a crisis in his adult life, looks back to an incident in his childhood when he first became aware of his vocation as a poet. The structure of the poem owes a great deal to music, particularly grand opera, which Whitman loved. He once said that without opera he could not have written *Leaves of Grass,* and an anonymous review in the *Saturday Press* in 1860 (which was actually written by Whitman himself) commented, "Walt Whitman's method in the construction of his songs is strictly the method of Italian opera."

The musical quality of the poem can be seen in the opening section of twenty-two lines, with its incantatory rhythms and wavelike quality, the latter suggesting the restless motion of a turbulent sea. This is most notable in the buildup of pressure in lines 8 to 15, each of which begins with the word "from"; the effect is like the inexorable rising of a powerful wave before it crests, breaks, and laps quietly onto the shore in the final half-line ("A reminiscence sing"). The meaning of the opening section is simple: Under moonlight on an autumn evening, the poet, caught in a moment of personal despair, has returned to a place on the seashore that he had known as a young boy. The scene reminds him of a moment of great significance in his life.

The next nine lines are the equivalent of the recitative (or narrative portion) in opera. The poet recalls that as a boy he spent many days one spring on Paumanok (the Indian name for Long Island), closely observing the nest of two mockingbirds. Recitative now alternates with the arias of the mockingbirds, who at first sing of their togetherness. One day the she-bird disappears, and all summer long the boy listens to the solitary song of the remaining bird.

The boy interprets the song as the bird calling for his absent mate, and now as a man he claims that he, a poet and a "chanter of pains and joys," understands the meaning of the lonely song better than other men. Lines 71 to 129 are a long, unashamedly sentimental lament by the mockingbird; the natural world seems to be rejoicing in love, but he cannot do so. He convinces himself that every vague shape in the distance must be his mate, and then he persuades himself that he has heard her responding to his song. Finally, however, he realizes that his quest is useless, and he ends sorrowfully.

The boy listens to the aria in ecstasy and in tears because he feels that its meaning has penetrated to his soul. From that moment, he is awakened; he knows his purpose and his destiny, and a thousand songs—poems—begin to stir within him. He, too, will sing of unsatisfied love and explore "the sweet hell within,/ The unknown want."

Then a new revelation comes as the boy learns to listen to the sea. All night long the sea whispers to him only one word, "the low and delicious word death," and this has a profound effect on him (which is emphasized in the poem by the repetition of the word nine times). The knowledge of the universality and inevitability of death—that all of nature is a field of death—comes upon him not with anguish but like a gentle, loving caress. The final, immensely evocative image is of the sea "like some old crone rocking the cradle." The image is striking because it suggests both age and infancy; it makes clear that the first stirrings of life are also a movement toward death. The sea, although it perpetually whispers "death," is a mother nevertheless (elsewhere in the poem, the sea is referred to as a "fierce" and "savage" "old mother"), and the rocking of a cradle is a soothing and comforting motion.

Whitman has been called the poet of death—although such a description hardly does justice to the massive life-affirming vision of his greatest poems—and sometimes this poem has been interpreted psychoanalytically as a regressive wish to return to the unconscious, to the undifferentiated security of the womb. It might also be argued that such a conclusion runs contrary to the poem's main theme, which, in the terms used by psychologist Carl Jung, records an important moment in the process of the individuation of the self: The poet discovers his personal destiny.

"WHEN LILACS LAST IN THE DOORYARD BLOOM'D"

First published: 1865 (collected in *Drum-Taps*, 1865)
Type of work: Poem

This work elegizes President Abraham Lincoln.

Whitman wrote "When Lilacs Last in the Dooryard Bloom'd" in the months following the assassination of President Lincoln on April 14, 1865. Whitman felt the loss of Lincoln personally. He had observed the president on a number of occasions in Washington, D.C. Once he saw him chatting with a friend at the White House and commented, "His face & manner . . . are inexpressibly sweet. . . . I love the President personally." The elegy contains many of the elements that make up the traditional pastoral elegy, including the expression of grief and bewilderment by the poet, the sympathetic mourning of nature for the dead person (expressed by means of the pathetic fallacy), the rebirth of nature, a funeral procession, the placing of flowers on the bier, and finally, reconciliation and consolation.

Whitman's elegy is also about how the poet transmutes his sorrow, which at the outset is so great that it prevents him from writing, to the point where he can once more create poetry.

The elegy centers around four symbols: the lilac, the evening star, spring, and the hermit thrush, a bird that sings in seclusion. These symbols recur in varied forms throughout the poem, like musical motifs. The poet first declares his grief and invokes Venus, the evening star, which has now fallen below the horizon and left him in darkness and sorrow. He then develops the lilac symbol: In the dooryard of an old some farmhouse, a lilac bush blossoms. Each heart-shaped leaf (a symbol of love) he regards as a miracle, and he breaks off a sprig. The fourth symbol, the thrush that sings a solitary song, is introduced in section 4.

Section 5 describes the coffin of Lincoln journeying night and day across the country (as it did in reality on its journey from Washington to Springfield, Illinois), as spring bursts through everywhere. Church bells toll, and as the coffin moves slowly past the poet, he throws his sprig of lilac onto it, although he makes it clear that this act is not for Lincoln alone (who is never mentioned by name in the poem) but for all who have died.

After an apostrophe to the evening star, which, in sympathy with the poet's state of mind, is sinking in woe, the poet returns to the song of the hermit thrush. Although he hears and understands the call, he cannot yet sing with the thrush, because the star (now clearly associated, as "my departing comrade," with Lincoln) still holds him. Eventually, as he looks out one spring evening on a serene landscape, an understanding of the true nature of death comes upon him like a mystical revelation. He personifies the knowledge of death, and his own thoughts about death, as two figures walking alongside him. Now he is able to interpret the song of the bird as a "carol of death." A long aria, reminiscent of the song of the bird in "Out of the Cradle Endlessly Rocking," follows. Death is described as soft, welcome, delicate, blissful, and as a "strong deliveress."

In section 15, the poet sees a surrealistic vision of a battlefield, on which lie myriad corpses and whitened skeletons. The poet sees that the dead are at rest and do not suffer; it is only those left behind—families and comrades—who suffer. He leaves the vision behind and is also able to leave behind the birdsong, the lilac, and the evening star. The meaning of all these symbols now remains a permanent part of his awareness, however, so the elegy can move to its stately and moving close: "For the sweetest, wisest soul of all my days and lands— and this for his dear sake,/ Lilac and star and bird twined with the chant of my soul,/ There in the fragrant pines and the cedars dusk and dim."

"PASSAGE TO INDIA"

First published: 1871 (collected in *Passage to India*, 1871)
Type of work: Poem

This poem celebrates the progress of human civilization and the spiritual evolution of the human race.

"Passage to India" is a salute to the idea of the evolutionary progress of the human race; it celebrates the scientific achievements of the age, looks forward to the imminent dawning of an era in which all divisions and separations between people, and people and nature, will be eliminated, and heralds the spiritual voyage of every human soul into the depths of the inner universe. Whitman himself described the meaning of his poem, saying "that the divine efforts of heroes, and their ideas . . . will finally prevail, and be accomplished, however long deferred."

The poem begins by celebrating three achievements of contemporary technology: the opening of the Suez Canal in 1869, the laying of the transAtlantic cable, and the growth of the American transcontinental railroad. These achievements outshine the Seven Wonders of the Ancient World; however, the poet still hears the call of the ancient past, embodied in the myths and fables of Asia, with their daring reach toward an unfathomable spiritual truth. The refrain "Passage to India" therefore suggests the theme of inner as well as outer exploration.

Section 3 elaborates on two of the new wonders, picturing the opening ceremony of the Suez Canal and the grand landscapes through which the American railroad passes. The poet has been careful to establish that the great works of the present should be celebrated not merely for the human skill and knowledge to which they testify but also because they mark an important stage in the fulfillment of the divine plan: the human race coming together in unity. The section ends by flashing back to the past and invoking the name of Christopher Columbus. Whitman liked to present himself as an idealized Columbus figure, exploring new literary and psychic worlds, yet rejected by his countrymen. Perhaps he had in mind Thoreau's injunction in the conclusion to *Walden* (1854): "[B]e Columbus to whole new continents and worlds within you, opening new channels, not of trade, but of thought."

Section 5 is central to the poem because it conveys Whitman's vision of the role of the poet in human evolution. Whitman first stretches the reader's awareness by evoking the vast earth "swimming in space/ Cover'd all over with visible power and beauty." He then describes the troubled history of the human race; the myriad restless, dissatisfied, questing lives. He alludes to the Transcendentalist idea that humankind and nature have become separated. No connection is perceived between the human, feeling subject and the apparently unresponsive external world: "What is this earth to our affections? (unloving earth, without a throb to answer ours . . .)." Yet the divine plan remains and shall be achieved, with the help of the poet, who is the "true son of God."

Coming after the inventors and the scientists, the poet will justify them (a deliberate echo of seventeenth century English poet John Milton, who wrote that he sought to justify the ways of God to humankind) by fully humanizing a mechanized world: He will soothe hearts, open all secrets, and join nature and humans in unity. Whitman thus reiterates the poetic manifesto contained in the preface to the 1855 edition of *Leaves of Grass*: "Folks expect of the poet more than the beauty and dignity

which always attach to dumb real objects . . . they expect him to indicate the path between reality and their souls."

After section 6 has presented a panorama of some of the great events in human history and again invoked Columbus, section 7 develops the theme implicit earlier in the poem, of the poet as spiritual explorer. This theme carries the poem through to its conclusion. The poet must journey, in partnership with his soul, to "primal thought," beyond all limitations of the physical body, to the infinite regions of the cosmic mind. The restless desire to expand, to voyage on the ocean of Being, becomes more and more urgent in the final section of the poem. The poet and his soul have lingered long enough. Now is the time to be bold and reckless, for the cosmic seas are safe: "[A]re they not all the seas of God?"

"SONG OF THE REDWOOD TREE"

First published: 1876 (collected in *Complete Poetry and Selected Prose*, 1959)
Type of work: Poem

A dying redwood tree sings of the night and virtue of the coming human civilization.

In "Song of the Redwood Tree," the poet injects himself into the consciousness of a century-old California redwood as it is being felled. In a musical structure that Whitman often used, the song of the tree is presented as a grand operatic aria, and it alternates with passages of recitative in which the poet repeats and expands upon the message that the great tree imparts. The poem testifies to Whitman's belief in the evolutionary growth of the universe toward perfection, culminating in the new land and peoples of America. These themes are particularly evident in Whitman's poems written after 1865, such as "Song of the Universal," "Pioneers, O Pioneers," and "Passage to India."

In Whitman's universe, consciousness pervades everything, even vegetable and mineral forms, and the sensitive soul of the poet can tap into the consciousness of the nonhuman world and interpret its meanings. Thus the death chant of the tree, which is accompanied by wood spirits who have dwelt in the woods of Mendocino for a thousand years, is unheard by the workers who are felling the tree, but the poet hears it.

The tree chants not only of the past but also of the future. It sings of the joy it has known throughout all the changing seasons in its long life—it has delighted in sun, wind, rain, and snow. It confirms that it, too, has consciousness and a sense of selfhood, as do rocks and mountains. The tree declares that it and its companions are content to abdicate their position to make room for the arrival of a "superber race," for which they have been long preparing.

The tree then gives expression to Whitman's belief in the special destiny of the American people. The new race has emerged peacefully to inherit a new empire. It has not come from the old cultures of Asia and Europe—the latter, stained with the blood of innumerable wars, is particularly unfit to give birth to a new kind of men and women. The building of America is the fruition of a long process of hidden growth. Deep within the continent has lain a secret, national will, working below the turbulence of surface events in order to manifest itself. Here in California, sings the tree, may the new man grow and flourish in freedom, "proportionate to Nature," acting on his own inner promptings, not bowing to the moral formulas and creeds of others. A new woman will emerge also, and she will be the nourishing source of life and love.

Listening in the woods, the poet catches the message of the "ecstatic, ancient and rustling" voices of the tree and its accompanying dryads, and in sections 2 and 3 he takes up and amplifies their themes. He celebrates America, with its fields and mountains bathed in healthier air, from Puget Sound to Colorado. He praises the new race that arrived after "slow and steady ages" in which the earth was preparing itself for them. He lauds American civilization but states that the achievements of American technology are useful only because they help to push the race on to a state of perfection in which the ideal (the spiritual level of life) is lived in the midst of the real (the material world).

SUMMARY

"The proof of a poet is that his country absorbs him as affectionately as he has absorbed it," wrote Whitman in his letter to Emerson that prefaced the second edition of *Leaves of Grass*. According to this criterion, Whitman has indeed proved himself many times over, as it is hard to imagine twentieth century American poetry without him. His influence has extended to poets such as William Carlos Williams, Hart Crane, Robinson Jeffers, Carl Sandburg, and Allen Ginsberg. Their admiration for Whitman is a tribute to the universal appeal of his long song of himself: his transcendental metaphysics, his emotional honesty and complexity, his lyric skill, and his faith in the future of his country.

Bryan Aubrey

BIBLIOGRAPHY

By the Author

POETRY:
Leaves of Grass, 1855, 1856, 1860, 1867, 1871, 1876, 1881-1882, 1889, 1891-1892
"Song of Myself," 1855
Drum-Taps, 1865
Sequel to Drum-Taps, 1865-1866
Passage to India, 1871
After All, Not to Create Only, 1871
As a Strong Bird on Pinions Free, 1872
Two Rivulets, 1876
November Boughs, 1888
Good-bye My Fancy, 1891
Complete Poetry and Selected Prose, 1959 (James E. Miller, editor)

LONG FICTION:
Franklin Evans, 1842

SHORT FICTION:
The Half-Breed, and Other Stories, 1927

NONFICTION:
Democratic Vistas, 1871
Memoranda During the War, 1875-1876
Specimen Days and Collect, 1882-1883
Complete Prose Works, 1892
Calamus, 1897 (letters; Richard M. Bucke, editor)
The Wound Dresser, 1898 (Bucke, editor)
Letters Written by Walt Whitman to His Mother, 1866-1872, 1902 (Thomas B. Harned, editor)
An American Primer, 1904
Walt Whitman's Diary in Canada, 1904 (William S. Kennedy, editor)
The Letters of Anne Gilchrist and Walt Whitman, 1918 (Harned, editor)

MISCELLANEOUS:
The Collected Writings of Walt Whitman, 1961-1984 (22 volumes)

About the Author

Allen, Gay Wilson. *A Reader's Guide to Walt Whitman.* New York: Farrar, Straus and Giroux, 1970.

_____. *The Solitary Singer: A Critical Biography of Walt Whitman.* Rev. ed. New York: New York University Press, 1967.

Asselineau, Roger. *The Evolution of Walt Whitman.* Expanded ed. Iowa City: University of Iowa Press, 1999.

Gold, Arthur, comp. *Walt Whitman: A Collection of Criticism.* New York: McGraw-Hill, 1974.

Greenspan, Ezra, ed. *Walt Whitman's "Song of Myself": A Sourcebook and Critical Edition.* New York: Routledge, 2005.

Kaplan, Justin. *Walt Whitman: A Life.* New York: Simon & Schuster, 1980.

Miller, James E., Jr. *Walt Whitman.* Rev. ed. Boston: Twayne, 1990.

Pearce, Roy Harvey, ed. *Whitman: A Collection of Critical Essays.* Englewood Cliffs, N.J.: Prentice-Hall, 1962.

Reynolds, David S., ed. *Walt Whitman.* New York: Oxford University Press, 2005.

Sowder, Michael. *Whitman's Ecstatic Union: Conversion and Ideology in "Leaves of Grass."* New York: Routledge, 2005.

Woodress, James, ed. *Critical Essays on Walt Whitman.* Boston: G. K. Hall, 1983.

Zweig, Paul. *Walt Whitman: The Making of a Poet.* New York: Basic Books, 1984.

DISCUSSION TOPICS

- Consider "Out of the Cradle Endlessly Rocking" as a poem about personal destiny.

- What features of *Song of Myself* make it clear that the poem is not merely an exercise in egotism?

- What is there about grass that inspired Walt Whitman to use the title *Leaves of Grass* for his book?

- What makes "Crossing Brooklyn Ferry" a timeless poem despite the passing of this particular ferry service?

- What qualities make "When Lilacs Last in the Dooryard Bloom'd" superior to Whitman's other poems on Abraham Lincoln's death, including the well-known "O Captain, My Captain"?

- What are the predominant images of "When Lilacs Last in the Dooryard Bloom'd," and how does he connect them in the poem?

- How free are the rhythms of Whitman's free verse?

JOHN GREENLEAF WHITTIER

Born: Haverhill, Massachusetts
December 17, 1807
Died: Hampton Falls, New Hampshire
September 7, 1892

Though notable as a newspaper editor and writer of anti-slavery political prose, Whittier is best remembered as a poet of the New England Renaissance whose nostalgic depictions of rural life were embraced by an American society otherwise caught up in tumultuous change.

Library of Congress

BIOGRAPHY

John Greenleaf Whittier's family was of true old New England stock. His ancestors settled in the locality of his birth in 1638, and the house in which he was born was more than a century old in 1807. His parents, John and Abigail (Hussey), worked the rough New England soil, often suffering from indebtedness but never impoverished. Both were devout Quakers who raised their four children to seek the Inner Light and beware of dogmatic religious authorities. Though their nearest neighbors lived half a mile away, the Whittiers were very sociable and staunch believers in the connectedness of all people. Young John absorbed the values of Yankee independence and Quaker social justice, as well as an affection and healthy respect for the region's countryside and history. All of these influences—familial, religious, and geographic—would find their way into Whittier's poetry.

Labor on the farm was harsh, and John's body found it difficult to endure. He worked hard but was often sick from exhaustion. During the winter of 1814-1815, the Whittiers sent John to the district school, his only formal education until young adulthood. Nonetheless, he learned to read and consumed his family's small library, which centered on the Bible and Quaker religious works. In 1821, a traveling Scotsman stopped by the farmstead and sang a number of poet Robert Burns's

songs in return for sustenance. Later the same year, the local schoolmaster Joshua Coffin read a number of other poems to the family, and the taste for poetry was awakened in fourteen-year-old John. The simplicity of Burns's lyrics and their rural flavor spoke to John with immediacy. Whittier's earliest poems were largely derivative and sometimes even in Burns's own Scots dialect. By the time he was nineteen, Whittier recorded some thirty poems that reflected his rural environment, his religiosity, and the Romantic sensivity to nature that was in full bloom. His older sister Mary encouraged his writing and, in 1826, sent "The Exile's Departure" to the *Newburyport Free Press* for publication. The paper's editor, abolitionist William Lloyd Garrison, was so impressed that he visited the young poet, beginning a long and complex relationship. Within a year or so, Whittier had published seventy-six poems in local papers, including the *Haverhill Gazette*, whose editor echoed Garrison's call for more. In 1827, Whittier enrolled for the first of two terms at the Haverhill Academy, where he earned tuition by teaching and shoemaking. He learned an enormous amount, including much about classical culture and literature and also that he hated teaching.

In 1829, Garrison secured Whittier the position of editor of Boston's *The American Manufacturer.* He held the position for seven months and literally did everything to produce the paper. This experience directed Whittier's attention to the politics and social issues of the day. In 1830, Whittier returned home to edit the *Essex Gazette*, in which he editorialized for political and social reform and wrote on contemporary literature. In July, he moved to Hartford to edit the well-respected *New England Weekly Review* but resigned in exhaustion after eighteen months. In addition to his editorial work, he published more than fifty poems and his *Legends of New-England* (1831). The *New York Mirror*'s review (March 19) compared it favorably to Washington Irving's *Sketches* and declared, "As a poet Mr. Whittier possesses undoubted genius." By 1833, Whittier had written 288 poems. During this period, Whittier grew more deeply involved in national politics, supporting Henry Clay and then Daniel Webster and unsuccessfully seeking a congressional seat.

In 1833, Garrison drew Whittier directly into abolitionist politics, and the poet served as a delegate to the first American Anti-Slavery Convention. In June, he produced the pamphlet *Justice and Expediency: Or, Slavery Considered with a View to Its Rightful and Effectual Remedy, Abolition*, and in 1835 he began his single term in the Massachusetts State House. Increasingly vocal in what he considered America's great problem, he lobbied politicians in Concord and returned to the *Essex Gazette* in 1836, eventually resigning in frustration after eight months. In the same year, he sold the old farmstead and settled in Amesbury, Massachusetts, his home for the next fifty-six years. In 1837, Whittier briefly managed the antislavery *Pennsylvania Freeman*, whose offices were burned in mob violence in May, 1838. Time spent in New York (editing *The Emancipator*, June-August, 1837) expanded his abolitionist network, but he retired, again exhausted, to Amesbury in 1840.

Whittier and Garrison parted company when the poet helped found the Liberty Party, which eventually merged with the Free Soilers. During the 1840's, Whittier ran unsuccessfully for Congress, edited the Liberty Party's *Middlesex Standard*, and became a corresponding editor for the *National Era*. His political poetry from the early 1830's through the Civil War reflected his political agenda of abolition and social justice. Many of these poems combined this agenda with Quaker piety, which saw Jesus's Gospel as a cry for human freedom and dignity. Many were published as broadsides with vivid depictions of shackled slaves suffering inhuman torments. In 1838, his first authorized edition of poetry, titled *Poems*, appeared, followed rapidly by the collections *Lays of My Home, and Other Poems* (1843) and *Voices of Freedom* (1846). His fictional *Leaves from Margaret Smith's Journal* (1849), which depicted New England in 1678-1679 through a young Englishwoman's eyes, was his last major prose work. In the years leading to the Civil War and long thereafter, Whittier wrote for *Atlantic Monthly*, which gained him some financial stability and a wide readership.

However, it was only after the Civil War, as Americans from the South and North salved their many wounds, that Whittier's poetry really became popular. He turned from the Great Cause, which had been successfully defended, back to his roots in rural New England. *Snow-Bound* (1866), written in the shadow of the death of his dear sister Elizabeth in 1864, earned him true renown and the princely sum of ten thousand dollars. Six collections of his work followed, with a definitive edition of his poetry to date published by Houghton Mifflin in 1888-1889 under the title *The Writings of John Greenleaf Whittier*. At age eighty-three, he published the appropriately named collection *At Sundown* (1890). He died following a stroke at Hampton Falls, New Hampshire, on September 7, 1892. He left a will reflecting a fortune of more than $130,000 and is buried in Amesbury, Massachusetts.

ANALYSIS

"Who cares for the opinion of the twentieth century? Not I, for one." Whittier was often ambivalent about his poetry, remaining unconvinced of its quality and genuinely surprised at its success. While all of Whittier's poetry may well be considered highly personal, its ultimate sources are the greater environments that enveloped and inspired him. In his youth, these included rural New England, with its distinctive lore, history, and geography, as well as God and the divine presence in humans and nature. His early works were often derivative, reflecting biblical cadences as well as the lyrics of Burns and the poetry of Byronic Romanticism. Many found ready readers in the newspapers of his day, however, and this popularity reinforced his initial impulses. The results were often unpolished and naïve, sometimes painfully crippled by his lack of discipline and aversion to revision.

His best-known works of the 1830's and 1840's

were shaped by his ever-deeper involvement in antislavery politics. Their tone is intense and sincere, embodying the righteous, but rarely self-righteous, anger and indignation of the abolitionist and reformer. "Moral beauty" took pride of place to natural beauty. In "The Reformer" he admits that the betterment of society demands sacrifices, even of things held dear. American slavery offended Whittier on every level—spiritual, political, intellectual, emotional—and his abolitionist poetry employs every rhetorical stance and technique. The early "Hunters of Men" (1835) asks ironically, if somewhat clumsily, "What right have they [black people] here in the home of the White/ Shadowed o'er by our banner of Freedom and Right?" In the later and often anthologized "Massachusetts to Virginia" (1843) Whittier angered Southerners with his strident championing of Northern moral rectitude over Southern acceptance of moral evil. "No slave-hunt in our borders,—no pirate on our strand!/ No fetters in the Bay State,—no slave upon our land!" With "Ichabod" (1850) and its dirge for tainted New Hampshire senator Webster, Whittier hit a high point and entered the mature phase of his poetry.

Retirement from the political arena in the 1850's revived Whittier's rural muse and returned him to his old sources of inspiration. While his political activities had satisfied one side of his Quaker piety—the search for social justice and human equality—he now turned rather more spiritual. This often expressed itself in nostalgic works that mourned the passage of time and folkways in the face of the greater forces of nature and national growth. Many times he harnessed his keen powers of observation (though he was color-blind) and description to simple and lyrical tales of times gone by and deep joys lost in the passage. In "Telling the Bees" (1858) Whittier presents his characteristic use of local color and custom as backdrop to a sudden realization of personal loss. After several years he visits the rural residence of an old flame: "There is the house, with the gate red-barred,/ And the poplars tall;/ And the barn's brown length, and the cattle-yard,/ And the white horns tossing above the wall." As he proceeds, he notes that the beehive is covered: a local way of indicating a death in the family. At first, certain it is the grandmother who died, he soon discovers it is his young friend.

In his masterpiece "Snow-Bound," Whittier har-

nesses a scene from his youth—perhaps actual, perhaps composite, perhaps fictional—for a Romantic meditation on the value of family love and affection amid nature's cruelest season. He interlaces scenes of family activity, of work and leisure, with reflections on his own aging and the deaths of most of the characters. Long passages linger on the frozen scenery, the comfortable hearthside, and old tales told to pass the time. His specifics are regional and even personal, but they rise to universality in his language of loss. No one can stop the cycling of the seasons or the deaths of loved ones or societal change. Memory alone—and the poet's pen—can immortalize what was once and still is loved.

"ICHABOD"

First published: 1850 (collected in *The Poetical Works of John Greenleaf Whittier,* 1894)
Type of work: Poem

Abolitionist Whittier expresses his anger, sorrow, and pity over Daniel Webster's support for the Missouri Compromise.

On March 7, 1850, New Hampshire senator Webster gave a noted speech in which he supported the political settlement known as the Missouri Compromise, by which new slave states could enter the Union. Whittier had been a supporter of Webster since the early 1830's and was thunderstruck by his move, as were many abolitionists. In the *National Anti-Slavery Standard,* James Russell Lowell demanded rhetorically "Shall not the Recording Angel write *Ichabod* (inglorious one) after the name of this man in the great book of Doom?" Whittier adopted the biblical name as the title for his political denunciation of Webster but expressed his sorrow and anger in other biblical terms. "So fallen! so lost!" the poem opens, "the light withdrawn." Webster is the fallen angel of John Milton's *Paradise Lost* (1667), his "bright soul driven, . . . From hope and heaven!" He has lost honor and his followers' love, but Whittier counsels not "passion's stormy rage," "not scorn and wrath" but "pitying tears" and a "long lament" as the nation's response. The disillusioned poet calls his fellows to treat Webster—who is never named—as one who is dead and to "pay the reverence of old days/ To his dead fame. . . ." He ends by referencing the drunken Noah in Genesis, whose sons approached his shameful nakedness walking "backward, with averted gaze" to cover the patriarch's folly. By mentioning neither Webster nor his speech, Whittier universalizes his sense of betrayal in what many consider a classic American poetic political denunciation, also known as a philippic.

"SNOW-BOUND: A WINTER IDYL"

First published: 1866 (collected in *Snow-Bound*, 1866)
Type of work: Poem

The poet waxes nostalgic over a New England snowstorm and his now largely dead family's experience of love and fellowship in its midst.

Generally considered Whittier's masterpiece, "Snow-Bound" is dedicated to "the Household It Describes" and prefaced by a quotation from the Renaissance occultist Cornelius Agrippa on the powers of sunlight and firelight over "Spirits of Darkness," and a passage from Ralph Waldo Emerson's "The Snow Storm." Whittier wrote this work of high nostalgia shortly after the death of his beloved sister, Elizabeth, who had long taken care of him. This carefully crafted genre piece opens with a long, elegiac description of a December day in New England and the chores performed on his boyhood farm. The east wind brings a heavy snowstorm that roars on through the long night. The sunless morning reveals a transformed landscape of unfamiliar shapes and contours, and the call of "our father" to the "boys" (Whittier and his brother) to cut a path from house to barn. Whittier evokes both the shriek of "the mindless wind" and the silence of the usually babbling brook now encased in ice. With the first night comes the fire that transforms the tiny and isolated world inside the house. The gathered family with warmed bodies and hearts and mugs of hot cider bask in the glow, "What matter how the night behaved?" Whittier the narrator then indulges in a reflection on the

past-ness of the scene: "with so much gone; . . . The voices of that hearth are still." His family is largely dead and gone, but "Life is ever lord of Death,/ And Love can never lose its own!" In the poem's second part, stories are told to "sleepy listeners as they lay," by father, mother, uncle, aunt, and elder sister, now lately gone to the "holy

peace of Paradise," and subject of a second reflective interlude. A schoolteacher and an annoyingly religious woman appear and share the warmth, which lasts until the fire crumbles to embers and ash. In the third part, teamsters arrive carving a public path, a doctor calls for help, and the poet's once snowbound world gives way to the world at large, best encapsulated in the newspaper with its tales of war and "the pulse of life that round us beats." Whittier ends in an elegiac postlude calling for a pause to reflect in the midst of the bustle of a changing world.

"AMONG THE HILLS"

First published: 1869 (collected in *Among the Hills, and Other Poems*, 1869)
Type of work: Poem

A trip to the countryside reminds the poet of the civilizing value of rural life.

In his prelude, Whittier criticizes the New Englanders of his time as crippled prisoners of their own lack of vision, with starved spirits though they live in a rich land. Optimistically he calls them to reach out for the beauty and joy provided by God and to appreciate the beauty of nature that reflects the love of God. As the poem opens, summer's long cloudy disposition gives way to sunshine and the natural beauties it reveals as a couple drives through the countryside to a farmhouse to purchase butter. Here the housewife tells her tale of how she came to the farm and convinced the crusty New Englander that he needed a wife and that it should be she: "And so the farmer found a wife." He was thus transformed as a man both private and public, as his "love thus deepened to respect." She too was transformed to a simpler life and outlook, now shunning "the follies, born/ Of fashion and convention." The couple returns home as the sun sets. and the poet reflects on her story and how "To rugged farm-life came the gift/ To harmonize and soften."

SUMMARY

As a representative of the New England Renaissance, John Greenleaf Whittier gathered material from the region's history, folklore, landscape, piety, and politics in creating a collection of poems that marked him in his day as one of the era's most characteristically American poets. While early on deriving much from Burns and the English Romantics, he developed his own voice that bespoke his fine abilities of observation and description. While never abandoning the rural and historical trends of his youth, from his mid-twenties through his early fifties, Whittier used his pen as a weapon against the evils of slavery and related social ills, while editing and writing for numerous Yankee newspapers. Buoyed by his Quaker faith in the Inner Light, he remained optimistic of humankind's ability to reform itself and never fell into dark cynicism. After the Civil War, he returned to the range of regional themes and topics and produced a corpus of mature poetic works that placed him in the top tier of nineteenth century American poets. As tastes changed, however, Whittier's popularity and critical acceptance tended to wane.

Joseph P. Byrne

DISCUSSION TOPICS

- How did John Greenleaf Whittier's early life shape his later poetry?

- Which writers and books had an early influence on Whittier's poetry?

- In what ways did the fact that Whittier was a Quaker influence his political views and career as a newspaperman? How did it affect his poetry?

- How did Whittier use his poetry to help affect political events from 1840 to 1860?

- Why were Americans in the post-Civil War era so accepting of Whittier's nostalgic poetry?

- Though Whittier is considered a regional (New England) poet, why do his works have an appeal for Americans from many regions?

BIBLIOGRAPHY

By the Author

POETRY:
Legends of New-England, 1831
Moll Pitcher, 1832
Mogg Megone, 1836
Poems Written During the Progress of the Abolition Question in the United States, 1837
Poems, 1838
Lays of My Home, and Other Poems, 1843
Voices of Freedom, 1846
Poems, 1849
Songs of Labor, and Other Poems, 1850
The Chapel of the Hermits, and Other Poems, 1853
The Panorama, and Other Poems, 1856
The Sycamores, 1857
The Poetical Works of John Greenleaf Whittier, 1857, 1869, 1880, 1894

Home Ballads and Poems, 1860
In War Time, 1863
Snow-Bound: A Winter Idyl, 1866
The Tent on the Beach, and Other Poems, 1867
Maud Muller, 1869
Among the Hills, and Other Poems, 1869
Ballads of New England, 1869
Miriam, and Other Poems, 1871
The Pennsylvania Pilgrim, and Other Poems, 1872
Hazel-Blossoms, 1875
Mabel Martin, 1876
Favorite Poems, 1877
The Vision of Echard, and Other Poems, 1878
The King's Missive, and Other Poems, 1881
The Bay of Seven Islands, and Other Poems, 1883
Saint Gregory's Guest and Recent Poems, 1886
At Sundown, 1890

LONG FICTION:
Narrative of James Williams: An American Slave, 1838
Leaves from Margaret Smith's Journal, 1849

NONFICTION:
Justice and Expediency: Or, Slavery Considered with a View to Its Rightful and Effectual Remedy, Abolition, 1833
The Supernaturalism of New England, 1847
Old Portraits and Modern Sketches, 1850
Literary Recreations and Miscellanies, 1854
Whittier on Writers and Writing: The Uncollected Critical Writings of John Greenleaf Whittier, 1950 (Edwin H. Cady and Harry Hayden Clark, editors)
The Letters of John Greenleaf Whittier, 1975 (John B. Pickard, editor)

EDITED TEXTS:
The Journal of John Woolman, 1871
Child Life, 1872
Child Life in Prose, 1874
Songs of Three Centuries, 1876

MISCELLANEOUS:
Prose Works of John Greenleaf Whittier, 1866
The Writings of John Greenleaf Whittier, 1888-1889

About the Author

Kribbs, Jayne K. *Critical Essays on John Greenleaf Whittier.* Boston: G. K. Hall, 1980.

Leary, Lewis, and Sylvia Bowman. *John Greenleaf Whittier.* New York: Macmillan, 1983.

Pickard, John B. *John Greenleaf Whittier: An Introduction and Interpretation.* New York: Holt, Rinehart and Winston, 1961.

Pickard, Samuel T. *Life and Letters of John Greenleaf Whittier.* Reprint. New York: Haskell House, 1969.

Wagenknecht, Edward C. *John Greenleaf Whittier: A Portrait in Paradox.* New York: Oxford University Press, 1967.

Woodwell, Roland H. *John Greenleaf Whittier: A Biography.* Haverhill, Mass.: Trustees of the Whittier Homestead, 1985.

University of Wyoming

JOHN EDGAR WIDEMAN

Born: Washington, D.C.
June 14, 1941

A major literary voice since the mid-1960's, Wideman combines modernist and postmodernist metafictional techniques with African American themes in fictional as well as nonfictional explorations of social injustice and the violence it generates.

BIOGRAPHY

The oldest of five children born to Bette French and Edgar Wideman, John Edgar Wideman grew up in Homewood, a black community in Pittsburgh, Pennsylvania, whose history roughly parallels that of Wideman's family in the North. After attending racially integrated Peabody High School, where he excelled in sports and also graduated as valedictorian, John was awarded the Benjamin Franklin scholarship to the then-barely integrated University of Pennsylvania. There he was recruited for the varsity basketball team in 1959 and as a forward won All-Ivy League recognition as well as a place in the Philadelphia Big Five Basketball Hall of Fame—accomplishments that encouraged his dreams about playing in the National Basketball Association (NBA). At Penn, Wideman also excelled academically, earning election to Phi Beta Kappa and a Rhodes scholarship upon graduation. After earning a B.A. in English in 1963, he went on to earn a B.Phil. in 1966 as a Thoron Fellow at Oxford University, and his writerly fate was sealed.

Having distinguished himself as a writer even as an undergraduate, Wideman was accorded a Kent Fellowship to attend the University of Iowa Writers' Workshop in 1966 and published his first novel, *A Glance Away*, in 1967. Hired by his alma mater in 1966, he later headed Penn's Afro-American Studies program from 1971 to 1973 and rose to the rank of professor of English; he also served as assistant basketball coach from 1968 to 1972. Other academic appointments have included posts at Howard University; the University of Wyoming, Laramie; the University of Massachusetts, Amherst; Baruch College of City University in New York; and Brown University. He also holds an honorary D.Litt. from the University of Pennsylvania (1985). Named a Young Humanist Fellow by the National Endowment for the Humanities in 1975, he conducted a State Department lecture tour of Europe and the Near East in 1976 and also held a Phi Beta Kappa lectureship. Following the publication of *Philadelphia Fire* (1990), Wideman won the American Book Award for Fiction and became the first writer to receive a second PEN/Faulkner Award (1991). He also secured a Lannan Literary Fellowship in 1991 and a MacArthur "genius" grant in 1993. *The Cattle Killing* earned the James Fenimore Cooper Prize for historical fiction in 1996. In 1998, he was accorded the Rea Award for the Short Story in honor of his considerable accomplishments in the genre; in 2000, he earned an O. Henry Award for best short story of the year.

Wideman has candidly acknowledged that his early achievements came at a psychological cost, however. As a young man Wideman had distanced himself from the perceived constrictions of his African American identity, only to discover that the personal alienation thus produced mirrored the condition of doubleness described by W. E. B. Du Bois and others as the consequence of growing up black in twentieth century America. Wideman has made this odyssey away from and back to his roots a frequent theme of his writing, using it to affirm the contemporary African American intellectual as someone fully in touch with the wide range of expression defining his cultural traditions.

As a Rhodes scholar in England, Wideman had concentrated his studies on the eighteenth century origins of the novel, a field far removed from the cultural environment from which he had sprung—and which ill-prepared him for requests from African American students at Penn that, as a new faculty member in the mid-1960's, he teach courses in black literature. To accommodate them, he began investigating the rich tradition of black American literary expression that has energized his own creative choices ever since. Besides adapting black American and African mythologies, folk arts, and storytelling methods to create his distinctive narrative technique, he frequently publishes essays about black literature and cultural production involving such diverse figures as Du Bois, writer Charles Waddell Chesnutt, activist Malcolm X, musician Thelonius Monk, athlete Michael Jordan, actor Denzel Washington, and director Spike Lee. In doing so, he extends the synthesizing intellectual reach of Du Bois himself.

Married in 1965 to Judith Ann Goldman, Wideman has three children: Daniel, Jacob, and Jamila. Dan is a published writer, and Jamila a successful athlete whose leadership of Stanford's women's basketball team propelled her into the professional ranks of the Women's National Basketball Association (WNBA). Youngest son Jake has painfully complicated this family history since, as a mentally ill teenager, he committed a 1986 murder for which he received a life sentence in the Arizona penal system—a grim reprise of the crisis surrounding Wideman's youngest sibling, Rob, who is serving a life sentence in Pennsylvania's Western Penitentiary.

Wideman's first highly acclaimed memoir, *Brothers and Keepers* (1984), examines Rob's story as a vehicle for John's continued racial ambivalence as a self-made man compromised by the haunting mirror image that Rob presents. His son's tragedy has similarly entered into Wideman's writing: It provides a major frame of reference in the later memoir *Fatheralong* (1994), nominated for the National Book Award. The murder of nephew Omar Wideman, Rob's twenty-one-year-old son, inspired *Two Cities* (1998); Wideman dedicates the novel to the young man with the words "We didn't try hard enough." A third memoir, *Hoop Roots* (2001), lyrically evokes basketball's existential and aesthetic meanings for its author as its elegiac tone mourns not only his failing body but the end of his thirty-plus years of marriage.

Critics have long remarked on the striking juxtaposition of Wideman's sophisticated literary style (characterized by modernist and postmodernist complexities of voice, metaphor, and structure) with his graphically realistic subject matter. *A Glance Away* deals with the world of a drug addict. *Hurry Home* (1970) depicts the deeply divided sensibility of an upwardly mobile young man whose efforts to escape the ghetto through education yield to the purposeful recovery of his African American heritage. *The Lynchers* (1973) examines American racial terrorism. In *The Homewood Trilogy*—published as a set in 1985, its separate parts originally published as *Damballah* (1981), *Hiding Place* (1981), and *Sent for You Yesterday* (1983)—Wideman explores the origins and decay of a black urban community. *Reuben* (1987) interweaves the stories of a self-proclaimed attorney and two of his clients: a prostitute trying to secure custody of her child and a directionless former athlete implicated in a bribery scandal.

With *Philadelphia Fire,* Wideman emphasizes the place "the City of Brotherly Love" holds in his imagination alongside Pittsburgh. That novel recounts the horrific firebombing of the MOVE compound in 1985 by the city's first black administration under Mayor Wilson Goode. *The Cattle Killing* explores older historical tragedies from Philadelphia's racial past, while *Two Cities* literally draws together his two "hometowns"—Pittsburgh and Philadelphia—as a comparative matrix for the varieties of national neglect that have exacerbated the crises of African American urban life.

ANALYSIS

Over the course of his writing career, Wideman has composed fiction that synthesizes twentieth century aesthetic concerns with the thematic emphases of the African American literary tradition. His stylistic indebtedness to T. S. Eliot, James Joyce, and William Faulkner demonstrates modernist preoccupations with myth and ritual, fractured narrative, surreality, and polyphonic voicings. Wideman maps the creative possibilities of colliding the two traditions. In *Philadelphia Fire*, for instance, the protagonist Cudjoe, his name and sensibility rich in Africanist associations, assiduously updates William Shakespeare's *The Tempest* to expose the shared dispossession of diasporan Africans both within and beyond the United States.

Wideman also has a postmodernist affinity for fantasy and deconstructive self-reflexiveness as means of conveying how the psyche processes the incoherencies of daily life, particularly those generated by the irreconcilable paradoxes of racism. A fusion of fiction and autobiography regularly marks his work, although he pointedly insists that his life and his writing are distinctive and separate frames of reality that he does not confuse—he knows and enforces the distance between them, however naïvely reviewers may conflate the two.

Wideman's preoccupation with the consequences of racism actually prevents his wholesale adoption of postmodernist sleight of hand. While he documents the mind's entrapment within its own subjective fabrications, his fiction does not withdraw into apolitical minimalism or self-enclosed fabulation apart from the social matrix in which his characters exist. Moving beyond the realist or naturalistic mode of previous generations of black writers, Wideman's postmodernism identifies concepts of racial difference as divisive and deluding cultural fictions, and it dramatizes the equally powerful role of the imagination in dismantling such fallacies. By collapsing traditional distinctions between narration and dialogue, he creates a fluid linguistic matrix that does not try to approximate the "reality" of the psyche so much as the power of language to fuse different modes of experience.

Wideman's literary techniques also express his belief in the accessibility of a collective African American racial memory kept alive through networks of family, community, and culture. Thus his narratives often juxtapose disparate time frames to emphasize the organic relationship between past and present—particularly as it is embodied across generations within the same family, as in *The Homewood Trilogy* and *Brothers and Keepers*. This same structuring device produces a free-floating, transchronological consciousness in novels such as *The Cattle Killing*, which dramatizes time's mythic

recurrences—a mixed message of hope alongside despair. The cri de coeur that suffuses *Philadelphia Fire* makes clear that what most profoundly concerns Wideman at the turn of the twenty-first century is the escalating rupture of that consciously nurtured connection across generations of African American families—a rupture born of increasing dysfunction among those persecuted and abandoned by the larger society's greed and racist indifference.

Similarly, Wideman elides the voices and thoughts of characters who share a given narrative, producing a continually shifting kaleidoscope of perspectives that evokes the dense interior lives of his subjects. Among those voices, the writer himself often steps from behind the mask of narrator to discuss directly the challenges posed by a subject, character, or plot, particularly in relation to an immediate personal crisis with which he himself, as John Wideman, is also wrestling. In doing so he crafts a fluid, uninhibited voice that merges the linguistic plasticity of Joycean stream of consciousness with the lyrical soarings of jazz improvisation and hip-hop playfulness.

Wideman has proven adept across genres ranging from the short story to the novel to the memoir to the essay, all of them infused with a characteristic linguistic fluidity reviewers regularly compare to a soaring jazz solo. The short story allows him to pursue separate character analyses that, when juxtaposed within the covers of a single text, comment upon one another thematically. While following the same polyphonic construction, his novels integrate seemingly disparate narrative strands into more tightly unified patterns. In both forms he explores the thesis that the imagination can generate potentially healing linkages and discover illuminating echoes among fragments—an activity always complicated, however, by the suspicion that the cloudedness of human vision makes real communication among individuals flawed, if not impossible.

The clearly autobiographical subtexts informing so much of his fiction erupt full blown in Wideman's highly acclaimed memoirs, where he confronts more openly the elusiveness of actual experience and his imaginative need for invention to redress life's brutal gaps and incoherencies. Wideman explains in *Hoop Roots*, his meditation on the meaning of basketball in his life, that in

Writing autobiography, looking back, trying to recall and represent yourself at some point in the past, you are playing many games simultaneously. There are many selves, many sets of rules jostling for position. . . . I still want more from writing. . . . More than the [fiction-making] puppeteer's invisibility. . . . Want to share the immediate excitement of process, of invention, of play. . . . Seeking more means self-discovery. Means redefining the art I practice. . . . [W]anting to compose and share a piece of writing that won't fail because it might not fit someone else's notion of what a book should be.

THE HOMEWOOD TRILOGY

First published: 1985 (includes *Damballah*, 1981; *Hiding Place*, 1981; *Sent for You Yesterday*, 1983)

Type of work: Short-story collection and two novels

The three separate works united under this title record the human history of a black neighborhood in Pittsburgh through several generations of the Hollinger/French family.

The Homewood Trilogy collects in a single volume works originally published individually but conceptualized as interdependent fictions about the specific African American community in Pittsburgh where Wideman was raised. Originally published in the early 1980's, they resulted from Wideman's rediscovery, while attending his grandmother's 1973 funeral, of his childhood community's richly evocative history. To keep faith with his source material, he initially chose to issue these three volumes as Avon paperbacks rather than in hardcover to improve their accessibility to the black reading public he hoped to reach. The third volume in that series brought Wideman his first PEN/Faulkner Award for Fiction.

Each volume draws from the family lore surrounding Wideman's maternal grandfather John French and his descendants, including two brothers who mirror the author and his youngest brother Rob. The trilogy resulted from Wideman's discovery that the stories of Homewood's inhabitants offered him an untapped reservoir of literary raw material. By recovering those stories, he sought to demonstrate "that Black life for all its material impoverishment continues to produce the full range of human personalities, emotions, aspirations." Moreover, Wideman uses racial experience to challenge delimiting racial categories: "Homewood is an idea. . . . [It] mirror[s] the characters' inner lives, their sense of themselves as spiritual beings in a realm that rises above racial stereotypes and socioeconomic statistics."

Recalling Faulkner's Yoknapatawpha County, the trilogy opens with an elaborate family tree mapping the relationships that provide the work's imaginative spine. The texts it spawns also become metafictions, absorbing into themselves the many oral forms which have kept the past alive while drawing attention to the writer's self-conscious difficulties in bending them to his aesthetic design.

The twelve short stories of *Damballah* demonstrate the human diversity of Homewood's landscape. Its title derives from African myth: Damballah, the "good serpent of the sky," proves a benevolent paternal deity whose detachment and wisdom shape the cosmos into a transcendent family. The title story involves an African-born slave named Orion whose spiritual strength rests upon native religious beliefs which he communicates to a slave boy through the repetition of Damballah's name. When Orion is brutally executed after being falsely accused of sexual misconduct, the child returns his severed head to the natural world he had so revered.

In "The Beginning of Homewood," the collection's final tale, Wideman expands the historical context of the present by tracing his maternal ancestry to an escaped slave, Sybela Owens, and her master/lover, whose flight north brought them to Bruston Hill, the symbolic umbilicus of Homewood. Juxtaposed time frames abound in the volume, and Sybela's tale appears within a contemporary meditation written to "Tommy," the narrator's brother, now in prison for murder. His situation raises the same issues of freedom, escape, and spiritual survival addressed in the slave's story and prompts Wideman to metafictional musings on the act of writing and its relationship to lived events.

Those two tales frame ten other stories of black men and women struggling to maintain or recover an authentic existence in the face of unrelenting danger or disappointment. Among them are John

French, the hard-drinking, tough-minded patriarch whose emotional presence dominates the twentieth century history of the French/Lawson clan; Freeda Hollinger French, his wife, whose violent act to save John's life resonates through the text and expresses the complex emotional dynamic that Wideman maps between black men and women; Lizabeth French Lawson, the narrator's mother and another heroic embodiment of the integrity and strength of black women facing crushing familial pressures; Reba Love Jackson, a gospel singer whose faith and artistry combine to create the song of a people; and Tommy Lawson, French's grandson, whose reliance on drugs and crime dramatizes Homewood's collapse beneath the mounting hopelessness of its citizens and the cynical indifference of the larger society. Based on Wideman's brother Rob, to whom *Damballah* is dedicated, Tommy offers an early fictional examination of the varied family crises that recur in Wideman's writings.

Hiding Place, the second volume in the trilogy, provides a novelistic interpretation of Rob's story. Expanding his characterization of the aged "Mother" Bess Simkins, introduced in "The Beginning of Homewood," Wideman elaborates on her relationship with a young man that had been previously sketched in that story. The granddaughter of Sybela Owens, Bess still lives on Bruston Hill as the novel opens, but while she signifies Tommy's family heritage, she long ago retreated from any real intercourse with the community.

Bess's isolation ends when Tommy, fleeing capture following an abortive robbery/murder, seeks refuge in her home. Like her, Tommy is hiding on many levels as he avoids honestly assessing his own responsibility for his circumstances. In Bess he encounters a hostile critic and responds by withdrawing into sleep. Still, through their confrontational exchanges, both recognize the need to reenter life, with all its attendant grief and outrage.

The alternating voices that structure the text include a youth named Clement whose simplemindedness offers another version of the self-involved, solipsistic dreaminess into which the other two characters retreat. Yet as Bess's errand boy he not only links her to the outside world she has shunned but also expands the human geography of the novel. Because Clement intuits realities that are obscured or falsified by the defensive facades constructed by other individuals in the novel, he offers an implicit critique of the ruses that thwart authenticity in the ghetto.

Wideman's sword thus cuts two ways in his examination of Homewood. Intensely aware of the role played by racism in the deterioration of his old neighborhood and the loss of spiritual purpose among its inhabitants, he just as sharply insists on the need for black men and women to attend to their own souls by rejecting the duplicities by which they distort the truth and cheapen their lives. Bess and Tommy both undergo this kind of soul-searching, a process that leads them to turn away from the "deadness" of their lives. Tommy chooses to return to town and confront whatever awaits him, and Bess, seeing the police corner him on the water tower outside her home, decides to leave Bruston Hill to testify on his behalf. The closing scene is apocalyptic; searchlights cut the darkness, and bullets fly as the police pursue Tommy. Bess's shack bursts into flames while she plans her departure. Violence serves as the companion and catalyst to their respective existential reckonings.

Sent for You Yesterday, the novel earning Wideman's first PEN/Faulkner Award, opens with an epigraph announcing that "[p]ast lives live in us, through us." As in the preceding works of the trilogy, Wideman intertwines narratives belonging to different generations and spun out of individual memories. This time he solidifies the imaginative sensibility that unites them into a character nicknamed Doot, who also happens to be Tommy's older brother. Doot is actively engaged not only in collecting the stories of his familial past but also in clarifying his own temporal and emotional relationship to them as a means of reversing his estrangement from Homewood. Tommy's crisis becomes one axis of the trilogy; Doot's penetrating self-scrutiny as an equally remorseful prodigal son seeking return provides another. Each revolves around the imaginative model of black manhood represented by John French.

At the heart of the novel is Albert Wilkes, a legendary Homewood musician whose affair with a white woman leads to the killing of her policeman husband (Wilkes's guilt is still highly contested in the community). Seven years later, he returns to Homewood and is gunned down by white lawmen in the house where he was raised, sitting at the piano he had always instinctively known how to play.

Among those who embody Wilkes's legacy is Brother Tate, an orphan adopted by the same couple who raised Wilkes and who, as a young man, spontaneously demonstrates the same musical genius.

Its title, *Sent for You Yesterday,* taken from a blues song, signals up front how deeply involved the novel is with the musical legacy through which African Americans have documented and interpreted their experience. Because Brother is an albino, his incongruous "white blackness" serves as an ironic metaphor for a society fixated on racial categorizations. When his young son Junebug is finally killed by his half siblings for his inherited surface difference, Brother confronts the fratricidal character of all racism and its violent consequences for the human family.

Brother's story intersects with that of his adoptive sister Lucy and his closest friend, Carl French, Doot's uncle. Through Lucy and Carl, lifelong lovers whose failure to marry seems the natural consequence of their intimate knowledge of one another, Doot untangles the narrative skeins that make up the novel's fabric, on which he embroiders his own imaginative designs.

Carl's history painfully forecasts a recurrent twentieth century pattern. A war veteran, Carl returns to a country which short-circuits the ambitions of eager young black men and women. His art school lessons are abandoned when a "helpful" instructor warns that there are no jobs for him, and his best friend withdraws into silence and apparent suicide following Junebug's racist persecution. All three—Carl, Lucy, and Brother—descend temporarily into drug addiction, with Carl's cure incomplete given his continued dependence on methadone. Yet Doot develops a keen respect for their resiliency and spirit. Wideman balances his determination to validate the lives and sufferings of such individuals with the need to show them wrestling with their own demons in a struggle to maintain their dignity. *The Homewood Trilogy* poignantly evokes the deeply felt humanity of a community by resisting the naturalistic reductionism so often resorted to by writers to "explain" the lives of the disenfranchised.

BROTHERS AND KEEPERS

First published: 1984
Type of work: Memoir

Writing about his youngest brother's crime and punishment, Wideman investigates many interrelated personal and social issues.

Brothers and Keepers demonstrates Wideman's complex personal, sociological, and artistic response to his brother Rob's life sentence for murder in 1978. In it he sees writ large the pathological interplay of white exploitation, racist neglect, and internal despair that have intensified, rather than lessened, in America's cities since the 1960's. Like the narrator of *The Homewood Trilogy,* Wideman presents himself with a bittersweet awareness that, in contrast to Rob, his lifelong efforts to straddle black and white cultural expectations have made him an incongruous figure in both worlds. The book opens in 1976 with the writer in the doubly white world of a snowy late winter in Laramie, Wyoming, where he teaches at the university, waiting intuitively for word from his fugitive younger brother even as he also deals with the aftermath of his infant daughter Jamila's traumatic birth.

In facing Rob when he does arrive, and in their subsequent meetings in jail over the years, Wideman recognizes that their polarized circumstances provocatively express the duality of the African American's psychological legacy in the United States. Ironically, each has pursued a path he has equated with the American Dream of material success and personal self-definition: John in the "safe" and deracinated terms of career and family championed by white society, Rob along more dangerous lines that challenge racist obstacles through illegal channels promising the glamor of the outlaw. Both men, despite their very different choices, now find themselves fumbling to recover what they sacrificed in pursuit of America's elusive seduction of "making it." Wide-

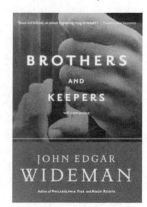

man also contextualizes his personal and familial anguish within a layered analysis of the American penal system that renders imprisonment a political, cultural, and existential condition.

With a characteristically self-referential technique, Wideman rachets up the complexity of his narrative by making his own suspect motives in writing Rob's story one of his themes: he understands the exploitative potential of what he is doing and takes great pains to circumvent it. This study of two brothers caught in a tragedy that brings them back into meaningful relationship to one another also documents Wideman's complex struggle to subordinate his voracious fictionalizing imagination and colonizing ego so as to allow his brother's emergent voice to take ownership of his own story. The resultant text employs numerous linguistic styles as Wideman searches for a medium that will do justice to its disparate sensibilities.

John himself speaks in differing voices, sometimes using the formal constructions of standard English and other times employing black spoken vernacular. Rob himself enters the text from equally various directions. While Wideman freely admits to adopting fictional strategies in re-creating conversations held with Rob at the prison, he also includes letters and poems his brother has actually written, as well as a speech Rob gave upon receiving his associate's degree through a prison education program. Moreover, John confesses that Rob's critiques of his older brother's usurping tendencies prompted John to rewrite an earlier draft of the memoir.

Thus chastised, Wideman tries to shake off the writer's tricks with which he typically makes a subject his own, Yet he invariably relies on just such tricks to construct a powerful narrative with the power to move and elucidate even as they inevitably distort Rob's heroic efforts to come to terms with the life he has led and the future he now faces. In a potent echo of *The Autobiography of Malcolm X* (1965), Rob's story becomes the familiar existential odyssey of the individual who, in losing his life, finds it—one that Wideman doubts he himself could survive. While the book initially provokes the obvious question as to why one brother has "gone bad" when another has "made good," it finally asserts Rob to be the better man, possessing far greater spiritual courage and stamina than his publicly accomplished sibling.

Wideman cannot manipulate the facts to construct a satisfactory resolution to Rob's tale—no amount of authorial skill can overturn Rob's sentence or the governor's refusal of a pardon, and John's published testament to Rob's strength cannot ensure that he will escape the ravages of encroaching despair or the very real threats posed by hostile guards and other inmates. The book's abrupt ending dramatizes the limits of the writer's imagination to effect real change in his brother's life, a realization bleakly consonant with Wideman's postmodernist skepticism in the ultimate reach of those imaginative fabulations which form his own raison d'être.

"FEVER"

First published: 1989 (collected in *Fever,* 1989)
Type of work: Short story

A minister struggles to transcend racist injustices while providing care for victims of Philadelphia's 1793 yellow fever epidemic.

"Fever," the title story in Wideman's 1989 collection of short fiction, provides an illuminating metaphor for the various episodes of racial antagonism depicted in the volume. As one of the story's narrative voices explains, "Fever grows in the secret places of our hearts, planted there when one of us decided to sell one of us to another. The drum must pound ten thousand thousand years to drive that evil away."

The narrative focus of the tale reflects Wideman's desire to correct the inaccurate historical record about the role of African Americans during the 1793 yellow fever epidemic that devastated Philadelphia. He dedicates the story to the author of one such fraudulent account and relies instead upon the eyewitness record left by black commentators. Among the chorus of voices in the text are those of two black men, one of them the historical Richard Allen and the other his fictionalized brother Thomas, whose differing perspectives on the disaster and its resultant hypocrisies work in counterpoint.

Allen, a former slave, a minister, and the founder

of the African Methodist Episcopal Church, is a deeply spiritual man who identifies his vision of the mass emancipation of slaves with the promise of Christianity. Allen has been ordered to serve a Dr. Rush in his ministrations to and autopsies of plague victims. After performing exhausting labor among white people, he turns to the destitute habitations of poor black people whom the disease ravages with equal savagery. There he devotes himself to their spiritual and physical health, despite their contempt.

Like many other elements of the narrative, Thomas's story further documents the presence of black people in the public sphere of American history: Thomas fought with the rebels in the American Revolution and, as a prisoner of the British, recognized the degree to which he had been denied participation in the society whose ideals he championed. His embittered outlook on the situation now facing black people in the plague-ridden city stems from the opportunistic shifts of white opinion during the epidemic. While slaves were initially blamed for importing the disease following a bloody revolt in the Caribbean, black people were later declared immune from its ravages and coerced to serve sick and dying white people. Each of these civic fictions exposes the denial of humanity responsible for the broader cultural pathology which is Wideman's principal target.

Philadelphia operates as symbolic setting for this story on religious as well as political grounds. Its Quaker egalitarianism does not preclude Allen's being refused a place at the Communion table with white Christians, nor does the city's birthing of the young republic ensure that its African American citizens will be accorded the same economic opportunities available to the waves of European-born newcomers. Rather than boasting a vigorous democratic climate, Wideman's Philadelphia festers in a stagnant environment whose waters breed contagion both literally and metaphorically. Nor is water the only sinister natural element pervading the landscape; apocalyptic fire fills the streets of the city as a grim purgative for its soul-sickness.

Added to the individualized voices of Richard and Thomas Allen is the combative monologue of Abraham, a dying Jewish merchant who describes his own experiences with bigotry as he aggressively challenges Allen's continued attentions to the white Christian populace. Abraham alludes to the Lamed-Vov, or "Thirty Just Men" of Judaic tradition, designated by God "to suffer the reality humankind cannot bear" and pay witness to the bottomless misery and depravity of existence. Richard Allen stands as one such figure among many in these stories whose compassion in the face of unbearable injustice and grief offers the only hope for salvation that Wideman can envision.

Wideman's fractured narrative perspectives jarringly emphasize that no one "story" exists independent of the wider human drama playing itself out across time. Within his textual montage, he melds such disparate elements as a newly enslaved African making the Middle Passage, a series of scientific descriptions of the fever and its assumed insect carriers, and a report of autopsy results documenting the physical devastation visited upon black and white plague victims alike. This polyphonic orchestration of voices links slave and freedman, black and white, Christian and Jew, historian and eyewitness.

To underline the timeliness of this meditation, Wideman introduces toward the end of the story the voice of a contemporary black health care worker contemptuous of his elderly white charges and the society that has discarded them. Finally, within a single paragraph, Wideman links the disease wasting Philadelphia's citizens in the late eighteenth century to the actual 1985 bombing of a black neighborhood ordered by the city's first black mayor, Wilson Goode, to eradicate the black counterculture group MOVE. About "Fever," Wideman claimed that "I was teaching myself different ways of telling history." With the publication of *Philadelphia Fire* in 1990, he returned to the MOVE incident as evidence of the worsening of America's continued "national schizophrenia" about race.

PHILADELPHIA FIRE

First published: 1990
Type of work: Novel

Drawing together personal and societal tragedies—his younger son's ongoing imprisonment and the 1985 firebombing of an outlier community in Philadelphia—Wideman indicts an America whose brutal indifference to the disenfranchised, especially children, is achieving new levels of murderousness.

Philadelphia Fire, the work for which Wideman won an unprecedented second PEN/Faulkner Award, seethes with its author's indignation over fifty years of unabated neglect and outright hostility toward African American inner-city communities by political elites and average citizens alike. Yet neglect alone does not explain the central event commemorated in the novel: the city government's 1985 firebombing of a West Philadelphia working-class neighborhood to eradicate a group calling itself MOVE, which had become a profound embarrassment to the administration of its first black mayor, Wilson Goode. The conflagration that resulted from this police action killed eleven people, five of them children; it also burned fifty-three homes to the ground and rendered 262 members of the larger community homeless.

Having spent much of his own young manhood in "the City of Brotherly Love," Wideman clearly took personally the failure of African American leaders to recognize the desperate need for hope and connection that had driven persons such as his fictional Margaret Jones—a hardworking single mother of two—into the realm of "the King," James Brown, the charismatic MOVE leader whose antiestablishment stance and lifestyle voiced a challenge to the injustice with which so many of his followers had been raised: "He be preaching what Jesus preached except it's King saying the words. Bible words only they issuing from King's big lips. And you know he means them and you understand them better cause he says them black, black like him, black like you. . . ."

Wideman does not make the MOVE compound itself the focal point of his narrative, however. His protagonist, a middle-aged African American ex-patriate named Cudjoe, offers another variation on the Widemanesque artist-intellectual estranged from his community but brought jarringly back to reclaim it in the wake of catastrophe: in this case, after watching Philadelphia's globally televised apocalypse from the other side of the world. Specifically, Cudjoe has been drawn back to the United States by the tale of a child who fled the ruins of the MOVE compound only to disappear into the bowels of the city. Determined to find the orphaned boy named Simba, he leaves behind the Greek island where he himself had abdicated the demands of family, career, and art. Recovering "Simmie" thus serves not only as a symbolic self-rescue but also as personal and collective mea culpa for the criminal neglect of children by adults entrusted with their well-being.

Investigating the subcultures where Simmie might have landed, Cudjoe learns of Kaliban's Kiddie Korps, a gang-like enclave of youngsters—"gangsters"—whose ironic "KKK" signature graffiti also includes the slogan "MPT" (for "Money Power Things"). Given that their elders' active sabotaging of the next generation's health, safety, and humanity has left them to fend for themselves, they in turn enthusiastically embrace a predictably brutal war against their elders, of whom they say "Olds are Vampires. They suck youngs' blood."

The gang's Shakespearean allusion to Caliban, malcontent enslaved "native" of *The Tempest*, offers only one of the play's vectors operating in the novel. Cudjoe himself had tried in the mid-1960's to stage an early postcolonial reinterpretation of the play, casting inner-city children in the roles. His history—withdrawal into his own island existence—evokes comparison to the play's magician-despot Prospero, whose confession ("This thing of darkness/ I acknowledge mine.") provides one of the intertextual sutures between Cudjoe's story and the autobiographical material into which Wideman moves mid-novel.

In this fiction lamenting failed fathers and blasted children, Wideman makes his own grieving confusion over son Jake's ongoing incarceration and mental decay part of the fabric of the text. Moving back and forth between first and third person (as he also does in Cudjoe's sections), as he contemplates his own artistic struggles with tumultuous material, he finds the comforts available to him in working with brother Rob to compose

Brothers and Keepers elude him in Jake's case: "How does it feel to be inhabited by more than one self? Clearer and clearer, in my son's case, that he is more and less than one. . . . To take stock, to make sense, to attempt to control or to write a narrative of self—how hopeless any of these tasks must seem when the *self* attempting this harrowing business is no more reliable than a shadow, a chimera. . . . " Clearly, Jake too has affinities with the lost Simba for whom Cudjoe desperately searches on the ravaged streets of Philadelphia.

Finally, then, it is Philadelphia's iconic status as birthplace of the American Dream—and emblem of its profound betrayal—that gives shape to the mélange of personal disasters with which Wideman is wrestling.

Opening with an epigraph drawn from William Penn's 1681 injunction on the city's founding— "Let every house lie placed . . . that it may be a greene Country Towne which will never be burnt, and always be wholesome"—it ends with a nod to James Baldwin's 1960's warning of further racial cataclysm to come: Caught amid a mob "Screaming for blood," at it moves "over the stones of Independence Square," Cudjoe recalls "The dreadlocked man promised more fire next time."

FATHERALONG: A MEDITATION ON FATHERS AND SONS, RACE AND SOCIETY

First published: 1994
Type of work: Memoir

Returning to the memoir form, Wideman spins a web of imaginative reconnection to his emotionally remote father, Edgar, and his psychologically damaged son Jake.

Fatheralong begins as a meditation on the lifelong shallowness that Wideman perceives in his ties to his own father, Edgar, and his recent efforts to redress the situation by cultivating a belated understanding of him. He hopes that such understanding might also foster the recovery of a larger male kinship across generations to reverse the psychic fatherlessness that he has come to regard as the normative condition of black sons in white America.

Two-thirds of the way into the text, however, John briefly alludes to his own imprisoned son—a situation he now shares with Edgar, father of Rob— the title subject of Wideman's celebrated 1984 work *Brothers and Keepers*. In a horrific extension of the family tragedy that had seen Rob given a life sentence for a murder resulting from a bungled robbery, John's younger son Jake had, at age sixteen, inexplicably murdered another teenager in an Arizona motel and had been given his own life sentence. Once again, then, the memoir form permits Wideman an imaginative vehicle to help contextualize his pain and confusion. In *Fatheralong*, he eventually dissolves all pretense of narrative distance by composing an open letter directly to Jake, the mystery of whose psychotic self-destruction "all these father stories" have, he admits, been an attempt to elucidate.

Fatheralong announces virtually from the outset Wideman's hard-won faith in the restorative power of recovered stories. It juggles heterogeneous autobiographical materials in an attempt to have the pieces glance off of and illuminate each other in unpredictable ways made possible through the creative process itself, now seen by Wideman as a locus of healing as well as linkage: "I'm setting down part of a story, a small piece of what needs to be remembered so when we make up the next part, imagine our lives, our history, this piece will be there, among the fragments lost, found, and remembered." Here the shaping sensibility of the memoirist seems humbler than in *Brothers and Keepers*, a measure in part of Wideman's having passed the half-century mark by the time of its composition— a milestone to which he repeatedly alludes.

A text grounded in his journey with his own father to investigate the Wideman family's ancestral home, all too conveniently located in Promised Land, South Carolina, it is first and foremost a book about time and history and the ways in which the latter can buffer the ravages of the former, so long as the stories of the past are sustained in living relationship to the present. It is in trying to fathom the loss of generational continuity between black fathers and sons—the absence of fathers in the contemporary cultural imagination of African Americans—that Wideman confronts the enigmatic "race paradigm" with which all black intellectuals have had to wrestle, and by which they know their own psyches are profoundly distorted. As he laments, "How can we talk about ourselves without falling into the trap of race, without perpetuating the terms of the debate we can't win. . . . " Thus, although John's father's life story, his parents' separation, his older son Dan's wedding, his younger son Jake's imprisonment, his wife's loss of her father, and his own aesthetic musings fill *Fatheralong*, it also offers a compelling example of the paradoxes that fill African American autobiographical writing: The story of the self—in fact, the story of necessarily multiform selves—recapitulates the story of the race, even today and even in texts that embrace postmodern indeterminacy. Yet a determination to achieve interracial as well as intraracial discovery also informs the text. During his book tour for this work, Wideman frequently noted that "the failure to get inside each other's skins" remains the most profound problem in American cultural life. By turning his entire familial history into a text-in-progress, Wideman makes a significant personal contribution to redressing American cultural dissociation.

THE CATTLE KILLING

First published: 1996
Type of work: Novel

This self-reflexive fiction examines the soul-crushing and recurrent consequences of racism across American history as well as the potential of religion and art as alternative means of sustaining the faith necessary for personal survival.

Told in a complex intertexual layering that juxtaposes the Philadelphia of the late eighteenth century with that of the 1990's, *The Cattle Killing* provides Wideman with an opportunity to reconfigure a common theme in his writing: the mythically resonant patterning of experience across history that can provide clues by which the past may explain—and potentially redeem—the present. The title derives from a legend detailing how the Xhosa people of South Africa allowed false prophecy to dupe them into killing their cattle herds to effect the departure of the white imperialists destroying their world. Tragically, their action furthered the white agenda by depriving the Xhosa of the staples upon which their way of life depended. For Wideman, the analogy to contemporary urban youth violence could not be clearer: Once again, a people desperate for rescue are sacrificing the lifeblood of their society in a pernicious receptivity to the wrong messages.

Wideman offers another example of such cultural miscalculation by dramatizing the racist consequences attending the 1793 yellow fever epidemic in Philadelphia. Having earlier published a short story entitled "Fever" (1989) on the same subject, this time Wideman adds to the picture of white scapegoating of black people with a study of how the contagion at the city's core spins into outlying areas beyond the metropolis: No amount of segregation or withdrawal from the collectivity can counter the essentially organic nature of the social order, and disease infecting one group will inevitably damage others.

In working out these themes, Wideman tells a story within a story. The frame narrative belongs to Isaiah, a contemporary African American writer much like Wideman himself who has completed a new book that he sets out to share with his father and son. The book actually closes with the son's analytic response via a letter, contributing a bit of information that Wideman then spins into one final collaborative twist. At the center of the manuscript is the storytelling activity of an unnamed eighteenth century former slave and itinerant preacher—storytelling to which he now resorts as an alternative to the religious faith that once sustained him but can no longer convincingly counter the brutal realities and waves of human misery that he has witnessed as a result of the plague. The love that he bears for a bedridden woman whom he intends to keep alive with his stories about his past provides a touchstone for him in the present. The woman herself is shrouded in mystery, with the narrative never explicitly naming her but associating her variously with the preacher's earlier encounters with a ladies' maid named Kathryn, as well as a slave who had delivered herself and a dead child into a lake, either drowning or "disappearing" in the process.

Long a practitioner of postmodern textual acrobatics—polyphonic narratives, unmediated disjunctions of time and place, elusive and elliptical voicings akin to jazz solos—Wideman also makes clear once again his doubts about the potential of art to relieve the artist's egotism or conjure up the audience with which he wishes to communicate. Yet he avoids repudiating the claims of artistic "meaning" altogether by appealing to the countervailing influences upon him of African American culture, with its faith in storytelling as a conduit for hope. In her defense of the novel's difficulty, reviewer Joyce Carol Oates called it "a work of operatic polyphony that strains to break free of linguistic constraints into theatrical spectacle."

SUMMARY

Wideman's writing, from fiction to memoir to literary criticism, testifies to his deeply felt commitment to document the African American experience by subjecting it to the illuminating lens of art. His work combines a personal journey to recover a cultural tradition he had once shunned with postmodernist literary methods.

Wideman dramatizes the challenges facing black men in a racist society that continually compromises their masculinity and demands ingenious strategies for reinventing male integrity. Family and community provide the bedrock of that integrity, and history is the fluid medium through which it must travel.

Barbara Kitt Seidman

BIBLIOGRAPHY

By the Author

LONG FICTION:
A Glance Away, 1967
Hurry Home, 1970
The Lynchers, 1973
Hiding Place, 1981
Sent for You Yesterday, 1983
The Homewood Trilogy, 1985 (includes *Damballah, Hiding Place,* and *Sent for You Yesterday*)
Reuben, 1987
Philadelphia Fire, 1990
The Cattle Killing, 1996
Two Cities, 1998

SHORT FICTION:
Damballah, 1981
Fever: Twelve Stories, 1989
All Stories Are True, 1992

DISCUSSION TOPICS

- How do familial and cross-generational relationships provide a counterforce to the impacts of racism on the minds and souls of John Edgar Wideman's protagonists? How redemptive do they prove to be, and why?

- Wideman evokes Northern inner-city landscapes and the existential struggles faced by their inhabitants. What driving forces shape the characters' lives and choices? What personal struggles do they undergo? How does Wideman fuse the personal and sociological as factors in the conditions of their lives?

- In what ways does Wideman illuminate the relationships between and among African American men—as fathers and sons, siblings, team members, musicians, and homeboys? What defines these varied bonds, and what threatens or even dissolves them?

- For Wideman, the ties between mother and son keep young African American males functioning in a hostile world. Where does that pattern emerge among his characters? Where does it break down?

- The sexual and emotional dynamics between men and women engage Wideman's imaginative scrutiny. What obstacles stand between them? What role does race play in their capacity for partnership?

- In *Brothers and Keepers,* prison serves as an arena of personal existential struggle for Rob Wideman. How much does John attempt to stay true to that struggle and avoid easy platitudes about his brother's situation? In *Philadelphia Fire* and *Fatheralong,* how have his meditations on prison deepened, given his son Jake's incarceration?

The Stories of John Edgar Wideman, 1992
God's Gym, 2005

NONFICTION:
Brothers and Keepers, 1984
Fatheralong: A Meditation on Fathers and Sons, Race and Society, 1994
Conversations with John Edgar Wideman, 1998 (Bonnie TuSmith, editor)
Hoop Roots, 2001
The Island: Martinique, 2003

EDITED TEXTS:
The Best American Short Stories, 1996
My Soul Has Grown Deep: Classics of Early African-American Literature, 2001
Twenty: The Best of the Drue Heinz Literature Prize, 2001

About the Author

Baker, Lisa. "Storytelling and Democracy (in the Radical Sense): A Conversation with John Edgar Wideman." *African American Review* 34, no. 2 (Summer, 2000): 263-272.

Bell, Bernard W. *The Afro-American Novel and Its Tradition.* Amherst: University of Massachusetts Press, 1987.

Bennion, John. "The Shape of Memory in John Edgar Wideman's *Sent for You Yesterday.*" *Black American Literature Forum* 20 (1985): 143-150.

Byerman, Keith E. *John Edgar Wideman: A Study of the Short Fiction.* New York: Twayne, 1998.

Callaloo 22, no. 3 (Summer 1999). Special issue on Wideman.

Coleman, James W. *Blackness and Modernism: The Literary Career of John Edgar Wideman.* Jackson: University Press of Mississippi, 1990.

Hume, Kathryn. "Black Urban Utopia in Wideman's Later Fiction." *Race & Class* 45, no. 3 (January-March, 2004): 19-34.

Lucy, Robin. "John Edgar Wideman (1941-   )." In *Contemporary African American Novelists: A Biographical-Bibliographic Critical Sourcebook,* edited by Emmanuel S. Nelson. Westport, Conn.: Greenwood, 1999.

Lustig, Jessica. "Home: An Interview with John Edgar Wideman." *African American Review,* Fall, 1992, 453-457.

Mbalia, Dorothea Drummond. *John Edgar Wideman: Reclaiming the African Personality.* Selinsgrove, Pa.: Susquehanna University Press, 1995.

Rushdy, Ashraf H. A. "Fraternal Blues: John Edgar Wideman's *Homewood Trilogy.*" *Contemporary Literature,* Fall, 1991, 312-345.

TuSmith, Bonnie. *Conversations with John Edgar Wideman.* Jackson: University of Mississippi Press, 1998.

RICHARD WILBUR

Born: New York, New York
March 1, 1921

Wilbur published some of the finest poetry of the mid-twentieth century; he was appointed poet laureate of the United States by the Library of Congress in 1987.

Stathis Orphanos

BIOGRAPHY

Richard Wilbur was born in New York City on March 1, 1921, the son of Lawrence L. Wilbur, a portrait painter, and Helen R. (Purdy) Wilbur, a daughter of an editor of *The Baltimore Sun*. He attended public schools in Essex Falls, New Jersey, and North Caldwell, New Jersey, and attended Montclair High School, where he was editor of the school paper.

In 1938, he matriculated at Amherst College; there he wrote editorials for and was chairman of the student newspaper, *The Student*, and was a contributor to *The Touchstone*, the student magazine. He once said that there he submitted an awful poem about a nightingale, a bird that he had never seen. He received a dollar for it. He received his A.B. at Amherst College in 1942, but before he could continue his studies, he was drafted into the Army. He served until 1945, when he was discharged with the rank of technician third class. He then went on to get his A.M. in religion at Harvard University in 1947. He had married Charlotte Ward in 1942; they had four children, Ellen, Christopher, Nathan, and Aaron.

After he received his master's degree at Harvard, he was elected junior fellow there from 1947 to 1950. In 1950, he became an assistant professor of English at Harvard, where he remained until 1954. In that year he became associate professor of English at Wellesley College, where he was promoted to professor in 1957; he taught there until 1977. Unlike many other poets of his generation, he did not look down on teaching as a job that spoiled his writing. Indeed, he pointed out in an interview given to Peter Stitt that the constant reading and the necessity of understanding one's reading very clearly were good exercises for the mind. In 1977, he was appointed writer-in-residence at Smith College, a position he held until 1986. He has since retired from teaching.

In 1947, while he was at Harvard's graduate school, a friend sent a sheaf of his poetry to Reynal & Hitchcock, whose editors liked it so much that they published it under the title *The Beautiful Changes, and Other Poems* (1947). Other books of original poetry followed: *Ceremony, and Other Poems* in 1950; *Things of This World* in 1956; and *Advice to a Prophet, and Other Poems* in 1961. A paperback collection, *The Poems of Richard Wilbur*, put out by Harvest Books, came out in 1963. *Walking to Sleep: New Poems and Translations* was published in 1969 and *The Mind-Reader: New Poems* in 1976. In 1988, a collection of poems from all of his books was published under the title *New and Collected Poems*. A more recent book of poetry is *Mayflies: New Poems and Translations* from 2000. In 2004, Wilbur released *Collected Poems, 1943-2004*.

Wilbur has augmented his original poetry with his many translations from the French. In 1955, he translated Moliére's *Le Misanthrope* (pr. 1666, pb. 1667; *The Misanthrope*, 1709). It was first played by the Poet's Theater in Cambridge, Massachusetts, in 1955 and was performed Off-Broadway at Theater East in 1956-1957. Wilbur's version is now the standard for performance. Later he translated Moliére's *Tartuffe* (pr. 1664, revised pr. 1667, pb. 1669) in 1963, for which he was the corecipient of the Bollingen Prize. He published *L'École des femmes* (pr. 1662, pb. 1663) as *The School for Wives* in 1971 and *Les Femmes savantes* (pr., pb. 1672) as *The Learned Ladies* in 1978. More recent translations from Moliére include *L'École de maris* (pr., pb. 1661) as *The School for Husbands* in 1991; *Sganarelle: Ou, Le Cocu imaginaire* (pr, pb. 1660) as *The Imaginary Cuckold: Or, Sganarelle*) in 1993; *Amphitryon* (pr. 1668; pb. 1668) in 1995; *Dom Juan* (pr. 1665; pb. 1682) as *Don Juan* in 2001; and *L'Etourdi* (pr. 1654?, pb. 1663) as *The Bungler* in 2000. Wilbur's translations from Jean Racine, the seventeenth century classic French tragedian, include *Andromaque* (pr. 1667, pb. 1668) as *Andromache* in 1982; *Phèdre* (pr., pb. 1677) as *Phaedra* in 1986; and *Les Plaideurs* (pr. 1668, pb. 1669) as *The Suitors* in 2001. His more recent books of poetry include translations from Voltaire, Dante, and Charles Baudelaire.

Among Wilbur's works for children are *Loudmouse* (1963), *Opposites* (1973), *More Opposites* (1991), *Runaway Opposites* (1995), *The Disappearing Alphabet* (1998), *Opposites, More Opposites, and Some Differences* (2000), and *The Pig in the Spigot* (2000). He wrote or rewrote most of the lyrics for *Candide* (pr. 1956) by Leonard Bernstein, the famous modern American composer, which was published by Random House in 1957, and the lyrics for a cantata, *On Freedom's Ground* (pr., pb. 1986) composed by William Schuman, a prominent musician and educator. He produced an edition of Edgar Allan Poe's poetry for Dell in 1959 and later edited the *Selected Poems* of Witter Bynner in 1978 and *Shakespeare: Poems* in 1966. He also published a book of literary criticism, *Responses: Prose Pieces, 1953-1976*, in 1976 (expanded edition, 2000) and another prose collection, *The Catbird's Song: Prose Pieces, 1963-1995* (1997).

Wilbur is the winner of many awards, the chief of which are the National Book Award and the Pulitzer Prize (both for his book of poems *Things of This World*), the Bollingen Award for his translation of *Tartuffe* in 1971, a second Pulitzer Prize for *New and Collected Poems*, and the National Medal for the Arts in 1994. He served as poet laureate of the United States in 1987-1988.

ANALYSIS

Summing up Richard Wilbur's poetic achievement seems at first very easy. Throughout his career, he has excelled at writing beautiful short poems about the surrounding natural world. However, a close look at some of his poems and a glance at his translations and other interests will find a writer more important than a painter of pretty pictures. He does, certainly, enjoy the world of living creatures. "Cicadas," the very first poem in his first book, is more than a clever rendering of the humming of cicadas. A close reading proves it to be about nature's ironies: These insects fill the world with song but are themselves deaf.

Animal titles are sprinkled throughout his work: There is "Still, Citizen Sparrow" "The Death of a Toad," "All These Birds," "The Pelican," and the delightful "A Prayer to Go to Paradise with the Donkeys," translated from the French of Francis Jammes, a modern French poet. Yet these animals are chosen because they provide a key to understanding the surrounding world. "Still, Citizen Sparrow" is really about how the vulture (and all it stands for) is needed in the world; "The Death of a Toad" shows how all death is tragic, and "Grasshopper" helps to distinguish the peace that is death from that which is contentment in activity.

Many critics think of Wilbur as a poet uniting flesh and spirit, discerning both, glorifying both. In "Running," he describes a day when his body as a boy was in perfect shape and the run he had was a glory of perfect control. "Thinking of happiness," he says, "I think of that." In "The Juggler," after lamenting the pull of gravity on a rubber ball, he praises the juggler for keeping the balls, brooms, and plates played by whirling in air. He discovers how people resent the weight that holds them to the earth, both physically and spiritually; he thereby discovers the reason for juggling, for dreams of flying, and perhaps for all the earth's restless desires.

Perhaps Wilbur's most characteristic poetic gift is his uncanny ability to pinpoint the essential interplay between humans and nature. "On the Marginal Way" begins, in a sedate six-line stanza ending with a final couplet, to describe a beach littered with boulders; they remind the poet first of naked women but then of a beach full of dead people, whose story he begins to imagine. He pulls himself short by exclaiming: "[It is] the time's fright within me which distrusts/ Least fancies into violence." He reminds himself that though it was "violent" volcanic action that created these boulders, it is a beautiful day, and joy comes with the faith, however momentary, that "all things shall be brought/ To the full state and stature of their kind."

In the short poem "Seed Loves," Wilbur patiently describes a phenomenon that every gardener knows: The first two leaves of every plant are always the same. The plant is in a state of pure potency, and it both wishes and fears to grow. Then the third and fourth leaves come out, and the plant resigns itself to be itself. A simple botanical fact echoes deep inside the human spirit.

There are more direct approaches, as in "Advice to a Prophet," which counsels a doomsayer not to predict a nuclear holocaust or the end of humankind on earth: "How should we dream of this place without us?" Reach us instead, he says, by telling how all the beautiful things in nature will disappear. In "A Summer Morning," he tells how the cook and the gardener, because their rich young employers got in late, enjoy the beautiful big gardens and house on a sunny morning, "Possessing what the owners can but own," bringing a moral insight to a small incident that would gladden Saint Francis.

The critics insist that Wilbur is a classic rather than a romantic poet. While often used vaguely, the words "classic" and "romantic" can indicate general tendencies. If "classic" points toward public themes, wit, and an intellectual acceptance of the human condition, "romantic" implies subjectivity, fierce emotions, and yearning after transcendent goals, then Wilbur is on the classic side. Even his choice of poets to translate is headed by the French classicists, Molière, Racine, and Voltaire, the eighteenth century satirist and political commentator. Perhaps a single Wilbur poem will illustrate. In "A Wood," a parable emerges from Wilbur's observation of the forest. It is an oak forest, an impressive place, but someone looking carefully, he points out, would notice dogwood and witch hazel fighting to keep their places in the forest. Classically enough, he provides a moral—"no one style, I think, is recommended"—but the true meaning in the poem is the feeling of sympathy for the underdog trees trying to survive in a forest of important oaks.

Wilbur's later work reveals a willingness to dwell on the dark side of nature, as in "A Barred Owl."

His poetic diction has become less mannered and ornate than in his earlier work. His style now favors the simple and direct statement. Changes in style, however, only highlight a sense of continuity with earlier work. He still remains a poet drawing inspiration and insight from nature. Thus in "Mayflies," the poet's sight of a swarm of transient mayflies, "those lifelong dancers of a day," leaves him feeling "alone in a life too much my own" until he realizes that he is "one whose task is joyfully to see," to continue with his poetic calling.

Finally, at least occasionally, Wilbur is a Christian poet. Biographers list his religion as Episcopalian, but his overtly devotional works are few and very generic. "A Christmas Hymn," for example, presents a brief history of salvation, with the refrain "And every stone shall cry" leading the reader from the stable through Palm Sunday and the crucifixion to Jesus' presence in glory. Nevertheless, the whole of Wilbur's poetry can be called, at least in a transferred sense, sacramental. Like a medieval poet, he reads the Book of the World, and all of its aspects—vegetable, mineral, animal, and human—are rife with meaning, which he, as a patient anatomist, discovers with care and love.

"A WORLD WITHOUT OBJECTS IS A SENSIBLE EMPTINESS"

First published: 1950 (collected in *Ceremony, and Other Poems*, 1950)
Type of work: Poem

The poet tries to discern which is the true human goal, spirit or flesh.

The poem's title is a quote from Thomas Traherne, a seventeenth century mystic and poet. The poem is written in a stanza form which would certainly be commonplace in the seventeenth century, with four-line stanzas rhyming *abab*, though some of the rhymes are slant rhymes. Line 1 is trimeter; line 2, pentameter; line 3, hexameter; and line 4, trimeter.

The central metaphor or conceit of the poem is that the search for Traherne's "sensible emptiness" is a camel caravan, leaving the security of the oasis for a "desert experience." It "move[s] with a stilted stride/ to the land of sheer horizon." The camels search for a place where there is nothing but sand and sky. This central metaphor uses the ambiguous connotations of desert and oasis to structure the poem into a statement on the search for spiritual perfection. The desert is traditionally both a place where the ascetic goes to find God and the very image of hell, the dry place without rejuvenating water. Similarly, the oasis is the place of refreshment, the goal of the desert traveler, while at the same time it is the desert saint's place of temptation, a return to the "Fleshpots of Egypt." In fact, the archetype here is the exodus, the stately camels leaving the oasis to find God in the desert.

The speaker plays on the ambiguity of the imagery, however; the camels, the "Beasts of my soul," are "slow and proud" and "move with a stilted pride." He suggests that the camels are not ascetics but aesthetes, calling them "connoisseurs of thirst," but what they thirst for is "pure mirage." The goal of their quest seems to be an illusion.

The poet in stanza 4 refuses this goal of mirage and nothingness. He insists that "all shinings need to be shaped," and he appeals to "painted saints" and "merry-go-round rings." He exhorts these camels to turn away from the sand and the desert to (in stanza 6) "trees arrayed/ in bursts of glare," and then names other green and substantial things—country creeks and hilltops illuminated by the sun. Stanza 7 advises the searcher/camels to watch "the supernova burgeoning over the barn" and then pronounces the true goal "the spirit's right oasis, light incarnate."

The poem, then, interprets the ambiguous associations in its own way. It takes the title's quote as a mere description, which the "camels of the spirit" have mistaken for a spiritual goal. It rejects the desert as an ascetic goal, because to conquer it as the camels seek to do is not a humane act but an example of pride, an attempt to overrun the limits of human nature; a human cannot pursue a goal where there are no objects. The last line hints at the incarnational theology that honors both body and spirit. Each object to be sought at the end of the poem is bathed in the "spiritual" light of the sun.

"LOVE CALLS US TO THE THINGS OF THIS WORLD"

First published: 1956 (collected in *Things of This World*, 1956)
Type of work: Poem

The poet tries to describe and then deal with the moment between sleeping and waking, when life seems glorious and beautiful.

"Love Calls Us to the Things of This World" is one of a precious few poems in the English language that operates as a perfectly delightful rendering of an experience that rides joyfully just outside the rational world. It can be seen as a companion piece to some of the poems of Wallace Stevens, the great modern American poet, such as "The Emperor of Ice-Cream" or "That November off Tehuantepec."

The stanza is of five lines of alternating trochaic and iambic patterns, with the second and fourth lines tending toward rhyme. The poem opens with a reference to a "cry of pulleys" as an unseen neighbor puts laundry out on the line; the pulleys may also be an allusion to the poem "The Pulley" by George Herbert, the seventeenth century English religious poet. In that poem, the pulley is an emblem of the means by which God draws humankind to himself—in that case, by making humans dissatisfied with life here on earth. In Wilbur's poem, the moment being described is the moment between sleeping and waking, when the world is in a state of perfect delight. Fitting in with the slightly non-rational tinge of the poem, the central conceit used here is that the moment is like laundry.

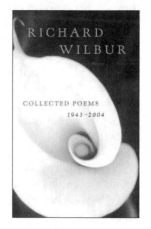

This strange moment is described in terms of the laundry hanging on the line outside the window. "Angels" in sheets, blouses, and smocks abound; they rise "together in calm swells/ Of halcyon feelings." In stanza 3, they perform the astounding feat of flying at top speed while not moving— "staying like white water"—

and then become so quiet that "nobody seems to be there." The soul begins to be aware of its situation, however, and in stanza 4 it looks forward with fear to the prospect of waking up to "the punctual rape of every blessed day" and cries out irrationally, "Oh, let there be nothing on earth but laundry."

As stanza 5 acknowledges, the day must come, the sleeper must fully awake, and the soul must "in bitter love/ . . . accept the waking body." What, then, can be gained from this pre-waking experience? The last stanza is a prayer—an eloquent one—asking that the laundry that bundles the angels in the vision become part of everyday life: "clean linen for the backs of thieves," new clothes for lovers so that they may "go fresh and sweet to be undone," and "dark habits" for "the heaviest nuns," who are "keeping their difficult balance." Significantly, love ends the dream of the angels and forces one to wake up from the insubstantial dream world. One is called now, to the things of this world, not to dreams of the next.

"IN THE FIELD"

First published: 1969 (collected in *Walking to Sleep: New Poems and Translations*, 1969)
Type of work: Poem

This poem compares the feelings aroused by looking at the stars with those caused by viewing a field of flowers.

The title "In the Field" is an ambiguous reference to the two halves of the poem. The poem chronicles two walks in the same field, the first at night (the speaker looks at the stars), and the second one on a sunny day (the speaker looks at the flowers of the field). The poem has both a speaker and someone spoken to, who is probably a wife or lover, and the poem is a looking back at the events delineated there.

The simple stanza form—four lines each of trimeter, pentameter, tetrameter, and trimeter, rhyming *abab*—gives the poem a classical feel with a personal twist. It may be said to have as its subject the fear of Blaise Pascal, the seventeenth century French philosopher and mathematician, of the immensity of the universe. It relates this topic not as an abstract concept but as one resulting from a personal discovery of the poet and his beloved.

The poem opens as the two are walking through the field on a moonless night looking at the stars. The imagery of stanzas 1 and 2, however, suggests that they are wading in the sea, their "throw-back heads aswim." The meditation begins with discussions of anciently named constellations, pointing out that Andromeda no longer fears the sea even though she moves "through a diamond froth of stars." Nor does she need Perseus, her godlike savior in the myth, or even Euripides, the famous ancient Greek tragedian, to preserve her memory. The dolphin of Anon, the legendary Greek bard, is still there, as flawless as he was in ancient times.

Stanza 5 turns the poem in a new direction. The speaker, as if discovering what he had forgotten, says that none of the legends written in the stars "are true." He explains by noting that the stars have moved slightly since ancient times: The pictures visible to the ancients are "askew" and, therefore, meaningless. The heavens have burst "the cincture of the Zodiac" and "shot flares" (meteors), and they no longer have anything to say.

So the two of them talk in modern astronomical terms—star magnitude, nebulae, and star clusters—which is fine until the imagination gets into the act with a "nip of fear." It fakes "a scan of space/ Blown black and hollow"; perhaps the imagination thinks of a time ahead when the stars go out, an intimation of apocalypse. The air becomes chill, and the two go home to bed.

The second half of the poem describes the field in sunlight. The stars are gone; the "holes in heaven have been sealed." The only galaxies they see are "galaxies/ Of dream flowers," images that populate stanzas 16 and 17. Yet what do they mean? Do they refute the fear felt in the night walk? No, that would be a mistake. In a complicated answer, the poet discovers the "heart's wish for life." He opines that this wish "pounds beyond the sun" and "is the one/ Unbounded thing we know."

When one has finished analyzing the poem, one finds that the ambiguous title "In the Field" now has a third meaning. Besides indicating the dark field of the stars and the bright sunny field of flowers, it indicates that speaker has taken a "field trip": an experience that backs up an abstract idea, Pascal's fear, which his mind had already grasped. The stars are frightening and the flowers comforting, but the infinite wishes of the human heart are the only "unbounded thing" humankind has from experience.

"THE MIND-READER"

First published: 1976 (collected in the *Mind-Reader: New Poems*, 1976)
Type of work: Poem

A dramatic monologue in which the speaker tells the poet how he became a mind reader and what are his thoughts on the human mind.

"The Mind-Reader" is a dramatic monologue in the tradition of Robert Browning, the nineteenth century British poet, written in blank verse. It is the statement of a mind reader, one perpetually ensconced in a café somewhere in Italy. He talks to the poet about how he came to be a mind reader, how he practices his "craft," and how he feels about what he does.

The poem begins with nineteen lines exploring what it means when something is really lost. Not till the end of the poem does the reader really find out why he speaks of these things. He begins with an image of a young lady's hat being blown off a parapet and sailing endlessly down into a vast ravine with a river at the bottom. He tells of a pipe wrench falling out of a pickup truck into a brook or culvert, then of a book slipping out of the hand of a reader on a cruise ship and into the sea. These things are "truly lost." Four mysterious lines follow which declare that it is another thing to be caught inside the prison of someone's head. (Was he so imprisoned? Was it traumatic?)

He explains in the next twenty-one lines that he, as a child, had a gift of finding things that others had lost. He tries to describe how it felt to be able to do this. He uses a metaphor of a moon bumping through a deep forest, through

> paths which turned
> to dried-up stream-beds, hemlocks which invited
> Through shiny clearings.

All of a sudden the lost object would be there, shining.

Perhaps he feels that this metaphor does not quite make the process clear, for he tries again. He says that it is like a train with fogged windows coming into a station where a young woman is waiting for you (his listener) to come, though she does not know what you look like. He alludes to the saying "out of sight, out of mind" and seems to imply that it is not precisely true. "What can be wiped from memory?" Nothing, he answers, no matter how mean or terrible the event. That is presumably why he, with his gift, can always find the thing that was misplaced. Everything is still there.

This arcane skill leads him to become the mind reader at the corner table of the café. He describes the credulous people who come to have their futures predicted, even though he cannot predict the future, and the skeptics who are afraid that if he can read minds, all the old superstitions will come rushing back. They are his "fellow-drunkards."

He describes his method: They write a question on a piece of paper, and he lays his hand on theirs and goes into a frenzy; he describes his act (for so it is) in terms that resemble the routine of the Delphic Oracle, the smoke from his cigarette substituting for the incense in the oracle's tripod. It is easy, he says, to know what they are thinking—everyone is the same. Sometimes he cheats, but remember, he says, every other skilled worker (a tailor, for example) can make a mistake and still be trusted. If he makes one, he is a fraud. Then he concludes with images of squalor: His mind is filled with anger, insomnia, mutterings, complaints, and "flushings of the race."

His gift is to find in others' minds their own misplaced questions, but, as he admits, he has no answers. He gives them answers that are the stock-in-trade of palm readers and astrologers everywhere, each bit of advice prefaced with a commonsense "if," each prediction based on a commonsense understanding of how life is led. He describes his stock answers as lies and evasions, although he believes that his clients are happy that he read their desire. These people are filled with "selfish hopes/ And small anxieties." True virtue and heroism are rare indeed. Maybe, he says, he simply cannot hear that part of them; maybe there is "some huge attention" which "suffers us and is inviolate," which "remarks/ The sparrow's weighty fall." The speaker seems oblivious to the reference to Christ's Sermon on the Mount, and he declares that he would be glad to know this if it were so.

The poem concludes with his own desire "for that place beyond the sparrow" and to find those things that are truly lost, which were mentioned in the opening of the poem—the falling hat, the wrench in the ditch, and the book in the sea. The listener apparently offers to buy him a drink, and he replies, perhaps smiling, "You have read my mind." Perhaps Wilbur, in this poem, wishes to illustrate what the human mind and its desires are like, apparently trivial and squalid like those the mind reader finds in his clients, yet perhaps containing way down the true desires, the infinite desires, symbolized by the lost hat, wrench, and book.

"TROLLING FOR BLUES"

First published: 1987 (collected in *New and Collected Poems*, 1987)

Type of work: Poem

The act of fishing inspires a wry meditation on the pitfalls of metaphor and humanizing the nonhuman.

"Trolling for Blues" could be styled a work whose metaphor takes over the poem and changes it into something other than what it started out to be. It is written in a five-line stanza of loose pentameters without rhyme. As it begins the poet talks to himself about metaphors: The "dapper terns" and the cloud that "moils in the sky" like an embryo are seen in human terms—humanity is projected upon them. (Only a person could be "dapper.") Wilbur then analyzes his fish-is-like-man metaphor. Humans make the fish, he points out, a "mirror of our kind." Immediately he begins to mock the poet in everyone: The fish is human only if, he says, one sets aside the fish's "unreflectiveness," his habit of leaping up out of the water, and his strange practice of swimming a hundred miles out to sea to spawn.

One conceives of the fish, the poet says, as blue, "which is the shade/ Of thought." He becomes at this point a symbol of the intellect "on edge! To lunge and seize with sure incisiveness." The fish, however, does not cooperate with the poet; suddenly he strikes the lure and dives into the deep, "Yanking imagination back and down/ Past recognition" to the dark places at the bottom of the water. There the fish becomes a symbol of the unconscious, of the place where there is no intellect. He is also a symbol of the evolutionary past—the dark, mindless Devonian age when there were no people. This is where humanity began, coming up from the depths to find the cool, blue intellect.

This poem, then, by a whimsical, circuitous route, mocking the poetic power that created it, sets up an allegory of human psychology. This fact begins to explain the title—as usual in Wilbur, a play on words. If one thinks of the fish as "blue," one is trolling for "blues," but if one thinks of the fish as intellect, one is trolling for a kind of melancholy reflection; the reader catches the idea that humankind's "roots" are far from intellectual, that its beginnings are at the bottom of the sea in "the unlit deep/ Of the glass sponges, of chiasmodon." The poem also reveals the dangerous human habit of projecting humanity onto things which only remotely resemble humans: In humanizing everything, it may be that one begins to fail to understand one's own humanity.

"A FINISHED MAN"

First published: 1985 (collected in *New and Collected Poems*, 1987)

Type of work: Poem

The poem teasingly draws out the smugness with which an old man views his "triumph."

The poem has five stanzas of four iambic pentameter lines each in rhymed couplets, allowing the poem a style well suited for gentle satire, for which Wilbur's familiarity with Molière suits him. In the poem, an old and wealthy man reminiscences during the dedication ceremony of a college gymnasium named after him. The poem's title plays with the connotations of the word "finished." The old man's wealth and prestige have brought him to a highly polished "finish" like a statue. He can even feel "the warm sun sculpt his cheek." His vanity shows in his hope that with time and money "he may be perfect yet." Yet "finished" can also mean that old man's life is over and done.

The poem's first three stanzas relate some embarrassing past incident of the old man's life, whether being "caught . . . in a lie" or being laughed at for an "appalling gaffe." These incidents still rankle the old man and lessen his self-esteem. He is delighted to have outlived the people who have seen him in a bad light. Wilbur suggests, however, that the old man is insecure. In old age, youthful embarrassments still have a hold on him.

"THE BARRED OWL"

First published: 1992 (collected in *Mayflies: New Poems and Translations*, 2000)
Type of work: Poem

The poem presents two images of an owl, suggesting that language can invest the same creature with opposite meanings.

The poem has two stanzas of six iambic pentameter lines each in rhymed couplets. As with much of Wilbur's poetry, this poem observes nature in order to interpret human life. In the first stanza, a child is awakened at night by an owl's hooting. The speaker explains to the child that the owl is just asking "Who cooks for you?" In the second stanza,

however, the nighttime visitor asking about cooking becomes a fearsome predator "with some small thing in a claw/ Borne up to some dark branch and eaten raw." This juxtaposition (cooked versus "eaten raw") occurs in the final lines of the two stanzas and forces the reader to see opposite views of nature.

The speaker sees language as working in two ways: to "domesticate a fear" and to "make our terrors bravely clear." The first stanza domesticates the owl, a friendly creature asking a question. In the second stanza, the owl is the predator who eats small creatures. The title "A Barred Owl" both names a particular species of owl and hints that natural terrors such as the owl have been "barred" from the child's imagination. Yet Wilbur's imagination, unlike the child's, can comprehend "bravely" nature's more frightening forms, perhaps responding to critics who have judged his work as too safe and too easy.

SUMMARY

Wilbur began his poetic career when a friend submitted some poems to a publisher. He continues, modestly writing poem after poem showing profound insights into how the human imagination delves into humankind's relationship with nature and civilization. To this achievement can be added Wilbur's skill in translation, especially in the area of French classical drama, an effort which has gracefully rendered these remote masters accessible to an American audience. Wilbur has probed the world with a keen, calm voice filled with wisdom and insight.

Robert W. Peckham; updated by Anthony Bernardo, Jr.

BIBLIOGRAPHY

By the Author

POETRY:
The Beautiful Changes, and Other Poems, 1947
Ceremony, and Other Poems, 1950
Things of This World, 1956
Poems, 1943-1956, 1957
Advice to a Prophet, and Other Poems, 1961
Loudmouse, 1963 (juvenile)
The Poems of Richard Wilbur, 1963
Walking to Sleep: New Poems and Translations, 1969

Digging for China, 1970
Opposites, 1973 (juvenile)
The Mind-Reader: New Poems, 1976
Seven Poems, 1981
New and Collected Poems, 1988
More Opposites, 1991 (juvenile)
Runaway Opposites, 1995 (juvenile)
The Disappearing Alphabet, 1998 (juvenile)
Mayflies: New Poems and Translations, 2000
Opposites, More Opposites, and Some Differences, 2000
    (juvenile)
The Pig in the Spigot, 2000 (juvenile)
Collected Poems, 1943-2004, 2004

DRAMA:

Candide: A Comic Operetta, pr. 1956 (lyrics; book by
    Lillian Hellman, music by Leonard Bernstein)

TRANSLATIONS:

The Misanthrope, 1955 (of Molière)
Tartuffe, 1963 (of Molière)
The School for Wives, 1971 (of Molière)
The Learned Ladies, 1978 (of Molière)
Andromache, 1982 (of Jean Racine)
Four Comedies, 1982 (of Molière)
Phaedra, 1986 (of Racine)
The School for Husbands, 1991 (of Molière)
The Imaginary Cuckold: Or, Sgarnarelle, 1993 (of Molière)
Amphitryon, 1995 (of Molière)
The Bungler, 2000 (of Molière)
Don Juan, 2001 (of Molière)
The Suitors, 2001 (of Racine)

NONFICTION:

Responses: Prose Pieces, 1953-1976, 1976, expanded 2000
On My Own Work, 1983
Conversations with Richard Wilbur, 1990 (William Butts, editor)
The Catbird's Song: Prose Pieces, 1963-1995, 1997

EDITED TEXTS:

A Bestiary, 1955
Modern America and Modern British Poetry, 1955 (with Louis Untermeyer and Karl Shapiro)
Poe: Complete Poems, 1959
Shakespeare: Poems, 1966 (with Alfred Harbage)
The Narrative Poems and Poems of Doubtful Authenticity, 1974
Selected Poems, 1978 (of Witter Bynner)
Poems and Poetics, 2003 (of Edgar Allan Poe)

DISCUSSION TOPICS

- How does imagery from the natural world shape Richard Wilbur's poetry?

- How does the poet's "praiseful eye," as Wilbur calls it, appear in his poetry?

- Does Wilbur's religious faith shape his poetic concerns? If so, how?

- Wilbur is famous for avoiding literary trends, but what poetic influences seem important to his work?

- How does Wilbur's formal verse (rhyme, meter, and so on) enhance what he has to say?

- Wilbur is sometimes thought to be an "easy" poet—too graceful, too formal, unwilling to accept risk or tragedy. How fair is this assessment?

About the Author

Bixler, Frances. *Richard Wilbur: A Reference Guide.* Boston: G. K. Hall, 1991.

Edgecombe, Rodney Stenning. *A Reader's Guide to the Poetry of Richard Wilbur.* Tuscaloosa: University of Alabama Press, 1995.

Hougen, John B. *Ecstasy Within Discipline: The Poetry of Richard Wilbur.* Atlanta: Scholars Press, 1994.

Michelson, Bruce. *Wilbur's Poetry: Music in a Scattering Time.* Amherst: University of Massachusetts Press, 1991.

Reibetang, John. "What Love Sees: Poetry and Vision in Richard Wilbur." *Modern Poetry Studies* 11 (1982): 60-85.

Salinger, Wendy, ed. *Richard Wilbur's Creation.* Ann Arbor: University of Michigan Press, 1983.

Stitt, Peter. *The World's Hieroglyphic Beauty: Five American Poets.* Athens: University of Georgia Press, 1985.

LAURA INGALLS WILDER

Born: Pepin, Wisconsin
          February 7, 1867
Died: Mansfield, Missouri
          February 10, 1957

Wilder's Little House series, based on her own experiences, provides a unique look at daily frontier life in the United States following the Homestead Act of 1862.

Herbert Hoover Presidential Library

BIOGRAPHY

Laura Elizabeth Ingalls Wilder was born in Wisconsin in 1867. She was the second child of Charles and Caroline Ingalls. She had three sisters as well as a brother who died in infancy. Laura's young life was spent on America's frontiers. Before she was thirteen her family had moved at least six times, re-establishing their home and fortunes in the states of Missouri, Iowa, and Minnesota, and twice into territories: Indian Territory, which later became Kansas, and the Dakota Territory, which later became South Dakota. In many of those places, the Ingallses had to build their own home and barn and dig wells as they provided food for themselves.

In each location, the Ingalls family members depended on their wits and ingenuity to survive. Charles Ingalls was a trapper, hunter, and experienced carpenter. He used all these skills to support his family. Caroline Ingalls had been a teacher before marrying, and she was an expert seamstress. Later in her life, she and Laura sewed to augment the family income. When the family lived in Iowa they managed a hotel, and they made their final move to Dakota Territory when Charles Ingalls found work with the Chicago and Northwestern Railroad as a timekeeper and bookkeeper.

Laura's school attendance was sporadic, but she was an avid student. She completed her studies and passed her teaching examinations when she was living in De Smet, South Dakota. She never formally graduated. Her last teacher held her back to graduate the following year with her whole class. Instead, Laura married Almanzo Wilder in August of 1885 and never returned to school for a formal graduation, despite completing all the requirements and passing her teaching examination.

Laura and Almanzo spent four years trying to prosper on Almanzo's claim near De Smet. Their daughter Rose was born in 1886. In the following three years, Almanzo suffered diphtheria, which left him lame. Their newborn son died in 1889, and their house burned to the ground. The financial strains brought on by bad weather and cash outlay for equipment overcame their efforts to support themselves. Between 1890 and 1894, they moved several times, attempting to find a permanent home in a good climate. In 1894, they settled in Mansfield, Missouri, where they remained for the rest of their lives.

At their Rocky Ridge Farm, they had a large apple orchard, and Laura had great success with her flock of chickens. Numerous speaking engagements about her hens brought her to the attention of the editors of the *Missouri Realist*, and she began writing for them in 1911. She served as their home editor from 1912 to 1923.

Wilder spent her life in hard work. She was a high-spirited woman who loved the outdoors and cherished her life of independence and rigorous labor with Almanzo. As she aged, she realized she had lived through a whole cycle of American westward expansion and that her life spanned a unique historical period. She wanted to tell her story in order to give young people a sense of how America developed and what the settlers on the frontier had endured to develop the middle region of the United States.

Her daughter Rose was a reporter for the *Bulletin* in San Francisco, and during a visit to Rose and her husband in 1915, Wilder began the collaboration which eventually led to her publishing the Little House series of nine books published between 1932 and 1943. Rose encouraged her mother, read her manuscripts, and introduced her to an agent. During the years Laura worked on her books, she and Rose carried on an extensive correspondence, which included suggestions from Rose about style and discussions of the manuscripts, which Rose edited.

Wilder died in 1957, having lived a long, productive life. She left a legacy of personal experience captured in her Little House books which paid tribute to the strength, determination, and faith that sustained the pioneers on American's frontier after the Homestead Act of 1862. The Little House series, published during the Depression, became widely popular. Five of the books after—and including—the fourth, *On the Banks of Plum Creek* (1937), were selected as Newbery Honor Books. *By the Shores of Silver Lake* (1939) was chosen for the Pacific Northwest Library Young Reader's Choice Award in 1942.

In 1954, the American Library Association instituted the Laura Ingalls Wilder Award and presented it to her for her contribution to children's literature. After 1960, this award was given every five years to "an outstanding author or illustrator of children's books." The 1974-1982 television series based on Wilder's books brought her experience and vision of the American frontier to millions of children and their parents long after the books were written.

ANALYSIS

Wilder produced nine books in the Little House series. Eight of these were based on her experiences growing up in various places on the American frontier, and one, *Farmer Boy* (1933), tells of her husband, Almanzo's, boyhood on a farm in New York State. Each novel can be understood without reading the others, but taken together they form a cyclical tale which follows the Ingalls family from Laura's early childhood to her marriage.

In keeping with the development of Laura, the reading difficulty and sophistication of ideas increases with each book. All are narrated by Laura, but they are not first-person narratives, nor are they autobiographical. Wilder employs a limited omniscient point of view. In all the Little House books except *Farmer Boy*, this means Laura's consciousness determines the tone of the story. Not writing in the first-person voice allows Wilder to use details freely. She is able to combine occurrences and relax the chronology to make her story stronger without worrying about the precise order in which events took place.

The series champions family life as the source of stability, encouragement, and safety on the frontier. The descriptions of daily work, physical challenges, shared meals, singing and storytelling on winter evenings, and dangers overcome together form the structure of the novels. Domestic rhythms are bolstered by the seasonal shifts in land and work which mark the completion of a year. Cyclical activities emphasize the relation of life inside the Ingallses' cabin to life outside—on the prairie, on a claim, or in town. The tension of completing harvesting, hunting, or building while the weather allowed these tasks stresses the urgency of each day's work for pioneer families. Wilder's coordination of outdoor work and family growth emphasizes the communal and environmental nature of life on the Ingalls homestead.

Wilder captures the essence of the pioneer spirit in her books, affirming the independent determination of Ralph Waldo Emerson's 1841 essay "Self Reliance" by comments like Ma's, that "a body makes his own luck" in *These Happy Golden Years* (1943). Pa's determination to prove up on his claim in De Smet, Dakota Territory, after years of loss and relocation is a testimony to his unbreakable spirit, one that Laura emulates in her own endeavors.

Throughout the novels, the Ingallses and their neighbors display a sense of entitlement to land. They believe that they have the right to take land they can prove up on according to the terms of the Homestead Act of 1862. Their beliefs reflect the popular nineteenth century doctrine of Manifest Destiny, which asserted the United States' right to settle all the land between the Atlantic and Pacific shores. This philosophy cast American Indians as a danger to settlers' rights as well as their lives because both groups laid claim to the same land. The plight of American Indians is filtered through the fears of Laura as a child and her parents' and their neighbors' comments. Charles Ingalls and Laura recognize the inequity of what is being done, but Pa offers no alternative and continues to assert his right to the land he has settled.

Wilder also draws on the American pastoral tradition, which attributes soul-expanding power to the landscape. Throughout the series Laura glories in the outdoors. She remarks on the songs of dickey birds on the prairie when she first sees the wide open expanse. She longs to run in the sunshine during her housebound winter months. She wades in the creek and helps plant seeds and water the family's gardens and fields.

The outdoors is not all wonder and allure. It contains danger and can menace the Ingalls family by drought or force. As a mature woman, Laura, on a buggy ride with Almanzo, watches the approach of a ferocious rainstorm which ravages farms for miles as well as the town of De Smet. Wilder captures the drama of rolling black clouds sweeping across the plains, sending down fingers to touch the ground as the storm roars past, leaving the joyriders untouched. In an early episode in *Little House on the Prairie* (1935), the new cabin, without windows or a solid door, is surrounded by a pack of wolves howling and snuffling at the cabin's sides during the night. Wilder is not naïve. She expresses the complex relationship of frontier people to the land. It both nurtures and haunts them, offering grand, healing vistas and the sense of space and possibility, along with infinite chances for harm to crops, animals, or the settlers themselves.

Wilder's declarative style suits the narrator and main character Laura's young and developing personality perfectly. It translates her practical and spunky spirit and aptly describes the ordinary tasks, celebrations, and concerns that made up frontier life in the mid- to late nineteenth century. The author's straightforward structure comes out of the Puritan emphasis on plain speaking, as does Laura's introspection about her motives and desires. Wilder's clear style epitomizes the Ingalls family's no-nonsense approach to relationships and work and also allows for the lyrical descriptions of landscape throughout the works. Her coordination of style and subject make the Little House series a suite of books that transforms America's westward expansion into a human drama. Laura and her family embody the sense of possibility which sparked migration to unsettled lands. Wilder's tone rings democratic, celebratory, and serious—a testimony to her commitment to passing along her pride and delight at being a pioneer who lived to tell her tale.

LITTLE HOUSE IN THE BIG WOODS

First published: 1932
Type of work: Novel

The book relates a year of Charles and Caroline Ingalls's life in a log cabin in the Wisconsin woods with daughters Mary, Laura, and Caroline.

"Once upon a time, sixty years ago, a little girl lived in the Big Woods of Wisconsin, in a little gray house made of logs." Thus begins the first of nine books based on the frontier existence of the Ingalls family, fixing the time at 1873 and introducing the main character of the series. The simplicity of presentation fixes Laura's perspective as the lens for the story, and all facets of the tale remain true to a child's point of view. Wilder's use of capital letters heightens Laura's wonder at her surroundings.

It is fall, and the snug Ingalls home bursts with harvest foods, colorfully cataloged. The themes of family safety and self-reliance emerge as central to this book and to the whole series. Complete but easy-to-understand descriptions of building a smokehouse and slaughtering a pig make it clear that even children knew the basics of preparation for winter. This recitation of essential frontier knowledge became one of the most valuable and interesting aspects of Wilder's contribution to later understanding of pioneer life.

Small details deepen the sense of the cares and dangers of such a life, as well as Ma's determination to create some beauty for her family:

Ma sat in her rocking chair, sewing by the light of the lamp. The lamp was bright and shiny. There was salt in the bottom of its glass bowl with the kerosene, to keep the kerosene from exploding, and there were bits of red flannel among the salt to make it pretty. It was pretty.

Small touches which helped make life lovely are highlighted in this and all the following books.

Pa's fiddling, singing, and storytelling on winter nights establish him as the reassuring center of folklore and continuity. A spring dance celebrating syrup-making at Laura's grandparents' home, summertime cheese-making, and honey collecting round out the year's progress toward harvest and reinforce the satisfaction this family feels with their remote life in the woods. Without glossing over danger or hard work, Wilder has managed to portray frontier life appealingly, with warmth and confidence at its core.

LITTLE HOUSE ON THE PRAIRIE

First published: 1935
Type of work: Novel

The Ingalls family moves from Wisconsin to Indian Territory, settles on a claim, encounters Indians, and decides to move on when they believe the government will expel settlers.

As the second book of the series begins, Ma reluctantly agrees to leave the sheltering woods and house for the frontier. The family is to cross the Mississippi River in the cold, early spring, before the ice breaks. Despite her reservations, she nurtures her girls. "In firelight and candlelight she washed and combed them and dressed them warmly" for the trip. Family as the heart and source of security continues to anchor the story to come. After their wagon nearly capsizes crossing a stream, and their dog Jack is feared drowned, the isolation and vastness of the prairie emerges in stark contrast to the last safe morning at home. "Not even the faintest trace of wheels or tracks could be seen. That prairie looked as if no human eye had ever seen it before. Only the tall wild grass covered the endless empty land and a great empty sky arched over it."

Chronologically, the prairie adventure covers a year, this time from spring to spring. However, the narrative relates far more strenuous activities, focusing on rudimentary survival. For the first five chapters, the Ingallses trek cross-country by wagon, camping. They live in a tent home while Pa builds their log house literally from the ground up. Before the house has a solid door or windows, a wolf pack surrounds the family on a full-moon night and howls and snuffles against the cabin walls until dawn. Pa digs a well so the family does not have to haul water from the creek.

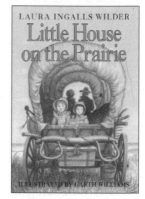

In this book a neighbor joins the family circle, even walking into town in dangerous weather to make sure the girls have presents from Santa on their first prairie Christmas. Several episodes focus on encounters with Indians, whom Ma finds terrifying, Pa respects for their ability to live on the prairie, and Laura endlessly wonders about. The nearby Osage extend peaceful forbearance toward white settlers but appear and take whatever food and tobacco they can find from the Ingalls house several times when Pa is gone.

The prairie holds other terrors. The family barely survives malaria, called "fever 'n' ague." A scream in the night proves to be a panther Pa barely escapes as he searches for the terrified "woman" they thought they heard. As spring approaches, the Indians have what Pa calls a jamboree with a full week of drumming, dancing, and "chopping with their voices." After sleepless nights for the Ingallses, the Indians disperse.

Following the jamboree, a prairie fire threatens the Ingalls home, and watching the last peaceful band of Osages file grimly out of sight leaves the family depressed and listless. The complicated mix of distrust, fear, and respect for Indians recurs throughout this book with no real answer as to the morality of white settlers usurping Indian land.

Finally, the disheartening rumor that soldiers may put the settlers off Indian land prompts Charles to load his family in the wagon again and head toward another new beginning. Laura still has hope. "They were all together, safe and comfortable under the starlit sky." Pa's strength, combined with Ma's steadfastness, provides the central force that propels the family into their future. Laura remains its heart.

THESE HAPPY GOLDEN YEARS

First published: 1943
Type of work: Novel

The book chronicles family life and Laura's teaching career in three schools beginning in 1882 and culminates with her marrying Almanzo Wilder in 1885.

This book in the series chronicles Laura's coming-of-age. She leaves her family to teach in a nearby settlement town, a dismal place with three claim shanties and only five students. The central motif for this book is Almanzo Wilder's courtship of Laura, which begins immediately. Her first week of teaching goes well, but squalid lodgings in an unhappy home depress her. Almanzo prevents a wretched weekend by coming for her with his team and cutter. Throughout the novel, Almanzo and Laura ride out together. Their courtship jaunts have ups and downs and some wild rides behind

unbroken colts, but they culminate in an engagement.

Laura teaches to help her family financially and proudly adds her first two salaries to the family coffer. Her third salary she divides, using part of it for fabric to sew the bed linens and clothes she needs as a new bride; the other is her final contribution to Ma and Pa. Her earnings help pay Mary's expenses at a college for the blind and buy an organ for Mary to play when she returns home.

This book completes several series themes. Frontier isolation is reduced. The growing town of De Smet seems full of strangers and population shifts. The Ingalls family remains rooted there; within a year the homestead claim will be theirs for good. Laura works outside her home to support the family. Most strikingly, she leaves her childhood home, beginning her own circle with Almanzo. The final volume mentions events from earlier times, incorporating the past, and continues Laura's compelling descriptions of landscape and sky which help explain the endless seduction of western lands despite the fact that, "everything changes."

SUMMARY

Wilder's works gave Americans firsthand knowledge of frontier family life following the Homestead Act of 1862. The Little House series covers the years 1873-1885, presenting daily life in a contented pioneer family through a fictionalized Laura Ingalls's eyes. Wilder captures the essence of the lure of the West, the overwhelming difficulty of routine work necessary for homesteaders to thrive, the deep strength of a committed family core, the dangers and unpredictability of wild places and weather, and her boundless love of the land. Her work draws on American pastoral traditions and the habit of plain speaking. She eloquently expresses the paradox of America's wild Eden which needs taming but is the source of restorative natural power, figuring forth its allure and the demands it made on pioneer sojourners.

Karen L. Arnold

BIBLIOGRAPHY

By the Author

CHILDREN'S LITERATURE:
Little House in the Big Woods, 1932
Farmer Boy, 1933
Little House on the Prairie, 1935
On the Banks of Plum Creek, 1937
By the Shores of Silver Lake, 1939
The Long Winter, 1940
Little Town on the Prairie, 1941

These Happy Golden Years, 1943
The First Four Years, 1971

NONFICTION:

On the Way Home: The Diary of a Trip from South Dakota to Mansfield, Missouri, in 1894, 1962

West from Home: Letters of Laura Ingalls Wilder, San Francisco, 1915, 1974

A Little House Sampler, 1988 (with Rose Wilder Lane)

Little House in the Ozarks: The Rediscovered Writings, 1991

Laura Ingalls Wilder: A Family Collection, 1993

About the Author

Anderson, William. "The Literary Apprenticeship of Laura Ingalls Wilder." *South Dakota History* 13 (Winter, 1983): 285-331.

Erisman, Fred. *Laura Ingalls Wilder.* Boise, Idaho: Boise State University Press, 1994.

Mac Bride, Roger Lea. *New Dawn on Rocky Ridge.* Illustrated by David Gilleece. New York: HarperCollins, 1997.

Spaeth, Janet. *Laura Ingalls Wilder.* Boston: Twayne, 1987.

Walner, Alexandra. *Laura Ingalls Wilder.* New York: Holiday House, 1997.

DISCUSSION TOPICS

- Laura Ingalls Wilder shows that life on the frontier demanded stamina and courage in the face of harsh weather, hard work, and isolation. What do the Ingallses do to keep their spirits up?

- How important was neighborliness to pioneer families? How was it defined?

- Laura and Mary show different attitudes toward pioneer life. How does each girl's personality equip her to succeed? Which one seems more likely to succeed? Why?

- What attitudes toward American Indians are expressed by members of the Ingalls family?

- Define a good citizen on the frontier. Are such qualities important today? Why?

- Discuss the difficulty of acquiring an education in early frontier settlements.

THORNTON WILDER

Born: Madison, Wisconsin
April 17, 1897
Died: Hamden, Connecticut
December 7, 1975

Considered one of America's most important, versatile, and innovative writers, Wilder wrote plays that rank him as one of America's top dramatists.

Thornton Wilder Society

BIOGRAPHY

Thornton Niven Wilder was born in Madison, Wisconsin, on April 17, 1897. He was a surviving twin, and all of his life he searched for the alter ego lost at birth. He had an older brother by two years, Amos Niven, a well-known theologian, professor, and writer. He also had three sisters: Charlotte, born in 1898; Isabel, born in 1900, a writer who devoted her life as confidant and secretary to Thornton; and Janet, born in 1910.

Thornton was named for his mother, the talented Isabella Thornton Niven, daughter of a Presbyterian minister; his brother Amos was named for their father, Amos Parker Wilder. Their father, a handsome, robust individual, held a doctorate in political science and was editor of the *Wisconsin State Journal*. He was a strict Congregationalist whose moral rectitude and constant career moves placed hardships on his wife and family. These served as important influences on Wilder, infusing him with a sense of unworthiness that haunted him all of his life.

Amos Parker Wilder was an uncompromising man whose strong editorial opinions clashed with those of Wisconsin's powerful senator, Robert M. La Follette. By 1906, Amos believed it was time to leave the state and accepted the appointment of American consul in Hong Kong. After living there six months, Isabella and Amos agreed to a temporary separation. She returned to the United States with the children, to live in Berkeley, California. Over the following eight years, Thornton attended various schools as he moved back and forth across the Pacific Ocean, finally completing his high school education at Berkeley High School in 1915. Amos forced Thornton to attend Oberlin College for two years and then transferred him to Yale University, his own alma mater.

Wilder began his writing career in college. Several of his pieces appeared in the *Oberlin Literary Magazine* and the *Yale Literary Magazine*. After he graduated from Yale in 1920, he traveled to Rome and attended the American Academy, where he worked on his first novel, "The Memoirs of a Roman Student." Thornton returned to the States to teach French at Lawrenceville Academy during the early 1920's. He also attended Princeton University and graduated with an M.A. degree in 1926.

The same year, Thornton saw the publication of his novel, now retitled *The Cabala*. In 1927, his first play, *The Trumpet Shall Sound*, was produced. Both creative efforts met with an indifferent reception. Not so his second novel, *The Bridge of San Luis Rey* (1927), which was an immediate success and won for him his first Pulitzer Prize. A number of one-act plays, written over a twelve-year period, were published in 1928 under the title *The Angel That Troubled the Waters, and Other Plays*. The sixteen brief plays offer a fascinating glimpse into Wilder's outlook on philosophy, literature, and history, and

2725

into his concept of theatricality that found mature expression in his later works.

The 1930's was a very busy decade for Wilder. In 1930, he wrote a novel, *The Woman of Andros*, based on Roman playwright Terence's *Andria* (166 B.C.E.; English translation, 1598). In 1931 he published *The Long Christmas Dinner, and Other Plays in One Act*, continuing his experiments in nontraditional theater. He adapted two works for the stage—André Obey's *Le Viol de Lucrèce* (called *Lucrece*) in 1932 and Henrik Ibsen's *A Doll's House* in 1937—as showcases for actresses Katherine and Ruth Gordon, respectively. He also found time to teach one semester each year from 1930 to 1936 at the University of Chicago and to publish the novel *Heaven's My Destination* in late 1934, a work hailed by Gertrude Stein as the quintessential American novel.

Stein's praise of Wilder initiated a correspondence between them that ripened into friendship. Her positive influence on Wilder's further writings is inestimable. Wilder tired of his teaching responsibilities and in 1936 resigned his position at the University of Chicago. He was then free to concentrate on writing, traveling, and visiting with friends. Two years later, he wrote the Pulitzer Prize-winning *Our Town*, arguably the United States' favorite, most-produced, and most-read play. The production opened to indifferent reviews but soon won over the public.

In 1938, Wilder opened another Broadway production, titled *The Merchant of Yonkers*, based on Johann Nestroy's *Einen Jux will er sich machen* (1842). Not an immediate hit, it was revised and retitled *The Matchmaker* in 1954. The play enjoyed successful revivals in London, Edinburgh, and New York. Later, the work was revised again and became the hit musical comedy *Hello Dolly!* The original Broadway production ran for only thirty-nine performances, compared with 486 for the 1955 New York production of *The Matchmaker* and almost three thousand for *Hello, Dolly!*

During World War II, Captain Wilder (later Lieutenant Colonel Wilder) of the Intelligence Corps of the United States Army Air Corps opened his play *The Skin of Our Teeth* in 1942, despite misgivings by some of the people involved in the production because of the play's surreal structure. The public loved it, however, and the comedy earned for Wilder his third and final Pulitzer Prize. In 1947, he wrote a short dramatic burlesque called

Our Century, which had limited distribution, followed by a novel based on the last days of Julius Caesar titled *The Ides of March* (1948), widely praised abroad but not in the United States.

During the last years of his life, Wilder received numerous awards, including the 1963 United States Presidential Medal of Freedom and the 1965 National Medal of Literature. He wrote two more novels, *The Eighth Day* (1967), a much-praised work that he believed was a disappointment, even though it earned the National Book Award, and his final fiction, *Theophilus North*, published in 1973, a novel more admired by his devoted readers than by critics. Two years later, on December 7, 1975, he died, suffering from the ravages of old age and a debilitating stroke that had partially blinded him.

ANALYSIS

Wilder achieved a successful career as a writer of both fiction and drama. His success is especially remarkable given his small literary output over the five decades that he wrote. In theater, for example, he is considered one of America's best playwrights, yet his fame rests squarely on three full-length plays and a handful of shorter ones. He wrote seven novels and received numerous awards, including a Pulitzer Prize in fiction. Wilder achieved national success and celebrity status with his second novel, at age thirty, *The Bridge of San Luis Rey*; he remained in the public eye during the rest of his literary career, although he wrote only five more novels during the last forty years of his life.

Wilder was heavily influenced at the beginning of his career by the nonrealistic movement of the 1920's that was quite popular abroad. Unlike the American writers Theodore Dreiser, Sinclair Lewis, and Eugene O'Neill, who were championed by such influential critics as H. L. Mencken and Edmund Wilson, Wilder found himself alone in his search for a new humanism that affirmed the dignity of humankind.

In his first novel, *The Cabala*, published in 1926, Wilder introduced a theme that recurred in his later work: the possibility that an American could travel abroad, partake of the cultural experiences that Europe had to offer, and return enriched but not overwhelmed. Wilder believed that America could benefit from the Old World but was still the land of golden opportunity. This concept ran counter to the thinking of the so-called lost generation of writers, who could not reconcile themselves to their homeland. Wilder was able to fuse the humanistic spirit of the past with the temper of the present.

In his work, Wilder explored moral and religious themes and tried to capture the complex chemistry of human life. He believed in the absolute mystery of life, the workings of which defy rational explanations. Wilder also believed in a higher power of love that did not simply spring from sexual desire. For Wilder, love was an indispensable part of life and a moral responsibility. One of the characters in *The Bridge of San Luis Rey*, who could be commenting on Wilder's work, observes:

> But soon we shall die . . . and we ourselves shall be loved for a while and forgotten. But the love will have been enough; all those impulses of love return to the love that made them. Even memory is not necessary for love. There is a land of the living and a land of the dead and the bridge of love, the only survival, the only meaning.

The eternal optimist, Wilder firmly believed that the human race, despite its ignorance, cruelty, self-destructive nature, and subjection to natural disasters, will always manage to survive.

Wilder's deep philosophical beliefs, along with the quiet encouragement of his friend Gertrude Stein, propelled him on a quest for the universal and the eternal. Perhaps that is why he often turned to the theater. In his preface to a collection of plays published in 1957, he wrote: "The novel is pre-eminently the vehicle of the unique occasion, the theater of the generalized one." His convictions found their deepest expression in the theater, where he could stretch the boundaries of convention. He made it clear that the small, ordinary events of daily life can take on a great significance. This concept runs through most of his early plays, but *Our Town* elevates it to the highest level. Wilder stresses that humans fail to understand and appreciate the priceless value of everyday events, wasting their lives by not valuing every moment of them.

What is remarkable about Wilder's work is the innovative spirit that animates it. From the first, Wilder tried to explore unique ways of presenting his ideas. In his early collection, *The Angel That Troubled the Waters, and Other Plays*, and in his 1931 *The Long Christmas Dinner, and Other Plays in One Act*, for example, Wilder was already experimenting with the conventions of theatricality, experimentation that found its artistic fulfillment in the Pulitzer Prize-winners *Our Town* and *The Skin of Our Teeth*. Both acclaimed and condemned for his nonrealistic approach, Wilder remained absolutely unapologetic. He stated, "I became dissatisfied with the theater because I was unable to lend credence to such childish attempts to be 'real.'"

Wilder's literary life was fairly serene. He cultivated a large and adoring public but on two occasions came under vicious attack. He was accused in 1942 of plagiarizing *The Skin of Our Teeth* from Irish writer James Joyce's *Finnegans Wake* (1939); it became an unpleasant affair that lasted for months.

The first and perhaps most damaging incident, however, temporarily dimming his national reputation, occurred in 1930 when Michael Gold, a Communist journalist and writer, excoriated the rising young writer. In an article in *The New Republic* titled "Wilder: Prophet of the Genteel Christ," he attacked Wilder for his "new humanism" principles (emphasizing classical restraint associated with the ancient Greek tradition) at a time when the United States had plunged into the Depression.

Examining Wilder's work to date, Gold criticized *The Bridge of San Luis Rey* as a "daydream of homosexual figures in graceful gowns moving archaically among the lilies." (Wilder was a confirmed homosexual, although he never had a long-term sexual relationship in his life.) Gold then switched his attack to Wilder himself, derisively calling him "this Emily Post of culture . . . always in perfect taste." Gold taunted Wilder about writing a book to "reveal all his fundamental silliness and superficiality." Angered and hurt by the criticism, Wilder rose to the challenge, and his reputation and credibility returned slowly.

Wilder's work remains eminently readable today. He enjoyed writing novels and plays and always cherished a deep love of humanity. Perhaps Chrysis, one of the characters in his novel *The Woman of Andros*, said it best: "Remember some day, remember me as one who loved all things and accepted from the gods all things, the bright and the dark. And do you likewise. Farewell."

THE BRIDGE OF SAN LUIS REY

First published: 1927
Type of work: Novel

Five strangers plunge to their deaths on a rope bridge near Lima, Peru, and their lives are reexamined by a Catholic priest who witnessed the tragedy.

Wilder's second novel, *The Bridge of San Luis Rey*, published in November, 1927, rocketed the modest author to celebrity status. Its extraordinary public reception and favorable reviews caught Wilder by surprise. Critics hailed it as a "work of genius," a "little masterpiece" with a "deceptive clarity of style that marks pellucid depths." The novel was viewed as a breath of fresh air as opposed to the downbeat realistic works of Upton Sinclair and Theodore Dreiser. Wilder was awarded the Pulitzer Prize on May 7, 1928. In 1929, and again in 1944, the novel was adapted on film, but both were disappointing ventures.

Wilder's writing was influenced by two important factors. First was the historical figure of Camila Perichole. A famous actress in late eighteenth century Lima, Peru, she had played the central character in Prosper Merimee's play *La Carosse du Saint-Sacrament* (1829), dazzling audiences with her performances. She became the mistress of the viceroy and donated his gifts to the Church to help the poor and dying. In *The Bridge of San Luis Rey*, Camila is a pivotal character who appears in all three main stories, coming in contact with every important character. The second influence concerned a real rope bridge that had been built in Peru in 1350, which collapsed centuries later, plunging people to their death.

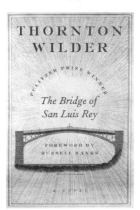

The Bridge of San Luis Rey is set in early eighteenth century Peru. The novel opens simply: "On Friday noon, July the twentieth, 1714, the finest bridge in all Peru broke and precipitated five travellers into the gulf below." The tragic accident is witnessed by Brother Juniper, a rational theologian, who attempts to piece together the story of the victims—why they were at the bridge at the same time and whether it was an accident or God's will. The victims include a young boy, an adolescent, a young man, a middle-aged man, and an old noblewoman.

The Bridge of San Luis Rey is divided into five sections, with the shorter opening and closing chapters serving as a framing device. The first major story involves the old, ugly Marquesa de Montemayor, her grief-ridden relationship with her unloving daughter, and the devoted servant Pepita. The middle tale concerns two inseparable twins, named Manuel and Esteban, who share a telepathic closeness. They suffer an estrangement when Manuel falls in love with the actress Camila; he later dies from blood poisoning. The final story is the love-hate relationship of Uncle Pio and Camila, his protégé, whom he has tutored to be Peru's finest actress. Wilder shows that all five sufferers were victimized in life not only by the falling bridge but also by loving someone who could not or would not love them in return. All five realize their folly at the end and set out to start their lives in new directions.

After telling his tale of the five doomed travelers, Wilder focuses on the survivors, those whose unrequited loves are not destroyed by falling bridges. He makes the final point that they have lost individuals very precious to them and yet have gained something in return, the bridge of love drawing together the living and the dead.

Wilder raises many questions about why these people were killed, including whether it was simply an accident, whether they were responsible for their own lives, or whether they were part of some divine plan and were doomed to die together. He does not answer any one question but suggests that it may have been a combination of all four, reaffirming his central belief that life's mysteries cannot be divined. Wilder ends the book with Brother Juniper, after years of research, attempting to publish his findings; the work, however, is declared heretical, and he and his research are burned by the Inquisition.

Wilder's Christian humanism is clearly evident in *The Bridge of San Luis Rey*. The concepts of wastefulness, sinfulness, and the failure to appreciate one's life—recurring themes in later works, particularly *Our Town*—are presented here forcefully and without sentimentality. The author's straightforward prose style, combined with an intriguing plot structure and compelling central characters, makes it Wilder's most successful fiction and his most widely read novel.

OUR TOWN

First produced: 1938 (first published, 1938)
Type of work: Play

Life, love, and death are seen through the lives of residents of a small New Hampshire town in early twentieth century America.

In the drama *Our Town*, Wilder would find the fullest expression of his humanistic convictions, pouring all of his genius into it. The play, which opened on Broadway on February 4, 1938, reaffirmed his deep-seated belief that eternal human truths can be observed in American life. Today, the play is regarded as an American classic. It was a different matter, however, in the beginning.

The play had a rocky out-of-town reception by the critics before opening in New York City, but thanks to the strong support of doyen Brooks Atkinson, it caught on with the public and ran for 336 performances. It was made into a film in 1940, which, despite a serious change in plot structure, was almost as popular as the stage presentation. Even though denied the prestigious New York Drama Critics Circle Award, the play did garner a second Pulitzer Prize for Wilder.

Wilder believed that he could achieve in drama what he failed to do in the novel. He opens *Our Town* simply: "No curtain. No scenery." He soon introduces the people of Grover's Corner, New Hampshire, on specific days during the period from 1901 to 1913. The almost nonexistent plot revolves around two neighboring households—the Webbs and the Gibbses. Both families, eventually united by marriage, are unremarkable, and nothing very special happens to them or the other characters.

What makes *Our Town* unique is the character of the Stage Manager, who narrates the play, a technique Wilder had previously used in his one-act play *The Happy Journey to Trenton and Camden* (1931). Wilder's innovative use of this device sets him apart from contemporary dramatists; the device draws its strength and roots from the chorus concept employed by William Shakespeare and earlier by the Greeks. The character is not only a stage manager and narrator but also a philosopher, druggist, Congregational minister, and wise seer. He represents a distillation of all of Wilder's wisdom, a fact not lost on the playwright, as he often played the role himself in various stage productions.

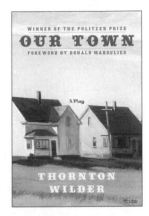

The Stage Manager embodies the spirit of the town by introducing a large number of characters and presenting the scenes chronologically to demonstrate his basic themes. Act 1 is called "Daily Life" and gives a glimpse of the people living in Grover's Corner and the two families. In act 2, titled "Love and Marriage," it is three years later. The eldest child of each household—Emily Webb and George Gibbs—are married. The events leading to that happy occasion, including their first date and declaration of love, are dramatized. The act concludes with the wedding ceremony.

Act 3 occurs nine years later and is called "Death." It is set in the town's cemetery, with dead townspeople sitting in chairs. Emily Webb Gibbs has died in childbirth, and she soon joins the others. Here Wilder cleverly brings past and present together by having Emily go back to Grover's Corner one more time to relive her twelfth birthday with her family. She quickly realizes that it is a mistake to be back among the living and cries out: "It goes so fast. We don't have time to look at one another." Wilder presses the point by having her also ask, "Do any human beings ever realize life while they live it?" The Stage Manager replies: "No. The saints and poets, maybe—they do some."

In *Our Town*, Wilder points out the precious gift of life and the value of even the most common and everyday events. Unaware of this, the people of Grover's Corner seldom scratch beyond the surface of their lives, the banal and the beautiful.

Artistically, Wilder manages to make his point by

taking the ordinary events and making them price-less. By focusing on growing up, love, marriage, and death and providing a running commentary via the Stage Manager on each phase, Wilder portrays life as trivial and absurd as well as significant and noble.

With *Our Town*, Wilder taps into a mythic vision of America and presents his characters, foibles and all, with love. He presents an ideal America that believes in the dignity of the human spirit. The playwright captures the essence of human nature, dramatizing the spirit of the eternal residing in the collective human psyche.

THE SKIN OF OUR TEETH

First produced: 1942 (first published, 1942)
Type of work: Play

This humorous and allegorical work looks at the survival of the family unit as it evolved during the prehistoric, biblical, and modern eras.

Wilder's last great play was *The Skin of Our Teeth*, which opened on Broadway on November 18, 1942. The play, with its allegorical mixture of contemporary and biblical events, confused some of the critics but proved delightful to audiences and ran for 355 performances. The play has been revived frequently and in 1961 was given an international tour by the U.S. State Department with Helen Hayes and Mary Martin in the leading roles.

What Wilder dramatizes in *The Skin of Our Teeth* is the struggle of humankind to survive, a conceit much appreciated by wartime audiences. Again the author focuses on the family unit to make his point—in this case, the Antrobus (*anthropos* meaning story of humans) family living in Excelsior, New Jersey. The play does not have a continuous action. Although the settings are contemporary, each act is structured around a historic catastrophe: the Ice Age, the Flood, and modern war. Respectively, humans must pit themselves against nature, the moral order, and, finally, themselves. Wilder's play can also be seen as units of time: geologic, biblical, and recorded.

Wilder's characters in *The Skin of Our Teeth* are all allegorical figures and exist on three planes: Amer-ican, biblical, and universal. Mr. and Mrs. Antrobus are the simultaneous embodiment of Adam and Eve, Everyman and Everywoman, and an average American couple. Mr. Antrobus has created the wheel, the alphabet, and the lever; his spouse has contributed the apron. They keep as pets a dinosaur and mammoth. Their motto is Save the Family. Daughter Gladys becomes increasingly slut-tish and by play's end has an illegitimate baby. Son Henry (his name had been Cain but it was changed) accidentally kills his brother and now combs his hair to hide the mark on his forehead. In opposition to the Antrobus family is Lily Sabina (combination of Lilith and the Sabine women), who moves in and out of their lives in a variety of roles including that of a servant, a beauty contestant, and a Jezebel out to snare Mr. Antrobus.

As he did in *Our Town*, Wilder is able to employ in *The Skin of Our Teeth* a nontraditional, theatrical approach. By this device, the playwright draws the audience directly to the characters as individuals, at the same time making them function as representatives of the human race. To achieve this effect, Wilder has the characters drop their characterizations from time to time and reveal the performers hired to play the roles. He is thus able to present various personalities within each character.

The Skin of Our Teeth generally received favorable reviews, particularly for the acting of Tallulah Bankhead, who played Sabina. Unfortunately, the play also plunged Wilder into an unpleasant controversy. Three months after the play opened, Joseph Campbell and Henry M. Robinson wrote "The Skin of Whose Teeth?" in *The Saturday Review of Literature*, charging in the article that Wilder had borrowed the theme and technique of his play from James Joyce's *Finnegans Wake*, thus accusing him of plagiarism. Many writers and critics came to Wilder's defense, and *Time* magazine, while not liking the play, asserted the attackers were "trying to make headlines out of what should have been footnotes." Wilder said nothing at the time, but in the 1957 edition of *Three Plays*, he admitted in the preface that he owed a debt to Joyce and slyly noted that he hoped "some author should feel similarly indebted to any work of mine."

As in other works, Wilder demonstrates an appreciative view of life in *The Skin of Our Teeth*. He shows how the human race can survive disasters, both natural and human-made. It is Wilder's humanity ending in faith that suffuses the entire play. Again, Wilder concentrates on the family, an emphasis technique found in his plays but not his other work. He skillfully juggles the serious and comic elements, telescopes time, and conveys his philosophic and poetic ideas. Wilder presents truth through the use of artifice and theatricality.

THEOPHILUS NORTH

First published: 1973
Type of work: Novel

A meddling good-hearted stranger comes to Newport, Rhode Island, in the 1920's and proceeds to change the lives of all the people he meets.

Theophilus North, which was published in October, 1973, turned out to be Wilder's last novel published while he was still alive. Wilder's publishers, knowing their market, took out a full-page ad promoting the novel in *The New York Times,* an honor most authors never realize. The publicity did its job, and the novel received very favorable comments from the critics. *Theophilus North* was a huge success with Wilder's adoring public. The book remained on the best-seller list for twenty-one weeks. It is a nostalgic piece with many autobiographical elements.

Wilder's brother, Amos, in his critical study *Thornton Wilder and His Public* (1980), believed that the author was haunted throughout his life by his missing twin, his alter ego. Amos suggested that "North" represented an anagram for Thornton, and "in this way he was able to tease both himself and the reader as to the borderlands between autobiography and fable." *Theophilus North* is labeled a novel but is really a collection of short stories held together by a narrator who willingly participates in all the events he describes. Wilder labeled the book fictionalized memoirs, an autobiography, and a novel. The central character did indeed have similar experiences to those of Wilder, but the author reshaped the material so much that the work should be viewed as a series of tales in the tradition of works by Lucius Apuleius, Geoffrey Chaucer, or Giovanni Boccaccio.

Early in the book, the reader is told by Theophilus North that he had many ambitions in life. He proceeds to enumerate them in the following order: saint, anthropologist, archaeologist, detective, actor, magician, lover, and a free man. The narrator is quick to point out that he never wanted to be in business or politics. A few pages later, North describes Newport, Rhode Island, as if he were the archaeologist Heinrich Schliemann commenting on the fabled Troy's nine cities piled on top of one another. Each of North's "cities," beginning with the first seventeenth century village, becomes increasingly complex until he reaches the eighth level, full "of camp-followers and parasites—prying journalists, detectives, fortune-hunters . . . wonderful material for my Journal."

The narrator's series of adventures varies according to his involvements. He comes to Newport in 1926 to teach tennis to children, give language instruction, and read classical literature to older people. North is quickly drawn into the social life of the very rich because he is a Yale University man and a Christian. In short order, he thwarts an elopement between an heiress and a divorced athletic instructor, removes the taint of ghosts from a beautiful haunted mansion, brings back to health a retired diplomat being manipulated by his children, shrewdly exposes a gang of counterfeiters, and fathers a child for a married woman whose husband is sterile. Both praised and despised, North becomes a manipulator for good in people's lives.

Wilder makes it clear that Theophilus North is a liberating influence who can mend broken marriages and inspire men and women to achieve their most secret desires. North never changes despite his myriad experiences, the numerous people he has helped, and the beautiful woman with whom he is intimate. He is a superior creature with no apparent flaws. He remains to the end an idealized boy scout who proves that good can overcome evil.

Theophilus North would be Wilder's last happy affirmation of life. He created a character who enjoyed life to the fullest and, in some ways, honestly reflected the author's views of life. To the end of his literary career, Wilder was still concerned about injustice, the achievement of the human spirit, and the positive values of humanistic belief in individual responsibility.

SUMMARY

Wilder remains one of America's most beloved novelists, dramatists, and persons of letters. His books and plays are widely read and staged, continuing to give enjoyment and intellectual stimulation. Wilder was the first author to win Pulitzer Prizes in both fiction and drama. His work includes both a large dose of human suffering and the belief that life is a miraculous gift to be cherished. Wilder was a mature humanist who reaffirmed the dignity of the individual and the uniqueness of American democracy. His classic work *Our Town* has been performed many thousands of times since its premiere in 1938.

Terry Theodore

DISCUSSION TOPICS

- What is the symbolic import of the bridge in *The Bridge of San Luis Rey*?

- In what ways does the Stage Manager of *Our Town* resemble the traditional dramatic device of the chorus?

- How does Thornton Wilder avoid sentimentality in *Our Town*?

- Wilder does not make many overt classical allusions in his writing, but in fact he was steeped in the Greek and Roman classics. How does this background reveal itself in his works?

- *The Skin of Our Teeth* was first produced in 1942. In what ways is it both a timely and a timeless play?

- Is the title character of *Theophilus North* a plausible human being, or is he to be considered primarily a literary device?

BIBLIOGRAPHY

By the Author

LONG FICTION:
The Cabala, 1926
The Bridge of San Luis Rey, 1927
The Woman of Andros, 1930
Heaven's My Destination, 1934
The Ides of March, 1948
The Eighth Day, 1967
Theophilus North, 1973

DRAMA:
The Trumpet Shall Sound, pb. 1920, pr. 1927
The Angel That Troubled the Waters, and Other Plays, pb. 1928 (includes 16 plays)
The Happy Journey to Trenton and Camden, pr., pb. 1931 (one act)
The Long Christmas Dinner, pr., pb. 1931 (one act; as libretto in German, 1961; translation and music by Paul Hindemith)
The Long Christmas Dinner, and Other Plays in One Act, pb. 1931 (includes *Queens of France, Pullman Car Hiawatha, Love and How to Cure It, Such Things Only Happen in Books*, and *The Happy Journey to Trenton and Camden*)
Lucrece, pr. 1932, pb. 1933 (adaptation of André Obey's *Le Viol de Lucrèce*)
A Doll's House, pr. 1937 (adaptation of Henrik Ibsen's play)
The Merchant of Yonkers, pr. 1938, pb. 1939 (adaptation of Johann Nestroy's *Einen Jux will er sich machen*)
Our Town, pr., pb. 1938
The Skin of Our Teeth, pr., pb. 1942
Our Century, pr., pb. 1947
The Matchmaker, pr. 1954, pb. 1956 (revision of *The Merchant of Yonkers*)
A Life in the Sun, pr. 1955, pb. 1960 (in German), pb. 1977 (in English; commonly known as *The Alcestiad*; act 4 pb. as *The Drunken Sisters*)
Plays for Bleecker Street, pr. 1962 (3 one-acts: *Someone from Assisi; Infancy*, pb. 1961; and *Childhood*, pb. 1960)
The Collected Short Plays of Thornton Wilder, pb. 1997-1998 (2 volumes)

SCREENPLAYS:
Our Town, 1940 (with Frank Craven and Harry Chantlee)
Shadow of a Doubt, 1943 (with Sally Benson and Alma Revelle)

NONFICTION:
The Intent of the Artist, 1941
American Characteristics, and Other Essays, 1979
The Journals of Thornton Wilder, 1939-1961, 1985

TRANSLATION:
The Victors, 1948 (of Jean-Paul Sartre's play *Morts sans sépulture*)

About the Author

Blank, Martin, ed. *Critical Essays on Thornton Wilder.* New York: G. K. Hall, 1996.

Blank, Martin, Dalma Hunyadi Brunauer, and David Garrett Izzo, eds. *Thornton Wilder: New Essays.* West Cornwall, Conn.: Locust Hill Press, 1999.

Bloom, Harold, ed. *Thornton Wilder.* Philadelphia: Chelsea House, 2003.

Burbank, Rex J. *Thornton Wilder.* 2d ed. Boston: Twayne, 1978.

Castronovo, David. *Thornton Wilder.* New York: Ungar, 1986.

Goldstein, Malcolm. *The Art of Thornton Wilder.* Lincoln: University of Nebraska Press, 1965.

Goldstone, Richard H. *Thornton Wilder: An Intimate Portrait.* New York: Saturday Review Press, 1975.

Harrison, Gilbert A. *The Enthusiast: A Life of Thornton Wilder.* New York: Ticknor and Fields, 1983.

Lifton, Paul. *"Vast Encyclopedia": The Theatre of Thornton Wilder.* Westport, Conn.: Greenwood Press, 1995.

Simon, Linda. *Thornton Wilder: His World.* Garden City, N.Y.: Doubleday, 1979.

Walsh, Claudette. *Thornton Wilder: A Reference Guide, 1926-1990.* New York: G. K. Hall, 1993.

Wilder, Amos Niven. *Thornton Wilder and His Public.* Philadelphia: Fortress Press, 1980.

TENNESSEE WILLIAMS

Born: Columbus, Mississippi
March 26, 1911
Died: New York, New York
February 25, 1983

One of the United States' major dramatists, Williams, also a poet and writer of short stories, is considered the poet of the American theater; he is to drama what William Faulkner is to the American novel.

Sam Shaw/Courtesy, New Directions Publishing

BIOGRAPHY

Thomas Lanier Williams, known as Tom during his boyhood and later as Tennessee, was born in his maternal grandparents' home, an Episcopalian rectory in Columbus, Mississippi, on March 26, 1911, to Edwina Dakin and Cornelius Coffin Williams. His mother came from a prominent old Mississippi family and his father from an equally prominent old Tennessee family with a proud military and patriotic background. Williams was immediately thrust into a conflict between the genteel Puritanism of his mother and the cavalier lifestyle of his father.

From his father's origins, he was given his nickname, and he chose to use it for the rest of his life. Because of his father's continual absence from home during Williams's boyhood, he developed an unusual closeness to both mother and sister and a distance from, and sometimes hostility toward, his father. His escape from his family was, ironically, similar to that of his father, even though it was a result of the classical conflict between the restrictions of the conventionally polite southern upbringing and the necessary freedom of the artistic life.

His boyhood experiences included many happy hours of reading spent in the library of his maternal grandfather, with whom Williams maintained a close relationship until his grandfather's death in his nineties. Williams had strong support, as well, from his maternal grandmother, who would send him money from time to time.

Few dramatists write so autobiographically as did Williams in *The Glass Menagerie* (1944). Williams based the character of Amanda Wingfield on his mother. Her husband, a shadowy but important character who does not appear in the play (except for his picture hanging on the wall), is referred to as having run away as a result of a love affair with long-distance telephone wires.

Williams's father once worked briefly for a telephone company before becoming a traveling salesman for the International Shoe Company. The fragile, introverted character of Laura Wingfield is drawn from his sister, Rose, the victim of a cruel prefrontal lobotomy, an event that left its psychological mark on her brother.

Tom Wingfield, like the real-life Tom, leaves home, but wherever he travels for the rest of his life, he is haunted by the memory of Laura. Finally, there is the shabby St. Louis apartment in which the Wingfields live, like the progressively downscaled residences of the Williams family as their financial condition declined. Considered by many Williams's best play, *The Glass Menagerie* is one of the three most famous plays about the American family. The other two are Eugene O'Neill's *Long Day's Journey into Night* (1956) and Arthur Miller's *Death of a Salesman* (1949), the Catholic and Jewish versions, respectively, of Williams's Protestant family. Williams's other plays, although not so closely autobiographical, also draw on his experiences and, for all their theatricality, have the ring of authenticity.

Williams's nomadic life began during his university years. Having won literary prizes at the University of Missouri and then having been withdrawn from the university by his father for failing a Reserve Officers Training Corps course, he worked as a shoe company stock clerk for three years. Finding the work intolerably boring, he returned to university, this time enrolling at Washington University in St. Louis, where he soon found congeniality with a theater group, the Mummers. In still another move, he transferred to the famous writers' school at the University of Iowa, from which he graduated in 1937.

After his first produced play (in Memphis, 1935), a farce titled *Cairo, Shanghai, Bombay!*, Williams had two plays produced by the Mummers in St. Louis in 1936. Soon, grant money began coming in from the Group Theater, the Rockefeller Foundation, and the American Academy of Arts and Letters. Williams also received money from Hollywood in the form of a six-month contract with Metro-Goldwyn-Mayer. Among the many ironies of his life, one of the earliest is MGM's turning down of his writing, including *The Glass Menagerie*, in 1943. He continued, however, to be paid for the six months of his contract.

There is hardly a year after 1944 (when *The Glass Menagerie* opened in Chicago) in which a new play, a revised play, a play adapted from a short story, a film, or a collection of poems or short stories of Williams was not produced or published. In New York, *The Glass Menagerie*, *A Streetcar Named Desire* (1947), and *Cat on a Hot Tin Roof* (1955) won prizes such as the Drama Critics Circle Award, the Pulitzer Prize, and the Sidney Howard Memorial Award.

With the influx of success and money, Williams's nomadic life included trips to Paris and Italy and various residences in New York, Nantucket, Key West, and New Orleans. Like his boyhood, his adult life included bouts with illnesses, some of them nervous breakdowns. These were complicated by drink, barbiturates, and his rebelliously bohemian lifestyle as a homosexual in a puritanically repressed society. Late in life, Williams converted to Roman Catholicism.

In his *Memoirs* (1975), Williams reveals with graphic detail his intimate personal and professional experiences. His most enduring and serious

relationship was with Frank Merlo, whose death from cancer in the 1960's devastated Williams. Among his long-standing friendships from the theater world were those with his New York agent, Audrey Wood, and actresses Maureen Stapleton and Anna Magnani. His plays and films attracted the major acting talents of his time, among them Margaret Leighton, Vivien Leigh, Vanessa Redgrave, Geraldine Page, Katharine Hepburn, Elizabeth Ashley, Paul Newman, and Jason Robards. On stage, Laurette Taylor in *The Glass Menagerie* and the duo of Marlon Brando and Jessica Tandy in *A Streetcar Named Desire* became legends in their own time. An important part of those legends was director and personal friend Elia Kazan, who was involved in the direction of a number of Williams's plays.

The awards heaped on his three most successful dramas, however, avoided many of Williams's other plays. Consequently, disappointment and bitterness with critics took their toll on him physically and psychologically. In *Small Craft Warnings* (1972), Williams even acted in a small role, hoping thereby to prolong the play's run.

The circumstance of Williams's death is ironically trivial. On February 25, 1983, he was found in his New York apartment, choked by a plastic bottle cap, evidently in an attempt to ingest barbiturates. Despite his nomadic lifestyle, Williams had a constant need for some permanent human attachment—provided early by his maternal grandparents, his mother, and sister, and later by Merlo. All but Rose were gone at the time of his death. One is reminded of the loneliness of many of his characters and of what is one of the most famous lines in his plays, pronounced by Blanche DuBois in *A Streetcar Named Desire*, a line referring to her constant dependence on the kindness of strangers.

ANALYSIS

Among the four generally acknowledged major American dramatists—Eugene O'Neill, Tennessee Williams. Arthur Miller, and Edward Albee—Williams holds the distinction of being the poet in the theater. The same year, 1944, that *The Glass Menagerie* opened in Chicago, some of his poems were published in *Five American Poets*. Revised, some of these poems reappeared in a later volume, *In the Winter of Cities* (1956). Williams's poems contain many of the themes, images, and musical qualities that dominate the style of his plays. One of his most famous characters, Tom Wingfield, was nicknamed Shakespeare by his fellow workers in a shoe factory because, as a loner, he wrote poems rather than join in their social amenities.

Williams's most prominent and all-inclusive theme is the effect of an aggressively competitive society on sensitive characters such as Laura and Tom Wingfield (*The Glass Menagerie*), Blanche DuBois (*A Streetcar Named Desire*), Brick and Maggie Pollitt (*Cat on a Hot Tin Roof*), Alma Winemiller (*Summer and Smoke*, 1947), Catharine Holly and Sebastian Venable (*Suddenly Last Summer*, 1958), and The Reverend Shannon and Hannah Jelkes (*The Night of the Iguana*, 1961)—all social outcasts in society.

Related to the theme of the outcast is that of the poet-artist. Laura has her collection of glass animals, Tom his poetry, Blanche and Alma that extraordinary delicacy of Williams's heroines which made irreconcilable the conflict between mind and body, Sebastian his poetry, and Hannah (the daughter of a ninety-seven-year-old poet) her portrait painting. Basic to the artistic nature is the insistence on, indeed passion for, truth and an equally persistent hatred of hypocrisy. The consequence of this love-hate duality is the doomed fate of the artist, who is therefore frequently depicted in Darwinian images of fragile creatures devoured by monstrous animals in the fight for survival of the fittest.

The dominance of the strong over the weak and of the "normal" over the poetic friend finds its most recurrent expression in Williams's work in repressed, perverse, or abnormal sexual experiences, demonstrated most delicately in the life of Laura and most violently in that of Sebastian. Between these extremes are found Blanche, Brick and Maggie, Alma (a "white-blooded spinster"), and Shannon and Hannah (a strong and practical support of her nonagenarian poet-father).

The landscapes of the plays are as important as are the characters and the themes; all are inextricably bound upon one another. The world of Laura and Tom is that of the 1930's, in which the atrocities of the Spanish Civil War, suggested in a reference to what is generally regarded as the most famous painting of the twentieth century, Picasso's *Guernica*, are ignored by a United States described as a school for the matriculation of the blind. More

immediately, the Wingfield family is imprisoned in a shabby apartment described as resembling a cage (a symbol that evokes the same situation in O'Neill's 1922 play *The Hairy Ape*).

Blanche's New Orleans is dominated by the images of two streetcars, one named Desire and the other Cemeteria, with Blanche's stop on that famous streetcar ride being the Elysian Fields. The landscape inhabited by Alma Winemiller includes a statue of Eternity in a public square—wings outstretched—and the office of a doctor: the eternal pitted against the ephemeral, the idealistic or spiritual against the physical. In their separate battles for survival, Brick and Maggie, a childless couple, find themselves in a southern mansion, opposing the insensitivities of a normal family with the famous "no-neck monsters."

The most exotic of Williams's landscapes, perhaps, is the veritable hothouse of *Suddenly Last Summer*—a luxuriant, junglelike profusion of an Henri Rousseau painting, again in New Orleans—created by Sebastian's mother in order to provide her son with the necessary seclusion and atmosphere for his poetry writing. Like Blanche, Sebastian and his mother travel, but their journey takes them to the Galápagos Islands (or the Encantades, the "enchanted isles"), where Galápagos sea turtles flee from flesh-eating birds, and then to Italy, where the symbolic eating of human flesh occurs.

Williams's themes are dramatized in three major styles in *The Glass Menagerie*, *A Streetcar Named Desire*, and *Suddenly Last Summer*. These styles—poetry, theatricality, and lush symbolism—at their strongest, are found, respectively, in the realistic expressionism of *The Glass Menagerie*, the naturalistic theatricality of *A Streetcar Named Desire*, and the exotic surrealism of *Suddenly Last Summer*. Perhaps the least successful of the styles he employed is illustrated in *Small Craft Warnings*, written in the mode of Maxim Gorky's *Na dne* (1902; *The Lower Depths*, 1912) and O'Neill's *The Iceman Cometh* (1946). A gathering of a variety of social outcasts in a California oceanside bar, a means to examining a cross-section of society, becomes a pale reincarnation of characters in his earlier plays.

Attacked in the 1950's by *Time* magazine and by some critics, such as George Jean Nathan and Mary McCarthy, for his increasing violence, depravity, and vulgarity, Williams found his critical stature bolstered not only by prestigious awards but also by other critics and by scholars whose analyses have offset what seem, in retrospect, like incredibly puritanical earlier views. In 1971, Ruby Cohn wrote that although she regards Williams's plays as narrow in range and his heavy reliance on symbols as weakening the drive of some plays, in his best work "Williams expands American stage dialogue in vocabulary, image, rhythm, and range." It is the impact of Williams's poetic language and imagery on the American stage that remains his distinctive contribution to American drama, even though they are extravagantly overdone in his lesser plays.

C. W. E. Bigsby, a British scholar of American drama, contends that with the single exception of the plays of O'Neill, those of Williams, Miller, and Albee are undoubtedly "the outstanding achievement of the American theatre." In his obituary on Williams, Frank Rich, a critic for *The New York Times*, places Williams second only to O'Neill.

The Glass Menagerie

First produced: 1944 (first published, 1945)
Type of work: Play

In the Depression era, an unhappy St. Louis family of three—mother, son, and daughter—is caught in a struggle between economic survival and keeping some semblance of beauty in their lives.

Williams begins *The Glass Menagerie* with a comment by Tom Wingfield, who serves as both narrator of and character within the play: "Yes, I have tricks in my pocket, I have things up my sleeve. But I am the opposite of a stage magician. He gives you illusion that has the appearance of truth. I give you truth in the pleasant disguise of illusion." In one sentence, Williams has summarized the essence of all drama. To the very end of the play, he maintains a precarious balance between truth and illusion, creating in the process what he contends is the "essential ambiguity of man that I think needs to be stated."

Williams suspends the audience of his interplay between reality and illusion by having Tom, who has run away from home, serve as a storyteller. As he remembers bits of his past, he fades from the role of narrator into the role of character and then back again, providing a realistic objectivity to a highly subjective experience. The transitions between past and present are accomplished by the use of lighting, legends (signs), and mood-creating music. Both outsider and insider, Tom cannot escape from the memories that haunt him; traveling in some foreign country, he sees or hears something that reminds him of his past. In writing a memory play, Williams successfully balances past with present, illusion with reality, fragility with brutality, mind with body, freedom of the imagination with imprisonment of the real world, and other unresolvable paradoxes of life. The combining of narrator and character in one person is itself a paradox, as Tom tells his story both from the outside looking in and vice versa.

Tom Wingfield's story is about himself, a young man who finds himself working as a stock clerk in a shoe factory to provide a living for his mother, Amanda, and his sister, Laura. The father has long since deserted the family. Only his larger-than-life photograph hangs on a wall to remind Tom of a father "who left us a long time ago" because, as a telephone man, he had "fallen in love with long distances . . . and skipped the light fantastic out of town."

Both the photograph and the family's economic plight serve to remind Amanda of the many "gentleman callers" she might have married instead of her ne'er-do-well husband. She escapes into the past even as she attempts to make things happen in the present, supplementing Tom's income by selling women's magazines over the telephone. She also attempts to provide Laura with some means of earning a living by sending her to a business school to learn typing. Rather than having Laura become a barely tolerated spinster among her relatives, Amanda wishes to see her able to support herself. Amanda's instinct for the preservation of the family (reality) and her memories of her girlhood and the many gentleman callers (illusion) give her life a balance in a world that otherwise would be overwhelming in its dreariness.

Laura, a victim of her family situation, is painfully conscious of her "crippled" condition, one leg being shorter than the other. She throws up from nervous indigestion in her early days at Rubicam's Business College and, after that experience, spends her time walking in the park and visiting the art museum, the zoo, and the "big glass house where they raise the tropical flowers." She herself is a hothouse flower, needing special care. In the family apartment, she has still another escape, her collection of glass animals, the most singular of which is a unicorn, a nonexistent animal. In a Darwinian world, her survivability, like the unicorn's, is questionable.

Like his mother and sister, Tom, suffocated by the mindlessness of his job, has created his own world, writing poetry at work and earning the nickname "Shakespeare" from his fellow workers. He spends his evenings attending motion pictures, which in the 1930's also included live acts, frequently those of a magician.

All three family members hold in precarious balance their respective worlds of reality and illusion. In an ironic sense, all three are like the husband and father who sought escape.

The catalyst for a change in the family situation is Laura's inability to continue in business college and Amanda's decision that a gentleman caller must be found for Laura. Much against his better judgment, and after many emotional arguments with Amanda, Tom gives in to her repeated requests that he invite a fellow worker, Jim, to dinner. On that fateful day, a rather ordinary one which Williams succeeds in making extraordinary, Jim arrives.

Predictably, Amanda has bought new furnishings—a floor lamp and rug—and new clothes for Laura. Appearances, so important to Amanda, have improved, but ironically Laura is seized with a nervous attack. To make matters worse, the electricity goes off during the dinner, Tom having failed to pay the electric bill.

Candles, however, save the day. Laura recovers a bit, and in one of the most touching scenes in American drama, she enjoys a brief romantic moment with Jim—a dance and kiss. In that dance, however, the unicorn, swept off its shelf, is broken, a symbol of Laura's shattered dream when she is told by Jim that he is already engaged to someone else.

Following one final, desperate argument with the bitterly disappointed Amanda, who shouts to him to "go to the moon," Tom runs away, not to the moon, as he says, but "much further—for time is the longest distance between two places." He attempts "to find in motion what was lost in space."

Williams's techniques, in addition to the use of a narrator, are those made famous by Bertolt Brecht, a German dramatist whose expressionism influenced many modern dramatists. Among the Brechtian techniques found in *The Glass Menagerie* are its use of lighting, the signs (legends) that provide the audience with information, and music that enhances either the romance or the harshness of the mood of the moment. Brechtian techniques make for a loosely told story in episodic scenes rather than a tightly knit sequence of actions that produce high drama.

A STREETCAR NAMED DESIRE

First produced: 1947 (first published, 1947)
Type of work: Play

In a run-down 1940's New Orleans French Quarter setting, Blanche DuBois, Williams's most famous Southern belle finally resolves a lifetime of psychological and cultural conflicts.

On a streetcar named Desire, Blanche DuBois travels from the railroad station in New Orleans to a street named Elysian Fields, where her sister, Stella, pregnant and married to Stanley Kowalski, lives in a run-down apartment building in the old French Quarter. Having lost her husband, parents, teaching position, and old family home—Belle Reve in Laurel, Mississippi—Blanche has nowhere to turn but to her one remaining close relative.

Thirty years old, Blanche is emotionally and economically destitute. The most traumatic experience in her life was the discovery that her husband—a poet whom she had married at the tender age of sixteen—was a homosexual. Soon after she had taunted him for his sexual impotence, he committed suicide. Their confrontation had occurred in Moon Lake Casino, ubiquitous in Williams's plays as a house of illusions. In her subsequent guilt over his death, she found temporary release in a series of sexual affairs, the latest having involved one of her young students and resulting in her dismissal.

She is horrified at the circumstances in which her sister Stella lives and at the man to whom she is married. Polish, uneducated, inarticulate, and working class, but sexually attractive, he has won Stella by his sheer masculinity. Stella, according to production notes by director Elia Kazan, has been narcotized by his sexual superiority. A fourth important character, Stanley's poker-playing companion Mitch, is attracted to Blanche. She is attracted to his kindness to her, for he is gentle in his manner, as Stanley is not. Blanche refers at one point to having found God in Mitch's arms, a religious reference frequently made by Williams's characters at important moments in their lives.

The action of the play, then, as in Greek tragedy, consists of the final events in Blanche's life. Tensions grow between her and Stanley, even as her physical attraction to him becomes palpable. She expresses her contempt for his coarseness and animality. In scene after scene, she reminds him constantly of their cultural differences. Their hostilities develop into a Strindbergian battle of the sexes for the affection of Stella. Blanche eventually loses not only Stella but also Mitch, a possible husband.

The theatrically ironic climax occurs on Blanche's birthday while Stella is in the hospital giving birth to her baby. Blanche has prettied up the apartment for her birthday. Drunk and inflamed by Blanche's taunts into proving his superiority, Stanley rapes her in what is Williams's most famous and most highly theatrical scene. Simultaneously repulsed and attracted by his sheer rawness, Blanche acts out her final rebellion against her genteel but sexually repressive background, as though to punish herself for violating her "soul." Her struggle with Stanley is the last in a series of losses in Blanche's life. Her delicate sensibility already strained to the breaking point when she had first arrived, she breaks down and at the end is led away to a mental institution.

As in *The Glass Menagerie*, there are candles, these on Blanche's birthday cake. Like the lights that go out in Laura's life and that forever after haunt Tom, Blanche's are symbolically extinguished. In the red pajamas that Stanley wears for the occasion, the blue candles on the cake, the extravagantly old-fashioned dresses that Blanche wears, the festive decorations, and Williams's use of music and lights, the illusions of Blanche's world are highlighted. In contrast, the repulsive vulgarity and the attractive animality of Stanley's world are symbolized in details such as the opening scene in which Stanley throws Stella a package of raw meat

and the famous beer-bottle-opening scene at the birthday party. Such violently opposing images are the hallmarks of Williams's highly theatrical poetry.

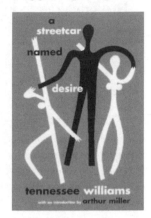

Even more than in *The Glass Menagerie*, when Tom descends the staircase of the Wingfields' St. Louis apartment for the last time, Blanche's arrival at the Kowalskis' home suggests a descent into the lower regions. It is her final descent into a mythical underworld, in which, like Orpheus, she is psychologically mutilated and eaten. In this modern American variation of the Greek myth, which Williams dramatizes more directly in *Orpheus Descending* (1957) and more violently in *Suddenly Last Summer,* one of the stops the streetcar makes is Cemetery; the Elysian Fields, ironically, is Blanche's last stop before her insanity and death.

The play's strongest effects can be found in Williams's use of language and in the many symbols. The lines remaining in the memories of those who have seen *A Streetcar Named Desire* epitomize the strong contrasts which lie at the center of the play: Stanley's bullish bellowing of "Stella, Stella" and Blanche's confession, "I have always been dependent on the kindness of strangers." Brutishness and reason, body and soul, mastery and dependency vie for survival within Stanley and Blanche.

In the loss of Belle Reve and the acceptance by Stella of a new life—the world of Stanley and of the kind but inarticulate Mitch—Williams, like Anton Chekhov in *Vishnyovy sad* (1904; *The Cherry Orchard,* 1908), dramatizes the replacing of one era by another. Like August Strindberg in *Fröken Julie* (1888; *Miss Julie,* 1912), Williams sees the social aristocracy being replaced by a coarser but more vital one. Social Darwinism is the basis for the change. As Stella rejects the old values and asserts dominance, audience sympathy for Blanche's vulnerability grows measurably. Regarded generally as Williams's most compactly constructed play, *A Streetcar Named Desire* is a dramatization of a heroine with few, if any, peers in her impact on the consciousness of the American theatrical tradition.

SUMMER AND SMOKE

First produced: 1947 (first published, 1948)
Type of work: Play

Alma Winemiller finds the irreconcilability of the conflict between body and soul impossible and eventually gives up one for the other.

Stylistically, *Summer and Smoke* is Williams's realistic compromise between the poetic expressionism of *The Glass Menagerie* and the violent theatricality of *A Streetcar Named Desire*. Although *Summer and Smoke* is more conventionally realistic than the other two, it is also his most allegorical statement on the conflict between the soul and the body, between innocence and experience, and between eternity and life—themes taking various forms in all of Williams's plays. The play is also one of Williams's three treatments of a character named Alma, the other being an earlier short story, "The Yellow Bird," and a later play, *The Eccentricities of a Nightingale* (1964).

Its allegorical realism consists of Williams's apparently simple and clear portraits of three women, the most important of whom is Alma (her name means "soul"), the daughter of a minister and his increasingly senile wife. Like Laura Wingfield, Alma has a deformity. Hers is of the soul rather than of the body: a chastity of mind that in the early years of her life repressed her sexuality. Slowly it has developed into a revulsion against the physicality of sex and then, later in the play, becomes an unconventional (for her) appetite for the physical aspects of sex.

Rosa Gonzales, on the other hand, the daughter of the owner of Moon Lake Casino (a recurrent symbol of the pleasures of the body in Williams's plays), is the embodiment of physical (sexual) attraction, the allegorical opposite of Alma's chastity-dominated soul. A third character, Nellie Ewell, a former piano pupil of Alma, represents a balance between the extremities represented by Alma and Rosa. Eventually, she marries Dr. John Buchanan, the young doctor who has been, at various times, attracted to Alma and Rosa. As a character, Nellie is even less developed than is Stella in *A Streetcar Named Desire* and is much less interesting dramatically. Even their names suggest their world of respective fates: Alma, purity; Rosa, the glow of life; and John and Nellie, normality.

Alma, the minister's daughter who has grown up next door to John, and John, the son of a doctor, are representative small-town American characters. John had his taste of an exciting life away in medical school, but Alma retained her small-town interests. Still in love with John, she has remained the product of the polite and conventional southern white, Protestant ethic. Her life consists of participation in local events, such as the town picnics at which she sings.

John, just graduated from medical school, returns home, still sowing his wild oats. He is attracted sexually to Rosa and, in one brief and unsuccessful encounter, to Alma. Characters change, as John slowly settles into the domestic and professional routines of a doctor's life, and Alma reverses dramatically, giving herself up to the claims of the body. She is seen at the end leaving for Moon Lake Casino with Archie Kramer, a traveling salesman. Roger Boxhill, in his 1985 study of Williams's plays, sees John's change as developmental and Alma's as fundamental.

The mixture of the realism of small-town life with allegorical symbolism contrasts with the artistry of *The Glass Menagerie* and *A Streetcar Named Desire*. Symbols and their meanings tend to have a one-to-one ratio, a characteristic of the allegorical style. There is, for example, the opening scene at the fountain square, with the statue of an angel of eternity, her wings outspread and her hands cupped as through ready to drink. Lights flash on and off the statue at various points in the play, indicating the change that is happening to Alma. At the end, as she walks away with the salesman, she waves her hand in what seems like a good-bye, first to the angel and then to her house. Seen by some as an allegorical treatment of the conflict between body and soul, the play is seen by others as a painfully sensitive farewell by Alma to the values of her southern small-town legacy. The world to which she bids farewell is a variation of that of Amanda and Laura Wingfield, Blanche DuBois, and women characters in later plays.

The young Dr. Buchanan is one of Williams's rare healthy survivors in the conflicts generated between body and soul. Like Stella, Nellie married. Unlike Stella, her marriage represents an ascent, rather than a descent. As decent and "normal" human beings, Dr. Buchanan and Nellie are juxtaposed against the pathetic Alma. With its theatricality and poetry muted by the allegorical style, *Summer and Smoke* is less forceful than *The Glass Menagerie* and *A Streetcar Named Desire*, but it is nevertheless a moving drama.

CAT ON A HOT TIN ROOF

First produced: 1955 (first published, 1955)
Type of work: Play

In a wealthy southern ancestral home, a family celebration becomes the scene of major confrontations.

In *Cat on a Hot Tin Roof* the cat is Maggie Pollitt, married to Brick, the favorite son of a wealthy plantation owner, Big Daddy, and the hot tin roof is the desperate measure she takes to regain her husband's sexual interest and to lay claim to her husband's family fortune. Opposing her are Gooper Pollitt, Brick's brother, and Gooper's family, consisting of his pregnant wife and their five children (Williams's famous "no-neck monsters"). Finally there is Big Mama, whose current status with her husband is much like Maggie's with Brick.

The estrangement between the silently suffering Brick and his loquacious father is the result of Brick's dropping out of professional football and sportscasting and his turning to alcohol. Pained by the suicide of his best friend, Skipper, Brick says he must drink until he hears a "click" in his head, a guarantor of relief from his pain. Big Daddy's inability to understand Brick is fueled by rumors that Brick and Skipper's closeness was homosexual in nature. The strain between Maggie and Brick is caused by Maggie's having gone to Skipper to confront him with his possible homosexuality. Shortly thereafter, Skipper committed suicide. Brick's loss of Skipper is intensified by Maggie's having made something dirty of what he said was a pure love.

Contrasting strongly with Brick, Gooper is successful both as a lawyer and as a prolific breeder of children. Gooper's family, particularly his wife, resents Big Daddy's favoritism regarding Brick and take advantage of every opportunity to change the situation. Thus the battle lines are drawn on what

was to be a festive occasion, a celebration of Big Daddy's sixty-fifth birthday. Maggie, playing on Big Daddy's favoritism, lies about being pregnant and then attempts to seduce Brick into making her pregnant. In a climactic scene between Big Daddy and Brick, the latter drops a bombshell: the true prognosis of his father's cancerous condition.

The play exists in several versions, the original having been altered by Elia Kazan for the premiere in New York in 1955. The original version was partly restored in 1974 and completely performed in 1990. In the three major productions, Barbara Bel Geddes, Elizabeth Ashley, and Kathleen Turner, respectively, played Maggie, the different versions allowing each to play distinctively different Maggies. In the original version, Brick does not support Maggie in her lie to Big Daddy, and it is uncertain whether Maggie has wooed Brick from his alcoholism and whether in his own mind Brick was convinced that his feeling for Skipper was platonic. Also, Big Daddy does not reappear on stage after his big scene with Brick.

The play's structure is unwieldy and irregular, in contrast with the rhythmically expressionistic structure of *The Glass Menagerie* or the rapidly developing tensions in *A Streetcar Named Desire*. Maggie's long speeches are like operatic arias, accompanied by the equally long silences of Brick. Similarly, the towering role of Big Daddy seems at times to vie with Maggie's. Both have the same purpose: to rescue Brick and to rehabilitate him.

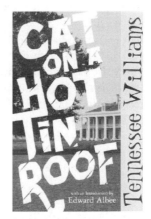

Despite Maggie's titular role, her sexual attractiveness, and her sympathy-evoking, if "mendacious," attempts to triumph over Gooper's family, it is the strong emotional honesty between Big Daddy and Brick for which Williams writes his most compelling moment in the play. Big Daddy's sudden and unexpected confrontation with the imminence of his death (at a time when he was looking forward once more to testing his sexual prowess) and Brick's silent suffering of pain and guilt over Skipper's death brilliantly counterpoint Maggie's attempt to create life, even when that attempt involves a distant husband and a lie that she hopes to turn into a truth.

The big scene between Big Daddy and Brick is magisterial in the former's disclosure of all the lies he has put up with all of his married life and his true feelings toward Big Mama, Gooper, Mae, and their five noisy children. Torn between his hatred of them and his reluctance to make Brick, an alcoholic, the legatee of his will, he insists on honesty from Brick regarding his drinking and his relationship with Skipper. It is Big Daddy's reference to homosexual innuendoes regarding Skipper that causes Brick to disclose Maggie's jealousy of his clean friendship with Skipper during their road trips as professional football players. He accuses Maggie of destroying Skipper by suggesting to him a "dirty" relationship. Big Daddy, however, refuses to allow Brick to "pass the buck," whereupon Brick, inflamed, taunts Big Daddy with the irony of the requisite happy returns of his sixty-fifth birthday "when ev'rybody but you knows there won't be any."

One truth after another tumbles from the opera-like duet between father and son, replacing the lies with which both have lived. Big Daddy's anger is that of a man betrayed, as he leaves the stage howling with rage. Although he does not appear in act 3, he is heard offstage crying out in pain. The scene between Big Daddy and Brick is one of two legendary father-son confrontations in American drama, the other being that between Biff and Willy Loman in Arthur Miller's *Death of a Salesman*.

With much of the humor and theatricality of *A Streetcar Named Desire*, but without its compact structure, *Cat on a Hot Tin Roof* remains a compelling play. The names of Big Daddy, Maggie, and Brick have been imprinted permanently on the American stage along with those of Amanda, Laura, and Tom Wingfield; Blanche DuBois; and Stanley Kowalski.

SUDDENLY LAST SUMMER

First produced: 1958 (first published, 1958)
Type of work: Play

Catharine Holly, despite the threat of a lobotomy, finds peace when she is finally able to tell the truth of the fate of her cousin, Sebastian Venable.

"Suddenly last summer" is a refrain that runs through the many interrupted attempts of Catharine Holly to tell a psychologist the truth about what happened to Sebastian Venable along the harbor of an Italian resort, Cabeza de Lobo. He had been protected all of his life by his mother, and he had used her the last few years of his life to procure partners for his sexual appetite. On her part, Mrs. Venable will go to any length to preserve the reputation of her son as a poet, for to her "the work of a poet is the life of the poet" and vice versa. Together, she and Sebastian traveled widely and luxuriously for twenty years. During each summer, he composed a poem, which Mrs. Venable had compiled into a gilt-edged volume. Then one summer he suddenly stopped writing. It is what happened this summer, the final one in Sebastian's rapidly deteriorating life, that Catharine, like Samuel Taylor Coleridge's ancient mariner, must tell.

When Mrs. Venable had a stroke one summer, Sebastian asked Catharine Holly, his cousin, to travel with him in his mother's place. Loving her cousin, even when she realized that she was being used as a lure to attract homosexual partners for him, she subsequently witnessed his physical mutilation by a mob of hungry young Italians who tore at his flesh, stuffing their mouths as they did so.

The play is set in the Garden District of New Orleans, a contrast with the old French Quarter setting of *A Streetcar Named Desire*. The setting includes the surrealistically lush, fantastic garden "which is more like a tropical jungle." Everything about the garden is violent—its colors, its harsh and sibilant noises that resemble "beasts, serpents and birds, all of a savage nature." Throughout the play, harsh noises as background underscore the harshness of the action.

In this setting, one year after her son's death, 1936, Mrs. Venable, in an attempt to preserve her son's memory, threatens to contest her son's will, which leaves a substantial amount of money to Catharine. Suffering from the trauma of witnessing the death of Sebastian and from her inability to stop his mutilation, she has been under intense psychological stress. The plot of the play involves the arrival of Catharine, her mother, her brother, a doctor, and a Catholic sister at the Venable residence. The psychologist has come to discover the truth and Mrs. Venable to preserve her illusion about Sebastian.

When Catharine finally reveals all, with the help of a drug, her revelation includes an even more lurid detail: Mrs. Venable had, like Catharine later, been a procuress for her son's sexual habits. The play concludes with Mrs. Venable's attempt to strike Catharine upon the latter's concluding her story with the graphic details of Sebastian's mutilation.

At one point, Catharine's need to tell the truth, a truth so horrible that even God could not change it, is a contrapuntal theme to Mrs. Venable's talk about Sebastian's search for God, whom Sebastian had once tried to find in a Buddhist monastery. That search is linked with another trip on which she had taken Sebastian—to the Galápagos Islands, where they witnessed giant sea turtles (after being hatched) fleeing from flesh-eating vultures. Most turtles did not survive. In that experience, she says, Sebastian had seen God. Ironically, that Galápagos image, Mrs. Venable's legacy to her son, became a fulfilled prophecy.

The action of the play, consisting of Catharine's many attempts to tell the truth, ends with that truth finally being told and with her finally finding some respite from the mental torture of living with her story for the past year, unable to utter its horror.

THE NIGHT OF THE IGUANA

First produced: 1961 (first published, 1961)
Type of work: Play

In a seedy Mexican tourist hotel during the off-season, three expatriate Americans are caught up in a private war among themselves and with a group of tourists.

Set during World War II, *The Night of the Iguana* features three main characters. Shannon, a defrocked

minister and recovering alcoholic, now a tour guide for a cheap Texas-based travel agency, and Hannah Jelkes meet at a shabby Mexican tourist hotel that is run by an oversexed American expatriate, Maxine. As one of Williams's survivor characters, Maxine supports herself, hoping some day to return to the United States to manage a motel.

Shannon's battles are internal, involving his dismissal from the church for reasons of alcoholism and sexual promiscuities. Throughout the play, he attempts to write a letter to his superior for reinstatement in the church. His failure even as a tour guide emphasizes the illusionary nature of his attempt at reinstatement. The play opens with a conflict between him and his tour group—ladies from a Baptist college in Texas—regarding their hotel for the night. Shannon insists that they stay at Maxine's rather than, as the tour brochure states, in the town below. Their arguments are protracted through the length of the play.

Arriving penniless at the hotel at the same time as Shannon are Hannah Jelkes and her nonagenarian grandfather, Nonno, who make their living in their travels, she by drawing portraits of tourists and he by reciting poems that he writes in his memory. Hannah has a purity and strength of character which is not of the world she inhabits.

In her behavior and her many conversations with Shannon, she is a painful reminder to him of lost ideals. Her honesty and courage contrast with the conventional hypocrisy of the American women and the smug complacency of the Germans at the hotel, one of whom constantly listens to his radio for reports on Adolf Hitler's success in bombing England (the play is set during World War II).

Hannah, a sharp contrast to the Americans and Germans, cannot endure seeing a creature, human or otherwise, suffering. At the end, she convinces Shannon to untie a captive iguana, which has been kept tied for the next meal at the hotel. Against Maxine's wishes, Shannon frees the iguana, just as he had earlier freed himself in his rebellion against his tour group. His act is a triumphant assertion of Hannah's religion of kindness to all living things and of his own former beliefs. Nonno then dies, having composed his last poem, which, for once, he had Hannah write down.

With their dependencies gone—Hannah's grandfather and Shannon's illusions as tour guide and minister—they are free, yet they are also alone.

For Shannon, there is only one possibility: to stay with Maxine and help her manage the hotel. For Hannah, there is a return to her nomadic existence. Even the nymphomaniacal Maxine, to Shannon's surprise, becomes poetical as she invites him down for a swim in the "liquid moonlight." When Hannah lights her cigarette, Shannon stares at her, wanting to remember her face, which he knows he will not see again.

Each of the three main characters has her or his "spooks" (Shannon's word). His are professional failure and alcoholism; Maxine's are loneliness and the Mexican "beach boys" she employs for business and personal reasons; Hannah's is her spinsterish lifestyle, which she endures in crucial moments by stopping to inhale deeply. All three have met life on their terms, and all three have survived. Shannon's freeing of the iguana is a metaphor for the resolutions of the private wars of the three main characters.

Structurally, the play's actions are loosely plotted, consisting mostly of episodic conversations between two of the three main characters. The moral landscape is that of World War II and of the petty lives of the German and American tourists, insulated from the cruelties of the public and private battles being waged around them.

SUMMARY

Several other plays that are important to the Williams canon include *Camino Real* (1953), *The Rose Tattoo* (1951), *Orpheus Descending* (1957), *Sweet Bird of Youth* (1959), and *The Milk Train Doesn't Stop Here Anymore* (1963). Williams's stylistic distinction consists of his theatrically poetic language. His main thematic concerns are his sympathetic portraits of women (sometimes his alter egos), his creation of what Ruby Cohn calls "garrulous grotesques," who have left indelible impressions on the American consciousness, his rebellion against the repressiveness of puritanical attitudes, and his use of Darwinism's "nature red in tooth and claw" as a metaphor for the cruelty of repressive, conventional attitudes.

Susan Rusinko

BIBLIOGRAPHY

By the Author

SHORT FICTION:
One Arm, and Other Stories, 1948
Hard Candy: A Book of Stories, 1954
The Knightly Quest: A Novella and Four Short Stories, 1967
Eight Mortal Ladies Possessed: A Book of Stories, 1974
Collected Stories, 1985

LONG FICTION:
The Roman Spring of Mrs. Stone, 1950
Moise and the World of Reason, 1975

DRAMA:
Fugitive Kind, pr. 1937, pb. 2001
Spring Storm, wr. 1937, pr., pb. 1999
Not About Nightingales, wr. 1939, pr., pb. 1998
Battle of Angels, pr. 1940, pb. 1945
This Property Is Condemned, pb. 1941, pr. 1946 (one act)
I Rise in Flame, Cried the Phoenix, wr. 1941, pb. 1951, pr. 1959 (one act)
The Lady of Larkspur Lotion, pb. 1942 (one act)
The Glass Menagerie, pr. 1944, pb. 1945
Twenty-seven Wagons Full of Cotton, pb. 1945, pr. 1955 (one act)
You Touched Me, pr. 1945, pb. 1947 (with Donald Windham)

Summer and Smoke, pr. 1947, pb. 1948
A Streetcar Named Desire, pr., pb. 1947
American Blues, pb. 1948 (collection)
Five Short Plays, pb. 1948
The Long Stay Cut Short: Or, The Unsatisfactory Supper, pb. 1948 (one act)
The Rose Tattoo, pr. 1950, pb. 1951
Camino Real, pr., pb. 1953
Cat on a Hot Tin Roof, pr., pb. 1955
Orpheus Descending, pr. 1957, pb. 1958 (revised of *Battle of Angels*)
Suddenly Last Summer, pr., pb. 1958
The Enemy: Time, pb. 1959
Sweet Bird of Youth, pr., pb. 1959 (based on *The Enemy: Time*)
Period of Adjustment, pr. 1959, pb. 1960
The Night of the Iguana, pr., pb. 1961
The Milk Train Doesn't Stop Here Anymore, pr. 1963, revised pb. 1976
The Eccentricities of a Nightingale, pr., pb. 1964 (revision of *Summer and Smoke*)
Slapstick Tragedy: "The Mutilated" and "The Gnädiges Fräulein," pr. 1966, pb. 1970 (one acts)
The Two-Character Play, pr. 1967, pb. 1969
The Seven Descents of Myrtle, pr., pb. 1968 (as *Kingdom of Earth*)
In the Bar of a Tokyo Hotel, pr. 1969, pb. 1970
Confessional, pb. 1970
Dragon Country, pb. 1970 (collection)
The Theatre of Tennessee Williams, pb. 1971-1981 (7 volumes)
Out Cry, pr. 1971, pb. 1973 (revision of *The Two-Character Play*)
Small Craft Warnings, pr., pb. 1972 (revision of *Confessional*)
Vieux Carré, pr. 1977, pb. 1979
A Lovely Sunday for Creve Coeur, pr. 1979, pb. 1980
Clothes for a Summer Hotel, pr. 1980
A House Not Meant to Stand, pr. 1981
Something Cloudy, Something Clear, pr. 1981, pb. 1995

SCREENPLAYS:
The Glass Menagerie, 1950 (with Peter Berneis)
A Streetcar Named Desire, 1951 (with Oscar Saul)
The Rose Tattoo, 1955 (with Hal Kanter)
Baby Doll, 1956
The Fugitive Kind, 1960 (with Meade Roberts; based on *Orpheus Descending*)
Suddenly Last Summer, 1960 (with Gore Vidal)
Stopped Rocking, and Other Screenplays, 1984

POETRY:
In the Winter of Cities, 1956
Androgyne, Mon Amour, 1977
The Collected Poems of Tennessee Williams, 2002

DISCUSSION TOPICS

- Tennessee Williams is often called a poetical playwright. What is poetical about his plays?

- What techniques does Williams use to blend illusion and reality in *The Glass Menagerie*?

- What is the relevance of the symbolic names in *A Streetcar Named Desire*?

- Is Blanche DuBois of *A Streetcar Named Desire* Williams's most fully realized character?

- Compare the father-son confrontation in *Cat on a Hot Tin Roof* with that in Arthur Miller's *Death of a Salesman* (1949).

- Consider *The Night of the Iguana* as a play about survival.

NONFICTION:
Memoirs, 1975
Where I Live: Selected Essays, 1978
Five O'Clock Angel: Letters of Tennessee Williams to Maria St. Just, 1948-1982, 1990
The Selected Letters of Tennessee Williams, 1920-1945, 2000

About the Author

Bloom, Harold, ed. *Tennessee Williams*. Philadelphia: Chelsea House, 2003.

Crandall, George W. *Tennessee Williams: A Descriptive Bibliography*. Pittsburgh: University of Pittsburgh Press, 1995.

Heintzelman, Greta, and Alycia Smith Howard. *Critical Companion to Tennessee Williams*. New York: Facts On File, 2005.

Kolin, Philip, ed. *Tennessee Williams: A Guide to Research and Performance*. Westport, Conn.: Greenwood Press, 1998.

_____. *The Tennessee Williams Encyclopedia*. Westport, Conn.: Greenwood Press, 2004.

Leverich, Lyle. *Tom: The Unknown Tennessee Williams*. New York: Crown, 1995.

Martin, Robert A., ed. *Critical Essays on Tennessee Williams*. New York: G. K. Hall, 1997.

Pagan, Nicholas. *Rethinking Literary Biography: A Postmodern Approach to Tennessee Williams*. Rutherford, N.J.: Fairleigh Dickinson University Press, 1993.

Rader, Dotson. *Tennessee: Cry of the Heart*. Garden City, N.Y.: Doubleday, 1985.

Roudané, Matthew C., ed. *The Cambridge Companion to Tennessee Williams*. New York: Cambridge University Press, 1997.

Spoto, Donald. *The Kindness of Strangers: The Life of Tennessee Williams*. Reprint. New York: Da Capo Press, 1997.

Thompson, Judith. *Tennessee Williams' Plays: Memory, Myth, and Symbol*. Rev. ed. New York: P. Lang, 2002.

Tischler, Nancy Marie Patterson. *Student Companion to Tennessee Williams*. Westport, Conn.: Greenwood Press, 2000.

Williams, Dakin, and Shepherd Mead. *Tennessee Williams: An Intimate Biography*. New York: Arbor House, 1983.

Woodhouse, Reed. *Unlimited Embrace: A Canon of Gay Fiction, 1945-1995*. Amherst: University of Massachusetts Press, 1998.

WILLIAM CARLOS WILLIAMS

Born: Rutherford, New Jersey
September 17, 1883
Died: Rutherford, New Jersey
March 4, 1963

One of the most accomplished and influential writers of the twentieth century, Williams developed distinctly modern poetic forms through which he expressed the American idiom and landscape.

BIOGRAPHY

A first-generation American, William Carlos Williams was born in Rutherford, New Jersey, on September 17, 1883. His father, William George Williams, of English ancestry, had been born in England and raised in the West Indies. His mother, Raquel Hélène Rose Hoheb Williams, whose ancestry contained elements of French, Spanish, and Jewish cultures, had been born in Puerto Rico.

With his younger brother, Edward, Williams went to public schools in his hometown. When he was fourteen, he went with his family to Europe for two years, where he attended school first near Geneva, Switzerland, and later in Paris. When his family returned to the United States, he was sent to Horace Mann High School in New York City. He commuted daily from Rutherford by streetcar and Hudson River ferryboat. Williams entered medical school at the University of Pennsylvania in 1902. While there, because of his interest in poetry, he met the poets Ezra Pound and H. D. (Hilda Doolittle) and the painter Charles Demuth, all of whom became his lifelong friends.

After his graduation from medical school in 1906, Williams interned at the old French Hospital and the Nursery and Child's Hospital in New York City. His first volume of poetry, *Poems*, published at his own expense, appeared in 1909. That same year he went to Europe again, where he did postgraduate work in pediatrics in Leipzig, Germany. While in Europe he renewed his friendship with Ezra Pound, and through him was introduced to many writers and artists of prewar London.

After brief trips to Italy and Spain, Williams returned to Rutherford in 1910 to begin the practice of medicine. In 1911, he married Florence Herman, the "Flossie" of his poems. During the next few years, Williams became the father of two boys, William and Paul. In 1913 he bought the house at 9 Ridge Road in Rutherford which would be his residence for the rest of his life. His second volume of verse, *The Tempers*, was published in England that same year. Williams was a very active pediatrician with a wide practice among the industrial workers of northeastern New Jersey. Nevertheless, he continued to be a deeply committed poet and literary man eagerly involved in the artistic life, publishing ventures, and general creative climate of Greenwich Village in the years of World War I and after.

During the 1940's, Williams contributed to numerous magazines, including *The Glebe, Poetry, Others* (of which he was associate editor for a time), *The Little Review, The Dial*, and *Broom*. He became acquainted with Walter Arensberg, Kenneth Burke, Marsden Hartley, Alfred Kreymborg, Marianne Moore, Charles Sheeler, and other poets and painters. Williams published his third collection of poems, *Al Que Quiere!*, in 1917 and *Kora in Hell: Improvisations*, an experimental collection of poetry and prose, in 1920. From 1920 until 1923, Williams edited *Contact* with the publisher Robert McAlmon and during these years published three daring experiments in prose and poetry: *Sour Grapes* (1921), *Spring and All* (1923), and *The Great American Novel* (1923).

In 1924 Williams went to Europe with his wife for six months and savored the expatriate life of the most important members of the American "lost generation" and their French counterparts. He was guided again by Ezra Pound, along with McAlmon, and through them Williams associated with such writers and artists as George Antheil, Sylvia Beach, Kay Boyle, Ford Madox Ford, Ernest Hemingway, James Joyce, Man Ray, Gertrude Stein, and such French writers as Valery Larbaud and Philippe Soupault.

Williams published one of his most influential prose works, *In the American Grain*, in 1925, a collection of essays on American history. During the following decade he contributed to *transition*, *The Exile*, *Blues*, *Front*, *Pagany*, *Alcestis*, and other magazines. In 1926 he received the Dial Award for Services to American Literature. Still a full-time pediatrician with a large private practice among the working class of Rutherford, he joined the staff of the Passaic General Hospital, while maintaining his general practice.

In 1927 he made another European visit when he and his wife escorted their two sons to school in Switzerland. While his wife remained with their sons in Switzerland for a year, Williams returned to his medical practice and to writing in New Jersey. During that time, he wrote a novel, *A Voyage to Pagany* (1928), based on the family's visit to Europe.

Williams continued in the following years to write prose (short stories, essays, novels, and an autobiography), poetry, and plays. Despite the pressures of constant professional demands and intrusions in those years, he published more than twenty volumes. Collected editions of his poems were published in 1934 and 1938. In 1941 and ensuing years, as his literary reputation grew, Williams lectured at the University of Puerto Rico, Harvard University, Dartmouth College, and elsewhere. In 1946 Williams began publication of *Paterson*, his long verse masterpiece. Individual books of the poem were published in 1946, 1948, 1949, 1951, and 1958. Notes for a sixth book were published posthumously.

Williams received the first National Book Award for Poetry (for *Paterson*, Book III and the 1949 collection *Selected Poems*) in 1950. His autobiography, published in 1951, shows the extent of his association with the avant-garde of American letters, especially during the years between 1910 and 1930.

In 1952, Williams was appointed consultant in poetry to the Library of Congress, a position roughly equivalent to poet laureate. The appointment was withdrawn before he could take office, however, partly because of accusations about his supposed leftist sympathies, owing much to his long friendship with Ezra Pound, who had been accused of being a traitor to the United States during World War II. Williams was subsequently reappointed to this position, but because of ill health he was never able to take it up.

A series of strokes that eventually made him a semi-invalid forced Williams to turn over his medical practice to his son William in the 1950's. He continued to devote himself to writing, however, and made frequent appearances at colleges and universities to lecture and to read his poems. In spite of periods of difficulty with his vision and his speech, he continued to live a vigorous creative life and to travel in the United States and, on two occasions, to the Caribbean region.

During the forty years he practiced medicine in Rutherford, Williams wrote in his autobiography, he saw a million and a half patients and delivered two thousand babies. Meanwhile, scribbling or typing rapidly between patients, jotting down images and ideas on prescription blanks between house calls, and typing late into the night after his workday as a pediatrician was over, he laid the foundation of the most extensive one-man body of literature in American history: a total of forty-nine books in every possible literary form. He wrote about six hundred poems, four full-length plays, an opera libretto, fifty-two short stories, four novels, a book of essays and criticism, his autobiography, a biography of his mother, an American history, and a book of letters.

When Williams died at the age of seventy-nine, on March 4, 1963, his reputation as a major poet was firmly established. He had won numerous awards during his lifetime, and two months after his death he was posthumously awarded the Pulitzer Prize in poetry for *Pictures from Brueghel* (1962) and the Gold Medal for Poetry of the National Institute of Arts and Letters.

ANALYSIS

Williams's writing is one of the major achievements in twentieth century American literature. As a significant representation of the modern American consciousness, it must be placed with that of four other poets born between 1874 and 1888: Robert Frost, Wallace Stevens, Ezra Pound, and T. S. Eliot. Williams's work complements theirs in important ways. He was less ready than they to maintain traditional techniques or assimilate the discoveries made in other literatures, but he was more genuinely open and responsive to both the fullness and the emptiness of contemporary life in the United States.

He listened more keenly to the dance rhythms and the flat cadences of American speech, observed more accurately the degradation and the unexpected beauties of its cities and countrysides, and explored more intensely the immediate historical ground on which Americans stood. He did all this, moreover, without slighting the spiritual emptiness that has haunted twentieth century writing. Williams may well be, of those five poets, the most important influence on the development of the American idiom in poetry during the last years of the twentieth century.

His work in both poetry and prose combines great technical ability with a passionate humanity. The major beauty of Williams's art is perhaps that of a hard-won honesty, achieved through his attempt to isolate individual experience, to make the distinctions necessary to its proper perception, yet to acknowledge at the same time the continuity of all experience.

The content of Williams's writing tends toward "pure poetry." He seldom moralizes or indulges in philosophical or religious sermonizing. Criticism of capitalism is sometimes found in his fiction (for example, in the story "Jean Beicke") and other prose (as in parts of *In the American Grain*) but almost never in his poetry. ("The Yachts" is one notable exception.)

The same is true of Williams's medical background. He uses his scientific training and his experience as a doctor frequently in his fiction (as in his fine 1932 short-story collection, *The Knife of the Times, and Other Stories*), but it seldom appears in his poetry, except in an occasional term or phrase borrowed from medicine. As a writer of fiction—he published four novels and a number of first-rate short stories—Williams's style is more conventional than in his poetry, but it is often ironic, sometimes even apparently callous, in attitude. His medical stories contain some of the most powerful descriptions of disease and suffering in modern fiction. In his fiction, as in his poetry, however, Williams is objective rather than indifferent. He shows the sympathetic detachment of a man who combined the writing of literature with a full-time career as a practicing physician.

Williams united a lifelong dedication to writing with a medical practice in New Jersey by writing emphatically about the life around him—the ordinary, and even apparently uninteresting, people, events, and landscapes that he encountered during his daily routine. His writing embodies two major tendencies. The first is vigorous formal experimentation in poetry and prose, frequently in the direction of abandoning traditional forms and, in his poetry, of mastering the possibilities of free verse, of which he remains the most influential practitioner.

The second is a plain-speaking directness of manner well suited to his native subjects and settings—for example, city streets, vacant lots, workers and their tools, a wheelbarrow, scraps of conversation, a sheet of paper rolling along in the wind, pieces of broken glass behind a hospital, the number five on a speeding fire engine. Nature, especially as represented by flowers and trees, is also an active presence in his poems, and it is celebrated without ever being idealized; it is puddles rather than lakes, sparrows rather than nightingales, weeds rather than roses. Everything is presented tautly, with a minimum of comment or judgment, in the simplest language and according to a lifelong preference for the concrete as expressed in his famous motto: "No ideas but in things."

Early in his career, Williams rejected the literary heritage of the Victorian era, particularly its trite diction and stultified verse forms. He strove constantly to achieve the brusque nervous tension, the vigor and rhetoric, of American speech. Although he avoids slang, his language is thoroughly idiomatic. He seldom uses a word that is beyond the vocabulary of the ordinary reader, and the rhythm and intonation of his language are those of common speech. A careful study of his typography and punctuation shows that they, too, are intended to reproduce the rhythm—the pauses and emphases—of ordinary speech.

Williams's poetry may be the most accessible and humane in modern American literature. He had a special knack for using natural speech poetically and an unusual appreciation of how other people feel and think. Virtually all of Williams's lyrics illustrate his determination to develop in poetry the rhythm, diction, and syntax of the language actually spoken in Rutherford, New Jersey. Many of his lyrics are about poetry—what it is, how to write it—but a poem about poetry is also, for Williams, about how to live, for poetry is essentially the direct "contact"—the fresh perceiving and feeling by which life becomes worth living.

The music of Williams's poems seems at first to be a deliberate absence of music, and it takes some time to perceive the finely controlled dance that the hesitations and abruptnesses of the free-verse lines accomplish. Reading them aloud should include experimentation with the pauses to be found on the page and listening for the plain, emerging music. The recognition of this unlikely lyricism involves the same kind of delighted surprise that can be experienced from Williams's ways of finding beauty in unexpected places. Subject and style have the same aims, and an aesthetic of discovery through reduction and directness lies behind everything Williams did. To put it in terms of the visual analogies that very much interested him, his poems combine the freshness and daring of cubist painting and the candor and unmediated confrontations of photography.

Williams's revolutionary ideas led him to write poetry that was simple, direct, and apparently formless. He seemed to be a "nonliterary" writer, yet his poetry, for all its freshness and seeming spontaneity, was the result of constant rewriting and refinement. Like nineteenth century American poet Walt Whitman, Williams used commonplace American scenes and speech to portray contemporary urban America. Like Whitman, he was a significant force in the freeing of poetry from the restraints and predictive regularity of traditional rhythms and meters. Williams was a prime literary innovator in prose and poetry, and he was the poet of the twentieth century most sensitive to the teeming squalor of modern America.

In all of his work, Williams carried forward a revolutionary heritage that was welcomed by younger writers responsive to his example and influence. While steadfastly supporting the principle of free organic form, he also helped refresh and renew the language of poetry by freeing it from stereotyped associations. In his passionate equalitarianism, he has been more attractive to younger generations of poets than the more aristocratic Pound and Eliot. Williams's writing reveals an openness to experience of all kinds and a refusal to accept doctrinaire theories and solutions. While insisting upon the authenticity of his own vision, he has at the same time insisted upon the relativity of all knowledge and the inadequacy of dogma. To this extent at least, despite his distance from the confident rationalism of the Enlightenment (which he also distrusted), his work as a whole supports the Jeffersonian principle of "eternal hostility to every form of tyranny over the mind of man."

"TRACT"

First published: 1917 (collected in *Al Que Quiere!*, 1917)
Type of work: Poem

While describing how to conduct a funeral, Williams's speaker gives advice that applies to many communal activities.

"Tract," from *Al Que Quiere!*, Williams's second book of poetry, appears at first to be a frankly didactic poem in which the speaker attempts to teach the proper way "to perform a funeral." The speaker gives advice in four areas: hearse, flowers, driver, and bereaved.

In stanzas 1 through 3, objecting to the usual funeral, with its standardized conventions which insulate mourners from the meaning of death, the speaker would substitute for the polished black hearse a "rough dray" to be dragged over the ground, with no decoration other than perhaps gilt paint applied to the wheels for the occasion. In stanza 4, in place of the usual wreaths or hothouse flowers, the speaker recommends "Some common memento . . . / something he prized and is known by:/ his old clothes—a few books perhaps—/ God knows what!" In stanza 5, he would have the driver pulled down from his seat to "walk at the side/ and inconspicuously too!" His final admonition, in stanza 6, is to the mourners:

> Walk behind—as they do in France,
> seventh class, or if you ride
> Hell take curtains! Go with some show
> of inconvenience; sit openly—
> to the weather as to grief.
> Or do you think you can shut grief in?
> What—from us? We who have perhaps
> nothing to lose? Share with us
> share with us—it will be money
> in your pockets.
>   Go now
> I think you are ready.

By such simplicity and show of inconvenience, the poem holds, the townspeople "are ready" to conduct a funeral properly.

At first glance, "Tract" seems to be a poem of direct statement: The speaker attempts to reform his neighbors' ideas about the proper conduct of a familiar ritual by setting forth specific precepts. The speaker's impulse to reform, however, reveals a preoccupation with the idea of form that goes beyond the subject of funerals. The fact that the funeral is a common ritual is a reminder that any such group activity is inevitably symbolic and, in Williams's view, a kind of art. From this perspective, the speaker's injunctions apply not only to one rite but also to a whole range of symbolic activity in which members of a community may be involved.

Metaphorically, the "tract" becomes a statement of an aesthetic as the poet asserts his commitment to certain principles of form which he urges upon his unenlightened townspeople. These are, not surprisingly, the familiar tenets of an organic theory in which rigid, predetermined conventions are rejected in favor of forms that are free and functional and adapted to the circumstances from which they arise. The separate assertions of what had seemed a poetry of statement are revealed to be integral parts of a more comprehensive, dramatically unified symbolic art.

"THE RED WHEELBARROW"

First published: 1923 (collected in *The Collected Poems of William Carlos Williams: Volume I, 1909-1939*, 1986)
Type of work: Poem

Williams discovers an aesthetic pattern and sensory pleasure in an ordinary wheelbarrow and a few chickens.

"The Red Wheelbarrow" is perhaps one of the shortest serious poems ever published by an American poet. The structure is rigidly formal. The poem consists of four miniature stanzas of four words each.

> so much depends
> upon
>
> a red wheel
> barrow
>
> glazed with rain
> water
>
> beside the white
>
> chickens.

Three images are involved: the wheelbarrow, described simply as red, the qualifying adjectival phrase "glazed with rain/ water," which relieves the excessive severity of the second stanza, and the contrasting white chickens of the final stanza. The first line is colloquial and open in its invitation; the second line, the preposition "upon," prepares the reader for the specifics to follow. Each two-line stanza has two stressed syllables in the first line and one in the second, and yet there is lively variation in where the stresses fall.

In "The Red Wheelbarrow," Williams discovers an aesthetic pattern and sensory pleasure in an ordinary sight. The poem—or the moment of perception it reports—evokes no cultural traditions or literary associations. The absence of these is strongly noticed, however, for if the poem is an immediate experience, it is also a demonstration and argument. "So much depends," it says, on the object being there, but it also means that so much depends on the reader's response to what is seen. If one's response is dull, the world takes on this quality, and the converse is also true. Thus, although Williams believed that the American environment offered a new challenge and possibility to poetry, his deeper meaning was that anything, however familiar or even drab, would become significant and moving when met with a full response.

"SPRING AND ALL"

First published: 1923 (collected in *The Collected Poems of William Carlos Williams: Volume I, 1909-1939*, 1986)

Type of work: Poem

Williams celebrates the struggle of all new life to assert itself and discover its innate form.

"Spring and All" is a poem of only twenty-seven lines, yet it echoes some of the imagery as well as the concepts of T. S. Eliot's *The Waste Land* (1922) and is filled with Williams's desire to break with poetic tradition. The poem reveals this in the second and third words of the title. Spring is one of the most traditional themes of poetry; "and All" deflates it.

The poem corrects poetic notions of spring—those one finds, for example, in Geoffrey Chaucer's famous opening of *The Canterbury Tales* (1387-1400), in which he describes the "sweet" season of flowers, bird songs, and balmy winds. Beginning with a description of a bleak winter scene on a road through muddy fields, the poem turns (in stanza five) to the tentative awakening of spring and the "naked,/ cold, uncertain" leaves of grass which are the first evidence of the return of life to the world. At first unconscious, the spring plants gradually acquire awareness as they come to life: "rooted, they/ grip down and begin to awaken."

Thus the poem depicts the cyclical rebirth of life, which is here, through the allusion to the "awakening" and awareness of plants, connected to intelligence and thus to humanity. A deft touch is the transition from winter images to images of spring, achieved in only seven words in the fifth stanza; the two lines of the stanza are connected organically to the preceding passage by one word,

"lifeless," which echoes "leafless" in the fourth stanza. The poem's simple and understated ending is typical of Williams's pared-down style. Through Williams's sensitive concentration on the new life of trees and shrubs struggling into being in the cold spring wind, "Spring and All" celebrates the struggle of all new life to assert itself.

"THE YACHTS"

First published: 1935 (collected in *The Collected Poems of William Carlos Williams: Volume I, 1909-1939*, 1986)

Type of work: Poem

Despite its beauty, a yacht race during the Depression reminds Williams's speaker of social inequality and injustice.

In "The Yachts," Williams's more typical penchant for imagistic presentation coexists with a tendency toward symbolism. Halfway through the poem, there is an interesting and unusual shift from an imagistic to a symbolic mode. The occasion is a yacht race in a bay protected from the "too-heavy blows/ of an ungoverned ocean."

During the preparations for the race, the speaker is impressed by the physical beauty of the graceful craft, "Mothlike in mists, scintillant in the minute/ brilliance of cloudless days, with broad bellying sails." Although the appeal is primarily imagistic, there is a metaphoric suggestion in the observation that the yachts, surrounded by more clumsy "sycophant" craft,

> appear youthful, rare
>
> as the light of a happy eye, live with the grace
> of all that in the mind is feckless, free and
> naturally to be desired.

As the race begins, however, after a delaying lull, the scene changes ominously. The waves of the roughening water now seem to be human bodies overridden and cut down by the sharp bows of the yachts: "It is a sea of faces about them in agony, in despair/ until the horror of the race dawns staggering the mind." The original appeal of the beautiful spectacle of pleasure boats is broken and then displaced by the revelation of deeper meaning. The race is finally shown to be a symbol of human struggle, in which the masses are cut down and destroyed.

There remains a question as to the nature of the struggle. Is it to be understood simply as a common battle for survival in nature, in Darwinist terms, or does it have more specific social implications? The yachts inevitably suggest a privileged life. As the fruits of surplus wealth acquired within a protected socioeconomic preserve (like an enclosed bay), the leisure and beauty of the life they represent exists at the expense of an exploited class. For all its seductive appeal, supported by long custom and tradition, the spectacle of the yacht race in a poem of the Depression period (the poem was written in 1935) must be a reminder of social inequality and injustice.

The movement of the poem from imagistic charm to symbolic horror is in accord with the shift in the poet's perception from a preoccupation with sensuous phenomena to an awareness of human meaning and value—the necessary movement, in short, from image to metaphor, without which the poetic presentation of such an event would remain an innocuous imagistic diversion.

PATERSON

First published: 1946-1958
Type of work: Long poem

Paterson *envisions the epic development of that New Jersey town and its inhabitants as representative of modern urban America.*

Paterson is a long poem originally in four parts, or books, published separately in 1946, 1948, 1949, and 1951, although sections of them had existed in various forms in earlier works. Williams added a fifth part in 1958, and fragments of the incomplete Book VI were published posthumously (1963) as an appendix to the collection of the first five parts. According to most critics, *Paterson* is one of Williams's greatest works and one of the finest long poems written by an American.

Like most long modern poems that abandon traditional narrative forms, *Paterson* is not easy to follow. One must first understand its basic and arbitrary symbols. The protagonist, Paterson, is a city, man, doctor, and poet. The land (sometimes personified as a woman) is not only that waiting to be civilized but also the poet's raw material. The river is both language and the natural movement of historical life. Thus, before the poem begins, the author's note declares, "A man in himself is a city, beginning, seeking, achieving and concluding his life in ways which the various aspects of a city may embody—if imaginatively conceived—any city, all the details of which may be made to voice his most intimate convictions."

Although primarily a book-length poem, the work also incorporates prose passages from historical documents, newspaper accounts, geological surveys, literary texts, and personal letters. As subject, Williams uses the city of Paterson on the Passaic River near his hometown of Rutherford, New Jersey, so as to bring forth the universal from a local setting. The poem presents local history and the natural scene (particularly Passaic Falls and Garrett Mountain) as well as the consciousness of a gigantic, mythic man (Paterson) and of the author—poet and doctor.

Paterson's struggle to interpret the language of the falls, his search for an expressive American language, is the major motif of the poem. *Paterson* swarms with characters, incidents, impressions, and dramatic passages, bound together by the work's wide-ranging introspective and associative process and its quest: "Rigor of beauty is the quest. But how will you find beauty when it is locked in the mind past all remonstrance?" Williams dissociated and consciously recombined these narrative, descriptive, and lyric elements in the manner of a montage or cubist painting. The jagged, juxtaposed collage effects are one way Williams hopes to break through contaminated words to reality.

Although there are echoes of both Pound and Eliot, the poem's basic technique is that of Irish novelist James Joyce's *Finnegans Wake* (1939). Williams took certain historical places and events (the town of Paterson, the Passaic River, and events recorded in local histories and newspapers) and forged them into a myth. The poem's general theme is the decay of life in a small eastern town meant to mirror American society. The falls above the town suggest both the possibility of good and healthy life and the correlative health of native speech. True to both history and myth, however, the river below the falls becomes polluted by industry, and the people's language and the people themselves take on a parallel dirtiness, loss of purpose, and inability to communicate. The process of decay, however, is not irreversible, as Williams indicates late in Book IV of the poem, when he insists that the sea (into which the river issues) is not humankind's true home.

Book I, "The Delineaments of the Giants," mythologizes the early history of Paterson in an effort to define the "elemental character of the place" and introduces the city (a masculine force), the landscape (a feminine principle), and the vital, unifying river. In this book, the city is linked with the as-yet-undiscovered identity of the poet. The river, which "comes pouring in above the city," is the stream of history and of life as well as the stream of language from which the poet must derive his speech:

> (What common language to unravel?
> .   .   combed into straight lines
> from that rafter of a rock's
> lip.)

Book II, "Sunday in the Park," concerned with "modern replicas" of the life of the past, meditates on failures in communication through language, religion, economics, and sex. The park, "female to the city," brings the poet into contact with the immediate physical world, the sensual life that he must transform. Here the Sunday crowd, the "great beast" (as Alexander Hamilton had called the people), takes its pleasure, pursues its desires among the "churring loves" of nature and within the sound of the voice of an evangelist, who vainly tries to bring them into the truth through the language of traditional religion, which Williams regards as outworn and simply another block to expression. Williams suggests, however, that redemption is possible through art, imagination, and memory.

In Book III, "The Library," the poet turns in his search for a common language from his immediate world to the literature (broadly interpreted) of the past. He moves from the previous section's "confused uproar" of the falls to find that "books will give rest sometimes"; they provide a sanctuary for "dead men's dreams." The past, however, represents only desolation, destruction, and death. Paterson's quest for beauty must continue. He says, "I must/ find my meaning and lay it, white,/ beside the sliding water: myself—/ comb out the language—or succumb."

Book IV, "The Run to the Sea," treats the polluted water below Passaic Falls in terms of corruption by modern civilization, while recognizing innovations in science, economics, and language. Finally, however, the identity of the river is lost in the sea, although the individual man (Paterson) survives and strides inland to begin again.

Book V, published seven years after Book IV, reveals a substantial continuity of image, theme, and metrical form, but there are significant differences in Williams's attitudes and in the treatment of certain themes carried over from the earlier books. Untitled, but dedicated to the French Impressionist artist Henri Toulouse-Lautrec, Book V is like a separate work, an oblique commentary on the poem by an aged poet from a point of view more international and universal than local. As for the poem's quest for beauty, this book shows that the only beauty that persists is art. Of the various Patersons (Paterson the Sleeping Giant; Paterson, New Jersey; Paterson Williams), *Paterson*, Book V is most intimately concerned with Paterson as Williams himself. The first four books found the place; it is himself the poet must now find—or rather, find again.

Paterson is a complex and difficult poem, yet it is honest and uncompromising. Williams lives in a world in which wholeness is intellectually indefensible; thus he makes no suggestion of the possibility of a wholeness representative of a systemized worldview. In this respect, *Paterson* is more modern and representative of its science-minded, skeptical age than myth-oriented poems such as *The Waste Land* of Eliot and *The Bridge* (1930) of Hart Crane, which depend for their basic organization upon the pattern of the rebirth archetype. On a much larger scale than in Williams's other poetic works, *Paterson* is a vigorous effort to discover the "common language" shared by the poet and the American people.

"THE CLOUDS"

First published: 1948 (collected in *The Collected Poems of William Carlos Williams: Volume II, 1939-1962*, 1988)
Type of work: Poem

Clouds take on many meanings in this poem about individual expression and expression and the life of the imagination.

Williams's insistence upon the freedom of the mind and hatred of conventional restraints is powerfully expressed in "The Clouds," a four-part poem in which the central image is the march of the ever-changing clouds across the sky. As natural phenomena, the stuff on which the mind and imagination feed, they symbolize the shifting flux of experience in which one must find human significance if one is to be more than a turtle in a swamp.

Clouds also represent the "unshorn" minds of free spirits such as Francois Villon, Desiderius, Erasmus, and William Shakespeare, who "wrote so that/ no school man or churchman could sanction him without/ revealing his own imbecility." These minds, like the skeptical Socrates, "Plato's better self," accepted the fact of human mortality and devoted themselves to the life of the mind and imagination—a life to which Williams gives precedence: "The intellect leads, leads still! Beyond the clouds."

In a brief and lively "Scherzo" (part 3 of the poem), Williams remembers coming as a tourist upon a priest in St. Andrew's in Amalfi, Italy, "riding/ the clouds of his belief," as he performed a Mass, "jiggling upon his buttocks to the litany":

I was amazed and stared in such manner

that he, caught half off the earth
in his ecstasy—though without losing a beat—
turned and grinned at me from his cloud.

Although he recognizes the ritual to be an act of the imagination, to Williams, the priest's cloud is not enough. In its regularity and neat order, reassuring though these may be to believers, it stands in contrast to "the disordered heavens, ragged, ripped by winds," which the poet, who accepts a naturalistic outlook, must confront in his search for form and meaning. The "soul" is the precious burden of the life of the imagination that each individual has a share in carrying forward, humanistically, from generation to generation: "It is that which is the brotherhood:/ the old life, treasured."

IN THE AMERICAN GRAIN

First published: 1925
Type of work: Essays

Williams attempts to discover the essential qualities of the American character by focusing on the lives and words of major and minor figures in American history.

Williams's collection of essays *In the American Grain*, first conceived in the early 1920's, was undertaken, the writer said, "to try to find out for myself what the land of my more or less accidental birth might signify" by direct examination of the original records of American founders. His hope was to rediscover the unmediated truth about the founders, the makers, and the discoverers of America. "In letters, in journals, reports of happenings," he says, "I have recognized new contours suggested by old words so that new names were constituted."

Williams divided *In the American Grain* into twenty chapters ranging in time and place from the settlement of Greenland, through the voyages of Christopher Columbus, to the exploration of Kentucky and the Civil War. In form, the essays include dramatic narratives, lyric interludes, brief character sketches, whole sections of Columbus's journals, Cotton Mather's *The Wonders of the Invisible World* (1693), Daniel Boone's autobiography, and excerpts from John Paul Jones's letters and log entries.

Taking his subjects in chronological order, Williams begins with the exploration and settlement of Greenland by Erik the Red and his son, Leif Erikkson; he ends with a prose poem on Abraham Lincoln during the Civil War. The collection includes sketches of such major or representative historical figures as Columbus, Hernán Cortés, Sir Walter Ralegh, Benjamin Franklin, George Washington, and Edgar Allan Poe.

In addition, Williams wrote essays on minor figures, such as Ponce de León, Hernando de Soto, Père Sebastian Rasles, Aaron Burr, and Sam Houston. Most of these apparently minor figures, especially Rasles, assume heroic proportions after Williams's assessment of their encounters in the New World. Williams's meditations on America's discoverers also include consideration of attitudes toward violence, sports, and commerce in the United States of the 1920's as well as such blights on the American conscience as the slaves ("Poised against the *Mayflower* is the slave ship . . . bringing another race to try upon the New World") and the suppression of women ("So Jacataqua gave to womanhood in her time, the form which bitterness of pioneer character had denied it"). Williams's hope in these essays is to restore his readers' awareness of the past.

Even the original records distort the truth about the past, Williams claims, so that it must be re-

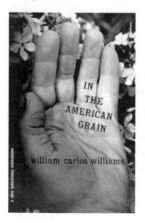

searched and reconstituted in new writing in order to be understood. In his attempt to get back to "the strange phosphorus of the life" that precedes every effort made to record it, he therefore metaphorically repeats or imitates the action of his subjects, who abandoned the advanced culture of Europe in order to go back to the beginning again, back to the forces and conditions that precede culture.

In order to restore a past lost through use of the wrong words to describe it, Williams often employs the words of his subjects so as to convey their ways of vision and expression. He attempted to compose each chapter in a style suited to its subject, copying and using what that subject had recorded. In "The Discovery of the Indies," for example, Williams makes extensive use of Columbus's journals.

In some chapters Williams allows his subjects to speak for themselves, verbatim. "Cotton Mather's *Wonders of the Invisible World*" consists entirely of excerpts from that book. A major theme of *In the American Grain* results from Williams's strategy of exploring, through myriad voices, ways in which his subjects viewed new worlds. Williams contends that history is as much a matter of language and imagination as of data; the past may be falsified by a misuse of language, failure to recognize its nuances, failure to perceive "new contours" in "old words." His use of sources is somewhat like his friend Ezra Pound's approach to translation. Williams is not afraid to compress, adapt, or modify in order to express more strongly and succinctly the spirit of his subjects; he does not feel it necessary to provide scholarly footnotes explaining his method.

To Williams, then, American history is not a result but a process. Because history is what is alive or dead in a present mind, any fixed idea of the past that one might hold is a fixation in oneself. That is why Williams urges, "History must stay open, it is all humanity." In order to keep history open, Williams orchestrated a conversation of many voices, dramatizing the continuing discovery (of the past and of oneself) that may occur as one pays attention to his historical ground.

From the beginning of his series of essays, Williams is aware of a dichotomy, of two types of people. On one hand were those, the Indians and some explorers, travelers and settlers, whose contact with the new continents of North and South America was positive. On the other hand were those who voyaged to the new land to prey upon it and either to return to the Old World with their plunder or, somewhat later, to settle on the land, as the Puritans did, and yet reject contact with it and inhibit the contact of others.

Another keen observer of the American spirit, D. H. Lawrence, expressing what he had learned from Williams's books, identified two major ways that Americans react to their continent. The first, and most common, is to recoil into individual smallness and insentience, and then to gut the great continent in mean fear. It is the Puritan way. The second way is to touch America as it is; to dare to touch it. This is the heroic way. Thus Williams's true heroes are those, like Columbus, Rasles, Boone, and the American Indian, who had embraced the gritty, fearful truth of America and had loved it.

In the American Grain is not a history book but an act of discovery, in which Williams attempted to "find out for myself what the land of my more or less accidental birth might signify." In its treatment of the makers of American history, ranging from Erikkson to Lincoln, *In the American Grain* has impressed many as Williams's most succinct definition of America and its people. The collection of essays is an exhilarating effort to reexamine the key figures, historical events, and documents that reveal the essence of America's myth about itself and its underlying psychological pressures. With Lawrence's *Studies in Classic American Literature* (1923), it stands as a pioneering effort in critical thinking.

SUMMARY

For most of his life Williams waged war against reductiveness—the tendency of human beings to mistake the part for the whole or the explanation for the reality. He wrote lyric poems, an epic, short stories, novels, essays, a remarkable volume of American history, and an autobiography, consciously reshaping these literary forms in the hope of engaging readers more directly and fully with experience. The cultural impact of Williams's achievements was registered slowly, but his influence on major poets of the succeeding generation has been pivotal, and a sense of the importance of his example continues to increase.

James W. Robinson, Jr.

DISCUSSION TOPICS

- What neglected virtues does William Carlos Williams encourage in "Tract"?

- What is the explanation of the fascination felt by so many readers of Williams's very short poem "The Red Wheelbarrow"?

- Does *Paterson* succeed as an American equivalent of T. S. Eliot's *The Waste Land* (1922)?

- Consider Williams as a poet of understatement.

- Williams brought the experiences of a practicing physician to many of his short stories. Identify several of these stories.

- What "essential qualities of the American character" are revealed in *In the American Grain?*

BIBLIOGRAPHY

By the Author
Poems, 1909
The Tempers, 1913
Al Que Quiere!, 1917
Kora in Hell: Improvisations, 1920
Sour Grapes, 1921
Spring and All, 1923
Last Nights of Paris, 1929 (translation of Philippe Soupault; with Elena Williams)
Collected Poems, 1921-1931, 1934
An Early Martyr, and Other Poems, 1935
Adam & Eve & The City, 1936
The Complete Collected Poems of William Carlos Williams, 1906-1938, 1938
The Broken Span, 1941
The Wedge, 1944
Paterson, 1946-1958
The Clouds, 1948
Selected Poems, 1949
Collected Later Poems, 1950, 1963
Collected Earlier Poems, 1951
The Desert Music, and Other Poems, 1954
A Dog and the Fever, 1954 (translation of Pedro Espinosa; with Elena Williams)

Journey to Love, 1955
Pictures from Brueghel, 1962
Selected Poems, 1985
The Collected Poems of William Carlos Williams: Volume I, 1909-1939, 1986
The Collected Poems of William Carlos Williams: Volume II, 1939-1962, 1988

LONG FICTION:
The Great American Novel, 1923
A Voyage to Pagany, 1928
White Mule, 1937
In the Money, 1940
The Build-up, 1952

SHORT FICTION:
The Knife of the Times, and Other Stories, 1932
Life Along the Passaic River, 1938
Make Light of It: Collected Stories, 1950
The Farmers' Daughters: The Collected Stories of William Carlos Williams, 1961
The Doctor Stories, 1984

DRAMA:
A Dream of Love, pb. 1948
Many Loves, and Other Plays, pb. 1961

NONFICTION:
In the American Grain, 1925
A Novelette, and Other Prose, 1932
The Autobiography of William Carlos Williams, 1951
Selected Essays of William Carlos Williams, 1954
The Selected Letters of William Carlos Williams, 1957
I Wanted to Write a Poem: The Autobiography of the Works of a Poet, 1958
The Embodiment of Knowledge, 1974
A Recognizable Image, 1978
William Carlos Williams, John Sanford: A Correspondence, 1984
William Carlos Williams and James Laughlin: Selected Letters, 1989
Pound/Williams: Selected Letters of Ezra Pound and William Carlos Williams, 1996 (Hugh Witemeyer, editor)
The Humane Particulars: The Collected Letters of William Carlos Williams and Kenneth Burke, 2003 (James H. East, editor)
The Correspondence of William Carlos Williams and Louis Zukofsky, 2003 (Barry Ahearn, editor)

TRANSLATIONS:
Last Nights of Paris, 1929 (of Philippe Soupault; with Raquel Hélène Williams)
A Dog and the Fever, 1954 (of Francisco de Quevedo; with Raquel Hélène Williams)

MISCELLANEOUS:
The Descent of Winter, 1928 (includes poetry, prose, and anecdotes)
Imaginations, 1970 (includes poetry, fiction, and nonfiction)

About the Author

Axelrod, Steven Gould, and Helen Deese, eds. *Critical Essays on William Carlos Williams.* New York: G. K. Hall, 1995.

Beck, John. *Writing the Radical Center: William Carlos Williams, John Dewey, and American Cultural Politics.* Albany: State University of New York Press, 2001.

Bremen, Brian A. *William Carlos Williams and the Diagnostics of Culture.* New York: Oxford University Press, 1993.

Copestake, Ian D., ed. *Rigor of Beauty: Essays in Commemoration of William Carlos Williams.* New York: Peter Lang, 2004.

Fisher-Wirth, Ann W. *William Carlos Williams and Autobiography: The Woods of His Own Nature.* University Park: Pennsylvania State University Press, 1989.

Gish, Robert. *William Carlos Williams: A Study of the Short Fiction.* Boston: Twayne, 1989.

Laughlin, James. *Remembering William Carlos Williams.* New York: New Directions, 1995.

Lenhart, Gary, ed. *The Teachers and Writers Guide to William Carlos Williams.* New York: Teachers & Writers Collaborative, 1998.

Lowney, John. *The American Avant-Garde Tradition: William Carlos Williams, Postmodern Poetry, and the Politics of Cultural Memory.* Lewisburg, Pa.: Bucknell University Press, 1997.

Mariani, Paul. *William Carlos Williams: A New World Naked.* 1981. Reprint. New York: W. W. Norton, 1990.

Vendler, Helen, ed. *Voices and Visions: The Poet in America.* New York: Random House, 1987.

Whitaker, Thomas R. *William Carlos Williams.* Boston: Twayne, 1989.

David Cooper/Courtesy, Yale Repertory Theatre

AUGUST WILSON

Born: Pittsburgh, Pennsylvania,
April 27, 1945
Died: Seattle, Washington
October 2, 2005

Wilson's award-winning plays earned him acclaim as one of the leading playwrights of his time by offering authentic accounts of the black experience in twentieth century America.

BIOGRAPHY

August Wilson was born in Pittsburgh, Pennsylvania, in 1945. The son of a white father who was rarely around his family and a black mother who struggled to raise her six children on welfare and her meager income from janitorial jobs, Wilson learned at first hand about the hardships and prejudice facing black people in American society.

When the family moved to a predominantly white neighborhood, bricks were thrown through their windows, and Wilson's schools days at Central Catholic High School were clouded by the racial epithets he often found scrawled on his desk. Wilson's mother, a proud, determined woman who insisted that her children spend time each day reading, imbued young August with a sense of pride and self-esteem.

Wilson's formal schooling ended in the ninth grade. Refusing to believe that a well-researched and footnoted paper that Wilson submitted could be his own work, his teacher gave him a failing grade. Wilson tore up the paper and never returned to school, choosing instead to educate himself at the local public library, where he read extensively on a wide range of subjects. There, he discovered for the first time the works of black authors such as Langston Hughes, Ralph Ellison, and Richard Wright.

Wilson's teens were for him a time of great anger and frustration, which found occasional release in outbursts of rage as he and his friends smashed the black lawn jockeys that they found in front of white homes. During the 1960's, Wilson joined several Black Power organizations, and for many years he adopted a militant stance toward society's racial injustices.

He supported himself during this period with a brief stint in the Army and by working as a short-order cook and a stock clerk. A keen observer of the world around him, he also began storing up the details of life in the black community that would later inform his plays, lending to them the authenticity that has made them successful.

Wilson's career as a writer began almost by chance when he was twenty. His older sister paid him twenty dollars to write a college term paper for her, and he used the money to buy himself a used typewriter. Still supporting himself with odd jobs, Wilson began writing poetry and became associated with the Black Arts movement in Pittsburgh. In 1968, he and playwright Rob Penny founded the Black Horizon Theater, where he worked as a producer and director.

Wilson began writing one-act plays in the early 1970's, but it was not until 1978 when he moved to St. Paul, Minnesota, that he began writing his first full-length play, *Jitney* (1979), the first entry in his ten-play dramatic cycle about African American life in the twentieth century United States. It was also during this period that Wilson met and married his second wife, Judy Oliver. From his earlier marriage he had a daughter, Sakina.

In 1979, Wilson began submitting plays to the O'Neill National Playwrights Conference. When his first four submissions were rejected—the conference rejected *Jitney* twice—Wilson found himself reassessing his previous efforts and embarking on a new project that would test the true depth of his writing talents. The result, *Ma Rainey's Black Bottom*, was accepted by the O'Neill Conference and given a staged reading in 1982.

It was there that Wilson met the conference's artistic director, Lloyd Richards. A powerful force within the American theater community, Richards was for many years the dean of the Yale University School of Drama and the director of the school's acclaimed repertory theater, as well as the first African American ever to direct a play on Broadway. Their meeting led to an ongoing collaboration between writer and director that would contribute greatly to Wilson's subsequent work.

At Richards's urging, Wilson applied for and received numerous grants and fellowships that allowed him to concentrate his efforts solely on his writing. Wilson's plays had their original stagings under Richards's direction at the Yale Repertory Theater before moving on to other regional theaters and to Broadway.

Ma Rainey's Black Bottom opened on Broadway in 1984 and received the New York Drama Critics Circle Award, and Wilson followed it in 1987 with *Fences*, which received four Tony Awards, the Drama Critics Circle Award, the first American Theater Critics Association New Play Award, and the Pulitzer Prize in drama.

Fences was followed by *Joe Turner's Come and Gone* in 1988 and *The Piano Lesson* in 1990, both of which received the Critics Circle Award. *The Piano Lesson* also brought Wilson his second Pulitzer Prize. In 1992, *Two Trains Running*, which received the Critics Circle Award and the American Theater Critics Association New Play Award, opened on Broadway.

In 1997, his early play *Jitney* was revived at the Crossroads Theatre in New Brunswick, New Jersey, and received enthusiastic reviews. The following year, Wilson received the Edward Albee Last Frontier Playwright Award. He collaborated with Victor Walker and others to form the African Grove Institute at Dartmouth College, where he also taught during the 1998 academic year.

In 1999, Wilson completed *King Hedley II*, which had its premiere at the Pittsburgh Public Theatre. The play went on to Broadway, where it was about to be closed after twenty-four preview performances and seventy-two regular performances. When it was nominated for a Tony as best play of 2001, however, its run was extended for another ten weeks.

Wilson completed the last play of his ten-cycle, decade-by-decade assessment of African American life in the United States, *Radio Golf*, within months of his death. It was presented at the Mark Taper Forum in Los Angeles in September, 2005. Wilson succumbed to liver cancer on October 2, 2005.

ANALYSIS

Since he first gained recognition with the Broadway production of *Ma Rainey's Black Bottom* in 1984, Wilson was hailed by critics as one of the most important writers to appear in the American theater in the late twentieth century. His work has received numerous awards, including two Pulitzer Prizes, and Wilson himself was the recipient of several grants and fellowships, including the McKnight Fellowship in Playwriting, the Whiting Writer's Award, and Bush, Rockefeller, and Guggenheim Fellowships. He was hailed by *The New York Times* as "the theater's most astonishing writing discovery in this decade" and by William A. Henry III, the theater critic for *Time*, as "certainly the most important voice to emerge in the Eighties, maybe the most important in the last thirty years or so."

Wilson brought to the American theater a fresh perspective on a subject he knows intimately: the lives of African Americans struggling to survive in a society riddled with prejudice and hatred. Declaring that "language is the secret to a race," Wilson gave voice in his plays to the rhythms, cadences, and phrasings heard in the homes and on the streets of the black community, bringing to life characters whose experiences had previously been given little exposure outside of that community.

From Troy Maxon in *Fences*, who opposes his son's athletic scholarship because he believes it will lead only to disappointment, to Levee, the jazz musician in *Ma Rainey's Black Bottom* who sells the rights to his music to a white recording company, to Hambone in *Two Trains Running*, who has been driven to the point of madness by his obsessive quest for the ham that he is owed in payment by a white employer, Wilson's characters capture the pain and struggle of the African American experience with a complexity and power that transform everyday life into compelling drama.

Wilson believed firmly that the road to empowerment for African Americans must include a willingness to embrace their heritage and draw on the sense of history it provides. He urged black America to study its complex legacy, from the culture of Africa itself through slavery, segregation, and the Civil Rights movement, and search there for the examples of courage and endurance that lie at the heart of any people's sense of pride and self-awareness.

In a 1987 interview, Wilson said, "Blacks in America want to forget about slavery—the stigma, the shame. That's the wrong move. If you can't be who you are, who can you be? How can you know what to do? We have our history. We have our book, which is the blues. And we forget it all." As a playwright, Wilson set out to explore African American history, in all of its diversity, through dramatic means.

Beginning with his earliest full-length work, *Jitney*, he embarked on an ambitious cycle of plays, each set in a different decade, focusing on different aspects of the black experience in the twentieth century. The plays were not written in chronological order; *Jitney*, although the first written, is set in the 1970's. It concerns Pittsburgh's black jitney bus drivers, who created jobs for themselves by driving fares into black neighborhoods where white cab drivers refused to go.

Ma Rainey's Black Bottom is set in a 1920's Chicago recording studio, where a great blues singer is working in a setting seething with racial tensions. *Fences*, the next play in the cycle, depicts the conflicts within a black family in the 1950's, as a father and son clash over the son's future.

Joe Turner's Come and Gone is set in 1911 and tells the story of a man who has made his way to Pittsburgh after enduring years of illegal enforced servitude in the South. *The Piano Lesson* takes place in the 1930's and focuses on the Charles family and their conflict over a piano that represents the family's heritage.

Two Trains Running is set in a Pittsburgh restaurant and explores the lives of urban black people amid the turmoil of the 1960's. *Gem of the Ocean* is set in 1904, the earliest setting of the plays in Wilson's cycle.

These plays examine widely differing facets of the black experience, yet similar themes and messages pervade all of them: the destructive results of racial discrimination; the need for courage, determination, and pride in the face of the staggering legacy of black history; and an appreciation for black culture itself—both artistic and social—as a means of survival.

Wilson's characters are frequently flawed and always complex, their individual personalities shaped by the experiences that have made up their lives. Their despair and hardships can be traced to the crushing denial of their worth by the dominant white society, and their salvation comes only through self-reliance and self-acceptance. In many of Wilson's plays, rage and frustration that remain unresolved are directed not at white people but at other black people, perpetuating the destructive cycle.

Like all great writers, Wilson himself was influenced by other artists whose work he admired. His early influences included the poets Dylan Thomas and John Berryman as well as Ralph Ellison, author of *Invisible Man* (1952). Wilson named as his principal inspirations a quartet he termed "my four B's": playwright Amiri Baraka, the Argentinean writer Jorge Luis Borges, the artist Romare Bearden (whose paintings inspired both *Joe Turner's Come and Gone* and *The Piano Lesson*), and, heading his list, the blues.

MA RAINEY'S BLACK BOTTOM

First produced: 1984 (first published, 1985)
Type of work: Play

A group of blues musicians in the 1920's deal with the effects of racial injustice.

Ma Rainey's Black Bottom, the first of Wilson's plays to win wide acclaim, is among his finest work. Set in a recording studio in the 1920's, the story takes place over the course of an afternoon, as a group of musicians and the legendary blues singer Ma Rainey record several songs. Much of the play takes the form of discussions and arguments among the four musicians, each of whom brings his own perspective to questions of prejudice and the problems facing black people in American society.

Toledo, a thoughtful, serious man, speaks of racial pride and the need for self-determination. Cutler places his trust in religion. Slow Drag is uncomplicated and unwilling to question his lot too deeply. Levee believes that his musical talent will bring him respect and power. Ma Rainey is outspoken, demanding, and well aware that she will be tolerated only as long as her records make money for her white producers.

Ma Rainey's Black Bottom contains many of the themes that run throughout Wilson's subsequent work: the devastating effects of racial discrimination, the callous indifference with which white society has traditionally regarded black Americans, and the idea that the key to black self-reliance and salvation lies in developing a sense of heritage and history. The play's central message is contained in a comment made by Toledo: "As long as the colored man looks to white folks to put the crown on what he say . . . as long as he looks to white folks for approval . . . then he ain't never gonna find out who he is and what he's about. He's just gonna be about what white folks want him to be about."

Ma Rainey is as aware as Toledo of the harsh realities of black life in American society, commenting that "they don't care nothing about me. All they want is my voice." Fiercely determined to play her hand well for as long as it lasts, she demands star treatment and respect from her producers, knowing that she can expect nothing from them when her popularity wanes.

For Toledo and Levee, however, Toledo's words will have tragic repercussions. As Levee sees his dreams of fame and success dissolve into the reality of the producer's offer to pay him five dollars per song to "take them off your hands," his anger turns to murderous rage against Toledo, who has accidentally stepped on his shoe. The opening Levee thought he saw in the white power structure was an illusion, and it is Toledo who pays the price for his despair.

FENCES

First produced: 1985 (first published, 1985)
Type of work: Play

A black family is torn apart by the father's adultery and his refusal to let his son accept a football scholarship.

Wilson received his first Pulitzer Prize for *Fences*, which also won several Tony Awards during its Broadway run. The powerful family drama is set during the 1950's, when the first hints of change in race relations often gave rise to generational conflicts between hopeful young black men and their wary, experience-scarred parents.

The play was inspired by Wilson's memories of his own stepfather, a onetime high school football player who had hoped to win an athletic scholarship and study medicine, only to find that no college in Pittsburgh would give a scholarship to a black player.

In *Fences*, Wilson's stepfather, Troy Maxson, is a proud, hardworking garbageman who once played baseball in the Negro Leagues. Embittered by the disappointments of his own life, Troy refuses to believe that times have changed when his son, Cory, is offered a football scholarship. Certain that athletics hold no hope of a better life for his son, Troy refuses to sign the necessary papers, effectively denying Cory his chance at a college education. Troy also deeply angers his wife when she learns that he has fathered a child by another woman, an act that destroys the bond that has held the couple together throughout their bleak life together.

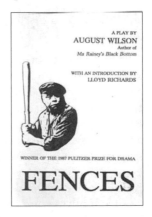

At the heart of the play's father/son conflict is an unbridgeable disparity between Troy and Cory's abilities to believe that society can indeed change the way it treats black Americans. Although Troy's unbending harshness often casts him in an unsympathetic light, Wilson grounds his character's personality in the frustrations and injustices that have shaped the course of his life. Cory is unable to understand the full impact of the events that have influenced his father's attitudes, and the two men ultimately engage in a showdown that destroys their relationship.

Fences is also a story about relationships between husbands and wives, and in Rose Maxson, Wilson has created one of his strongest female characters. Rose's rage at her husband's betrayal, her articulate refusal to accept his justifications as valid, and her painful decision to raise Troy's illegitimate daughter as her own all mark her as a complex and remarkable character.

Wilson's plays are notable for the powerful voice given to black women as well as black men, and nowhere is this more in evidence than in the compassionate, impassioned characterization of Rose. Her words speak for a generation of black women, just as her husband's life embodies the hardships faced by black men.

THE PIANO LESSON

First produced: 1987 (first published, 1990)
Type of work: Play

A brother and sister argue over a family heirloom, a piano that represents their heritage as the descendants of slaves.

The Piano Lesson brought Wilson his second Pulitzer Prize in drama, and, as in *Fences*, its subject is a family conflict. The story is set in 1930's Pittsburgh, where Doaker Charles lives with his niece, Berniece, and her young daughter, Maretha. The arrival of Berniece's brother, Boy Willie, from Mississippi sets the plot in motion, as Boy Willie declares his intention of selling a piano that holds a unique place in the family's history.

Originally owned by a man named Sutter, who had received it in payment for Doaker's grandmother and father, the piano was carved by Doaker's grandfather with scenes depicting the family's life in slavery. Berniece refuses to part with such a powerful symbol of her family's terrible history, while Boy Willie hopes to earn enough from the sale to buy Sutter's land from his descendants.

At the center of the pair's disagreement is the is-

sue of confronting rather than rejecting the African American heritage of slavery. For Berniece, the piano is a source of strength; it reminds her of the courage and endurance shown by her ancestors, and she believes that selling the piano would be a denial of that history. Boy Willie believes in looking only to the future, and he cannot understand his sister's refusal to part with the instrument.

An unexpected dimension is added to the story with Berniece and Doaker's declarations that they have seen the ghost of Sutter's grandson, whom Berniece believes Boy Willie murdered in order to get his land. The ghost is a very real presence in the play; Wilson was not afraid to incorporate aspects of the supernatural in his work and also did so in *Joe Turner's Come and Gone*.

In both plays, phenomena that might be dismissed as fantastic are embraced as an outgrowth of African culture and are incorporated into the story in imaginative and effective ways. *The Piano Lesson*'s dramatic conflict is resolved when Boy Willie does battle with the ghost as Berniece draws on the power of the piano itself to exorcise the spirit. The action is both dramatically compelling and a stunning symbolic evocation of the power that black history can bring to those who embrace it.

TWO TRAINS RUNNING

First produced: 1992 (first published, 1993)
Type of work: Play

Wilson identifies the two trains in his title as two inevitabilities that humans face: life and death.

Part of his ten-play cycle, one for each decade of the century, *Two Trains Running* takes place in Pittsburgh in 1969 during a period of both hope and despair for African Americans.

Early in the decade, Jackie Robinson was elected to the Baseball Hall of Fame, the first black player to achieve such an honor. Registration of southern black voters reached new levels. Dr. Martin Luther King, Jr., was awarded the Nobel Peace Prize in 1964 and the following year led three thousand people on a fifty-four-mile protest march between Selma and Montgomery, Alabama. Thurgood Marshall became the first black Supreme Court Justice in 1967, and in 1968 the Civil Rights Act was passed by Congress.

Despite such progress, civil rights workers, black and white, were murdered as they attempted to secure equal rights for southern black people. Dr. King was murdered in 1968, as Malcolm X had been three years earlier. It is against such a backdrop that Wilson sets his play, which takes place in Memphis Lee's homestyle family restaurant, a gathering place for black people that faces demolition as the neighborhood in which it is located encounters urban renewal.

The regulars at Lee's are a mortician, a bookie, a street philosopher, and a man who is disturbed by petty injustices. Into the setting Wilson interposes Sterling, an African American who wants to preserve the spirit and philosophy of Malcolm X.

Sterling, a former convict, begins to hit on Risa, the restaurant's sole waitress and cook, who has disfigured herself to discourage the sorts of advances that Sterling is making. Meanwhile, Memphis Lee has larger concerns, most notably his struggle with city hall to get at least a fair price for his restaurant if and when it is razed.

In this play, Wilson forces his characters to look into themselves and to discover who they really are and what they really want. Memphis certainly is ambiguous. He would like to keep his restaurant, but he also is plotting to feather his nest if he cannot do so, which is only prudent. In this play, Wilson illustrates convincingly that people are the stories that they tell. Their very identities lurk in the stories, both fictional and nonfictional, that they create.

SEVEN GUITARS

First produced: 1995 (first published, 1996)
Type of work: Play

Five friends remember a murdered man just after his funeral.

The play opens with five friends—Canewell, Vera, Red Carter, Hedley, and Louise—gathered in the backyard of a Pittsburgh house. They have just returned from the cemetery where they paid their final respects to their friend Floyd "Schoolboy" Barton, mysteriously murdered at thirty-five. It is 1948.

Ironically, his death occurs at precisely the time that his first blues records is fast becoming a hit. The scene is somber until Louise, Floyd's landlady, erupts with a ribald song, which imparts a joviality to what had been a sad event.

As the play develops, Floyd's assembled friends recount memories of him and, in a series of flashbacks through which much of the play is revealed, elements of their lives and of Floyd's are presented and assessed.

Some of the people who attended the funeral swear that they saw angels at the cemetery. Vera insists that she saw six angels, one for each of the mourners and one for Floyd. Louise doubts the presence of angels at Floyd's funeral, but hers is a minority opinion.

Wilson uses the angels to represent the roles that Floyd's friends played in his life and the role Floyd played in the lives of his friends who are assembled in his memory. Wilson points to the exploitation that African Americans suffer at the hands of white society. Floyd has been exploited, but now that success is palpable, he will not be alive to enjoy it.

Part of the success of *Seven Guitars* is attributable to Wilson's intimate knowledge and understanding of African American society. In one of the flashbacks, Wilson reveals to the audience that Vera and Floyd were once lovers but that their romance was tempestuous. Floyd, in his frequent trips to Chicago, had become involved with Pearl Brown, the knowledge of which drives a wedge between him and Vera.

Floyd attempts to remove this wedge by sending

Vera a love letter. Not trusting himself to write a sufficiently beguiling letter to her, however, he turns to a friend at the workhouse who specializes in writing letters for others. He pays him fifty cents to produce a letter that he hopes will bring about a reconciliation with Vera.

Floyd, who has been in the workhouse, has kept records of what will be owed him upon his release for the work he did there. He hopes to start a new life with the paltry sum that he is owed. He dreams of getting out of pawn the electric guitar that he hocked earlier. Upon his release, he finds that the documentation he needs to receive what is due him has disappeared and that the payment date to redeem his guitar has passed.

Floyd's situation is comparable to that of playwright Jonathan Larson, whose play *Rent* (1996), having been rejected by several producers, was finally accepted for a production at a 150-seat Off-Broadway theater. During rehearsals, Larson complained of chest pains and, twenty-four hours before *Rent*'s premiere, died of an aortic aneurysm. His play was highly successful and was moved to Broadway for a long run. Larson's situation was in the forefront of Wilson's mind as he wrote *Seven Guitars*.

KING HEDLEY II

First produced: 2001 (first published, 2005)
Type of work: Play

Set in Pittsburgh's Hill District in the 1980's, the play focuses on King Hedley, recently granted a parole from prison, where he has been confined after being convicted of killing a youth who had slashed him in a knife fight.

King Hedley II is the eighth play in August Wilson's ten-play cycle that, decade by decade, examines African American life in the United States during the twentieth century.

King Hedley's wish, now that he has returned to Pittsburgh from prison, is to support himself by selling refrigerators and to start a family. Some of the characters in this play were presented earlier in *Seven Guitars*; this leads to a bit of confusion, as Wilson anticipates that audiences will remember these characters from a play produced seven years earlier. If they fail to remember them, then they may at times be bewildered by a lack of information about them in the present play.

Despite this limitation, *King Hedley II* is a remarkable achievement. In the play, Wilson reached new pinnacles of expression, writing at times with the lyricism that he had been developing in his earlier work but that he had never achieved to quite the extent that he does in *King Hedley II*. One reviewer compared the structure of the play to that of a Gothic cathedral, with its intricate design, flying buttresses, and multipurpose gargoyles.

The play is set during the Reagan administration, with its emphasis on supply-side economics aimed at providing trickle-down benefits to all Americans. Most African Americans are still awaiting the trickling down that is supposed to improve their economic conditions.

The new parolee, King Hedley, has left prison with the resolve to control his temper, which has gotten him into trouble in the past. He is also determined to become legitimate, but not before he has, through illegal activity (notably selling stolen refrigerators), accumulated a nest egg so that he can settle down and start a family.

Hedley becomes haunted by this past when his mother, Ruby, suggests that King Hedley I might not have been his father. He also must cope with having impregnated Tonya, whose own seventeen-year-old daughter is an unmarried mother. Tonya wants to terminate her pregnancy, but King wants an heir and will not consent to an abortion for her. To add stability to their economic situation, King robs a jewelry store, leading to his downfall.

Wilson deals in this play, as in many of his other plays, with the inability of many African Americans to better themselves because the dominant society has stacked the cards against them. In *King Hedley II*, audiences are presented with the consequences of this social disbalance.

GEM OF THE OCEAN

First produced: 2003 (first published, 2006)
Type of work: Play

Set in 1904, this play is chronologically the earliest in Wilson's ten-play cycle.

This ninth play in August Wilson's ten-play cycle examining African American life in the United States during the twentieth century had one of the shortest runs of any Wilson play. The play, which originally ran for over three hours, was reduced to a two-and-a-half hour production when it was brought to Broadway after its Los Angeles premiere.

Audiences are immediately forced to suspend their disbelief when they learn that the play's protagonist, Aunt Ester Tyler, is 287 years old. She was born when the first slave ships left Africa for the New World, has survived more than two centuries of slavery, and now experiences a freedom legally granted by the Emancipation Proclamation but withheld by most of the dominant, white society.

The characters that Wilson creates in this play are arresting. Besides Aunt Ester, in whose house in Pittsburgh's Hill District much of the play takes place, there is Solly, a slave who escaped to Canada but returned at his own peril to help slaves escape via the Underground Railroad. He points to sixty-two slaves whom he has helped to free in this way. Citizen Barlow is a troubled character who has committed a murder that was pinned on an innocent man, who drowns himself rather than face prosecution in white-dominated courts.

Much of the action of the play involves discontent among black mill workers. This unrest results in the torching of the mill by Solly and Citizen Barlow, who have to flee from Caesar, the constable out to find the perpetrators of the unrest and subsequent fire.

As in all the plays in this cycle, *Gem of the Ocean* exudes an irony that demonstrates how it is almost impossible for poor African Americans to lead ethical lives in a society that is unwilling to grant them equal opportunities. If black people commit crimes far in excess of those committed by white people, then it is largely because their backs are to the wall in an unjust society.

SUMMARY

Wilson's groundbreaking cycle of plays chronicling the black experience in the twentieth century brought a vital new voice to the American theater. The stories that he told and the complex characters that he created offered powerful dramatic portraits of lives that have often been marginalized or forgotten altogether. Believing that only by embracing their history can African Americans find a true sense of their heritage, Wilson drew on important periods in black history as background material for his plays. His poetic explorations of African American lives and culture embodied the sentiment that he once expressed in an interview: "Claim what is yours."

Janet Lorenz; updated by R. Baird Shuman

BIBLIOGRAPHY

By the Author

DRAMA:
Ma Rainey's Black Bottom, pr. 1984, pb. 1985
Fences, pr., pb. 1985
Joe Turner's Come and Gone, pr. 1986, pb. 1988
The Piano Lesson, pr. 1987, pb. 1990
Two Trains Running, pr. 1990, pb. 1992
Three Plays, pb. 1991
Seven Guitars, pr. 1995, pb. 1996
Jitney, pr. 2000, pb. 2001
King Hedley II, pr. 2001, pb. 2005

Gem of the Ocean, pr. 2003, pb. 2006
How I Learned What I Learned, pr. 2003
Radio Golf, pr. 2005

NONFICTION:
The Ground on Which I Stand, 2000

TELEPLAY:
The Piano Lesson, 1995 (adaptation of his play)

About the Author

Bogumil, Mary L. *Understanding August Wilson.* Columbia: University of South Carolina Press, 1999.

Booker, Margaret. *Lillian Hellman and August Wilson: Dramatizing a New American Identity.* New York: Peter Lang, 2003.

Clark, Keith. *Black Manhood in James Baldwin, Ernest J. Gaines, and August Wilson.* Urbana: University of Illinois Press, 2002.

Elam, Harry J., Jr. *The Past as Present in the Drama of August Wilson.* Ann Arbor: University of Michigan Press, 2004

Elkins, Marilyn, ed. *August Wilson: A Casebook.* New York: Garland, 2000.

McDonough, Carla J. *Staging Masculinity: Male Identity in Contemporary American Drama.* Jefferson, N.C.: McFarland, 1997.

Pereira, Kim. *August Wilson and the African-American Odyssey.* Urbana: University of Illinois Press, 1995.

Poinsett, Alex. "August Wilson." *Ebony,* November, 1987, 68-71.

Wolfe, Peter. *August Wilson.* New York: Twayne, 1999.

DISCUSSION TOPICS

- Discuss the role that irony plays in the plays by August Wilson that you have seen or read.

- Do you consider Wilson an angry playwright or merely a realistic one?

- Discuss the roles of women in the Wilson plays that you have seen or read.

- Aristotle placed considerable emphasis on the unities of time and place in evaluating drama. Discuss these unities in the Wilson plays with which you are familiar.

- What do you consider the three most important social issues in the black communities about which Wilson writes?

- Discuss the part that parentage plays in Wilson's writing.

- Abraham Lincoln's Emancipation Proclamation freed the slaves in 1863. According to Wilson, were African Americans really free in the twentieth century United States?

LANFORD WILSON

Born: Lebanon, Missouri
April 13, 1937

One of the most prolific and accessible of major American dramatists, Wilson successfully bridges the distance between repertory, regional, Off-Broadway, and mainstream Broadway theater.

BIOGRAPHY

Lanford Wilson was born on April 13, 1937, in Lebanon, Missouri, a locale he would later use as the setting for his cycle of plays about the mythical Talley family. When he was five years old, his parents divorced, and his mother took him to live in Springfield, Missouri. The search to establish a relationship with an absent father would constitute an important motif in a number of his plays, most notably in the autobiographical memory play *Lemon Sky* (1970) and in *Redwood Curtain* (1992), in which a half-Vietnamese girl tracks down her American father.

When Wilson's mother remarried in 1948, the family moved to a farm in Ozark, Missouri. While a high school student there in the mid-1950's, Wilson received his formative experiences in the theater, acting the role of the narrator, Tom, in a production of Tennessee Williams's *The Glass Menagerie* (1944) and attending a production of Arthur Miller's *Death of a Salesman* (1949) at Southwest Missouri State College.

In 1956, Wilson went to California for an unsuccessful reunion with his father. While there, he studied art history at San Diego State College, claiming it made him aware of "what our heritage was, and what we are doing to it," which becomes a pivotal concern in several works, particularly *The Mound Builders* (1975).

In the late 1950's, Wilson, by then an artist working for an advertising firm in the Midwest, enrolled in a playwriting class offered by the University of Chicago and began working in the one-act form. He moved to New York in 1962 and settled in Greenwich Village. Early the following year, he saw a production of an absurdist work by Eugène Ionesco at the Off-Off-Broadway Caffe Cino; the play's blend of the funny and the serious greatly affected the young playwright.

Over the next few years, Caffe Cino and Ellen Stewart's La Mama Experimental Theater Club would provide a hospitable home for many of Wilson's short works, including *The Madness of Lady Bright* (1964), which dramatizes the descent of an aging homosexual queen into insanity and remains an impressive contribution to the development of gay theater, and *The Rimers of Eldritch* (1966), which might be seen as Wilson's dark version of Thornton Wilder's *Our Town* (1938). Wilson's first full-length work, *Balm in Gilead*, focusing like many of his plays on society's down-and-outers, opened in 1965.

With dissections of two marriages, a troubled interracial one in *The Gingham Dog* (1968) and a middle-aged disillusioned one in *Serenading Louie* (1970), Wilson branched out into regional theaters, a movement then burgeoning in importance for developing playwrights. In 1969, Wilson and three others, including the director Marshall Mason, organized the Circle Repertory Company, which became the home for the premiere productions of virtually all of Wilson's plays. His *The Hot l Baltimore* (1973) captivated audiences for more than a thousand performances and won for Wilson his first New York Drama Critics Circle Award for Best American Play.

Wilson's later plays continued to open at Circle Repertory or regional theaters, eventually moving on to Broadway. *Angels Fall* (1982), for example, began at the New World Festival in Miami, while *Burn This* (1987) was first seen at the Mark Taper Forum in Los Angeles.

Wilson continued to receive accolades and awards, including a Pulitzer Prize in drama for *Talley's Folly* (1979). As befits an artist for whom the image of the garden—either lost or restored—is a potent symbol and for whom the preservation of the past is an overriding concern, Wilson's hobby is tending the gardens around his restored house in Sag Harbor, Long Island.

ANALYSIS

Although Wilson has often been spoken of as a distinctively midwestern playwright in the tradition of William Inge, he is by no means a narrow regionalist. His canvas is all of America, rural and urban, East and West as well as Midwest, with characters from every socioeconomic stratum. Of his first half-dozen long plays, only *The Rimers of Eldritch* occurs in a small town.

Reminiscent of the Welsh poet Dylan Thomas's *Under Milk Wood* (1954), Wilson's play tells of the murder of the village idiot/outsider Skelly as he tries to prevent a rape. Wilson's town of Eldritch has more in common with the poet Edgar Lee Masters's Spoon River than it does with *Our Town*'s pristine Grovers' Corners, as Eldritch contains small-town narrowness, repression, and hypocrisy. The symbolic hoarfrost (rime) blights all, and the ritual killing of the scapegoat accomplishes no regenerative purpose.

The Rimers of Eldritch, a threnody for voices, is as much readers' theater as traditional play. It employs several techniques that Wilson uses in other works from the same period: a montage or collage structure, featuring multiple protagonists involved in simultaneous actions; direct address, monologues, and overlapping voices; and an almost cinematic use of lighting to achieve effects analogous to film close-ups and fade-outs.

Such devices appear again in *Balm in Gilead* and *The Hot l Baltimore*, both of which have urban settings—a corner lunchroom and a hotel lobby— that should be sanctuaries fostering a sense of community and belonging but that are instead places peopled by society's outcasts and underclass: prostitutes and pimps, drunks and drug dealers, the lost and lonely and dislocated.

Wilson, a former graphic artist, is especially adept at handling theater space; more than anything, it is the setting of *The Hot l Baltimore* that establishes the link between Wilson and the Russian master Anton Chekhov. The locale of *The Hot l Baltimore* is the lobby of a once-elegant railroad hotel now ready for the wrecker's ball. Wilson comments that "the theater, evanescent itself, and for all we do perhaps disappearing here, seems the ideal place for the representation of the impermanence of our architecture," thus alerting the reader of change and decay as central motifs.

The play's action occurs on Memorial Day and builds on the dichotomy between past and present, permanence and progress, and, as in Chekhov, culture and materialism, beauty and use. The characters decry the diminishing countryside, the decline of the railroads, and the environmental pollution destroying the land—all effects of the greedy "vultures" who glorify financial gain.

Even though Wilson's language may lack the elegiac poeticism of some other literary descendants of Chekhov such as Tennessee Williams, in his use of place as symbol to convey meaning visually, as well as in his recurrent emphasis on the rape of culture and civilization by an amoral business class, Wilson remains the chief Chekhovian dramatist writing in modern America—as David Storey is in Great Britain.

The Chekhovian patterns also foretell other works in the Wilson canon: These include *Fifth of July* (1978), in which a family faces the prospect of seeing its ancestral home bought for use as a recording studio and its land turned into an airstrip, and *Redwood Curtain*, in which a family always careful to balance its business dealings with the need to preserve the environment is powerless to resist the huge conglomerate that will cut down the ancient trees—a direct allusion to Chekhov's *Vishnyovy Sad* (1904; *The Cherry Orchard*, 1908).

As in Chekhov's play, the destruction of the forest is linked to the disintegration and dispersal of the family unit. Trees hacked off at the ground are like a family denied its collective memory, left with no sense of rootedness or identity.

Although Wilson does not push as incessantly as Arthur Miller the notion of the debasement of the American Dream by the drive for unlimited success through competition and aggression, this criticism remains implicit in his Chekhov-like questioning of what has been sacrificed or lost in order to achieve material gain.

An integral part of the formulation of the American Dream has always been the promise of a New Eden, the restored garden to the West. The California in Wilson's *Lemon Sky*, however, is a sterile wasteland, both environmentally and emotionally, where nothing is "naturally" green; rather, everything is autumnal, "umber, amber, olive, sienna, ocher, orange."

While gardens, literal and symbolic, proliferate in Wilson's work, they are just as likely to be dying out (as in *The Hot l Baltimore* and *Redwood Curtain*) as growing or thriving (as in *Fifth of July*). When the garden is healthy, it is usually because an artist tends and nurtures it. Even the creative imagination seems to atrophy when cut off from garden places.

Artists and artist figures—often estranged from their fathers—abound in Wilson's plays. In *Lemon Sky* an adolescent writer-son is rejected by a long-lost father, who suspects him of homosexuality. In *Burn This*, a choreographer learns that the creative process necessarily involves drawing upon personal experience; eradicating the line between life and art can give rise to a representation that somehow mysteriously transcends life. In *Redwood Curtain*, a young pianist who discovers her identity through music expresses disillusionment with a public increasingly lacking any interest in art.

In the apocalyptic *Angels Fall*, set in a southwestern mission church under threat of radioactive fallout in a postnuclear "garden" surrounded by a uranium mine, a reactor, and a missile base, the concept of artist expands to include all who recognize their vocations—be they teachers, painters, priests, doctors, or athletes.

Once one hears the call and decides "what manner of persons who ought to be," then "magic . . . happens and you know who you are." Each of these characters, in the face of the pervasive danger of annihilation, goes forth from this temporary sanctuary committed to doing his or her work in a perilous world.

If the determination to work that one finds at the end of a Chekhov play sometimes seems but a hollow response to fear of facing the void, when such a determination occurs in Wilson's work (for

example in *Angels Fall* or in *Fifth of July*), it reflects instead a hard-won resolve, a positive renewal of oneself to active fellowship in the community of humankind.

THE MOUND BUILDERS

First produced: 1975 (first published, 1976)
Type of work: Play

An archeological excavation pits scientists against land developers, uncovering not only a primitive god-mask but also human greed, jealousy, and violence.

The most complex treatment of Wilson's themes appears in *The Mound Builders*, probably his most impressive achievement. The action occurs in "the mind's eye" of Professor August Howe, who recalls an archeological dig he led the preceding summer in southern Illinois that unearthed an ancient burial ground of the Temple Mound People. Howe (accompanied by his wife, Cynthia, and their daughter) and his young assistant Dan Loggins (accompanied by his pregnant wife, Jean) come into conflict with the owner of the property and his twenty-five-year-old son, Chad, who hope to make a great deal of money by selling the land for a vacation resort.

Chad, who is carrying on an affair with Cynthia Howe, had saved Dan from drowning the summer before but now tries unsuccessfully to lure Jean away from him. Thwarted both personally in his desire for Jean and financially because laws prevent developing the property, Chad eventually kills Dan, bulldozes the excavation, and kills himself, leaving the god-king mask to be reburied by the mythic flood waters.

Wilson's dramaturgy in this memory play approximates that of Williams in *The Glass Menagerie*. The playing area might be seen as August's mind, with the slides of the precious artifacts that are projected onto the back wall prompting his remembrances. The central conflict is between the preservation of a culture, on one hand, and commercial progress on the other; between a past age of poetry and a present age of facts. The scientists stand poised between commercial promoters and creative artisans, capable of bending either way.

Whereas the ancient tribe sought its immortality through gorgeous works used in rituals, modern humans seek theirs through material gain. When Dan holds the death mask from the god-king "up to his face, and almost inadvertently it stays in place," it is perhaps an act of hubris, revealing his lack of sufficient awe for the primitive culture and leading unwittingly to his death at the hands of the sexually jealous and money-crazed Chad.

The modern artist who arrives in this midwestern "garden of the gods" is Howe's sister Delia. The author of one successful novel, she has been unable to summon up the creativity necessary to produce a second book. The source of her writing block was the death of her father and her separation from her paternal home.

If the heritage of the past, whether childhood home or ancient burial site, serves as a creative spur to the artist, then once these places are lost or defiled, judged as worthless or anachronistic except when exploited for profit, all that remains are "syllables, not sense." Lack of adequate respect for the past results in a present beset by greed and violence and a decline into savagery.

FIFTH OF JULY

First produced: 1978 (first published, 1978)
Type of work: Play

Three generations of a family and four friends from the Vietnam War era gather to replay the past and decide on a direction for the future.

The first of Wilson's plays about the Talley family, *Fifth of July* explores two of the playwright's preoccupations: the need to preserve the past in order to live humanely in the present and the importance to both self and society of embracing one's vocation. Although *Fifth of July* is an ensemble piece

with several protagonists, the focal character is Kenny Tally, who arrived back from the Vietnam War with five citations for bravery but without his legs.

It is 1977, and Kenny is determined not to return to his calling as a high school teacher. Feeling discomfort over coming home alive, although maimed, from the war, Kenny senses the invisibility imposed upon veterans of an unpopular cause when others refuse to look at them out of shame or guilt.

Joining Kenny at the family homestead are his Aunt Sally Friedman, who has come back to spread the ashes of her deceased husband, Matt (the story of their courtship is later told in the 1979 play *Talley's Folly*), Kenny's sister June, who was a flower child in the 1960's, and June's daughter, Shirley, an aspiring writer.

Also visiting are John Landis, a record promoter who wants to buy the Talley property, and his wife, Gwen. They had attended the University of California at Berkeley with Kenny and June but had deliberately gone to Europe without Kenny, leaving him behind to be drafted. Tending the grounds of the Talley home has been Jed, Kenny's homosexual lover.

Jed has gradually been replanting the property in the manner of a traditional English garden that will take years to mature; recently, he has rediscovered a lost rose that once again will be propagated at Sissinghurst Castle in England, "the greatest rose garden in the world." Jed, in his planting of the garden and his caring for and loving the disabled Ken, is the new Adam who inspires a sense of purpose and restores a feeling of community after the Fall.

Both Sally, a representative of the oldest generation of Talleys onstage, and Shirley, a member of the family's youngest generation, join Kenny in resisting the lure of spatial dislocation to answer instead the pull of the ancestral home. If necessary, Sally will buy the Talley place so that it will not go out of family control and become a cement airstrip, especially now that she and Jed have spread Matt's ashes among the roses.

While Shirley commits the younger generation to renewing the Talley clan, Kenny—once he has learned how to understand the virtually unintelligible speech of his young half cousin through creatively having the boy record a story—overcomes the temptation to give up teaching and recommits himself to his "mission" in life. On all levels—the archetypal, the natural, the familial, and the individual—the movement of *Fifth of July* is thus from despair and death to renewal and rebirth.

TALLEY'S FOLLY

First produced: 1979 (first published, 1979)
Type of work: Play

Two misfits approaching middle age and discovering they are made for each other pledge love and commitment despite the opposition of a prejudiced family.

Set on July 4, 1944, *Talley's Folly* concerns two characters who are revealed largely through exposition and lengthy monologues: Sally Talley, a nurse headed for self-imposed spinsterhood, and Matt Friedman, a liberal Jewish accountant fond of using comedy routines to mask his vulnerability.

The "folly" of the play's title and the locale for the action is a boathouse that Sally's Uncle Everett constructed in place of a gazebo he had hoped to build. Wilson opens the play using a Wilder-like frame, with Matt as narrator/stage manager conspiratorially explaining to the audience that they are about to witness a "once-upon-a-time" romance that could happen only in the theater.

When Matt narrates the history of his family—of a Prussian father and Ukrainian mother "indefinitely detained" by the Germans in World War I; of a Latvian sister tortured by the French so their father would divulge information he never had; and of himself, born in Lithuania and arriving as a refugee with his uncle from Norway via Caracas—he distances the painful story by narrating it in the third-person voice.

Because of his wandering family's past, Matt considers himself non-nationalistic, feeling little allegiance to any political cause or "ism." Although he escaped the draft because of his age, he is not unaffected by the war (which, he believes, governments deliberately prolong for economic reasons). Uncertain that there will ever be a time after this war, he refuses to bring another child into the world "to be killed for political purposes," and thus he hesitates to marry Sally.

Sally yearns on this Independence Day to break free from a restrictive family that is anti-liberal, anti-Semitic, and anti-German—and, therefore, anti-Matt. Yet political, religious, and racial intolerance are not all that prevent her marriage. Years before, she was engaged to her high school sweetheart; their marriage portended a merger of two prominent families, but her father committed suicide during the Depression.

Finally, she reveals to Matt (and to the audience waiting to hear her secret) that an illness has left her sterile. Once her misconception that Matt is only claiming that he would never father a child in order to spare her the burden of not being able to give him one is cleared away, these two can unite.

The boathouse "folly" has always been, for Sally, a green world, a place of escape and magic. Matt and Sally leave the boathouse to return to a family and a community unprepared to accept them and ready to ostracize them, just as Matt, the stage manager again at play's end, sends the audience out from the theater exactly ninety-seven minutes later into their imperfect world.

A dissonance exists between what Matt calls the "waltz" or "valentine" of this fairy tale the audience has been watching and the prejudice that pervades their world. Sally Talley's folly, shared by Matt, is the courage to choose love in spite of the world's unwillingness to dissolve barriers of class, nationality, politics, and religion.

TALLEY AND SON

First produced: 1985 (first published, 1986)
Type of work: Play

This play in Wilson's Talley cycle deals with father-son relationships in three generations of Talleys.

This play, produced relatively late in Lanford Wilson's Talley cycle, actually had its first Broadway airing in 1981, when it was produced as *A Tale Told*. This early version of the play was not a notable success, although it received some encouraging critical attention. After it closed on Broadway, it enjoyed a continued run Off-Broadway.

Wilson has a habit of working and reworking plays that do not please him, and he reworked *A*

Tale Told for four years, bringing it to Broadway with the new title *Talley and Son*. The play has a complicated plot, but Wilson provides one character, the ghost of Timmy Talley, to serve the function of the chorus in Greek plays, that of giving the audience the details that they need to follow the action.

The play opens at sunset on the fourth of July, 1944. Timmy Talley's ghost returns to his home on a rise overlooking Lebanon, Missouri, Wilson's birthplace. Timmy, a member of the United States Marine Corps, was granted a furlough to come home from the South Pacific, where he was stationed, to attend the funeral of his grandfather, Calvin. Ironically, the old man has rallied to the point that he sneaks out in his son's Packard automobile for a drive. Timmy was killed before he was able to leave the battle area. His brother, Buddy, who is serving in the armed forces in Italy, having received a similar furlough, arrived home a day earlier.

Talley & Son

A PLAY BY LANFORD WILSON

The play's first act juggles four separate lines of narrative. Most of the characters have appeared earlier in other Wilson plays relating to the Talleys, and Wilson uses Timmy, in his role as chorus, to fill in needed details.

The Talley family has secrets that are gradually revealed as the play evolves. The grandfather, Calvin, is aware that his son Eldon impregnated the family's washerwoman, Viola Pratt, eighteen years earlier. Avalaine Pratt, the child born of Eldon's union with Viola, is now seventeen. Calvin tries to bribe her to marry Emmet Young, a handyman whom he employs.

Avalaine realizes her parentage and demands her part of the family fortune. Eldon, who has been running Talley & Sons, is under pressure from Delaware Industries to sell the company. Calvin is in favor of selling, but Eldon is stalwartly opposed to doing so. Calvin thinks he can prevent the impending sale, but Eldon has his father's power of attorney, and, by using it in accordance with his own preferences rather than his father's, he can thwart the takeover.

In this play, Wilson deals effectively with crucial intergenerational relationships as well as with the dog-eat-dog environment of big business. He also shows the effect of a prolonged war on a family whose sons are involved directly in it. The play seethes with the small-mindedness of a midwestern town. It deals also with the manipulation of the little people by those in power.

REDWOOD CURTAIN

First produced: 1992 (first published, 1993)
Type of work: Play

One of the recurring themes in Lanford Wilson's plays is the search for the father, which underlies the entire action of this play.

The play's main character is Geri, a seventeen-year-old whose mother is a Vietnamese florist and whose father, an American GI, impregnated his lover and then disappeared. Another American soldier found Geri and took her to the United States. This soldier, Laird Riordan, and his wife, Julia, adopted Geri and raised her in California. Geri develops into a concert pianist who has a promising career before her. At seventeen, she already has a lucrative record contract with Sony.

Laird has carefully groomed Geri for the musical career that is now within reach for her. An alcoholic, Laird suffers from post-traumatic stress disorder that, in part, accounts for the heavy drinking that leads to his death just as Geri's career is beginning to take off. After Laird's death, Julia sets out for Europe, leaving Geri in the care of her Aunt Geneva, who lives in a sequoia forest.

It is here among the redwoods of the play's title that Geri puts her concert career on hold to search for her biological father. She has little information about him, although she does remember her birth mother telling her that he had one brown and one blue eye.

The redwood forest near Geneva's house is home to a contingent of homeless war veterans who survive on their meager disability checks. Among this motley throng is Lyman Fellers. Because he has one brown and one blue eye, Geri is convinced that he is her father, although he actually is not.

Nevertheless, Geri pursues him relentlessly. Lyman, who just wants to be left alone, is the only one of the homeless veterans whom the audience meets, but he comes to represent all such veterans. Geri eventually redeems him somewhat unconvincingly by playing Erik Satie's "Gymnopedies" for him.

Wilson introduces into the play one of his favorite topics—the rape of the land by an industrial society. Lumber companies unconscionably destroy centuries-old redwoods for quick profits. For Wilson, such destruction represents the destruction of familial roots as well. Wilson, in much of his work, introduces gardens and plants, which he contends can be saved only by artists. He uses them as props to shed light on the role of artists in society.

Redwood Curtain was not well received on Broadway. Because he did not want his audiences to be distracted at any point in its development, Wilson insisted that the play, long on diatribe and short on action and more than two hours in length, be presented without an intermission.

In addition, *Redwood Curtain* was pieced together from two of Wilson's shorter, earlier plays. The joining of the two stories was, in this case, not seamless. Despite these reservations, *Redwood Curtain* is an important play in the Wilson canon because it reveals some of the artist's most consuming social concerns.

In 1995, the American Broadcasting Company (ABC) presented a two-hour adaptation of the play on prime-time television. This version was better received than the Broadway version had been.

DAY

First produced: 1995, as part of *By the Sea by the Sea by the Beautiful Sea* (first published, 1996)

Type of work: Play

This play served as one act in a three-part drama by Wilson and two other playwrights as an experiment in collaboration.

Members of the Bay Street Theatre Festival Committee in Long Island's Hamptons hatched the original idea for *By the Sea by the Sea by the Beautiful Sea*. The community, the heart of which is Sag Harbor, is home to many writers, actors, and other celebrities. The committee proposed involving three of the area's most notable playwrights—Terrence McNally, Joe Pintauro, and Lanford Wilson—in a collaborative effort that would eventuate in three one-act plays having to do with the sea and the beach. The plays would all take place on one day, respectively in the morning, at noon, and at sunset.

Wilson's contribution to this collaborative effort is the middle play, "Day." Pintauro wrote "Dawn," and McNally wrote "Dusk." The great challenge was to have a unified work rather than merely three one-act plays. The authors gathered to decide what the setting of each play would be, and they finally decided that the beach would become the unifying setting. After it was decided that dawn, day, and dusk would be times of the plays, the three playwrights drew straws to determine which time frame each would use. Each play was to have three characters, two women and one man, but they were to play different roles in the plays, each of whose characters was different.

Originally, one of the plays took place at a lifeguard station, one on a dock, and one on a stretch of beach. Finally, however, to increase the unity of the production, it was decided that all of the plays would take place on a stretch of beach and that there would be no identifying references to actual places so that the beach in each play would have a universality.

Pintauro's play begins in the very early morning and continues until dawn. It is about a sister, a brother, and the brother's wife who come to the beach to spread the ashes of their dead mother. Wilson's contribution takes place during the lunch hour and involves a man who does landscaping, his girlfriend, and a mysterious woman writer. McNally's contribution takes place at sunset and involves two woman vying for the attention of one man.

Wilson's play is unique in the trio because it begins with a clean slate and is heavily plot-oriented. The audience knows nothing about Ace, his male character, so his whole story is unfolded without reference to any past history. Such is not the case in the other two plays. Writing within the one-act format, Wilson has to develop his play quickly, as do the other two collaborators.

The women characters in the three acts contrast

sharply to each other. Mace, the writer, is reserved and, on the surface, more proper than Bill, Ace's girlfriend. She also appears to be better educated. Ace himself is reserved and enjoys being alone, but not to the extent that Mace does.

At one point, Bill engages in a shouting match with Ace, during which all three characters talk heatedly and simultaneously. They get into a discussion about the immigration of Latins to the United States. Ace points out that a twenty-seven-year-old pharmacist from Columbia works with him planting trees and doing landscaping for the affluent because he can make more money doing that than he can ever hope to make in Colombia pursuing his profession.

This experiment was extremely creative in its conception. It also was remarkably creative in its execution on Broadway under the splendid direction of Leonard Foglia.

SUMMARY

Partly because Wilson has chosen to premiere his plays at Circle Repertory or in regional theaters, he has seldom attracted the sustained media attention accorded such contemporaries as David Rabe, Sam Shepard, and David Mamet. Yet Wilson's works are among the most distinctively American dramas of the late twentieth century. Wilson's emphases closely reflect issues at the heart of the United States' survival: tolerance for the have-nots and out-

DISCUSSION TOPICS

- To what extent do you think it is accurate to identify Lanford Wilson as a regional playwright?

- Discuss the uses that Wilson makes of ancestry and family cohesion in his writing.

- Do you find any pervasive and recurring symbols in Wilson's writing? If so, how does he use them?

- Discuss the father/son, mother/son relationships in Wilson's work and consider what they reveal about family structure.

- Consider Wilson's commentaries on contemporary society. Identify and discuss three or four of his major social concerns.

- Quest is a major element in most drama. In Wilson's writing, what are some of the quests that motivate the characters?

siders, respect for the multicultural heritage of the past, the need to preserve beauty in the face of technological advance, the value of work in defining one's self, and the importance of community for instilling a sense of belonging and rootedness.

Thomas P. Adler; updated by R. Baird Shuman

BIBLIOGRAPHY

By the Author

DRAMA:
So Long at the Fair, pr. 1963 (one act)
Home Free!, pr. 1964, pb. 1965 (one act)
The Madness of Lady Bright, pr. 1964, pb. 1967 (one act)
No Trespassing, pr. 1964 (one act)
Balm in Gilead, pr., pb. 1965
Days Ahead: A Monologue, pr. 1965, pb. 1967 (one scene)
Ludlow Fair, pr., pb. 1965 (one act)
The Sand Castle, pr. 1965, pb. 1970 (one act)
Sex Is Between Two People, pr. 1965 (one scene)
This Is the Rill Speaking, pr. 1965, pb. 1967 (one act)
The Rimers of Eldritch, pr. 1966, pb. 1967 (two acts)
Wandering: A Turn, pr. 1966, pb. 1967 (one scene)
Untitled Play, pr. 1967 (one act; music by Al Carmines)

The Gingham Dog, pr. 1968, pb. 1969
The Great Nebula in Orion, pr. 1970, pb. 1973 (one act)
Lemon Sky, pr., pb. 1970
Serenading Louie, pr. 1970, pb. 1976 (two acts)
Sextet (Yes), pb. 1970, pr. 1971 (one scene)
Stoop: A Turn, pb. 1970
Ikke, Ikke, Nye, Nye, Nye, pr. 1971, pb. 1973
Summer and Smoke, pr. 1971, pb. 1972 (libretto; adaptation of Tennessee Williams's play; music by Lee Hoiby)
The Family Continues, pr. 1972, pb. 1973 (one act)
The Hot l Baltimore, pr., pb. 1973
Victory on Mrs. Dandywine's Island, pb. 1973 (one act)
The Mound Builders, pr. 1975, pb. 1976
Brontosaurus, pr. 1977, pb. 1978 (one act)
Fifth of July, pr., pb. 1978
Talley's Folly, pr., pb. 1979 (one act)
A Tale Told, pr. 1981 (revised and pb. as *Talley and Son,* 1986)
Thymus Vulgaris, pr., pb. 1982 (one act)
Angels Fall, pr., pb. 1982
Balm in Gilead, and Other Plays, pb. 1985
Say de Kooning, pr. 1985, pb. 1994
Talley and Son, pr. 1985, pb. 1986
Sa-Hurt?, pr. 1986
A Betrothal, pr., pb. 1986 (one act)
Burn This, pr., pb. 1987
Dying Breed, pr. 1987
Hall of North American Forests, pr. 1987, pb. 1988
A Poster of the Cosmos, pr. 1987, pb. 1992 (one act)
Abstinence: A Turn, pb. 1989 (one scene)
The Moonshot Tape, pr., pb. 1990
Eukiah, pr., pb. 1992
Redwood Curtain, pr. 1992, pb. 1993
Twenty-one Short Plays, pb. 1993
Collected Works, pb. 1996-1999 (3 volumes; Vol. 1, *Collected Plays, 1965-1970;* Vol. 2, *Collected Works, 1970-1983;* Vol. 3, *The Talley Trilogy*)
Day, pr. 1995, pb. 1996 (one act; part of *By the Sea by the Sea by the Beautiful Sea*)
A Sense of Place: Or, Virgil Is Still the Frogboy, pr. 1997, pb. 1999
Sympathetic Music, pr. 1997, pb. 1998
Book of Days, pr. 1998, pb. 2000
Rain Dance, pr. 2000

TRANSLATION:
Three Sisters, 1984 (of Anton Chekhov's play *Tri sestry*)

TELEPLAYS:
One Arm, 1970
The Migrants, 1973 (with Tennessee Williams)
Taxi!, 1978
Sam Found Out: A Triple Play, 1988
Lemon Sky, 1988
Burn This, 1992
Talley's Folly, 1992

About the Author

Barnett, Gene A. *Lanford Wilson*. Boston: Twayne, 1987.

Bryer, Jackson R., ed. *Lanford Wilson: A Casebook*. New York: Garland, 1994.

Busby, Mark. *Lanford Wilson*. Boise, Idaho: Boise State University, 1987.

Dasgupta, Gautam. "Lanford Wilson." In *American Playwrights: A Critical Survey*, edited by Bonnie Marranca and Gautam Dasgupta. New York: Drama Book Specialists, 1981.

Dean, Anne M. *Discovery and Invention: The Urban Plays of Lanford Wilson*. Rutherford, N.J.: Fairleigh Dickinson University Press, 1994.

Gussow, Mel. "A Playwright at Home with Life's Outsiders." *The New York Times*, September 15, 2002, p. AR1.

Herman, William. *Understanding Contemporary American Drama*. Columbia: University of South Carolina Press, 1987.

Hornsby, Richard Mark. "Miscarriages of Justice." *The Hudson Review* 56 (Spring, 2003): 161-167.

Schvey, Henry I. "Images of the Past in the Plays of Lanford Wilson." In *Essays on Contemporary American Drama*. edited by Hedwig Bok and Albert Wertheim. Munich: Max Huber Verlag, 1981.

Williams, Philip Middleton. *A Comfortable House: Lanford Wilson, Marshall W. Mason, and the Circle Repertory Theatre*. Jefferson, N.C.: McFarland, 1993.

LARRY WOIWODE

Born: Carrington, North Dakota
October 30, 1941

Novelist, short-story writer, and poet, Woiwode is credited with reviving the genre of the family chronicle in postwar American letters.

© Nancy Crampton

BIOGRAPHY

Larry Alfred Woiwode was born in Carrington, North Dakota, on October 30, 1941, and spent his early years in nearby Sykeston, a predominantly German settlement amid the rugged, often forbidding north-midwestern terrain. No doubt the beauty as well as the stark loneliness of this landscape heightened the author's appreciation for the effect of nature upon individual character. At the age of ten, he moved with his family to Manito, Illinois, another evocatively midwestern environment capable of nurturing the descriptive powers of a budding fiction writer.

He attended the University of Illinois for five years but failed to complete a bachelor's degree, leaving the university in 1964 with an associate of arts degree in rhetoric. He met his future wife, Carol Ann Patterson, during this period and married her on May 21, 1965. After leaving Illinois, Woiwode moved to New York City and supported his family with freelance writing, publishing in *The New Yorker* and other prestigious periodicals while working on two novels.

During his career, Woiwode has been known primarily for his longer fiction, but he has frequently published short stories in such prominent literary periodicals as *The Atlantic Monthly* and *The New Yorker*, and he published a well-received collection of poems, *Even Tide*, in 1977. Several of his short

stories have been chosen for anthologies of the year's best. Woiwode's first novel, *What I'm Going to Do, I Think*, won for him the prestigious William Faulkner Foundation Award for the "most notable first novel" of 1969 and brought him immediate critical attention. It reached the best-seller list and has been translated into several foreign languages.

His second novel, *Beyond the Bedroom Wall: A Family Album* (1975), actually begun before *What I'm Going to Do, I Think*, was nominated for both the National Book Award and the National Book Critics Circle Award. It became an even bigger commercial and critical success than his first novel.

Woiwode's third novel, *Poppa John* (1981) was less successful commercially and critically; it departed from his signature, the midwestern prairie setting, and located its protagonist, an aging soap opera actor, in New York City. *Born Brothers* (1988), the long-awaited sequel to *Beyond the Bedroom Wall*, returned readers to the unfolding lives of a quintessential midwestern family, chronicling the tensions of two Neumiller brothers, Charles and Jerome. *The Neumiller Stories* (1989), a collection of reworked short stories about the Neumiller clan, expanded the "snapshot album" of narratives about this family and continued Woiwode's refinement of the psychic landscape first begun as episodes in his novel *Beyond the Bedroom Wall*. Woiwode's novel *Indian Affairs* (1992) continued the marital saga of Chris and Ellen begun in *What I'm Going to Do, I Think*. His collection of short stories *Silent Passengers* (1993) featured families and their relationships to the land and to each other on the upper plains.

Departing from fiction, Woiwode penned *Acts: A Writer's Reflections on the Church, Writing, and His*

Own Life (1993), a meditation connecting the Gospel of Luke to the author's decision to depart academia in order to relocate his family to a farm in North Dakota. *Aristocrat of the West: The Story of Harold Schafer* (2000) is a biography of Woiwode's North Dakota hero. *What I Think I Did: A Season of Survival in Two Acts* (2000) is the first of a planned three-part autobiography.

In 1977, Woiwode was awarded an honorary doctor of letters degree from North Dakota State University. Woiwode's oeuvre has merited numerous awards, including the 1991 John Dos Passos Prize, the 1992 Nelson Algrew Short Fiction award, the 1995 Award of Merit from the American Academy of Arts and Letters, and the 1999 Associated Writings Program Award. In academic life, Woiwode has served as a writer-in-residence at the University of Wisconsin, Madison, and has held extended teaching posts at Wheaton College (Illinois) and at the State University of New York, Binghamton, where he served as faculty member and Writing Program director for four years. He continues to conduct writing workshops in the United States and abroad. Woiwode lives with his family on a 160-acre farm in North Dakota, where he raises quarter horses and writes. In 1995, he was named North Dakota Centennial Poet.

ANALYSIS

Woiwode's quirky, family-centered narratives signal the rehabilitation of the venerable genre of the family chronicle, a kind of fiction once pervasive in American novel writing but regarded by many critics as defunct. In the family chronicle, a writer basically builds a narrative around the history of one family, often an immigrant family whose daughters and sons fight to establish their own identity in the "new world" to which their parents or grandparents have brought them. Authentic and engaging family chronicles normally depend upon adherence to a meticulous realism that requires careful attention to the nuances of family life and conversation. Woiwode is equal to this task, and he unabashedly admires the traditional nuclear family. Consequently, his fiction underscores the value of finding one's way in the modern world by retracing one's steps in his or her family legacy.

Woiwode refuses to drown his characters in the angst-ridden excesses that have become so conventional in the modern American novel. Even to readers accustomed to cynical and world-weary protagonists preoccupied with discovering the mysteries of life in the squalor of the city while involved in some illicit relationship, Woiwode can make such old-fashioned values as family loyalty seem startlingly fresh and appealing.

His characters are not helpless victims of their times but participants in them. They are accountable not so much for what has happened to them but for what they do in response to their circumstances. This is a world that registers as authentic to the reader precisely because of Woiwode's gift for psychological realism, made more engaging because of his command of the role of human memory in shaping one's perception of one's relationships.

Woiwode's characters eventually recognize that the answers to their dilemmas are only partly in themselves. In the reestablishment of personal trust in friendships and the nostalgia of forgotten familial relationships, they recover a sense of balance and worth in themselves. However obliquely, each major Woiwode character finds himself or herself in a quest for a transcendent moral order— a renewed trust in God and humankind that would provide a reference point for his or her life. This quest animates their rejection of narcissism and a search for a love and security that only marital and familial relationships can foster.

Woiwode's willingness to affirm that these relationships are central to self-fulfillment and to the stability of true American culture makes him unique among a generation of writers whose thematic concerns tend to focus on their characters' dehumanization in society, their alienation from family life, and their eschewing of marital fidelity. Woiwode thus belongs in the company of self-consciously moralistic writers such as Walker Percy and Saul Bellow, writers more interested in the ways human beings survive and thrive in a fallen world than in the ways they capitulate to it.

His characters' conflicts, from Chris Van Eenanam's enigmatic search for manhood in *What I'm Going to Do, I Think* to Poppa John's drive to recover his identity, are not merely contrived psychological dramas played out inside their own consciousness. They are compelling confrontations with the very concrete world of everyday life.

Despite his solid reputation in modern letters, Woiwode's career, especially when compared with other writers of his caliber, does not represent the work of a particularly prolific author. In the two decades after he ended his abortive college career to pursue freelance writing, he produced few major works: one long, rather complex family chronicle, one medium-length novel, one short novel, a short-story collection, and a book of poems. Yet two of his three novels were critically acclaimed, national best sellers and are arguably among the best American novels written since 1960.

A highly acclaimed first novel can often prove to be a mixed blessing, as it can overshadow a writer's subsequent efforts. *Poppa John*, Woiwode's third novel, was greeted with some disappointment; that reaction, coupled with a long period in which Woiwode published nothing, led some critics to wonder about his commitment to his vision. After the period of relative inactivity following the success of his first two novels nearly twenty-five years earlier, Woiwode returned to the family chronicle in *Born Brothers, The Neumiller Stories*, and *Indian Affairs*. Their appearance seems to have answered the concerns of his critics.

Woiwode's recent foray into autobiography with the introspective *Acts* and the publication of *What I Think I Did*, with plans for two additional autobiographical volumes, suggests that in his sixties Woiwode began to move into a new phase of his life's work, one involving looking back on his writer's journey; certainly, with his continued literary productivity, it does not imply that his journey is anywhere near its end.

WHAT I'M GOING TO DO, I THINK

First published: 1969
Type of work: Novel

A newlywed couple search together for meaning and purpose against the bleak, faithless landscape of the late 1960's.

Woiwode's first novel, *What I'm Going to Do, I Think*, is an absorbing character study of two newlyweds, each of whom is originally drawn to the other as opposites proverbially attract. Chris Van Eenanam, the protagonist, is a listless mathematics graduate student, an unhappy agnostic preoccupied with his unsure footing in the world. Put simply, he lacks vocation or a consuming vision of what he should do with his life. The novel's title thus accentuates his self-doubt and indecision, echoing something Chris's father once said in observing his accident-prone son: "What I'm going to do, I think, is get a new kid." Ellen Strohe, his pregnant bride, is a tortured young woman, dominated by overbearing grandparents who raised her after her parents' accidental death. Neither she nor Chris can abide her grandparents' interference and meddling.

Little action takes place "live" before the reader, as Woiwode's psychological realism deploys compacted action and flashbacks and the patterned repetition of certain incidents to carry the reader along as effortlessly as might a conventionally chronological narrative. The reader learns "what happens," primarily as events filter through the conversations and consciousness of Chris and Ellen during their extended honeymoon at her grandparents' cabin near Lake Michigan. This tantalizing use of personal perception and vaguely unreliable memory has become a trademark of Woiwode's characterization. It permits him wide latitude in choosing when and how to reveal his characters' motivations and responses to the events that shape their lives.

In their retreat from the decisions that Chris chooses not to face, the couple, now intimate, now isolated, confront a grim modern world that has lost its faith in a supreme being fully in control of the created universe. This loss is exemplified most dramatically in the lives of Chris and Ellen as they try to sort out the meaning of affection and fidelity in their new relationship as husband and wife and as potential parents. Ellen's pregnancy is, at first, a sign of a beneficent nature's approval of their union, but later, as each has a premonition of their unborn child's stillborn delivery, it becomes a symbol of an ambivalent world's indifference to their marriage and its apparent fruitlessness.

In the absence of a compensatory faith even in humankind (a secondary faith arguably derived from faith in God), Chris and Ellen come to realize that they have lost their ability to navigate a hostile world with a lasting, meaningful relationship. The "student revolutions" of the 1960's had promised social enlightenment and unadorned love, a secure replacement for the tottering scaffold of religious faith and civic duty that undergirded their parents' generation. They discover, however, that neither science, as represented in Chris's mathematics pursuits, nor nature, as a metaphor for the modern world's hostility to metaphysical certainty, can fill the vacuum left by a waning faith in God or humankind. Such a committed faith, whose incessant call is to fidelity and perseverance, cannot survive without passion or understanding in the perplexity of the young married couple's inexperience in living.

In a suspenseful epilogue that closes the novel with an explanation of what has happened to them in the seven years following their marriage, Chris and Ellen return to their honeymoon cabin. Chris retrieves the rifle that he has not touched in many years, and, as the action builds toward what will apparently be his suicide, he repeats to himself the beginning of a letter (perhaps a suicide note) that he could not complete. *"Dear El, my wife. You're the only person I've ever been able to talk to and this is something I can't say. . . . "*

As he makes his way to the lake, he fires a round of ammunition into a plastic bleach container half-buried in the sand. In the novel's enigmatic final lines, Chris fires "the last round from his waist, sending the bullet out over the open lake." This curious ending seems intended by Woiwode to announce Chris's end of indecision, a recognition that his life can have transcendent meaning only in embracing fully his marriage commitment to Ellen.

BEYOND THE BEDROOM WALL

First published: 1975
Type of work: Novel

A sprawling chronicle of an immigrant family's vitality and enduring faith despite the obstacles to its survival in the modern world.

The expansiveness and comic twists of Woiwode's second novel, *Beyond the Bedroom Wall: A Family Album,* offer a marked contrast to *What I'm Going to Do, I Think.* In *Beyond the Bedroom Wall,* Woiwode parades sixty-three characters before the reader by the beginning of chapter 3. True to its subtitle, "A Family Album," *Beyond the Bedroom Wall* is a rather impish and gangly work of loosely connected snapshots of three generations of the German Catholic immigrant Neumiller family. Woiwode straightforwardly invites the reader to leaf through this "album" not as a rigorously chronological narrative but as a curiosity piece, pausing at particular episodes and events.

From sentimental scenes of a father telling his children stories and the poignancy of a child fighting a nearly fatal illness to the agonizing grief of losing one's spouse, *Beyond the Bedroom Wall* is an engaging homage to the seemingly evaporating family unit at the end of the twentieth century. Nevertheless, the novel's "plot" is nearly impossible to paraphrase, consisting as it does of some narrative, some diary entries, and even its protagonist Martin Neumiller's job application for a teaching position. Woiwode had published nearly a third of the forty-four chapters of *Beyond the Bedroom Wall* as self-contained short stories in *The New Yorker;* thus it is no surprise that the book reads as a discontinuous montage of events, images, and personalities. Woiwode reworked many of these episodes, foregrounding other characters and character traits, for his collection *The Neumiller Stories.*

Part 1 of the novel opens with the funeral of Otto Neumiller, a German immigrant farmer who had brought his family to the United States, and it continues, to part 5, with stories of the third generation of Neumillers, concluding in 1970, thus bringing members of the Neumiller family full circle from birth to life to death. Otto Neumiller had emigrated to America in 1881, relocating in the plains of North Dakota. As the reader meets him at the end of his life, he stands poised between two worlds, knowing neither the love nor the admiration of his neighbors, but seeking to bequeath something of value to his son, Charles. The farm he tended and leaves behind becomes emblematic, not of his success as a man of the soil but of his life as a devoted father who has sown and reaped a loyal and steadfast family, one whose strength is not in great friendships or possessions but in mutual love.

After setting this context, Woiwode moves the narrative forward quickly, introducing the family of Charles's son, Martin, who is the "family album's" true focal point. Martin Neumiller, like his father and grandfather, is a God-fearing, devoutly Catholic man and proud son of North Dakota whose ordinary adventures and gentle misadventures give the novel any formal unity it possesses. "My life is like a book," he says at one point, "There is one chapter, there is one story after another."

To see his life as a story, written by God in the gives and takes of everyday life, Martin must accustom himself to finding profundity and sustenance in the painfully ordinary patterns and repetitions of life and not in the frantic and guilt-ridden excesses of sophisticated city life or Hollywood romanticism. To accentuate this resolution, Woiwode peoples the novel with odd folks who serve as Martin's extended family, a naturally burlesque troupe of characters who boisterously sample both the joys and the sorrows of life on Earth within the confines of small-town America.

The Neumiller family over which Martin presides is hardworking, intelligent, and generally steady; they are manifestly not extraordinary when measured against the typical families of traditional, rural, midwestern life. Martin, like Woiwode, revels in their normality. Driven to resign as an underpaid and underappreciated small-town teacher and principal, Martin takes on odd jobs as a plumber and insurance salesman to provide an income while waiting for another opening. Hearing of a principalship in the small Illinois town where his parents live encourages him to move there from North Dakota. Completely loyal to his wife, Alpha, Martin clearly treasures her and the six children they have. They have committed themselves to each other "till death parts them."

The move to Illinois is disastrous, however, as anti-Catholic bigotry denies Martin the job he sought, and Alpha subsequently dies abruptly. The reader discerns, with Martin, that it was his break from "ordinariness," from typical family patterns of mutual decision-making—found in his uncharacteristically sudden decision to move his family east—that has animated most of the tension and diversion within the novel and which ultimately delivers its theme. Left to serve as "father, mother, nurse, teacher, arbiter, guardian, judge," Martin appears to shrivel up inside. Outwardly stoic about his life's ups and downs, he continues to be resolute about how to face disappointments and discouragements: "A man should be grateful for what he gets and not expect to get one thing more."

Using this "family album" approach, Woiwode lends concreteness to his notion that reality is a fragile construction, one that sometimes cannot bear scrutiny "beyond the bedroom wall"—that is, beyond the dreamy world of sleep, of its visions of what might be. Woiwode intimates that whatever hope there may be for fulfilling one's dreams, it is anchored in "walking by faith, and not by sight," by trusting in and actively nurturing family intimacy.

The rather sentimental, "old-fashioned" quality Woiwode achieves in this family chronicle, his evocation of once-embraced and now-lamented values, prompted critic and novelist John Gardner to place Woiwode in the company of literature's greatest epic novelists: "When self-doubt, alienation, and fashionable pessimism become a bore and, what's worse, a patent delusion, how does one get back to the big emotions, the large and fairly confident life affirmations of an Arnold Bennet, a [Charles] Dickens, a [Fyodor] Dostoevsky? *Beyond the Bedroom Wall* is a brilliant solution."

Woiwode's eye for the rich details of daily life enables him to move through vast stretches of time and space in executing the episodic structure in this novel. His appreciation for the cadences of Midwestern speech and his understanding of the distinctiveness of prairie life and landscape and its impact on the worldviews of its inhabitants recalls other regional writers such as Rudy Wiebe and Garrison Keillor at their best.

POPPA JOHN

First published: 1981
Type of work: Novel

An aging actor fights to regain his self-respect and recover his own identity after his soap opera character dies.

When compared with the massive *Beyond the Bedroom Wall, Poppa John* is shockingly short and is more a finely wrought character study than a novel. Consequently, Woiwode relies on subtle symbolism and poignant imagery to convey the story's essentially religious themes. The book takes its title from the character that aging actor Ned Daley has played for many years on a popular television soap opera. With his character's immense personal popularity beginning to overshadow the show itself, he is eventually written out of the show in a dramatic "death." Now close to seventy, outspoken, and Falstaffian in appearance and behavior, he seeks to recover his identity as "Ned," which has been sublimated during his twelve years as the imperious Poppa John.

Poppa John's compressed action takes place on two days in the Christmas season, a Friday and a Sunday—nakedly separated by a vacant and voiceless Saturday—and the novella is thus divided into two parts, decisively marked by the calendar: Friday, December 23, and Sunday, December 25. As in his other fiction, Woiwode is concerned that the reader discover the nature of his characters' predicaments by "listening" to their own thoughts and memories as they recall them, rather than by intrusive exposition by an omniscient narrator. Progressively but achronologically, one learns the relevant facts of Ned's past; recollection, in fact, dominates present action in the evolving narrative.

Therefore, in responding to the novella, it is important to recognize the character traits that Ned has sought to embody in Poppa John for twelve television seasons. Part King Lear, part Santa Claus, Poppa John evinces a kind a tragic benevolence, resolving contrived soap opera dilemmas with well-chosen biblical verses. Though easily spouting Scripture while in character, Ned rarely discerned its significance for himself, nor has the sage presence of Poppa John transferred any benefits to his own relationships. In this portrayal, Ned found inspiration in his own grandfather, a fiery evangelical preacher scandalized when his daughter, Ned's mother, married a Catholic and converted to this alien faith. His father, a vaguely corrupt policeman, had died a violent death that Ned himself overheard taking place while hiding in a warehouse—a signal event that drove him into an adult acting career that has prevented him from becoming the unique individual he was born to be.

Consequently, Ned has a complex and paradoxical relationship to religious faith. It at once circumscribes his life and distances it from its reality. The "Scriptures," Woiwode's narrator opines, "had given him slivered glimpses into the realm of time, from the vantage of his years, where a central pureness . . . held the continual revolving of days into weeks—into months, into ages—in balance with the compiled weight of the ages revolving beneath the particular minute of each day." When Poppa

John dies, Ned's own life begins to unravel, and he is increasingly forced to face his own inconsistencies, his doubts, and even his sins.

The novel opens as Ned and his devout and devoted wife, Celia, dress for a day of Christmas Eve shopping. Ned has been out of work for more than a year, and the couple must withdraw money from savings to fund any gift buying for each other. "Ned" only to his wife (he is "Poppa John" to everyone else), he is lost in the malevolent nostalgia of growing old without a true self or true self-respect. Ned is tentative about this trip uptown; he has been in analysis, seeking to exorcise the ghost of Poppa John from his psyche. He no longer knows how to "be himself."

As he strolls the streets of New York, he moves intermittently in and out of his Poppa John identity, conversing amiably with strangers who recognize him, all the while employing the gestures and intonations his adoring fans have come to expect. He is simultaneously a captive of the public who gave him his livelihood and the victim of a medium that rewards popularity by "killing" its source.

The more his casual acquaintances offer their condolences for his fictional death, the more self-pitying he becomes. After he and his wife agree to split up so each can shop for the other, Ned succumbs to an old temptation, alcohol. In a neighborhood bar, he allows himself to be "picked up" by an admiring fan and would-be dancer who takes him to her apartment. When her roommate returns to find the drunken and blubbering old man, she persuades the dancer to return him to the bar whence they came, and eventually they send him on his way in a cab. Exiting at the next block, Ned wanders the streets and eventually collapses in a street mission, which he mistakes for the homely Catholic cathedral of his youth. The next face he sees, now on Christmas morning, is that of his wife. Confined to a hospital psychiatric ward, Ned is "coming to himself," realizing that he, after all these years, does believe in God and therefore can come to believe in himself.

In minimizing the action of the novella and compressing it into only two days, Woiwode places special weight on two different and compelling Christian images he seeks to juxtapose: the joyful incarnation of the baby Jesus, foregrounded in the Christmastime setting; and Christ's crucifixion and resurrection, a dark Friday and a buoyant

Easter Sunday separated by a bleak, lost Saturday. As Christ is in the grave, his fate unknown, Ned/Poppa John is also buried and left for "dead" in his drunken stupor. When he awakens to receive his wife's Christmas gift of a briefcase bearing his initials N. E. D., his life as Ned Daley is restored, and he is thereby enabled to embrace a future he despaired of finding again. What Woiwode offers in *Poppa John* is a modern parable of life, death, and rebirth.

BORN BROTHERS

First published: 1988
Type of work: Novel

The continuing saga of the Neumiller family, whose characters were introduced first in Beyond the Bedroom Wall.

Woiwode calls this novel a "companion volume" to *Beyond the Bedroom Wall,* and it returns to the characters and setting of that work. Beginning in the middle of the twentieth century, *Born Brothers* is filtered through the perceptions of Charles Neumiller; through his memories, he is seeking a meaning and purpose for his life. As elsewhere, Woiwode eschews chronological narrative, and the present is submerged deeply into the past. The novel progresses through various memories of Charles. To speak of a plot or setting is unhelpful; to force Woiwode's uniquely fashioned version of family chronicle into such misleading categories is to misconstrue Woiwode's vision—that lives do not neatly fit into prescribed, sequential patterns. Family members appear in a seemingly random way that shows Charles's quest for an answer to the plaintive cry of his heart: Is there life after childhood?

A gifted raconteur and orator, Charles has followed his voice into a New York career as a "voice-over" in commercials and as a "radio personality" focused on small-town life. He is thus accustomed to creating illusions and re-creating forgotten, homely images in the minds of his listeners. In fact, he is incapable of conceiving of a meaningful world outside the psychic landscape of his own family structure. Having endured assaults on his marriage and having struggled with alcohol, Charles leaves New York behind for his beloved North Dakota. A suitable anthem for Charles Neumiller's life can be drawn from his own musings: "Imagination is, indeed, memory—that is more profound than any fantasy." The events and relationships of the past are as concrete as any the present can offer him.

His childhood and his own fatherhood have profoundly shaped his life in ways that preclude other influences and forces from engaging his life. The minutest detail of a past experience is recalled and rehearsed in Charles's mind as the reader is invited to share vicariously in its warmth and vitality. Errant smoke from a father's cigar, a mother's bedtime stories, a life-threatening fall—each of these recollected events breathes life into Woiwode's protagonist as he searches for an anchor to hold onto in the storms of modern life.

The thematic key to the novel may be found in a recognition that Charles longs for a restored bond of brotherhood he once shared with his elder brother, Jerome—drawn from a childhood which the adult Charles visits frequently, once again inhabiting what now seems an idyllic Garden of Eden in North Dakota, free from the cares and motivations of prurient, polluted, industrial life. That Charles's radio job comprised the roles of both the interviewer and the interviewee encapsulates his need for conversion, of freedom from self. He needs an outside, a reference point, which, implicitly, he seeks in Jerome— an affirmation he anticipates but does not truly realize in a New York reunion in a dingy hotel room. If their memories  are not "mutual," he fears, "I might have invented our love." Ultimately, Woiwode hints, Charles will find "a place to stand" only through a renewed faith in the transcendent, and eventually Charles concedes that the only proof of God's existence "is God's existence in you for eternity."

At times, the tedious details of Charles's recollections are dizzying, even unedifying. Yet it is the totalizing effect, the sheer volume of Charles's "unedited" introspections, that gives the novel its weight and its merit. In part, it is Woiwode's intent to lay the blame for American society's apparent moral disintegration—rampant promiscuity, unwanted pregnancy, and divorce—to the absence of strong family ties, but he leaves open the question of whether Charles's captivity to the past is the solution or part of the problem. In the end, *Born Brothers* can perhaps be received as fiction's most ambitious, if not most successful, attempt since the work of French novelist François Mauriac to capture the vagaries of the active conscious mind and tortured spirit within the linearity of print.

INDIAN AFFAIRS

First published: 1992
Type of work: Novel

This is the second installment in the chronicles of Chris and Ellen Van Eenanam, the young married couple first introduced in What I'm Going to Do, I Think.

Chris and Ellen Van Eenanam are still adjusting to life together as a couple, to the death of their stillborn child, and to the changes inevitable in young adulthood. Chris needs to complete the writing of his dissertation, the final step in attaining his Ph.D. in mathematics. In an isolated cabin in upper Michigan, Chris intends to concentrate on his writing and his marriage.

Chris Van Eenanam is of mixed blood (Lakota on his grandfather's side) but has always considered himself more white than red, having been raised and educated in New York. His relocation will prove to be cultural as well as geographic, personal as well as regional, as he grapples with issues of self-identity. His move inland toward the center of the nation positions him closer to his heritage in a type of reverse migration. Through encounters with other American Indians, Chippewa whom he initially disdains, Chris gradually sees a reflection of himself and acknowledges his Indian heritage, but it comes at a cost—increasing estrangement from his wife, Ellen.

In this novel of personal reversals, Chris makes a final identity shift. His decision to return to New York at novel's end suggests an abandonment of his newly acquired American Indian persona and a return to the assimilated mainstream Chris Van Eenanam, the selfsame character that he was at the novel's beginning. In the final analysis, Chris appears to don identities as he dons clothing, wearing that which is most conducive to the social and geographic climate at hand. Woiwode seems to propose that in an age of uncomplicated travel and increasingly merged ancestries, a clear sense of self becomes difficult to sustain. That a unified Chris could emerge with a hybrid identity, one both white and Indian simultaneously, unfortunately is not an option.

"SILENT PASSENGERS"

First published: 1993 (collected in *Silent Passengers: Stories,* 1993)
Type of work: Short story

Together the Steiner family recovers from a tragic accident that renders their son comatose.

Set on a high-plains ranch, the summer retreat of a Silicon Valley family, "Silent Passengers" explores personal tragedy from a perspective that is intimate and introspective. Ostensibly the Steiners have purchased their summer home to enable Mr. Steiner to spend quality time with his children, nine-year-old James and twin daughters, but on the afternoon in question he lies isolated in the twins' bedroom, napping off the aftereffects of excessive beer consumption while his family visits a neighboring ranch to ride horses.

After Steiner's wife, Jen, and their children dismount from their ride, one of the horses, an Apache, hooves James in the chest, and the boy is knocked unconscious when his head strikes the ground. Apprised of the accident by a neighbor's phone call, Steiner recalls the final words that he spoke to James, a dismissive "I don't care" in response to his son's query about whether to go with the girls or remain with his father to help repair a broken tractor. As he races to the emergency room, this memory torments Steiner, as does his regret about drinking, a habit he had promised to avoid while on vacation.

Ultimately, this is a story about caring, hope,

love, and resurrection. The father who said he did not care cares deeply. Following a doctor's pronouncement that James will likely remain comatose, Steiner and his wife fall to their knees in an anguished embrace suggestive of physical if not verbal prayer. When they rise in unison, Steiner's next action is to lift James out of his labyrinth of tubes and deliver him to his mother's lap, where Jen cradles her son. Instinctively, the boy raises his arms to clasp his mother's neck. On the day following their reenactment of his conception and birth, James attempts speech. Steiner, awakened as well, realizes that he and his wife have been silent passengers on their son's quick descent into and slow deliverance from darkness. Though he may never return to mental and physical wholeness, James's awakening to consciousness is sufficient cause for Steiner's joy: "That's enough, he thought. . . . it was enough to have the child with them, alive."

Following a week of physical therapy, their son is brought home to the ranch to continue his recovery. Wearing a harness to aid mobility, a wobbly James is attached to his mother's steady hand by a leather strap, a symbolic umbilical cord. Undeterred, the boy runs downhill, mother in tow, in the direction of their own grazing horses. The image panics Steiner, who still fears his son's mortality. A sudden gust of wind raises skyward the hair on the heads of his family members, and this natural phenomenon, suggestive of threads connecting earth to heaven, and emblematic of life after death, transforms Steiner's parental dread to one of benevolent acceptance.

WHAT I THINK I DID

First published: 2000
Type of work: Autobiography

This first volume of a projected three-part autobiography is set in two contrasting landscapes: the North Dakota prairie and the New York publishing world.

The title of Woiwode's memoir, *What I Think I Did*, is a playful variation of the title of his 1969 novel, *What I'm Going to Do, I Think*. The autobiographical work is structured in two parts separated by an in-

termezzo that functions more like a pause than a transition. The first section contains the author's memories of his childhood, including the death of his mother; his changing relationships with his own children at various ages; his connection to the prairie and, by extension, to nature; and the development and nurturing of his craft as a writer.

Central to act 1 is Woiwode's account of surviving the North Dakota winter of 1996, the most severe on record. That dark season provides an emotional backdrop upon which he projects memories that, like snowdrifts, shape and reshape themselves. Storm temperatures, wind chills reaching negative triple digits, are potentially lethal, Woiwode recounts. His purchase, construction, and maintenance of a wood-burning furnace to heat the buildings on his ranch become a metaphor for both maintaining human life and relationships and fueling the writing process. Woiwode struggles to assimilate the childhood loss of his mother with the direction of his adult life: "Her death, the calamitous event I've tried in different ways to put into the hands of fictional characters, hoping to leave it with them, sometimes returns." Exploring the events surrounding her death and 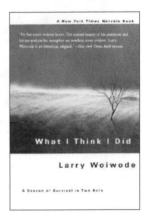 seeking the information denied him as a child, it is his inquisitiveness that characterizes Woiwode as a writer and propels him toward his chosen career. His search for answers both practical (How did she die?) and spiritual (Why did she die?) continues in act 2 as he explores his apprenticeship as a young writer in New York City.

Aptly titled "Intermission," the middle of Woiwode's autobiography offers a break between parts 1 and 2 and acts as a spatial divide between prairie and city. The words attach themselves to no single place, and the section is startling in its physical disconnectedness, so dissimilar to what comes before and after. A description of walking through a crowded art gallery melds into a boyhood hike through solitary woods. Eventually, the section abandons terra firma altogether to become a powerful soliloquy whose intended audience is no longer solely the reader, but the ear of God. In this manner, "Intermission" becomes what it aims to be: a spiritual, not material, discourse.

The second section of his memoir locates Woiwode away from the prairie landscapes of his youth and middle age, landing him first on the campus of the University of Illinois in Urbana and later in the concrete cityscape of New York. Woiwode's college days are complicated by his falling in love simultaneously with acting, writing, and a young woman, all three competing passions connected by their reliance on words to communicate emotions. Out of school and in New York, he befriends a young Robert De Niro, the actor, when they appear in an Off-Broadway play, but it is the page, not the stage, that holds the greatest appeal for Woiwode. In pursuit of this avocation, he is guided by William Maxwell, an editor at *The New Yorker*, who becomes Woiwode's mentor. The culminating scene in act 2 depicts both men spilling tears at the news of the young author's inaugural publication.

In this first installment of his life story, Woiwode avoids a strictly linear approach to narration; instead, he offers readers insight into significant scenes as they appear to cross his mind. Memories of events, places, and people are enhanced by Woiwode's philosophical musings, commentary on both what he recalls thinking at the time and what he presently discerns of a recollected situation. His writing style, as it shifts forward and backward, mimics the powerful winds that wreaked havoc on the plains in the first section. *What I Think I Did* is part *Bildungsroman*, the story of a young writer's emergence, and part elegy, a tribute to his mother and others who gave birth to his dream. It is a chronicle of life, death, survival, relationships, and writing. The author looks not so much within, but around himself, to acknowledge the sources of his craft.

SUMMARY

While believing that the most important human questions are, in fact, spiritual ones, Woiwode rejects the notion that there can be legitimate, compelling "novels of ideas." Woiwode handles such questions by creating authentically ordinary characters and settling them into the concrete and mundane world of daily life as filtered through human imagination and memory. Woiwode's prose is consistently active, alive, and unassuming, with a finely tuned lyricism. His keen eye for the extraordinary ordinariness of life makes his narrative vision compelling and believable. Woiwode thus stands out as a moderating influence among contemporary novelists, an advocate for restoring a moral, even spiritual voice to modern letters.

Bruce L. Edwards; updated by Dorothy Dodge Robbins

BIBLIOGRAPHY

By the Author

LONG FICTION:
What I'm Going to Do, I Think, 1969
Beyond the Bedroom Wall: A Family Album, 1975
Poppa John, 1981
Born Brothers, 1988
Indian Affairs, 1992

SHORT FICTION:
The Neumiller Stories, 1989
Silent Passengers: Stories, 1993

POETRY:
Poetry North: Five North Dakota Poets, 1970 (with Richard Lyons, Thomas McGrath, John R. Milton, and Antony Oldknow)
Even Tide, 1977

NONFICTION:

Acts, 1993

Aristocrat of the West: The Story of Harold Schafer, 2000

What I Think I Did: A Season of Survival in Two Acts, 2000

My Dinner with Auden, 2006

About the Author

Connaughton, Michael E. "Larry Woiwode." In *American Novelists Since World War II,* edited by James E. Kibler, Jr. Detroit: Gale Research, 1980.

Dickson, Morris. "Flight into Symbolism." *The New Republic* 160 (May 3, 1969): 28.

Gardner, John. Review of *Beyond the Bedroom Wall,* by Larry Woiwode. *The New York Times Book Review* 125 (September 28, 1975): 1-2.

Gasque, W. Ward. Review of *Acts,* by Larry Woiwode. *Christianity Today,* March 7, 1994, 38.

Marx, Paul. "Larry (Alfred) Woiwode." In *Contemporary Novelists,* edited by James Vinson. 3d ed. New York: St. Martin's Press, 1982.

O'Hara, Barbara. Review of *What I Think I Did,* by Larry Woiwode. *Library Journal,* June 1, 2000, 128.

Pesetsky, Bette. Review of *Born Brothers,* by Larry Woiwode. *The New York Times Book Review* 93 (August 4, 1988): 13-14.

Prescott, Peter S. "Home Truths." *Newsweek* 86 (September 29, 1975): 85-86.

Woiwode, Larry. "An Interview with Larry Woiwode." *Christianity and Literature* 29 (1979): 11-18.

_____. "An Interview with Larry Woiwode." Interview by Ed Block, Jr. *Renascence: Essays on Values in Literature* 44, no. 1 (Fall, 1991): 17-30.

_____. "Interview with Woiwode." Interview by Shirley Nelson. *The Christian Century,* January 25, 1995, 82.

_____. "Where the Buffalo Roam: An Interview with Larry Woiwode." Interview by Rick Watson. *North Dakota Quarterly* 63, no. 4 (Fall, 1996): 154-166.

Discussion Topics

- Larry Woiwode's characters tend to have a strong connection to place. How would you describe their relationship to the land?

- The search for meaning, for a spiritual life, is a motif in many of Woiwode's novels and stories. Where does Woiwode suggest this spiritual life be found?

- Intragenerational relationships play a role in *Beyond the Bedroom Wall* and *The Neumiller Stories.* What do younger family members learn from their elders (and vice versa) that stresses the importance of maintaining communication between the generations?

- Woiwode has said that he incorporated his mother's death into a number of his works as an exercise in coming to terms with his early loss. What do these scenes reveal about the grieving process?

- Woiwode's fiction and nonfiction both seem dedicated to preserving or reviving a way of life. Based on the work or works that you have read, how would you characterize that way of life?

Library of Congress

THOMAS WOLFE

Born: Asheville, North Carolina
    October 3, 1900
Died: Baltimore, Maryland
    September 15, 1938

By recasting in a fictional guise characters and events from his own life, Wolfe created situations that evoked the underlying, quintessential ethos of southern and American ways of life during the period of his youth and early manhood.

BIOGRAPHY

Because so much of his writing was based upon his own background and upbringing, critics and biographers have often interpreted the novels of Thomas Wolfe by reference to the author's personal life. Although occasionally his fictional vision diverged from the realities of Wolfe's life, often the correspondence between literary narration and actual events was so close that the sources of his works could easily be traced to his own experiences.

The last of eight children, Thomas Clayton Wolfe was born in Asheville, North Carolina, on October 3, 1900. His parents, Julia Elizabeth Westall Wolfe and William Oliver Wolfe, were of widely contrasting temperaments. While his father, a stonecutter, was an ingratiating sort who nevertheless was prone to angry outbursts and wild drinking sprees, his mother was of a practical turn; she was somewhat avaricious, and she became involved in local real estate ventures. She doted on her youngest son, however, and it would seem that Thomas Wolfe's attachment to his mother was part of the basis for that element of fondness with which he later recalled the years of his childhood. A family business, a boarding house called the Old Kentucky Home, was opened in 1906; it was managed by Julia Wolfe. From relatively early, Thomas Wolfe acquired some notions about the sorts of people who had settled

in the area or who stayed there during their travels in the region.

In 1905, Wolfe entered the Orange Street Public School in Asheville; in 1912, he was enrolled in the private North State Fitting School. He was an avid, incessantly curious boy who combed the shelves of the local public library for reading material. Because of his aptitude for academic work, it was decided (after he had set his hopes on out-of-state schools) that he should attend the University of North Carolina in Chapel Hill. Although he experienced some difficulties in adjustment when he entered as a freshman in 1916, Wolfe later became well known at the university for his involvement with campus organizations and literary projects. For a time he edited the school's newspaper.

In 1919, *The Return of Buck Gavin*, a play he had written for one of his courses, was staged by the local Carolina Playmakers; Wolfe performed in it and delighted many with his extravagant portrayal of the title character. As a college student, his consuming determination to read as widely as possible continued unabated. In many courses he did well. Wolfe was often regarded as showing particular promise; by 1920, when he began graduate studies at Harvard University, he seems to have become settled in his ambition to be a writer. In addition to studies that brought him into contact with leading specialists on English literature, such as John Livingston Lowes, he was associated with a well-known theater workshop group. He received a master's degree in 1922, and in 1923 his play *Wel-*

come to Our City was performed. During this period, however, he was deeply saddened by the loss of family members; in 1918 his brother Ben died of tuberculosis, and after a prolonged struggle with cancer his father died in 1922.

In February, 1924, Wolfe accepted a position as an instructor in English at New York University, and he taught there intermittently for about six years. In October, 1924, he set off on the first of seven journeys to Europe. On his return, in August, 1925, he met a wealthy married woman, Aline Bernstein, who was about nineteen years older than he. A strange and turbulent love affair followed, which lasted until 1932, a year after his wife apparently tried to resolve matters by threatening suicide. All along, Wolfe worked steadily at composing prose fiction. After three years of work, the manuscript of his first novel had been prepared; it was partly because of the extraordinary efforts of Maxwell Perkins, the editor for the publisher Charles Scribner's Sons in New York, that *Look Homeward, Angel* could be published in October, 1929. The success of this work, and the award to Wolfe of a Guggenheim Fellowship in 1930, which supported further travel overseas, instilled in him added confidence to continue writing.

Wolfe published important works of short fiction during the early 1930's, and beginning in 1933, he was assisted by Elizabeth Nowell, who served as his literary agent and found journals that would publish his stories. With the invaluable aid of Maxwell Perkins during some protracted and arduous editing sessions, Wolfe's second novel, *Of Time and the River,* appeared in 1935. Wolfe traveled widely during this time, both in the United States and abroad. While on a visit to Germany during the Berlin Olympic Games of 1936, he developed a deeply felt antipathy to Nazi ideology, and he subsequently presented this theme with great effect in his fiction.

Back in New York, complications about his dealings with his publisher broke into the open; in particular, there were quarrels over the handling of legal matters, and there were some recriminations about a royalty agreement which Wolfe considered unsatisfactory. In 1937, he signed a contract with Harper and Brothers and entrusted further manuscripts to Edward C. Aswell, the editor for that firm. The following year he traveled extensively in the United States, and he delivered an important lecture, which was later published, at Purdue University. He visited Western states, and in Seattle he came down with pneumonia. A latent tubercular lesion had been opened, and tuberculosis of the brain set in.

Although he was taken finally to the Johns Hopkins Hospital in Baltimore, doctors found his condition beyond hope of treatment, and he died on September 15, 1938. His last two novels, *The Web and the Rock* (1939) and *You Can't Go Home Again* (1940), were published posthumously, as was some of his other prose fiction. Over a period of several decades, the publication of personal letters, collected interviews, plays, and other literary fragments he had left cast further light on his outlook and interests.

ANALYSIS

Typically, Wolfe composed his novels as vast, sprawling narratives which, beginning with the origins, early childhood, or youth of his protagonists, would recount in abundant detail memorable impressions and episodes from his past. Those who knew Wolfe personally and who had heard him speak described him as capable of extraordinary, vivid, and tumultuous outpourings of words that could be prompted spontaneously by suitable occasions. This quality may be seen in much of his writing. Many of the particularly evocative passages in his novels display descriptive powers that he developed at some length, and which in turn were related to the thematic currents underlying his works. His writings were particularly effective in conveying sights and sounds of locales that were familiar to him. Inner reactions and the subjective life of his fictional alter egos were also depicted in depth.

Resonant and seemingly universal in their appeal were Wolfe's evocations of the timeless joys and travails of childhood and youth and the many-faceted manifestations of the American spirit. He also had a definite sense for the specific characteristics of certain regions and groups; in some passages he would contrast southern ways with those that prevailed in other parts of the United States. Often he would indulge in written mimicry of dialects, whether southern or northeastern, and sometimes he attempted to reproduce the intonations of English spoken with an Italian, French, or German accent. He also had a satirical bent and was wont to portray those who seemed typecast in somewhat overblown guises.

Some parts of his works have been taken as suggesting tolerance of racial prejudices, and it would appear that he also had ambivalent—and at times not necessarily sympathetic—feelings about Jews, but as such matters are handled in his novels, attitudes of this sort could also be regarded as to some extent characteristic of the times during which he lived. Otherwise, however, in many respects Wolfe s protagonists could be considered as expressing, in a somewhat larger-than-life form, the yearnings and ambitions of many who might feel that in America a quest for learning, love, or fulfillment might be realized.

It would appear that, among the numerous authors, classical and modern, with whom Wolfe was familiar, he was probably influenced as much by the works of James Joyce as by any other writer. Wolfe's writings were known to most of his contemporaries, as well as to the wider reading public; in particular, Sinclair Lewis esteemed his work highly—in the speech he delivered when he won the Nobel Prize, Lewis took particular note of Wolfe's attainments. In a somewhat cryptic vein, William Faulkner pointed to Wolfe as a failure but a failure on a magnificent scale which others of their generation had not reached.

Readers and reviewers of Wolfe's time, and later, often enough were prone to complain of the extreme wordiness that burdened all of his major works. It has also been maintained that because of the all but limitless concern Wolfe had for his protagonists, his writing bordered on the overwritten, the puerile, and the mawkish. His defenders, both during his lifetime and subsequently, have contended, however, that even where his efforts were flawed and overly effusive, the scale and depth of his achievements still could not be denied.

LOOK HOMEWARD, ANGEL

First published: 1929
Type of work: Novel

Family life and self-discovery are among the themes that punctuate the story of a young southerner during the first twenty years of his life.

As childhood may be composed, in part, of the recollections and impressions passed along by parents, so it may seem not to have a precisely fixed beginning or end. *Look Homeward, Angel: A Story of the Buried Life*, the story of Eugene Gant, commences not with the boy's first conscious sensations but with the origins of his father and mother.

William Oliver Gant, whose ancestors had settled in Pennsylvania, had been apprenticed to the stonecutter's trade. He moved eventually to the South and, after two marriages, he came to the rural mountain city of Altamont, the fictional equivalent of the author's native Asheville. There he met Eliza Pentland, who came from an established, if somewhat eccentric, family of that region, and after some courtship he married her. Even then, Gant was a wild and exuberant sort, who was capable of epic drinking bouts; he also possessed a certain untamed vitality, and by the end of the nineteenth century, when he was nearly fifty years old, his wife had conceived their last child.

By way of this oddly retrospective narrative introduction, the circumstances of Eugene Gant's early years are set forth, and events from his life even as a small child are then recorded at some length. For example, from the age of six he could recall the many colors of bright autumn days, and he was aware of the many smells of food in all its varieties, and of wood and leather. He was alive to the crisply etched sights of furniture, hardware, trees, and gardens that were to be found around his home and in the city. Once he had learned to read, he became enchanted with tales of travel and adventure, and indeed with the very power of words themselves, but there was also a worldly and earthy element to his character.

At the age of eight he had some vague appreciation for bawdy rhymes and crude jokes told by the older boys. He could also recall the blunt racial slurs that were routinely used by those in his neighborhood. Beyond that, however, there was a contemplative and inward-looking aspect to his cast of mind. He could remember that before he was ten years old he would brood upon what seemed to be tantalizingly unanswerable contradictions that went to the very nature of the human spirit.

Various themes and motifs seem to characterize Eugene's adolescent years. He has a literary curiosity of prodigious proportions, and he reads books of all sorts, many at a time. He has great energy and considerable zest for sports, even though he is awkward and ungainly on the baseball diamond. An imaginative boy, he is prone to indulge in vividly embroidered daydreams which cast an idealized counterpart of himself as an invincible hero. He has some awkward misadventures with women, which seem later to arouse further longings in him. During this period there occur some richly comic episodes, as when Eugene's father prepares an elegant stone angel as a burial monument for a prostitute. There are also some hints of events in the wider world beyond them; on one occasion William Jennings Bryan visits the town and makes some suitably politic replies to questions from local admirers.

As the youngest member of his family, Eugene feels more closely drawn to his brother Ben than to others around him. Another brother, Steve, turns out to be a ne'er-do-well. Their brother Luke has a particular talent for earning money from odd jobs of any kind but has little aptitude for academics; after some study at a college and a technical school he becomes a worker in a boiler factory. Meanwhile, their father has become sallow and aged; prostate cancer has set in, and his vigorous, exuberant manner seems to have become subdued and petulant. In Eugene's life, a major change comes when he enrolls in the state university and for the first time lives away from home. By this juncture it is recorded that, just short of the age of sixteen, he remains still very much a child at heart; great but vaguely felt ideals of beauty and order are still largely untempered by contact with the world beyond.

The university has a distinctive, unforgettable charm and resembles an oasis of learning in a provincial wilderness. Here Eugene's education begins in earnest; while previously he had been simply a precocious, somewhat pampered boy with vast and undefined ambitions, during his college work his impulse to read widely and in depth assumes somewhat clearer contours. At the outset he feels isolated and disoriented, but he eventually becomes initiated in college ways. He visits a prostitute in a neighboring city and comes down with a verminous affliction which must be cured by a local doctor when he returns home for Christmas. Later he feels stirred by impulses that are both romantic and erotic. During a summer he spends back home in Altamont, he meets Laura James. She is a pert, attractive woman five years older than Eugene, and she has already become engaged to another man; for the time being she has come to stay at the Gants' boardinghouse. Eugene has a brief but intense affair with her which, while loosely based on events in Wolfe's life, seems here to have been reworked considerably in order to emphasize the romantic prowess of the protagonist.

For a period during World War I, Eugene, who is too young for active service, goes to work at a Navy yard in Virginia, not too far from Laura James's original home; he is disappointed that, after their brief sojourn together, he does not hear anything further from her. Other and more distressing troubles soon confront Eugene and his family, for Ben, Eugene's favorite brother, who had defended him during family disputes, has been stricken with a fatal illness of the lungs. As his all-too-brief life draws to a close there are scenes that are alternately petty and poignant. At the hospital, their father suddenly begins complaining about medical costs, to the discomfiture of the others. On the other hand, Eugene, who has never been particularly religious, fervently begins to pray when it appears that Ben has passed beyond recovery. He reflects unhappily that somehow in death Ben has meant more to the family than when he was alive. Toward the end, when Eugene has graduated from college and is preparing to go on to Harvard University, it seems to him in some imagined way that out of the past Ben's ghost has come back and is asking him where he is going on his life's journey.

OF TIME AND THE RIVER

First published: 1935
Type of work: Novel

The adult years of Wolfe's fictional counterpart are depicted in this lengthy narrative of his quest for personal fulfillment in the United States and abroad.

In much of Wolfe's writing, lengthy descriptions of train journeys impart a sense of movement and change. In *Of Time and the River: A Legend of Man's Hunger in His Youth,* his hero, Eugene, embarks upon a trip northward. Having left college in his native state, Eugene believes that he has become a witness to a vast and panoramic series of images which, taken together, reveal the many faces of America itself. There is to him a sensation of escape from the dark and mournful mystery of the South to the freedom and bright promise of the North, with its shining cities and extravagant hopes. The plains, peaks, and valleys that shape the landscape over which he passes, as well as the innumerable towns and cities along the way, bespeak to him the limitless diversity of the United States.

Other images, mainly from the past, are called up within Eugene when he stops in Baltimore to visit the hospital where, in his fatal illness, his father is being treated. The old man seems yellow, wan, and exhausted, and only the stonecutter's

THOMAS WOLFE

Of Time and the River
New Introduction by Pat Conroy

hands, of a massive size and grace, seem still to suggest the strength and dignity with which he had once carried out his chosen calling. Otherwise, old Gant appears to have wasted away, and his sullen self-pity indicates that little remains of his once vibrant spirit. Somewhat later, in some graphic passages, the old man is left drained and enfeebled by sudden and vast outpourings of blood; he dies in the midst of numerous relatives and friends who have come by during his last days.

Wolfe's second novel is divided into parts bear-ing allegorical allusions; the figure most readily identified with his fictional hero is portrayed in the second section as "young Faustus." At least as much as during earlier times, when he was a boy or an undergraduate student, Eugene Gant is propelled by an immense and boundless striving to read anything and everything he can and to encompass all known learning and literature in a self-imposed regimen that goes well beyond the limits of formal study. At Harvard's library he prowls about in the stacks, taking down volumes he has not seen before and timing with a watch how many seconds it takes to finish one page and read the next before moving on. Eugene also walks the streets alone, mainly for the sake of gathering in sights and sounds that are still new and not entirely familiar to him. He marvels at the lonely, tragic beauty of New England, which he has come to believe differs from his native South and yet resembles it in ways that distinguish both regions as essentially American.

Eugene, like Wolfe himself, for a time devotes unstinting energies to writing plays for a workshop which absorbs his energies, but later he recoils from such efforts as constraining and imposing limits upon his creative self. At times he expresses his disdain for productions that he thinks others had tried to make overly fashionable or artistic. Wolfe often was given to expressing his hero's observations and aspirations quantitatively, in large numbers, to suggest some great and unrealizable vision of the nation and of human culture, in its immeasurable richness: While at Harvard, Eugene yearns to read one million books, to possess ten thousand women, and to know something about fifty million of the American people. Such strivings convey the great elemental yearnings of Wolfe's protagonist, whose very being seems set upon not the satisfaction but the pursuit of his unending quest.

For a time, however, he must provide for himself as best he can, and this he does by teaching college-level English courses in New York. All the while, the growing discontent fed by this routine breeds in him wants of another sort. As was the case with Wolfe himself, travel for Eugene seems to open vistas on several levels. One autumn he sets forth to see the great cities of the Old World.

In England, Eugene feels some affinity with a people who share with him a common language and literature; indeed, his admiration for British culture seems favorably to predispose him toward those he meets. Though England seems drab and colorless in some ways, and the cooking turns out to be for the most part bland and disappointing, at the end he senses a bond of affection has been established which transcends any outward differences. On the other hand—and in some respects it would seem that Wolfe regarded Europe as a measure by which those qualities most distinctive about America could be grasped anew—Eugene cannot but be struck by the atmosphere and attitudes which contrast with those of his own country. In France he feels overwhelmed by the Faustian urges that had beset him earlier; he wants to learn and read everything about Paris and its people. Not quite attracted or repelled, he becomes fascinated and at times awestruck by his surroundings.

Some episodes having less to do with cultural matters prove diverting and at times distressing. When he encounters a man he had known from his Harvard days and two American women, their brief camaraderie turns to bitterness and recrimination when Eugene, somewhat put out by what he regards as their affected Boston ways, becomes involved in a fight with his erstwhile friends. After some spirited quarrels, he leaves the others. Once out of Paris, he is befriended by some odd older women from noble families; in the end, as he has chronically been on the verge of exhausting his money altogether, his travels on the Continent must be brought to a close. Having traveled about at length, more and more he has become beset with a longing for home, and indeed he is eager for the sight of anything that might hint of America. When the journey of this modern Faust has been completed, he also—in a state of some wonderment—comes upon a woman for whom he has been longing, on the return voyage home.

THE WEB AND THE ROCK

First published: 1939
Type of work: Novel

In another retelling of events from the author's youth, Wolfe recounts the travails of love and creative writing.

In the preface to this novel, written approximately four months before his death, Wolfe announced that he had turned away from the books he had written in the past; he had intended rather to create a hero whose discovery of life and the world takes place, by his standards, on a more objective plane. Other ways in which the pattern of his earlier works had been varied are evident. Although *The Web and the Rock* was based upon his early life and experiences, those portions dealing with childhood and adolescence were allotted comparatively less space. There is correspondingly more emphasis on events from the author's early adulthood that had not been discussed in the previous novels. The protagonist and Wolfe's final hero, named George Webber, outwardly does not resemble the author to the same extent as does Eugene Gant, though there can be little doubt that, in the same way as Gant, Webber was meant to be the spokesman for Wolfe's thoughts and ideas.

In the first part of the novel, the style also is somewhat more terse and less free-flowing than had been the case in previous works, though later the narrative tends more to resemble that which had been used earlier. It should be mentioned as well that, while it has sometimes been asserted that Wolfe's last two books were to a significant extent adapted by (and indeed, partly written by) his second editor, Edward Aswell, specialists have found that in their essential features the works conformed in most ways to the form in which Wolfe originally had cast them.

The Web and the Rock begins in another fictional version of Wolfe's native city, this time named Libya Hill; his central character, George Webber, is the son of a stonecutter who had migrated to the South many years before. George's early life is described from about the age of twelve. Because of his short, stocky, crouched bearing, George has a vaguely simian appearance; he is called "monkey," or "Monk." While physically he differs noticeably from his creator, he otherwise has much in common with Wolfe. In the early portions of the novel there is a great deal of attention paid to sports and games and other pastimes. Friendships and confrontations with other boys occupy much of his time, and indeed those he had known from this period seemed destined later to appear in his life at unexpected junctures. On the other hand, the boy could not but be fascinated by the dark and violent underside of southern small-town life. On one occasion, a black man he had come to know inexplicably has gone berserk and kills several people with a rifle before being brought down by a sheriff's posse; his bullet-riddled corpse is left on display at a local undertaker's establishment. Such incidents underscore the fragile balance between orderliness and destructive impulses.

When George is about sixteen, the reader learns, his father has died, and George has become a student at a state school named Pine Rock College, where he comes upon some quaint and rustic characters. Nevertheless, he feels that even with its provincialism and its austerity, his school is more than a match for the renowned private institutions of northern states. The events of George's college years are set forth among some evocations of the atmosphere that pervades the campus. In classes there is an earnest, though at times not self-consciously serious, effort to appreciate the better works of literature.

Students also have time enough for carousing and wild sports rallies that seem to have a primitive, earthy vitality of their own. The peculiar status of college football heroes, who appear to hold sway in a domain all their own, is depicted in some vignettes of George's friend Jim Randolph, who seems possessed of extraordinary powers on the playing field but later proves incapable of accomplishing great things in the wider world. For George, however, new and portentous changes are ushered in when he moves to New York; the contrast between his obscure provincial background and outlook and the grandeur and squalor of the great city, in its massive and manifold forms, is particularly striking to the young man.

After living with friends for a while, and after a lonely and desperate year spent by himself, George's inchoate quest and his innermost yearnings are answered, after a fashion, much as they were in Wolfe's own life. The remaining portions of the novel have to do largely with a prolonged love affair which takes place prior to the publication of his first book.

On a return trip from Europe he meets a certain Esther Jack (who has generally been regarded as a fictional rendition of Aline Bernstein), and quickly he becomes infatuated with her. This strange and, for a time, overwhelming passion is described as the result of longing which had created in her an idealized form of woman—indeed, the embodiment of someone she never was or possibly could never have been. In one light she is described as middle-aged, even matronly, though full of energy and still attractive. In his enamored vision, he regards her as the supremely beautiful and sublime embodiment of his desires, and when he perceives her later as falling short of this extravagantly conceived image, quarrels and differences arise. There are as well some remarks on her Jewish origins and on the clannish, insular, but also generous character of her people.

On a directly personal level, he seems attracted to her because of her solicitude and sympathy during his travails as an aspiring but as yet unrecognized writer; her concern for his well-being is quite touching and leads to some memorable scenes where their affection is expressed during the enjoyment of succulent meals she has prepared for him. She also lends her considerable moral support to his work on his first novel, a bulky manuscript ten inches thick, which he has started showing to publishers in the city. After this work has been unceremoniously rejected by the satirically, if infelicitously named, firm of Rawng and Wright, she consoles him and encourages him to look elsewhere.

Soon thereafter, however, discord sets George and Esther apart. He suggests that she has a penchant for younger lovers and becomes tormented by jealousy and distrust. Her sophisticated, urban mannerisms begin to grate harshly upon his rather less refined sensibilities. Remonstrances and countercharges fly back and forth, and claims that Christians cannot tolerate Jewish ways, or the converse, are bandied about. George apparently resents his dependence upon Esther. For her part, stricken by his sudden outbursts of suspicion and hostility, she threatens to end her own life.

As the situation seemingly has become intractable, George finally sets off for Europe, thinking that she will write him or make some effort to settle their differences. He travels in England and on the Continent, increasingly troubled by loneliness and doubts. He feels that he is a foreigner in lands where even American tourists seem strange and out of place. He tells himself finally, when he is in a hospital in Munich recovering from wounds he received in a fight, that "you can't go home again." This reflection sets the tone for the next and final series of his adventures and experiences.

YOU CAN'T GO HOME AGAIN

First published: 1940
Type of work: Novel

Triumphs and troubles in the later life of the author are set forth in this work which also depicts social and political turmoil in America and abroad during the 1930's.

From among the several million recorded words that Wolfe wrote during his career, the phrase that concludes one work and was chosen as the title for this novel has been probably the best-known of all the expressions he ever used. The adage "you can't go home again" evidently was suggested first by Ella Winter, the widow of the writer Lincoln Steffens. This phrase seems apt, not on the most obvious literal level but rather in the sense that, in the flux of time and life, old ties and associations cannot remain the same, unchanged. Once they have been outgrown or cast off, old ways must be set aside as part of a past which cannot easily again be recaptured.

Wolfe's last novel opens with George Webber's return to New York, where Esther Jack receives him. He is apprised that his manuscript has been favorably reviewed by a well-known publishing house, which has sent an advance check for five hundred dollars. He also learns that his aged maiden aunt has died, and he travels southward, to return home for the first time in many years. On the way he meets Nebraska Crane, a friend and companion from his boyhood days who, though he has made a name for himself as a professional baseball player, feels that the best period of his career is behind him.

When George arrives in Libya Hill, he is treated by some as a visiting local celebrity. In newspapers, he is quoted with some inventiveness as expressing the fondest sentiments possible about his native city. Libya Hill has been overtaken by frenetic speculation in real estate and, in fact, in all realms of business, which temporarily has transformed it into a boom town. There is a pervasive atmosphere of change, both superficial and permanent. George, who feels oddly isolated even on native ground, comes to sense that his visit has been an act of farewell more than a homecoming.

Somewhat later, after his novel has been published, George ruefully, but with some amusement, notes the reaction it has stirred up among local people. Because much of his book was essentially based upon real characters, he has received letters complaining with some vehemence of the shame and disgrace he has brought upon those who once were his neighbors and friends. One anonymous writer threatens to kill him. On the other hand, someone else has offered to provide him with even more salacious material should he care to inquire.

By this time, George's affair with Esther has run its course; after some oddly harrowing scenes at one of her social gatherings, he decides that he can turn away decisively from what he regards as her artificially cultivated, high-society circles and way of life. He turns instead to other women for short periods of time but finds none of them particularly endearing or even compatible. All the while, he has also become aware of changing fortunes all around him, brought about by the onset of the Great Depression. He learns that in Libya Hill land values have collapsed suddenly, with resulting hardships and uncertainty. In much of New York, signs of destitution and desperation can be seen at first hand; some moving passages describe dejected homeless men and the discovery of a suicide victim in the street. In spite of the many signs of desolation around George, and despite recurrent brooding loneliness, Wolfe's hero is moved to reaffirm his faith in life and creation.

In describing the only enduring friendship from this period of his hero's life, Wolfe paid unusual tribute to his editor Maxwell Perkins, whom he recast here as Foxhall Edwards. George Webber, who much earlier had lost his own father, is described as benefiting from a sort of spiritual adoption that provides him with needed guidance. To be sure, the editor depicted here seems in some ways foppish and has some strangely idiosyncratic habits. He also has a knack for getting around problems that seems at once cunning and guileless, but he is portrayed as fundamentally tolerant and fair-minded in ways that others of his profession are not.

Another fictional portrait from life of a well-known literary figure appears in the course of George's further travels. During a visit to London he has the opportunity to meet the writer Lloyd McHarg, who was modeled upon Sinclair Lewis.

When a newspaper story reports that McHarg has warmly praised George's work, the young author manages to arrange a meeting with the great man. Although McHarg receives George on friendly, even cordial, terms, the younger man is struck not merely by his unprepossessing, in some ways ugly, appearance: In McHarg, he also believes that he can detect the trials and disappointments of fame and recognition. The widespread acclaim that McHarg had earned seems only to demonstrate that writers could not be satisfied merely with public acceptance. McHarg, in the sheer surfeit of his triumphs, has taken to constant traveling and drinking to allay the numbing boredom and loneliness that have befallen him.

Earlier in his career, Wolfe had shown some fondness for Germany, where he had traveled and where his first book, in translation, had been favorably received. Later, however, much had changed, and a sizable portion from the last part of this novel has to do with some striking and rather horrifying impressions that were gathered during travels under the Nazi regime. Although George Webber, as was Wolfe himself, is treated as an eminent foreign writer, he feels a pronounced uneasiness which sets in almost as soon as he arrives in Berlin. The Olympic Games held in the German capital are flanked by regimented demonstrations of marching men which hint strongly of preparations for war. People George meets are curiously reticent on political matters, though dark and unseemly rumors surface from time to time. The atmosphere of fear and compulsion seems more ubiquitous and more oppressive than any of the killings, gangster plots, or other manifestations of hatred and violence that America had ever known.

During a train trip to the west, George and some other travelers meet a curiously nervous little man, who is afraid he will be detained for currency violations. He presses upon George and the others some coins he had hidden away. When they change trains at the frontier, they discover that the man, who is Jewish, is attempting to escape while smuggling much of his money out of the country. In a brutal, wrenching confrontation with Nazi police, he is apprehended. The others must, helplessly, leave him to his fate. The novel concludes with George's return to New York, where he writes a long letter to Foxhall Edwards, summarizing his beliefs and setting forth his artistic credo. Though he will work no longer under his former editor and friend, he believes that some explanation—and some exposition of the directions his life has taken—is required. At the end, George maintains that the forces of time and change cannot be resisted and that the past he had known must be put behind him.

SUMMARY

Wolfe's ability to present personal experiences and memories in a manner that has inspired many readers to identify with the fictional characterizations of the author has contributed much to the appeal of his major works. Although to some his approach has appeared overly centered on the self, indeed narcissistic, he was able to transform impressions and ideas into forms of expression that are broadly representative of the American ethos, both during his own day and for later generations. The continuing attraction of his writings has been derived partly from his powers of description and characterization, but perhaps more than that from the extent to which the personal and the specific were made to appear universal in his great novels.

J. R. Broadus

BIBLIOGRAPHY

By the Author

SHORT FICTION:
From Death to Morning, 1935
The Hills Beyond, 1941
The Complete Short Stories of Thomas Wolfe, 1987

LONG FICTION:

Look Homeward, Angel, 1929
Of Time and the River, 1935
The Web and the Rock, 1939
You Can't Go Home Again, 1940
The Short Novels of Thomas Wolfe, 1961 (C. Hugh Holman, editor)

DRAMA:

The Mountains, pr. 1921, pb. 1970
Welcome to Our City, pr. 1923 (pb. only in Germany as *Willkommen in Altamont,* 1962)
Mannerhouse, pb. 1948

POETRY:

The Face of a Nation: Poetical Passages from the Writings of Thomas Wolfe, 1939
A Stone, a Leaf, a Door: Poems by Thomas Wolfe, 1945

NONFICTION:

The Story of a Novel, 1936
Thomas Wolfe's Letters to His Mother, 1943 (John Skally, editor)
The Portable Thomas Wolfe, 1946 (Maxwell Geisman, editor)
The Letters of Thomas Wolfe, 1956 (Elizabeth Nowell, editor)
The Notebooks of Thomas Wolfe, 1970 (Richard S. Kennedy and Paschal Reeves, editors)
The Thomas Wolfe Reader, 1982 (C. Hugh Holman, editor)
The Autobiography of an American Novelist: Thomas Wolfe, 1983
Beyond Love and Loyalty: The Letters of Thomas Wolfe and Elizabeth Nowell, 1983 (Kennedy, editor)
My Other Loneliness: Letters of Thomas Wolfe and Aline Bernstein, 1983 (Suzanne Stutman, editor)
To Loot My Life Clean: The Thomas Wolfe-Maxwell Perkins Correspondence, 2000 (Matthew J. Bruccoli and Park Bucker, editors)

DISCUSSION TOPICS

- Thomas Wolfe wrote in a letter to his editor that he felt that he "belonged to the land." How do his novels confirm this feeling?

- How much of an impediment to the reader is the wordiness of which Wolfe has often been accused?

- Which of Wolfe's two protagonists—Eugene Gant or George Webber—most resembles Wolfe?

- Consider Wolfe's evocation of childhood in his novels.

- Wolfe's last novel is titled *You Can't Go Home Again.* Are the reasons for this assertion embodied in the novel? If so, what are they?

About the Author

Bassett, John Earl. *Thomas Wolfe: An Annotated Critical Bibliography.* Lanham, Md.: Scarecrow Press, 1996.

Bloom, Harold, ed. *Thomas Wolfe.* New York: Chelsea House, 2000.

Donald, David Herbert. *Look Homeward: A Life of Thomas Wolfe.* 1987. Reprint. Cambridge, Mass.: Harvard University Press, 2003.

Evans, Elizabeth. *Thomas Wolfe.* New York: Frederick Ungar, 1984.

Field, Leslie A., ed. *Thomas Wolfe: Three Decades of Criticism.* New York: New York University Press, 1968.

Idol, John Lane. *Literary Masters: Thomas Wolfe.* Detroit: Gale, 2001.

Kennedy, Richard S. *The Window of Memory.* Chapel Hill: University of North Carolina Press, 1962.

McElderry, Bruce R. *Thomas Wolfe.* New York: Twayne, 1964.

Phillipson, John S., ed. *Critical Essays on Thomas Wolfe.* Boston: G. K. Hall, 1986.

Rubin, Louis D., Jr., ed. *Thomas Wolfe: A Collection of Critical Essays.* Englewood Cliffs, N.J.: Prentice-Hall, 1973.

Tom Wolfe

Born: Richmond, Virginia
March 2, 1931

Courtesy, Author

A skilled satirist and social critic, Wolfe began his career as a journalist, was a founder of the movement called New Journalism, and later became a satirical novelist. He argues in favor of the large-scale, realistic novel, reflecting the society from which it emerges, as opposed to the spare, mannered novel, which emphasizes style above all other elements.

BIOGRAPHY

Thomas Kennerly Wolfe, Jr., was born on March 2, 1931, in Richmond, Virginia, to businessman and scientist Thomas Kennerly and Helen (Hughes) Wolfe. Wolfe graduated cum laude from Washington and Lee University in 1951 and went on to earn a Ph.D. in American studies from Yale University in 1957. From 1956 until 1959, he was a reporter for *The Union* in Springfield, Massachusetts, then worked at *The Washington Post* from 1959 to 1962. During the 1960's, he began to chronicle the foibles of his generation in a breathless, exciting style that was exuberant and distinctively his own, working as contributing editor for two major magazines: *New York* and *Esquire.*

In 1978, he married Sheila Berger, the art director of *Harper's* magazine, where he has also worked as a contributing artist. His drawings and caricatures, some of which are reproduced in his first collection of essays, have been exhibited. Wolfe studied creative writing at Washington and Lee (a classmate has remembered Wolfe's then preference for writing baseball stories and a fascination with *Gray's Anatomy*) before turning to American studies at Yale.

Wolfe's involvement with New Journalism began in 1963, after he had been assigned to write a newspaper story on the Hot Rod and Custom Car Show at the coliseum in New York. *Esquire* later sent him to cover the custom car scene in California; the essay he wrote for *Esquire*, a benchmark for New Journalism, supplied the title for his first published collection of essays, *The Kandy-Kolored Tangerine-Flake Streamline Baby* (1965).

Other collections followed: *The Pump House Gang* and *The Electric Kool-Aid Acid Test* appeared in 1968. Wolfe continued to produce essay anthologies with flamboyant titles—*Radical Chic and Mau-Mauing the Flak Catchers* (1970) and *Mauve Gloves and Madmen, Clutter and Vine* (1976). In 1973, along with E. W. Johnson, Wolfe edited an influential anthology titled *The New Journalism,* published by Harper & Row, in which he attempted to describe the style of the movement, which combined objective description with a sense of "the subjective or emotional life of the characters."

Wolfe has always been obsessed with the icons of wealth, power, status, and fashion. In two books, *The Painted Word* (1975) and *From Bauhaus to Our House* (1981), he examined examples from painting and architecture. His work covers social and political as well as cultural criticism—the government-sponsored poverty program criticized in "Mau-Mauing the Flak Catchers," for example. Wolfe has been criticized for writing such lightweight articles as "The Girl of the Year" while the Vietnam War was in full swing, but he finally caught up with Vietnam in "The Truest Sport: Jousting with Sam and Charlie," which concerned Navy pilots who flew missions over North Vietnam; it was first published in *Esquire* in October of 1975 and was later included in *Mauve Gloves and Madmen, Clutter and Vine.*

Wolfe's major achievement during the 1970's was *The Right Stuff* (1979), an animated history of the American space program and the esprit de corps of the first astronauts, which won both the Columbia Journalism Award and the American Book Award for 1980. This nonfiction achievement was later matched by his sprawling satirical novel *The Bonfire of the Vanities* (1987), which became a best seller. It was followed by two more novels, also heavily plotted in the Victorian manner: *A Man in Full* (1998) and *I Am Charlotte Simmons* (2004). *Hooking Up* (2000) is a collection of short pieces, taking its title from the term for the casual sexual encounters that have replaced dating among America's young people.

ANALYSIS

Wolfe is the ultimate decadent stylist of the late twentieth and early twenty-first centuries. He invented his psychedelic style as if by accident, as he explained in the introduction of *The Kandy-Colored Tangerine-Flake Streamline Baby*. As a reporter, he had covered the Hot Rod and Custom Car Show in New York for the *Herald Tribune* in a conventional newspaper story, yet he sensed that his coverage had somehow missed the spirit of the event.

Customizing cars as a folk art form, he believed, was culturally important, yet conventional journalism could not describe it adequately. He agreed to do a longer piece for *Esquire*, and his editor sent him to California. Up against a deadline, Wolfe concluded that he could not write the piece but told *Esquire* he would pass on his notes to Bryon Dobell, the managing editor, so that other writers could shape them into a story. Dobell simply printed Wolfe's forty-nine pages of notes under the title "The Kandy-Kolored Tangerine-Flake Streamline Baby," and Wolfe's career as a stylist and chronicler of popular culture—and of what Wolfe himself called "Pop Society"—was born.

His natural exuberance became the lynchpin of his flamboyant style, which could be used for either satire or praise. In *The Right Stuff*, for example, Wolfe indulges in satire when he writes about President Lyndon Johnson and the foibles of the astronauts and the space program, but many of his most energetic and remarkable passages are obviously meant to celebrate the achievements of the program and to praise the raw courage and determination of America's pioneers in space. The book,

then, becomes a celebration of patriotism, individuality, and heroism.

The genius of this book is that it manages to humanize the technological achievements of contemporary American science while also fortifying the myth of American inventiveness and ingenuity through heroic examples of individual courage. The astronauts are made vividly distinct—Wolfe describes them as though they were characters in a novel, a grand national epic of daring discovery. *The Right Stuff* is history embellished with psychology, history wedded to journalism and creative writing, history made subjective and personal. It is history brought to life.

In *The Right Stuff*, Wolfe did for history what he had earlier done for journalism. The conventional historian, like the conventional journalist, traditionally works under the constraints of objectivity. Wolfe's contribution was that he brought to the task of writing history and journalism a unique voice and point of view. He invaded the minds of his subjects as if he were portraying fictional characters, applying New Journalism techniques to history.

In *The Kandy-Kolored Tangerine-Flake Streamline Baby*, for example, Wolfe is especially effective when he writes about the South. One of the best profiles in this collection concerns the "legend" of North Carolina stock-car racer Junior Johnson, whom Wolfe characterizes as "The Last American Hero," much admired for his skill, courage, and recklessness, virtues similar to those of test pilot Chuck Yeager in *The Right Stuff*. This local hero is a risk taker who developed his driving skills while delivering moonshine and outrunning federal agents on the back roads of his native state. Heroes are rarely found in the writings of Tom Wolfe; Johnson and Yeager are among those few.

Wolfe is a master of hyperbole, which he uses more often to denigrate than to praise, as when he describes Baby Jane Holzer as "the most incredible socialite in history." Wolfe understands vanity and folly, ego and excess, image-making and fame, money and power, and the quest for status, which is a dominant motif in his writing.

Wolfe's novel *The Bonfire of the Vanities*, which he describes as being "realistic" fiction, can and should be read as a sociological satire on status—how it is achieved and how it can be lost. It is also a treatise on power and politics, exposing the decadent and corrupt nature of New York City. Clearly, Wolfe knows his territory, having lived there and having earned his own literary status in the nation's most brutally competitive city.

Curiously, the nightmare vision of New York exactly fits the stereotype of provincial America's most negative impression of New York as a corrupt dystopia, an alien territory populated by greedy, egocentric, materialistic monsters. Wolfe's antihero, Sherman McCoy, is too seriously flawed by arrogance, vanity, licentiousness, and craven fear to have much tragic dimension, though he does seem capable of learning from his misfortune at the end. In general, one looks in vain for admirable characters, finding only emblems and caricatures. Wolfe may consider his style "realistic," but it often appears rather to be symbolic, allegorical, and savagely satiric. In *A Man in Full*, he turns his attention to the foibles of Atlanta, emblem of the New South.

THE KANDY-KOLORED TANGERINE-FLAKE STREAMLINE BABY

First published: 1965
Type of work: Essays

This collection of essays on cultural trends and figures is shaped by New Journalism to resemble short stories.

This pioneering anthology established a model for the personal, subjective style of New Journalism. The first essay attempts to capture the spirit of the city of Las Vegas and is typical of Wolfe's self-conscious satirical method. Fascinated by the vulgar spectacle of Las Vegas, Wolfe was able to fashion a verbal style to suit the substance, a style that is itself excessive and prolix, repeating key words and motifs. The essay herniates itself in the first paragraph, for example, where the word "hernia" is repeated fifty-seven times, catching the babble of a casino zombie at the craps table. Wolfe piles words on top of one another to create a verbal cascade; he fractures syntax for effect; he overpunctuates, overloading his sentences, as in the title of his lead essay, "Las Vegas (what?) Las Vegas (can't hear you! too noisy) Las Vegas!!!"

At the end of the book, Wolfe describes "The Big League Complex" of New Yorkers with the wonderment of an outsider. Years later, in *The Bonfire of the Vanities*, he reworks this theme from the vantage point of an insider who has achieved status and tasted its hollowness.

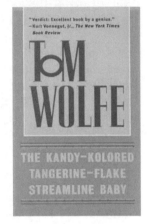

Wolfe later coined the phrase "The Me Decade" to describe the 1970's, after having helped to create the style of that decade. Each tirade of excess, every verbal spasm of his decadent and psychedelic style, is designed to capture the reader's attention with the unstated but insistent plea: Look at me!

Throughout the book, Wolfe is fascinated by cultural eccentricity. In "Clean Fun at Riverhead," he profiles Lawrence Mendelsohn, who created and then promoted the notion of the demolition derby as a new "sport." Other selections reveal a fixation on automobiles and car culture. The title essay concerns customized cars and the celebrities of this subculture, such as Hollywood customizer George Barns, who paints his "creations" with "Kandy Kolors." One of the book's longest and most effective pieces, "The Last American Hero," profiles stock-car racing celebrity Junior Johnson, explaining the man, his sport, and its cultural context in such a way as to convince the reader that Johnson may be convincingly heroic.

Junior Johnson is a regional celebrity. Elsewhere in the book, Wolfe profiles national celebrities: motion-picture star Cary Grant, in "Loverboy of the Bourgeoisie," for example, in which Wolfe contends that Grant is "an exciting bourgeois" rather than "an aristocratic motion picture figure," and heavyweight champion Cassius Clay (later Muhammad Ali), in "The Marvelous Mouth," famous for making vulgar and extravagant claims about other contenders such as Sonny Liston.

Most of the book concerns celebrities and status. Many of the celebrities have faded into obscurity, such as celebrity model Baby Jane Holzer, "The Girl of the Year," once the darling of New York café society, now hardly a pop-cultural footnote. Perhaps more enduring is celebrity disc jockey Murray the K, "The Fifth Beatle," the "king of the Hysterical Disc Jockeys," famous for inventing a much-imitated goofy announcing style, who managed to befriend the Beatles during their first American tour and gained a measure of immortality by fortunate association.

Wolfe is fascinated by the offbeat. In "Purveyor of the Public Life," he profiles Robert Harrison, the publisher of "the most scandalous scandal magazine in the history of the world," *Confidential* (1952-1958), and a specialist in what Wolfe calls the "*aesthetique du schlock*." Wolfe cheerfully explores culture, high and low. On one hand, he treats rock-and-roll magnate Phil Spector ("The First Tycoon of Teen"); on the other, he takes on Huntington Hartford and his Gallery of Modern Art ("The Luther of Columbus Circle") and the Museum of Modern Art ("The New Art Gallery Society").

Emblems of status abound: an executive's brown Chesterfield and his "Madison Avenue crash helmet" (in "Putting Daddy On"), fashionable interior decorators ("The Woman Who Has Everything"), tailor-made suits ("The Secret Vice"), and exclusive neighborhoods ("The Big League Complex"). Like F. Scott Fitzgerald, Wolfe is fascinated by the rich and powerful. Only rarely does he pay attention to the underclass, the have-nots, as he does in "The Voices of Village Square." Those voices come from the Women's House of Detention at 10 Greenwich Avenue. This is the author's choice, and it is apparently even his fixation.

THE RIGHT STUFF

First published: 1979
Type of work: Nonfiction

The book is an example of New Journalism, written like a novel in which the first astronauts and their wives are the principal characters.

Tom Wolfe begins *The Right Stuff* by introducing Pete Conrad, who did not become an astronaut until the second round of selections, and Chuck Yeager, who was never an astronaut. Still, both men have always possessed the "right stuff," especially Yeager, "the most righteous of all the possessors."

From the third chapter onward, the worth of every astronaut is implicitly measured against that of Yeager, the acknowledged king of the fighter pilots turned test pilots. Wolfe defines the right stuff as the Fighter Jock's combination of courage, competence, insouciance, and unshakeable self-confidence. Wolfe compares the astronauts' right stuff to the defining quality of the Elect. In Calvinistic theology, the Elect are those fortunate souls who are predestined for salvation from the beginning of time. If one is not among the Elect, then one cannot get to be. If one does not already possess the right stuff, then one cannot get it.

The incidents in *The Right Stuff* are factual, but the author gives them a novelistic treatment. He does not, like some of his fellow New Journalists, fabricate conversations to which he was not privy, but he does chronicle the thought processes of the astronauts and their wives at length. He devotes detailed chapters to the suborbital flights of Alan Shepard and Gus Grissom, to the increasingly sophisticated orbital flights of John Glenn, Scott Carpenter, Wally Schirra, and Gordon Cooper. As usual, Wolfe is fascinated by the minutiae of his subject matter. He describes every feature of the space capsule, from the fans and the gyros to the inverters, and every segment of each flight. However, *The Right Stuff* is really more the story of who the astronauts were than of what they did.

The press has decided at the outset that the astronauts are America's finest. So fawning is its coverage of them that Wolfe refers to the press as the "consummate hypocritical Victorian gent." Reporters ignore the differing personalities among the first seven astronauts chosen for the program. They also ignore the astronauts' penchant for bouts of drinking, late-night car racing, and womanizing. The astronaut who best fits the all-American ideal is Glenn. He is a master at playing the press. No one will be surprised when he enters politics. He immediately becomes the group's star and, understandably, is not universally admired by his six colleagues. He is given the ironic title Galactic Single-

Combat General. Although he is only the third American to fly in space, and his successors flew far more orbits than he did, he remains the iconic astronaut. For example, Colonel Glenn Road is an important artery in Little Rock, Arkansas, to which John Glenn has no attachment whatever, either biographical or geographical.

Wolfe has no interest in reportorial objectivity. He grossly exaggerates for comic effect. An example is the astronauts' reception in Houston, Texas. He uses the heat and Texas heartiness to create what is clearly a caricature, albeit an amusing one. With the publication of *The Right Stuff*, Hollywood discovered Wolfe, and the book was adapted as a highly successful motion picture.

THE BONFIRE OF THE VANITIES

First published: 1987
Type of work: Novel

A Wall Street high roller is involved in a hit-and-run accident and is eventually brought to justice.

The Bonfire of the Vanities provides an interesting contrast to Wolfe's earlier work. It is a huge, sprawling novel that runs to more than 650 pages, yet it reveals the same fascination with wealth, power, and status that dominated *The Kandy-Kolored Tangerine-Flake Streamline Baby*, his first book. In the novel, which was a long time in the making, Wolfe skillfully introduces a large and diverse cast of characters representing many levels of New York society while setting multiple, intersecting plots in motion. It begins as a meticulously constructed work. It is entertaining as satire and fascinating because of the way it weaves multiple satiric sketches into a unified but cumbersome plot that gains momentum like a runaway train. When it finally grinds to a halt, it seems to have run out of steam, almost dying of exhaustion.

The plot is so densely textured that it resists easy summary. The main plot follows the fortunes of Sherman McCoy, a thirty-eight-year-old, Yale-educated bond dealer on Wall Street who considers himself a "Master of the Universe." He lives in the "right" neighborhood, in a tenth-floor duplex on Park Avenue. He has a perfect wife and child, as well as a Mercedes and a mistress. The latter two possessions serve to bring about his ultimate downfall and disgrace.

Maria, his mistress, is married to a very wealthy husband. She is a well-traveled, ill-bred, faithless cracker bimbo. Maria spends a week in Italy, and Sherman agrees to meet her return flight at Kennedy Airport. Driving back to Manhattan, Sherman makes a wrong turn and ends up in the South Bronx. He gets lost in the land of the have-nots, and he and Maria end up in a blocked cul-de-sac. Getting out of his Mercedes to remove an obstacle, he notices two approaching black youths, one of whom offers help. Believing they are "setting him up," Sherman scuffles with them. In a state of panic, he then runs for the car to effect a getaway. Maria, who is now driving, is also in a state of panic. She crashes the car into the boys, who have retaliated to Sherman's attack. One of them, Henry Lamb, suffers a concussion and lapses into a coma. The muckraking press describes Lamb as an "honor student" and screams for racial justice.

Eventually Sherman will find himself charged with hit-and-run manslaughter, though, realistically, the wheels of justice turn slowly. At first, all that is known is that the boy was hit by a Mercedes registered in New York. The Reverend Reginald Bacon, an opportunist who chairs the "Harlem-based All Peoples's Solidarity" movement, makes the most of the incident's political implications.

The exploitive press, represented by a sleazy alcoholic British tabloid hack named Peter Fallow, thrives on the issue. Abe Weiss, a Jewish district attorney who is up for reelection, and his deputy, Lawrence Kramer, have a political stake in bringing Sherman to justice. Wolfe follows these and other characters through the protracted investigation, while Sherman sweats. It was his Mercedes, and he knows that Maria cannot be trusted to support him or even tell the truth about what happened. In the end, Sherman loses everything—his wife and child, his job, his Park Avenue apartment, his money, his power, and his status.

The novel ends in an epilogue in the form of a feature in *The New York Times* thirteen months after the accident; it informs the reader that Henry Lamb died and Sherman was arraigned for manslaughter. Bronx District Attorney Richard A. Weiss gets reelected as a result of his "tenacious prosecution." Albert Vogel, a radical-chic lawyer representing the victim, wins a $12 million settlement against Sherman. The sleazy Peter Fallow wins a Pulitzer Prize for his coverage of the affair. In short, all the corrupt characters come out winners.

Sherman, who is technically innocent, gains dignity and human dimension through his tribulations, once his career and his ego have been demolished; the only other potentially decent character, Thomas Killian, Sherman's defense attorney, also finds himself the target of litigation and on the skids financially. Lisa Grunwald, profiling Wolfe for *Esquire*, argued that the writer is more significant as a storyteller than as a social critic, but this is an arguable conclusion if one measures the achievement of *The Bonfire of the Vanities*. Wolfe sets a complicated plot in motion and sustains a heavily textured narrative for hundreds of pages, but the same skill and brilliance that is amply in evidence at the beginning is not sustained at the conclusion, which seems rushed, forced, and curiously flat. It is a well-designed first novel, but a truly outstanding storyteller might have provided a more effective conclusion.

Supremely self-confident, Wolfe sees himself as a writer of realist fiction and has dared to compare himself with novelists Honoré de Balzac, Émile Zola, and Charles Dickens. As a latter-day naturalist, he may be able to justify this claim to an extent, but the comparison with Dickens is questionable. Dickens could be a master of sentiment, but Wolfe's flair for satire does not allow for sentiment in this epic tale of greed, vanity, and folly in contemporary New York. Dickens could draw characters that touched the hearts of his readers, but it is difficult to find characters in Wolfe's novel who are sympathetic or even likable; his characters are consistently deeply flawed.

Rather than Dickens, Wolfe is closer in tone and spirit to Henry Fielding, whom he might begin to rival as a satirist. Even Fielding, however, was able to create the formidable Parson Adams—flawed, perhaps, by vanity, but essentially an honorable and honest man—in the novel *Joseph Andrews* (1742). There is no character of his dimension of humanity in *The Bonfire of the Vanities*.

The novel quickly became a best seller and was hugely successful. It was not without its critics, however. Reviewing Wolfe's novel for *The Nation*, John Leonard wrote that "only Tom Wolfe could de-

scend into the sewers of our criminal justice system and find for his hero a white victim in a city where Bernie Goetz gets six months [for shooting a black youth he thought was threatening him in the New York subway]. . . . Only Wolfe could want to be our Balzac and yet not notice the real-estate hucksters and the homeless." Nevertheless, whatever its limitations, *The Bonfire of the Vanities* is an intricately plotted work of social observation, and as Wolfe's first foray into full-length fiction, it is an impressive achievement.

A MAN IN FULL

First published: 1998
Type of work: Novel

The author examines New South society under a piercing light. The novel is centered in Atlanta, Georgia, but the plot expands, in typical Wolfe fashion, to span the country.

A Man in Full is another massive Wolfe effort, 742 pages in length, which reveals his indebtedness to the nineteenth century French naturalists and Victorian realists. There are two major plot lines, several significant subplots, and literally hundreds of characters. The dual protagonists are Charles "Charlie" Croker, a once powerful businessman whose real estate empire is rapidly crumbling around him, and Conrad Hensley, young, married, father of two, whose straits are even more desperate than Charlie's. Charlie has overbuilt a large office complex and has gone deeply into debt in the process. As a result, one of Charlie's allied businesses, Croker Global Foods, near Oakland, California, must lay off workers. Conrad Hensley is one of these employees. The two protagonists' fortunes spiral downward simultaneously.

The construction of the narrative is reminiscent of Leo Tolstoy's *Anna Karenina* (1878), wherein the stories of Anna and Levin proceed separately and do not really converge until almost page 700 of an 800-page novel. Similarly, for most of *A Man in Full*, Charlie is fighting for his fortune and the life that he has known in the Southeast, while Conrad suffers on the West Coast. Both stories are rich in incident and reflect Wolfe's attitude toward fiction—

why, with the wealth of material America affords (race relations, sexual mores, regional and class distinctions, the cult of celebrity, fortunes won and lost, politics, sports, show business, and more) would any novelist limit himself or herself to a narrow, inward-looking stylistic approach?

Charlie has a family which, if not dysfunctional, at least complicates his life. He has an ex-wife, Martha, who got a generous divorce settlement; a trophy wife, Serena, thirty-two years younger than he; an eleven-month-old daughter; and three children from his first marriage, two of whom are older than his wife.

Wolfe reintroduces the theme of racial conflict with which he has dealt since the publication of *Radical Chic and Mau-Mauing the Flak Catchers.* Fareek "the Cannon" Fanon, Georgia Tech's star running back, is accused of raping the daughter of a prominent white Atlantan. As racial tensions are close to bursting into violence, Fanon, an inner-city product, is defended by Roger White II, a successful light-skinned black lawyer, who has been derisively labeled "Roger Too White." As Roger frets over his suspension between the two races, Wolfe is one of the few white writers daring to deal with the question of what makes a person an "Authentic Black."

While Charlie is dying, economically and socially, the death of a thousand cuts in Atlanta, Conrad, through a series of misadventures and downright injustices, is jailed in Alameda County, California. By mistake, he is sent as reading material *The Stoics,* and he soon becomes a disciple of the philosopher Epictetus. An earthquake strikes, the correctional facility collapses, and Conrad escapes. Mai, a member of an underground railroad for illegal Asian aliens, sends him to Atlanta, where it is believed that he will be safe. Conrad meets Charlie, becomes his "man," and sticks with him after all others have left. Conrad converts Charlie, who becomes a highly successful evangelist of Stoicism throughout Georgia, Florida, and Alabama.

The title of the novel is nicely ambiguous. It may simply mean that each of the heroes has been studied from every possible angle, or it may mean that it is only when Charlie and Conrad are united that the reader sees "a man in full."

I AM CHARLOTTE SIMMONS

First published: 2004
Type of work: Novel

A brilliant, innocent young woman from the rural South experiences a painful voyage toward self-discovery during her first year at college.

The eponymous heroine of *I Am Charlotte Simmons* is the most brilliant student ever graduated from Alleghany High School in tiny Sparta, located high in the Blue Ridge Mountains of North Carolina. Although she is beautiful of face and form, her academic seriousness has always distanced her from her classmates. She wins a scholarship to Dupont University in Chester, Pennsylvania, "on the other side of the Blue Ridge." Dupont is an elite institution, ranked second in the nation by *U.S. News & World Report.* Her mother tells her that, if faced with a temptation she knows is wrong, she need only remind herself, "I'm Charlotte Simmons." The novel explores whether she *is* the Charlotte Simmons of the opening chapters and, if not, what Charlotte Simmons has she become?

Charlotte has dreamed of living the life of the mind at Dupont, but she finds it very different from what she expected. Charlotte is one of the few freshmen who attended a public high school. Even so, the men in her coed bathroom are purposely disgusting. These sons and daughters of privilege are habitually foul-mouthed, drunk, and sexually promiscuous. Beverly Amory, Charlotte's anorexic roommate from Sherborn, Massachusetts, is patronizing and sarcastic in her manner, sluttish in her behavior. Disguised by the university's imposing gothic exterior are gloomy corridors and "worn and exhausted" rooms. Dupont's colors are mauve and yellow. Wolfe cleverly uses the royal connotations of purple to comment ironically on the degenerate lives being led by America's best and brightest.

On campus, Charlotte is pursued by three very different Dupont men. Joseph J. (Jojo) Johanssen is a six-foot, ten-inch, 250-pound power forward on the Dupont Charlies basketball team. Charlotte urges Jojo to become a real student, as opposed to just a student-athlete, and he responds as well as he can. Adam Gellin (originally Gellininsky) is hired by the Athletic Department to be Jojo's tutor; he also delivers pizzas and writes for the campus newspaper, *The Daily Wave*. He is intellectually pretentious, but Charlotte is drawn to him and his little clique of social misfits because they seem more interested in ideas than in sports, keg parties, and "hooking up." Hoyt Thorpe is the acknowledged leader of the Saint Ray fraternity boys. He is a handsome, charming sexual predator. He seduces Charlotte. It is her first, and a very unpleasant, sexual experience. She falls into a deep depression, which nearly dooms her Dupont career.

The plot weaves three narrative lines together. First, there are Charlotte's travails in her first semester at Dupont. Second, as Hoyt and his fraternity brother Vance Phipps are walking through the Grove beneath a full moon, they stumble upon the governor of California—a Dupont alumnus on campus to give an address—having sex with a student. Third, Adam has written a history paper for Jojo (before the latter's academic conversion). Jojo's professor, Jerome (Jerry) Quat, an activist and an avowed enemy of the Athletic Department, has taken the first steps toward having Jojo and Adam dismissed from Dupont. The narrative threads converge in the final chapters, and the conflicts are resolved in a manner that was skillfully foreshadowed. Hoyt is bribed with the promise of a good job with an IB (investment banking firm) after graduation, but he is betrayed by a disgruntled fraternity brother, who gives the story to the press. Adam gets the scoop for *The Daily Wave*. Quat, who hates the Republican governor of California, is so pleased with his exposure that he drops his charges against Adam and Jojo. Hoyt's job offer is withdrawn. In the final chapter, Charlotte has become the unlikely girlfriend of Jojo Johanssen.

The most memorable features of the novel, however, are the richly detailed character studies and Wolfe's rather disturbing portrayal of American higher education in the twenty-first century.

SUMMARY

Wolfe revitalized American journalism with his first collections of essays. With *Bonfire of the Vanities*, *A Man in Full*, and *I Am Charlotte Simmons*, he has attempted to reform postmodern fiction by imitating the nineteenth century realist masters in a manner that has more in common with eighteenth century satire. Like his earlier essays, Wolfe's first novel is fascinated with what he has called "status details," but the result of accumulating such details in a "realistic" setting is finally a novelistic comedy of manners pushed to the threshold of bitter satire. Though skilled as a storyteller, Wolfe's major contribution to American letters is that of a supreme stylist and satirist. After the publication of *A Man in Full*, he engaged in a spirited, and sometimes acrimonious, literary debate with several of America's most prestigious novelists. Undeterred by their reputations, Wolfe attacked—as he saw it—the vapidity of their minimalist fiction.

James M. Welsh; updated by Patrick Adcock

BIBLIOGRAPHY

By the Author

NONFICTION:
The Kandy-Kolored Tangerine-Flake Streamline Baby, 1965
The Pump House Gang, 1968
The Electric Kool-Aid Acid Test, 1968
Radical Chic and Mau-Mauing the Flak Catchers, 1970
The New Journalism, 1973
The Painted Word, 1975
Mauve Gloves and Madmen, Clutter and Vine, and Other Stories, Sketches, and Essays, 1976
The Right Stuff, 1979
In Our Time, 1980
From Bauhaus to Our House, 1981
The Purple Decades: A Reader, 1982
Hooking Up, 2000

LONG FICTION:
The Bonfire of the Vanities, 1987
A Man in Full, 1998
I Am Charlotte Simmons, 2004

About the Author

Edwards, Thomas R. "The Bonfire of the Vanities." *The New York Review of Books* 35 (February 4, 1988): 8-9.

Ewers, Justin. "Wolfe on Campus [Thomas Wolfe and his new novel, *I Am Charlotte Simmons*]." *U.S. News & World Report* 137, no. 17 (November 15, 2004): 78-80.

Kamp, David. "The White Stuff." *Vanity Fair* 457 (September, 1998): 284-287.

Leonard, John. "Delirious New York." *The Nation* 245 (November 28, 1987): 636-640.

McGrath, Charles. "Wolfe's World." *The New York Times Magazine*, October 31, 2004, 34-39.

Powers, Thomas. "Wolfe in Orbit." *Commonweal* 106 (October 12, 1979): 551-552.

Will, George F. "Tom Wolfe's Rooftop Yawp [*A Man in Full*]." Newsweek 132, no. 21 (November 23, 1998): 96.

Wolfe, Tom, and E. W. Johnson, eds. *The New Journalism.* New York: Harper & Row, 1973.

DISCUSSION TOPICS

- Does Tom Wolfe appear to be a "conservative" writer, as some have characterized him? If so, in what ways?

- Should actual events, such as those in *The Right Stuff*, be enhanced for literary effect? If not, why not?

- Wolfe writes very long books. Do his subjects warrant the extensive treatment that he gives them?

- Would you agree with Wolfe's assertion that the realistic novel should still be the major fictional form in the twenty-first century?

- The eighteenth century satirists believed that their purpose was to identify and to correct through ridicule human error. Is there evidence in Wolfe's work that he, like these satirists, is a moralist?

- Some have argued that a seventy-three-year-old writer was ill prepared to write about contemporary college life in *I Am Charlotte Simmons*. How well do you think Wolfe accomplished this task?

- In what ways, if any, does *The Right Stuff* predict the form of Wolfe's later fiction?

- Wolfe has often introduced black characters into both his fiction and his nonfiction. What does his work seem to say about race relations in America?

TOBIAS WOLFF

Born: Birmingham, Alabama
June 19, 1945

In short stories, novellas, memoirs, and a novel, Wolff narrates with bleak, unsparing, but sometimes comical detail the moral struggles of characters confronting situations that threaten to overwhelm them physically or emotionally.

© Jerry Bauer

BIOGRAPHY

Tobias Jonathan Ansell Wolff was born June 19, 1945, in Birmingham, Alabama, to Rosemary Loftus and Arthur Saunders "Duke" Wolff. His older brother, Geoffrey, also became a writer of fiction and memoirs. When Wolff was four years old, his parents separated; he lived with Rosemary while his brother stayed with their father. In 1955, Wolff and his mother moved to Seattle, where she remarried. The stressful period of this marriage is described in Wolff's 1989 memoir, *This Boy's Life*. Wolff managed to escape to a boarding school in Pennsylvania, from which he was expelled in 1963. Shortly afterward, he entered the armed services and served in Vietnam from 1964 to 1968. A few years after his military service, he attended Oxford University in England, earning a B.A. and M.A. in English language and literature. In 1975, he married Catherine Dolores Spohn. Further study took him to Stanford University, where he was a Wallace Stegner fellow in creative writing and earned an M.A. in English in 1978.

Following graduation from Stanford, Wolff began teaching at colleges and universities, including Goddard College in Plainfield, Vermont (1978); Arizona State University (1979); Syracuse University in New York (1980-1997); and, beginning in 1998, at Stanford University in Palo Alto, California. Throughout his teaching career, he has published dozens of short stories as well as his novella

The Barracks Thief (1984), his memoirs *This Boy's Life* and *In Pharaoh's Army: Memories of the Lost War* (1994), and his autobiographical novel, *Old School* (2003). His principal collections of short stories are *In the Garden of the North American Martyrs* (1981), *Back in the World* (1985), and *The Night in Question* (1996).

Wolff's early life was marked by a sense of confusion about his identity, in part because of his separation from his father, who was a rather mysterious figure himself, as Geoffrey Wolff discloses in his memoir, *The Duke of Deception* (1986). His mother's remarriage exposed him to a difficult stepfather, and his own rebellious personality led to a fascination with the kinds of things children are most encouraged to avoid, such as smoking, guns, and lying. His rebellious traits warred with his natural intelligence and literary gifts, leading to his expulsion from prep school (an incident fictionalized in *Old School*) and subsequent enlistment in the armed forces during the Vietnam War. Wolff has expressed surprise that from such beginnings he has ended up leading a productive and relatively sedate life as a writer and teacher.

ANALYSIS

Wolff emerged as a short-story writer in the generation following the authors of so-called experimental fiction, such as Robert Coover, Donald Barthleme, and John Barth. His stories, along with those of his contemporary Raymond Carver, were less concerned with form and structure and more interested in questions about moral choice in daily life. In this respect, Wolff follows a tradition established by earlier American short-story writers going back through John Cheever, Flannery O'Connor, and Nathaniel Hawthorne, and such European predecessors as Anton Chekhov and James Joyce. However, unlike these writers, Wolff's moral questions rarely revolve around adultery or religion; instead they examine the grave difficulty people often have in telling the truth. It could be said that Wolff's great subject is the many reasons for lying and all the ripples of consequence that come from each lie. In his memoirs and in *Old School*, Wolff's protagonists eventually recognize the effects of their lying and accept any punishments (such as being expelled from school) with some humility. In the short stories, the recognition of error is more often left to the reader, though there are exceptions, as in "An Incident in the Life of Professor Brooke" (1980), in which a man who has been judgmental toward a colleague realizes that his own conduct deserves similar scrutiny.

Many stories touch on the theme of social class, or more specifically, social climbing. Although Wolff spent much of his youth in the blue-collar town of Chinook, Washington, he was aware that his father had attended prestigious schools and aspired to an Ivy League lifestyle. In fact, Wolff's brother Geoffrey (who lived with their father after the parents' divorce) attended Princeton University and encouraged his younger brother to apply to a private boarding school. Once there, Wolff encountered evidence of the class stratification and anti-Semitism that becomes an important theme in *Old School* and in short stories, such as "Smokers" (1976), which have a prep school setting.

In general, the settings of Wolff's stories mirror the stages of his own life: the rural, blue-collar world of Chinook, the elite prep school environment, the military experience in Vietnam, and finally, life as a professor of English. Despite the variety of these settings, the themes and narrative style of the works remain very similar. The voice of the narrator often appears objective but in fact is always ready to reveal the damning detail about both protagonist and antagonist. For example, this dynamic characterizes much of *This Boy's Life* in its portrayal of the rebellious Jack and his bullying stepfather, Dwight.

"IN THE GARDEN OF THE NORTH AMERICAN MARTYRS"

First published: 1976 (collected in *In the Garden of the North American Martyrs*, 1981)
Type of work: Short story

A depressed college professor delivers a startling lecture when she discovers that she has no chance of being offered the position she desired.

"In the Garden of the North American Martyrs" tells the story of Mary, a college professor who has grown increasingly depressed since her longtime employer, Brandon College, closed. At Brandon, Mary made herself as agreeable as possible and rarely expressed her own opinions. Now marooned at an inadequate school in Oregon, Mary is thrilled to be invited by a former colleague, Louise, to apply for a job at Louise's university in upstate New York. When Mary arrives for her interview, however, Louise's behavior is unsettling. At the last minute she unexpectedly tells Mary she must give a lecture after her interview. Later, Mary discovers that at least one female candidate must be brought in for every open position. She rightly suspects that she has been misled by Louise into thinking there was a chance for her to get the job. Stunned by the betrayal, she improvises a dramatic lecture that details the tortures inflicted on two Jesuit priests by the Iroquois tribe. Despite protests by the faculty in the audience, Mary turns off her hearing aid as she begins to narrate the religious advice of the dying Jesuit, including the admonition to "turn from power to love." Her story rebukes the cold brutality of Louise and the hiring committee who invited her for a sham interview. She has finally learned that being agreeable ultimately serves little purpose. Her shocking monologue pushes the genre of the story from realism to parable.

THE BARRACKS THIEF

First published: 1984
Type of work: Novella

The bond among three army recruits stationed at Fort Bragg during the Vietnam War is shattered when one becomes a thief.

The Barracks Thief begins with a short prologue introducing the character who will narrate much of the tale. Philip Bishop, the elder son of a marriage that has ended badly, impulsively enlists in the Army, leaving behind his worried mother and vulnerable younger brother. At this point, the story shifts into the first person to recount Philip's military experiences. Philip meets Hubbard and Lewis when he arrives at Fort Bragg. Ignored by the rest of the company, the three newcomers reluctantly become companions and form a bond when they are assigned to guard an ammunition dump together. They each reveal something about their prior lives at home. Hubbard focuses on his two closest buddies and their shared love of cars. He confesses that he could never kill anyone and worries about being sent to Vietnam. In contrast, Lewis presents himself as a tough guy and experienced womanizer. He makes light of an incident where he hesitated to rappel down a cliff during training exercises. Lewis was particularly offended when the sergeant on duty called him "Tinkerbell." Their conversation is interrupted by the appearance of a car bearing two local policemen. Warned that a forest fire might ignite the dump, the soldiers rudely turn away the men, and recklessly decide to stand by their post, developing an illusory sense of power and bravery.

Soon after, some men in the company are dispatched to Oakland to await assignments overseas. One day they are assigned crowd-control duty during an antiwar protest and find themselves rattled by facing down people their own age who despise the idea of the Vietnam War. After the protest, Lewis invites the others to a Bob Hope film but they decline. In the following days, three wallets are stolen in the barracks. The third victim of theft is Hubbard, who is punched in the face by his attacker. Although he is not seriously hurt, the injury hits hard because Hubbard has just learned that his two best

friends from home were killed in an accident. At this point, the narrative shifts back to third person, and the focus becomes specifically on Lewis, who decides to go to the film by himself. He gets a ride with an elementary teacher who works at the post. The teacher helps him apply calamine lotion to his swollen hand, and they have a quiet moment of connection. Later, during the film, Lewis becomes enraged when the cartoon figure of Tinkerbell appears. He becomes determined to have sex with a woman and ends up with a weary prostitute. After spending one night with her, he becomes the barracks thief in order to pay for return visits. He steals Hubbard's wallet without knowing whom he has attacked. Opening the wallet, he finds the poignant letter from Hubbard's mother describing the deaths of his friends. Tossing the wallet away, he keeps the letter, leading to his later capture when the sergeant insists on emptying the pockets of all the men in the barracks.

In the last section of the story, Philip describes Lewis's collapse when confronted with the crime he had committed against a friend. Readers learn that Lewis receives a dishonorable discharge, while Hubbard eventually deserts the Army. In contrast, Philip goes to Vietnam and is a good soldier and later a better husband than his own father had been. He draws a connection between the suffering face of Lewis and the expressions he has seen on the face of Vietnamese prisoners, and on his brother during his troubled life. Unlike Hubbard and Lewis, he draws some measure of solace in being part of a group and doing the things that society approves.

THIS BOY'S LIFE

First published: 1989
Type of work: Memoir

A young boy tyrannized by his stepfather develops antisocial habits as a form of rebellion.

In *This Boy's Life*, Wolff offers a detailed, highly subjective portrait of himself and his family from the time that he was ten until he leaves for boarding school at fifteen. He develops a portrait of himself as someone with a passion for self-invention, beginning with his decision to change his name to "Jack," upon his arrival in a new town with his mother, Rosemary, in 1955. However, his new name does not appease the nagging sense of unworthiness he carries with him everywhere nor his tendency to invent stories about himself. Jack's existence is complicated by his mother's love life. First, he is subjected to her jealous boyfriend, Roy, who appears

to young Jack as a "man's man." Roy buys him a rifle and teaches him to shoot. The gun proves to be a dangerous temptation to the lonely young boy, who likes to aim it out the window and once shoots a squirrel. When Rosemary decides that they are going to leave Roy and travel to a new town, Jack insists on taking the rifle with him, to his mother's displeasure. His attachment to the gun foreshadows his attraction to certain kinds of risky and even antisocial behavior, which continue once the duo move to Seattle and Rosemary embarks on another tempestuous relationship.

A few months after arriving in Seattle, Rosemary begins to date Dwight, a mechanic with three teenagers of his own, who lives three hours north in the town of Chinook. Despite her mild reservations and Jack's strong resistance, Rosemary agrees to consider Dwight's proposal of marriage, with an unusual condition: She wants Jack to live for several months with Dwight and his children while she continues to work in Seattle. If it looks like they can make a go of it as a family, she will agree to marry him. She is partly motivated by the desire to get Jack out of his current school, where he already has a reputation as a troublemaker. Thus begins a period of great stress for Jack, mixed in with some positive memories of time spent with Dwight's children: pathetic Pearl, restless Skipper, and pretty Norma. Dwight takes control of Jack's spare time, enrolling him in the Boy Scouts, securing him a paper route, and assigning him an array of petty chores. Despite his aversion to Dwight, Jack is reluctant to let his mother know his real feelings, and

within a few months, Dwight and Rosemary are married.

The bulk of the memoir details the poisonous atmosphere of life with Dwight, along with the growing sense of restlessness and amorality that lead Jack to accept Dwight's assessment of him as a liar and a thief. He lies so often that he begins to believe his own fabrications, and his thefts progress from filching candy to taking Dwight's possessions and pawning them. The only label that makes him uncomfortable is that of "sissy," which derives in part from Jack's friendship with a sensitive, unusual boy named Arthur, who is in some ways his best friend yet whom he often rejects. Jack's other companions are generally drinkers and troublemakers. Jack is so unhappy with his life that he plots various avenues of escape. Eventually, Jack's alienation from Dwight is so complete that Rosemary arranges for him to live instead with the family of a friend, Chuck Bolger. Although Chuck is generous and at times shows signs of a good heart, he is also a heavy drinker and reckless about sex. Just at the point when Chuck is accused of statutory rape, Jack hears that he has been accepted at the Hill School in Pennsylvania with a scholarship covering most of the costs. There is little question in his mind that he wants to go, although he is harboring a secret: The transcript and letters of recommendation he sent with his application were faked. They represented him as an A student, when in reality he was earning Cs. He wrote the letters based on an image of himself that he felt could have been true, if only circumstances had been different.

This Boy's Life concludes with a quick overview of the months before Jack's departure for boarding school, when he lived briefly with his father and brother in California, followed by a summary of only a few paragraphs about his time at the Hill School. We learn that Jack continued to have trouble following rules and ultimately was asked to leave the school, whereupon he enlisted in the army, returning to the world of guns and uniforms familiar to him from his Boy Scout days. Like Mark Twain's character Huckleberry Finn or a confidence man from a Herman Melville novel, Jack is a liar, yet he gains the reader's trust and inspires attention to the story of his boyhood.

"FIRELIGHT"

First published: 1992 (collected in *The Night in Question*, 1996)
Type of work: Short story

Accompanying his mother to look at apartments, the narrator gets a glimpse of family life around the fire that will follow him to adulthood.

OLD SCHOOL

First published: 2003
Type of work: Novel

Having lied in order to gain admission to prep school, the narrator thrives there until his untruthful habits result in his expulsion.

"Firelight," narrated in the first person, describes a cold Seattle evening spent by a mother and son much like Wolff and his mother. The boy is old enough to imagine that he can pass for a student when the two of them walk around the local university. In fact, they are out investigating possible apartments to rent, looking forward to the time when they can leave the noisy boardinghouse that fits within their current limited budget. At their last stop of the day, they encounter an intellectual couple and their teenaged daughter, who is lying by the fire reading. The boy is drawn into the warmth, almost mesmerized by the firelight as the couple discusses the apartment with his mother. From time to time he realizes that the man is bitterly criticizing the university. Later he speculates that perhaps the man had been denied tenure and that was why the family was giving up the apartment to be rented to someone else. He falls into a dreamy state, almost imagining that he lived there and had a family larger than just himself and his mother. At the end of the story, the narrator shifts to his adult life, when he does in fact have a wife and two children and a fireplace to call his own. He is content and yet a fear nags at him that if he becomes complacent, he will wake up and find his happiness a dream. Perhaps he identifies with the man in the apartment who had a warm home and a happy family yet had turned bitter. Perhaps he simply remembers the time he had to leave the firelight to walk back into the cold, facing another night at the boardinghouse.

Although Wolff calls *Old School* a novel, its plot follows the events of his own life beginning with his enrollment at prep school (in other words, it begins where *This Boy's Life* leaves off). The narrator of the story, Wolff's stand-in, is intimidated by the class snobbery at his school, particularly the hint of anti-Semitism that he senses. (The narrator's father, like Wolff's, is Jewish.) He struggles with most of the academic material at school, but finds his niche in English classes and on the staff of the literary magazine. He becomes caught up in a school tradition—the chance to have a one-on-one meeting with a famous visiting writer. These writers include Robert Frost, Ayn Rand, and Ernest Hemingway, said to be a friend of the school's dean. When the time comes to compete for the Hemingway prize, he struggles to produce a worthy submission. In the end, he plagiarizes a story from another school's literary magazine, changing only a few details. In the story, "School Dance," a prep-school girl hides her Jewish identity in order to attend a country club party. The narrator's version of the story (with the protagonist changed to a boy) is initially praised by everyone at school, but before long his deception is uncovered, and he is  expelled the same day. His acceptance to Columbia University is withdrawn, and he drifts for a few years before enlisting in the army.

The last section of *Old School* tells the story of Dean Makepeace, who left his post for a year at the time of the planned Hemingway visit. It turned out that the dean had never, in fact, known Hemingway, but he had allowed this misconception to circulate on campus for many years. When he finds out not only that Hemingway will visit campus, but also that a student is going to be expelled for dishonesty, he impulsively resigns from his position. Although he eventually returns, his decision to separate himself from the false persona he had formerly allowed to stand reflects the novel's emphasis on the fluid process of identity creation.

SUMMARY

Given the emphasis in Tobias Wolff's writing on lies and the construction of identity, it is fitting that his literary reputation rests on both fiction and memoir. His fiction often draws from his life, and his memoirs admittedly contain some subjective recreations of the truth. A theme of self-doubt and, at times, self-blame, runs through much of Wolff's writing; his descriptions of the many ways people disappoint one another contain elements of apology but also of forgiveness. Although his work is never overtly religious, some stories include confessions of sin and an expressed desire to reform and to make amends. Others, however, are portraits of people struggling with a half-realized sense of inadequacy, which often takes the form of coldness or hostility toward others. Wolff's chiding of human failure includes sympathy and rarely becomes simply satire.

Diane M. Ross

DISCUSSION TOPICS

- How is Tobias Wolff's *This Boy's Life* related to other American narratives about childhood, such as Mark Twain's *Adventures of Huckleberry Finn* (1884)?

- How does Wolff develop themes of friendship and the betrayal of friendship?

- In what ways does Wolff explore the theme of conformity versus rebellion?

- Many of Wolff's characters tell lies. What is the moral status of lying in his work?

- Wolff's short stories have sometimes been called "realistic" or "minimalist." Are these useful terms for describing his work?

BIBLIOGRAPHY

By the Author

SHORT FICTION:
In the Garden of the North American Martyrs, 1981
Back in the World, 1985
The Stories of Tobias Wolff, 1988
The Night in Question, 1996

LONG FICTION:
The Barracks Thief, 1984
Ugly Rumours, 1975
Old School, 2003

NONFICTION:
This Boy's Life, 1989
In Pharaoh's Army: Memories of the Lost War, 1994

EDITED TEXTS:
Matters of Life and Death: New American Stories, 1983
The Picador Book of Contemporary American Stories, 1993
The Vintage Book of Contemporary American Short Stories, 1994
The Best American Short Stories, 1994, 1994
Best New American Voices, 2000
Writers Harvest 3, 2000

About the Author

Challener, Daniel D. *Stories of Resilience in Childhood: The Narratives of Maya Angelou, Maxine Hong Kingston, Richard Rodriguez, John Edgar Wideman, and Tobias Wolff.* New York: Garland, 1997.

Cornwall, John. "Wolff at the Door." *Sunday Times Magazine* (London), September 12, 1993, 28-33.

DePietro, Thomas. "Minimalists, Moralists, and Manhattanites." *Hudson Review* 39 (Autumn, 1986): 487-494.

Hannah, James. *Tobias Wolff: A Study of the Short Fiction.* New York: Twayne, 1996.

Lyons, Bonnie, and Bill Oliver. "An Interview with Tobias Wolff." *Contemporary Literature* 31, no. 1 (Spring, 1990): 1-16.

Wolff, Geoffrey. *The Duke of Deception.* New York: Viking Press, 1986.

© Nancy Crampton

CHARLES WRIGHT

Born: Pickwick Dam, Hardin County, Tennessee
August 25, 1935

With respect to both substance and style, Wright has written some of the most distinctive and original poetry of the second half of the twentieth century.

BIOGRAPHY

Charles Wright was born in a rural section of northeast Tennessee, not far from the city of Kingsport near the Virginia state line. His family lived in Oak Ridge during World War II, where his father worked for the Tennessee Valley Authority as a civil engineer, then settled in Kingsport during Wright's primary school years. Wright attended a school with eight students in Sky Valley, North Carolina, prior to graduating from the Episcopal Boarding School in Arden, North Carolina, in 1953. Wright recalls that "both of these schools made a profound impression on me, and gave a lot to write about later, mostly in *Hard Freight* (1973) and *Bloodlines* (1975)." He enrolled in Davidson College intending to major in history and spent what he describes as "four years of amnesia, as much my fault as theirs, probably more," trying to write fiction during that time, "sketches . . . which were never more than extended descriptions of landscape."

Wright joined the Army for four years after graduating in 1957, training at the Army Language School in California where he wrote "what I thought was a journal . . . really only whining and inarticulate pang." In Verona, Italy, where he was stationed in 1959, Wright read Ezra Pound's poem "Blandula, Tenulla, Vagula," an evocation of the supposed place of Catullus's villa on the tip of the Sirmione Peninsula, a place "more beautiful than Paradise," and he felt that at that moment, "My life was

changed forever." What Wright calls "the continuous desire to write that I had since I was a senior in high school had finally found its form: the lyric poem." Wright regards Pound as "a tremendous influence, the first poet I ever read seriously," and would follow Pound, who had just returned to Italy following his incarceration in St. Elizabeth's in Washington, D.C., through the streets of Venice without feeling able to actually introduce himself.

Following four years in the army's intelligence division, where he "drifted into the Italian landscape, and was never the same again," Wright entered the Graduate Poetry Workshop at the University of Iowa in 1961, explaining with wry humor that he was admitted since he "applied in August and no one happened to read my manuscript." He felt that this was the first time that he truly began studying poetry, by being involved with the distinguished Iowa faculty, including writers such as Donald Justice, the director of the program, who Wright feels "had a major effect on my life." Wright remembers the atmosphere in class as "electric, insatiable, the feeling that you were at the center of the most important thing going on anywhere on earth." Although the poets Wright was encouraged to concentrate on at Iowa were well-known American modernists such as Robert Lowell and John Berryman, he also discovered Chinese poetry though Pound's *Cantos*, leading toward the ideogrammatic imitations of *China Trace* (1977) and other Asian-oriented poems such as his versions of Han Shan and the Zen stylings of poems such as "Looking Outside the Cabin Window, I Remember a Line by Li-Po."

Wright had translated Eugenio Montale's motets while in Iowa, where he earned an M.F.A. in

1963, and his application for a Fulbright Scholarship to pursue this interest was successful. He spent the next two years at the University of Rome, studying with Maria Sampoli, an expert on Montale's work, leading to his 1978 translation of Montale's *La bufera, e altro* (1956; *The Storm, and Other Poems*) which then won a P.E.N. Translation Prize. Wright taught at the University of Iowa in 1965 and 1966 and joined the faculty of the University of California at Irvine in 1966. He traveled to Europe periodically while living in California, returning to Italy as a Fulbright Lecturer at the University of Padua in 1968 and again in the summer of 1985—a trip that inspired "Journal of the Year of the Ox" in *Zone Journals* (1988)—and visiting London in 1983, which became the subject for "A Journal of English Days." Wright remained in Irvine until 1983, where he and the photographer Holly McIntire were married in 1969. They have lived in Charlottesville, Virginia, since 1983 when Wright accepted a position at the University of Virginia; here he was named the Souder Family Professor of English.

Wright began to publish poetry at Iowa when his first small volume, *The Voyage*, was issued by the Patrician Press in 1963. His first major publication was *The Grave of the Right Hand* (1970) from the prestigious Wesleyan University Press poetry series. His next book, *Hard Freight*, was nominated for a National Book Award, leading to a National Endowment for the Arts Grant in 1974 and a Guggenheim Fellowship in 1976. *Bloodlines* won the Edgar Allan Poe Award from the Academy of American Poets, and with *China Trace*, the three books formed what David Young, who with Stuart Freibert interviewed Wright at Oberlin College in 1977, called a "carefully planned trilogy (dealing roughly with past, present and future)." *Country Music: Selected Early Poems* (1982) won the National Book Award in 1983. *The Southern Cross* (1981) is a single, sustained poem in twenty-five sections, while *The Other Side of the River* (1984) follows "the Pilgrim" from Laguna Beach where Wright lived while he taught at Irvine backward toward the past (the American South and Italy) and onward to parallel places (Montana) in the present. *Zone Journals* dealt with close examinations of places (England and Italy) where Wright spent extended periods of time. Wright's work has continued to receive national honors, notably the Ruth Lilly prize in 1993, the Lenore Marshall Prize for *Chickamauga* (1995) in 1996, and the Pulitzer Prize in poetry for *Black Zodiac* (1997) in 1997. *Chickamauga* and *Black Zodiac* paired with *Appalachia* (1998) constitute another trilogy. Wright was named a Chancellor of the Academy of American Poets in 1999.

ANALYSIS

It is both a testament to the originality and power of Wright's poetry—as well as its singular peculiarities and distinctive features—that fellow poets and serious critics have strained to describe and define its qualities and characteristics from its initial appearance. The elements that account for Wright's voice and that make up his primary fields of interest seem too disparate to allow for an ultimate coherence. His language ranges from the invitingly colloquial to the formidably classic in ways that provide jolts of energy that are intriguing and startling, and his employment of a wide range of formal arrangements has not provided any specifically Wrightian structure that can be easily identified. Inspired by the infinitely fascinating aspects of landscape viewed and recorded with evocative images, Wright stubbornly resists the understandable temptation to turn the terrain into a pantheistic source of comfort and persists in an extensive and extended meditation on the mysteries of an indescribable and elusive deity who is, nonetheless, for the poet, a distant but discernible presence in human endeavor.

Particularly articulate about his work, Wright stated some of his core principles concerning composition in an essay titled "Improvisations on Form and Measure," the title itself proclaiming his commitment to a thoughtful, carefully constructed poetic design. His observation: In poems, all considerations are considerations of form, the fundamental principle from which all others follow. Proceeding in this fashion, Wright insists "The line is a unit of Measure: measure is music: the line is a verbal music," a direct exposition of the approach to poetry that he learned from his reading of Pound. Pound's utilization of a lyric mode is the grounds for Wright's determination to maintain a verbal music in his poems, a strategy built on the query-response: "Do poems have to sing? No. Do good poems have to sing? Probably. Do great poems have to sing? Absolutely." However, in an apparent contradiction to Pound's well-known definition of literature as "news that stays news," Wright observes,

"What you have to say—though ultimately all-important—in most cases will not be news. How you say it just might be." It is an indication of his respect for, but not slavish devotion to, Pound, or any of the other historical figures (including painters Paul Cézanne and Giorgio Morandi, author Thomas Hardy, or Chinese poet Han Shan) who Wright regards as so crucial to his work that he has said they are "great ghosts we need to seance with."

Regarding the "great ghosts" from his personal pantheon, Wright told Calvin Bedient that "I always thought that what I wanted to be was Walt Whitman in Emily Dickinson's house, but now what I see I really want to do is be Emily Dickinson on Walt Whitman's road," explaining that he aimed for Whitman's "length of line and expansiveness of life gusto with her intelligence walking along, and her preoccupations, which are my preoccupations." To order the line, Wright has worked with a number of structuring possibilities, using what he calls "a tight free verse off an iambic base," and stating that he counts "every syllable and every stress in every line I write" to make sure "that they differ."

As important as form is for Wright, it does not take precedence over his frequent reference to John Keats's comment that poetry is about "soul making," and one of Wright's more revealing comments about poetry is his insistence that "the destination is the cross, and all that implies." His use of familiar Christian terminology is a conscious choice, but Wright's religious focus has always been a search unconstrained by any kind of doctrinal certainty. Instead, it is a spiritual journey born of an unusual geographic juxtaposition, linking Wright's upbringing where "I was formed by the catechism in Kingsport, the evangelical looniness at Sky Valley Community in North Carolina, and by country songs and hymns," with the historical and theological depth of Dante and the Italian Renaissance. This linkage is described by Wright in metaphorical terms as "a connection, a lushness, in my mind between my east Tennessee foliage and the Venetian leafage that keep coming out in my poems," and is exemplified by Wright's frequent use of the language and rhythms of country music pioneers such as his neighbors from childhood, the famed Carter family, whom he calls the "all-time great American poet-singers" and whose "song lyrics themselves (are) traditional and oddly surreal at the same time." This inclination toward the vernacular is Wright's way of maintaining a close contact with the region that left an indelible imprint and which, in the mountains of the Blue Ridge near his home in Charlottesville, continues to offer what seems like an infinitely varying landscape and skyscape for contemplation and rumination.

"BLACKWATER MOUNTAIN"

First published: 1973 (collected in *Hard Freight*, 1973)
Type of work: Poem

"Blackwater Mountain" is a vivid lyric, drawing on a memory of an experience with someone who the poet wished to understand and impress, and who is now recalled and revived in poetic time.

"Blackwater Mountain" begins with a powerful evocation of a landscape recalled and reconstructed from memory, the setting heightened and deepened by the play of the poet's mind on the elements of the natural world and on his relationship with an important person in his life. Like many of the poems in *Hard Freight*, "Blackwater Mountain" is rooted in a relived past, built on an autobiographical impulse which depends on a kind of memory that Wright has defined as "the invisible end of a vanishing rope" and an autobiography which develops through "fragmental accretions." The first of three stanzas—"This is what I remember"—presents the phenomena of the natural world as a display of sensory excitements, a tableau of sound ("When the loon cries") and light ("when the small bass/ jostle the lake's reflections"), which transforms the terrain into almost a sentient entity ("When lily and lily pad/ Husband the last light") that the poet responds to with a deep sense of pleasure.

Then, shifting the focus toward a distinctly personal perspective, the poet addresses his companion, continuing to use details to make the person real ("The moon of your face in the fire's glow") and his own reactions poignant ("Young,/ Wanting approval, what else could I do?") both in recollection and in recreation. The frustration of his inadquate response is emphasized by his thoughts of a "thicket as black as death," where he struggled

"Without success or reprieve" to act in accordance with some expectation he could not satisfy. The final stanza is a drawing back from the immediacy of the moment, recapitulating an important event now shadowed by the passage of time, with the details of the present establishing the link to the past, "a black duck" which "shows me the way to you," and then "shows me the way to a different fire," symbolized by the "black moon" that illuminates a dark vision fusing eras that overlap in the poet's consciousness.

"HOMAGE TO PAUL CÉZANNE"

First published: 1981 (collected in *The Southern Cross*, 1981)
Type of work: Poem

This poem serves as a meditative exposition on one of the poet's central concerns, wherein the style of Cézanne's painting is examined in terms of the poet's relationship to the past.

In the pantheon of great artists who Wright admires, Paul Cézanne has a primacy of place. "I'd like to be able to write poems the way he painted pictures," Wright says, and Cézanne is most prominent among the "great dead" with whom Wright feels he must converse in his work. Eight pages long, a section per page, and sixteen lines per section, "Homage to Paul Cézanne" opens *The Southern Cross*, establishing an elegaic ethos that permits Wright to interweave the ghostly and the tangible (as David Walker puts it). The separate sections of the poem are not numbered, but are not "haphazard or substitutable," Wright explains, their order "accumulative," thus functioning like brushstrokes or the layering of paint on a canvas, a technique which Wright likens to his poetic method and which he illustrates in action with an image like "The dead are a cadmium blue/ We spread them with palette knives in broad blocks and planes."

As the poem opens, Wright states one of his essential themes, a proposition that is a factor in his work even when it is not directly addressed. Speaking of "the dead," the poet states, "Like us, they refract themselves. Like us/ They keep on saying the same thing, trying to get it right./ Like us, the water unsettles their names." This direct corre-

lation removes a barrier, mingles modes, and leads to a series of propositions that David Young describes as "triggers, opening moves" in a "painterly succession of meditative stanzas." Each section is an enlargement of the concept that "the dead" are telling, "through clenched teeth," their story, "*Remember me, speak my name.*"

For Young, this means that "the dead are of course finally us," although one could also follow Edward Hirsch's formulation that "the dead are always with us, an ancestral presence—refracted and transfigured," or Bruce Bond's suggestion that throughout the poem, "the dead, as emissaries of the unseen, emerge incarnate in an archetypal, 'primitive' world." These interpretive conceptions are necessary because the effect of Wright's approach is to avoid the too-specific while reaching for the tangible, and through the eight sections of the poem, an alteration between an exterior essence and an interior dimension prevents the poem from becoming too programmatic or in any way rephraseable. As Cézanne worked with his materials, Wright depends, with relish, on words, and thus it is the language and its forms that constitute the homage.

"APOLOGIA VITA SUA"

First published: 1997 (collected in *Black Zodiac*, 1997)
Type of work: Poem

"Apologia Vita Sua" is the first poem in Wright's Pulitzer Prize-winning volume, providing a balancing frame for the book with "Disjecta Membra" (scattered parts), the final poem.

Apologia pro vita sua literally implies "the explanation of life," a paradoxical use of the familiar phrase since in Wright's cosmos, such an explanation must be incomplete and finally frustrating if certainty and closure are sought. The poem is divided into three sections: a philosophic excursion recapitulating ideas and insights from the past, a recollection of moments of intense being in Wright's life as autobiographical fragments organized in terms of places of consequence, and a

third section that attempts to penetrate as deeply as possible into a Self that is revealed through constant questioning, with an occasional assumption of insight that requires further qualification and testing. Tentatively, but not without some confidence, the poet is ready to present a few thoughts that he can rely on:

Affection's the absolute

everything rises to,

Devotion's detail, the sum of all our scatterings,

Bright imprint our lives unshadow on.

However, even this lyric effusion is followed by the observation, "Easy enough to say now, the hush of late spring/ Hung like an after-echo," to emphasize how the temporal splendor of the landscape—very prominent element of all of Wright's work—can momentarily distract or disarm doubt. The "after-echo" testifies to the persistence of this feature while acting as a commentary on the perceptual aspects of the poet's mind.

"STRAY PARAGRAPHS IN FEBRUARY, YEAR OF THE RAT"

First published: 1998 (collected in *Appalachia*, 1998)
Type of work: Poem

This poem serves as a reaffirmation of the continuing importance of terrain for the poet.

In "Stray Paragraphs in February, Year of the Rat," the third line, "A love of landscape's a true affection for regret, I've found," conveys Wright's characteristic contradictory vision of landscape as a tableau of endless fascination as well as a source of discontent—"outside us, yet ourselves" as Wright sees it. The pattern of counterstatements contin-

ues: "Renunciation, it's hard to learn, is now our ecstasy," with Wright's doubt-driven faith operating as a foundation for some deep-winter expressions of yearning and uncertainty. As in many later poems, Wright's sense of a deity is darkened by an almost existential mood of resignation. "[I]f God were still around," Wright poses, "he'd swallow our sighs in his nothingness."

Following four stanzas in this fashion, Wright directly addresses the season as if it were a manifestation of divine power: "February, old head turner," he implores, "cut us some slack," his use of a vernacular making the plea personal. The "melancholy music" of the season (and the era, significantly the "Year of the Rat") is pervasive, but Wright hopes that some force, internal and/or external, will "Lift up that far corner of the landscape," which he now designates as "toward the west" where the "deep light" of day's end might provide some reason for hope and the revival of life—"the arterial kind"—that the advent of spring promises.

The following poem, "Stray Paragraphs in April, Year of the Rat," augments this expectation with its conclusion that "The soul is air, and it maintains us."

SUMMARY

The process of the poem "Black Zodiac" is an illumination of Wright's practice, a testing, measuring and searching, always with an attitude of awareness and curiosity. "Unanswerable questions, small talk,/ Unprovable theorems, long abandoned arguments—" are the elements of a poetic journey, and the poet knows he "has got to write it all down." After a series of images that convey the feeling of a vast field for contemplation, the poet muses about the difficulties of reaching any kind of conclusion, calling himself and his company "Calligraphers of the disembodied, God's word-wards"—as close to a compliment to his profession as he will allow himself. His task is to "Witness and walk on," remaining modest with respect to a muse or deity that is called upon to "Succor my shift and save me . . . ." This is the poet's creed, and his faith, as in all his work, is in his power to see and say something about the ineffable. "Description's an element, like air or water" he asserts, and concludes the poem with an echo of the most powerful of biblical utterances: "That's the word."

Leon Lewis

BIBLIOGRAPHY

By the Author

POETRY:

The Dream Animal, 1968
The Grave of the Right Hand, 1970
The Venice Notebook, 1971
Hard Freight, 1973
Bloodlines, 1975
China Trace, 1977
The Southern Cross, 1981
Country Music: Selected Early Poems, 1982, 2d ed. 1991
The Other Side of the River, 1984
A Journal of the Year of the Ox, 1988
Zone Journals, 1988
Xiona, 1990
The World of the Ten Thousand Things: Poems, 1980-1990, 1990
Chickamauga, 1995
Black Zodiac, 1997
Appalachia, 1998
Negative Blue: Selected Later Poems, 2000
A Short History of the Shadow, 2002
Buffalo Yoga, 2004
The Wrong End of the Rainbow, 2005

TRANSLATIONS:

The Storm, and Other Poems, 1978 (of Eugenio Montale)
Orphic Songs, 1984 (of Dino Campana)

NONFICTION:

Halflife: Improvisations and Interviews 1977-1987, 1988
Quarter Notes: Improvisations and Interviews, 1995

About the Author

Andrews, Tom, ed. *The Point Where All Things Meet: Essays on Charles Wright.* Oberlin, Ohio: Oberlin College Press, 1995.

Bourgeois, Louis. "An Interview with Charles Wright." *The Carolina Quarterly* 56 (Spring/Summer, 2004): 30-37.

Lewis, L. H. "*Buffalo Yoga.*" In *Magill's Literary Annual, 2004,* edited by John Wilson and Steven G. Kellman. Pasadena, Calif.: Salem Press, 2005.

Wright, Charles. *Halflife: Improvisations and Interviews, 1977-1987.* Ann Arbor: University of Michigan Press, 1988.

_____. *Quarter Notes: Improvisations and Interviews.* Ann Arbor: University of Michigan Press, 1995.

DISCUSSION TOPICS

- Charles Wright has said that in his latter poems, he has tried to combine a "longer line with a condensed subject matter." How does this technique work in books such as *Appalachia* or *A Short History of the Shadow*?

- Wright insists that "If you're not going to write in the historical meters of English language verse, you'd better know what they are and why not." In what ways does Wright use traditional forms in his work?

- Wright claims that he likes "prose poems a lot." Which of his poems might be regarded as efforts in this genre?

- Apply Wright's comment "When the finger of God appears, it's usually the wrong finger" to his extensive exploration of religious themes.

- Examine how Wright's idea that "the poet is engaged in re-creating the familiar through introducing the unfamiliar" operates in his work.

JAMES WRIGHT

Born: Martins Ferry, Ohio
December 13, 1927
Died: New York, New York
March 25, 1980

One of the most admired and widely read poets of his generation, Wright was particularly noted for his formal dexterity, grace of phrasing, and humane themes.

© Nancy Crampton

BIOGRAPHY

James Arlington Wright was born and reared in Martins Ferry, Ohio, near Wheeling, West Virginia, a small town on the Ohio River that provides the setting and background for a number of his poems. Following high school, he served for three years in the U.S. Army in the aftermath of World War II. Upon his return he attended Kenyon College in Ohio, where he began writing poetry. After graduation he spent a year in Austria as a Fulbright fellow and then entered graduate school at the University of Washington, where he obtained both M.A. and Ph.D. degrees.

He began teaching at the University of Minnesota in 1957, later moving to Macalaster College in St. Paul. Yale University Press in 1957 published his first book, *The Green Wall*, in its Yale Younger Poets Series, a remarkable achievement for a writer still in graduate school. The volume received positive reviews, especially for its skillful versification and formal facility. A second book, *Saint Judas*, appeared in 1959, the year Wright completed his Ph.D. dissertation; this volume, too, gained critical applause. These first two books are noteworthy in that some of Wright's best-known and most often reprinted pieces appeared in them, particularly "Arrangements with Earth for Three Dead Friends," "A Winter Day in Ohio," and "The Alarm." These books also established Wright's characteristic settings and themes—notably of loneliness and alienation; these remained constants throughout his career.

During his Minnesota period, Wright came in contact with the poet and editor Robert Bly, who had a significant influence on him. Bly had remained largely aloof from the formalist-traditionalist schools that had dominated poetry during the first half of the twentieth century. He advocated instead an intuitive, subjective approach that sought elemental responses and their expressive equivalents rather than abstract formal patterns and rhetorical cleverness. This movement, eventually called the "deep image" school of the 1960's and 1970's, had special affinities with the highly subjective, language-distorting work of the Central American writers Pablo Neruda and César Vallejo, who were in turn strongly influenced by Spanish Surrealism and Futurism. Although Wright later denied that Bly had been more than a catalyst to an internal process already begun, these forces combined to modify Wright's style extensively. His next book, *The Branch Will Not Break* (1963), shows the extent of the change.

This change was pivotal in Wright's career; it turned him in the direction in which he would find his characteristic voice. His earlier poems were directed toward realizing a fine exterior beauty, toward shaping exquisite verbal structures—poems as works of art, to which the poet was largely subordinate. They are mainly poems of the mind. The newer poems come from the heart; they attempt literally to put feelings into words, almost as if they are just in the act of becoming aware of themselves.

As if to symbolize his development, Wright moved at this time from the Midwest to become a professor at the City University of New York, where he would remain for the rest of his life. While there he published *Shall We Gather at the River* in 1968; in that volume, he carries the personalization of his poetry one step further. Wright forces his readers to look at aspects of their civilization that are typically ignored and compels them to recognize neglected parts of humanity.

Wright's larger poems—both the Wright "New Poems" included in *Collected Poems* (1971) and those gathered in *Two Citizens* (1973) (which he later repudiated), *Moments of the Italian Summer* (1976), *To a Blossoming Pear Tree* (1977), *The Temple in Nimes* (1982), and *This Journey* (1982)—move back to a more affirmative position, yet they do not abandon Martins Ferry and his typical subjects. An extended visit to Europe, especially Italy, opened a remarkable new vein, meditations on monuments of antiquity, especially in contrast with modern behavior. These show, at times, a rare geniality. While working on these materials, Wright contracted cancer and died on March 25, 1980, at the age of fifty-two.

ANALYSIS

Wright proceeded through three rather distinct phases in his poetic career, in all of which he produced work so commendable that he is considered one of the half-dozen best poets of his generation. He is also one of a few poets to have gathered a kind of popular following. For several years after his death, a group of devotees met annually in Martins Ferry on the anniversary to hold a memorial reading and reminisce about Wright's life and work.

His first phase persists through the early volumes *The Green Wall* and *Saint Judas*. The poems of this period are very much in the style fashionable at the mid-twentieth century: composed in strict formal patterns, witty and ironic in tone, integrating a battery of rhetorical devices into a fused, weighty whole. The poems have substance; they are made objects, conspicuous for the fineness of their finish.

In keeping with the dictum that the poet should incorporate as much of his poetic heritage as he could, they reflect, draw on, and add to the long, unbroken line of English poetry. Wright's background and education suited him well for this kind of work. In the middle of the twentieth century,

American sympathies were stridently pro-British; the United States had fought two wars that rescued and preserved the British cultural heritage.

Furthermore, although Wright came from a working-class background, his education reinforced traditional British values. Kenyon College sponsored *The Kenyon Review*, one of the most influential literary quarterlies of the time—and one particularly associated with the dissemination of the New Criticism, which emphasized the idea of the poem as a cultural object. Further, Wright had earned a Ph.D. in English literature, his dissertation on Charles Dickens. He was steeped in British culture.

Thus, many of these poems are conventional. Yet this does not mean that they are negligible; several are among the finest of the period. "Arrangements with Earth for Three Dead Friends," for example, is so good as to be almost timeless. For a variety of reasons, however, Wright came to feel that this approach to poetry was limited; intellectualism and formalism had not cornered the market.

This opened his second phase, which appears full-blown in *The Branch Will Not Break*. The change is much less thematic than stylistic. Wright's characteristic attitudes and motifs persist. He remains the poet of the downtrodden in mind and body, the castaways of society, the commonplace victims trapped in the poor streets. The subjects—the natural and human victims of a vicious society—remain constant, but the difference of orientation makes them seem more personal. Wright had always concerned himself with loneliness, despair, and death, but he had seemed to escape from them in his poems. The new poems make the loss felt.

In this respect, he shares the capacity of Walt Whitman for sympathizing with the multitudes; he seems uniquely able to tune in to the secret loneliness, the inward emptiness, the gut-filling sense of loss that allow all of humanity to relate to the concept of the Everyman and his fate. Yet, Wright's formal strategy has been transformed. In place of the highly wrought verbal textures and patterns of his earlier verse, Wright turns to a poetry that speaks simply, in relaxed breaths, from the heart. If the earlier poems were perceptions turned to elegant filigree and lace, these are states of feeling just finding their first stage of articulation into words and images.

One celebrated poem that reveals this is "Autumn Begins in Martins Ferry, Ohio." In it, Wright brilliantly contrasts the empty lives of three kinds of fathers with the superficially highlighted ones of their adolescent sons. The lives of the fathers are over; all that is left for them is to dream about the heroism they have become too old to enact. At the same time, their football-player sons sacrifice their bodies in the vain—or at best temporary—quest for athletic glory. The conjunction is a compounding of futility; yet this is the best that can be hoped for in these degenerate times. In this poem, Wright creates a delicate equilibrium between the objective and the subjective, the head and the heart.

Wright's next volume, *Shall We Gather at the River,* carries the negativism of his new vision to extreme points, opening up a third phase. It seems almost as if once the poet began listening to the murmurs of his heart, he found it impossible to exercise restraint. The book, as a result, is a gallery of monologues and portraits of people broken by the world. In "Before a Cashier's Window in a Department Store," for example, he creates the state of mind of a derelict standing on the street staring at a cashier and manager in a store filled with merchandise completely irrelevant to his state of need. They ignore him, of course; worse than negligible in their world, he feels their glances pass through him, as if he were dead.

He likens himself to corpses picked over on a battlefield, an image that sums up the dominant feeling of the volume. Even when he works in regular stanzaic patterns, harking back to his beginnings, his vision remains desolate, inconsolable—as in "Two Postures Beside a Fire," in which he returns to his boyhood home to spend an evening with his father and discovers that he brings nothing that can light up the life of the aged man.

The emotional desolation of the speakers of these poems is palpable, to the extent that the book has been referred to by several critics as painful, even unbearably so. The pain comes from Wright's uncanny ability to create images of those broken by the ruthless strains of modern life—in his phrase, of "the poor washed up by the Chicago winter." The book offers little respite from the unrelenting disclosure of suffering. It does, however, provide a kind of relief. These are powerful poems; Wright sometimes penetrates the heart of despair and catches the anguish residing there.

THE GREEN WALL

First published: 1957
Type of work: Poetry

Wright's first book of poems demonstrates sophisticated command of formal design, delicate phrasing, and evocative images, especially those of death and suffering.

A first book of poetry usually lays a mere foundation; with *The Green Wall,* James Wright built an entire structure for a poetic career. Moreover, as several of these poems continue to be anthologized half a century after composition, they continue to constitute a significant part of his achievement. In these poems, Wright displays an unusual sureness of touch, as if he had always known what his themes were going to be and had only waited for the right opportunity to state them.

"The Fishermen," for example, juxtaposes the carefree carelessness of two young men drinking beer by the beach with the chronic, age-old sadness of old men fishing there. By bringing these images together, Wright manages to fuse them, to show their essential identity: They are two stages of the male experience. Then Wright extends the fusion; men have always been like this, and in drawing near the sea, they near their primordial roots. The sea is their end, the natural entity they will join after death, just as it had been their beginning.

This theme of the community of all living things in death permeates the book, of which "Three Steps to the Graveyard" could stand as its center. The "three steps" are actually three stages of visitation, three arcs that constitute a circle in life, all commemorating death. The speaker records three visits; one in the spring, one in summer, and one at the end of autumn. In spring, the boy's father shelters him but then leaves him in darkness and "bare shade." In autumn, everything, even the field mice, trembles in anticipation. The three steps span life, bringing it to death, as is fitting.

This theme culminates in "Arrangements with Earth for Three Dead Friends," Wright's most famous poem. In it, Wright dares to write about the death of children. In doing so, he creates a masterpiece. Moreover, he does it in exactly the way his seventeenth century predecessor Ben Jonson did—by so formalizing his treatment that the poem takes on the impersonal objectivity of a carving in stone. The restraint is managed so delicately that it turns personal grief into a tribute of felt beauty, the enduring note of this volume.

SAINT JUDAS

First published: 1959
Type of work: Poetry

In this collection, Wright consolidates the gains of his earlier work, expands into the region of love, and deepens his vision of the omnipresence of death.

The title figure of *Saint Judas,* the paradox of the consecrated villain, reflects much of the spirit of this book. The poems are arranged in three sections which, at first, do not seem to have much connection: "Lunar Changes," "A Sequence of Love Poems," and "The Part Nearest Home." They ultimately disclose continuity, both internally and with Wright's previous work. Formally and thematically, the links to the past are quite clear. Wright is still working primarily with traditional formal patterns, still approaching poetry as if it consisted of art objects carved carefully by the artist out of all the resources of language. His subjects remain death, loss, the suffering intrinsic to life, and the way these experiences bind all life into a single sheaf.

Near the end of "Lunar Changes," one poem, "The Revelation," provides a key. The speaker is meditating about his dead father, recalling how anger continues to divide the two of them. Even as he feels the anger rising again, a beam of moonlight illuminates a vision of his father weeping and reaching out to him. As they embrace, formerly barren apple boughs shed petals. Love can overcome even the separation of death; through love, death can be a solvent for life, unifying all living things in its embrace. Death may even be necessary for the existence of love.

This bridges into "A Sequence of Love Poems," which needs the title, because otherwise few readers would identify these as such. "In Shame and Humiliation," for example, is overtly about the distinctly human act of cursing, especially the way in which males define themselves by that act. "A Breath of Air" similarly seems a lissome mood piece, but its connection to love seems tenuous. Eventually, Wright instills his point: These are love poems not because they celebrate love—though some do, in quite unconventional ways—but because they create the possibility of love. They record stages of self-awareness that must precede love. Thus "A Girl Walking into a Shadow" creates a sympathetic projection of a girl barely noticed in passing and shows that this act of imaginative identification is itself an act of love, one that further qualifies the speaker for loving.

"The Part Nearest Home" returns to the familiar territory of Wright's home themes. It includes works on death-row inmates, funerals, visits to his father's grave, all integrated under the signs of the community of the living and the dead. The sonnet "Saint Judas" acts as a centerpiece for the set. It is a stunning evocation of a ready-made image perfect for Wright: the villain in spite of himself, the man who betrays Christ because he is doing God a kindness. This Judas brings about the death of Christ, to be sure, but he does it as an act of love, because it will make salvation possible for humans, otherwise desolate.

Wright sets up a striking scenario to reveal this aspect of Judas and fit him into his vision of the relation of death and love. He presents Judas as on his way to killing himself when he finds a man being beaten by thieves. Immediately, he leaves his business to rescue the victim. Judas, in other words, becomes the Good Samaritan, the figure Christ himself set up as the ideal Christian. Yet—and this is thoroughly Wright—he also presents Judas as becoming aware that not even this act of charity can remove his guilt. The book is complex, but it deepens Wright's vision.

James Wright

THE BRANCH WILL NOT BREAK

First published: 1963
Type of work: Poetry

In this volume, Wright turns to simpler, more personal forms and to a more uncompromising vision of the sufferings generated by human indifference.

The title of *The Branch Will Not Break* seems to disclose the spiritual and emotional state Wright had reached at the time it was written. He had been confronting the strains and stresses of modern life throughout his career. Now he was making a statement of his fitness: Whatever the pressure, he could stand up to it, as if determined to prove that

James Wright
THE BRANCH WILL NOT BREAK

his central theme of the coexistence of death and life, suffering and love, was more than just a pious hope.

Recognizing this has led many critics to misemphasize the impact of some aspects of these poems. By consensus, these works show the solidification of Wright's despair before the absolute bleakness of his defining work, *Shall We Gather at the River*. There is, however, more wit, vitality, humor, and variety in this book than that judgment would indicate.

These poems are much less formal than Wright's earlier work and much more personal and intimate. The voice speaks from within rather than assuming a public posture. There is less apparent artifice and polish, more spontaneity, more emphasis on the words of the heart. "Autumn Begins in Martins Ferry, Ohio," for example, has nothing like the strict stanzaic forms characteristic of his previous poems. The lines are arbitrary, broken apparently according to whim; they suggest the almost inarticulate murmurings that proceed just beyond the range of conscious recognition.

They also re-create the scene in graphic detail, neatly conflating the dreams of two generations, the older people caught in the act of deflecting their hopes to their offspring, the younger ones oblivious of any frame of reference more encompassing than daily frivolity. Overriding all, however, is the idea that both generations are more profoundly interconnected than they realize, and that this interconnection foreshadows the path of salvation.

The volume contains several masterpieces, but "A Blessing" would outshine galaxies. In apparently effortless breath-units, Wright depicts an encounter between two travelers and two wild horses. The lines ripple, as if imitating the movements of the horses. Wright fuses the horses' dancing, the excited breathing of the men, and the pacing of the lines into the same rhythm, so that all become part of the whole. The poem becomes an act of communion. Wright catches the rapt commingling of the speaker with the animals through direct description. It comes as no surprise when he likens the filly's ear with the "skin over a girl's wrist" or expresses his desire to embrace her. This merely anticipates the final transformation, which then appears simply natural: The poet offers to leave his body—which in the poem he has already done—and realizes that if he does, it will put forth blossoms. Wright has used this image before, to symbolize his reconciliation with his dead father; here, he signifies his fusion with the natural universe.

SUMMARY

By all measures, Wright deserves his ranking as one of the foremost American poets of the twentieth century. He is honored by annual convocations in his name held by common readers. He will long be remembered for his heart-wrenching realizations of animals, children, and familiar but rarely perceived states of mind.

James Livingston

BIBLIOGRAPHY

By the Author

POETRY:
The Green Wall, 1957
Saint Judas, 1959
The Branch Will Not Break, 1963
Shall We Gather at the River, 1968
Collected Poems, 1971
Two Citizens, 1973
Moments of the Italian Summer, 1976
To a Blossoming Pear Tree, 1977
This Journey, 1982
Above the River: The Complete Poems, 1990

NONFICTION:
Collected Prose, 1983
Wild Perfection: The Selected Letters of James Wright, 2005 (Anne Wright and Saundra Rose Maley, editors)

TRANSLATIONS:
Twenty Poems of George Trakl, 1961 (with Robert Bly)
Twenty Poems, 1962 (of César Vallejo; with Bly and John Knoepfle)
The Rider on the White Horse and Selected Stories, 1964 (of Theodor Storm)
Twenty Poems of Pablo Neruda, 1967 (with Bly)
Poems, 1970 (of Hermann Hesse)
Wandering, 1972 (of Hesse; with Franz Paul Wright)

About the Author

Dougherty, David. *James Wright*. Boston: Twayne, 1987.
_____. *The Poetry of James Wright*. Tuscaloosa: University of Alabama Press, 1991.
Roberson, William. *James Wright: An Annotated Bibliography*. Lanham, Md.: Scarecrow Press, 1995.
Smith, Dave. *The Pure Clear Word: Essays on the Poetry of James Wright*. Urbana: University of Illinois Press, 1982.
Stein, Kevin. *James Wright: The Poetry of a Grown Man*. Athens: Ohio University Press, 1989.

DISCUSSION TOPICS

- What is the justification for calling Judas a "saint"?

- What does James Wright's poetry gain from his abandonment of the formal stanzas, meter, and rhyme that he employed in his early poems?

- What compensations do Wright's afflicted characters receive in return for their troubles?

- In Wright's "A Blessing," what is the blessing? What does the phrase "break into blossom" at the end of the poem signify?

- How do individual poems of *The Branch Will Not Break* fulfill that suggestive title?

- Find examples of Wright's precise observations of external nature.

Jay Wright

Courtesy, Yale University

Born: Albuquerque, New Mexico
May 25, 1935

By incorporating cross-cultural themes into his poetry about the African American experience, Wright has distinguished himself from his contemporaries.

Biography

Jay Wright was born on May 25, 1935, in Albuquerque, New Mexico, to Leona Dailey, a Virginian of black and American Indian heritage, and George Murphy, an African American from Santa Rosa, New Mexico, who claimed to be of Cherokee and Irish descent. Soon after Jay's birth, his father, a construction worker and handyman, adopted the name Mercer Murphy Wright and relocated to California. Jay lived with his mother until he was three years old, when she gave her son to a black Albuquerque couple, Frankie and Daisy Faucett, who were known for taking in children. The Faucetts were a religious couple, and they exposed Wright to African American church tradition while he lived in their home.

Wright attended Albuquerque public schools until he was in his early teens, when he went to live with his father and later his stepmother in San Pedro, California. During his high school years, he began to play organized baseball and upon graduation worked as a minor-league catcher for several California teams. During those years, he also learned to play the bass guitar, and this interest in music later led him to explore rhythm and style. Wright joined the Army in 1954 and served in the medical corps until 1957. He was stationed in Germany, and he took the opportunity to travel widely throughout Europe, where he encountered a variety of cultural traditions.

A year after he returned to the United States, he enrolled at the University of California at Berkeley, where he studied comparative literature. He received his A.B. in 1961, and the next fall attended Union Theological Seminary in New York City on a Rockefeller grant. He left Union in 1962 and began graduate study in literature at Rutgers University, taking a brief leave to teach English and history at the Butler Institute in Guadalajara, Mexico.

Returning to Rutgers in 1965, he spent the next three years there, completing all the requirements for the doctoral degree except the dissertation, and received an M.A. degree in 1966. While studying at Rutgers, he lived and worked in Harlem, where he met other African American writers, including Larry Neal and Amiri Baraka, who were also exploring black tradition. In 1967, Wright was awarded a National Council on the Arts grant to further his studies. That same year, his early poems were published in a chapbook, *Death as History*.

In 1968, Wright married Lois Silber, and the couple moved to Mexico. They lived briefly in Guadalajara and then in Jalapa, where they stayed until 1971. During this time, Wright occasionally returned to the United States, spending brief periods as a writer-in-residence at Tougaloo College in Mississippi in 1968 and Talladega College in Alabama in 1969-1970. Beginning in 1970, he wrote plays on a Hodder Fellowship at Princeton University. In 1971, Wright's second book of poetry, *The Homecoming Singer*, was published. Appearing at the height of interest in modern black writing, the book received considerable critical acclaim.

In 1971, the couple left for Scotland, where Wright spent the next two years as a fellow at Dundee University. Returning to the United States, they lived in New Hampshire on and off from 1973 to 1978. In 1975, Wright began teaching at Yale University, where he remained until 1979. During this period, Wright published three books of poetry, all of which refine the mythology and continue the autobiographical themes he began in the early books. In these books, he also synthesizes the results of his studies in African, Latino, and American Indian cultures. His *Soothsayers and Omens* and *Dimensions of History* both appeared in 1976, *The Double Invention of Komo* in 1980.

In 1979, Wright settled in New Hampshire and began teaching at Dartmouth College; he has also taught at the Universities of Utah, Kentucky, and North Carolina. He has traveled extensively throughout the Americas and Europe, and with a writers' group, he visited the People's Republic of China in 1988. In the 1980's, Princeton University Press published three more books of his poetry: *Explications/Interpretations* in 1984, *Selected Poems of Jay Wright* in 1987, and *Elaine's Book* in 1986. *Boleros* appeared in 1991.

Wright is also the author of several one-act plays based on African myths, including *Balloons* (pb. 1968) and *The Death and Return of Paul Batuata* (pb. 1984). His full-length plays include a version of the poem *Death as History* (1967). In the 1960's, a Berkeley radio station performed a number of his dramatic works. His poetry has appeared in numerous periodicals and anthologies, including *Black World*, *Evergreen Review*, *New American Review*, *New Black Voices*, *The Nation*, and the *Yale Review*.

ANALYSIS

In a 1983 interview, Wright stated, "For me, multi-cultural is the fundamental process of human history." In this respect he differs from such other African American writers of his generation as Amiri Baraka, who in the late 1960's and early 1970's favored a black cultural nationalism. Wright looks for his spiritual roots not only in African traditions but also in the links between these and other cultural traditions of the West and East. This quest for intellectual and spiritual identity extends throughout his poetic career. It is his main theme.

In his early poetry, Wright uses conventional English autobiographical poetic narrative. As his search expands to the myths and traditions of other cultures, he integrates styles and allusions from these cultures into the poems. Some, because

they use obscure references and rhythms, are difficult. These techniques, however, enhance the thematic material and emphasize the complex relationship between the African American present and past. Few writers have such an extensive background to contemplate cross-cultural themes as does Wright.

Readers get their first real glimpse of Wright's magnitude in *Soothsayers and Omens*, where he looks for his personal roots in African tradition and culture. Poems such as "Sources" use both West African and pre-Columbian mythologies. Two poems about the eighteenth century African American scientist Benjamin Banneker integrate elements of Dogon theology, an African ritual Wright also works into many of his later poems. *The Dimensions of History*, however, is the book in which he fully explores the idea that all cultural traditions are part of the African American cultural heritage and collective memory. The book is arranged in the format of an initiation ritual involving separation, transition, and reincorporation. Wright delves into cultural traditions throughout time and space and explores how, in each myth, the dead relate to the living.

This awareness that the dead have something to say to the living propels Wright on his quest to find spiritual order personally and collectively. Many of his poems in *The Homecoming Singer* (1971) examine the relationship between his ancestors and himself, between his biological father and his foster father. He also grounds his search in the southwestern places of his early childhood as he explores Native American mythology. In "An Invitation to Madison County," he looks to the American South for a sense of community with black tradition. In "The Albuquerque Graveyard," he tries to find answers to his personal past by contemplating his dead relatives.

He also searches for his place in a collective past. His book-length poem *The Double Invention of Komo* is based on a male initiation ceremony of the Komo society of the Bambara tribe. Poetically describing this ritual, which has 266 signs relating to gods, enables Wright to synthesize its elements and values with other patterns he has found during his quest, thus making him individually a part of a collective community of like spirits. Feeling a part of a cosmology, he has the security to venture further into the unknown. The alienation he expresses in his earlier work is gone; by understanding the complexities of his past, he has regained his identity and come to realize his authentic cultural and spiritual heritage.

Wright uses more challenging references as he delves deeper into his quest and discovers cultural links. In "Homecoming," from *Soothsayers and Omens*, Wright intersperses quotations from Dante with images from West African mythology. Later poems become even more complex. In the second part of *Dimensions of History*, Wright mixes allusions to Aztec, Egyptian, Mayan, Incaic, Arabic, Christian, Yoruba, Akan, Dogon, and Bambara mythologies.

He also incorporates rhythms from other cultures. He believes that a poem ought to employ the rhythm of the culture it portrays. In *Explications/Interpretations*, he makes poetic use of the beat of African American music. In "Twenty-two Tremblings of the Postulant" ("Improvisations Surrounding the Body"), he arranges a complex blues structure into twenty-two stanzas; each corresponds not only to a part of the body but also to a specific musical chord. This interest in music corresponds to Wright's search for forms that embody the rhythms of all African American cultural groups.

In Wright's poetry, music and dance forms open the way to understanding not only the African cultural heritage but also many other traditions. By recording his search for knowledge throughout cultures, Wright is unique in uncovering the links among cultures. These links imply kinship, and despite the difficulty of some of the poems, Wright's explorations, built around the single theme of self-discovery, represent a unique perspective in African American literature.

"AN INVITATION TO MADISON COUNTY"

First published: 1971 (collected in *The Homecoming Singer*, 1971)
Type of work: Poem

Searching for his identity, the African American poet discovers links to his past in the traditions of a black family in rural Mississippi.

"An Invitation to Madison County" comes from *The Homecoming Singer*, Wright's second book of poetry. In many poems in this work, he portrays places he

has lived or visited. He uses these autobiographical materials as springboards from which to launch his search for identity. "An Invitation to Madison County" relates his experiences in rural Mississippi when he toured the South on a fellowship in the 1960's.

When he first arrives, the poet feels alienated. At the end of the poem, however, he visualizes a common tradition as he begins to communicate with a rural black family. The first three stanzas express the tension the poet feels in Mississippi, far away from the familiar environment of New York City. He is anxious, trying to write in his "southern journal," but "can't get down the apprehension,/ the strangeness, the uncertainty" that he feels in the small town. He envisions southern white racism, but nothing happens: "No one has asked me to move over/ for a small parade of pale women,/ or called me nigger, or asked me where I'm from."

His host picks him up at the airport, and they drive silently through the quiet streets. The speaker is still apprehensive as they approach the small college campus, that, like the poet, seems alien to the environment. Even the conversations of young students and instructors do not break the invisible wall surrounding him; he still feels "not totally out of Harlem." He wonders how he will let his hosts know that he does not want to listen to pleasantries but rather wants them to teach him something about what it means to be black.

His anxiety begins to dissipate in the next three stanzas, after he meets a young woman who "knows that I can read" and who simply accepts him for what he is. Chatting naturally about the land and her life, she takes him to her home, "a shack dominated by an old stove." He meets her mother, who treats him as she would any stranger, politely but warily. Despite her dismissal, he stays. After watching him sniff the food and observe her nine-year-old son, the woman senses that he is searching for something. She is right. He is fantasizing about how she is preparing her son to go to the big city and perhaps meet someone like him, a poet "who will tell him all about the city," and who will understand the boy because he understands his background. The poet, though, does not yet understand these people and their cultural link to himself, so he is "still not here,/ still can't ask an easy question." He cannot tell the family why he is here or speak of his preconceived notions about the South.

In the last three stanzas, the poet begins to get beyond his own feelings. He places himself "in Madison County,/ where you buy your clothes, your bread,/ your very life, from hardline politicians." He sees the road, the escape route to the city, where uncertainty lies. He puts himself in the southern blacks' place, "listening for your apprehension,/ standing at the window in different shadows," and finally perceives some of their feelings.

Seeing the similarity of their tensions and fears to his own prepares him to understand what happens when the father comes home from work in the field to have a meal. With only a nod, the man surveys his home and everyone in it and performs the daily ritual: "His wife goes in, comes out with a spoon,/ hands it to you with a gracious little nod,/ and says, 'Such as . . . '" With this phrase, the poet realizes the sense of community for which he has come. He recalls hearing the phrase from his own mother when she invited anyone in to eat, from black waitresses in the Southwest, and from people in the Harlem ghetto, "when people, who have only themselves to give,/ offer you their meal."

Throughout his poetic career, Wright returns many times to such places as Mississippi to record the experiences that have given him clues to his identity as an African American. Yet his alienation not only from white society but also from the more conventionally rebellious posture of black artists pushes him to explore cultural traditions other than African, that eventually will provide spiritual and intellectual answers to his questions.

"THE ALBUQUERQUE GRAVEYARD"

First published: 1976 (collected in *Soothsayers and Omens*, 1976)
Type of work: Poem

Discovering his past enables the poet to see himself as part of an order rather than as an isolated, alienated individual.

"The Albuquerque Graveyard" comes from the middle section of Wright's third book, *Soothsayers and Omens*, a volume that marks his first steps to-

ward defining a spiritual order and his place in it. In these poems, Wright explores African creation myths that have become a part of the cross-cultural collective memory. Using this new perspective, he revisits the Mexico and New Mexico of his earlier work.

"The Albuquerque Graveyard" is typical of the transitional poems in the second and third parts of the four-part volume. In it, the poet returns to a cemetery he has visited many times, but this time with a new challenge: understanding himself in the context of past generations of African Americans.

He begins the poem by commenting about the difficulty of getting to the cemetery: "It would be easier/ to bury our dead/ at the corner lot"; that way, he would not have to get up before dawn and take several buses. The search follows a familiar routine. On the way to the rear of the cemetery, he passes the opulent graves of white people and remarks that "the pattern of the place is clear to me."

The poet articulates what that pattern means in the next four lines: "I am going back/ to the Black limbo,/ an unwritten history/ of our own tensions." He refers not only to the cemetery's physical layout but also to a historical pattern. In the poem, "limbo" has two meanings: Blacks are in limbo, an area of uncertainty and neglect where their struggles have not been articulated; moreover, they must consciously maintain a tense balance, as a person does when doing the limbo, the dance created on the crowded slave ships. The poet wants to write the history that has been forgotten and to unwrite that which has been done in error. He wants to solidify the place of the African American—the dead as well as the living—in Western culture.

The poet sees the cemetery's occupants lying "in a hierarchy of small defeats." He stops by individual graves and recalls the people buried there: a man who saved pictures of the actor and singer Paul Robeson and who dreamed of acting the part of Othello; a woman who taught him to spell so that he would become the writer she could never be. Yet the memories of these "small heroes" bother him, because he cannot put them and himself in a larger, more significant context.

He ends the poem by describing the uneasy search for his relatives, the "simple mounds I call my own." He finds them, drops his flowers on the graves, and heads for home. He confronts his relatives' graves still feeling alienated. The experience of connecting with his personal past is pivotal in Wright's poetic development, however; it paves the way for his process of conversion by enabling him to see himself as an integral part of an order in the world rather than an unconnected life.

"Coda"

First published: 1991 (collected in *Boleros,* 1991)
Type of work: Poem

To live an authentic life, a person must understand spiritual connections between past and present.

"Coda" is the last poem in Wright's collection *Boleros,* a book he dedicated to his wife, Lois. Like a coda that ends a musical composition by summarizing main themes and variations, the poem forms a definitive ending to a volume in which Wright continues his spiritual and intellectual quest. This quest takes many biographical and mythological forms. He tells of places he has lived—both physically, such as Mexico, and spiritually, such as India. He reinvents stories and explores new poetic forms. In "Coda," Wright uses meter and rhyme reminiscent of the

bolero dance, with its triple meter and staccato endings. He uses an open stanza form, incorporating lines from popular Latin American songs into an English-language environment. The form of the poem thus enhances its content, which concerns the search for culture cross-currents.

"Coda" is a good example of Wright's continuing effort to transform language and cultural visions into new forms that emphasize themes from the body of his poetry. The three stanzas all use eight lines, with a conventional paired rhyme scheme. A refrain, repeated three times at the end, finishes the poem. Allusions to Latin American culture deepen the density of the poetic context. Poems such as "Coda" challenge the reader to enter the world of an original poet who is continuing his quest for identity.

Summary

In his introduction to *Selected Poems of Jay Wright* (1987), the critic Robert Stepto stated that Wright's distinction as a poet is that he explores not only American patterns of community and history but also the larger body of transatlantic traditions. In doing so, Wright "enables us to imagine that breaking the vessels of the past is more an act of uncovering than of sheer destruction, and that we need not necessarily choose between an intellectual and a spiritual life, for both can still be had."

Wright's poetry is a record of his quest to understand personally and collectively the patterns of both these lives and the relationships between them. His cross-cultural approach to his quest makes him one of the most original voices in contemporary literature.

Louise M. Stone

Bibliography

By the Author

POETRY:
Death as History, 1967
The Homecoming Singer, 1971
Soothsayers and Omens, 1976
Dimensions of History, 1976
The Double Invention of Komo, 1980
Explications/Interpretations, 1984

Elaine's Book, 1986
Selected Poems of Jay Wright, 1987
Boleros, 1991
Transfigurations: Collected Poems, 2000

PLAYS:
Death as History, 1967
Balloons, pb. 1968
The Death and Return of Paul Batuata, pb. 1984

About the Author

Callaloo 6 (Fall, 1983). Special issue on Jay Wright.

Doreski, C. K. "Decolonizing the Spirits: History and Storytelling in Jay Wright's *Soothsayers and Omens*." In *Reading Race in American Poetry: An Area of Act*, edited by Aldon Lynn Nielsen. Urbana: University of Illinois Press, 2000.

Harris, Wilson. *The Womb of Space: The Cross-Cultural Imagination*. Westport, Conn.: Greenwood Press, 1983.

Kutzinski, Vera M. *Against the American Grain: Myth and History in William Carlos Williams, Jay Wright, and Nicolás Guillén*. Baltimore: Johns Hopkins University Press, 1987.

Okpewho, Isidore. "From a Goat Path in Africa: An Approach to the Poetry of Jay Wright." *Callaloo: A Journal of the African American and African Arts and Letters* 14 (Summer, 1991): 692-726.

Stepto, Robert. "After Modernism, After Hibernation: Michael Harper, Robert Hayden, and Jay Wright." In *Chant of Saints: A Gathering of Afro-American Literature, Arts, and Scholarship*, edited by Michael S. Harper and Stepto. Urbana: University of Illinois Press, 1979.

_____. Introduction to *Selected Poems of Jay Wright*. Princeton, N.J.: Princeton University Press, 1987.

Welburn, Ron. "Jay Wright's Poetics: An Appreciation." *MELUS* 18 (Fall, 1993): 51-70.

DISCUSSION TOPICS

- How does Jay Wright explore links between African, African American, and other cultures?

- How does Wright use myth to convey his themes?

- How does Wright use musical techniques?

- In "The Albuquerque Graveyard," how does Wright attempt to solidify the place of African Americans in Western culture?

- How have Wright's poetic techniques changed over the course of his career?

RICHARD WRIGHT

Born: Roxie, Mississippi
September 4, 1908
Died: Paris, France
November 28, 1960

Wright, one of the first African American writers to win a large white as well as black readership, indicted racism and wedded his protest against social injustice to an existentialist philosophy and a championing of developing nations against colonialism.

Library of Congress

BIOGRAPHY

Richard Wright was the first of two sons born to sharecropper Nathan Wright and former school-teacher Ella Wilson Wright in a village outside Natchez, Mississippi; all four of his grandparents had been slaves. After a move to Memphis, Tennessee, and his father's desertion before Richard was five, the family's circumstances became increasingly difficult as their poverty deepened. When, in 1915, Ella became unable to support her sons, they were temporarily placed in the Memphis Settlement House, a Methodist orphanage.

Subsequent relocations moved Richard back and forth between the rural and urban South. In Elaine, Arkansas, in 1917, he encountered first-hand the virulence of southern racism when his uncle was lynched. His mother experienced her first stroke when Richard was ten, and the crisis precipitated their removal to her parents' home in Jackson, Mississippi, where Richard chafed under the strict constraints placed on his behavior by the religious fundamentalism of his grandmother. Richard set out on his own in 1925, upon graduating as valedictorian from the ninth grade. Heading first to Memphis, he spent two years saving the funds to move his family to Chicago.

Wright lived in Chicago from 1927 to 1937 and held a number of jobs, ranging from busboy to insurance salesman to youth counselor to day laborer. In 1935, he secured a position with the Illinois Federal Writers Project, where he worked with other literary apprentices such as Margaret Walker, Nelson Algren, and Arna Bontemps.

While working at the post office in Chicago, Wright befriended several Communists and was recruited in 1933 for the John Reed Club, a leftist organization with a literary as well as political emphasis. The fellowship Wright found there provided his first sense of shared purpose with like-minded individuals; moreover, he found in Marxism a systematic explanation for the oppressive circumstances that had defined his own experience.

In late 1933 Wright joined the Communist Party, and he became an eloquent spokesman for its attacks on racial and class injustice. For almost a decade, the party's doctrines and aims provided the theoretical skeleton upon which Wright's fiction and journalism were built; he sought to arouse white readers to a fuller awareness of the degradation caused by institutionalized bigotry and to awaken the black masses to their own revolutionary potential. The effect of Wright's party affiliation upon his creative work is debated among critics, some arguing that it subjected his writing to a doctrinal straitjacket, and others pointing to the coherence that Communist doctrine gave to his perceptions of reality. Wright privately broke with the party in 1942, disillusioned with its attempts to curtail the individual freedom of the artist and its criticism of his novel *Native Son* (1940) as a counterrevolutionary work.

His more public renunciation in 1944 resulted from the Communist Party's wartime compromise on the question of civil rights. For the rest of his life, Wright was attacked by the international Communist press. He conceded, nevertheless, that the party's teachings had encouraged him to envision a wholesale reconfiguration of the social order, fueling a passionate idealism about the purposes of his writing. Moreover, through the party he met both of his wives: Dmihah Rose Meadman, whom Wright married in 1939 and divorced soon after, and Ellen Poplar, whom he married in 1941 and with whom he had two daughters, Julia and Rachel.

The decade between 1935 and 1945 was the most productive period in Wright's creative career. His dedication to nurturing black aesthetic expression prompted his founding of the South Side Writers Group in 1936. Wright moved to New York City in 1937, where he was soon employed as editor for the Harlem bureau of the Communist *Daily Worker.* In 1938, he published a collection of short fiction about southern racism titled *Uncle Tom's Children* and won first prize in a Works Progress Administration (WPA) competition. He soon completed *Lawd Today,* his first effort to mine the autobiographical experience of southern black migrants in Chicago, published posthumously in 1963.

After receiving a Guggenheim Fellowship in 1939, Wright completed *Native Son* and in 1941 was awarded the prestigious Spingarn Medal of the National Association for the Advancement of Colored People (NAACP). *Twelve Million Black Voices,* a nonfictional "folk history" of black America composed in collaboration with photographer Edward Rosskam, appeared in that same year, as did a successful stage adaptation of *Native Son.* The publication of *Black Boy* (1945) cemented Wright's international celebrity as the preeminent black author of the decade.

Along with Wright's increasing literary reputation grew his sense of besieged isolation as an intellectual black artist at odds with factions that sought either to coopt or silence him. He eagerly accepted a 1946 invitation from the French government to visit that country under the sponsorship of his good friend Gertrude Stein. In Paris he exulted in the freedom from racist categorization that had plagued him in the United States, and with a second trip to France in 1947, he became an expatriate.

There Wright immersed himself in existentialism, befriending Jean-Paul Sartre, Simone de Beauvoir, and Albert Camus, and committed himself to a humanistic politics. The primary literary result of this philosophical odyssey was the novel *The Outsider* (1953).

Wright's expanded metaphysical concerns matched his political preoccupations with the efforts of people in developing nations to throw off colonial domination. The rationale for his support lay in his discovery of an intellectual and spiritual affinity with nonwhite people. They alone, he argued, possessed the moral force to resurrect the West from the soullessness of modern industrialism and totalitarianism. Wright devoted considerable energy during the 1950's to the encouragement of black solidarity in the arts as well as politics. He became involved in the "negritude" movement exploring the black aesthetic sensibility, and in 1952 he helped organize the First Congress of Negro Artists and Writers. Similarly, he attended and reported upon conferences on the liberation of developing countries and social reconstruction in such works as *Black Power* (1954), *The Color Curtain* (1956), *White Man, Listen!* (1957) and *Pagan Spain* (1957).

Wright's creative efforts also continued during this time, although critics concede that they lack the power of his earlier fiction. In addition to *The Outsider,* Wright published *Savage Holiday* (1954) and *The Long Dream* (1958). Shortly before his death he published *Eight Men,* a collection of short fiction that appeared in the United States in 1961. In addition, he became deeply involved in a 1951 film adaptation of *Native Son,* for which he wrote the screenplay and in which he played Bigger Thomas.

The events surrounding Wright's sudden death in 1960 have received considerable investigation. As an expatriate, he suffered harassment by the U.S. State Department, Central Intelligence Agency (CIA), and Federal Bureau of Investigation (FBI) as a result of his former Communist membership, his outspoken criticism of American foreign policy during the Cold War, and the hysteria of the Joseph McCarthy era.

The stresses of a faltering publishing career, financial difficulties, internal hostilities within the African American community abroad, and recurrent health problems had put Wright in the hospital for extensive tests when a heart attack killed him on November 28, 1960. Conspiracy theories have surfaced, but biographers conclude that while the American government bears responsibility for intensifying the strains on Wright's health, no evidence of foul play exists.

ANALYSIS

Wright's most significant achievement as a writer was his ability to render the particulars of American racism from the point of view of its victims. He powerfully chronicles the historical injustices that black Americans have suffered: physical abuse and emotional degradation, the denial of meaningful opportunities to cultivate and benefit from their native abilities, stifling living conditions dictated by segregation and poverty, and a compromised legal system.

In Wright's fiction, as in his own life, characters respond to such outrages first with rebellion and finally with flight, because escape alone seems to offer a real alternative. Yet his depictions of the northern migration undertaken by thousands of southern black people in the twentieth century always include the disorientation and rootlessness they suffer in their new urban milieu, and his expatriates continue to struggle with the psychological wounds—rage, anxiety, and self-doubt—engendered by earlier bigotry.

The various philosophical positions Wright assumes in his work spring from his hunger to see the African American's experience as a metaphor for the modern human condition. Having learned to interpret the world through a deterministic lens, he finds in literary naturalism a congenial intellectual apparatus upon which to build the compelling logic of his narratives. The antidote to naturalistic despair in Wright's early fiction is provided by Communism, which explains the degradation of racism as part of a worldwide pattern of class exploitation whose remedy is assured through the historical inevitability of revolution. The Marxist hopefulness of *Uncle Tom's Children* and Max's anguished social protest in *Native Son* reflect this orientation. Even in *Native Son*, however, Wright is straining toward a less mechanistic interpretation of black universality—one which equates the negation of self experienced under racism with a cosmic spiritual alienation that is humanity's existential fate.

The symbolic import of black people rests on their outcast status in relation to the dominant white culture. Denied their own identities by the racist premises determining their lives and precluded from entering the culture on any other terms, they become metaphysical outlaws estranged from the moral codes of society and continually testing the limits of individual moral freedom in search of self-definition.

Wright's fictions, from *Native Son* to *The Long Dream*, employ criminal melodrama not only because of the taste Wright developed for it as a boy but also because tales of violent crime dramatize his vision of modern humans' existence in a godless universe. Wright's protagonists regularly find themselves faced with choosing between affirmation of their bond with others and assertion of their own egotism at the expense of such ties. The equation mirrors Wright's intellectual contradictions as well, for while he espouses a belief in Enlightenment rationalism (embodied first in Marxism and later in a committed existentialist individualism), his creative energies are most engaged when examining the psyche's dark, demoniac side. Wright demonstrates a fascination with psychoanalytic theory that takes a variety of forms.

Such interests explain his increasing resistance later in his career to being categorized as a writer of racial themes—the troubled sensibility of *The Outsider*'s Cross Damon, for example, is attributed to something other than his race. Ironically, a crucial source of Wright's outcast sensibility lay in his hostility to the southern black community from which he had sprung, and much of his work indicts the elements therein that stifle rational thinking and thwart personal aspiration toward a better way of life. As Wright's international experience grew, he became aware of the presence of intellectuals such as himself in preindustrial societies worldwide.

While his fiction explores the tragic condition of these "marginal men" caught between cultures, Wright's political writings of the 1950's charge them with the responsibility for transforming their homelands into modern industrial societies and insist that Western nations responsible for the colonization of the so-called Third World materially assist them to that end. Wright also recorded his own divided responses to black cultures in Africa and the Caribbean region, revealing an emotional empathy for the spiritual cohesiveness of such communities as well as a deep skepticism of the tribal and religious traditionalism that hampered what the West would term progress.

His report from Ghana in *Black Power* reflects that tension, which leads him to concede that history has transformed the African American into a Westerner. Wright's overarching literary vision springs from a philosophical extrapolation of that fact; he considered himself a cosmopolitan humanist grounded in secular rationalism but was convinced that only the nonwhite peoples of developing nations could redeem Western civilization. This view explains his willingness to devote so much energy in the last decade of his life to documenting the potential of developing nations.

NATIVE SON

First published: 1940
Type of work: Novel

An angry black teenager in the Chicago ghetto commits two murders which liberate him from his own victimized mind-set at the same time they feed the societal racism that has defined his life.

Native Son triggered Wright's emergence into the foreground of American literature; the book became a best seller and was selected as the first Book of the Month Club offering by an African American. It immediately initiated controversy: Many within the black bourgeoisie condemned its depiction of a violent, white-hating black youth as the embodiment of white racist fantasies about the Negro "threat." Wright's fellow Communists disliked its racial preoccupations and reactionary emphasis upon the misdirected rebellion of a lone individual.

The novel also garnered high praise, however, often from those same audiences: The NAACP awarded Wright the Spingarn Medal, and critic Irving Howe suggested that Wright had transcended strictly aesthetic evaluations, saying, "The day *Native Son* appeared, American culture was changed forever." Wright's avowed intention was to force readers to confront the full "moral horror" of American racism.

In the essay "How Bigger Was Born," Wright explains that *Native Son*'s protagonist, Bigger Thomas, is the composite of innumerable young black men Wright had encountered throughout his life; their outrage at being denied the American Dream explodes into unfocused violence that is as much a consequence of modern America's urban industrial rootlessness as it is their racial grievances. Wright's perspective rests on the Marxist tenet that the race question is intimately linked to the class exploitation at the heart of capitalism. Chicago's notorious 1938 Nixon case, in which a black teenager was tried for the robbery and murder of a white mother of two and which influenced Wright in some of his fictional choices, provided topical validity for a story whose larger truths Wright had been pondering for years.

The novel rests upon elaborate philosophical and aesthetic underpinnings. Wright composed *Native Son* in three "acts," titled "Fear," "Flight," and "Fate," each of which blends naturalism, symbolism, and ideology. "Fear" deals with Bigger's circumstances as the eldest son in a fatherless household dependent on government assistance. It also depicts the emotional volatility with which he responds to the grinding poverty of his family members' lives, his mother's expectations of rescue through accommodation to the system, and the repeated evidence of the futility of his ambitions in a racist culture. Among Wright's influences was Theodore Dreiser's *An American Tragedy* (1925), with which *Native Son* shares a bleak naturalism: The biological and environmental factors propelling Bigger's actions as a human "organism" subject him to the machinery of impersonal cosmic and societal forces poised to crush those who misstep.

Bigger's automatic impulse is a chilling propensity for violence. The opening scene functions both as naturalistic parable and symbolic forecast. While trying to rescue his terrified family from a rat, his fear energizes him to an instinctual assault on the animal, which responds with equal fierceness until it is killed with a frying pan. The boy gloats over his kill, enjoying an efficacy denied him in daily life: To kill, he intuits, is paradoxically to live.

To placate his desperate mother, Bigger grudgingly takes a chauffeur's job with the wealthy Dalton family and is immediately thrown into a setting that arouses his deepest fears by putting him into constant, unpredictable contact with white people. When he is befriended by the Daltons' daughter Mary, whose political sensibility reflects that of her Communist boyfriend Jan Erlone, Bigger is both attracted and repelled. He hates the danger in which she so unthinkingly puts him, for he knows the cultural taboos their contact violates, yet he is imaginatively and erotically fascinated by her for the same reason.

He has no illusions concerning Mary and Jan's idealistic but implausible claims of solidarity with his race; they know nothing of his life and only compound his anxiety by their naïve efforts at egalitarianism. They tragically place Bigger in the most compromising position possible to a black man: He finds himself alone with a drunken white woman, responding tentatively to her vague sexual invitation. When he hears someone outside her bedroom door, his terror prompts him to suffocate her, after which he disposes of her body by decapitating and burning her in the basement furnace; such lurid details transform the realistic facade of the narrative into something surreal.

In "Flight," Bigger's efforts to deflect his guilt serve only to ensure his entrapment. He concocts a scheme to disguise the crime as a kidnapping and ransom committed by Communists, but the black idiom of the ransom note betrays the killer's race. Media attention leads to his exposure when a reporter camped out at the house discovers Mary's bones as he stokes the furnace. Bigger's decision to seek the help of his girlfriend Bessie backfires when she reveals her inability to handle such pressure, and Bigger decides—this time quite coldbloodedly—to kill her as well.

With this second act, which Wright included despite friends' urgings to omit it, Bigger moves beyond the naturalism defining the first section of the novel and into the existential realm of moral experimentation reminiscent of another of Wright's literary influences, Russian novelist Fyodor Dostoevski's *Prestupleniye i nakazaniye* (1866; *Crime and Punishment*, 1886).

Ironically, while Bigger is far more responsible for Bessie's murder than for Mary's arguably accidental death, it is of virtually no importance to the white society which will eventually put him on trial. It becomes a footnote in his prosecution, the real target of which is his presumed violation of white womanhood. Bigger's killing of Bessie contributes to the chain of events springing his trap: It not only costs him the ransom money but also moves him steadily toward capture as the police dragnet confines him to the ghetto and finally isolates him on a rooftop water tower, in a scene recalling the rat episode.

"Fate" deals with Bigger's trial and his yearning to know what his life has meant before he dies. Wright uses verbatim Chicago newspaper accounts of the Nixon trial to demonstrate the inflammatory racist lens through which a crime such as Bigger's is projected before the public. This effort at verisimilitude gives way to competing ideological analyses of Bigger's situation, the tensions between them indicative of the struggle within Wright between Communist Party doctrine and existentialist individualism.

The speech of Bigger's eloquent lawyer, Max, argues that the jury recognize the moral culpability of a society that produces boys filled with such hate and violence. Max also follows Marxist doctrine in pointing out the inevitable collision between classes in an exploitive capitalist system that pits haves against have-nots. Max's defense, while unheeded by the jury which sentences Bigger to death, has a profoundly liberating effect on Bigger, who is stunned into recognizing that his humanity is confirmed, not denied, by his acts, which alone can define him: He declares, "What I killed for, I am!"

Bigger refuses to subordinate his identity to ideological symbolism and instead embraces his outlaw behavior as evidence of his vitality, not victimization. One might also argue that he is severing meaningful connection to collective societal values when he celebrates his act of murder as life-affirming. As the jail door swings shut on the doomed youth, Wright transforms Bigger from racial icon to representative existential man, responsible for determining the meaning of his own life in a cosmic void where death is the only absolute.

BLACK BOY

First published: 1945
Type of work: Autobiography

A sensitive and rebellious black American survives a life of poverty, familial strife, and southern bigotry to pursue his goal of becoming a writer in the North.

Black Boy, which was another immediate best seller, is often considered Wright's most fully realized work. Ostensibly a description of the first twenty-one years of Wright's life, the book derives its aesthetic design from two distinct but interwoven narrative skeins: the African American exodus motif, in which a character's movement from south to north suggests a flight from oppression to freedom, and the *Künstlerroman*, or novelistic account of the birth of the artist—in this case, a "portrait of the artist as a young black American." In the process, Wright analyzes how poverty, intolerance, and racism shaped his personality but also fed his creativity, enabling him to view his pain as an embodiment of the existential human condition.

As a chronicle of family life, *Black Boy* presents a grim portrait of violence, suffering, and disintegration. While the veracity of every event related in the text is questionable, one cannot deny the authenticity with which Wright has documented the emotional truths of his childhood and their devastating psychological consequences. The central motif of the work is the gnawing hunger defining every facet of Richard's existence: physical hunger born of his family's worsening poverty after his father's abandonment; emotional hunger rooted in that abandonment, compounded by his mother's prolonged illnesses, and resulting in his alienation from other black people; and intellectual hunger exacerbated by his limited formal schooling and the repressive religious fundamentalism of his maternal relatives. Wright had initially chosen "American Hunger" as his title, and it was later applied to the second volume of his autobiographical writings, published posthumously in 1977.

Richard's responses to the conditions of his life are, from the first, a volatile combination of rebellion, anger, and fear. *Black Boy* opens with a bored and peevish four-year-old Richard retaliating against his mother's demand for quiet by experimenting with fire until he sets the house ablaze. He then hides under the burning structure until he is pulled free by his enraged father and beaten unconscious. The episode provides a paradigm for Richard's young life: willful self-assertion repeatedly produces self-destructive consequences and crushing rejection by those closest to him. His renegade or outlaw sensibility is in dangerous conflict with the arbitrary tyranny of the authority figures dominating his youth, particularly males. Rather than offering a buffer against the injustices of the Jim Crow South, Richard's home is the crucible of his lifelong estrangement from the human community.

In childhood, Richard learns that the essential law of existence is struggle against forces deterministically operating to extinguish the weak; this view explains the pervasive naturalism of *Black Boy*. The lesson remains the same whether he is observing the casual violence of nature, confronting street urchins, or battling wits with prejudiced white people. Surrounded by hostility directed at him from all quarters, including the supposedly Christian adults who regularly beat and humiliate him, Richard rejects religion as fraudulent in its premises and hypocritical in its practices. He allows himself to be baptized only because of the emotional blackmail of his abject mother and the friends whose camaraderie he desperately seeks.

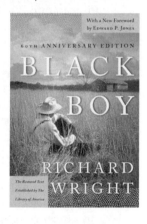

He craves an analytic vantage point that will illuminate the random pointlessness of experience.

After he graduates from the ninth grade and begins working in Memphis, he finds in the works of H. L. Mencken, Theodore Dreiser, and Sinclair Lewis evidence not only that his own insights into the brutal nature of existence are valid but also that they are potentially the stuff of serious literature. Years earlier, he had discovered the explosive power of language and the raw emotional energy generated by melodramatic narrative, and he had vowed to become a writer. As a young man, he becomes consumed with literature's promise to give him a voice in counterpoise to all those forces that have worked so systematically to silence him, and he finds therein the purpose that will save and direct his life after the nightmare of his southern childhood. Wright's naturalism, Marxism, and existentialism coalesce in *Black Boy*, particularly in his analysis of American racism.

On the most basic level, Wright depicts the situation confronting the African American male in the first quarter of the twentieth century as literally life-threatening: By the age of fifteen, he had known an uncle lynched for being "too" successful and knew of a black youth murdered for forgetting the strict sexual taboos surrounding interchanges between black men and white women. He had been personally assaulted without provocation by white youths and had participated in street battles between white and black adolescents. His insistent pursuit of a way out of the South is thus a reaction to the physical terrorism exercised against the black community. It is also a repudiation of the psychological condition that racism fosters in its victims.

Richard has already suffered for years from the debilitating anxiety caused by trying to predict the behavior of white people, and he has often felt the impact of their displeasure, repeatedly losing jobs when they resent his manner or ambition. He chafes under the dehumanizing stereotypes they superimpose on him: "The White South said that it knew 'niggers,' and I was what the white South called 'nigger.' Well, the white South had never known me—never known what I thought, what I felt." Richard's exodus from the South is triggered as much by a spiritual hunger to define his own personhood, free of racist categorizations, as it is by a pursuit of greater material opportunity.

Wright asserts that his personality bears permanent scars as a southern black man—scars that explain his emotional and philosophical alienation as well as his unresolved anger. Significantly, however, they also serve as the creative wellspring of his powerful artistry.

Wright leaves no doubt about his resentment of the white racist social order that defined his youth; what is more difficult to resolve is the ambivalence toward black people that permeates *Black Boy*. By the time he reaches adulthood, Wright finds himself estranged from the black community by his dismissal of religion, his resistance to strategies for manipulating white people behind the mask of stereotype, and his contempt for passive acquiescence in response to white terrorism. That estrangement becomes central to his depiction of black people and explains his vacillation between analytic detachment and deeply personal condemnation.

Nevertheless, a key source of *Black Boy*'s narrative tension—and its author's positioning of himself as existential outcast—lies in his antipathy to the world that failed to nourish him. One might also argue that Wright's impulse to repudiate the past is very much in keeping with the American literary paradigm of "making oneself" anew in a new world. Richard sets out to define himself according to his own proclivities and talents in the unknown future of Chicago, toward which he is rushing by train at the close of the book.

SUMMARY

Wright's career marked the first time that an African American's work so forcefully commanded the attention of the American literary establishment. It did so through uncompromising depictions of the social and moral crisis that racism had precipitated in the United States. In harnessing his anger and alienation into creative channels and giving the oppressed a voice, Wright inspired the following generation of black writers, including Ralph Ellison, Chester Himes, and James Baldwin. Ironically, the militant racial activism of the 1960's led to a temporary rejection of Wright's achievement, despite his courageous political stances. More recently, however, writers and critics are recovering Wright's legacy and recognizing him as a man ahead of his time.

Barbara Kitt Seidman

BIBLIOGRAPHY

By the Author

SHORT FICTION:
Uncle Tom's Children: Four Novellas, 1938 (expanded as *Uncle Tom's Children: Five Long Stories*, 1938)
Eight Men, 1961

LONG FICTION:
Native Son, 1940
The Outsider, 1953
Savage Holiday, 1954
The Long Dream, 1958
Lawd Today, 1963

DRAMA:
Native Son: The Biography of a Young American, pr. 1941 (with Paul Green)

POETRY:
Haiku: This Other World, 1998 (Yoshinobu Hakutani and Robert L. Tener, editors)

NONFICTION:
Twelve Million Black Voices: A Folk History of the Negro in the United States, 1941 (photographs by Edwin Rosskam)
Black Boy: A Record of Childhood and Youth, 1945
Black Power: A Record of Reactions in a Land of Pathos, 1954
The Color Curtain, 1956
Pagan Spain, 1957
White Man, Listen!, 1957
American Hunger, 1977
Richard Wright Reader, 1978 (Ellen Wright and Michel Fabre, editors)
Conversations with Richard Wright, 1993 (Keneth Kinnamon and Fabre, editors)

MISCELLANEOUS:
Works, 1991 (2 volumes)

DISCUSSION TOPICS

- What explains the unusual amount of recognition that Richard Wright received as an African American writer as early as the 1940's?

- How does Wright succeed in inducing sympathy for the violently antisocial Bigger Thomas in *Native Son*?

- Ralph Ellison compared Wright's work to the blues. What characteristics of this form of music find their parallel in Wright's novels?

- Consider the significance of hunger, both literal and metaphorical, in *Black Boy*.

- What circumstances caused Wright to be simultaneously vilified by both communists and federal agencies combating communism?

- To date, Wright's reputation as a novelist has fluctuated. What characteristics of his work are most likely to entitle him to the rank of major American writer?

About the Author

Baldwin, James. *The Price of the Ticket: Collected Nonfiction, 1948-1985*. New York: St. Martin's Press/Marek, 1985.

Bloom, Harold, ed. *Richard Wright*. New York: Chelsea House, 1987.

Butler, Robert. *"Native Son": The Emergence of a New Black Hero*. Boston: Twayne, 1991.

Fabre, Michel. *The Unfinished Quest of Richard Wright*. Translated by Isabel Barzun. New York: William Morrow, 1973.

Felgar, Robert. *Richard Wright*. Boston: Twayne, 1980.

Hakutani, Yoshinobu. *Richard Wright and Racial Discourse*. Columbia: University of Missouri Press, 1996.

Kinnamon, Keneth, ed. *Critical Essays on Richard Wright's "Native Son."* New York: Twayne, 1997.

_____. *A Richard Wright Bibliography: Fifty Years of Criticism and Commentary: 1933-1982*. Westport, Conn.: Greenwood Press, 1988.

Rand, William E. "The Structure of the Outsider in the Short Fiction of Richard Wright and F. Scott Fitzgerald." *CLA Journal* 40 (December, 1996): 230-245.

Walker, Margaret. *Richard Wright: Daemonic Genius*. New York: Warner, 1988.

AP/Wide World Photos

PAUL ZINDEL

Born: Staten Island, New York
May 15, 1936
Died: New York, New York
March 27, 2003

Widely recognized for his plays, Zindel is also credited with pioneering a new kind of fiction for young adults in which the crises of adolescence are portrayed with seriousness and candor.

BIOGRAPHY

Paul Zindel was born in Staten Island, New York, on May 15, 1936, the son of Paul and Beatrice Mary Frank Zindel. His father, a policeman, deserted his family when Paul was two years old, leaving Beatrice with the responsibility of raising Paul and his sister, Betty, who was two years older. The breakup of the family left Paul with a deep-seated feeling of resentment toward his father, who ignored his children and failed to make any financial contribution to their support.

Following her husband's desertion, Zindel's mother worked in a variety of jobs, supplementing her salary at times by stealing small items from her clients. Since many of these jobs were short-term practical nursing assignments, the family moved frequently. As a result, Zindel's childhood was rootless and lonely. This loneliness was intensified when he developed tuberculosis at age fifteen and was forced to spend eighteen months in a sanatorium, where most of the patients were adults.

After his recovery and return to high school, Zindel, who had shown an interest in writing plays, entered a playwriting contest sponsored by the American Cancer Society. He was awarded a silver ballpoint pen for his drama about a pianist who recovers from a serious illness to play Frédéric Chopin's *Warsaw Concerto* at Carnegie Hall.

During his senior year in high school, feeling what he called a "teenaged angst," Zindel dropped out of school and traveled to Miami, Florida, where he tried unsuccessfully to find a job. After two weeks and the total exhaustion of his financial resources, Zindel returned to New York, where he finished high school in 1954, one year late. He then applied to five colleges, without any clear idea of what he wanted to do. He was accepted by several prestigious schools but decided to attend Wagner College on Staten Island, a move he believes was prompted by low self-esteem and social insecurity, legacies he attributes to his mother.

Zindel majored in chemistry at Wagner but maintained his interest in writing. He served as editor for the school newspaper and wrote an original play as his term paper for a continental drama course. During a visit to New York to cover a writers conference (an assignment he had given himself), Zindel came under the spell of Edward Albee, a playwright best known for his play *Who's Afraid of Virginia Woolf?* (1962). Zindel signed up for a course taught by Albee and under his famous teacher's direction completed a play, *Dimensions of Peacocks* (unpublished). Produced in 1959, the play, about a disturbed teenager whose domineering mother is a practical nurse who steals from her patients, anticipates much of Zindel's later work.

Zindel was still uncertain about a career when he graduated from Wagner College. He needed a job, but he wanted to write, and he compromised by accepting a technical writing position with Allied Chemical. Six months later, bored and tired of commuting, he returned to Wagner to complete a master's program in education.

In the fall of 1959, he was hired to teach physics and chemistry at Staten Island's Tottenville High School. He continued at the school until 1969, spending his summers writing plays. His second play, *Euthanasia and the Endless Hearts* (unpublished) was produced in 1960 and was followed in 1964 by *A Dream of Swallows* (unpublished). Neither play attracted critical attention.

During the summer of 1963, Zindel wrote *The Effect of Gamma Rays on Man-in-the-Moon Marigolds*, a play inspired by Zindel's memories of his mother. The play, which won the Pulitzer Prize in 1971, was first produced in 1965 by Houston's Alley Theater. A year later, Zindel took a one-year leave of absence from teaching to accept a Ford Foundation playwright-in-residence award at Alley Theater.

When he returned from Houston, Zindel became discouraged with teaching and resigned so that he could spend more time writing. Encouraged by Charlotte Zolotow, a children's book editor at Harper & Row who had been impressed with teenagers Ruth and Tillie in *The Effect of Gamma Rays on Man-in-the-Moon Marigolds*, Zindel began exploring the possibility of writing a young adult novel. After careful research, Zindel decided he wanted to attempt a novel of this type. *The Pigman*, which many consider a groundbreaking novel, was published in 1968 and was followed quickly by a second young adult novel, *My Darling, My Hamburger* (1969).

Zindel's third novel, *I Never Loved Your Mind*, was published in 1970, a year that marked the beginning of one of the most intense periods in his life. By 1973, he had completed three plays, *And Miss Reardon Drinks a Little* (1967), *The Secret Affairs of Mildred Wild* (1972), and *The Ladies Should Be in Bed* (1973), besides working on several screenplays. Two of Zindel's plays, *Let Me Hear You Whisper* (1970) and a shortened version of *The Effect of Gamma Rays on Man-in-the-Moon Marigolds*, were produced by National Education Television (NET) during this period. Shortly after this flurry of activity, Zindel had a breakdown and entered psychoanalysis.

On October 25, 1973, Zindel married Bonnie Hildebrand, who had helped in his recovery from his breakdown, and the couple moved to New York. The Zindels' first child, David, was born in 1974,

and their second, Lizabeth, was born in 1976. The arrival of children may have prompted Zindel to write a children's picture book, *I Love My Mother* (1975). This was followed by three more young adult novels, *Pardon Me, You're Stepping on My Eyeball!* (1976), *Confessions of a Teenage Baboon* (1977), and *The Undertaker's Gone Bananas* (1978). A play, *Ladies at the Alamo*, was produced in 1975.

In 1978, Zindel, seeking to earn more money, moved to Beverly Hills, California. By his own admission, money was his main motivation for writing during his California period. After writing three so-called potboilers—*The Pigman's Legacy* (1980), *The Girl Who Wanted a Boy* (1981), and *When a Darkness Falls* (1984)—Zindel returned to the style of writing found in his earlier novels. *Harry and Hortense at Hormone High* (1984) and *A Begonia for Miss Applebaum* (1989) are both in *The Pigman* tradition of Zindel fiction. In 1985, Zindel, feeling that he was losing both artistic and moral perspective, moved his family back to New York. It was in that city that he died in 2003 of cancer at the age of sixty-six.

ANALYSIS

To understand the themes that preoccupy Zindel, one must have a working knowledge of his personal life, because it infused most of what he wrote. His plays, for example, reflect his "virtually desperate" search for meaning in life. His young adult novels, on the other hand, reflect an attempt to resolve, through the creative process, problems left unresolved by an adolescence interrupted by a number of events.

The relationship between Zindel's personal life and his writing may also be seen in the way he worked when writing. He usually began by creating what he calls an "inspirational homunculus." This is a basic idea for a character, which was always based on a "life model" or "living image" (a real person Zindel had known). As his characters developed, Zindel identified closely with them as he placed them in situations in which they must resolve one or more of his own unresolved conflicts. Every situation is based on Zindel's own experience. His young adult novels are usually constructed around what he considered four fundamental themes of adolescence: the search for identity and meaning, the youthful questioning of traditional values, the loneliness of an individual in a crowd, and the difficulty of communication.

With minor variations, Zindel's stories follow an established formula. There is a principal protagonist, usually a dominant, wise-cracking male teenager, who is joined by a second teenager, always of the opposite sex. The second character may also bear part of the responsibility for telling the story, as he or she does in *The Pigman* and *A Begonia for Miss Applebaum*. The couple are usually drawn together as a result of the isolation of each.

They are basically two people who are lonely because they are unable to communicate with their parents, their teachers, and, sometimes, with their peers. In some instances, their isolation is a result of their instinctive, superior, youthful wisdom which makes them oddities at home, at school, and in the community. Thus thrown together, the two proceed to wrestle with the problems associated with growing up. In the process, they learn valuable lessons and gain new insights.

Zindel's novels are written in a style which has been praised by some as "the authentic voice of the modern teenager." To others, Zindel's teenagers sound like Holden Caulfield, in J. D. Salinger's *The Catcher in the Rye* (1951). They acknowledge that the style is entertaining and suitable to the situations Zindel created but question whether anyone actually talks like a Zindel character.

Unlike the novels, Zindel's plays are written for adult audiences and feature few nonadult characters (*The Effect of Gamma Rays on Man-in-the-Moon Marigolds* is an exception). They are mostly about troubled women who do not seem to have Zindel's teenagers' knack for resolving their problems. The plays tend to exaggerate and embellish the themes of the novels. Many of the plays' female characters resemble the parental authority figures in the novels, but in the plays the women are more likely to be perversely crazy or mindlessly destructive to those around them. They often repeat the strange behavior of the adults in the novels; in the plays there is something bizarre about the way they act.

For example, both Lorraine Jensen (*The Pigman*) and Tillie Frank (*The Effect of Gamma Rays on Man-in-the-Moon Marigolds*) are kept out of school to do housework, but when the demand is made by Tillie's mother it is tinged with an element of lunacy. Mrs. Jensen's excuse is simply that she needs Lorraine's help. She "can't go out and earn a living" and keep house, too. Betty Frank, however, manages to encapsulate into her demands frustrations and hatreds dating back to her own high school days.

Like the novels, Zindel's plays are related to his personal life. Each play is, in a sense, a result of his search for "some sign, for any bit of hope, or reason, to make being a human sensible."

During an interview, Zindel once said that remembering that he was composed of matter which came from the sun a long time ago was a thrilling experience. "The idea of being linked to the universe by these atoms," he said, gave him a "feeling of meaning." This discovery of a form of cosmic resolution, arrived at through a knowledge of science, is frequently echoed in Zindel's plays and novels. *Pardon Me, You're Stepping on My Eyeball!*, for example, ends with the words, "At last there were the stars set in place." This sentiment is repeated in *Confessions of a Teenage Baboon*, which concludes: "I began to look past the moon, past all the great satellites of Jupiter, and dream upon the stars."

THE EFFECT OF GAMMA RAYS ON MAN-IN-THE-MOON MARIGOLDS

First produced: 1965 (first published, 1971)
Type of work: Play

An alcoholic single parent, a teenage daughter subject to seizures, and another daughter interested in science attempt to find meaning in life.

The Effect of Gamma Rays on Man-in-the-Moon Marigolds, which won a Pulitzer Prize in 1971, was inspired by Zindel's memories of his mother's "charmingly frantic" get-rich-quick schemes. In its focus on the crazy world of a severely troubled woman, and in its resolution in one of the characters' discovery of self-importance through science, *The Effect of Gamma Rays on Man-in-the-Moon Marigolds* anticipates both the plays and young-adult novels that Zindel would later write.

The Effect of Gamma Rays on Man-in-the-Moon Marigolds, like most of Zindel's plays, intensifies the themes and characters that appear in his young-adult novels. Two teenagers, Ruth and Tillie, live in a world dominated by a single parent whose life has been a tragic disappointment. Like Zindel's mother, Beatrice, Betty Frank has been left with two children to support. She does this by providing nursing care in her home for elderly clients such as the ancient "Nanny," who is a resident at the time the play takes place.

Betty Frank, who was known as "Betty the Loon" during her high school career, is an unsympathetic exaggeration of some of the parents in Zindel's novels. Selfishly preoccupied, slightly alcoholic, and frequently lost in a dream world of preposterous schemes to make money and fantasies about what she might have been if she had not made the mistake of marrying and getting saddled with two kids, Betty Frank is capable of mindlessly destroy-

ing both her own and her daughters' worlds. With Ruth, who is subject to convulsions, Betty Frank is at times carelessly indulgent, at times a skillful nurse capable of talking Ruth out of an attack, and at times the most diabolically destructive force in Ruth's life. Her chloroforming of the girls' rabbit appears to be a calculated attack on Ruth's sanity.

With Tillie, on the other hand, Betty Frank exhibits none of the careless indulgences afforded Ruth. Tillie's passion is learning, and her mother, like some of the mothers in Zindel's novels, places a very low value on education. Because Ruth's ability to learn is limited, Betty Frank is content to allow her to attend school regularly, but Tillie's interest seems to challenge her mother to find ways of placing stumbling blocks in the way of her daughter's education. Cleaning up rabbit droppings, to Betty Frank's thinking, is far more important than anything Tillie might discover at school. The final expression of her disapproval of education comes at the end of the play, when she refuses to attend an awards night event after Tillie wins the science competition for her experimentation with seeds exposed to radiation.

Underlying the action of the play is Zindel's "virtually desperate" search for something to "hang onto," something "to make being a human sensi-

ble." Unfolding against the backdrop of a senseless world like the Franks', Zindel attempts to find the "grain of truth" which will make it sensible. In *The Effect of Gamma Rays on Man-in-the-Moon Marigolds*, it is science that provides the "grain of truth" for Tillie.

Zindel often uses science as a metaphor for or a source of meaning and harmony, but it should be noted that his respect for science and for scientific experimentation is a qualified one. He disapproves of the use of animals for scientific research, and this disapproval is reflected in Ruth's indignation over Janice Vickery's boiling a live cat to study its anatomy. Zindel expanded on this theme later in *Let Me Hear You Whisper*, a play about a dolphin who refuses to talk when he learns the purpose of the experiment in which he is involved.

It is in the conclusion of *The Effect of Gamma Rays on Man-in-the-Moon Marigolds*, however, that Zindel makes his strongest statement about the value of science as a solution to the meaninglessness of being human. In a speech that shows the close relationship between Zindel's personal life and his writing, Tillie Frank says that the most important benefit of her experimentation is that it has made her feel important. "Every atom in me," she says, "has come from the sun—from places beyond our dreams."

THE PIGMAN

First published: 1968
Type of work: Novel

Two high school sophomores, a boy and a girl, learn a valuable lesson through their experiences with a lonely old man.

The Pigman, Zindel's first young adult novel, has been called a groundbreaking work. Zindel's portrayal of high school students struggling with their own problems in their own environments introduced a new type of adolescent fiction. *The Pigman* was revolutionary in that Zindel moved away from more cautious traditional juvenile fiction to a kind of writing that depicted teenagers and their problems with candor and seriousness. *The Pigman* established a style of writing for young adults which became almost a formula for teen novels (including Zindel's own) after 1968.

The Pigman records the adventures of two high school students whose search for fun leads to the death of a lonely old man. Like Zindel's novels that follow, it is written in a style which has been described as an accurate capturing of the "bright, hyperbolic sheen of teen-age language."

The two teenagers who tell the story, John Conlan and Lorraine Jensen, assume responsibility for alternating chapters in what they call an "epic."

Characteristically, John is the dominant personality. As in most of his novels, the principal characters are two teenagers of opposite sex, with the male typically taking the leading role. In novels such as *My Darling, My Hamburger,* the boy serves as narrator, but in *The Pigman* and *A Begonia for Miss Applebaum* the task is shared, with each narrator responsible for alternating chapters. Notes, drawings, and reproductions of clippings are interspersed throughout the text, a device that Zindel uses less than successfully in some of his later novels.

The adults in *The Pigman* are treated unsympathetically, as they are in Zindel's plays. They are frequently unable to establish an adequate home environment, and they find most of the interests of the young either uninteresting or unimportant. Even school is categorized as unimportant. Lorraine's mother, like Betty Frank, often attempts to keep Lorraine at home to clean house, as she sees no practical advantage in an education. When Lorraine says that a Latin test is important, her mother responds by saying she is sure that later in life Lorraine will be using Latin daily.

Parents are referred to derisively and in most instances are portrayed as being far less astute than their children, who, unlike their parents, are able to perceive the sources of problems, solve them, and in the process gain new insights hidden from their parents and other adults in the stories. Perhaps because of his own experience, Zindel sometimes appears unable to appreciate parental effort. In an introduction to *The Effect of Gamma Rays on Man-in-the-Moon Marigolds*, Zindel referred to his mother's efforts to support her family as "an endless series of preposterous undertakings." John Conlan reflects Zindel's attitude when he refers to his father as "the Bore" and assumes that Mr. Conlan is interested only in stocks.

The boys in Zindel's novels often follow John's practice of referring to their parents only by a derogatory nickname. In *I Never Loved Your Mind,* for example, Dewey Daniels refers to his parents as "the Engineer" and "the Librarian." The use of sobriquets underscores Zindel's portrayal of adults as one-dimensional, monomaniac figures; it explains why teenagers such as John and Lorraine must seek their fun outside the family circle. Excitement may be found only among their peers, or in the company of adults such as Mr. Pignati, who is capable of varying from dull routine and can find fun in doing simple things.

Following his habit of using "life models" for the characters in his novels and plays, the characters in *The Pigman* are based on people Zindel has known. Lorraine's mother, like Betty Frank in *The Effect of Gamma Rays on Man-in-the-Moon Marigolds*, is modeled after Zindel's mother. Like Beatrice Zindel, Mrs. Jensen is a single parent working as a practical nurse, and, like Zindel's mother, Mrs. Jensen restocks her kitchen and bathroom shelves with items stolen from her clients.

Zindel has admitted that it was his own "interrupted adolescence" that prompted him to write for young adults and that his stories, in the main, are his own attempts to resolve problems left over from those years. As a result of this compulsion to solve problems, Zindel's novels always place the main characters in situations requiring the solution of a major youth-related problem. As the problem is solved, Zindel's teenagers (and Zindel himself) learn lessons and gain new insights. When the lesson does not seem obvious, Zindel may spell it out at the end of the novel, as he does in *The Pigman.* Speaking through John Conlan, Zindel says that life is what the individual makes it. Ultimately, there is "no one else to blame." People, like baboons, "build their own cages."

MY DARLING, MY HAMBURGER

First published: 1969
Type of work: Novel

Four high school seniors struggle with issues such as casual sex, contraceptives, and abortion.

My Darling, My Hamburger, Zindel's second young adult novel, was the first to use the type of offbeat title which would become a kind of Zindel trademark. Eventually, the Zindel bibliography would grow to include titles such as *Pardon Me, You're Stepping on My Eyeball!, Harry and Hortense at Hormone High,* and *The Amazing and Death-Defying Diary of Eugene Dingman* (1987). Zindel was again concerned with four basic themes—identity and meaning, the questioning of traditional values, the loneliness of the individual, and the difficulty of communication. *My Darling, My Hamburger* goes beyond these concerns to deal with subjects such as casual sex, the use of contraceptives, and abortion as an alternative to unwanted pregnancies. These subjects are dealt with realistically and with candor.

Zindel departs from the format used in *The Pigman* and other novels by focusing on four teenagers rather then his usual two. These four, like the young people in the other novels, learn through their own experiences, without much help from adults. In My *Darling, My Hamburger,* the lesson appears to be that carefree living has risks and that people must account for their actions. Zindel also departed from *The Pigman* formula by using a third-person omniscient narrator to tell the story; the language used in the dialogue is similar to that used in his other novels. As in *The Pigman,* Zindel accompanies the text with facsimiles of letters and announcements, reproductions of lesson assignments, and copies of surreptitious notes, allowing for a more personal treatment of the characters.

As *My Darling, My Hamburger* develops it becomes apparent that Zindel believed that at least a part of the cynicism expressed by his teenage characters must be attributed to their sense of having been betrayed by adults. These adults might have provided something for young people to fall back on at critical times in their lives. Instead, as Miss Fanuzzi does, they give "dumb" and impotent advice. Miss Fanuzzi, for example, recommends suggesting going for a hamburger when a boy is pressuring a girl to "go all the way." Her students realize that this advice is useless, and there is a sense of frustration, as well as betrayal, in the observation that "she needs a little more experience with men."

One of the strengths of *My Darling, My Hamburger* is Zindel's realistic portrayal of the pressures faced by adolescents. The impotence of adult advice in the face of this pressure is dramatized by his division of the book into two parts. Each of the divisions is given half the book's title, which is based on Miss Fanuzzi's advice for handling sexual stimulation. The first part, "The Darling," deals primarily with the pressures to yield to the male's sexual advances, and it ends with one of the main characters, Liz, yielding. The second part, "The Hamburger," is primarily concerned with the consequences; the title is ironic, because Miss Fanuzzi's advice has failed.

In most of his novels, Zindel's characters gain new insights and learn lessons as a result of their experiences. In *My Darling, My Hamburger,* the lessons are obvious to the reader, but many readers believe that Zindel diluted the impact of the novel by concluding with a weak ending. After all has been said and done, the novel ends in some commencement address platitudes. There is a hint that, when it comes to problems related to casual sex, contraceptives, and abortion, Zindel has little more to offer than Miss Fanuzzi.

I NEVER LOVED YOUR MIND

First published: 1970
Type of work: Novel

A teenage high school dropout discovers the value of education as a result of a disappointing romance with a hippie-type coworker.

I Never Loved Your Mind, Zindel's third young adult novel, was written after the author had spent six months in Taos, New Mexico, following his decision to quit teaching. Zindel had taken a leave of absence from teaching to spend a year as playwright-in-residence at Houston's Alley Theater, and when he returned to the classroom he quickly became disillusioned with teaching. After his resignation, he went to Taos, where he lived in a house given him by a friend. When he returned from Taos and had to have an appendectomy, he commented that he was grateful to have a "traditional doctor . . . rather than someone at Hot Springs commune."

True to form, *I Never Loved Your Mind* is essentially a summarization of Zindel's own experiences, with characters drawn from life models. The model for Dewey Daniels was a "nasty and a little preppy" student of Zindel, while Yvette Goethals is a composite. The primary model for Yvette was an orphan Zindel had befriended, but Zindel's mother may be seen in Yvette's habit of stealing something at the end of each shift she works.

After using the third-person omniscient narrator format in *My Darling, My Hamburger,* Zindel returned to first-person narrative in *I Never Loved Your Mind.* He also returned to the style of writing that characterizes the John Conlan chapters of *The Pigman.* Some readers, however, feel that Zindel placed too much reliance on hyperbole in constructing Dewey's narratives. They point out that at times Zindel seems to arbitrarily opt for exotic, grotesque, or ridiculous imagery when plain language would serve. Dewey's description of Yvette provides one example of Zindel language excesses. Dewey begins by saying simply that Yvette's shape is "not too fat, not too slim." He then adds, "Best of all was a commendable frontal insulation of the respiratory cage." This description is followed by an asterisk, which points to a footnote explaining that Yvette "had some pair of peaches." The footnotes, intended as comic devices, tend to intensify a labored quality of the writing, giving many readers the impression that Zindel is trying too hard.

The story that Dewey Daniels sets out to tell is a variation on the old boy-meets-girl theme. Dewey is a high school dropout who works as an inhalation therapist in a local hospital. One of his coworkers is Yvette Goethals, a hippie type who is also a high school dropout. Yvette is a vegetarian and lives with a rock band. Dewey manages to convince himself he is in love with Yvette; it is Yvette's disclaimer that she never loved his mind after she and Dewey have slept together that provides the title for the novel. His brief, one-sided, and disillusioning love affair eventually leads Dewey to a decision to return to school. Yvette, significantly, moves on to a hippie commune near Taos, New Mexico.

In most of Zindel's young adult novels, his characters are searching for answers to disturbing questions or are seeking resolution of some of the disturbing problems of adolescence. *I Never Loved Your Mind* touches on these problems—Dewey is confronted with the need for an education—but the novel is primarily an expression of Zindel's frustrations with teaching and of his distaste for the hippie subculture of the 1960's. Neither the hippies nor the students in Zindel's science classes were interested in things of the mind, and Yvette's parting words to Dewey become, for Zindel, the distasteful motto for the world he re-creates in the novel. Society, as a whole, appears to be saying to scientist and educator alike, "I never loved your mind."

For Zindel, who often uses science as a metaphor for harmony and meaning, this is a particularly tragic situation, as his reproduction of Yvette's illiterate letter at the end of the novel shows. The letter is symbolic of what society can expect from those who do not love the mind. Fortunately, Dewey comes to his senses, and his understanding of the need for the mind is reflected in his concluding words. While he has no idea what he is going to do, he is sure it is not going to be Yvette's "Love Land crap." Neither is he "going to give civilization a kick in the behind." John realizes that he, like the author, "might need an appendectomy sometime."

SUMMARY

"Whatever I do," Zindel once said, "becomes summarized in my writing." The result of this summarization is a series of plays and novels constructed around Zindel's search for meaning and the resolution of problems left over from his adolescence. The plays, which are written for an adult audience, are most often about troubled women, and they contain some attempt to find a reason behind a seemingly senseless life. The novels, on the other hand, are directed toward a young adult audience and are designed to provide both entertainment and insight. In each of Zindel's novels his characters, and perhaps his readers, learn a lesson.

Chandice M. Johnson, Jr.

BIBLIOGRAPHY

By the Author

DRAMA:

Dimensions of Peacocks, pr. 1959
Euthanasia and the Endless Hearts, pr. 1960
A Dream of Swallows, pr. 1964
The Effect of Gamma Rays on Man-in-the-Moon Marigolds, pr. 1965, pb. 1971
And Miss Reardon Drinks a Little, pr. 1967, pb. 1972
Let Me Hear You Whisper, pb. 1970
The Secret Affairs of Mildred Wild, pr. 1972, pb. 1973
The Ladies Should Be in Bed, pb. 1973
Ladies at the Alamo, pr. 1975, pb. 1977
A Destiny with Half Moon Street, pr. 1983
Amulets Against the Dragon Forces, pr., pb. 1989
Every Seventeen Minutes the Crowd Goes Crazy!, pr. 1995, pb. 1996

LONG FICTION:

When a Darkness Falls, 1984

SCREENPLAYS:

Up the Sandbox, 1972
Mame, 1974
Runaway Train, 1983
Maria's Lovers, 1984

TELEPLAYS:

Let Me Hear You Whisper, 1966
Alice in Wonderland, 1985 (adaptation of Lewis Carroll)
A Connecticut Yankee in King Arthur's Court, 1989 (adaptation of the novel by Mark Twain)

CHILDREN'S LITERATURE:

The Pigman, 1968
My Darling, My Hamburger, 1969
I Never Loved Your Mind, 1970
I Love My Mother, 1975
Pardon Me, You're Stepping on My Eyeball!, 1976
Confessions of a Teenage Baboon, 1977
The Undertaker's Gone Bananas, 1978
A Star for the Latecomer, 1980 (with Bonnie Zindel)
The Pigman's Legacy, 1980
The Girl Who Wanted a Boy, 1981
To Take a Dare, 1982 (with Crescent Dragonwagon)
Harry and Hortense at Hormone High, 1984
The Amazing and Death-Defying Diary of Eugene Dingman, 1987
A Begonia for Miss Applebaum, 1989
The Pigman and Me, 1992 (autobiography)
Attack of the Killer Fishsticks, 1993
David and Della, 1993

DISCUSSION TOPICS

- How do Paul Zindel's young adult novels differ from those by other writers in this genre?

- Explain how Zindel's works question traditional values.

- Compare Zindel's treatment of loneliness in his plays and his fiction.

- How does Zindel use science as a metaphor?

- Discuss the treatment of child abuse in Zindel's works.

- Discuss the influence of J. D. Salinger's *The Catcher in the Rye* (1951) on Zindel's fiction.

- Is the bizarre behavior of Zindel's adult characters realistic, exaggerated for artistic purposes, or a weakness in his art?

- How is *The Effect of Gamma Rays on Man-in-the-Moon Marigolds* the seed for most of Zindel's later works?

Fifth Grade Safari, 1993
Fright Party, 1993
Loch, 1994
The 100 Percent Laugh Riot, 1994
The Doom Stone, 1995
Raptor, 1998
Reef of Death, 1998
Rats, 1999
The Gadget, 2001
Night of the Bat, 2001
The Surfing Corpse, 2001
The Scream Museum, 2001
The E-mail Murders, 2001
The Lethal Gorilla, 2001
The Square Root Murder, 2002
The Phantom of 86th Street, 2002
The Gourmet Zombie, 2002
Death on the Amazon, 2002

About the Author

DiGaetani, John L. "Paul Zindel." In *A Search for a Postmodern Theater: Interviews with Contemporary Playwrights,* edited by DiGaetani. New York: Greenwood Press, 1991.

Forman, Jack Jacob. *Presenting Paul Zindel.* Boston: Twayne, 1988.

Megyeri, Kathy A. "Paul Zindel." *English Journal* 93 (November, 2003): 12-13.

Rees, David. *The Marble in the Water: Essays on Contemporary Writers of Fiction for Children and Young Adults.* Boston: Horn Book Press. 1980.

Smith, Grant T. "The Pigman's Story: Teaching Paul Zindel in the 21st Century." In *Censored Books, II: Critical Viewpoints, 1985-2000,* edited by Nicholas J. Karolides. Lanham, Md.: Scarecrow, 2002.

Strickland, Ruth L. "Paul Zindel." In *Twentieth-Century American Dramatists, First Series,* edited by John MacNicholas. Vol. 7 in *Dictionary of Literary Biography.* Detroit: Gale Research, 1981.

GLOSSARY OF LITERARY TERMS

Absurdism: A philosophical attitude underlining the alienation that humans experience in what absurdists see as a universe devoid of meaning; literature of the absurd often purposely lacks logic, coherence, and intelligibility.

Act: One of the major divisions of a play or opera; the typical number of acts in a play ranges from one to four.

Agrarianism: A movement of the 1920's and 1930's in which John Crowe Ransom, Allen Tate, Robert Penn Warren, and other southern writers championed the agrarian society of their region against the industrialized society of the North.

Allegory: A literary mode in which a second level of meaning (wherein characters, events, and settings represent abstractions) is encoded within the narrative.

Alliteration: The repetition of consonant sounds focused at the beginning of syllables, as in "Large *m*annered *m*otions of his *m*ythy *m*ind."

Allusion: A reference to a historical event or to another literary text that adds dimension or meaning to a literary work.

Alter ego: A character's other self—sometimes a double, sometimes another side of the character's personality, sometimes a dear and constant companion.

Ambiguity: The capacity of language to sustain multiple meanings; ambiguity can add to both the richness and the concentration of literary language.

Angst: A pervasive feeling of anxiety and depression, often associated with the moral and spiritual uncertainties first arising in the twentieth century.

Antagonist: The major character or force in opposition to the protagonist or hero.

Antihero: A fictional figure who tries to define himself and to establish his own codes, or a protagonist who simply lacks traditional heroic qualities.

Apostrophe: A poetic device in which the speaker addresses either someone not physically present or something not physically capable of hearing the words addressed.

Aside: A short passage generally spoken by one dramatic character in an undertone, or directed to the audience, with the idea that it is not heard by the other characters onstage.

Assonance: A term for the association of words with identical vowel sounds but different consonants; "star, " "arms," and "park," for example, all contain identical "a" (and "ar") sounds.

Atmosphere: The general mood or tone of a work: it is often associated with setting but can also be established by action or dialogue. *See also* Tone.

Autobiography: A form of nonfiction writing in which the author narrates events of his or her own life.

Avant-garde: A term describing works intended to expand the conventions of a genre through the experimental treatment of form and/or content.

Bardic voice: A passionate poetic voice modeled after that of a bard, or tribal poet/singer, who composed lyric or epic poetry to honor a chief or recite tribal history.

***Bildungsroman*:** Sometimes called the "novel of education," the *Bildungsroman* focuses on the growth of a young protagonist who is learning about the world and finding his place in life; typical examples are James Joyce's *A Portrait of the Artist as a Young Man* (1916) and Thomas Wolfe's *Look Homeward, Angel* (1929).

Biography: Nonfiction that details the events of a particular individual's life.

Black humor: A general term of modern origin that refers to a form of "sick humor" that is intended to produce laughter out of the morbid and the taboo.

Blank verse: Lines of unrhymed iambic pentameter; it is a poetic form that allows much flexibility, and it has been used since the Elizabethan era.

Caesura: A pause or break in a poem; it is most commonly indicated by a punctuation mark such as a comma, dash, semicolon, or period.

Canon: A generally accepted list of literary works; it may refer to works by a single author or works in a genre. The literary canon often refers to the texts that are thought to belong on academic reading lists.

Catharsis: A term from Aristotle's *De poetica* (c. 335-323 B.C.E.; *Poetics*, 1705) referring to the purgation of the spectators' emotions of pity and fear as aroused by the actions of the tragic hero.

Character: A personage appearing in any literary or dramatic work.

Chorus: An individual or group sometimes used in drama to comment on the action; the chorus was used extensively in classical Greek drama.

Classicism: A literary stance or value system consciously based on classical Greek and Roman literature; it generally denotes a cluster of values including formal discipline, restrained expression, reverence for tradition, and an objective rather than a subjective orientation.

Climax: The moment in a work of fiction or drama at which the action reaches its highest intensity and is resolved.

Comedy: A lighter form of drama that aims chiefly to amuse and that ends happily; comedic forms range from physical (slapstick) humor to subtle intellectual humor.

Comedy of manners: A type of drama that treats humorously, and often satirically, the behavior within an artificial, highly sophisticated society.

Comic relief: A humorous incident or scene in an otherwise serious or tragic work intended to release the reader's or audience's tensions through laughter without detracting from the serious material.

Conceit: One type of metaphor, the conceit is used for comparisons which are highly intellectualized. When T. S. Eliot, for example, says that winding streets are like a tedious argument of insidious intent, there is no clear connection between the two, so the reader must apply abstract logic to fill in the missing links.

Confessional poetry: Autobiographical poetry in which personal revelation provides a basis for the intellectual or theoretical study of moral, religious, or aesthetic concerns.

Conflation: The fusion of variant readings of a text into a composite whole.

Conflict: The struggle that develops as a result of the opposition between the protagonist and another person, the natural world, society, or some force within the self.

Connotation: A type of meaning that depends on the associative meanings of a word beyond its formal definition. *See also* Denotation.

Conventions: All those devices of stylization, compression, and selection that constitute the necessary differences between art and life.

Counterplot: A secondary action coincident with the major action of a fictional or dramatic work. The counterplot is generally a reflection on or variation of the main action and is strongly integrated into the whole of the work. *See also* Subplot.

Couplet: Any two succeeding lines of poetry that rhyme.

Cubism: In literature, a style of poetry, such as that of E. E. Cummings and Archibald MacLeish, which first fragments an experience, then rearranges its elements into some new artistic entity.

Dactyl: A metrical foot in which a stressed syllable is followed by two unstressed syllables; an example of a dactyllic line is "After the pangs of a desperate lover."

Deconstruction: An influential contemporary school of criticism based on the works of the French philosopher Jacques Derrida. Deconstruction treats literary works as unconscious reflections of the myths of Western culture; the primary myth is that there is a meaningful world which language signifies or represents. The deconstructionist critic is often concerned with showing how a literary text tacitly subverts the very assumptions or myths on which it ostensibly rests.

Denotation: The explicit, formal definition of a word, exclusive of its implications and emotional associations. *See also* Connotation.

Denouement: Originally French, this word literally means "unknotting" or "untying" and is another term for the catastrophe or resolution of a dramatic action, the solution or clarification of a plot.

Detective story: In the "classic" detective story, the focus is on a crime solved by a detective through interpretation of evidence and clever reasoning. Many modern practitioners of the genre, however, have deemphasized the puzzlelike qualities, stressing instead characterization, theme, and other elements of mainstream fiction.

Determinism: The belief that a person's actions are essentially determined by biological and environmental factors, with free will playing a negligible role. *See also* Naturalism.

Deus ex machina: Latin, meaning "god out of a machine." In the Greek theater, it referred to the use of a god lowered by means of a mechanism onto the stage to untangle the plot or save the hero. It has come to signify any artificial device for the easy resolution of dramatic difficulties.

Dialogue: Speech exchanged between characters or even, in a looser sense, the thoughts of a single character.

Dime novel: A type of inexpensive book very popular in the late nineteenth century that told a formulaic tale of war, adventure, or romance.

Domestic tragedy: A serious and usually realistic play with lower-class or middle-class characters and milieu, typically dealing with personal or domestic concerns.

Donnée: From the French verb meaning "to give," the term refers to the premise or the given set of circumstances from which the plot will proceed.

Drama: Any work designed to be represented on a stage by actors. More specifically, the term has come to signify a play of a serious nature and intent that may end either happily (comedy) or unhappily (tragedy).

Dramatic irony: A form of irony that most typically occurs when the spoken lines of a character are perceived by the audience to have a double meaning or when the audience knows more about a situation than the character knows.

Dramatic monologue: A poem in which the narrator addresses a silent persona whose presence greatly influences what the narrator tells the reader.

Dramatis personae: The characters in a play; often it refers to a printed list defining the characters and their relationships.

Dramaturgy: The composition of plays; the term is occasionally used to refer to the performance or acting of plays.

Dream vision: A poem presented as a dream in which the poet-dreamer envisions people and events that frequently have allegorical overtones.

Dualism: A theory that the universe is explicable in terms of two basic, conflicting entities, such as good and evil, mind and matter, or the physical and the spiritual.

Elegy: The elegy and pastoral elegy are distinguishable by their subject matter, not their form. The elegy is usually a long, rhymed, strophic poem whose subject is meditation upon death or a lamentable theme; the pastoral elegy uses a pastoral scene to sing of death or love.

Elizabethan: Of or referring to the reign of Queen Elizabeth I of England, lasting from 1558 to 1603, a period of important artistic achievements; William Shakespeare was an Elizabethan playwright.

End-stop: When a punctuated pause occurs at the end of a line of poetry, the line is said to be end-stopped.

Enjambment: When a line of poetry is not end-stopped and instead carries over to the next line, the line is said to be enjambed.

Epic: This term usually refers to a long narrative poem that presents the exploits of a central figure of high position; it is also used to designate a long novel that has the style or structure usually associated with an epic.

Epilogue: A closing section or speech at the end of a play or other literary work that makes some reflection on the preceding action.

Episodic narrative: A work that is held together primarily by a loose connection of self-sufficient episodes. Picaresque novels often have an episodic structure.

Epithalamion: A bridal song or poem, a genre deriving from the poets of antiquity.

Essay: A nonfiction work, usually short, that analyzes or interprets a particular subject or idea; it is often written from a personal point of view.

Existentialism: A philosophical and literary term for a group of attitudes surrounding the idea that existence precedes essence; according to Jean-Paul Sartre, "man is nothing else but what he makes himself." Existential literature exhibits an awareness of the absurdity of the universe and is preoccupied with the single ethical choice that determines the meaning of a person's existence.

Expressionism: A movement in the arts, especially in German painting, dominant in the decade following World War I; external reality is consciously distorted in order to portray the world as it is "viewed emotionally."

Fabulation: The act of lying to invent or tell a fable, sometimes used to designate the fable itself.

Fantastic: The fantastic has been defined as a genre that lies between the "uncanny" and the "marvelous." All three genres embody the familiar world but present an event that cannot be explained by the laws of the familiar world.

Farce: A play that evokes laughter through such low-comedy devices as physical humor, rough wit, and ridiculous and improbable situations and characters.

First person: A point of view in which the narrator of a story or poem addresses the reader directly, often using the pronoun "I," thereby allowing the reader direct access to the narrator's thoughts.

Flashback: A scene in a fictional or dramatic work depicting events that occurred at an earlier time.

Foot: A rhythmic unit of poetry consisting of two or three syllables grouped together; the most common foot in English is the iamb, composed of one unstressed syllable attached to one stressed syllable.

Foreshadowing: A device used to create suspense or dramatic irony by indicating through suggestion what will take place in the future.

Formalism: A school of literary criticism which particularly emphasizes the form of the work of art—that is, the type or genre to which it belongs.

Frame story: A story that provides a framework for another story (or stories) told within it.

Free verse: A poem that does not conform to such traditional conventions as meter or rhyme, and that does not establish any pattern within itself, is said to be a "free verse" poem.

Genre: A type or category of literature, such as tragedy, novel, memoir, poem, or essay; a genre has a particular set of conventions and expectations.

Genre fiction: Categories of popular fiction such as the mystery, the romance, and the Western; although the term can be used in a neutral sense, "genre fiction" is often used dismissively to refer

to fiction in which the writer is bound by more or less rigid conventions.

Gothic novel: A form of fiction developed in the eighteenth century that focuses on horror and the supernatural.

Grotesque: Characterized by a breakup of the everyday world by mysterious forces, the form differs from fantasy in that the reader is not sure whether to react with humor or horror.

Half-rhyme. *See* Slant rhyme.

Hamartia. *See* Tragic flaw.

Harlem Renaissance: A flowering of African American writing, in all literary genres, in the 1930's and 1940's.

Hero/Heroine: The most important character in a drama or other literary work. Popularly, the term has come to refer to a character who possesses extraordinary prowess or virtue, but as a technical term it simply indicates the central participant in a dramatic action. *See also* Protagonist.

Heroic couplet: A pair of rhyming iambic pentameter lines traditionally used in epic poetry; a heroic couplet often serves as a self-contained witticism or pithy observation.

Historical novel: A novel that depicts past events, usually public in nature, and that features real as well as fictional people; the relationship between fiction and history in the form varies greatly depending on the author.

Hubris: Excessive pride, the characteristic in tragic heroes such as Oedipus, Doctor Faustus, and Macbeth that leads them to transgress moral codes or ignore warnings. *See also* Tragic flaw.

Humanism: A human-centered rather than god-centered view of the universe that usually stresses reason, restraint, and human values; in the Renaissance, humanism devoted itself to the revival of the life, thought, language, and literature of ancient Greece and Rome.

Hyperbole: The use of gross exaggeration for rhetorical effect, based upon the assumption that the reader will not respond to the exaggeration literally.

Iamb: The basic metric foot of the English language, the iamb associates one unstressed syllable with one stressed syllable. The line "So long as men can breathe or eyes can see" is composed of five iambs (a form called iambic pentameter). *See also* Trochee.

Imagery: The simulation of sensory perception through figurative language; imagery can be controlled to create emotional or intellectual effects.

Imagism: A school of poetry prominent in Great Britain and North America between 1909 and 1918. The objectives of Imagism were accurate description, objective presentation, concentration and economy, new rhythms, freedom of choice in subject matter, and suggestion rather than explanation.

Interior monologue: The speech of a character designed to introduce the reader directly to the character's internal life; it differs from other monologues in that it attempts to reproduce thought before logical organization is imposed upon it.

Irony: An effect that occurs when a writer's or a character's real meaning is different from (and frequently opposite to) his or her apparent meaning. *See also* Dramatic irony.

Jazz Age: The 1920's, a period of prosperity, sweeping social change, frequent excess, and youthful rebellion, for which F. Scott Fitzgerald is the acknowledged spokesman.

Künstlerroman: An apprenticeship novel in which the protagonist, a young artist, faces the conflicts of growing up and coming to understand the purpose of his life and art.

Leitmotif: The repetition in a work of literature of a word, phrase, or image that serves to establish the tone or otherwise unify the piece.

Line: A rhythmical unit within a poem between the foot and the poem's larger structural units; the words or feet in a line are usually in a single row.

Lyric poetry: Poetry that is generally short, adaptable to metrical variation, and personal in theme; it may explore deeply personal feelings about life.

Magical Realism: Imaginary or fantastic scenes and occurrences presented in a meticulously realistic style.

Melodrama: A play in which characters are clearly either virtuous or evil and are pitted against one another in suspenseful, often sensational situations.

Memoir: A piece of autobiographical writing that emphasizes important events in which the author has participated and prominent people whom the author has known.

Metafiction: Fiction that manifests a reflexive tendency and shows a consciousness of itself as an artificial creation; such terms as "postmodernist fiction," "antifiction," and "surfiction" also refer to this type of fiction.

Metaphor: A figure of speech in which two different things are identified with each other, as in the T. S. Eliot line, "The whole earth is our hospital"; the term is also widely used to identify many kinds of analogies.

Metaphysical poetry: A type of poetry that stresses the intellectual over the emotional; it is marked by irony, paradox, and striking comparisons of dissimilar things, the latter frequently being far-fetched to the point of eccentricity.

Meter: The rhythmic pattern of language when it is formed into lines of poetry; when the rhythm of language is organized and regulated so as to affect the meaning and emotional response to the words, the rhythm has been refined into meter.

Mise-en-scène: The staging of a drama, including scenery, costumes, movable furniture (properties), and, by extension, the positions (blocking) and gestures of the actors.

Mock-heroic style: A form of burlesque in which a trivial subject is absurdly elevated through use of the meter, diction, and familiar devices of the epic poem.

Modernism: An international movement in the arts that began in the early years of the twentieth century; modernism in general was characterized by its international idiom, by its interest in cultures distant in space or time, by its emphasis on formal experimentation, and by its sense of dislocation and radical change.

Monologue: An extended speech by one character in a drama. If the character is alone onstage, unheard by other characters, the monologue is more specifically referred to as a soliloquy.

Musical comedy: A theatrical form mingling song, dance, and spoken dialogue that was developed in the United States in the twentieth century; it was derived from vaudeville and operetta.

Myth: Anonymous traditional stories dealing with basic human concepts and fundamentally opposing principles; a myth is often constructed as a story that tells of supposedly historical events.

Narrator: The character who recounts the story in a work of fiction.

Naturalism: The application of the principles of scientific determinism to fiction. Although it usually refers more to the choice of subject matter than to technical conventions, conventions associated with the movement center on the author's attempt to be precise and objective in description and detail, regardless of whether the events described are sordid or shocking. *See also* Determinism.

Neoclassicism: The type of classicism that dominated English literature from the Restoration to the late eighteenth century. Modeling itself on the literature of ancient Greece and Rome, neoclassicism exalts the virtues of proportion, unity, harmony, grace, decorum, taste, manners, and restraint; it values realism and reason.

New Criticism: A reaction against the "old criticism" that saw art as self-expression, applied extrinsic criteria of morality and value, or gave credence to the professed intentions of the author. The New Criticism regards a work of art as an autonomous object, a self-contained universe. It holds that a close reading of literary texts will reveal their meanings and the complexities of their verbal texture as well as the oppositions and tensions balanced in the text.

New Journalism: Writing that largely abandons the traditional objectivity of journalism in order to express the subjective response of the observer.

Nonfiction novel: A novel that, although taking actual people and events as its subject matter, uses fictional techniques to develop the narrative; an example is Truman Capote's *In Cold Blood* (1966).

Novel: A long fictional form that is generally concerned with individual characterization and with presenting a social world and a detailed environment.

Novel of ideas: A novel in which the characters, plot, and dialogue serve to develop some controlling idea or to present the clash of ideas.

Novel of manners: Classic examples of the form might be the novels of Jane Austen, wherein the customs and conventions of a social group of a particular time and place are realistically, and often satirically, portrayed.

Novella, *nouvelle*, novelette: These terms usually refer to that form of fiction which is said to be longer than a short story and shorter than a novel; "novella" is the term usually used to refer to American works in this genre.

Ode: A lyric poem that treats a unified subject with elevated emotion and seriousness of purpose, usually ending with a satisfactory resolution.

Old Criticism: Criticism predating the New Criticism and bringing extrinsic criteria to bear on the analysis of literature as authorial self-expression (Romanticism), critical self-expression (impressionism), or work that is dependent upon moral or ethical absolutes (new humanism).

Omniscient narration: A godlike point of view from which the narrator sees all and knows everything about the story and its characters.

One-act play: A short, unified dramatic work, the one-act play is usually quite limited in number of characters and scene changes; the action often revolves around a single incident or event.

Opera: A complex combination of various art forms, opera is a form of dramatic entertainment consisting of a play set to music.

Original Sin: A concept of the innate depravity of humankind's nature resulting from Adam's sin and fall from grace.

Paradox: A statement that initially seems to be illogical or self-contradictory yet eventually proves to embody a complex truth.

Parataxis: The placing of clauses or phrases in a series without the use of coordinating or subordinating terms.

Pathos: The quality in a character that evokes pity or sorrow from the observer.

Pentameter: A line of poetry consisting of five recognizable rhythmic units called feet.

Picaresque novel: A form of fiction that involves a central rogue figure, or picaro, who usually tells his own story. The plot structure is normally episodic, and the episodes usually focus on how the picaro lives by his wits.

Plot: The sequence of the occurrence of events in a dramatic action. A plot may be unified around a single action, but it may also consist of a series of disconnected incidents; it is then referred to as "episodic."

Poem: A unified composition that uses the rhythms and sounds of language, as well as devices such as metaphor, to communicate emotions and experiences to the reader or hearer.

Point of view: The perspective from which a story is presented to the reader. In simplest terms, it refers to whether narration is first person (directly addressed to the reader as if told by one involved in the narrative) or third person (usually a more objective, distanced perspective).

Postmodernism: The term is loosely applied to various artistic movements that have followed so-called high modernism, represented by such giants as James Joyce and Pablo Picasso. The term is frequently applied to the works of writers (such as Thomas Pynchon and John Barth) who exhibit a self-conscious awareness of their predecessors as well as a reflexive treatment of fictional form.

Prose poem: A type of poem, usually less than a page in length, that appears on the page like prose; there is great stylistic and thematic variety within the genre.

Protagonist: Originally, in the Greek drama, the "first actor," who played the leading role. The term has come to signify the most important character in a drama or story. It is not unusual for there to be more than one protagonist in a work. *See also* Hero/Heroine.

Psychoanalytic theory: A tremendously influential theory of the unconscious developed by Sigmund Freud, it divides the human psyche into three components—the id, the ego, and the superego. In this theory, the psyche represses instinctual and sexual desires, and channels (sublimates) those desires into socially acceptable behavior.

Psychological novel: A form of fiction in which character, especially the inner life of characters, is the primary focus. The form has characterized much of the work of James Joyce, Virginia Woolf, and William Faulkner.

Psychological realism: A type of realism that tries to reproduce the complex psychological motivations behind human behavior; writers in the late nineteenth and early twentieth centuries were particularly influenced by Sigmund Freud's theories. *See also* Psychoanalytic theory.

Pun: A pun occurs when words that have similar pronunciations have entirely different meanings; a pun can establish a connection between two meanings or contexts that the reader would not ordinarily make. The result may be a striking connection or simply a humorously accidental connection.

Quatrain: Any four-line stanza is a quatrain; other than the couplet, the quatrain is the most common type of stanza.

Rationalism: A system of thought that seeks truth through the exercise of reason rather than by means of emotional response or revelation.

Realism: A literary technique in which the primary convention is to render an illusion of fidelity to external reality. Realism is often identified as the primary method of the novel form; the realist movement in the late nineteenth century coincided with the full development of the novel form.

Regional novel: Any novel in which the character of a given geographical region plays a decisive role; the southern United States, for example, has fostered a strong regional tradition.

Representationalism: An approach to drama that seeks to create the illusion of reality onstage through realistic characters, situations, and settings.

Revue: A theatrical production, typically consisting of sketches, song, and dance, which often comments satirically upon personalities and events of the day; generally there is no plot involved.

Rhyme: A full rhyme comprises two or more words that have the same vowel sound and that end with the same consonant sound: "Hat" and "cat" is a full rhyme, as is "laughter" and "after." Rhyme is also used more broadly as a term for any correspondence in sound between syllables in poetry. *See also* Slant rhyme.

Rhyme scheme: Poems which establish a pattern of rhyme have a "rhyme scheme," designated by lowercase letters; the rhyme scheme of ottava rima, for example, is *abababcc*. Traditional stanza forms are categorized by their rhyme scheme and base meter.

Roman à clef: A fiction wherein actual persons, often celebrities of some sort, are thinly disguised as characters.

Romance: The romance usually differs from the novel form in that the focus is on symbolic events and representational characters rather than on "as-if-real" characters and events. Character is often highly stylized, serving as a function of the plot.

Romantic comedy: A play in which love is the central motive of the dramatic action. The term often refers to plays of the Elizabethan period, such as William Shakespeare's *A Midsummer Night's Dream* (pr. c. 1595-1596) and *As You Like It* (pr. c. 1599-1600), but it has also been applied to any modern work that contains similar features.

Romanticism: A widespread cultural movement in the late eighteenth and early nineteenth centuries, Romanticism is frequently contrasted with classicism. The term generally suggests primitivism, an interest in folklore, a reverence for nature, a fascination with the demoniac and the macabre, and an assertion of the preeminence of the imagination.

Satire: Satire employs the comedic devices of wit, irony, and exaggeration to expose and condemn human folly, vice, and stupidity.

Scene: In drama, a division of action within an act (some plays are divided only into scenes instead of acts). Sometimes scene division indicates a change of setting or locale; sometimes it simply indicates the entrances and exits of characters.

Science fiction: Fiction in which real or imagined scientific developments or certain givens (such as physical laws, psychological principles, or social conditions) form the basis of an imaginative projection, frequently into the future.

Sentimental novel: A form of fiction popular in the eighteenth century in which emotionalism and optimism are the primary characteristics. The best-known examples are Samuel Richardson's *Pamela* (1740-1741) and Oliver Goldsmith's *The Vicar of Wakefield* (1766).

Sentimentalism: A term used to describe any emotional response that is excessive and disproportionate to its impetus or occasion. It also refers to the eighteenth century idea that human beings are essentially benevolent, devoid of Original Sin and basic depravity.

Setting: The time and place in which the action of a literary work happens. The term also applies to the physical elements of a theatrical production, such as scenery and properties.

Short story: A concise work of fiction, shorter than a novella, that is usually more concerned with mood, effect, or a single event than with plot or extensive characterization.

Simile: Loosely defined, a simile is a type of metaphor that signals a comparison by the use of the words "like" or "as." William Shakespeare's line "My mistress' eyes are nothing like the sun," establishing a comparison between the woman's eyes and the sun, is a simile.

Slant rhyme: A slant rhyme, or half-rhyme, occurs when words with identical consonants but different vowel sounds are associated; "fall" and "well," "table" and "bauble" are slant rhymes.

Slapstick: Low comedy in which physical action (such as a kick in the rear, tripping, or knocking over people or objects) evokes laughter.

Social realism: A type of realism in which the social and economic conditions in which characters live figure prominently in their situations, actions, and outlooks.

Soliloquy: An extended speech delivered by a character alone onstage, unheard by other characters. Soliloquy is a form of monologue, and it typically reveals the intimate thoughts and emotions of the speaker.

Sonnet: A traditional poetic form that is almost always composed of fourteen lines of rhymed iambic pentameter; a turning point usually divides the poem into two parts, with the first part presenting a situation and the second part reflecting on it.

Southern gothic: A term applied to the scenes of decay, incest, madness, and violence often found in the fiction of William Faulkner, Erskine Caldwell, and other southern writers.

Speaker: The voice that speaks the words of a poem—sometimes a fictional character in an invented situation, sometimes the author speaking directly to the reader, sometimes the author speaking from behind the disguise of a persona.

Stanza: When lines of poetry are meant to be taken as a unit, and the unit recurs throughout the poem, that unit is called a stanza; a four-line unit is one common stanza.

Stream of consciousness: The depiction of the thought processes of a character, insofar as this is possible, without any mediating structures. The metaphor of consciousness as a "stream" suggests a rush of thoughts and images governed by free association rather than by strictly rational development; the term is often used loosely as a synonym for interior monologue.

Stress: When more emphasis is placed on one syllable in a line of poetry than on another syllable, that syllable is said to be stressed.

Subplot: A secondary action coincident with the main action of a fictional or dramatic work. A subplot may be a reflection upon the main action, but it may also be largely unrelated. *See also* Counterplot.

Surrealism: An approach to literature and art that startlingly combines seemingly incompatible elements; surrealist writing usually has a bizarre, dreamlike, or nightmarish quality.

Symbol: A literary symbol is an image that stands for something else; it may evoke a cluster of meanings rather than a single specific meaning.

Symbolism: A literary movement encompassing the work of a group of French writers in the latter half of the nineteenth century, a group that included Charles Baudelaire, Stéphane Mallarmé, and Paul Verlaine. According to Symbolism, there is a mystical correspondence between the natural and spiritual worlds.

Syntax: A linguistic term used to describe the study of the ways in which words are arranged sequentially to produce grammatical units such as phrases, clauses, and sentences.

Tableau: A silent, stationary grouping of performers in a theatrical performance.

Terza rima: A rhyming three-line stanza form in which the middle line of one stanza rhymes with the first line of the following stanza.

Tetrameter: A line of poetry consisting of four recognizable rhythmic units called feet.

Theater of the Absurd: The general name given to plays that express a basic belief that life is illogical, irrational, formless, and contradictory and that humankind is without meaning or purpose. This perspective often leads to the abandonment of traditional theatrical forms and coherent dialogue.

Theme: Loosely defined as what a literary work means. The theme of W. B. Yeats's poem "Sailing to Byzantium," for example, might be interpreted as the failure of humankind's attempt to isolate itself within the world of art.

Thespian: Another term for an actor; also, of or relating to the theater. The word derives from Thespis, by tradition the first actor of the Greek theater.

Third person: Third-person narration is related from a point of view more distant from the story than first-person narration; the narrator is not an identifiable "I" persona. A third-person point of view may be limited or omniscient (all-knowing).

Three unities. *See* Unities.

Tone: Tone usually refers to the dominant mood of a work. *See also* Atmosphere.

Tragedy: A form of drama that is serious in action and intent and that involves disastrous events and death; classical Greek drama observed specific guidelines for tragedy, but the term is now sometimes applied to a range of dramatic or fictional situations.

Tragic flaw: Also known as hamartia, it is the weakness or error in judgment in a tragic hero or protagonist that causes the character's downfall; it may proceed from ignorance or a moral fault. Excessive pride (hubris) is one traditional tragic flaw.

Travel literature: Writing that emphasizes the author's subjective response to places visited, especially faraway, exotic, and culturally different locales.

Trimeter: A line of poetry consisting of three recognizable rhythmic units called feet.

Trochee: One of the most common feet in English poetry, the trochee associates one stressed syllable with one unstressed syllable, as in the line, "Double, double, toil and trouble." *See also* Iamb.

Unities: A set of rules for proper dramatic construction formulated by European Renaissance drama critics and derived from classical Greek concepts: A play should have no scenes or subplots irrelevant to the central action, should not cover a period of more than twenty-four hours, and should not occur in more than one place.

Verisimilitude: The attempt to have the readers of a literary work believe that it conforms to reality rather than to its own laws.

Verse: A generic term for poetry; verse also refers in a narrower sense to poetry that is humorous or merely superficial, as in "greeting-card verse."

Verse paragraph: A division within a poem that is created by logic or syntax rather than by form; verse paragraphs are important for determining the movement of a poem and the logical association between ideas.

Victorian novel: Although the Victorian period extended from 1837 to 1901, the term "Victorian novel" does not include works from the later decades of Queen Victoria's reign. The term loosely refers to the sprawling works of novelists such as Charles Dickens and William Makepeace Thackeray, which are characterized by a broad social canvas.

Villanelle: The villanelle is a French verse form assimilated by English prosody. It is usually composed of nineteen lines divided into five tercets and a quatrain, rhyming *aba*, *bba*, *aba*, *aba*, and *abaa*.

Well-made play: A type of play constructed according to a nineteenth century French formula; the plot often revolves around a secret (revealed at the end) known only to some of the characters. Misunderstanding, suspense, and coincidence are among the devices used.

Western novel: The Western novel is defined by a relatively predictable combination of conventions and recurring themes. These predictable elements, familiar from television and film Westerns, differentiate the Western from historical novels and other works that may be set in the Old West.

Worldview: Frequently rendered as the German *Weltanschauung*, it is a comprehensive set of beliefs or assumptions by means of which one interprets what goes on in the world.

CATEGORY LIST

LIST OF CATEGORIES

AFRICAN AMERICAN/ AFRICAN DESCENT

Ai
Maya Angelou
James Baldwin
Toni Cade Bambara
Amiri Baraka
Gwendolyn Brooks
Octavia E. Butler
Charles Waddell Chesnutt
Countée Cullen
Edwidge Danticat
Samuel R. Delany
Frederick Douglass
Rita Dove
Paul Laurence Dunbar
Ralph Ellison
Charles Fuller
Ernest J. Gaines
Nikki Giovanni
Alex Haley
Lorraine Hansberry
Michael S. Harper
Robert Hayden
Chester Himes
Langston Hughes
Zora Neale Hurston
Charles Johnson
James Weldon Johnson
Adrienne Kennedy
Jamaica Kincaid
Yusef Komunyakaa
Nella Larsen

Audre Lorde
Terry McMillan
Paule Marshall
Toni Morrison
Walter Mosley
Walter Dean Myers
Gloria Naylor
Suzan-Lori Parks
Ann Petry
Ishmael Reed
Ntozake Shange
Jean Toomer
Alice Walker
Margaret Walker
Phillis Wheatley
John Edgar Wideman
August Wilson
Jay Wright
Richard Wright

AMERICAN INDIAN

Ai
Sherman Alexie
Paula Gunn Allen
Louise Erdrich
Joy Harjo
Linda Hogan
N. Scott Momaday
Leslie Marmon Silko
Gerald Vizenor
James Welch
Jay Wright

ASIAN AMERICAN/ ASIAN DESCENT

Ai
Carlos Bulosan
Frank Chin
Garrett Hongo
David Henry Hwang
Gish Jen
Ha Jin
Cynthia Kadohata
Maxine Hong Kingston
Joy Kogawa
Chang-rae Lee
Bharati Mukherjee
Michael Ondaatje
Cathy Song
Amy Tan

CANADIAN

Margaret Atwood
Robertson Davies
Mavis Gallant
William Gibson (b. 1948)
Anne Hébert
W. P. Kinsella
Joy Kogawa
Stephen Leacock
Farley Mowat
Alice Munro
Michael Ondaatje
Gabrielle Roy
Carol Shields

GAY OR BISEXUAL
James Baldwin
Djuna Barnes
Elizabeth Bishop
Harold Brodkey
Truman Capote
Hart Crane
Samuel R. Delany
Robert Duncan
Allen Ginsberg
H. D.
Tony Kushner
David Leavitt
Audre Lorde
Carson McCullers
James Merrill
Frank O'Hara
Adrienne Rich
Gertrude Stein
Gore Vidal
Tennessee Williams

JEWISH
Saul Bellow
Harold Brodkey
Stanley Elkin
Edna Ferber
Allen Ginsberg
Jerzy Kosinski
Stanley Kunitz
Tony Kushner
Bernard Malamud
Arthur Miller
Clifford Odets
Cynthia Ozick
Robert Pinsky
Chaim Potok
Philip Roth
Neil Simon
Wendy Wasserstein
Nathanael West

LATINO
Julia Alvarez
Rudolfo Anaya
Jimmy Santiago Baca
Sandra Cisneros
Oscar Hijuelos
Rolando Hinojosa
Judith Ortiz Cofer

Gary Soto
Luis Miguel Valdez
Helena María Viramontes

NONFICTION WRITERS
Edward Abbey
Henry Adams
Paula Gunn Allen
Maya Angelou
Robert Bly
Joan Didion
Annie Dillard
Frederick Douglass
Ralph Waldo Emerson
Benjamin Franklin
Lillian Hellman
Zora Neale Hurston
Maxine Hong Kingston
Stephen Leacock
Frank McCourt
Peter Matthiessen
N. Scott Momaday
Wright Morris
Farley Mowat
Anaïs Nin
Judith Ortiz Cofer
Chaim Potok
May Sarton
Susan Sontag
Gertrude Stein
Hunter S. Thompson
Henry David Thoreau
Mark Twain
John Edgar Wideman
Tom Wolfe

NOVELISTS
Henry Adams
James Agee
Louisa May Alcott
Nelson Algren
Julia Alvarez
Rudolfo Anaya
Isaac Asimov
Margaret Atwood
Louis Auchincloss
Paul Auster
James Baldwin
Toni Cade Bambara
Djuna Barnes

John Barth
Donald Barthelme
Ann Beattie
Saul Bellow
Thomas Berger
Wendell Berry
Edward Bloor
Judy Blume
Paul Bowles
Kay Boyle
T. Coraghessan Boyle
Ray Bradbury
Richard Brautigan
Harold Brodkey
Pearl S. Buck
Charles Bukowski
Carlos Bulosan
Octavia E. Butler
Robert Olen Butler
James M. Cain
Erskine Caldwell
Truman Capote
Willa Cather
Raymond Chandler
John Cheever
Charles Waddell Chesnutt
Frank Chin
Kate Chopin
Sandra Cisneros
Tom Clancy
James Fenimore Cooper
Robert Coover
Robert Cormier
Stephen Crane
Edwidge Danticat
Robertson Davies
Samuel R. Delany
Don DeLillo
Philip K. Dick
James Dickey
Joan Didion
Annie Dillard
E. L. Doctorow
John Dos Passos
Rita Dove
Theodore Dreiser
Stanley Elkin
Ralph Ellison
Louise Erdrich
James T. Farrell

William Faulkner
Edna Ferber
F. Scott Fitzgerald
Richard Ford
William Gaddis
Ernest J. Gaines
John Gardner
William H. Gass
Kaye Gibbons
William Gibson (b. 1948)
Ellen Glasgow
Susan Glaspell
Mary Gordon
Alex Haley
Dashiell Hammett
Nathaniel Hawthorne
Anne Hébert
Robert A. Heinlein
Joseph Heller
Mark Helprin
Ernest Hemingway
Frank Herbert
Patricia Highsmith
Oscar Hijuelos
Tony Hillerman
Chester Himes
Rolando Hinojosa
S. E. Hinton
William Dean Howells
Zora Neale Hurston
John Irving
Shirley Jackson
Henry James
Gish Jen
Sarah Orne Jewett
Ha Jin
Charles Johnson
James Weldon Johnson
Cynthia Kadohata
Garrison Keillor
William Kennedy
Jack Kerouac
M. E. Kerr
Ken Kesey
Jamaica Kincaid
Stephen King
Barbara Kingsolver
Maxine Hong Kingston
W. P. Kinsella
John Knowles

Joy Kogawa
Jerzy Kosinski
Louis L'Amour
Nella Larsen
David Leavitt
Chang-rae Lee
Harper Lee
Ursula K. LeGuin
Madeleine L'Engle
Elmore Leonard
Sinclair Lewis
Jack London
Alison Lurie
Cormac McCarthy
Mary McCarthy
Carson McCullers
Ross Macdonald
Thomas McGuane
Terry McMillan
Larry McMurtry
Norman Mailer
Bernard Malamud
Paule Marshall
Bobbie Ann Mason
Peter Matthiessen
Herman Melville
James A. Michener
Henry Miller
N. Scott Momaday
Brian Moore
Wright Morris
Toni Morrison
Walter Mosley
Farley Mowat
Bharati Mukherjee
Walter Dean Myers
Vladimir Nabokov
Gloria Naylor
Anaïs Nin
Frank Norris
Joyce Carol Oates
Tim O'Brien
Flannery O'Connor
John O'Hara
Tillie Olsen
Michael Ondaatje
Judith Ortiz Cofer
Cynthia Ozick
Suzan-Lori Parks
Gary Paulsen

Walker Percy
Ann Petry
Jayne Anne Phillips
Sylvia Plath
Katherine Anne Porter
Charles Portis
Chaim Potok
J. F. Powers
Richard Powers
Reynolds Price
Thomas Pynchon
Ayn Rand
Ishmael Reed
Conrad Richter
Philip Roth
Gabrielle Roy
J. D. Salinger
William Saroyan
May Sarton
Ntozake Shange
Carol Shields
Leslie Marmon Silko
Upton Sinclair
Jane Smiley
Susan Sontag
Jean Stafford
Wallace Stegner
John Steinbeck
Robert Stone
Harriet Beecher Stowe
William Styron
Glendon Swarthout
Amy Tan
Jean Toomer
Scott Turow
Mark Twain
Anne Tyler
John Updike
Gore Vidal
Helena María Viramontes
Gerald Vizenor
Kurt Vonnegut
Alice Walker
Margaret Walker
Robert Penn Warren
James Welch
Eudora Welty
Nathanael West
Edith Wharton
John Edgar Wideman

Laura Ingalls Wilder
Thornton Wilder
Larry Woiwode
Thomas Wolfe
Tom Wolfe
Tobias Wolff
Richard Wright
Paul Zindel

PLAYWRIGHTS
Edward Albee
Amiri Baraka
Frank Chin
Robertson Davies
T. S. Eliot
Charles Fuller
William Gibson (b. 1914)
Susan Glaspell
John Guare
Lorraine Hansberry
Lillian Hellman
Beth Henley
David Henry Hwang
Adrienne Kennedy
Tony Kushner
David Mamet
Arthur Miller
Clifford Odets
Eugene O'Neill
Suzan-Lori Parks
William Saroyan
Ntozake Shange
Sam Shepard
Neil Simon
Luis Miguel Valdez
Wendy Wasserstein
Thornton Wilder
Tennessee Williams
August Wilson
Lanford Wilson
Paul Zindel

POETS
Ai
Sherman Alexie
Paula Gunn Allen
Maya Angelou
John Ashbery
Jimmy Santiago Baca
Amiri Baraka

Wendell Berry
John Berryman
Elizabeth Bishop
Robert Bly
Anne Bradstreet
Gwendolyn Brooks
Charles Bukowski
Hart Crane
Robert Creeley
Countée Cullen
E. E. Cummings
James Dickey
Emily Dickinson
Rita Dove
Paul Laurence Dunbar
Robert Duncan
T. S. Eliot
Ralph Waldo Emerson
Louise Erdrich
Philip Freneau
Robert Frost
Allen Ginsberg
Nikki Giovanni
Mel Glenn
Louise Glück
H. D.
Joy Harjo
Michael S. Harper
Robert Hayden
Anthony Hecht
Linda Hogan
Garrett Hongo
Langston Hughes
Randall Jarrell
Robinson Jeffers
James Weldon Johnson
Yusef Komunyakaa
Stanley Kunitz
Denise Levertov
Henry Wadsworth Longfellow
Audre Lorde
Robert Lowell
Edgar Lee Masters
Herman Melville
James Merrill
W. S. Merwin
Edna St. Vincent Millay
N. Scott Momaday
Marianne Moore
Frank O'Hara

Sharon Olds
Charles Olson
George Oppen
Judith Ortiz Cofer
Dorothy Parker
Robert Pinsky
Sylvia Plath
Edgar Allan Poe
Ezra Pound
John Crowe Ransom
Ishmael Reed
Adrienne Rich
Edwin Arlington Robinson
Theodore Roethke
Muriel Rukeyser
Carl Sandburg
May Sarton
Anne Sexton
Leslie Marmon Silko
Gary Snyder
Cathy Song
Gary Soto
William Stafford
Wallace Stevens
Jean Toomer
Mona Van Duyn
Margaret Walker
Robert Penn Warren
Phillis Wheatley
Walt Whitman
John Greenleaf Whittier
Richard Wilbur
William Carlos Williams
Charles Wright
James Wright
Jay Wright

SHORT-STORY WRITERS
Sherman Alexie
Nelson Algren
Paula Gunn Allen
Rudolfo Anaya
Sherwood Anderson
Isaac Asimov
Margaret Atwood
Toni Cade Bambara
John Barth
Donald Barthelme
Ann Beattie
Wendell Berry

Ambrose Bierce
Paul Bowles
Kay Boyle
T. Coraghessan Boyle
Ray Bradbury
Harold Brodkey
Octavia E. Butler
Robert Olen Butler
Raymond Carver
John Cheever
Charles Waddell Chesnutt
Kate Chopin
Sandra Cisneros
Robert Coover
Stephen Crane
Edwidge Danticat
Guy Davenport
Philip K. Dick
E. L. Doctorow
Paul Laurence Dunbar
Stanley Elkin
William Faulkner
F. Scott Fitzgerald
Richard Ford
Ernest J. Gaines
Mavis Gallant
William H. Gass
William Gibson (b. 1948)
Susan Glaspell
Bret Harte
Nathaniel Hawthorne
Mark Helprin
Ernest Hemingway
O. Henry
Chester Himes
Langston Hughes
Washington Irving
Shirley Jackson
Gish Jen
Sarah Orne Jewett
Charles Johnson
Garrison Keillor
Jamaica Kincaid
Barbara Kingsolver
W. P. Kinsella
Ring Lardner
Stephen Leacock
David Leavitt
Jack London
Bernard Malamud

Bobbie Ann Mason
Herman Melville
Bharati Mukherjee
Alice Munro
Joyce Carol Oates
Flannery O'Connor
John O'Hara
Tillie Olsen
Cynthia Ozick
Grace Paley
Dorothy Parker
Ann Petry
Jayne Anne Phillips
Edgar Allan Poe
Katherine Anne Porter
J. F. Powers
Reynolds Price
Thomas Pynchon
J. D. Salinger
William Saroyan
Jane Smiley
Gary Soto
Jean Stafford
Wallace Stegner
Gertrude Stein
James Thurber
Mark Twain
John Updike
Helena María Viramontes
Kurt Vonnegut
Alice Walker
Eudora Welty
John Edgar Wideman
Larry Woiwode
Tobias Wolff

WOMEN
Ai
Louisa May Alcott
Paula Gunn Allen
Julia Alvarez
Maya Angelou
Margaret Atwood
Toni Cade Bambara
Djuna Barnes
Ann Beattie
Elizabeth Bishop
Judy Blume
Kay Boyle
Anne Bradstreet

Gwendolyn Brooks
Pearl S. Buck
Octavia E. Butler
Willa Cather
Kate Chopin
Sandra Cisneros
Edwidge Danticat
Emily Dickinson
Joan Didion
Annie Dillard
Rita Dove
Louise Erdrich
Edna Ferber
Mavis Gallant
Kaye Gibbons
Nikki Giovanni
Ellen Glasgow
Susan Glaspell
Louise Glück
Mary Gordon
H. D.
Lorraine Hansberry
Joy Harjo
Anne Hébert
Lillian Hellman
Beth Henley
Patricia Highsmith
S. E. Hinton
Linda Hogan
Zora Neale Hurston
Shirley Jackson
Gish Jen
Sarah Orne Jewett
Cynthia Kadohata
Adrienne Kennedy
M. E. Kerr
Jamaica Kincaid
Barbara Kingsolver
Maxine Hong Kingston
Joy Kogawa
Nella Larsen
Harper Lee
Ursula K. Le Guin
Madeleine L'Engle
Denise Levertov
Audre Lorde
Alison Lurie
Mary McCarthy
Carson McCullers
Terry McMillan

Paule Marshall
Bobbie Ann Mason
Edna St. Vincent Millay
Marianne Moore
Toni Morrison
Bharati Mukherjee
Alice Munro
Gloria Naylor
Anaïs Nin
Joyce Carol Oates
Flannery O'Connor
Sharon Olds
Tillie Olsen
Judith Ortiz Cofer
Cynthia Ozick
Grace Paley
Dorothy Parker
Suzan-Lori Parks
Ann Petry
Jayne Anne Phillips
Sylvia Plath

Katherine Anne Porter
Ayn Rand
Adrienne Rich
Gabrielle Roy
Muriel Rukeyser
May Sarton
Anne Sexton
Ntozake Shange
Carol Shields
Leslie Marmon Silko
Jane Smiley
Cathy Song
Susan Sontag
Jean Stafford
Gertrude Stein
Harriet Beecher Stowe
Amy Tan
Anne Tyler
Mona Van Duyn
Helena María Viramontes
Alice Walker

Margaret Walker
Wendy Wasserstein
Eudora Welty
Edith Wharton
Phillis Wheatley
Laura Ingalls Wilder

Young Adult Authors

Edward Bloor
Judy Blume
Robert Cormier
Mel Glenn
S. E. Hinton
Cynthia Kadohata
M. E. Kerr
Madeleine L'Engle
Walter Dean Myers
Gary Paulsen
Laura Ingalls Wilder
Paul Zindel

MAGILL'S SURVEY OF
AMERICAN LITERATURE

Revised Edition

TITLE INDEX

AUTHOR INDEX